# The *Monarchia* Controversy

# The *Monarchia* Controversy

An Historical Study with Accompanying

Translations of Dante Alighieri's *Monarchia*,

Guido Vernani's *Refutation of the "Monarchia" Composed by Dante*,

and Pope John XXII's Bull *Si fratrum*

*by* Anthony K. Cassell

The Catholic University of America Press
Washington, D.C.

The paper used in this publication meets the minimum requirements of American National Standards for Information Science—Permanence of Paper for Printed Library
materials, ANSI Z39.48-1984.

∞

*Library of Congress Cataloging-in-Publication Data*

Cassell, Anthony K. (Anthony Kimber), 1941–

The monarchia controversy: an historical study with accompanying translations of Dante
Alighieri's Monarchia, Guido Vernani's refutation of the Monarchia composed by Dante
and Pope John XXII's bull, Si fratrum / by Anthony Cassell.

p. cm.

Includes bibliographical references and index.

ISBN 0-8132-1338-X

1. Dante Alighieri, 1265–1321. Monarchia.    2. Vernani, Guido, fl. 1327. Reprobatio.

3. Catholic Church. Pope (1316–1334 : John XXII). Si fratrum.    4. Italy—Politics and
government—476–1268.    5. Catholic Church—Italy—Political activity.    6. Church and
state—Italy—To 1500.    I. Title

PQ4311.D4 C34 2003

320'.01—dc21

2002015139

*For my old friend*
*Lawrence Paul Buck*

Dì oggimai che la Chiesa di Roma,
Per confondere in sé due reggimenti,
Cade nel fango, e sé brutta e la soma.

*Purgatorio* 16:127–129

La tua città, che di colui è pianta
che pria volse le spalle al suo fattore
e di cui e la 'nvidia tanto pianta,
produce e spande il maladetto fiore
c'ha disvïate le pecore e li agni
però che fatto ha lupo del pastore.
Per questo l'Evangelio e i dottor magni
son derelitti, e solo ai Decretali
si studia, sì che parea' lor vivagni
A questo intende il papa e' cardinali;
non vanno i lor pensieri a Nazarette
là dove Gabriello aperse l'ali.

*Paradiso* 9:127–138

# Contents

# Acknowledgments

It is a pleasure to thank Dr. John Harris for his essential help on the finer points of Latin and for his friendship during some very difficult times, and Dr. John Serembus of Widener University for his expert advice on matters of formal logic. In each case I learned much, but I have made my own decisions in composing and writing. Dr. Patricia Hollahan offered much precious advice on medieval ideas and on format. Larry Buck, expert on things ecclesiastical, generously read the manuscript and was a constant source of knowledge and inspiration, despite the fact that he had no idea that the book would be dedicated to him.

# List of Abbreviations

| | |
|---|---|
| *Æn.* | Vergil, *Æneid.* |
| Barnes | Aristotle, *The Complete Works of Aristotle: The Revised Oxford Translation*, edited by Jonathan Barnes, Bollingen Series 71, 2 vols. (Princeton, N.J.: Princeton University Press, 1984). |
| Carlyle and Carlyle | R. W. Carlyle and A. J. Carlyle, *Mediæval Political Theory in the West*, 6 vols. (Edinburgh: William Blackwood, 1903–1936; rpt. 1950). |
| *CIC* | *Corpus iuris canonici*, ed. Richter and Friedberg. |
| *Conv.* | Dante, *Convivio.* |
| *CSEL* | *Corpus Scriptorum Ecclesiasticorum Latinorum* (Vienna, 1866+). |
| *Dante Studies* | *Dante Studies and the Annual Report of the Dante Society.* |
| *DCD* | St. Augustine, *De civitate Dei.* |
| *DDJ* | *Deutsches Dante-Jahrbuch.* |
| *De cons. Phil.* | Boethius, *De consolatione Philosophiæ.* |
| *Inf.* | Dante, *Inferno.* |
| LCL | Loeb Classical Library (Cambridge, Mass.: Harvard University Press/London: William Heinemann). |
| *Meta.* | Aristotle, *Metaphysics.* |
| *MGH* | *Monumenta Germaniæ Historica.* |
| *Mon.* | Dante, *Monarchia.* |
| *Nic. Ethics* | Aristotle, *Nicomachean Ethics.* |
| *Par.* | Dante, *Paradiso.* |
| *PG* | *Patrologia græca*, in *Patrologiæ Cursus Completus*, ed. Jacques-Paul Migne (Paris, 1886–1912). |

| | |
|---|---|
| *Phars.* | Lucan, *Pharsalia.* |
| *PL* | *Patrologia latina,* in *Patrologiæ Cursus Completus,* ed. Jacques-Paul Migne (Paris, 1844–1864). |
| *Pol.* | Aristotle, *Politics.* |
| *Purg.* | Dante, *Purgatorio.* |
| *Ref.* | Vernani, *Refutation of the "Monarchia" Composed by Dante (De reprobatione).* |
| *ST* | St. Thomas Aquinas, *Summa theologiæ (Summa theologica).* |
| *Theb.* | Statius, *Thebaid.* |

All citations from the Bible are from the Vulgate and the Douay-Rheims versions, except where noted. All 221 volumes of *PL* can be accessed online through the *Patrologia Latina Database* at the University of Michigan, at http://ets.umdl.umich.edu/p/pld.

Passages from Vergil's *Æneid* are from H. Rushton Fairclough's edition and translation in *Virgil with an English Translation . . . in Two Volumes,* LCL (Cambridge, Mass.: Harvard University Press/London: William Heinemann, 1967).

Citations from *The Divine Comedy* in Italian and English are taken from the edition with translation and commentary by Charles S. Singleton, 6 vols., Bollingen Series 80 (Princeton, N.J.: Princeton University Press, 1970–1975); Singleton therein reproduces the Italian text of Giorgio Petrocchi's edition, *La Commedia secondo l'antica vulgata,* 4 vols., from *Le opere di Dante Alighieri,* Edizione nazionale 7 (Milan: Mondadori, 1966–1967).

I have not hesitated to alter the wording of any of the English translations of foreign works that I have consulted and listed in the Bibliography if I thought the citations were in need of correction or whenever I wanted to show wording parallel to other texts.

Dante's *Monarchia* and
Vernani's *Refutation*
in Context

# Prolegomena

## *The Crisis and Its Major Players*

When, in 1318, Dante Alighieri set his pen to the treatise he named *Monarchia*, or *Liber Monarchiæ*,[1] a savage controversy had erupted concerning Pope John XXII's refusal to recognize the election of Ludwig IV of Wittelsbach as Holy Roman Emperor. Conveniently, papal lawyers had agreed that during vacancies of the imperial throne, the pope became the true sovereign. The aged pope's power play crowned an effort made by preceding pontiffs to encroach ever more upon temporal control.[2] Dante's patron, Can Grande della Scala of Verona, was meanwhile defying the pope's prohibitions imposed by the bull *Si fratrum*, of 1316–1317,[3] by daring to retain and insist upon his lifetime title of "Vicar to the Emperor" bestowed upon him by the late emperor, Henry VII of Luxembourg, on March 7, 1311.[4] Pope John, while firing repeated interdictions and anathemas against the lord of Verona, then dispatched his protégé and legate, Cardinal Bertrand du Poujet, from Avignon on what was to be a declared armed crusade by the Guelphs, the pro-Church party, against the Ghibellines, the pro-imperial forces, in Italy.[5] In turn, Can Grande, one of the Ghibellines' three principals in the north of the peninsula, remained unintimidated and grew ever more confirmed in the justice of his case. Dante came to the aid of his friend and former patron,[6] applying his remarkable learning in theology, history, logic, and even canon law to compose a treatise baring the roots of the issue: the tangled question of papal interference in temporal affairs. The poet presents the resultant defense as an oasis of logic amid the tumult.

The story of how, after Dante's death in September 1321, the *Monarchia* came to be used as imperial propaganda—and how some seven years later that use led not only to the *Monarchia*'s prohibition and burning by the pope's cardinal legate, but to the risk that the late poet himself could be charged with heresy and that his bones, like those of so many others, could suffer postmortem public burning—is one that craves to be retold.[7]

By 1328, there entered into the murky picture an obscure and curiously rancorous Dominican, Friar Guido Vernani of Rimini, who was to become Dante's first antagonist. His acerbic *Refutation of the "Monarchia" Composed by Dante* of 1329,[8] which the friar sarcastically dedicated to the ardent Bolognese admirer of the *Commedia* Graziolo de' Bambaglioli, appears here for the first time in English, together with a new translation of its target, Dante's philosophical masterpiece, the *Monarchia*. A first English version of John XXII's infamous bull, which eventually caused blood to be shed upon the troubles, rounds out the documentation.

## CHAPTER I

# Tiara and Scepter

In broaching the problem of the separation and correlation of the priestly and the imperial powers, Dante bravely, knowingly, and carefully entered a controversy that had simmered in different guises for centuries. By the second decade of the fourteenth century, the question had reached yet one more deplorable crisis not only because certain "modern" theorists argued that the papacy had direct power and jurisdiction over the domain of temporal princes, but because the pope then reigning, John XXII, insisted on the precedent recently reiterated by Clement V that he, in fact, wielded imperial authority in the case of the death or deposition of the emperor.[1] While civil law, especially in the *Corpus Authenticorum,* clearly designated the two powers that presided over mankind as *sacerdotium* and *imperium,* proceeding from the same one, divine, ultimate cause,[2] hierocrats' treatises happily obfuscated what was "kingly" and what was "temporal" in both word and fact. Partisans of papal claims ignored passages in the *Decretum* that admitted Christ's own division of powers, even passages such as those of Pope Nicholas I (858–867): "Christ separated the right [*ius*] of both powers by his own acts."[3] Instead, Innocent III, in the bull *Venerabilem [fratrem nostrum, Arelatensis archiepiscopum]* of 1202, and in a great part of his official writings, had formalized Leo I's, Gelasius's, and St. Bernard's affirmation (in *On Consideration* 2:15) that the papacy had inherited all of Christ's "royal" *(regia)* authority as both "priest and king in the order of Melchisedech" (Gn 14:18; Ps 110:4; Heb 6:20, 7:1ff.) into a sweeping doctrine. As Christ's Vicar, the pope alone thus inherited not only the totality of spiritual power but also—although its exercise and effects were mostly delegated—of temporal, kingly jurisdiction. Innocent IV made it plain that he alone was head of the Christian world, not only Vicar of St. Peter but Vicar of Christ: "The Lord Jesus Christ, as very man and very God, so remaining true King and true Priest, according to the order of Melchisedech . . . has established in the apostolic throne not only a pontifical, but also a regal monarchy, committing to the blessed Peter and his successors the government of both an earthly and celestial empire."[4] All high-papalist supporters—to name but a few among the poet's contemporaries, Tolomeo da Lucca (writing ca. 1301), Giles of Rome, and the theologian Giacomo da Viterbo (or James of Viterbo, ca. 1303), broadcast the formula.[5]

In his opening paragraphs Dante is clear about his desire for the palm of success in describing the necessity, legitimacy, and especially the independence of imperial rule; he assumes an attitude of humble duty in prying out truths previously hidden. His insistence on what will turn out to be for some truths invidious and hateful, however, waxes ever bolder, until, in the third book, he foresees the bitterness of his opponents' replies:[6] "The truth of this problem . . . cannot emerge without bringing shame to some and will perhaps be the cause of some resentment against me" (*Mon.* 3:1:2). "The truth of this third question has so much contention surrounding it that, while in other matters, ignorance is usually the cause of strife, so in this, strife is rather the cause of ignorance" (*Mon.* 3:3:3). Dante, as we shall see, amid political chaos and in a bold and altruistic effort to ward off imminent danger to another, composed a work that was to suffer not only pillorying by the opportunistic Vernani, but official holocaust and centuries of proscription. Hostilities between the Catholic Church and the Holy Roman Empire, Guelphs and Ghibellines, rose to enmesh Dante both in life and in death.[7]

The Church's growing pretensions to temporal hegemony faced awkward biblical precepts. Christ had commanded, according to Matthew 22:21, "Render therefore to Cæsar the things that are Cæsar's; and to God the things that are God's." And in John 18:36, he had admonished, "My kingdom is not of this world. . . . My kingdom is not from hence."[8] Paul in 2 Timothy 2:4 declared: "No man, being a soldier of God, entangleth himself with secular affairs."[9] Early writers and apologists, such as St. Augustine of Hippo (354–430), had not even referred to any establishment of an ecclesiastical authority, let alone one that could challenge the Roman Empire. After the Edict of Milan of 313, early emperors had increased the prestige of the Church of Rome in order to consolidate their own power amid the turmoil of conflicting claims and doctrines;[10] the emperor Gratian in 378 supported the Roman bishop's claim to authority over all the other bishops in the Western Empire; Theodosius I (ruled 379–395) and his co-emperor son, Valentinian II, recognized the bishop of Rome as the guardian of the true Catholic faith and established Roman Catholicism as the state religion in 380; and in 445, the edict *Certum est* of the Emperors Valentinian III and Theodosius II gave the whole strength of Roman civil law to uphold the primacy of St. Peter's See over others, allowing the bishop of Rome to charge and summon all the rest to Rome for judgment, decreeing, "Let whatever the authority of the Apostolic See decrees, or shall decree, be accepted as law by all."[11] Considerations of prestige and piety through the centuries steadily downplayed and reinterpreted these raw, secular, and adjutative concepts of papal power. Forty-nine years later, Pope Gelasius I, in his letter to the eastern emperor Athanasius (*Epistula* 12, *Ad Imperatorem Anastasium*), codified the Church's growing claim that two powers, not one, ruled this world, a royal and a sacred authority, with the priestly power the more important.[12] Gelasius's letter was to tip the balance in favor of the Church's autonomy while affirming the transference of Church jurisdiction from heaven to earth, thus defining the relationship between the papal and the imperial prerogatives; he ironically set the grounds for centuries of contention: "I hope that it will not have to be said of a Roman emperor that he resented the truth being brought home to him. Two there are, August Emperor, by which this world is chiefly ruled, the sacred authority [*auctoritas*] of the priesthood and the royal power [*potestas*]. Of these the responsibility of the priests is more weighty in so far as they will answer for the kings and men themselves at the divine judgment."[13] Out of Gelasius's insistence on protecting episcopal independence in spiritual affairs there grew the acceptance that two powers, one priestly and the other earthly, supported Christendom, each divinely ordained and each assisting the other, respecting each other's boundaries of responsibility. Early canon law affirmed the view, but long thereafter papal decretalists[14] from the end of the twelfth century moved the direction of ecclesiastical power to ever greater earthly dominion.

As Dante was well aware, references to the emperor's authority as ordained directly by God punctuate the *Corpus iuris civilis*, consisting of Justinian's *Code, Novellæ, Digest,* and *Institutes*. Justinian, in his supplemental constitution of A.D. 535, the *Novellæ* VI, formulated the classical Byzantine theory of Church and State relations, affirming that God in his mercy had granted man two supreme gifts, the *sacerdotium*, caring for his divine part, and the *regnum*, directing the earthly part; both proceeded from one single God, and while the two were mutually interdependent, neither was subordinated to the other.[15] In the *Monarchia*, the poet agrees fundamentally with this civil tradition and insists on the *de jure* legitimacy of Roman imperial power throughout. We must remember, however, that the encoding of Roman law is itself historically post-Gelasian, and that this fact is essential for an understanding of Dante's final paragraph of *Monarchia* 3:16 concerning the spiritual, filial reverence that the emperor must ultimately bear toward the sacramental office of the pope. Though he expresses utter contempt for those who had betrayed their sacred office, the poet never, of course, writes against the Church itself, but strives to turn its governance back toward the spiritual purpose of its origins; he aimed always to renew the Church's primal apostolic integrity, sullied and compromised, as he saw it, by the unworthy involvements of incumbents in earthly greed and corruption.[16] We must concede that the poet's vision ultimately exceeds any simplistic conception of the separation of powers and actually defies our attempts to define him narrowly: for Dante the Holy Roman Empire itself was as sacred and divine as the Church of Christ and both must return to their primitive purity.

Historically, once a concept of two powers had entered the picture, thereafter their separation remained a muddy issue and antipathy inevitably grew as both canonists and civil legal minds set forth their theories of a double regulation of Christendom. From the start the temporal and the papal defenders had warily defined their positions. The split between them grew into a gulf as each asserted plenitude of dominion for itself. Both imperialists and papalists counterclaimed and justified their directly divine origin and the direct power of their respective authorities. By Dante's time the question finally became reduced to one critical question: Did power descend from the Godhead directly to both the independent Church and the independent Holy Roman empire at once, or did power only come to a subordinate empire by way of the Church?

Although the Church was to exercise, unquestioned, the greater spiritual force, ironically, its real practical, earthly power grew enormously in the legal sphere. A short time before 1140, the great "Father of Canon Law," Franciscus Gratianus (Gratian), whom Dante places in *Paradiso* 10:103–5, then a mere Camaldulese monk of San Felice of Bologna, codified some four thousand patristic texts, conciliar decrees, and papal edicts into his *Concordantia discordatium canonum (The Concord of Discordant Canons)*, which became known as the *Decreta*, or the *Decretum Gratiani*. Though Gratian intended it as a private compilation, it became the basic text of schools of canon law that grew up around it and upon which the masters—that is, the decretists—of the universities of Bologna, Oxford, and Paris lectured. The compilation formed the first part of the body of canon law, the *Corpus iuris canonici*, and created the conditions for the great jurist-popes of the thirteenth century to build their system of pontifical rescripts and constitutions that shifted authority from the old canons to the new decretals.[17]

In the twelfth century the papacy had based some of its claim to control the empire upon two events: first upon the spurious Donation of Constantine, by which that grateful emperor, cured of leprosy by Pope Sylvester (314–335), was supposed to have given control of the West, including Rome, Italy, and some major islands, to the papacy, and, second, upon the papal transfer *(translatio)* of the empire from the Greeks to the Germans in the eighth century.[18] According to Honorius Augustodensis's codification in the *Summa gloria* of circa 1123, the pope set up and constituted the *regnum*, or earthly power, and chose its emperor; however, Honorius made no specific case for the papacy's divinely holding the authority of both swords, the temporal and the spiritual, and therefore he framed no assertion of the papacy's radical possession of temporal power and of thus being its original source.[19] Even though it was not, in Dante's time, recognized as a clumsy forgery, the Donation was not the main rock upon which the high papalists built a false foundation for their Church: in fact, it provided a most feeble and flawed basis for authority, as both the decretalists and Dante clearly understood (*Mon.* 3:10). To have any force or practical value, it depended, after all, upon the emperor's having first given his worldly rule over to the papacy: the root of such power would remain imperial. The Donation was fundamentally contradicted by the more substantial Melchisedech doctrine of universal power with which the Church replaced it.[20]

With the competent and businesslike Innocent III, pope from 1198 to 1216, came the climax of medieval ecclesiastical power and the zenith of papal claims to the feudal overlordship of the Roman see. For Innocent, the superiority of the papacy was self-evident: he was the Vicar of Christ who had said in Matthew 28:18 "All power is given to me in heaven and earth."[21] In a letter to the nobles of Tuscany ten months into his pontificate he embellished one of the favorite, novel images he had found (despised and refuted by Dante), that of the sun and the moon, as analogies of pontifical authority and royal power: "Now just as the moon derives its light from the sun and is indeed lower than it in quantity and quality in position and power, so too the royal power derives the splendor of its dignity from the pontifical authority." In 1201, in his letter *Solitæ benignitas*, he reminded Alexius III, the usurping emperor of Constantinople, that just as the soul excelled the body, so the pope's binding and loosing of souls transcended the empire's earthly jurisdiction, excepting nothing "whatsoever."[22]

Innocent took to heart, perhaps more than any other pope, the enormous charge laid upon him as he accepted the triple crown on February 22, 1198:

"Know that Thou art Father of princes and kings, Ruler of the world and on earth Vicar of our savior Jesus Christ." In his extraordinary coronation sermon he reasserted those words, magnifying the title applied to bishops and abbots, none other than "the Vicar of Jesus Christ, the successor of Peter," and thus set over nations, both "King of Kings and Lord of Lords" and "the intermediary between God and man: beneath God, above man: less than God, more than man." The pope exercised "fullness of power"; judging all men, he was judged by none.[23] In his letters he claimed to share authority with the deity, for the pope did not exercise the office of man, but that of the true God on earth.[24] He cut the Gordian knot of all counterclaims by insisting that the popes' right to judge the *regnum* in temporal affairs depended upon their duty to control the moral conduct of rulers *"ratione et occasione peccati,"* "by reason of, and in case of sin."[25] Since no man was without sin, this obviously meant limitless jurisdiction.[26]

Innocent gave his policy its definitive formulation in his decretal to the bishops of France, *Novit*, of April 1204, drawn up to defend his interference in the English-French controversies.[27] He was extraordinarily successful not only in expanding the frontiers of his own papal states in central Italy, but also in his spiritual bullying of the emperors and the rulers of the principal states of Europe into vassalage—all those which Barbarossa had earlier haughtily termed the "provincial kingdoms" of the empire—along with the realms of Britain and Scandinavia, and, especially, after the creation of the Latin Empire in Constantinople in 1204, those formerly under the Eastern Church. His recognition of many religious orders—Franciscans, Dominicans, Humiliati, Trinitarians, and Hospitalers of the Holy Spirit—not only crushed the hydra of heresy but was gradually to extend Church influence, particularly with Franciscan missions, to the far coast of China.[28]

Having long delayed his support for the imperial claims of Otto IV of Brunswick (elected in March 1198), he then backed him vigorously, only later to align himself with Otto's opposition, Philip of Swabia (elected in June 1198), the brother of Henry VI. Finally, after the murder of Philip on June 21, 1208, and left with the now anti-papal and apparently rivalless Otto, Innocent excommunicated him on March 31, 1211, and crowned Frederick II of Hohenstaufen, the emperor Henry VI's only son, as king of the Romans in 1212. His twenty-year-long declared crusade against the Cathar-Albigensian heretics in the south of France wiped out entire communities, hamlets, and cities; not even those seeking sanctuary at the feet of their parish priest as he said mass at the altar of Bézier Cathedral were spared.[29]

Justifying his intervention, *ratione peccati*, Innocent assumed the right to settle the feudal quarrels between King John of England and King Philip-Augustus of France. After the death of Philip-Augustus's second wife, Isabel d'Hainault, after years of negotiations he finally compelled the king to reconcile with his repudiated first wife, Ingeborg of Denmark, in 1213, having forbidden him to marry a third, Agnes of Meran. By later supporting Philip-Augustus and Frederick, he was able to realize victory over the deposed emperor Otto at Bouvines on July 27, 1214, to the satisfaction of his allies. After a quarrel over the acceptance of his close schoolfriend, Stephen Langton, as archbishop of Canterbury, in 1213, by means of interdict, excommunication, and deposition, he forced King John of England to recognize the papacy as the feudal overlord of the Crowns of England and Ireland in exchange for absolution, and thus wrested from England a tribute of one thousand marks sterling each year.[30] He attempted to depose King Sverre of Norway through both interdiction and excommunication, urging the rulers of Denmark and Sweden to rid Norway of "that limb of the Devil." He granted the Duke of Bohemia the hereditary title of king in gratitude for his support, sending him a scepter and a diadem along with the permission to mint his own coinage,[31] and urging him at first to assist and seek coronation from Emperor Otto IV. In 1205, Peter of Aragon made his act of vassalage to the pope for the kingdom of Aragon with Innocent's asserting the papal right of coronation and delegating it in the future to the archbishop of Tarragona. Under papal duress, Alfonso IX of Leon put away his wife whom he had married against ecclesiastical canons. After a long-drawn-out controversy, the heir of the adamant Sancho I of Portugal, Alfonso II, also bowed to Innocent's ecclesiastical authority in the question of the clergy's immunity from taxation.

In 1208 Innocent dispatched a Latin archdeacon to Demetrius, prince of the Albanians, who wished, with all his people, to join the Roman Church. Innocent expended much effort to win the Slavs and other peoples beyond the Balkans to his fold: he strengthened the new church in Livonia (Latvia, Estonia); to keep Kalojan, king of Bulgaria, and his bishops within the Western Church, he granted that king's request for the crown and the right to strike money. King Imre placed his kingdom of Hungary, which Gregory VII had apparently exempted from papal jurisdiction, under the pope's paternal protection and submitted to Innocent's extensive judgments in many family and state affairs. On June 15, 1315, King John of England, coerced by his barons, signed the *Magna Carta* at Runnymede, relieving their payments and allowing them a share in his power by permitting his tutelage by twenty-five of their number. Innocent was among the first to disapprove of the document as un-workable, ignominious, and evil. In November of that same year, however, no Bulgarian, Armenian, or Ruthenian bishops heeded the pope's invitation to attend his Lateran Council. Innocent's involvement in the tragically diverted Fourth Crusade against Constantinople, as with his victorious bloody war against the Cathars, which had ended in the triumph at Muret in 1213, gave rise to centuries of slander and legend.[32]

In short, we have a picture of the highest personal convictions wedded to high-handed political intransigence. Regardless of any modern quibbling over the canonistic and theological bases for the unprecedented extent of this busy interference, the fact remains that, in practice, Innocent III manifested a meticulous and panoramic preoccupation with policing temporalities.

His bull on imperial elections, *Venerabilem fratrem* (*Decretales* 1:6:34), of March 1202, addressed to the Duke of Zähringen, asserted that, although the election of the emperor fell to the imperial electors, to the pope belonged the right and authority of examining the person elected as king in the empire: *"ius et auctoritas examinandi personam electam in regem ad imperium ad nos spectat."* The institution of an emperor came under the sphere of papal authority both principally and finally, *"principaliter"* and *"finaliter"*: *"principaliter"* because of the *"translatio imperii"* (transfer of the empire) from the Greeks to the Germans in 800 A.D., and *"finaliter"* because the scrutiny, benediction, coronation, and investiture of the emperor were the pope's prerogatives.[33]

From the mid-thirteenth century the papacy became ever more embroiled in European politics. In cases of the breakdown of governmental authority in any area, church courts, in an effort to dispense justice to all, became, ever increasingly, the venue of last resort even in civil matters: temporal cases choked its institutions. Plaintiffs and defendants who disagreed with the decisions of civil courts took their suits to the papacy for redress. By 1234 with this emergence of ecclesiastical legal powers and a *de facto* papal monarchy, came the promulgation of new law books under the authority of Gregory IX (1227–1241) called the *Decretals*, with their own fresh set of glossators, and, finally, the Rota romana instituted by Urban IV (1261–1264), the special papal court to administer the flourishing and soon overwhelming business. Historians have observed that only one saint, the unfortunate Celestine V, arose from the Chair of Saint Peter in the thirteenth and fourteenth centuries, preoccupied as it was with the day-to-day business of drafting and executing canon law; in fact, through the pontificates of Innocent III (1198–1216), Gregory IX (1227–

1241), Innocent IV (1243–1254), Boniface VIII (1294–1303), Clement V (1305–1314), and John XXII (1316–1334), every pope of any historical effectiveness was a canon lawyer.[34]

The idea of the empire's control of all men and their affairs had dimmed with the culmination of the penance of Henry IV before Gregory VII at Canossa in 1077. But what earlier had seemed a usurpation of imperial right by the papacy had, through vehement assertion and use, become hierocratic[35] principal.

A great jurist came to restate and define the separation: Uguccione da Pisa, Hugutio Pisanus, or Ferrarensis, familiarly known as "Huguccio" to the canonists who abbreviated his name to a simple "H." Uguccione had been a professor of law at Bologna where Lotario de' Segni, later Pope Innocent III, had spent about two of his student years. Clement III had named him bishop of Ferrara in 1190, and Innocent III, esteeming his abilities, employed him on many missions as judge-delegate.[36] Ironically, however, after Uguccione's death in 1210, and especially in the second half of the thirteenth century, fate destined the great jurist's theories to aid the imperialist side.[37] Uguccione became the recognized codifier of the doctrine known as *"dualitas,"* or "dualism," holding that the ecclesiastical and the secular governments were of independent origin, both receiving their authority directly from God.[38] His early decretist followers elaborated theories of Church-State relations upon his work that were far different from those that the later decretalists developed after the 1250s—those decretalists whom Dante assails in the *Monarchia* (esp. in 3:3) and in *Paradiso* 9:133–135.[39] In his *Summa decretorum* (or *Summa super decreta*), Uguccione had personally concluded and taught, in contrast to other canonists, but just as Dante would later, that the emperor received his powers from the imperial electors as spokesmen of God (cf. *Mon.* 3:16:13); the empire was historically precedent to the papacy; neither power was subordinated to the other: "Here it can be clearly gathered that each power, the apostolic and the imperial, was instituted by God and that neither is derived from the other and that *the emperor does not have the sword from the apostle. . . . I therefore believe that the emperor does not hold his power of the sword and his imperial dignity from the apostolic power but from the princes through his election and from the people . . .* there was an emperor before there was a pope and an empire before a papacy."[40]

Uguccione held that where temporal authority recognized no power superior (*superioritas*) to itself, removal of the ruler belonged solely to the subjects of his power, just as in the Church, where in case of deviation from the true faith or because of an election tainted by simony, the deposition of the pontiff belonged to the faithful in Christ.[41] The jurist, however, moderated his theory significantly, for in practice he believed that no *earthly* power, even one that was divinely instituted, was without a judge superior to it. The emperor, though not receiving his temporal sword from the pope, could only assume his title after unction, confirmation, and an oath of loyalty to the pontiff.[42] Although the emperor was greater in temporal matters, this did not extend to any judgment over the pope.[43] Thus *ratione defectus iustitiæ*—there being no other recourse of justice from a higher authority—the pope was superior to any earthly ruler who had no other *temporal* ruler above him, and while subjects, or rather in the case of the emperor, the princes, had the power to *begin* the procedure of deposing an emperor, of accusing and convicting him, the pope alone had the ultimate jurisdiction to issue the sentence to remove him from office.[44] Uguccione confirmed the pontiff as ordinary judge, that is, judge of ultimate resort, not only in spiritual but in these temporal cases when no other redress or appeal existed. Although no other ecclesiastic could remove the error or infamy committed by a secular judge, that power did belong to the pope.[45] The main difference between Uguccione and later extreme canonists was that he saw both powers originating directly and separately from God, and remaining independent while in close collaboration.[46] These points are essential for our understanding of Dante's, ironically, conservative, aristocratic, and quite reactionary *Monarchia*.[47] Though eclectic in its emphases, the treatise is dependent upon Uguccione's thought. Curiously, though, historical reception has been mixed. The treatise's traditionality has appeared to some readers as being quite servile in its return to the more "Gelasian" position hinted at in *Monarchia* 3:16:17, while on the other, its other emphases have appeared to others as exceptionally radical, especially in the light of Guido Vernani's sarcastic fury and its fanatic proscription by John XXII's cardinal legate in Bologna.[48]

Uguccione's theories had been a subject discussed in Florence among the papalist Dominicans at Santa Maria Novella, perhaps in Dante's presence; Remigio de' Girolami, the lector of theology there, gives the pertinent passages from Uguccione's *Summa super decreto* (also entitled the *Summa decretorum*) in his *Contra falsos ecclesie professores* (ch. 22–23), citing, "The emperor indeed has his power from God alone as far as temporals are concerned, nor is he subject to the pope concerning them; there was an empire before there was an apostolate."[49] He unequivocally interprets Matthew 16 and 22 as dealing purely with spiritual matters: "Therefore, temporals, as temporals, are not under the authority of the pope principally and directly."[50] Remigio was never thoroughly persuaded, however, that the pope could not intervene *"causaliter"* (occasionally) and directly in temporal affairs, especially in the case of sin; and, as Florentine opinion moved toward an intransigent support of papal monarchy after 1305, Remigio turned fiercely to reject his earlier pro-dualist statements.[51]

Thus, expecting a flurry of ensuing controversy, Dante attends to the origin of imperial power as he had come to understand it—even amid those with whom he was later forced to disagree. In *Epistola* 5:5:17, the poet described God as the sole source from which all authority derived independently: *"a quo velut a puncto bifurcatur Petri Cæsarisque potestas"* (Him from whom, as from a point, the power of Peter and Cæsar doth bifurcate).[52] And the poet agrees with Uguccione in stressing the quotidian necessity of cooperation and mutuality between the powers. We note that the poet avoids any mention in the treatise of imperial anointing and coronation (soon to be brought into comically sordid disrepute by Ludwig IV after the poet's death) and merely dismisses the contingency of an emperor's deposition. Dante only allows a glimpse of the relationship between pope and emperor as implying any ultimate papal superiority almost as a necessary high point of reconciliation at the very end of his treatise. There he follows a tradition that never doubted the philosophical necessity of the spirit's superiority over the earthly; as all theologians, canonists, and publicists of any stripe—monarchist, imperialist, or papalist—allowed and repeated, the temporal was always *"quodammodo"* (in some way) under the spirit.[53]

Uguccione da Pisa's arguments for the independent origin of the two powers had already become a powerful weapon in the arsenal of the French publicists who supported the autonomy of Philip the Fair against the claims of Boniface VIII. Those defending a radical dual originism included the anonymous French authors of the *Quæstio disputata in utramque partem* (*For and Against Pontifical Power*) and the *Quæstio de potestate Papæ* (*An Enquiry into the Power of the Pope*), also entitled *Rex pacificus* (*The King of Peace*), and the eminent Dominican theologian John Quidort of Paris, who all penned their treatises circa 1302. The unnamed author of the first states adamantly "that the powers are distinct and that the pope does not have lordship over all temporals is proved, first, by philosophical arguments; second, by theological arguments; third, by canon law; fourth, by civil law."[54] John of Paris agrees: "The episcopal and temporal powers are distinct not only in themselves, but they are to be distinguished also by the subject in which they are found. And the emperor, having no superior over him, is greater in temporal matters, as the pope is in spiritual matters." He insists that "royal power existed in its own right in both principle and practice before papal power and there were kings before there were Christians in France."[55] Logic demanded that if the origins were independent, so were the goals of the two regimes. The French partisans, despite this, continued to give lip service to the superiority of the spiritual, as does Dante, despite the complete distinction between the two jurisdictions that led to those two consecutive ends.[56]

Some extreme publicists of the empire, however, were later to repudiate Uguccione's dualism even to the point of asserting, as did a later supporter of the *Monarchia*, the jurist and defender of Dante Bartolo of Sassoferrato (1314–1357), that anyone who rejected the superior lordship of the emperor was a heretic.[57] With imprecations, Marsiglio of Padua defined the logical culmination of the Aristotelian-Ghibelline position in the *Defensor Pacis* (anathematized in 1327 by John XXII) three years after Dante's death: the emperor's supremacy over the pope was absolute and civil happiness was "the best of the objects of desire possible to man in this world, and the ultimate aim of human acts"[58]—radical anti-Augustinian conclusions that the "theologus-poeta" Dante could never have accepted.

In the wake of Innocent III's (d. 1216) extensions of temporal activity, and after the demise of the House of Hohenstaufen in 1265, hierocrats had even more to gain than imperialists in rejecting Uguccione's substrative dualism, and they insisted on the concept of divine origin for the papacy alone, with the emperor receiving his total authority indirectly through the pope. By 1327, Guido Vernani could confidently state, as an unquestioned premise and conclusion of chapter 10 of his *De potestate summi pontificis*, that "the temporal power proceeds from God *through the medium* of the spiritual power."[59] Decretalists began to tar Uguccione and all those who followed him with Ghibellinism; Egidio Spiritale (d. ca. 1338), a canonist from Perugia, was one of the few decretalists courageous—or immoderate—enough in his *Libellus contra infedeles* to label Uguccione's dualism heretical.[60] That such a charge was also to threaten the *Monarchia* is thus far less surprising.

Although these later papal publicists cleaved brazenly to the decretals, theological arguments were also to hold a decisive power for all sides, and therein decretalists found an additional formidable weapon to refine and redeploy. In his influential *De Sacramentis* (*On the Sacraments*) of 1134, Hugh of St. Victor (died ca. 1141–1142, widely renowned as *"alter Augustinus,"* "the second Augustine," and one of the authors whom Dante most closely read and respected) had maintained the primacy of the papacy both temporally and chronologically, and had stated that the spiritual power was both the initiator and the judge of the temporal power:

The spiritual power has also to establish the earthly power in order for it to exist, and it has to judge it, if it has not been good. Indeed, [the spiritual power] itself was established first by God and when it goes astray it can be judged by God alone, just as it is written: "The spiritual man judges all things; and he himself is judged of no man [1 Cor 2:15]." Now, it is manifestly declared among that ancient people of the Old Testament where the priesthood was first established by God that spiritual power, in so far as it looks to divine institution, is both prior in time and greater in God's order. Wherefore, in the Church sacerdotal dignity still consecrates regal power, both sanctifying it through benediction and forming it through institution. If then, as the Apostle says, "He who blesses is greater, and he who is blessed less" [Heb 7], it is established without any doubt that earthly power which receives benediction from the spiritual is thought inferior by law.[61]

Hierocrats echoed Hugh of St. Victor's doctrine and his important scriptural backing down through the next century. Alexander of Hales (ca. 1186–1245), the English founder of the Franciscan school of theology, reproduced the popular text in his unfinished *Summa theologica*, claiming that the pope could judge rulers given his powers as Christ's Vicar.[62] Enrico Bartolomei da Susa (Henry of Susa, or Segusio) the extremist known as "Father of the Canons," "fount and monarch of laws," and "star and brilliant light of the *decreta*," redefined the Victorine's doctrine in his immense *Summa aurea*. He had become cardinal bishop of Ostia in 1261 (d. 1271), and was thus universally called "Hostiensis." Enrico Bartolomei was indeed that very "Ostiense" of *Paradiso* 12:82–84, whom Dante has St. Bonaventure condemn for "neglecting true manna" and venally grubbing after worldly matters.[63] As did all his colleagues, Hostiensis pressed into service the verse of Jeremiah 1:10, "I have this day set thee over nations and over kingdoms," as the authoritative Old Testament *locus* prefiguring the "commission" of the keys to St. Peter, and claimed that the verse gave the popes the power to depose kings.[64]

Dante's contemporary, the curialist and adviser to Boniface VIII, Giles of Rome,[65] abandons his own youthful, more moderate political theories dealt with so thoroughly in his lengthy treatise *De regimine principum (On the Rule of Princes)*,[66] to cite Hugh in his hastily composed *De ecclesia potestate (On Ecclesiastical Power)* of circa 1302: "As Hugh [of St. Victor] has made clear, the spiritual power must institute the earthly power and must judge whether it be good; and this could not be so unless it could plant and uproot it" (1:4:1–2).[67] The theologian James of Viterbo echoes the Victorine in his *De regimine christiano (On Christian Government)*, circa 1303.[68] Hugh's words were to resound again in Boniface's bull *Unam sanctam* of November 18, 1302, which claimed the temporal subjection of the kingdom of France by reason of jurisdiction over sin: "The spiritual power has to establish the earthly power and to judge it, if it be not good. . . . If therefore the earthly power err, it shall be judged by the spiritual power; if the lesser spiritual power err, it shall be judged by the higher; but if the supreme spiritual power err, it could be judged solely by God, not by man; of which the Apostle is witness, 'The spiritual man judgeth all things; and he himself is judged by no man.'"[69]

When the decretalists included *Unam sanctam* in the *Corpus iuris canonici*, they prefaced it with a typical Hugonian rubric: "All faithful of Christ, by necessity of salvation, are subject to the Roman Pontiff who has both swords [that is, the temporal and spiritual], judges all, but is judged by no one."[70] In 1327, a year or so before he read Dante's *Monarchia*, Guido Vernani had cited the whole passage from Hugh, verbatim and at length, in chapter 6 of his *De potestate summi pontificis*;[71] he concluded: "From these words of the aforesaid Doctor, it is clear that according to Divine Law, the empire is under the pope, both as far as its institution and as far as its deposition [*quantum ad destitutionem*] are concerned." By the year 1327, the emperor Ludwig's undoing had become the political and military priority of the Church.[72]

Thus, while Philip's men had been toiling in Paris, so in the years 1302–1303 and thereafter, there poured from the Roman curia and elsewhere a storm of treatises and pamphlets defending papal plenipotency. Giles of Rome courteously dedicated his *De ecclesia potestate (On Ecclesiastical Power)* to Boniface, and, in all likelihood, was the one who drew from that text to compose the bull *Unam sanctam* on the pope's behalf.[73] After Dante's exile, in the now Black Guelph Florence, the inconsistent theorist and orator Fra Remigio de' Girolami swung with public opinion, or, at least, with the most powerful, and hardened in his high-papalist views, now proclaimed from the pulpit of Santa Maria Novella the doctrine of Innocent IV and Clement V that the pope was not only the source of all secular authority but was himself the true emperor.[74] Distant also from the curia, the ambitious Fra Guido Vernani, in venerable Bologna and in provincial Rimini, aped the early success of Giles with his own *De potestate summi pontificis (On the Power of the Supreme Pontiff)* and a commentary on the *Unam sanctam*. James of Viterbo, who like Giles also piously dedicated his treatise *De regimine Christiano (On Christian Government)* to Boniface, concluded that the Church not only had total temporal jurisdiction, but was also, itself, the *state*, catholic and universal. As with other papalists, Vernani among them, James's view of the Church oscillated among many configurations and definitions. At once it was, or could be, as argument necessitated, not only the mystical Body of Christ, encompassing all the faithful, but all Creation itself; as required, it was also Christ's kingdom, the Church Militant and Triumphant, and, more narrowly, yet more grandiosely, an earthly government constituted by the ordained priesthood.[75] Most of all, he affirmed, like his peers, what was said in Innocent III's *Venerabilem fratrem*, that the pope must have the ultimate say in the appointment of any temporal sovereign. Besides James, another of Giles's younger colleagues, the prolific and prolix Agostino d'Ancona (ca. 1270 or 1273–1328, known later as "Agostino Trionfi" and "Augustinus Triumphus" in the sixteenth century), the chaplain and counselor to the Guelph kings Charles and Robert of Naples, assembled the longest and most indigestible body of extreme curialist theory in his *Summa de potestate ecclesiastica (Summa on Ecclesiatical Power)* and completed the treatise in 1326, one year before Vernani's *De potestate summi pontificis* and five years after Dante's death. Agostino again asserted that the pope, the *"verus Imperator,"* should himself both elect the temporal emperor *("per ipsum possit imperatorem eligere")*, and have full authority to depose him, just as Vernani also maintained that "the Supreme Pontiff can coerce the Emperor into obedience and punish him if disobedient, and depose him if he is pertinacious."[76] In fact, for Agostino d'Ancona, no imperial law was valid without the pope's approval. In short, he posited both as his founding principle and his foregone conclusion that: "it follows therefore that both spiritual and temporal power reside in the Supreme Pontiff."[77] His deliberations like those of his faction loop in reactionary pirouettes, endlessly repeating the claim of papal precedence in worldly affairs, which history was soon to curtail.[78]

Given Dante's obvious dependence on the French publicists, it is surprising that he makes not even a passing reference in the *Monarchia* to the question of the sovereignty of the national monarchies of France and England. Despite his vituperations of Boniface VIII in each of the three canticles of the *Commedia*,[79] the poet is silent too about the desperate events that had occurred between the issuance of Boniface's bull *Clericis laicos* of February 24, 1296, and the pope's death on October 11, 1303. The shameful episode at Anagni of September 7, 1303, shocked Europe, as violence triumphed in the quarrel between Philip the Fair and the pope.[80] With the obsession of trying Boniface before a general council of his realm—even, if necessary, perhaps, post mortem, propping his cadaver up in papal garb—the king abandoned all reverence and ordered the pope's arrest.[81] One thousand footmen and three hundred knights led by the king's minister Guillaume Nogaret, allied with the aggressively ambitious Sciarra Colonna, seized Boniface in the town of his birth, assaulted him, and held him captive, hastening the pope's demise within a month, thus clearing the way for new heirs to the throne of St. Peter pliant to the throne of France. The outrage revealed the fragility and impotence of the papacy.[82]

Clement V, pope from 1305 to 1314, succeeding the short reign of the unremarkable Benedict XI, sought to muster lost strength by removing the curia formally to Avignon in 1309, not foreseeing that its enfeebling "Babylonish Captivity" would endure there until 1378.[83] Although by birth a Gascon, earlier archbishop of Bordeaux, and thus a subject and vassal of the English king Edward I, Clement had been consecrated in Lyons in the ominous presence of Philip the Fair, an event symbolizing the new papal subservience to French interests.[84]

In 1316, the intemperate and politically minded Jacques Duèse assumed the papal throne at the age of seventy-two, taking the name John XXII. Duèse was a native of Cahors—a city whose very name Dante identifies with usury at *Inferno* 11:50—and the candidate and former chancellor of the ardent Guelph Angevin Robert III, "the Wise," of Naples.[85] With this ascension of the fiscally brilliant John, whose amazing vigor and tenacity belied his sickly emaciated appearance, and whose reign lasted thirteen years after the poet's death, there erupted the major dispute over the Church's possession of temporal wealth: the truculent pope became immediately enmeshed in the quarrels splitting the Minorite Order over St. Francis's rule of apostolic poverty. By the bulls *Sancta Romana* of December 30, 1317, and *Gloriosam Ecclesiam* of January 23, 1318, declaring the Fraticelli, Beghards, Bizoches, and Brethren of the Life of Poverty excommunicated, John XXII suppressed the Franciscan Spiritual party; from the Franciscan chapter in Perugia, in 1323, he finally condemned as heretical the dogma of the absolute poverty of Christ and his Apostles held by the majority of Franciscans. The pope's intransigence made many charge that he opposed the very Gospels and was openly flaunting the avarice and corruption of the curia. The moderate Friars Minor, the Conventuals, acquiesced, but many of the zealous and militant among the Spirituals of the order, the "Fraticelli," revolted.[86] In Marseilles in 1317, after having tried twenty-five recalcitrants, John's Inquisition relinquished four of the most obdurate to the secular arm to be burned at the stake as heretics in May 1318.[87] The majority of Franciscans made obeisance to the pope by 1325, but scores of Minorites, among them the minister general Michael of Cesena and the philosopher William of Ockham (d. 1347), bolted to the protective Nuremburg court of Ludwig of Bavaria, whose 1314 election as Holy Roman Emperor the papacy was never to recognize.

While Innocent III had claimed that the Church was the supreme court of appeal in any imperial vacancy, Innocent IV and Hostiensis had developed this claim into a specific declaration that the pope, since he created the universal emperor and was himself the source of imperial power, thus logically not only retained the right to administer the empire when the emperor died or was deposed but actually succeeded the emperor in that event: *"Vacante regno et imperio succedit papa"* (When a kingdom and the empire are vacant, the pope succeeds).[88] The extreme claim became a cliché: in 1303 James of Viterbo takes for granted that "the Supreme Pontiff can intervene in temporal matters more directly, as is clear from the fact that he can exercise an immediate temporal jurisdiction when the Empire is vacant." By 1326 Agostino Trionfo would merely reiterate it as accomplished fact.[89] With his notorious decretal *Si fratrum*, written in mid-April and promulgated on March 31, 1317, John XXII had already declared the imperial seat vacant and asserted the power of the papacy to administer it as his hierocrats had set forth. In the words of the preamble it still bears in the *Corpus iuris canonici, Si fratrum* commands "that no one should retain, assume or reassume the title of Vicar of the Emperor or any other office whatsoever."[90] Although the issue was far from being a religious one, as we can read in the text printed at the end of this volume, the bull proclaimed excommunication for any who infringed the Church's right. By December 16, 1317, canonical proceedings were opened against the three major military lords of northern Italy, Can Grande della Scala of Verona; Matteo Visconti, who had assumed the title duke of Milan; and Passarino (Rainaldo) Bonaccolsi of Mantua. Emperor Henry VII's lifetime appointment of Dante's patron, Can Grande della Scala, as imperial vicar of Verona and Vicenza was thus in jeopardy.[91] On April 6, 1318, John excommunicated the three Ghibelline tyrants.[92] And on December 6, 1318, the papal court confirmed the charges against them and once more gave them the two months notice, as stipulated by the bull, to appear under pain of interdiction.[93] On June 17, 1320, the pope ordered his cardinal legate Bertrand du Poujet, then in Asti, to promulgate the excommunications against the rebels; in particular, the Lord of Verona, for naming himself "vicar," was now suspected of heretical depravity.[94] Can Grande had long resolved to resist and fight the injunction as necessary. Dante openly flouted the strictures of *Si fratrum* in the dedication of his *Epistola ad Canem Grandem* (*Letter to Can Grande; Epistola* 10 [13]), dating from the midst of the controversy, in its opening words: "To the magnificent and most victorious Lord, the Lord Can Grande della Scala, *Vicar-General of the most holy principality of Cæsar* in the city of Verona, and town of Vicenza."[95] And in 1220 the true measure of the poet's loyal tenacity emerges: on Sunday, November 20, two and a half months after Can Grande's defeat at Padua on August 26, 1320, where the great general was wounded and forced to flee, Dante was again to reaffirm his patron's claim to the title of imperial vicar, noting, at the end of his address on the *Questio de aqua et terra*, that his speech had taken place "under the dominion of the unconquered lord Can Grande in the name of the Sacrosanct Roman Empire."[96] Dante's position has hardened as he honors the empire not just with the normal *"sanctum"* (holy) but with the epithet *"sacrosanctum,"* the prerogative of the Church. We can imagine the long, militant applause. Dante's moving tribute to his patron in *Paradise* 17:76–91, whether completed before or after the *Questio,* attests to the continuing firmness of their mutual affection. Amid a political struggle generally fought without adherence to genuine principles, Dante thus became not merely an intellectual dissident, but a partisan in the construction of a Ghibelline ideology. From his refuge in Ravenna he saw his friend and former patron in dire need of moral, intellectual, and legal help; and thus, already a learned philosopher, theologian, and poet, he became a logician and canon lawyer to enter the arena as champion of the empire: he drafted the *Monarchia* to refute the claim of papal jurisdiction over temporal affairs.

## CHAPTER 2

# Dante in the Eye of the Storm

## THE LOGICIAN AND THE PROPHET

We know from the poet's affirmation in *Monarchia* 1:12 that he had, by the time of its writing, completed the *Paradiso* at least up to canto 5:22 where he had dealt with free will, *"de la volontà la libertate"*: "This liberty, or this principle of all our liberty, is the greatest gift to human nature conferred by God—as I have already said in the *Paradiso* of the *Comedy*." As recent scholars have concluded, we cannot disregard the remark or treat it, as many editors once did, as a mere scribal interpolation.[1] The passage, attested by all the manuscripts, is the only concrete internal evidence that we possess for dating the *Monarchia's* composition post-1314 and, most compellingly, for its completion in the last months of 1318.

Leaving the earlier political fervidness of the *Epistles* written in support of Henry VII's descent into Italy for coronation as Holy Roman Emperor (1310–1313), and the elegaic, tragic, and, occasionally, fulminating verses of the *Commedia*, the reader approaching this treatise is struck by Dante's authorial strategy of divorcing it as far as possible from the contingencies of contemporary history.[2] Except for one cause célèbre, the reference in *Monarchia* 3:16:14 to the unremitting controversy (1314–1356) caused by the split among the German electors in 1314,[3] the treatise differs from most of his works by its shrouding of references to contemporary affairs. Nowhere does the poet identify himself. No central players on the political scene, past or present, such as Innocents III or IV, Gregory IX, Frederick II of Hohenstaufen (d. 1250), Henry VII of Luxembourg, Boniface VIII, Nicholas III, Clement V, or John XXII ever appear directly. Most extraordinary is the absence of any reference to the strife that Henry VII had met in unsuccessfully asserting his overlordship over King Robert III, "the Wise," of Naples to gain full imperial power.[4] Reduced to accepting his crown from a bishop other than the pope in the "Sancta Sanctorum" chapel of the burned-out basilica of St. John the Lateran as a result of King Robert's machinations, Henry had ultimately lost his quest to be recognized as *"dominus mundi,"* "lord of the world," as the law books haughtily proclaimed. By the event of his untimely death at Buonconvento in 1313, he had failed to maintain his jurisdiction as emperor over the different communes and kingdoms that made up the Holy Roman Empire. Dante passes in silence over both the *Pastoralis cura,* Pope Clement V's bull that formally repudiated the supremacy of the medieval empire over the papal curia,[5] and passages of the *Corpus juris civilis* that validated kings of new national states as *de facto* and *de jure* independent of the emperor.[6] Although in Dante's own lifetime the emperor had ceased to be *"lex animata,"* law and justice personified,[7] the poet likewise ignores his contemporaries' bewailing of the juristic and actual—material and fiscal—weakness that threatened the empire's imminent demise.

In addition to the syllogistic method, we catch in the *Monarchia's* more tempered style other results of the poet's study of Aristotle in Moerbeke's staid translations, along with his reading of the dispassionate Latin commentaries of St. Thomas Aquinas.[8] He takes to heart Aristotle's specific warning in the *Nicomachean Ethics* that immature emotions can render the study and experience of political science profitless.[9] Most especially, Dante reflects the more rigidly impersonal tractates of the decretalists that had clearly been a constant study, perhaps from the inception of his exile. Critics have noted that the prose of the *Monarchia* bears an intimate similarity to the style and content of the *Epistola* 10 [13], the *Letter to Can Grande,* in which Dante dedicates the last canticle of the *Commedia* to his patron in April or May of 1320.[10] Wielding this polemical pretense of aloof objectivity, the author manipulates his reader into a sense of a text discarnate, creating the impression of a message beyond time, derived from man's divine reason and inspired by God's revelation. The author's own tactics thwart all historians' and critics' struggles to place the treatise at a date different from that indicated by the allusion to the fifth canto of the *Paradiso.*

But this calmer tone is one of maturer degree. Dante's aim in the *Monarchia* is overtly propagandist, as it was in his fiery political *Epistolæ.*[11] In those lay encyclicals he had not only employed the powerful rhetoric he had learned from the republican Brunetto Latini and the imperial letters of Pier della Vigna, but he imitated the papal decretalists' compulsive reliance upon biblical quotations and exaggerated their vehement tone as a partisan antidote.[12] In the *Monarchia* he again exploits the public nature of his rebuttal of papal claims—he will hurl his wicked and lying opponents from the arena of this debate "while the world looks on."[13] Indeed, the alternately imprecating, adoring, and imploring frenzy of those early political letters disappears in the *Monarchia*, and the poet generally maintains a studied detachment. In books 2 and 3, however, Dante does rise to the patriarchal pitch of a weary Old Testament prophet and psalmist, and at other places to a magisterial irritation and sarcasm.[14]

The other characteristic of the *Monarchia* is its dependence, especially in book 2, not only upon the Bible but even more firmly upon the classical record of pagan Rome interpreted by Roman epic poets and historians, between whom—oddly, only for the modern reader—the writer does not distinguish. He makes no mention of the Jews being the Chosen People in the times before Christ. Perhaps mindful of Pope Nicholas III's promulgation of 1278 in which the Romans of his day are titled *"gens sancta, populus electus"* (a holy race, a chosen people), the poet argues that God's attention and will manifested itself in the Romans' pursuit of dominion,[15] identifying ancient Rome with his own cherished anachronistic ideals. He looks back to a Golden Age of a temporal rule on earth, not, as did the hierocrats, to Christ's commission of St. Peter as foundation stone and head of the Church, but to the pagan dominion of the Romans, which God the Father had ordained and which his Son had humbly approved in the flesh.

St. Augustine of Hippo (381–430) had most persuasively propagated the early Christian Fathers' view that political life had been corrupted by mankind's inherited sin from the Fall. Government was a divine *poena et remedium peccati*, a coercive, punishing institution, a remedy to provide minimum order amid a world of sin. A prince, Christian or not, could only struggle to mitigate human drives for greed and power and to enforce a modicum of justice on the now errant but future damned, so that those of the Heavenly City, the future blessed, who dwelt beside the wicked on earth, could achieve their goal of eternal glory.[16] Aristotle, on the contrary, knew nothing of original sin and was concerned solely with the mortal happiness of the individual and the earthly welfare of political society. And although not overly sanguine concerning the creation of the perfect state,[17] the philosopher saw the possibilities of an education in virtue fautored by the polis. Man was a *zoon politikon*, a political animal, a creature made for the affairs and natural growth of the city-state.[18] Aristotle's treatment of some of the 158 forms of government in fourth-century B.C. Greece provided a shimmering contrast to feudalism and flashed a beam of recognition and opportunity to fourteenth-century theorists of the city-state in Italy. St. Thomas Aquinas had labored much to combine these two traditions and provide a synthesis for politics and law, approaching the formidable task of squaring Aristotle's immanent preoccupation with Augustine's transcendental goal through the principle that "grace does not contradict nature but perfects it." In Aristotle's concept of final causes Thomas had discovered the possibility of an answer: God creates man and all things so that they function for their perfect fulfillment.[19] Man is thus teleologically drawn by God to his goal of perfect beatitude. Thomas thus found Aristotelian consonance with Augustine's assertion in *Confessions* 1:1, "For You have made us for Yourself and our hearts shall not rest till they rest in You." In his first chapter of *De regimine principum* (*On Princely Government*), Aquinas declares that "man . . . has a destiny to which all his life and activities are directed." He adds to Aristotle's definition, saying that "man is naturally *a social* and political animal, destined more than other animals to live in a community," for, unlike other animals, his private resources are insufficient for the fullness of human life. For this God gave man reason and the gift of communication for the formation of a community fit to provide both his collective and his individual needs. The ruler directs this community of free men, masters of their own actions, toward the common good. The state thus has a positive role: the goals of nature and grace concur. In this the Aristotelians who dwelt in Florence—among them, not only Dante but Remigio de' Girolami and Tolomeo da Lucca—all agreed.[20]

Like the latter, in Thomas's wake, Dante also turns Augustine's negative interpretation of history in *The City of God* against itself. Whereas the Bishop of Hippo, with his follower, Paulus Orosius, writing in the early Christian tradition, had used pagan history as a series of negative exempla "against the pagans," seeing in Roman dominion over the known world only *"latrocinia magna,"* or "a great piracy,"[21] Dante records his own change of mind in the first chapter of *Monarchia* 2: "I indeed once used to wonder how the Roman people had been, without resistance at all, appointed to rule over the whole globe of the earth. . . . I judged that they had obtained this not *de jure* but merely by force of arms. But when I fixed the eyes of my mind to its innermost part, I came to understand by the most effective signs that divine providence had accomplished it." In spite of this, however, Dante agrees with Augustine in considering Roman history as a divine and not a human institution, one capable, as Augustine had affirmed, of valid inference and interpretation by men and recorded so that they might interpret God's actions in history and thus learn and teach the truth of God's plan.[22] History is for the poet—and thus central to his project of the *Monarchia,* and especially of book 2—a record of God's *positive* intervention to bring peace to the world in the fullness of time. Christ put his seal upon Rome's authority by his birth, by his enrollment in the census, and by his submission to its judges (*Mon.* 1:16, 2:11:3–7): as the poet had said in the *Epistola* 8:2 (*Epistle to the Italian Cardinals*), "Rome ... after so many triumphs and glories, Christ by word and deed confirmed the empire of the world."[23]

### DANTE'S FORENSIC PROCEDURE

By the thirteenth and fourteenth centuries, the employment of a severe technical method distinguished the treatment of philosophical and theological enquiry. Precise development of thought and rigor of expression followed a formalized deductive—syllogistic—procedure. As with the Ptolemaic system in astronomy, medieval and Renaissance scholars considered Aristotelian logic propædeutic and accepted it beyond question.[24] Francesco Petrarca was often to censure logic as a hobbling obsession of the Scholastics, yet in other instances he recommended it as a preparation for philosophical studies: he decried those who piqued themselves as "philosophers" and yet were no more than logicians, "shamelessly growing old in a study proper to schoolboys."[25] Francis Bacon attempted to undermine the foundations of Aristotelian reasoning in his *Novum Organon* of 1620, yet in 1787, in the final revised version of his *Critique of Pure Reason,* Immanuel Kant thought he could still claim that logic had not made a single advance since Aristotle's *Prior Analytics.*[26] Aristotelian logic, or what passed for it, held sway until, perhaps, the turn of the twentieth century. While we tend to view it in the twenty-first century, amid our extraordinary technical advances in symbolic language, perhaps not as wrong or misguided, but as simply inadequate, we cannot help finding it also overly abstruse and not a little tiresome.[27]

At the turn of the fourteenth century, Aristotle's *Organon* (I use anachronistically the name given to his six treatises on logic and dialectic after 1502) was the indispensable tool that underlay all areas of knowledge.[28] The philosopher had been the first to systemize logical questions fundamental to science by treating them apart from other divisions of philosophy.[29] His individual treatises comprising the *Organon* encompassed the field: the *Categoriæ* (*The Categories*), a treatise on the ten primary classes into which things are divided;[30] *De*

*Interpretatione (On Interpretation)*, on terms and propositions: the noun, the verb, the complete sentence, oppositions between contrary and contradictory propositions; the *Analytica priora (Prior Analytics)*, on inference or deduction; the *Analytica posteriora (Posterior Analytics)*, on logical analyses of science: how arguments demonstrate truth from statements that are certain; the *Topica (Topics)*, a handbook on the rules and method of dialectic reasoning if demonstrative proofs are unavailable; and *De sophisticis elenchis (Sophistical Refutations)*, on fallacious reasoning. Only the small treatise by Porphyry (Porphyrius, 233–304 B.C.), entitled the *Isagoge*, or the *Introduction to the Categories of Aristotle*, had been added to Aristotle's achievement.[31]

The *Categories* and *De Interpretatione* by Anicius Manlius Severinus Boethius (ca. A.D. 480–524/526), and that author's translations of the *Prior Analytics* and the *Posterior Analytics*, his three commentaries—on the *Categories (De sillogismis cathegoricis)*, the translation of and commentary on Porphyry's *Isagoge*, and the commentary on Cicero's *Topica (In topica Ciceronis* and *De topicis differentiis)*—and a series of short monographs on logic, including the *De hypotheticis syllogismis*, were to be the slim central core of logic texts, later known as the *"logica vetus"* (*"l'arte vecchia,"* or "the old art," as Dante calls it in *Conv.* 2:13:12) used by students and scholars of Western Europe from the sixth century on.

With the rediscovery of the rest of Aristotle's numerous works after the twelfth century, however, the West obtained an encylopædic outline of all known areas of knowledge and a whole new basis for university curricula. By the 1230s new Latin versions of his logical writings along with those of his Arab commentators, Avicenna (Ibn Sina, 980–1037) and Averroës (Ibn Rushd, 1126–1189), became widely available, and Scholastics began to build their system on stronger foundations. The *"logica nova"* (*"l'arte nuova,"* "the new art") then comprised Aristotle's two *Analytics*, his own *Topics*, and the *Sophistical Refutations*. Aristotle became "the master of Philosophers" (*Conv.* 4:8:15), "the master and guide of human reason" (*Conv.* 4:6:8), "the master of those who know" (*Inf.* 4:131). In consequence, for Dante and his contemporaries, Aristotle's syllogistic inference was equivalent to logic itself: there was no other. And while logic had its most powerful effect upon theology, it also formed the foundation of politics, grammar, rhetoric, and law, all the disciplines in which Dante roots his *Monarchia*.[32]

The most important effect of the Aristotelian conquest with the *"logica vetus,"* synthesized by Peter Abelard (ca. 1079–ca. 1142) and developed by his followers in the 1130s, had already been the institution and habit of dialectic, disputation, or litigation on any issue of importance; Scholasticism itself became identified with the practice of confronting apparently contradictory texts. At the end of the twelfth century logic, after the reintroduction of the lost treatises, when dialectic flourished as *"logica nova,"* debate took center stage; the University of Paris fully accepted its application in Scholastic theology. Especially with the reintroduction of the *De sophisticis elenchis,* terminist logic began to center upon the doctrines of fallacy.

Opposition at Paris to stem the tide of Aristotelian studies because of possible conflicts with Christian truth ultimately failed, but not without considerable upheaval. Despite St. Thomas Aquinas's efforts to demonstrate the compatibility of Greek thought with Christian revelation, such thinkers as Siger of Brabant (ca. 1240–1284) had held that both must be true, even if their conclusions led to contradictory results. This concept frightened the Church: in 1270, Etienne Tempier, bishop of Paris, condemned thirteen of Siger's propositions, and in 1277, he reiterated the ban, adding another two hundred and nineteen, including twenty that had been defended by St. Thomas, who had died three years earlier. Despite the fact that the Arab commentator Averroës held some views inimical to Christianity and even to his own Islam, his superb commentary on Aristotle became so major a guide to the philosopher in the schools that he was known simply by his honorific title "the Commentator." Dante, indeed, placed him in Hell, but provided an honored position for him within the Nobile Castello along with Aristotle and Virgil in Limbo, discoursing among those without faith and those unbaptized (*Inf.* 4:144); the Averroist Siger of Brabant he lauds and places in Heaven among the other great Doctors of the Church (*Par.* 10:136–138).[33] Such treatises as St. Albertus Magnus's *De unitate intellectus contra Averroistas (On the Unity of the Intellect against the Averroists)* (1256); St. Bonaventure's sermons; St. Thomas Aquinas's *De unitate intellectus contra Averroistas (On There Being Only One Intellect, Against the Averroists)* of 1270, and his earlier *Summa contra gentiles* of 1259–1264; and Giles of Rome's *Errores philosophorum (Errors of the Philosophers)* (ca. 1280–1290) had, amid stormy controversy, endeavored to solve the problems, particularly concerning Averroës's denial, or at least, ambiguity, on the immortality of the soul, by simply acknowledging and listing the Arab's philosophical errors as a warning.[34] By the beginning of the fourteenth century, such studies, profiting from William of Moerbeke's new translations of Aristotle from the original Greek (after 1263) and from St. Thomas Aquinas's twenty years of meticulous commentaries, were intended to preserve Aristotle's thought from any Arabianized, Neoplatonist interpretation inimical to Christianity.

While reading the *Monarchia* and the *Refutation,* we can reflect that, while the theologian-jurist Guido Vernani could confidently assume that all of Aquinas's writings were in the main orthodox, Dante had been intelligently and reverently digesting St. Thomas's thought long before Thomas's canonization in July 18, 1323 (two years after the poet died). Dante's argumentative and interpretative amplifications from the great Dominican thinker are essential for our understanding of the conservative erudite nature of his treatise. The contrast, therefore, between the two isolated interlocutors of the *Monarchia* debate can thus come into clear ironic focus: the daring intuition of Dante stands out against Vernani's derivative complacency. Whenever it suits him, as the friar boasts, he "scoffs with confidence, scrutinizes . . . and . . . demolishes" (*Rep.*, Dedication 6), even blithely and capriciously ignoring the times when the poet meticulously adheres to the methods, thought, and distinctions of the authorities he employs.

In dialectic, exercised as lively *disputatio,* the aim of participants, following strict, obligatory norms, was to continue debate, to find inconsistencies, and to make wrangling distinctions ad infinitum. In every field dialectic became vitriolic: polemicists scored points by attending to abstractions often quite divorced from concrete experience. We must remember that the custom of such contentiousness was to characterize science beyond the time of Galileo. The controversies that engaged the living Dante and those that prompted the severe censures in Vernani's *Refutation* after the poet was safely—and, perhaps, for Vernani, annoyingly—dead, certainly pose no exception.

In *Convivio* 2:12:2–7, the poet tells us that he frequented "the schools of the religious" and "the disputations of the *filosofanti.*" At the two major *studia* in Florence, at the Franciscan convent of Santa Croce, and, perhaps more so, at the *studium* of the Dominican Church of Santa Maria Novella during the 1290s,[35] Dante absorbed theology and philosophy and, especially, obtained a thorough Schoolman's knowledge of Aristotle's *Nicomachean Ethics* and acquired a passing acquaintance with the *Politics.* He assimilated dialectic not only through the writings of the Arab commentators, but also, and in a more digested way, through the works of Thomas Aquinas and Siger of Brabant. Given the plentiful number of extant copies of Boethius, Porphyry, and Aristotle's *Old Logic* and *New Logic* from Dante's time now in Florentine libraries, we know that they were found on the shelves at Santa Croce, and, from the records of lectures offered at Santa Maria Novella, we can obviously conclude that they were there too for ready consultation.[36]

After first seeing dialectic as veiled and difficult (*Conv.* 2:13:12),[37] Dante began to see the subject gleam when he experienced his first exposure to Peter of Spain's popular commentary on Aristotle's *Prior Analytics*,[38] the *Summulæ logicales*, and to digest the simple maxims to which that master reduced the complicated system of the syllogism.[39] Recalling his efforts to master the *Summulæ*'s twelve books, in *Paradiso* 12:134–35 he celebrates Peter's placement in the Heaven of the Sun amid the sages: *Pietro Ispano, / lo qual giù luce in dodici libelli* (Peter of Spain, who down below shines in twelve books).

The author of that primer, born Pedro Juliano Rèbolo in Lisbon, rose in the Church to reign as Pope John XXI from 1276 to 1277. In fact, the most eminent and daunting experts in the field populate Dante's intellectual world, and especially those whom he sees in opposition. Among them are Giles of Rome, the prior general of the Augustinians and archbishop of Bourges, who penned a commentary on the *Posterior Analytics*, and his younger follower, Agostino d'Ancona, professor of theology at Paris and regent of the Augustinian Studium Generale, who was to write both the *Scriptum seu expositio Analyticorum Priorum Aristotelis* (*Exposition on Aristotle's Prior Analytics*) and the now lost *Commentarium in libros Analyticorum Posteriorum Aristotelis* (*Commentary on Aristotle's Posterior Analytics*).[40] Thus as Dante girds himself to refute papal encroachments in the *Monarchia*, he is fully aware that major defenders of hierocracy have been, and still are, towering experts in the field of logic. Facing such odds, he strides into the wrestling ring for the championship.

Thus the *Monarchia* is, as it had to be, an outstanding example of Aristotelian thought, proceeding from a first principle (each of the three books proceeds thus) and developing topics discussed in a concatenation of polysyllogisms consisting of prosyllogisms (syllogisms to form fundamental premises), syllogisms, and episyllogisms (syllogisms borrowing premises to deduce corollary consequents) building one upon the other, as the conclusion of one becomes the premise of the next.[41] These deductions may often surprise our modern uninitiated eyes as rather odd—not because Dante works them out invalidly, but because we judge his premises as not merely utopian or outdated but, for us, unsound. Indelibly central to the *Monarchia* is his cherished ideal of a paragon monarch-judge of the world, a "DXV" or "515" in an Eden regained (*Purg.* 33:43), untainted by ignorance and concupiscence (*Mon.* 1:11), one who would thus be, according to the poet's polemics, "the purest subject for justice among mortals."[42] Dante's hope was chiliastic and he fully knew the impossibility of its realization without divine intervention since in theology these two flaws constituted the very postlapsarian condition of man, the very *vulneratio naturæ,* the "wounding of man's nature," sullying all men with the sole exception of Christ.[43] Since scarcely few of us, studying the cataclysms of the last century, could entertain the idea of a world ruled by a single potentate, to be fair to Dante's reasoning we can only put aside our own horizon of expectations in political thought with toleration and try as best we can to view his millenialism and methodology from a fourteenth-century perspective.[44]

The syllogistic method dominated all contemporary compendiums of logic, though few hands found it conducive to the development of an engaging writing style or to original perception. While its scientific advantages are clear, its literary limitations are unavoidably tedious. It is remarkable how Dante masters its clumsiness in the *Monarchia.*

The schools taught the syllogism, or "deduction," as a process of inference by which, from two given propositions, one could proceed to a third proposition whose truth followed from these as a necessary consequence. For example (in *barbara* mood), "All humans are mortal; all Americans are humans; ergo, all Americans are mortal." Or, to put it in formal terms: to argue validly, one must deduce and support the conclusion of any syllogism by two premises. The first of these, called the major premise (*major propositio:* e.g., "All humans are mortal"), contains the major term (C; *terminus maior:* e.g., "mortal") that is the predicate of the conclusion. The second premise, the minor premise (*minor propositio*), contains the minor term (B; *terminus minor:* e.g., "Americans") that is the subject of the conclusion. The "middle term" (A; *terminus medium*) must be common to both, and that term ("humans" above, actually used as a principle) is excluded from the conclusion—that is, in the simplest form, all *A* (middle term) is *C* (major term); all *B* (minor term) is *A*; therefore, all *B* (minor term) is *C* (major term).

Error enters, for example, if there are more than three terms in the first two premises. This violation of the basic rule of structure of the syllogism is called "the fallacy of four terms" (*quaternio terminorum*);[45] for example, were I to use a word for the middle term in a double or ambiguous sense, I would actually be surreptitiously introducing a fourth term (and thus changing my basic principle) to produce an invalid consequent. For example, if I say, "Whatever is right is useful; only one of my hands is right; therefore only one of my hands is useful," I am using the word "right" in two different senses in the premises. I have therefore used more than three terms and my syllogism is not categorically genuine.

We shall see below how Dante reveals the formal errors in his opponents' arguments through a detailed examination of the contents of the *Monarchia*. Dante charges that his adversaries would habitually commit not only the elementary fallacy of four terms (three times, in fact, in *Mon.* 3:4:22, 3:5:3, and 3:7:3.),[46] but also far more egregious errors, such as that of confusing accidents with substances (*fallacia accidentis;* 3:4:12–15, 3:12:3), of taking "a noncause as a cause—(*fallacia secundum non causam ut causam;* 3:5:1–5),[47] or of erroneously applying (in the language of logicians, "distributing") terms (3:8:6). In many instances Dante's arguments are so professionally convincing and effective that Guido Vernani will find it easier not to respond. For our part, however, we must not forget that *the syllogisms that the poet ascribes to his adversaries are actually of his own fabrication*—straw men he sets up only to demolish—and realize that the literal-minded friar from Rimini, despite his own warnings in the *Refutation*'s dedication to Graziolo de' Bambaglioli, totally succumbs himself to the poet's mesmerizing fictions not in terza rima, but in the awkward rhythms of logic. Especially in book 2, we will see how Dante's clever use of the enthymeme lays a minefield of rhetorical ploys and diversions for his unwary opponents; his craft permits him to win his points against those such as Vernani even post mortem.

## THE PERILS OF POSTHUMOUS BURNING

At the age of fifty-six, during the night of September 13–14, 1321, the poet died in the odor of sanctity. We do not know what caused his death; the unfounded guess that it was malaria is probably the result of the historian Filippo Villani's attempt to make a condign parallel with the tragic death of his first friend, Guido Cavalcanti. Dante had served that summer, perhaps from the end of July or the beginning of August, as part of an embassy on behalf of his last patron, Guido da Polenta, to Doge Giovanni Soranzo, trying to quell the differences and small skirmishes that had flared up between the two city-states.[48] As Giorgio Petrocchi observes, Dante had wished to demonstrate in his senior years that he was a man of peace (the principle of the *Monarchia;* cf. 1:4:5 and 3:16:16–17). During his life, because of the powerful message of his "sacred poem"—whose lines, so Petrarch complained, were everywhere alive even upon the lips of society's unwashed members—the poet had been popularly considered one headed directly for the glory of Heaven. Boccaccio informs us that Guido Novello da Polenta, Dante's last patron, arranged a contest for the finest epitaph in his honor among the mourning poets of Romagna.

The real threat posed by the *Monarchia* came to be sensed only later in the papacy of John XXII when, suddenly, a storm broke against the great Florentine to threaten his memory with false charges of heresy. During the Church's shameful politically motivated campaign in Lombardy and Romagna, both Dante's works and the poet's very remains were to be imperilled by the flames.

On July 23, 1319, John XXII appointed as papal legate in Lombardy a young compatriot and graduate in decretal law whom he had elevated to the key cardinalate-bishopric of Ostia, the capable Bertrand du Poujet (ca. 1280–1352). By July 10, 1319, or at least by June 1320,[49] the pope had dispatched him to the peninsula on a crusade to "punish the heretics according to the laws of Frederic II." The infamous law in the *Liber Augustalis* of 1231, prepared for the emperor by his logothete and chief justice Pier della Vigna, declared that heretics "committed to the flames should be burned alive in the sight of the people."[50] The cardinal's mission was, in other words, to crush the Lombard Ghibellines whom the pope had excommunicated the year before, to bring their leaders to trial for heresy, and, if possible, to have them consigned to the stake publicly by the secular authorities. He was thus to ensure the victory of Guelph forces during the propitious vacancy of the imperial throne that his close familiar and protector John XXII had himself conveniently declared.

In February 1327, Ludwig IV of the Bavarian house of Wittelsbach began belated preparations to receive the crown in Rome in the face of the inveterate hostility of the Holy See. Ludwig's election had been messy, as were his sundry coronations. He had been chosen long before on October 20, 1314, by a clear majority of five of the seven German electors, the very day after Frederick the Fair of Austria had been chosen by only two, to wit, Henry, the archbishop of Cologne, and Rudolf, count palatine of the Rhine. Amid the official discord, both candidates had been crowned king of the Germans on November 25, 1314, with Ludwig consecrated in the traditional place, Aix-la-Chapelle, but by the untraditional archbishop of Mainz,[51] and with Frederick anointed, untraditionally, in the convent of the Friars Minor in Bonn, but, as tradition warranted, by the archbishop of Cologne.[52] The substance of the conflict can best be represented by John XXII's first threat of excommunication against Ludwig, dated October 8, 1323. The process listed Ludwig's three offences: first, that he had dared to assume his royal title without papal approval, although his election had been *in discordia;* second, that he had undertaken administrative actions in the realm and the empire despite the fact that the latter seat was vacant; and, third, that he had shown favor both to "Galeazzo Visconti of Milan and his brothers," lately condemned for heresy, and to other rebels against the Church.[53] The issue was sovereignty, not spirituality, and the charges were unanswerable. Ludwig could not yield to the papal threat. John not only excommunicated him on March 23, 1324, but declared him deposed on July 11 of that year.

In dire need to consolidate his throne, Ludwig arrived in Trent to convene a congress of Italian Ghibellines who, despite mutual distrust and animosity, had banded together under his protection;[54] these included Marco Visconti, who represented Milan; ambassadors from Castruccio Castracane of Lucca and from King Frederic II (d. 1337) of Trinacria (Sicily); Passarino de' Bonaccolsi of Mantua; Obizzo d'Este of Ferrara; Guido de' Tarlati di Pietramala, bishop of Arezzo and Città di Castello; and Can Grande della Scala of Verona. Before his departure from Trent on March 13, Ludwig reacted to the papal sentences by declaring John XXII illegitimate and heretical because of the pope's condemnation of ecclesiastical poverty.[55] Ten days later it was John's turn to declare Ludwig a heretic and to place any city that dared to welcome the emperor under interdict. Ludwig paused to enjoy Milan until August 12. Here, he first reconfirmed the imperial vicar of Milan, and on May 31 he entered St. Ambrose Cathedral, together with his wife, Marguerite d'Hainault, as consort, to receive the iron crown, not from the hands of the archbishop of Milan, who had fled, but from the excommunicate Guido, bishop of Arezzo, assisted by the similarly contumate bishops of Trent and Brescia.[56] Francesco dei Bonaccolsi and Passarino's son, Rinaldo d'Este, attended the ceremony. Can Grande, who seven years before had sworn fealty to Ludwig's rival, Frederick of Austria, and had, in exchange, obtained a renewal of his vicariate on March 16, 1317, did not attend.[57]

Meanwhile, Ghibelline factions in Rome had banished Napoleone Orsini and Stefano Colonna, the two Guelph heads of rival noble factions reputed to be partisans of the pope's vassal, King Robert of Naples. The unique, notorious, and now aging Sciarra Colonna—the assailant of Boniface at Anagni—seized his opportunity to be elected "captain of the people" and set to rule the city with fifty-two advisers.[58] A Roman embassy to Avignon handed Pope John the ultimatum of choosing either his immediate return to the Holy City or Rome's submission to the execrate Ludwig. The pope demurred, and Rome refused entry to his second papal legate, Giovanni Orsini, who, in retaliation, placed the city under interdict.

On January 7, 1328, Ludwig, with Castruccio Castracane, now newly named count palatine, by his side, left his quarters at Santa Maria Maggiore and entered Old St. Peter's amid cheering throngs.[59] On Sunday, January 17, 1328, as an adverse tradition holds, after the consecration by two partisan cardinal bishops in St. Peter's, Sciarra della Colonna, as the people's representative, placed the imperial crown on Ludwig's head.[60] To replace Pope John's representative, the emperor then named Marsiglio of Padua ecclesiastic vicar of the city. The latter—who had accompanied Ludwig from Nuremburg to Rome and upon whose principles, earlier published in the *Defensor pacis* (1324),[61] the emperor had conducted his irregular coronation—immediately set about the governance of the city's clergy, coercing them implacably into disregarding the papal ban.

As Ludwig prepared to depose the pope, John proclaimed a crusade against the emperor on March 21, pronounced his coronation null and void on March 31, and began an ecclesiastical suit against the Romans. Marsiglio of Padua took his revenge on recalcitrant clergy who observed the papal ban; in one case, he had the prior of the Augustinian monks at San Trifone thrown to caged lions on the Capitol.[62] Then, at the culmination of his brief sojourn in the Holy City, on April 18, 1328, Ludwig declared "the priest, Jacques of Cahors, who calls himself Pope John XXII" guilty not only of heresy, but of lèse majesté. A Roman mob burned John in a straw effigy dressed in papal garb, and ten days later Ludwig condemned the pope to death. On May 12, 1328, the emperor arranged the election of a minor friar from the convent of Ara Coeli in the Abruzzi, Pietro Rainalducci da Corbara, as antipope Nicholas V. Then, in a superfluous and desperate effort to ensure his legitimacy and redress his perennial dearth of due consecration, he had that pontiff recrown him during the papal coronation ceremony on May 22.[63] The usurping and foolish Nicholas, unrecognized even by Ludwig's ally Frederic II of Trinacria and most Ghibelline cities, pursued at least two of Pope John's adherents to the stake and began, whether because of his hypocrisy, his ostentation, his moral corruption, or his simple stupidity, to become the butt of public hatred. On April 22, another member of the fractured Colonna family, this time Jacopo Colonna, a canon of St. John the Lateran, allied to du Poujet, had been able to give a daring public reading of John's bull excommunicating Ludwig and condemning him as a heretic, to defiantly affix the document to the sheltering door of the cardinal legate's own church of San Marcello, and to escape Rome unscathed back to Palestrina on horseback. Finally, mob jeers of

"Heretics!" and "Death!" accompanied the forced departure of Ludwig and his retinue from Rome on August 4. By August 8, the second papal legate, Giovanni Orsini, had entered Rome, and a people's parliament annulled the Bavarian's every act and edict.[64] Pietro da Corbara was soon to renounce his errors to John XXII, and, after three years of easy detention, to die forgotten on October 16, 1333, only a year before the clouded demise of his briefly triumphant rival.[65]

Just how deeply Dante's elegant, poetical, and theological *Monarchia*, commandeered by Ludwig's propagandists, influenced these historic charades we can only conjecture, but we do know how it suffered.[66] Giovanni Boccaccio's two redactions of the *Trattatello in laude di Dante (A Short Treatise in Praise of Dante)* give us precious information concerning the early vicissitudes of the treatise's reception.[67] In the first decade after the *Monarchia*'s appearance, its relative moderation and traditional arguments had prompted little attention; only by its exploitation after the divulgation of Marsiglio's *Defensor pacis* (1324), the ludicrous travesty of the coronations, and the installment of an antipope, was the *Monarchia* rocketed into notoriety. Ironically, until that moment, as Boccaccio tells us, the work "had hardly been heard of." In the first version of the *Trattatello in laude di Dante*, Boccaccio recounts the events as he had learned of them:

This book [the *Monarchia*] was condemned several years after the death of the author, by Lord Beltrando, Cardinal del Poggetto and papal legate in the regions of Lombardy during the pontificate of John XXII. And the reason for this was that Ludwig . . . (coming into Italy for his coronation in Rome against the wishes of the said Pope John, and then being in Rome), against the orders of the ecclesiatical authorities made a minor friar called Piero della Corbara pope . . . and there had himself crowned by this pope. And since there had arisen questions about [the emperor's] authority in many cases, he and his followers began to use many of the arguments found in that book in order to defend this authority and himself; for this reason, the book, which up till then had hardly been heard of, became quite famous . . . the said cardinal . . . obtaining the said book . . . condemned it publicly to the flames as containing heretical matters.[68]

In the second redaction, Boccaccio, now tactfully or perhaps fearfully omitting the title given in the first version (*"Monarcia"*), gives a shorter, firmer account of the perils and prohibitions, informing us that "the said book during the papacy of John XXII was condemned for containing heretical things by messer Beltrando, Cardinal del Poggetto, legate in Lombardy for the Church of Rome; and he prohibited anyone from studying it."[69]

The manuscript copies of the *Monarchia* proliferating on the imperial side was exceeded by the number ferreted out and consigned to the flames by Cardinal du Poujet and other opponents on the peninsula. Boccaccio adds that it was only through the brave and extraordinary efforts of the Florentine Pino della Tosa and Guido da Polenta's heir, Ostagio da Polenta of Ravenna,[70] who had gone to meet the papal legate personally in 1329, that Bertrand du Poujet's fury was somewhat assuaged and that the legate refrained from burning Dante's mortal remains.[71] Bartolo da Sassoferrato (Bartolus de Saxoferrato), the ardent Ghibelline, celebrated jurist, and supporter of Dante, reports the near-miss escape independently: "Dante debated three questions: one of which was whether the emperor depends upon the Church, and he held that he did not; but on this account after his death he was nearly condemned for heresy."[72] We know that an inquisitorial mentality had taken hold, with the extremist hierocrat Henry of Cremona, among others, warning in his treatise *De potestate papæ* that *even considering* a question of the pope's legitimacy in temporal power was heretical.[73] At the Dominican Chapter held at Santa Maria Novella in Florence on September 8, 1335, the reading and study of the *Commedia* and of the poet's minor works were forbidden to ecclesiastics of the province.[74]

We cannot ignore the fact that the poet had long and publicly advertised himself as a lightning rod for vengeful reprisal in his epistles. So often did Dante adopt the cry of the Old Testament prophets from Isaiah to John the Baptist that we cannot disregard the biblically implied consequences of popular scorn: suffering and martyrdom. He had, as far as we know, composed his postexile works in Ghibelline territory where the Inquisition was either weak or powerless. Maria Picchio Simonelli, writing of the terror that pervaded Italy from 1243 to 1342, that is, from the time of Innocent IV to that of Benedict XII, has reminded us that it was dangerous for a layman to speak at all of religious matters.[75] Hostiensis, like his imitator Vernani, had been the sworn enemy of poets, arguing that their "trifles" were dangerous to the immortal soul since they "multiplied lies and vain useless words."[76] The great canonist had, in fact, inserted a clause in his *Summa aurea* that had a serious effect on inquisitors' manuals from the late 1200s to the early 1300s: "No one, however much he declares that he has seen God in dream visions, is allowed to preach."[77] Particularly, in seeking signs of heretical divination, Bernard Gui's infamous *Practica* advises the inquisitor to ask suspects "what knowledge they have or had . . . about lost or damned souls . . . of the state of souls of those who have died . . . of the prophecies of future events. . . ."[78] By the time Dante composed the *Monarchia*, he had already placed Hadrian V in his *Purgatory* for avarice and had sent Celestine V—a pope who would be canonized in 1313— to the vestibule of Hell (ambiguously!) for his abdication (*Inf.* 3:58–60). Not only had he asserted the eternal punishment for simony of Boniface VIII in *Inferno* 19 at verse 53, that of Nicholas III at verses 70–73, and that of Clement V at verse 83, but he would also go on to condemn Clement V's and John XXII's thirst for Christian blood in *Paradise* 27: 58–59.[79] As he often repeated, the shepherds of the Church had become rapacious wolves; by affirming that imperial power derived directly from God and not from the papacy, he had set forth the very doctrine that was abominable to the Church. There exists, however, no record that the otherwise intransigent Cardinal du Poujet himself ever proceeded with an official inquisition against Dante: he neither sent the *Monarchia* to the papal curia in Avignon for examination, nor, after his intervention of 1328, did he pursue the poet post mortem as a heretic.[80]

John XXII, the second pontiff of the hated "Babylonish Captivity,"[81] was himself, ironically, destined, in his waning years, to be one of a tiny minority of popes to be accused of heterodoxy by Church authorities, and, obviously, given the number of his enemies, under clearly political motivations. But it was not, finally, as we might surmise, his condemnation of the doctrine of apostolic poverty (asserted at the General Chapter of the Franciscan Order in Perugia, 1323),[82] nor his temporal revocation of the imperial election, as Ludwig IV and others had charged, but, interestingly, six sermons of a different order, which, to his dying regret, he delivered between All Saints Day of 1331 and the Feast of the Ascension, May 4, 1334, that caused the flurry of scandal. John asserted to his congregation, contrary to received doctrine, but not to dogma, that after death and before the Resurrection of the Flesh and the Last Judgment, the saints did not enjoy the Beatific Vision, but only the Humanity of Christ; he further taught that neither the damned nor the demons were yet in Hell, nor were the angels or the souls, as yet unclothed with their bodies, yet in Paradise[83]—seemingly pointless revisionisms, yet ideas obviously made cogent by the 1328 condemnation of Dante's *Monarchia* by John's intimate and protégé Cardinal Bertrand du Poujet, and surely aimed at undermining the theological structure and astounding rival renown of Dante's *Commedia*, so authoritatively scathing to John and his predecessors in its most salient and memorable verses. The University of Paris condemned John's assertions in the first four sermons in the autumn of 1333. A little over a year later, on December 4, 1334, aged eighty-nine, the pontiff, practical and perspicacious to the end, recanted his much repeated statements on his deathbed in the presence of cardinals, saying that these errors were merely his personal opinions that he would easily abjure if they were contrary to the faith of the Church. He thus averted any punishments that may have afflicted his own corpse. His enemies made the most of his difficulties and many, including William of Ockham, rejected his recantation as false. But, as in the case of Dante, officials never pressed charges of heresy against him.[84]

We must emphasize that Dante wrote the *Monarchia* as a publicist document intended for pragmatic effect in both the political and the spiritual arenas, just as he often affirms within its lines and as the pamphlet's tumultuous history fully attests. The poet hews out an ethical defense on behalf of political justice, championing the right of the God-ordained empire to enjoy the mutual aid of a restricted ecclesiastical power within ideal traditional limits. He puts to shame those who would ambitiously defile the Church with the proud concerns of this world. Contrary to what many have held, Dante's *Monarchia* is far more than a late gothic dream from a horn of ivory, merely admirable, ethical, and poetic, divorced from effect and utterly visionary.[85] Dante was the first of the truly great fourteenth-century Italian thinkers to argue against papal aggression, usurpation, and its unjustified authoritarianism—while ironically strengthening foundations for justifying absolutism in the temporal field. The eventual struggles between the papacy and worldly powers were to be of wider scope and far different from anything the poet could have allowed or foreseen. The enfeebling clashes between Philip and Boniface and between Ludwig and John played a major part in shaping the future face of Europe: they portended the crumbling of the central powers, both the imperial and the papal; the eventual disintegration of a united medieval Christendom; the rise of national states; the theory of the divine right of kings; theories of a divine or historical determinism in political life; and, eventually, the ideal wall of separation between Church and State that Thomas Jefferson was to hold so dear. As Aldo Vallone has described him, Dante was, for the Church, the first of the accused and the first defendant in a continuing litigation.[86] Dante found a firm follower in Albericus de Rosate (ca. 1340–1360), who was among the first to define the *"potestas absoluta,"* or a prince's right to rule *de jure*, but quite arbitrarily; Albericus relied upon both Dante's *Monarchia* and John of Paris's *De regia potestate et papali* for his view of the separation between secular and ecclesiastical authority.[87] Other contemporaries, as we have seen, the more flamboyant Marsiglio of Padua (ca. 1275–1342), accursed of John XXII, and the controversial "Venerabilis inceptor," William of Ockham (ca. 1285–1347),[88] were even more avidly and radically involved in the international struggle.

The manuscript tradition of the *Monarchia* in its early years, that of the first two or three generations of copies proscribed, hunted out, and burned publicly, suggests that it suffered all but total elimination.[89] Although no official ever made a posthumous indictment of heresy against Dante, the perpetual dread that his departed father could be liable to such an accusation haunted Dante's son Pietro throughout his long and prosperous life.[90] The possibility that his father's *Commedia* could be found heterodox and that he himself could forfeit his patrimony and wealth drove Pietro to compose three versions of his commentary on the *sacro poema* to explain away its controversial verses.[91] Ironically, that threatening circumstance bequeathed to us the priceless gift of Pietro's intensive, several-times updated, interpretation of his father's masterpiece.

The scribe of the earliest surviving manuscript of the *Monarchia*, the Bini Codex from the Staatsbibliothek in Berlin (now in Tübingen), transcribed in Florence around 1334 or earlier, purposefully omitted the *incipit*[92] to avoid revealing either the title or the author of the forbidden work; a different hand waggishly entitled the treatise *"Incipit Retorica Dantis,"* "Here begins Dante's Rhetoric" (f. 89ʳ).[93] In the *explicit*, the main scribe could not resist hurling the following tantalizing derision in vernacular Florentine: *"Explicit. endivinalo sel voy sapere!"* (The end. If you've got to find out—try and guess!). But a third, fourteenth-century hand spoils the sport with *"monarcia Dantis."*[94] Two related manuscripts, one now in the British Library in London, Add. 28804 (fourteenth century), and one in Lucca's Biblioteca Canonica San Martino, Feliniano 224 (fifteenth century), protest the polemical title *"Liber Monarchia Dantis Aldigherii Christiani de Florencia"* (The Book of the Monarchia by Dante Alighieri the Christian of Florence).[95] Even the oldest copy of Vernani's *Refutation*, the friar's autograph copy from his convent in Rimini, now in the British Library, has had its title scraped away to avoid mention of Dante's work. Thus we find many of the earliest manuscripts of the *Monarchia* without the author's name, with false ascriptions, or with misleading titles, although, taking advantage of its brevity, scholars had copies bound with other works of a different kind to conceal it.[96] Notably, during the Church's pursuit and imprisonment of him as a rebel, the erstwhile Roman tribune and friend of Petrarch, Cola di Rienzo, penned an important commentary on the *Monarchia* in 1343.[97]

The *Monarchia* continued to be the perennial victim of harsh clerical polemics during the late Renaissance. Only in 1559 did the *editio princeps* of the original Latin appear amid a grouping of treatises on imperial authority by other hands—in reformed, post-Zwingli Basel.[98] Its proofreader was, more than likely, John Foxe, who assisted the publisher, Johann Herbst, "Joannes Oporinus." Interestingly, either to conceal the authorship, or by simple error, Herbst stated in his preface that the author, Dante Alighieri, was not the famous poet, but instead a certain fifteenth-century friend of Poliziano.[99] A German rendering of Ficino's Italian translation entitled *Monarchey*, probably by Johann Heroldt, also saw publication in that city in the same year.[100] Slightly modified by Simon Schard, who also corrected Herbst's attribution, the *princeps* had three reprints, a first in 1566, by Herbst himself, and then a second and a third in Strasbourg by Zetzner and his heirs, respectively, in 1609 and 1618. A victim of the Counter Reformation, the treatise was banned initially in Venice in 1554; then in 1564 it was placed on the *Index* that had been first promulgated in Rome in the last year of Pope Paul IV's pontificate (1555–1559). The first edition on Italian soil was a Venetian reprinting of Schard's revised *editio princeps* with Herbst's "Preface" in 1740 to complete Dante's *Opera omnia* initiated by G. B. Pasquali, but the place of publication was given as "Coloniæ Allobrogum" to escape the censors. The first acknowledged publication on the peninsular was the quarto edition by Antonio Zatta in Venice in 1757–1758, reprinted in octavo once in 1760 and twice in 1772.[101] Once transferred to Pius IV's *Index Tridentinus* of 1564, however, through inertia and reaffirmation, it remained on the Roman Church's *Index librorum prohibitorum* until its removal in 1881.[102] Yet at least four translations had been made into Italian during the Renaissance. Marsiglio Ficino's elegant Italian translation of 1457 (published first in Florence in 1839, edited by Pietro Fraticelli) soon replaced an anonymous flawed rendering of 1456[103] (though a copy of this appeared again at the beginning of the sixteenth century). Once again the work probably was used to defend a patron: this time, Cosimo de' Medici, threatened with excommunication for encroaching on the papacy's territorial rights claimed under the forged Donation of Constantine.[104] Ficino's translation, along with yet another version from 1461, can thus be classed as further strikes against the Donation's illegality, amid the successful attacks by Nicolas of Cusa (1433), Lorenzo Valla (1440), and Reginald Pecock (1450),[105] all of whom recognized the charter of the *Institutum Constantini* as a forgery. Pier Giorgio Ricci describes the fourth Italian translation of the *Monarchia*, dating, this time, from the sixteenth century.[106]

Abundant hand glosses in the earlier manuscripts and printed versions show that the work was avidly read by friends and foes alike. But the tradition of reliable early texts, as Ricci noted, and Prudence Shaw painstakingly confirms, is meager: Ricci counted a mere nineteen extant manuscripts when he made his edition for the Società Dantesca first published by Mondadori in 1965.[107] In 1969 Shaw described a major manuscript unknown to Ricci, which she had discovered in Uppsala; it too contained the famous reference to the *Paradiso*, reinforcing Ricci's later dating.[108]

We cannot resist the hope that further copies must await us in libraries and archives dislocated by secularly long upheavals from the Peasants' War to the end of the communist dominations.

## ECCLESIASTICAL AMBITION, TERROR, AND SPLEEN

Cardinal Bertrand du Poujet's military campaign on the pope's behalf had first met with considerable difficulties but then with great fortune in Lombardy and Romagna, for on June 5, 1326, Passarino abandoned his imperial vicarship of Modena to the triumphant du Poujet;[109] by September 30, 1326, the cardinal legate had become lord of Parma, and, by October 4, lord of Reggio for the duration of the empire's declared "vacancy." With these victories in hand and while Emperor Ludwig planned strategy in Trent with the Ghibellines, du Poujet, accepting an invitation for a visit to the Guelph stronghold of Bologna, entered the city in triumphal pomp on February 5, 1327. Accepting the absolute *signoria* of its government on February 8, Bertrand then established himself firmly in Bologna with effective harshness, by beheading conspirators and cutting out the tongues of at least two lawyers who opposed him.[110] He totally converted the city's republican constitution into a monarchic system, by abolishing the council of the people, imposing taxes for his war against Ludwig, quietly eliminating the political posts of *bargello* and *gonfaloniere*, and fusing the offices of supreme *podestà* and *capitano del popolo* into that of a single *rettore* (rector) totally subordinate to him (April 25).[111] In 1332, the pope made du Poujet count of Romagna.[112] And in the same year Pope John XXII contemplated, but had ultimately to reject, the removal of the Holy See to Bologna, where he could have reigned in greater security in the newly re-built Galliera castle, surrounded by Guelph partisans.[113] Neither the pope nor his favorite legate could foresee the sea change by the spring of 1333, when, af-ter du Poujet, with some assistance from Graziolo de' Bambaglioli, had formed an alliance with John I of Luxembourg, king of Bohemia,[114] Italian Guelphs and Ghibellines, angered at the threat that the alliance would pose to both parties, met in Castelbado near Padua and agreed to establish a league to drive the Bohemian from Lombardy. The Bolognese, despite their submission "in perpetuity" to the Church, assumed too that the pope had betrayed them by handing their city over to the king. Cardinal du Poujet was besieged by a furious mob in his new papal citadel and barely escaped from the city under the protection of three hundred Guelph horsemen urgently dispatched from Florence.[115] When the legate died, long after, in 1352, the poet Francesco Pe-trarca only noted the steep decline of Romagna after the legate's departure. Five years later, however, he disclosed his true, intimate feelings, describing du Poujet more frankly as a "brigand with a filthy temper," dispatched as a ma-rauder into Italy by the Pontifex Maximus "like a second Hannibal, not a sec-ond Peter."[116]

At the close of 1328, amid his earlier, extraordinary successes, and in reac-tion to the notorious coronations of Ludwig of January and May, and the in-solent election of an antipope in that year, du Poujet had judged the *Monarchia* an enemy pamphlet advocating the emperor's position and had it burned pub-licly in the main square of Bologna.[117] It is possible to imagine that the social-ly assertive Dominican canonist, Guido Vernani of Rimini, might have earlier received an appointment from ecclesiastics to investigate the *Monarchia*'s philo-sophical and theological weaknesses and any suspicious heretical content.[118] But no such documentation has come to light. Far more likely, Vernani volun-teered the censure on his own initiative to curry favor with the cardinal legate—for (it is historically important to note) even such luminaries as Gio-vanni Villani and Francesco Petrarca believed the rumor that the cardinal priest of San Marcello was John XXII's close blood relative, and probably not a nephew, but in reality the pope's own bastard son.[119] In 1325 Vernani had been given the task of reading and explaining to the laity and clergy Pope John XXII's bull of excommunication of Ludwig of Bavaria and Castruccio

Castracane.[120] The request must have added to his sense of self-importance. Having already tried to draw favorable interest from the papal curia with his commentary on Boniface's *Unam sanctam* in 1327, Vernani joined the publicist lists yet again: the promising beacon of an ecclesiastical career in canon law, and perhaps even of a prelacy through a toadying support of the legate's lordship and of John's papacy (soon, he had heard, to be transferred to Bologna) shone bright enough for the aggressive Vernani to pursue renown in a field in which he already had considerable experience. A set of very familiar circumstances—first, a pope with a powerful family protégé who was winning his own realm in Romagna, repeated in the Renaissance by the Borgias and the Medicis; and second, the intense desire for a political appointment—were to inspire a secretary of Florence to draft a treatise on principates two centuries later.

At all events, in 1329 the *Refutation* appeared, the first of an important number of *reprobationes* that the Guelphs were to promulgate in the first half of the century not only against Dante, but, more especially, against other imperial treatises such as those of Marsiglio of Padua and William of Ockham.[121] Leaving aside the anti-Dante mockery and philosophical attacks of Cecco d'Ascoli (burned at the stake for heresy in 1327) in *L'Acerba*, even the sainted archbishop of Florence, Antonino (1389–1459), who established the convent of San Marco with Cosimo de' Medici, followed the then-current Dominican tradition of speaking against the *Monarchia*.[122] In 1400 came two assaults: the first from a Franciscan, Guglielmo Centueri of Cremona, bishop of Piacenza and Pavia, who took up Vernani's cause in his theological *De iure monarchiæ* (the butt of his bitter reproach *"contra Dantem"* appears only identified in a marginal gloss), and the second from the Dominican Johannes Falkenberg (ca. 1365– ca. 1435), who wrote passages of vehement censure in his lengthy *De monarchia mundi*.[123]

Guido Vernani, O.P., our mysterious, well-spoken, high-papalist notary-canonist-theologian of whose origin no Dominican archive gives any notice whatsoever, appears first circa 1310 as a humble lector at the *studium*, or University of Bologna,[124] at the same time that his more famous colleague Cecco d'Ascoli taught philosophy, medicine and, later, astrology there.[125] Vernani appears to have passed the decade from 1310 to 1320 in that city, but to have lived most of his life at the convent of San Cataldo in the coastal city of Rimini where various records show he performed many notarial tasks.[126] Versed in Aristotelian thought, though not as intelligently as the "prodigious autodidact" Dante, Vernani penned three volumes on Aristotle, two on the temporal power of the popes, the treatise on the *Monarchia*—here presented for the first time in English—and, most probably, a discourse on ethics: his works are entitled *Summa de virtutibus secundum Aristotelis sententiam* (*A Summa on the Nicomachean Ethics*), known in six manuscripts; *Expositio libri Aristotelis de anima* (*A Commentary on Aristotle's On the Soul*), available only in one manuscript in Paris; *Sentencia rhetorice Aristotelis*, or *Summa super rethoricam Aristotelis* (*A Commentary on Aristotle's Rhetoric*), surviving in three manuscripts; *De potestate summi pontificis* (*On the Power of the Supreme Pontiff*), found in four manuscripts, one from the eighteenth century; *Expositio super decretali Unam Sanctam* (*A Commentary on the Papal Bull "Unam Sanctam"*), available in a codex in the Biblioteca Nazionale in Florence, published by Grabmann;[127] and, lastly, the attributed *Liber de virtutibus* (*A Book on Virtues*), contained in one extant manuscript.[128]

Especially in the treatise *De potestate summi pontificis* of 1327 and in his *Expositio super decretali Unam Sanctam*, we can read in published form the Dominican's exposition of the decretalist theories in those traditional formulas that he was to find again invaluable for his censure of Dante circulated two years later. The *Refutation* itself is extant in two manuscripts, the first, Guido's own copy on parchment without title or *incipit* in Codex Add. 35325, of the Philips Collection 6310, ff. 2$^r$–9$^v$ in the British Library,[129] and the second, Codex 335, ff. 65$^r$–69$^v$ "*Incipit Tractatus Fratris Guidonis Vernani Ordinis Predicatorum de Reprobatione Monarchie composite a Dante*," in the Biblioteca Comunale Classense. Versions of the *Reprobatio* and the treatise *De potestate summi pontificis*, both based on the undependable Classense Codex, were first printed together in 1746;[130] Matteini dutifully records the notice by Domaneschio of an earlier publication in Rome of 1741, but no copies have come to light.[131] R. Piccini prepared an edition of the *Reprobatio* accompanied by a bowdlerized Italian translation in 1906 under the title *Contro Dante*, and in 1938 Thomas Käppeli presented a carefully edited version as an article with German apparatus. Nevio Matteini in his edition of 1958 follows Käppeli's work extremely closely and with few emendments (even reproducing the text and footnotes without change, obscure abbreviations without expansion, and erroneous paginations without correction), but he brings new and interesting research in the details of various, elusive, and tenuous biographical references to the friar from Rimini. In fact, most of Matteini's detailed research establishes, ironically, Vernani's absence from the places where we would most expect to discover his name.

None of the friar's other works seem so far to have been printed.[132]

Vernani's dedication of the *Refutation* to the notary Bonagrazia de' Bam-baglioli (ca. 1291–ca. 1341),[133] called Graziolo, is of singular interest, especially for its rather sinister nastiness and unwarranted condescension. Bambaglioli, a poet of moderate fame in his own right, had enrolled in the Guild of Notaries in Bologna in 1311 and went on to occupy an honorable and onerous post in the chancellery of Bologna, the court of records and public archives, which was charged primarily with making copies of every communal law available in both Latin and Italian and with recording all costs and fines from legal cases.[134] By the terms of a law passed on July 26, 1321, the priors, ancients, consuls, standard-bearer of justice, praeconsul, notaries, functionaries, and legal advisers of the guilds had increased the number of chancellorships to two—considering that "the Office of the Chancery of the Commune of Bologna was burdened by the weight of so many documents to draw up that a single chancellor could not perfectly execute it."[135] These chancellors were to be elected by ballot in the Council of Four Thousand every six months, but the second, that to which Graziolo was specifically named as "continuing and diligent chancellor,"[136] was, in practice, of permanent tenure—that of instructing the four notaries chosen for every semester by the Society of Notaries on the basis of their excellent handwriting and knowledge of rhetoric. The law remained, unchanged by the cardinal legate's later constitutional reconstructions, until the single chancellorship was restored in 1335, on the pattern of the pre-du Poujet conditions of 1318.[137]

Sometime after assuming office of *"comunis Bononie cancellarius,"* Graziolo, pursuing his love of poetry, began the first self-dated Latin commentary on the first canticle of the *Commedia,* and he released this sympathetic and adulatory work in 1324, three years after the poet's death.[138] Only very shortly before, in 1322, had Dante's son Jacopo composed the first—most pedestrian and disappointing—commentary on his father's *Inferno* in the vernacular;[139] and in the same year Jacopo, together with his brother Pietro, had made public the entire sacred poem, presenting it to Guido Novello da Polenta of Ravenna. Vernani's decidedly patronizing malice in the *Refutation*'s opening pages, addressed to Graziolo, a man far above the friar's station in talent and position, metamorphoses into an admonition or, more ominously, into a warning to the Guelph chancellor about his supposedly disloyal interest. The friar aims his fulsome and duplicitous dedication so that the attack on Dante ricochets upon Bambaglioli. We have no record of the chancellor's reaction. But if it had been an attempt to oust him, it did not succeed. Graziolo was by ancient family tradition an entrenched Guelph; his family had been notaries by profession, and city records show that ten among them had engaged in that profession; the family had even given its name to a suburb. Graziolo himself had held several important but minor offices from 1316 on, until, in 1324, he was elected to the exclusive body of the "Anziani" of Bologna from whom political appointees were drawn, and he was to occupy his chancery post until 1334, when he was banished from Bologna and chose exile at the Guelph court of King Robert of Naples—the year of John XXII's death, and a year after the cardinal legate's expulsion from the commune.[140] That, precisely in 1328, surely unknown to Vernani, Cardinal du Poujet had also entrusted Bambaglioli with the secret military-intelligence position of notary to the Office of Spies for the Holy Roman Church certainly excludes the hand of the cardinal from any part in Vernani's dedication and thus of any official commission of the *Refutation*.[141] The *Monarchia* itself presents such diametrically opposite views to those which the friar cherishes in the *De potestate summi pontificis* and his *Expositio super decretali*[142] that it is easy to read the *Refutation* as a polemic motivated by opportunism, self-promotion, ambition, and a great deal of grandiose, oversensitive, personal vindication. We must observe, however, that when Vernani's fellow lector at the Bolognese *studium*, Cecco d'Ascoli, was burned for heresy in 1327, Vernani immediately dashed off his three pro-papalist works in hurried succession: the commentary on *Unam sanctam* (1327), the *De potestate summi pontificis* (1327), and the *Refutation* (1328). The friar knew that in the trial records of the Inquisition all classes of society were generously included: burghers and peasants, shepherds and tradesmen, intellectuals and nobles, rich and poor, laymen and clerics. Sympathy, comfort, or even mere contact with someone connected to a heretical sect constituted sufficient grounds for immediate condemnation.[143] We may easily infer some intimate relation of Vernani's activities to Cecco's condemnation that has not come into clearer light. In adopting his intransigent, hierocratic posture, Vernani may have urgently wished to distance himself from Cecco by posturing as more Guelph than the Guelphs; the peculiar tone of his dedication to Graziolo and his scathing remarks on Dante and his poem may be rooted not only in resentment and ambition but in servile terror. His retreat to his cell in Rimini may thus be quite understandable.

While Dante wields traditional arguments with a creative twist, turning even the reasonings of historic opponents of the empire to his own account, the hasty pedestrian attacks of the would-be papal publicist show little originality except in the vituperation of his dead victim. Throughout his condemnations the Dominican betrays a genuine fear and respect of Dante's persuasiveness and of his quarry's scholarly and popular renown. Friar Guido's polemics express far more fearful spleen than lofty disdain, although ironically his very spite makes his censure most compelling reading.

It is surely not the task of modern readers to palliate or excuse the uncharitable acrimony with which Vernani attacks Dante, nor the patent envy and malice with which he mistreats Graziolo; but we certainly can try Vernani on his own terms for his measure of Aristotelian-Thomistic precision in contrast to the extraordinary performance of Dante Alighieri. The farcical events, the motives, the tone, and the manner in which the attack from this first, irreconcilable opponent took place are themselves of great interest and substance; but of greatest value will be our increased appreciation of how Dante was received just after his death amid the full radiance of his *Commedia's* triumph among both intellectuals and the common people.[144]

## CHAPTER 3

# The *Monarchia* and Vernani's Censures

## ON BOOK I

Dante opens the *Monarchia* echoing the first words of Aristotle's *Metaphysics* 1:1, "All men desire to know," with which he had also begun the *Convivio*, and turns them to further, charitable, Christian purpose: all those whom God sealed with a love of truth must share their knowledge and experience with others. Thus he will himself be like the Psalmist's tree planted near running water (Ps 1:3), not only in blossoming, but in revealing the fruit of new knowledge and hidden truths for the public good.[1] He will not be like those who did not share or practice their knowledge and skill, or used it for ill, like all those he sees fittingly transformed by a literalized metaphor into barren, bleeding *"piante,"* or trees in a seared dark forest of their own making, running for no prize in a barren wilderness, roasted in flames in a barren ditch, or imprisoned like straws in the ice of Caina's depths—Guelphs and Ghibellines, moderns and ancients alike, all self-obsessively condemned to Hell in the first canticle of the *Commedia*.

The wide polysemousness of this first sentence and his expectations of contention thus belie the seemingly bucolic simile. In this debate with contemporary assailants of the empire, the opening paragraph already identifies the poet with the ancient sport and military champions of Rome and begins the bold rhetoric of temporal responsibility: he is a loyal Roman citizen vigilant for the common good; out of civic duty he aims to win "the palm of so great a prize" (1:1:5). In books 2 and 3, he will go on to describe the struggle of the Roman people and to announce his own firm advocacy of their empire in terms of an athletic contest and a blood duel.

In chapter 2:1, he presents his definition of temporal monarchy, "which they call empire," as "the one single principality placed over all men in time, or among and over those things that are measured by time," and then sets forth the principal questions with which he will deal in the three books of the

*Monarchia:* first, whether a single world governor is necessary for the good of the world; second, whether the Roman people appropriated the office of monarchy to itself *de jure;* and third, whether the authority of monarchy depends directly upon God or on some other minister or vicar of God.

Dante, as a true Scholastic Aristotelian who identifies the art of thinking with dialectic, sets out to build book 1 on human reason, relying on syllogistic propositions. Immediately, the process of such analytic deduction requires the establishment of a first principle upon which to substantiate all conclusions that will then spring from it; he thus devotes the next two chapters, 2 and 3, to a chain of truths searching to lay forth this axiom.

God, through Nature, called "God's art," creates all things for a purpose, a final goal, or a last end—that is, God creates nothing in vain, but creates it rather for the perfection of its functioning. His divine purpose must and will be fulfilled. The goal of humanity as a whole is the proper functioning of its essence, which is identified with the proper functioning of its intellectual potential (1:3:3), its "possible intellect" or "potential intellect"—named "possible" because, as man's highest part, it has possibilities or potentialities before any thinking even begins and capacities beyond what it may be presently putting into effect.[2] Thus, in chapter 4:1, Dante asserts that "the function proper to mankind taken in its totality is always to effect the whole potentiality of the possible intellect." And for this fulfillment man needs peace and tranquility. Thus the poet can finally sum up the foundation of book 1 as "universal peace, which we must take as a principle for all the arguments that are to follow" (1:4:5).[3]

Only in chapter 5 does Dante turn to the first of the three fundamental questions: "Whether temporal monarchy is necessary for the well-being of the world." He centers upon the question of man's *temporal* happiness, following Aristotle's definition of supreme happiness, in *Ethics* 1:10:1101a, as that attained by those *living* men whose activities are an expression of complete virtue, not simply at one given moment, but throughout their lives. For the poet, the peace and beatitude of this life can only be attainable when the right functioning of temporal rule is first achieved: a world monarch is necessary to achieve the total function of man's possible intellect by guiding man to what is right and good. This fulfillment involves not the intellect of one particular individual, but of all those upon earth in some future time when all thought and will shall be one.[4] For Dante, such a goal is achievable only under a single God-sent world prince placed over all men *"in time,* or among and *over those things that are measured by time"* (*Mon.* 1:2:1). The poet sees such immanent goals of secular happiness as a climbing pathway to higher ends: the end of the family is righteous living; that of the neighborhood or village, reciprocal aid; that of the city and the kingdom, harmonious and satisfying living. The poet does not conceive the justice achieved by the justness of a world ruler as an object in which to *rest* as a final goal, but as the greatest ethical goal *on earth* to strive for and conserve as a medium in which the intellect can grow. Beyond the full realization of human intellect, Dante gives little further precision concerning the "beatitude of this life," but, as we shall examine below, St. Thomas Aquinas himself allowed such a qualified twofold beatitude and saw the body as in some unspecifiable way as obviously necessary for the soul's well-being in its attainment.

Vernani begins his *Refutation* by imitating the language of indignant anathema and condemnation that had become familiar to canon lawyers from the sequence of decretals that Pope John XXII had recently drafted—decretals that evinced a thought and style markedly different from those used during the pontificate of Clement V. Exactly as Pope John's adversaries in the exordium of *Quia quorundum mentes*, for example, in Vernani's "Dedication" Dante is made the son of the "father of lies," poisoning men's minds with his "pernicious" and "pestiferous" doctrine, seducing both the wise and the simple into error.[5] The friar even manages to adopt the same grandiose tone of condescension typical of the aged reigning pontiff. Then, after the oily derogations of his greeting to Graziolo Bambaglioli, Guido Vernani tries to recapture the benevolence of his reader (whoever that intended reader may truly have been) by opening book 1 of the *Refutation* more reticently than he will its two following books, restricting his rebuttal mainly to Dante's chapters 3 and 9. The friar shows himself to be an opponent deeply familiar with the methods and writings of his quarry, but, even before he arrives at Dante's specific mention of the heretical Arab philosopher Averroës, in *Monarchia* 1:3:9, there already creeps within his polemics an obsessive suspicion and inquisitorial will to taint his opponent with heterodoxy. His intimations of heresy, however, while perfectly clear, are never overtly pronounced.[6]

Instead, for his censure of *Monarchia* 1:3, Vernani seizes upon four points that he terms merely "errors." He first insists that the individual and mankind have but one single goal: different parts do not have different ends, or ends that differ from the final goal of the whole. He therefore spurns (*Ref.* 1:23–26) the fittingness of Dante's analogy of the relation of the hand or the foot to the whole body with the relation of one man to the whole of mankind; to do so, he forces Dante's figure into corollaries unintended. Bodily members, says the poet, do have an end different from man as a whole. In his rebuttal the friar insists that, unlike man among mankind, parts of the body do not have a separate being; corporal members indeed have goals different from that of the whole but they are not analogous to the members of the human race, who, as *substantial* parts, singly and severally, have but one goal. We must note that Aristotle himself had used the very same hand-body metaphor in *Ethics* 1:30:1097b precisely to show a different purpose (i.e., the proper function) of the parts of the body from the purpose of the man entire, but nowhere did he extend it to differentiate one man's final purpose from another's—and neither, of course, ultimately, does Dante. The poet probably knew, for example, that Remigio de' Girolami, the Dominican lector of theology at Santa Maria Novella in Florence, had also insisted on the necessary participation of the individual in the whole human community to realize his full potential in action. Remigio had cited Aristotle to the effect that a man who is not a citizen is not a man, just as a hand cut from the body ceases to be a living hand: in both instances the function and the individuality cease to exist. For Fra Remigio, the well-being of the community is above that of the individual, and from the good of that community comes all the good of the individual.[7] Dante too insists that the potentiality of mankind cannot be fully realized in a single individual; he does not, of course, ever deny a common end for the individual man and mankind, but sees that, practically, there are *also* lesser, subordinate goals in addition to, and leading to, the supreme end. In *Monarchia* 1:2:8, after affirming the lesser goals of subordinate parts of a state, he concludes that "[i]t is indeed idiotic to think that there is one end for this, or that, community, but that there is no single end for them altogether." And, similarly, in *Monarchia* 1:4:2, he maintains that "[s]ince, inasmuch as *what is in the part is in the whole*, to the individual man it happens that 'by sitting and resting he may acquire perfection in prudence and wisdom,' it is obvious that in quietude, or in the tranquillity of peace, mankind is able to attend without hindrance or difficulty to its own proper functioning."[8] The end of all civil law and right is to pursue this common welfare, for Dante a vision of an eternally valid way of life, first earthly, but in preparation for the spiritual afterlife. The provincial Vernani narrowly refuses to understand that Dante describes a philosophically mature "both/and" approach to end goals, not an "either/or" ("if this, then not that") dichotomy. The friar's disagreement here is, at any rate, hardly damaging to Dante's ultimate points—the very conclusions that had also been reached by learned contemporary Dominican Aristotelians in Florence.[9]

In order to comprehend precisely why Vernani would claim so insistently that Dante "has shamefully erred" in holding that the end of the whole human race is differentiated from that of the individual man, we must attend to the friar's immediately preceding argument that denies any possibility of any true earthly happiness for man (*Ref.* 1:19–22).[10] Vernani is on firm ground when he criticizes Dante's differing from the strict Augustinian position in this regard, and the friar only follows a beaten path of tradition when he affirms that ultimate true beatitude can only be transcendent, for none other than the vision and enjoyment of God, the highest truth and the highest goodness, can quench man's thirst; the human heart can find no rest in anything immanent.

Vernani also sees fit (*Ref.* 1:26 on *Mon.* 1:3) to make an arbitrary distinction quite beyond the compass of Dante's subject at hand—that is, between a *qualitative* difference and a *quantitative* distinction in goals of ultimate beatitude, "in degree—but not in kind"; he thereby again hypothesizes transcendental conclusions that Dante does not reach or intend in his treatise. If the goals of each soul were *qualitatively* different, the friar argues, the actual goal for all mankind as a whole would be of a quality different from that for the individual: further, since that goal or purpose for all mankind would be autosufficient and autonomous, the value and individuality of human souls would perforce disappear.[11] Vernani's leaping extrapolations and extravagations prepare for his coup-de-grace imputation of heretical thought to Dante, that is, the theory of a world-soul into which all individual souls would meld indistinguishably after death.[12] The friar allows, ironically, however, that if the difference in the achievement of the goal of eternal happiness were merely *quantitative*, however, "only in degree," then Dante's argument would be correct. He well knows that the poet had composed his last canticle of the *Commedia* basing his conceptions on both the quantitative and the qualitative difference among eternal states of bliss enjoyed by individual souls after death. From Vernani's obvious familiarity with the poem, we know that the friar had read Dante's careful arguments for the distinctions in the hierarchy of beatitude outlined in *Paradiso* 2–4—of the souls' enjoyment of the ultimate goal of beatitude, the vision of God.[13] The poet, giving an elaborate palinode in *Paradiso* to his own earlier, erroneous views expressed in the *Convivio* 2:13:9, has Beatrice insist there (*Par.* 2:65) on the relation between "*quali*" ("of what kinds") and *"quanto"* ("how much"), in a round *rejection* of Averroës, insisting that the quantitative rarity and density of the heavens is insufficient to explain the differing luminosity of heavenly bodies, and by implication, the differing grades of blessedness of the souls in Heaven. In the glory of the Empyrean, according to the poet, *each soul enjoys both a quantitative and a qualitative difference in blessedness,* each to his or her capacity, thus allowing God's glory to shine more in some, in others less; and, notably, he expresses it here precisely in quantitative terms: ". . . *differentemente han dolce vita / per sentir* più e men *l'etterno spiro"* (All . . . have sweet life in different measure, by feeling *more and less* the eternal breath; *Par.* 4:35–36; my emphasis).

In the highest heaven the souls continue their individuality and enjoy different lots, *"più e meno,"* in beatitude.[14] By attacking this central principle upon which the poet constructs the whole hierarchy of the blessed in *Paradiso,* Vernani makes an overly nice distinction that Dante never intends; the friar may have slyly hoped, as would the reigning pontiff in his own sermons of 1331–1332 on damnation and the Beatific Vision, that the objection threatened the orthodox foundation of Dante's major and most popularly acclaimed work, those "poetical phantasms and fictions" the friar heard recited in triple rhyme around him daily by members of every social class.

In the case of the minor, second error that Vernani alleges concerning *Monarchia* 1:3:7; (*Ref.* 1:27ff.), however, the friar may be justified. The poet identifies being *(esse)* as one with understanding *(intelligere)* in spiritual substances, asserting that if spiritual substances—the angels—did not understand continuously and ceaselessly, they would not be sempiternal: *"Substantia que non semper intelligit, non potest esse sempiterna."* Vernani rebuts the argument by noting that human souls are also eternal, yet they do not, after all, have their intellects in ceaseless operation, and that, similarly, celestial bodies (i.e., all those above the sphere of the Moon and beneath the Empyrean) are sempiternal and yet they have no use at all of an intellect. Exploiting his righteous momentum, Vernani observes, incontrovertibly, but, perhaps quite beside the point, that only in God are intellect and will one, since God is pure act (*Ref.* 1:31). Although the friar labels Dante's argument an "intolerable error," he admits himself in the next two lines that he spends on this quibble that it is marginal to Dante's main argument (*Ref.* 1:32).

In the third case (*Ref.* 1:33ff.), Vernani simply jumps to wild conclusions to steal a premature victory as he accuses Dante of making a false affirmation: that the possible intellect cannot be actuated except by the whole human race.

This the friar censures as "the worst kind of error": "By such a statement, it clearly follows that there is one single intellect for all mankind; but to say and hear such a thing is to commit the flagrant error of its author and inventor, Averroës, to whom he refers."[15] Vernani had likely checked the translation of Averroës's *Commentary on the Soul,* and had found that precisely on the two occasions where the Arab philosopher had dealt with the "multitude of intellects," he mentioned the unity of the material and the speculative intellect in all men. Averroës indeed divorced his concept of the soul from any ideas of eschatological revelation or beatitude,[16] since, for him, there was no individual afterlife—an heretical tenet contrary not only to natural and moral philosophy but to the doctrines of both Christianity and Islam.

As Bruno Nardi recognized, Dante begins his formulation on the fulfillment of the possible intellect upon extrapolations from Aristotle: the philosopher had taught that because a single individual being was limited by time and space, its own separate capacities could not completely and forever realize the perfection of the whole species—the species being itself eternal; this naturally necessitated the existence of *many* (and we may note that Aristotle *himself* does not say *"all"*) individuals of the same species.[17] Averroës in turn had concluded that the goal could be reached by the procreation of other separate individuals who would contribute to the supreme goal of the whole.[18] In a most interesting development, theologians had actually adapted Aristotle and Averroës to explain the words of Genesis 12:28, "increase and multiply."[19] Dante can thus state with some authority, although with some lack of clarity:

Ergo, there is a particular function proper to all mankind to which *the totality of humanity in its great multitude is ordered* [*ad quam ipsa universitas hominum in tanta multitudine ordinatur*]; a function, indeed, to which neither a single man, nor a family, nor a neighborhood, nor a city, nor a particular kingdom can attain. . . . It is, therefore, obvious that the ultimate potentiality of mankind itself is its intellectual potentiality or power. And since this potentiality cannot be completely brought into action at one time through one individual man or by any of the particular communities defined above, it is necessary that there be *a multitude among mankind* [*necesse est multitudinem in humano genere*] through whom this potentiality can be actuated—just as it is necessary that there be a *multitude of generated things* so that all the potentiality of primal matter may always be found actuated, otherwise we would have to posit a separate potentiality, and this is impossible (and Averroës agrees with this opinion in his *Commentary* on the books of *The Soul*). The intellectual potentiality, then, of which I am speaking, does not concern only the universal forms or species, but also, through a certain extension, particular forms. (*Mon.* 1:3:4–9; my emphasis)

Only if no attention were paid to the context in which Dante merely affirms, correctly, *that pure potentiality cannot have its own existence,* for "a separate potentiality . . . is impossible," or to the last lines of the paragraph that contain further disclaimers, could the passage be misrepresented to appear damaging. We should observe that Dante does not cite the Arab philosopher as a source or authority here, but merely observes, in an offhand aside or afterthought, that Averroës's ideas on potentiality are in concord (*"concordat"*) with his view.[20] Vernani thus falsifies the true consistency of Dante's position with Christian-Aristotelian thought, for St. Thomas Aquinas himself had defined "multitude" as a "plurality" that itself could be divided into parts according to its potential—that is, he conceived of it as an aggregate, not as a monolith.[21] But there must be concord in the collectivity. Not only had St. Thomas affirmed that "the happiness of this life consists in an operation of the intellect, either speculative or practical,"[22] but he had insisted on Aristotle's dictum in the *Politics* that all pluralities themselves must be ruled by one to one end; as all knowledge and art as a unity is ordered to one goal—beatitude—so wisdom (*sapientia*) must direct all, and the wise must rule all others.[23] Human reason directs law to the common good: "Now the first principle in practical matters, which are the object of the practical reason, is the last end: and the last end of human life is bliss or happiness. . . . *Moreover, since every part is ordained to the whole, as imperfect to perfect;* and since one man is part of the perfect community, the law must needs regard properly the relation to universal happiness." St. Thomas then cites *Ethics* 5:1, to the effect that justice in legal affairs was that which was "adapted to produce and preserve happiness *and its parts* for the body politic."[24] St. Thomas not only agreed that man was a political animal, but added his own fundamental opinion that man was also *social,* that is, a being of charity; in the passages where Aquinas described his own view of a twofold beatitude for man, he insisted that man could not achieve these alone. Vernani was probably quite unaware that in Florence, his fellow Dominican, Fra Remigio de' Girolami, had come to a conclusion similar to Dante's in the *De bono communi* that a union of minds, constituting a rational concord of wills, formed the peace and *summun bonum* of the state: political community arose from "the union or conjunction of hearts, that is of wills willing the same thing." Remigio affirmed that "[p]erfect beatitude cannot exist in one individual man, since for that the participation of many are required."[25] Thus men must cooperate as social animals: "Men naturally bond together and make a city or other community for the sake of their common benefit in order to remedy the defect of human life which one individual cannot heal."[26]

Within Dante's paragraphs, cited above, the phrase "the totality [*universitas*] of humanity *in* its great multitude [or, in its great whole]" of 1:3:4, becomes, in 1:3:8, "a multitude *among* mankind among mankind through which this potentiality can be actuated," removing any possibility of an Averroistic totality. That "multitude *among* mankind" is a *"quoddam totum," "some totality* by relation to some parts" (*Mon.* 1:7:1), that is, not all men in all places from Adam to the Last Judgment, but clearly *only a plurality of given men united in will and intellect at a future time when the world would be one under the sway of one ruler.* To put it another way, the part, the family, the city, the realm, or the empire governed justly by one ruler ordained by God is isomorphic to, and, as it were, a synechdoche of, God's perfect rule of the universe, but they come as points occurring in linear time. "Just as the inferior parts of the whole of humanity fittingly correspond to this whole, so this whole is said to correspond fittingly to its totality" (*Mon.* 1:7:2). Such an aggregate body can reach the justice and peace of the earthly paradise.[27] While affirming, ideally, that all men *should* reach the goal in a restoration of empire, practically, Dante means to include only the vast number of those who would be alive at the time of such future fulfillment before the end of time, just as he believed a similar vast number had been alive in the fullness of time at Christ's Advent. We recall that the poet has insisted that his vision of empire only deals with "the one single principality placed over all men *in time,* or among and over *those things that are measured by time*" (*Mon.* 1:2:2), that is, as St. Thomas puts it, with "the happiness of this life," with temporality, and not with the next world; Dante's concept of this life's beatitude must per se be divorced from any alternate heretical concept of the individual's soul subsumed into a total world-soul *in the hereafter.* Need we really observe that, had the poet held any such notion, he would never have composed the *Commedia* whose whole edifice deals with the state of *personal, individual* souls after death?

Vernani ends his hostile construction of Dante's argument by citing Aristotle's words from *On the Soul* 3:4: the soul, that by which we live, feel, and think, and the intellect, that by which the soul knows and understands, are part of that individual soul—all reiterated, absurdly, as if Dante would not have been in complete agreement.

But to preserve the integrity of his argument in the *Monarchia,* Dante does have to struggle with an awkward handicap that he cannot openly admit. He is at pains to avoid the major association and definition of his "multitude," the *societas humana,* with one that would inevitably occur to the reader and undermine the arguments for empire: that is, its identification with the body of all Christian believers, cleric and lay indifferently, that form the one body in Christ—one of the major definitions of *Ecclesia*, the Church, in its earthly and heavenly form and one that the poet had assumed, for example, in his *Letter to the Italian Cardinals* (para. 10).[28] Dante's argument here cannot brook confusion of his concept of a "multitude" with the Church either as the mystical body of the *societas christiana* with one head (as *Unam Sanctam* proclaimed),[29] or as the hierocratic *sacerdotium*, the earthly corporate organization of ordained priests. Nor is Dante's plurality yet to be identified with the "City of God," comprising only of the past, present, and future blessed; in fact, one could correctly say that Dante must necessarily avoid such spoiling, Augustinian nomenclature in his reasoning. In fact, all arguments about a restoration of an *original* Edenic justice or right order in the soul and state, are, from an orthodox Catholic point of view, impossible; and, while *personal, individual justice* may be regained by individuals through redemption, grace, and the choice of accepting that grace, in point of fact neither a pope nor an emperor on earth could lead *all* of mankind, of all times, to beatitude: the very *fomes peccati*, "the tinder of sin," a necessary consideration in the doctrine of free will, meant that some individuals had already chosen, do choose, and will inveterately choose lesser goods instead of the Highest Good, and will go willingly and impenitently to Hell.[30] In *Monarchia* 1:3:4–9 ultimately, Dante's "multitude" is an associated whole, isolated at a particular time, and neither contains all individuals of mankind's ideal species, nor can it be identified here with the totality of the blessed—meaning those believers predestined for beatitude and including those already blessed in the hereafter. Dante's theory expressed in his second use of "a multitude *among* mankind," then, very like that of the state conceived by his fellow Florentine, Remigio de' Girolami, is of a polity that will not be a *totalitas universalis*—not a "universal totality"—but a *totalitas integralis*—an "integral totality"—binding together the intellects and will of a community of men to create a higher rationality.[31] We could only concur with Vernani's charge if we were to misconstrue Dante's statement not only as being teleological but also as being eschatological, and stubbornly ignore the fact that the poet's text attempts to deal with the goals of a collectivity of individual souls in the sublunar, material world, delimited by linear time.[32]

While Ernst Hartwig Kantorowicz made great advances in comprehending Dante's corporate notions of the body politic,[33] Michele Barbi and others, on the other hand, came to Dante's defense and "excused" him on the grounds that he was not a philosopher but, after all, a poet and publicist.[34] His thought on this point, they maintained with some justice, was not organic and consistent. Although Bruno Nardi believed in Dante's adherence to Christian doctrine, he held that some of the poet's Aristotelian views were pushed further than those of some of his contemporaries and saw that the *Monarchia* indeed conveyed certain Averroistic tenets akin to those expressed by Marsiglio of Padua a decade later.[35] Vernani's most recent editor, Matteini, thought that Vernani was speaking in good faith of an *"error pessimus,"* and "flagrant error" merely because the friar could not have understood the radical "laicism" of Dante; though Dante's thought was "consonant" with Christian doctrine, Matteini held, the friar was right to disagree.[36]

I believe it is obvious that the poet would have cleanly escaped the friar's calumny had he limited himself only to using the common (Averroistic!) term "possible intellect" that had long entered the mainstream of Scholastic thought to signify the highest part of the soul (*Mon.* 1:3:12–13). Dante's only misstep is not to have foreseen that merely bringing up the *name* of Averroës would inevitably cloud his argument.[37] In *Purgatorio* 25:61–78, while describing the creation of the individual soul in the foetus, the poet had, after all, avidly opposed the very idea of the separation of the possible intellect, and had censured that Arab thinker for the very fallacy of monopsychism:

> Ma come l'animal divegna fante,
> non vedi tu ancor; quest'è tal punto,
> che più savio di te fe' già errante,
> sì che, per sua dottrina, fe' disgiunto
> dall'anima il possibile intelletto,
> perchè da lui non vide organo assunto.
> (vv. 61–66)

But how from animal it becomes a human being you do not see yet: this is such a point that once it made one [Averroës] wiser than you to err, so that in his teaching he separated the possible intellect from the soul because he saw no organ assumed by it. (My translation)

Vernani who, when ambition suits him, demonstrates his thorough knowledge of the *Commedia*, conveniently disregards these verses.

In chapter 7, Dante goes on to contend that the human race can only achieve that future terrestrial fulfillment of the possible intellect when mankind on earth acts as one. That for this mankind needs a single governor, the *"mon-arch,"* the "sole-ruler," the poet argues from the firmness of meta-phoric tradition. The monad, the one, the sole, the unity, had always meant the Godhead, holiness, peace, and concord, while the dyad, plurality, the many, signified division and disintegration (made clear, later, in ch.15). For Dante the argument was not mere analogy: it was cause and fact. The numero-logical abstraction served to disembody his argument, concealing its human facture. In sum, since unity is the Deity; humanity, as microcosm in the like-ness and image of God, best resembles him as macrocosm when it is one (chs. 8–9). We, who might reject such analogies, recognize his argument's a priori circularity. Dante, however, believed and knew that he argued incontrovertibly, for in the traditional apologetics of Christianity the concept of the single world ruler did not merely *reflect* the axiom of unity: Christians had long used it as the major *proof* of monotheism.

When Etienne Gilson hastily asserted that "Dante was able to raise up a universal Monarch vis-à-vis the universal Pope only by imagining this mon-arch himself as a kind of Pope," he reversed the true historical process of Dante's thought.[38] The poet obviously recognized the parallel and knew that the canonists had emphasized the assimilation,[39] but the emperor-as-pope was a simile that his thesis could not afford; he knew, besides, that, historically, the papacy had derived its central plan from the empire and not vice versa. As modern readers we cannot, after all, ever forget Hobbes's wry derision in the *Leviathan*, "If a man consider the original of the great ecclesiastical dominion, he will easily perceive that the *Papacy* is no other than the ghost of the de-ceased *Roman Empire*, sitting crowned on the grave thereof."[40] At the moment of the *Monarchia*, Dante was only too keenly aware that the historical novelty lay in the *Church's* replacement of the temporal monarch with the pope, and not vice versa. Of course, the poet never argues for the singleness of the emperor upon the contemporary analogy of a unique spiritual Vicar of Christ, aware that it would destroy his position, but rather, directly upon the analogy of a unique Godhead. And, most important, in this he appeals to the legacy of monotheism ultimately stretching back to early Christianity.

Dante's pleas for world monarchy, in fact, exactly reflect the case made by the early Christian apologists who had grounded the worship of the one true God upon the uniqueness of a single Roman emperor. Particularly influential in this regard was the "Christian Cicero," Lactantius, who had outlined his ar-guments for monotheism in the *Divine Institutes* 1:3 (a.d. 304–311):[41] the paral-lels, even in tone, to Dante's argument are notable. Lactantius begins with the question, "Whether the world is ruled by the power of one god or many?," and then argues that the rule of many compels the weakness of many rulers:

For what need is there of many sustaining the government of the world? Unless, perhaps, we will think, if there are many, that each single one will have less of strength and power. Actually, this is what they do who maintain that there are many; because it is necessary for them to be weak, inasmuch as each individual one is not able to sustain the governance of such a great mass without the aid of the others. However, God, who is eternal Mind, is by all means in every way perfect and consummate in his power. Since this is true, it is necessary that He be one.[42]

Similarly, Lactantius's traditional argument for the indivisibility of God's power—"For ruling the world there is need of one with perfect power rather than many with weakness"[43]—lays the ground, directly or indirectly, for the shape of Dante's later argument (*Mon.* 3:10) against the division of the empire caused by the Donation of Constantine.

That a king stood to his realm in the same relation as God stood to the world was a commonplace in Hellenistic political philosophy as well as in the Pythagorean-Platonic traditions, and we find it echoed not only in Lactantius, but in Ambrosiaster (a.d. fourth century), and, most important, in John of Salisbury (ca. 1115–1180);[44] it appears as a matter of course in St. Thomas Aquinas's *De regimine principum* (*On Princely Government*) completed by Tolomeo da Lucca:

The greatness of kingly virtue becomes further apparent from another fact; that is from *a king's singular likeness to God* [my emphasis]; since a king does in his kingdom what God does in the universe. Hence in the book of Exodus the judges of the community are called gods; and, their emperors were called gods by the Romans. But a thing is more acceptable to God the nearer it comes to imitating Him: so the Apostle warns the Ephesians [5:1]: "Be ye imitators of God as most dear children."[45]

To inspire a sense of utter indisputability and confidence for his thesis, Dante simply assumes and inverts the earlier traditional analogy of the world monarch that Lactantius and other early Christian apologists had used to argue for the unity of the Godhead.[46]

Thus, in his fourth point of confutation, we can, perhaps, comprehend why Vernani becomes for an instant more generous, giving credit to Dante's outlining of monarchy's unity, for he could readily see its application to the single papacy. The friar cannot resist, however, charging contemptuously that his opponent's "foolish love for his own opinion obscured his wits" (*Ref.* 1:44).

We must note that, in the second chapter (pp. 53–54) of the friar's own earlier treatise, *De potestate summi pontificis (On the Power of the Supreme Pontiff)*, Vernani had, in fact, alleged similar Aristotelian arguments from the family, neighborhood, and kingdom parallel to Dante's in *Monarchia*, chapter 5, for a single, supreme ruler among men, but, as we would expect, with a radically different conclusion. Considering the conditions ordered in Genesis 3:16, "Thou shalt be under thy husband's power, and he shall have dominion over thee," not as a postlapsarian punishment but as a "natural order," the friar reasoned that the rule of the paterfamilias was analogous to the intellect's rule over the body, and that fatherly authority had thus to signify the superiority of the spiritual power over the temporal. In chapters 2–3, he continued inductively with the governance of the city and the republic, determining, of course, that the spiritual power in the person of the pope must dominate.

Clearly, Vernani had read the *Monarchia*'s inimical conclusions only after he had completed the *De potestate* and the *Expositio super decretali Unam Sanctam*, since his earlier arguments betray no pattern that would indicate any special, earlier preparation for refuting Dante, and he makes no reference to the poet or to his ideas within those treatises. Acutely aware, by 1329, of Pope John XXII's ambitions for dominion and of Cardinal du Poujet's successes in advancing them by rendering Bologna and its dominated territories into a monarchical realm suitable for the Holy See to nest within, Vernani admits that the poet's idea of a single monarch is in conformity with ecclesiastical and philosophical opinion: "Monarchy would therefore be optimum, if the whole human race kept the laws and the precepts of peace according to the teaching of the Gospel of our Lord Jesus Christ. And *whatever is correctly affirmed on this matter in this fellow's treatise fits our catholic and philosophical way of thinking consistently* . . ." (*Ref.* 1:52; my emphasis)—but Dante, he avers, did not understand that Jesus Christ was the true monarch alone, his power to be assumed by the Supreme Pontiff as monarch on earth. Vernani perhaps affects ignorance that the designation "Vicar of Christ" had been also the prerogative title of the emperor at least from the fifth century.[47]

Vernani's next minor quibble concerning chapter 9, where Dante describes how mankind must follow the cosmic order of the heavens, seems to argue more against Aristotle (*Physics* 2:2:194b13) than Dante: he insists "that man and the sun beget man" must be understood only in respect to the flesh, not to the soul of man directly created by God. The friar then passes over Dante's second set of arguments in the rest of book 1 in silence, for, as he must have realized, they too could apply equally well to an ecclesiastical ruler.

In those remaining chapters of *Monarchia* 1, Dante continues to examine the unity and perfection of imperial rule. In 1:10 he expounds his arguments concerning the emperor as peacekeeper over lesser princes: since wherever there is a dispute there must be a resolving judgment available, and since equals do not have dominion over equals, two rulers will always require a third higher jurisdiction. Ultimately, to avoid escalation to an "impossible" infinity, a supreme judge, who is the emperor, must always have final jurisdiction. Neither Dante nor Vernani, of course, see fit even to mention the ironical fact that the papal Rota romana was, in fact, used as a final court of appeal in both ecclesiastical and civil cases.

After showing, in chapter 11, that a world monarch, possessing all by reason of his office, would be uninfected by cupidity or greed, the poet proves in a series of involved syllogisms that such a ruler is both most willing and most powerful in justice, power and charity, and is thus necessary for the best world order. Among canonists, mutatis mutandis, the same reasoning could easily and equally be applied to the Roman pontiff.

In chapter 12 the poet syllogizes his concept of liberty: man is at his best, that is, at his happiest, when most free; and man is most free under a world ruler; ergo, man is at his best under a world ruler. The monarch serves for the sake of his citizens, unlike rulers in the three corrupt or crooked forms *("politie oblique")* of government (*"democratie"*—by which Dante means mob or demagogic rule—oligarchies, and tyrannies), in which those who rule serve their own selfish ends. The poet waxes his most idealistic in chapter 13, as he argues that only the emperor, as one who has no occasion for avarice, can be free of anything that is the opposite of justice. Owning all and being most free of cupidity, the emperor is thus capable of imparting justice to others and is therefore best disposed to lead others to virtue. In chapter 14, again proving the necessity of single rule, Dante tries to avoid any taint of the kind of ecclesiastical reasonings expressed in *Unam Sanctam,* and bases his tenet on the principle of Aristotelian economy, as well as, once more, on the common prejudices concerning the monad and plurality: when something can be performed sufficiently well by one agent instead of by two, he avers, the second agent is an evil redundancy against nature and divine will. Although law emanates from a single source, however, the emperor, following Moses' example in the Bible, ignores detail and deals only with general matters, leaving minor issues to subordinates who attend to regional customs and differences. Therefore, again, the single monarch is necessary for the well-being of the world. In chapter 15 the poet continues to avoid mention of the papacy even while arguing for the inseparability of unity and goodness; for mankind is at its best when all wills concòrd. In practicality, however, one will must rule and direct others to this unity; therefore, he concludes implacably, for mankind to be at its best, there must be one monarch and one monarchy for the well-being of the world.

Finally, in chapter 16, Dante sees this perfect harmony and peace as having once existed under the emperor Augustus at the moment of Christ's birth, for it is attested by both St. Paul and St. Luke, as well as in pagan historians and poets. Returning to the themes outlined in chapters 3 and 5, the poet ends this first book with a stirring exhortation to mankind, sick in its speculative and practical intellect and in its affections, to seek a cure by pursuing a unified goal following the guide of a single emperor. Although Vernani was in all probability unaware of the connection, Dante's soteric concept of the historical mission of Rome here bears a striking similarity to the sermons (and we might surmise, perhaps to the private conversations) of his fellow Florentine, Remigio de' Girolami—who also affirms that Christ chose the hour of his birth at the "fullness of time" to mark as his own the world's most perfect, complete and last sixth age when Octavian ruled the entire world in a reign of utter peace.[48]

## ON BOOK 2

To set forth his response to the second question of *Monarchia* 1:2:3, "Whether the Roman people appropriated the office of monarchy to itself *de jure*," Dante relies less on the deduction of truths and more on the persuasive eloquence of dialectic and rhetoric. He argues, as the traditions of logic allowed, both from authority and by enthymeme, that is, as Aristotle defined, by "rhetorical syllogisms" based on truisms, likelihoods or, especially, signs (*Mon.* 2:5:6).[49] Nevertheless, despite his reiterated claims of using "the light of human reason," we recognize, often with uneasy suspicion, that the arguments arise and spill ever more into his beloved and more familiar realm of poetry. The more pedestrian Friar Guido will be driven to a cannonade of frustration: "This fellow sets forth some bombastic rhetoric in which he promises something beyond the powers of his smug ignorance" (Ref. 2:1). But Vernani indulges in unfair objurgations, for he knows well that Dante appeals several times, in *Monarchia* 2:2:1, 2:2:7 and 2:5:6, to Aristotle's recognition at the beginning of the *Nicomachean Ethics* (1:3:7) that political science was not exact: "It is the mark of an educated mind to expect that amount of exactness in each kind which the nature of the particular subject admits. It is equally unreasonable to accept merely probable conclusions from a mathematician and to demand strict demonstration from an orator."[50] The processes of reasoning differ according to the class of question to be treated; when the subject and premises are merely generalities, it is sufficient to arrive at generally valid conclusions. Though Dante builds a case and Vernani sets out vainly only to destroy, we must, notwithstanding, keep in mind that both the poet and the friar in their contrasting ways obeyed Aristotle's observations of "much difference of opinion and uncertainty" in politics. Both knew that St. Thomas in his *Commentary* on Aristotle's passages had warned that "moral matters are variable and divergent, not having the same certitude each time," for "rhetoric . . . deals with political matters where a variety of views occurs."[51] Both followed the rules of dialectic whose very etymology was known to signify contradiction and dispute rather than demonstration or proof.[52]

Dante's major concern in book 2, although he never names Augustine outright in this connection, is to mollify the anti-Roman negativity of that saint's treatise *The City of God*, that had narrowed and transformed the primitive Christian acquiescence in "the powers that be," preached by both Christ and the Apostle Paul, into antagonism. Augustine's treatise embodied the most influential adverse doctrines against temporal government during the Middle Ages. Both he and his follower Paulus Orosius (in the treatise *Adversus paganos* [*Against the Pagans*]) had given scornful portrayals of the heroes of republican Rome. While Augustine conceded to the Romans courage and self-control— that they despised wealth and corruption—this did not alter the fact for him that their government was never a true republic in that it never pursued the common weal. Augustine wryly derided the ancients for the idolatry that led them to a proud and obsessive pursuit of worldly glory through war and gore. For the memory of all ages, he recounted the tale of Alexander's pirate captive where the cynical prisoner revealed that empires were no more than huge robber baronies or brigandage.[53] Nonetheless, for the Bishop of Hippo, God's providence was still the source of all empire, for even unjust rulers were divine chastisement for the sins of subjects.[54] Augustine's position was at best equivocal: though he mocked and vituperated Roman pride and paganism, he proclaimed in *The City of God* 5:21 that "the Roman rule [*Romanum regnum*] was established by God, from whom all power comes, and by whose providence all things are ruled."[55]

In *Monarchia* 2:2:2–6, Dante recounts his break with the Augustinian position, which he describes almost as a conversion. After having earlier accepted that the rise of the Roman Empire was merely a series of chance events compelled by force of arms, he changed his mind, recognizing certain convincing signs that its growth was the result of God's will and favor.[56] Already in *Convivio* 4:5, inspired by Anchises's account of Roman history in *Æneid* 6:756–853, Dante had enthusiastically expressed the thesis that Providence had directed the origin and development of the empire and had listed instances of Roman sacrifice and heroism. To accommodate Augustine to Aristotle and bring these two radical Western currents of opinion on the origin of earthly government into some concord, Dante had to reconcile the Christian's view of the state as God-ordained for the punishment and correction of sin[57] with the Greek's teachings on the state's natural origin for the beneficent education of the citizen. He embraced Augustine's providential origin of empire while radically substituting *ius*, law and right, for force: legitimate Roman rule and justice brought the world to peace. The poet thus was to hold the history of the Holy Roman Empire as sanctified and as soteric as biblical history.

From chapter 1, the poet launches his major appeal to "the divine ray of authority," and proceeds, in chapters 3 through 9, with a series of seven arguments using allusions to major Roman events to demonstrate that the directing and perfecting will and judgment of the Deity is as dominant and apparent in pagan affairs as it is in Holy Scripture. For the last two chapters, 10 and 11, he draws on the authority of Christian revelation.

*Monarchia* 2:2 lays out his initial thesis: since right [*ius*] exists in the mind of God, and since all that is here on earth is a likeness of God's unseen divine will, it follows that any right *gained* through right—anything done *de jure* for a righteous end—is such a reflection of his will: thus the Romans, acting righteously for a righteous goal, obtained their dominion *de jure*.[58]

In chapter 3:2, he contrives a syllogism: "It is fitting that the most noble people be preferred before all others; the Roman people were the most noble; ergo, it is fitting that they be preferred before all others." To prove the truism of the first premise and to give two diverse definitions, he first cites, probably at secondhand, from Aristotle's *Politics* 1, where nobility is said to proceed socially "from virtue and ancient riches," and then from Juvenal's *Satire* 8:20, where that poet declares that "nobility is the one and only virtue."[59] Dante here modifies and corrects his less informed stand in the *Convivio* where, in the dissertation on his *canzone* "Le dolci rime d'amor," reflecting a favorite topic of the *dolce stil nuovo* poets (such as that expressed in Guido Guinizelli's seminal "Al cor gentil ripara sempre amore"), he had insisted on the personal acquisition of nobility through virtue. He there had roundly rejected the idea that nobility could be inherited:

When asked how he would define nobility, Frederick the Swabian, the last emperor of the Romans, replied that it consisted in age-old wealth and pleasing manners. I go on: *Someone else, of a shallower cast of mind:* after much thought and reflection on this definition from every angle, this person dispensed with the last feature (pleasing manners), and restricted himself to the first (age-old wealth). As the text says with feigned hesitation, perhaps it was because this person did not himself possess pleasing manners, and yet did not want to forfeit his title to nobility, that he defined it in a way that suited him: the possession of age-old wealth. I go on to imply that this opinion is held by almost everyone, when I say that they all follow his lead who hold that anyone is noble simply because he belongs to a family that has been wealthy for a long time, for this is barked in almost universal chorus. It seems that these two opinions can draw on two very important sources for support (though, as I have said, one of these opinions simply does not merit attention). The first is the belief of the Philosopher that it is impossible that what the majority of people holds should be totally false [!]; the other is the authority of the emperor, which is to be held in the highest esteem. To bring out more clearly how convincing the truth is, which is superior to every authority, I shall now discuss exactly what bearing and weight each of these sources has. Since one cannot know what value to attach to imperial authority unless one traces this to its root, I shall first devote a special chapter to discussing this topic. (*Con.* 4:3:6–10)

Dante knew that Brunetto Latini in *Li livres dou Tresor* had argued eruditely against Aristotle on the matter:

A man is called noble on account of his noble and virtuous deeds, and from this is born originally the nobility of a gentle race, and not from ancestors, for to have a vulgar heart and high lineage is to be an earthen vessel gilded outside with gold. Of this says Solomon, "Happy is the land that has a noble lord." For reason which gives him nobility overcomes all evil. Seneca says, "Who is noble? He who is by nature suited to virtue." (*Tresor* 2:54)[60]

Now, in the *Monarchia*, passing in silence over his earlier ignorance in having attributed the opinion of nobility-as-birthright to Frederick II, Dante must firmly establish the inherited nobility of the Roman people by now accepting the importance of genealogical character traits and the moral example that ancestors can set. Following Tolomeo da Lucca and veiling in silence the fact that his second, minor, premise—that the *Roman* people were the most no-ble—diametrically rejects the Christian authority of St. Augustine, Dante in-duces his proofs from the pagan authority of Livy and Vergil.[61] Crucial cita-tions from the *Æneid* validate poetically first the nobility of Æneas himself, then that of his forbears, and lastly that of his three wives—one from each of the three known continents, Creusa from Asia, Dido from Africa (for Dante, a wife *de facto*), and Lavinia from Europe.

In his *Refutation*, Guido Vernani recalls Augustine's derision of Roman mo-tives and easily deflects that mockery upon the poet. We must observe, howev-er, that, unmoved by what a modern reader might term Dante's romantic whimsy, nowhere in this regard does the friar impugn Dante's logical methods, his topics, nor even his poetical authorities per se, but only the interpretations and conclusions that the poet induces. Well trained in rhetoric and logic him-self, Vernani simply responds in kind, giving his own array of opposing quo-tations to assert Roman corruption, picked in turn from Christian authorities, not only from Augustine, but from St. Paul, Valerius, St. Bernard, and St. Jerome. He concludes instead that the Roman people lay nefariously "in the perpetual whoredom of the idolatrous worship of the foulest demons" (*Ref.* 2:6); no nation showed greater greed than they. The Jews, after all, he reminds us, not the Romans, were the Chosen People. Vernani, as the zealous hierocrat, mines the negations of his own earlier treatise *De potestate summi pontificis (On the Power of the Supreme Pontiff)* where he had discounted the legitimacy of the Ro-man Empire on the grounds that "among the unbelievers there never was a true republic or any kind of emperor."[62] In chapter 4 of that work, Vernani had held that "[a]mong the infidel there was never a true republic nor was there a true emperor," and he had elaborated:

Never was there a universal empire, for never was the whole world placed under obe-dience to one man, nor to one house, one city nor to one people. And thus it appears that among the empire[s] of the Assyrians, Persians, Greeks and Romans, who held the dominion of all, they [all] possessed it through violence. Similarly . . . never was there a true emperor among unbelievers, because there was never any man of purity who was of such perfection that it could exceed the perfection of all his subjects; but this perfection was alone in Christ, and thus he himself is the only true Emperor . . . and consequently his Universal Vicar.[63]

Friar Guido here complies with the reasoning of other extreme decretalist de-fenders and, particularly, that of his favorite model, Giles of Rome: "That unbelievers are all unworthy of any possession, lordship or power."[64] Yet the friar knew well that these assertions were far from universally accepted at the time and, that, instead, according to many theologians and canonists, unbelief had no bearing at all on the legitimacy of temporal rule.[65] He conveniently ignores the authority of even such a vehement defender of papal jurisdiction as Innocent IV who had asserted, circa 1250, that government was necessary not only for Christians, but for all rational creatures. Indeed, Innocent III had allowed that "lordship, possession and jurisdiction can belong to infidels licitly and without sin."[66] Vernani is similarly unmindful of St. Thomas Aquinas's more cautious view, of which Dante was aware, that, since government has a positive role and moral justification, established infidel rulers may rule—even over the faithful: "We must observe that dominion and authority are institutions of human law, while the distinction between faithful and unbelievers arises from Divine law. Now the Divine law which is the law of grace, does not do away with human law which is the law of natural reason. Wherefore *the distinction between faithful and unbelievers, in itself, does not do away with dominion and authority of unbelievers over the faithful* [my emphasis]."[67]

For his second argument, Dante gives a further enumeration of authoritative texts on portentous events to prove that God's active will aided the Roman people's rise to dominion by miracles (*Mon.* 2:4): first, the fall of the peculiar buckler from the skies during the prayers of Numa Pompilius[68] that pointed to the very place where the Roman Empire should arise; second, the fortuitous cackling of a goose that preserved the Capitoline Hill from the Gauls' night assault; third, the hailstorm that halted Hannibal's invasion; and, fourth, the wondrous escape of the hostage Cloelia, who broke her bonds and swam the Tiber on horseback during Lars Porsenna's siege of the city. It is hard today not to see the poet's instances as preposterously quaint even while we inevitably admire the intensity of his personal persuasion. His arguments have, after all, nothing to do with claims of using the light of human reason or even of adducing credible authority.

Thus, at first we might almost be tempted again to acquiesce in Vernani's ridicule of the poet's examples (*Ref.* 2:18–41); but then we realize that his objections are very different from those which we might have put forth ourselves. Accepting the accounts as historical fact, the friar first distinguishes the "preceptive" from the "permissive" will of the Deity: God did not *cause* or desire these real events to occur, but, rather, *permitted* them to happen, just as he might (in his divine, ever-indulgent love) *permit* a man to sin. Vernani makes here the same division within God's will that he had made in chapter 5 of his

*De potestate summi pontificis,* where, citing Augustine, he had affirmed that God *permitted* the ancient Romans to rule for an ultimate benefit: "to test the patience of the good, to punish the iniquity of the wicked." God merely allows the devil to reign justly over the proud.[69] The friar proceeds by rejecting Dante's positive explication of the four incidents rather than by censuring them immediately, or at any point, as mere *fictio* or poetry. We are struck by the obsessive pessimism in Vernani's distinctions: the forces "permitted" by God according to the *Refutation* are not caused by his generosity and justice in regard to the free will of mankind, but by the opposition of a diabolical, near-Manichaean force of evil (the shield, the geese, and the hail). Yet the friar feels bound by Dante's procedure and follows in the very pattern set by his opponent, responding within its delimitations.

Citing Augustine's opposing interpretation of the Capitoline goose (Ref. 2:20, 35–38), the friar tries to mimic Augustine's theological manner:

The tale of the goose is even sillier because this goose was either a real, living creature or a fantastic one. If it was a real goose, a creature extremely alert by nature, and if it was sleeping, it awakened and cackled at the slightest noise; therefore the tale is not to be regarded as miraculous but ridiculous. Concerning this, the blessed Augustine speaks derisively . . . in *The City of God* 2[:22]. . . . *If, on the other hand, the goose was a phantasm, it was easy for the demons not only to shape it but also to speak through it, in just the way the devil spoke to our first parents through the serpent.*[70]

Miracles these were not, Vernani insists, even if they may have been, per se, beyond the wont of nature, for only God can perform miracles. Thus to rebut his opponent, the canon lawyer must discover other *supernatural* modes and causes by which these events might have occurred. Since it never occurs to Vernani to treat this goose tale as folklore, any foolishness must needs lie in deception by diabolic conjuration. His opinion of the pagan gods as malignant demons ensnaring the minds of human beings with false beliefs to drag them down to hell is, after all, in accord with St. Augustine's (*The City of God,* 2:22, 3:8, 2:10, 2: 25).[71] Vernani thus argues that these are not prodigies of God, but supernatural acts of Satan (such as, those indeed—although the friar does not mention it—which Dante has Buonconte da Montefeltro recount in Augustinian fashion in *Purg.* 5:109–29). In other words, Vernani cavils merely at Dante's *in bono* decoding of the events while tacitly acquiescing in their supernatural quality. The events derive from devilish causes: Dante's inferences that they are God-ordained, not his processes, are at fault.

In *Monarchia* 2:5:4, the poet sets forth the syllogism of his third argument: "It is therefore obvious that he who attends to the common weal, directs his thoughts to the goal of right. If the Romans attended to the common weal, ergo, it will be true to say that they directed their thoughts to the goal of right." After having shown sufficiently—by a single quotation from Cicero —that the Romans served the common good in their public assemblies, Dante then lists seven cases of republican (not imperial!) heroes who sacrificed themselves for liberty and for love of country: Cincinnatus, who, taken from the plough to be made dictator, returned to the poverty of his former estate; Fabricius, who, refusing the bribe of Pyrrhus, preferred his poverty; Camillus, the dictator triumphant over the Veii, and still condemned and banished by envious enemies, who humbly obeyed that sentence of exile until the Senate removed it; Brutus, as consul, who sentenced his own sons to death for treason; Mucius, brought before Porsenna after failing to kill him, who held his own left hand in the fire to demonstrate his dedication to liberty, his loyalty to Rome and his indifference to pain; the three Decii who all gave their lives for Rome in battle; and, lastly, Cato Uticensis, who preferred suicide to life under the tyranny of Julius Cæsar.[72] Dante derives all the instances except Cato's from book 5, chapter 8 of Augustine's *The City of God*. The names parallel but are not identical to the examples Dante had earlier given in *Convivio* 4:5 to extol divine providence and Latin political genius; there he had taken seven from Augustine's chapter—Fabricius, Mucius, Torquatus, Brutus, Cincinnatus, Camillus, and Regulus—and added the Decii, the Drusi, Curius, Cato, Scipio, and Cicero; in *Monarchia* 2:5, he omits Torquatus, Regulus, and the Drusi.

While Augustine had admitted that the heroes were models of fortitude and dedication, he had presented each deed as flawed by the wrongful motive of exaggerated overweening pride. Such sacrifices for a mere city upon earth should be not a source of vainglory but a source of shame. For example, citing Cincinnatus's dedication, Augustine had warned that Christians should imitate such an action "to obtain a place in the company of angels," not as the Romans did, "only to preserve their own glory." The saint saw Brutus as an example to Christians of the extremes that pagan honor could lead in contrast to the easy yoke of Christ: Brutus was a lesson to the foolish who might dare to believe that they could actually merit eternal glory.[73] Mucius's bravery in the absence of any promise of eternal life was an exemplum to more fortunate Christian martyrs. As for Cato's touted suicide, Augustine had obscured it with doubt in *The City of God* 1:23: "What can I say of this act, then, other than that certain of his friends, also learned men, but more prudent ones, tried to dissuade him from it? For they deemed suicide more the deed of a foolish spirit than of a proud one: an act demonstrating not honor forestalling villainy, but weakness unable to sustain adversity."[74]

In writing *Convivio* 4:5 and *Monarchia* 2:5, Dante was not the first to balk at Augustine's negativity and dour anti-Roman sermonizing. The poet read and absorbed *On the Government of Rulers*, the long supplement to or, perhaps, more correctly, completion of, St. Thomas Aquinas's *On Princely Government to the King of Cyprus*, written by his Florentine acquaintance, the Dominican pupil and personal traveling companion of Thomas, Tolomeo da Lucca (ca. 1236–1327), but the similarity of his thought to Tolomeo's may be due also to a more direct and personal contact. Tolomeo, compiling the treatise during his priorate of the Dominican convent of Santa Maria Novella in Florence, probably about 1301,[75] had incorporated and elaborated much material from an earlier treatise of his own, the *Libellos sive tractates de iurisdictione imperii*, better known as the *Determinatio compendiosa (Short Determination)*, completed some twenty-three years earlier.[76] In both his treatises, Tolomeo had asserted that "because the kings and rulers of the Roman world were more solicitous than any others for these things, God inspired them to govern well, and for this reason they deserved an empire."[77] While following Augustine in affirming, in the *Government of Rulers* 3:1, that "all dominion is from God," he converted Augustine's lukewarm ambivalence into consummate praise:[78] the Romans merited dominion because of their zeal for the fatherland (3:4) and the sacred laws that they passed down (3:5). Their pursuit of justice was essential in their assumption of imperial supremacy, for their rule was granted "to preserve peace and justice." Never mentioning Augustine's censures of the Romans' proud egoism and idolatry, Tolomeo proves instead that the highest of the three religious virtues, *caritas*, motivated Roman patriots, and he seeks thereby to prove that the Romans gained their power by their threefold effort: their devotion to country, their zeal for justice, and their good intent toward their society.[79] While agreeing with some of Augustine's ambivalent providential arguments from *The City of God* 5:18, he had reused, in an opposite and positive way, a number of the examples and anecdotes there (Brutus, Torquatus, Curtius, Regulus, Fabricius, and Curius) to prove how and why God had granted world rule to the Roman people.[80] Unlike Dante, Tolomeo held that the papacy had replaced the ancient empire as the successor to Christ as king: ancient Roman righteousness backed the modern papal claim. Although in his view of global government Tolomeo supported the contemporary hierocratic theories of the pope's temporal ascendence, in the civil realm of the commune he was revolutionary in treating kingship as despotism and advocating the mixed and balanced governmental form of the *"politeia"* of republican Rome. Dante's argument for the ancient historical *legality* of the ancient Roman's assumption of temporal power is thus, in essence, at one with Tolomeo's, but, quite unlike Tolomeo, Dante, whose central aim was to support the temporal heir of the Romans against the papal claim of unique power, makes no distinction between republican and imperial Rome because he believes that *all* Roman feats bore witness to the pursuit of the goal of right that led ultimately to the *pax Romana* under Divus Augustus.

As is clear, Dante's selection of examples from Augustine's chapter do not exactly match the choices of Tolomeo, and it is probable, rather, that both Tolomeo and the poet eagerly reflect the subject and tenor of political-philosophical conversations in Florence of 1290–1302 at Santa Croce and Santa Maria Novella[81]—the restricted community of the erudite, and especially of Aristotelian scholars in the city, meant that Dante, Prior Tolomeo, and the lector and popular public orator Fra Remigio de' Girolami would have had ample opportunity to exchange ideas. Remigio, from 1273 until a few years before his death in 1319, had taught philosophy and theology at the Dominican *studium,* and there wrote, among many other works, *De bono communi* ( *On the Common Weal;* 1302–1303), *De bono pacis* (1304), and his sermon-guide to future lectors, *Contra falsos ecclesie professores* (1305), in which he examines the extent of papal power.[82] Just as Tolomeo and Dante choose a varied listing in two works, so Remigio derives a similar, but not identical, number of heroes from *The City of God* 5:18 as examples of civic honor for his *De bono communi.*[83] All the while he too rejects, again without overt dialectic, Augustine's decisively negative interpretation of Roman *pietas.*[84]

With an enthusiasm that stirs our admiration and with the comforting (yet not unquestioned) precedents of his Tuscan colleagues, Dante sets out to show that the will of God was made evident in the growth of the Roman Empire by signs and miracles operating in the actions of its citizens.

Vernani's reaction to Dante's list is predictable: he determines simply to be unimpressed. The friar either is unaware of, or else slyly ignores, the work of his fellow Dominicans and attacks Dante's arguments primarily on another, more encompassing ground set by Augustine: that idolatry destroys all possibility of righteousness or legality in governance. Thus, for the friar, the poet's central syllogism fails both in the minor premise and in the consequent. First, the Roman people were not attentive to the common weal since the "good" can only be one with the worship of God—and the Romans had not only worshiped idols but had even sacrificed human lives to demons. Second, the Romans were bent not on the sole, true celestial beatitude in which the human heart can rest, but upon the restless pursuit of worldly glory. He resorts to name-calling: only a madman *(insanus)* could claim that they had ruled justly.[85]

Vernani then turns his assault upon Dante's sixth and central chapter *(Ref.* 2:55ff.), where the poet argues that nature, by necessity, had to provide one place and fit one people to rule all others with justice to bring about world peace: "What nature has ordained is preserved *de jure,*" Dante argues, and, "the Roman people were ordained by nature to rule" *(Mon.* 2:6:1, 4, 8). Thus the one people and one place chosen for the *de jure* rule of the world were "Rome and its citizens, or rather its people" (2:6:8). In "sufficient proof" of the last contention the poet had offered two stirring quotations from the *Æneid* on Æneas's fitness to rule Rome. Friar Guido affirms the contrary: that it is not nature but rather man's will that inclines man toward beatitude; what is more, however much man's will is inclined to blessedness, man cannot attain it under his own power, for, as Vernani proves through biblical quotations, only God's grace and his divine providence can bestow its achievement. Divine providence therefore brought about Rome's greatness, not Rome's own ethical choice. In fact, the Greeks had more natural disposition toward ethics. Noting Dante's omission of the Jews as Chosen People, Vernani argues that by the centrality of their land[86] and by their religion, the Jews ought more rightly to have ruled the nations. Perhaps realizing that this argument vainly contradicts the actual outcome of history, Vernani feels he must note how late the Roman Empire was in coming. The world had waited some 4484 years since Creation,[87] as the Jews measure it, and 715 years from the founding of the city of Rome, until the rule of the idolatrous, sexually perverted (and therefore unrighteous and unjust) Cæsar Augustus brought about the empire, which, as both Sallust and St. Augustine bear witness, had become "utterly foul and dissolute . . . disgusting and profligate."[88]

Dante's longer, fifth argument, which covers chapters 7, 8 and 9, deals with the various forms in which God reveals his will in the outcomes of secular history. Some judgments of God, the poet explains (2:7:2), are clear to all, such as the necessity of risking one's life for one's country (a subject, in fact, then much discussed in factional Florence).[89] Some will be forever hidden, such as that only faith in Christ can lead to salvation, even though one may never hear of Christ.[90] Some of them God reveals either spontaneously, with or without a sign, or else by the prompting of man's prayers (2:7:8). Some he reveals through the casting of lots (as in the selection of Matthias to replace Judas). And, lastly, still others does God reveal through the outcome of a contest *(certamen)*. This form of judgment, which becomes the central core of the argument, the poet divides into two: revelation by athletic contest and revelation by blood duel.[91]

Beginning with chapter 8, Dante sets out to prove that God's decision is manifest by the Roman people's "prevailing over all other athletic contestants in a struggle for world empire" to gain the prize or goal of dominion over all mortals. The efforts of the Assyrians, Egyptians, and Persians as recorded by Paulus Orosius all failed, as did Alexander the Great's attempts to cheat the Romans of their prize. Lines from Vergil, Lucan, and Boethius bear witness to the Roman victory. To crown his point the poet cites Luke 2:1 on Cæsar Augustus's census of "the whole world." The Romans, therefore, prevailed by God's will, gained power by God's will, and thus held their dominion *de jure*.

In the following chapter, Dante presents, however, the argument that readers have always found the weakest in the *Monarchia*, for while his syllogism is formally impeccable, his major and minor premises appear at once arbitrary and unsound. What is acquired by a duel, he claims, is acquired *de jure* (2:9:1); the Roman people acquired empire by duel (2:9:12); ergo, the Romans acquired empire *de jure* (2:9:20). Thus the outcome of a *duellum*, by which he means a blood duel between rival champions, or a trial by battle between any combatant parties, reveals the unmediated intervention of the Deity. He probably hoped that his adoption of the concept of *"disceptatio"* (meaning roughly "divine revelation through the decision or outcome of a contest" [2:9:3]) and the substance of his argumentation would lean heavily on the authority of Augustine expressed passim in *The City of God:* for both writers, "the duration and the outcome of wars depend on the judgment of God."[92] In his examples the poet omits all of Augustine's admonishments and censures of such contests, as well as the saint's vehement deploring of such Roman engagement as nothing but a sacrilegious squandering of life. Instead, he boldly extols the famed duel of the Horatii and Curatii despite the full knowledge that Augustine had denounced the fight, memorably, as an arrogant, ungodly waste.[93] Dante may have been unaware that the Germanic recourse to duels, despite the impossibility of its eradication, had been condemned by Cassiodorus under Theodoric circa 507–511, banned on Italian soil since at least 643, and forbidden, in tradition, by Pepo, the legendary eleventh-century father of Bolognese juridical studies. But for his forensic purposes, Dante certainly feigns ignorance of Pope Nicholas I's prohibition of such contests in 867, of Gratian's encoding of that proscription in the *Decretum*, of Celestine III's total abolishment (1191–1198) of duels, of Innocent III's prohibition of them at his accession,[94] and of Gregory IX's solemn reiteration of that ban that canonists entitled: "Duels and other popular expiations are prohibited, because most often he who should be absolved is condemned, and God is seen to be tempted."[95] The poet is making an appeal at once both overly erudite and popular: although dueling was outlawed often by both ecclesiastical and civil governances, we find the obstinate custom much attested into the thirteenth century, not only in traditionalist feudal communities, but especially in communal Florence.[96]

The validity of such a duel by two sets of champions or two armies, Dante cautions, must be guaranteed by strict norms: combat must be by common assent, be the last resort after all other means have failed, and be motivated only by zeal for justice, not bitterness or hatred (2:9:4). Surely, he conjectures, on the thinnest ground (2:9:5), that with the rules obeyed, would not the combatants have been gathered in God's own name (as Christ promises in Mt 18:19–20)? He then runs through a list of citations dealing with four major Roman wars, two of the early period, with the Albans and with the Samnites, and two of the later, with the Greeks and with the Carthaginians. The outcomes of all these duels (albeit among benighted pagans, we must emphasize), in the poet's contention, bear witness to the direct intervention of God.[97]

Vernani has easy grounds for rash refutation, but his attack here is deliberate: he even spares Dante easy mockery concerning the adducing of Matthew 18:20. If no victory is unjust, then, surely, the friar now asks with solid logic, how can the defeats that the Romans themselves suffered be unjust? Similarly, the argument that whatever is acquired as an outcome of war is acquired justly (*Ref.* 2:84ff.) is self-evidently false, for then any criminal assault or victory would be just. The poet has not only failed to distinguish just from unjust wars, but the overabundance of sins that bound the Romans—as in Saint Augustine's list, their gratuitous craving of harm, cruel revenge, obdurate rancor, barbarity in rebellion, and obsession for power—marred the righteous outcome of all their wars, tainting all legality of their triumphs. Taking his argument to its irresistible extreme, Vernani glowingly concludes that the Romans acted against the very law of nature.[98] But, like Dante, Vernani omits any reference to the prohibitions in ecclesiastic and civil law.

By chapter 10 Dante has concluded his first six arguments based upon his brief, idealistic overview of Roman history, what he terms, so curiously for us, "reasons that rest upon rational principles," and commences his "proofs by principles of the Christian faith," that is, by allusions to the major events of Christian redemption. But before making his final point, the poet first vents his moral outrage in an attack on his chief opponents: those who have had, in recent history, the greatest advancements in the papal hierarchy, the lawyer-prelates who, while professing their zeal for the Church, not only refuse to acknowledge the authority of the emperor, but advance their ambitions through nepotism, steal from the Church, and deny help to the poor. Dante surely wishes to appear respectful while actually recalling to the reader's memory St. Paul's censures in Romans 10:2–3: "They have zeal of God, but not according to knowledge. For they, not knowing the justice of God, and seeking to establish their own, have not submitted themselves to the justice of God." The poet was certainly aware that this one use of the word "zeal" in the Gospels came *as Christ cast out the sellers from the temple in John 2:17*: Christ's disciples thereupon recall Psalm 69:10: "The zeal of thy house hath eaten me up; and the reproaches of them that reproached thee are fallen upon me." The poet is actually hammering his point paraliptically: the fault lies at root in the Church's corrupting wealth and ambition for temporal power.

In *Monarchia* 2:10:4, Dante comes to what should be the climax of his argument, but, to our surprise, he changes his dialectical procedure to formally weaker antecedent-consequent statements such as he suggested in *Monarchia* 2:5:21: "Everything stands to its end as a consequent to its antecedent." He presents his question not in a complete syllogism, but as a conditional argument in the *modus tollens* form, or, as he says in *Monarchia* 2:10:9, "denying the consequent": "I therefore affirm that if the Roman Empire did not exist *de jure*, then Christ by His birth approved something unjust; the consequent is false; ergo, the contradictory of the antecedent is true." Most important for Vernani's rebuttal, the poet presents the proposition as an enthymeme, a choice that allows the omission of any tedious intermediate polysyllogisms or episyllogisms, that is, of any confusing antecedent premises and conclusions: Christ could not have approved something unjust, ergo the Roman Empire existed *de jure*. Dante intends the unspoken abhorrent implicit conclusion of an injustice sanctioned by Christ to compel our instant agreement. He thereby lays down a rhetorical minefield for future adversaries.

To be on logically safe footing himself (2:10:4), the poet cleverly adduces Aristotle's repeated affirmation that "contradictory judgments cannot both be true," in compliance with Peter of Spain's formulation in the *Summulæ logicales*: "The law of contradictories is such that if one thing is true, the other must be false and vice versa: in no question can things be true and false at the same time."[99] But as to its soundness rather than its logical validity, Dante's actual procedure becomes purely forensic. He knows that Aristotle himself had intentionally omitted the discussion of enthymemes in his *Rhetoric* 1:1, when the philosopher explained: "These writers [of *Rhetoric*], however, say nothing about enthymemes, *which are the substance of rhetorical persuasion, but deal with nonessentials. The arousing of prejudice, pity, anger, and similar emotions has nothing to do with the essential facts,* but is merely a personal appeal to the man who is judging the case."[100] In Dante's case, his argument is not logically substantial: it is a personal entreaty to the reader.

Dante's unspoken premise according to Christian faith is that "Christ never sanctioned anything unjust" or that "Christ only approved what was just." But the intermediate, unstated consequents/antecedents that his enthymeme leaps over are numerous, among them, necessarily: "Whatever Christ suffered he approved," to which, as we shall see, Vernani is drawn to give an erroneous and self-defeating rebuttal. Among the other intermediate steps necessary to prove that "Christ by His birth approved the Roman Empire," Dante would have had to deduce further that "the birth of Christ signified approval," that "Christ was born under the effective legitimacy of Cæsar's edict calling the census" and, most important, that "Cæsar's edict calling the census was not unjust." Vernani is, however, acute enough, at least, to attempt a disproof of this last missing element in his *Refutation* 2:98: "[Christ] did not approve of that edict, since two vices, of course, *avarice and vainglory, drove Cæsar to proclaim it*" (my emphasis).

Dante proceeds relentlessly with his argument, even though many of the faithful to whom he appeals, as strict followers of Augustine, would a priori refuse to transfer their belief in the uprightness of Christ to the presumed righteousness of the Roman Empire. The poet leads the reader into surrendering to the final arguments by concentrating on the fact, not of the empire's legality, but on the precedent that has been assumed from the start by faith—that of Christ's justness.

Vernani, correctly identifying Dante's argument with rhetoric[101] rather than with logic, should have become immediately more wary, but he gives, as we have seen, merely a facile rebuttal (*Ref.* 2:95–96), responding to the poet's unstated assumptions with a list of supposedly corollary absurdities: to argue Christ's approval of Cæsar's census by the timing of his birth would be the same as arguing that Christ had approved not only Pontius Pilate's condemnation, but also Judas's betrayal, the Jews' cry for crucifixion, and the soldiers' scourging. In this case again Friar Guido allows only the "permissive" will of the Deity: Christ did not *approve*, Vernani contends, but only *submitted* to all of these by his own will. Only Cæsar's sheer cupidity and vainglory motivated the proclamation of the census. Vernani strives vainly to demolish the argument, but as we shall understand, his attempt to reduce faith to pure logic is fatally flawed: in Christianity, God really did positively will and approve man's redemption in the extraordinary manner Dante sets forth. The friar forgets that even St. Augustine had feared lest indulging in excessive censures of the idolatry of the Romans might overshadow the message of God's overruling will and providence, and the friar fails to keep in mind that Augustine had corrected any such trap in *The City of God*.[102] As we shall see, Vernani neglects to consider that Christ's sacrifice was both beyond reason and itself glowed as the foolishness of the Cross.

Dante begins his final, seventh argument (chapter 11) by redoubling his daring leap of faith and logic: if the Roman Empire had not existed *de jure*, Adam's sin was not punished in Christ. The poet's rhetorical inversion seizes the reader's wonder at his method of arriving at this final point, for surely, again, the efficacy of Christ's sacrifice cannot be put in doubt. For the space of the argument the poet can blind us to the fact that it is the first, not the second, proposition that requires proof, and, consequently, he can slip into that which, for a believer, really needs no proof at all: had the Crucifixion not been a just punishment, man could not have been redeemed from Adam's sin. Fatally, Vernani will be led to reprove the proven and err in doing so.

After a paragraph seeking the true sense of punishment, omitting Christ's obvious lack of culpability, Dante reaches the almost self-evident and sound proposition that "if Christ had not suffered under an ordinary judge [one of last resort] that penalty would not have been a punishment." He then delves into the question of such a judge's power and authority to exact penalty. Adducing the undeniable and undoubted superabundance and perfection of Christ's redemption, he ends with a number of biblical quotations proving the legitimacy of Cæsar's and Pilate's authority. The very Bible is here the basis of the poet's belief in the right and law of the empire:[103] Adam had incurred sin for all of mankind; since the Roman Empire ruled all of mankind, it therefore had ultimate authority to impose sentence. Since Pilate was the vicar of Cæsar, therefore Pilate, and not King Herod, must have been the judge plenipotentiary with due jurisdiction. Christ therefore sanctioned the Roman Empire both at his birth and at his death: it therefore existed *de jure*. Thus Dante hopes to silence all opposition by invoking the supreme Christian example of direct divine intercession.

Here, in reaction, an embarrassed Vernani takes a crude cue from the poet's repeated citation of Psalm 2:1 on the raging of the nations, and attempts idle retribution by labeling Dante's "useless and ludicrous argument" as the "height of ... delirium." He flashes us a glimpse of the poet's writhing grotesquely in the paroxysms of an epileptic seizure (*Ref.* 2:101). The friar waxes a little more expansive and prolix, however, as he begins to savor the presumed integrity of his rebuttal. Surely, Vernani ratiocinates, the punishment for original sin could not lay in the power of any earthly jurisdiction; Christ's death was the Savior's obedience to God's will, not just punishment for the commission of sin, but for "the preservation of righteousness." Then to counter Dante's contention that Pilate was fully, *de jure*, judge ordinary in deciding Christ's death (*Mon.* 2:11:2–3) with full sacred power to inflict due punishment upon the Savior for the collective sin of mankind, the friar triumphantly caps his lucubrations by citing St. Augustine's *On True Religion* 16:31: "What greater injustice than that an innocent man be condemned."[104] But the friar completely misreads and misrepresents that quotation from Augustine's context, for the Bishop of Hippo there is opposing the humility and willingness of Christ to the incomprehension and pride of those putting him to death. Contrasting the ways of God to the ways of man, Augustine stresses the Jews' and the heathens' bafflement at the Savior's peerless sacrifice:

To heal souls, God adopts all sorts of means suitable to the times which are ordered by his wondrous wisdom.... The peoples, to their own destruction, sought riches that ministered to pleasures while [Christ] determined to be poor.... He suffered insults of every kind while they thought injuries were not to be endured: *"What greater injury can there be than that a just and innocent man should be condemned?"* They execrated bodily pain while he was beaten and tortured.... (My translation; my emphasis)

It was a matter of judgment and approval for Christ both as man and God that by his own will he suffered death on the Cross. The lawyerly Vernani, beguiled by Dante's rhetoric to concentrate upon truths proven, seeks to find some legal fault to disprove in the poet's presentation. But in the effort, Vernani quite obliviously places himself on the side of the unbelievers! We might, on the friar's behalf, add Isaiah's words that were taken as prophetic of Christ's death: "Surely he has borne our infirmities and carried our diseases. . . . the Lord had laid on him the iniquity of us all. He was oppressed, and he was afflicted, yet he did not open his mouth; like a lamb to the slaughter, and like a sheep that before its shearing is silent, so he did not open his mouth. *By a perversion of justice he was taken away*" (53:4–12). Yet Vernani does not cite this, and had he done so it would not matter. He could still only be correct if we were to rely solely upon the Old Testament as authoritative and ignore the fulfillment in the New. Besides, the friar's conclusion is dead wrong.

We note that Dante's reference is first to the high priest Caiaphas's prophesy of Christ's death (*Mon.* 2:11:6), second to Herod's obvious submission to Pilate's ultimate Roman authority on the sentencing (Lk 23:11), and, finally (as the poet had also noted in his *Epistle 5, To the Peoples and Princes of Italy*), to Christ's own words of recognition of Pilate's divinely ordained power in John's Gospel.[105] Not only is Caiaphas moved to give, unknowingly, the true prediction of God's redemptive will (as Bruno Nardi noted), "It is necessary that one die so that all others may not perish" (Jn 11:49–50, 19:10–11), the bound Christ's own words grant and affirm that Pilate indeed possessed God's full jurisdiction over him: "You would have no power over me *unless it had been given you from above.*"[106]

The poet thought such truths common knowledge and self-evident as a witness to Christ's love and had carefully planned his "denial of the consequent" argument accordingly. Vernani plays ironic foil to Dante's daring dialectic.

## ON BOOK 3

Dante's third book deals with a prevailing and intensely litigated question, "whether the authority of the Roman monarch, who is *de jure* the monarch of the world . . . depends directly on God, or on some vicar or minister of God." Whereas in book 1 of the *Monarchia*, we saw him proceed as a philosopher, by means of syllogisms, and in book 2, write in the guise of historian-poet-visionary, appealing to the precedents of pagan history and divine intercession, in book 3, he returns to Scholastic logical forms, speaking as a theologian and a canonist, proceeding carefully to confront the legalistic reasonings of the papal curia and correct its rhetorical and political abuses. This defense of the empire's autonomy is tactical and combative: his tone often swells with contained aggressiveness and his vocabulary waxes bellicose, as if he could foresee the imminent and tragic destruction that radical papal claims were to wreak. Once he completes his arguments, however, in chapter 16:17–18, he chooses to conclude his treatise on the peaceful, charitable note of shared love and reciprocal cooperation.

Dante brings nine arguments to bear in his rebuttal of decretalist claims (the symbolism of the poet's favorite number in these refutations is noteworthy): six are scriptural, with three each, in biblical order, from the Old and New Testaments, and then three are historical. When this corrective, negating, phase is complete, he then adds one more positive argument of his own based, he claims, on reason, to bring the total up to ten, the numerological symbol of perfection. Most revealing of the late medieval cast of Dante's thought is the process by which, even as he refutes false conclusions, he works within the prison of the system in which those conclusions were reached. He must refute analogical reasoning by analogical disputation, that is, by discrediting the similitude or, as it was then called, the "exemplum"—in short, by attacking the presumed causal soundness of the analogy, but not repudiating the accepted process of logic by analogy itself.[107]

Ironically, for the antagonistic reception that Guido Vernani gives book 3, Dante has returned there to agree with the earlier decretist, dualist positions that some papal canonists had once held—especially, as we have noted, those put forth by Uguccione da Pisa who had defended the discrete and distinct divine origin of the dual powers. Vernani gives these conclusions his most virulent rebuttal. Here especially, no appreciation of the poet's positions glimmers in the mind of this truculent adversary, no matter how close they may be even to the work of Dominican theologians whom the friar himself respected.

Dante is not using mere hyperbole, when, in chapter 1, in his opening citation from Daniel 6:22, and again in chapter 3:1–5, he recognizes the inquisitorial risks that antagonism to his defense of justice could incur. He fully expects the rancor of the opposition to be the bitter fruit of his labor. A new Daniel, trusting his own righteousness, ignoring self-interest, invoking the pure eloquence of Isaiah, and girded with Paul's breastplate of faith, he enters the metaphoric wrestling ring/lions' den of debate to hurl forth his opponents. The imagined and confused causal relation of Genesis's "two great lights" to the earthly and spiritual powers will be the center of his argumentation, and, more specifically, "whether the authority of the Roman monarch, who is *de jure* the monarch of the world . . . depends directly on God or on some vicar or minister of God who . . . is the successor to Peter and is truly bearer of the keys of the kingdom of heaven."

At first reading, chapter 2 appears as a rather involved interpolation, despite the fact that it establishes as the main principle "that God does not will anything that is repugnant to the intention of nature." This, however, will become fully and clearly cogent by the last chapter of book 3, as Dante spells out his fuller argument concerning man's dual end, which is both temporal and celestial. So that man may arrive at the first of these goals, God and nature therefore provide the means: the earthly emperor.

In chapter 3, he lists his three main groups of opponents, all of whom claim falsely that the emperor derives his power only indirectly through the papacy. The first are the pope and bishops, motivated, he grants ironically, by zeal for the Keys of Heaven and for the Church rather than by pride; the second, those motivated through greed or cupidity, by which he means those who, by exploiting their allegiance to the Guelph party,[108] stand to gain the greatest temporal benefits by their ascendancy in Italy; and the third, the decretalists who base their arguments only upon recent papal decrees. Dealing with the groups in typical chiastic, or reverse, order,[109] he first dismisses these last opponents. He insists, contrary to the official practices of canon law, that by precedence and authority among the various ecclesiastical writings before, during, and after the early Church, their texts hold the least weight of any: the Scriptures dating before the Church's founding, namely, the Old and New Testaments are of highest importance;[110] then, concurrent with the Church are the findings of the great councils working in the presence and inspiration of God—and with these belong also the writings of the early doctors, Augustine and others. But, in third place, long postdating the founding of the Church, are those writings recently given the name "traditions" which, though they are worthy of veneration for their apostolic authority (detractors of canon law were liable to a charge of blasphemy against the Holy Spirit, as Gratian had warned), are still to be assigned authority inferior to that of the fundamental Scriptures. Traditions come from the Church, not the Church from its traditions: Dante is especially exercised by the novelty of one insolent decretalist's recent claim "that the 'traditions' of the Church were the foundation of the faith" (*Mon.* 3:3:10, 16). The specific "traditions" to which Dante sarcastically refers here are not the original true "divine traditions" of the early Apostolic Church, but, as he makes clear, "those traditions that are called 'decretals'" (*Mon.* 3:3:14). The poet contemns the current, pompously hierocratic term "traditiones ecclesiasticæ" applied to such bulls as *Novit, Per venerabilem* and *Venerabilem fratrem* of Innocent III, and *Ausculta filii* and *Unam Sanctam* of Boniface VIII, a usage also ridiculed, for example, in contemporary manuscripts of the anonymous *Disputatio inter Clericum et Militem (A Debate between a Clerk and a Knight),* of 1302.[111]

The problem of the hierarchy of church texts, however, had already festered for almost two centuries. Gratian himself had affirmed, perhaps, for the time, rather astoundingly, that the decretals were to be preferred over the Church Fathers' theological exegeses in questions of faith. Henry of Susa (Hostiensis), the most adamant and influential of the "moderns" whom Dante so detested, had reaffirmed Gratian's position: "In all disagreements *it is better to believe canon law rather than the statements of the saints* or teachers [*in omnibus dissentionibus* magis est credendum legi canonicæ quam dictis sanctorum *vel magistrorum*], which are in conflict among themselves, for to the pope and to no other is given the interpretation of such doubtful matters."[112] Among the Franciscans, whose order had forbidden the teaching of medicine and law during the thirteenth century, the unfortunate Roger Bacon (ca. 1214–ca. 1292) had complained of the novelty of the "cavils and frauds of the jurists" in canon law, urging a return to the authority of theology.[113] Among the famous civil scholars of law, Dante's close friend Cino da Pistoia had been most acrimonious against ecclesiastical lawyers on the subject.[114] We might recall that Dante relegates the Bolognese Guelph jurist Francesco d'Accorso, who had written the *Glossa magna* to Justinian's *Pandects* and attributed higher value to the *Decretals* than to the Church Fathers' writings, to the teams of naked sodomites on the Plain of Fire (*Inf.* 15:110).

Thus in his daring rebuttal, Dante recalls that Christ himself taught that slavish attention to tradition was wrong and that it was to be given a lower place. Hence, those who hold this belief the poet throws first from the arena of argument. He likewise (*Mon.* 3:3:17) summarily dismisses the greedy Guelph hangers-on who call themselves "sons of the Church," yet are the devil's brood. They wear their feigned allegiance to mask their love of money. Dante censures their barratry and simony, evoking in the knowing reader his unforgettable picture of Pope Nicholas III (1277–1280) buried upside down in eternal punishment for simony in *Inferno* 19.[115] The conjoining of these two groups darkly colors the poet's exaggerated veneration in his treatment of his first, and now final, category of opponents, the prelates and the supreme pontiff (*Mon.* 3:3:18).

Thereafter, in *Monarchia* 3:4, the poet engages in a more extended combat with the hierocrats' grandiose analogy supposedly based on Genesis 1:14–19[116]—that the emperor receives his power from the pope just as the moon receives all its light from the sun: "The present question, which we will have to discuss, centers upon 'the two great lights,' namely, the Roman pontiff and the Roman prince."[117]

An important and telling version of the analogy of the "two lights" had appeared, not for the first time in ecclesiastical writing, but for the first time in a papal document, in Innocent III's letter *"Sicut universitatis conditor"*[118] to the prefect Acerbo Falseroni and the Tuscan nobility, of November 3, 1198: there Innocent affirmed that the moon, which was the royal power, belonged to and resided within the "firmament of the Church"; it was emphatically inferior in splendor, in quality, size, and power to the sun, which the Church-firmament also possessed completely:

Just as God, the founder of the universe, has constituted "two great lights" in the firmament of heaven, so that the greater light might preside over the day and the lesser light might preside over the night [Gn 1:16], in the same way *within the firmament of the universal Church,* which is signified by the name of Heaven, He established two great dignities, the greater to preside over souls, corresponding to the day, and the lesser to preside over bodies, corresponding to the night. These are the pontifical authority and the royal power. Thus, as *the moon receives its light from the sun* and for this very reason *is inferior both in quantity and in quality,* in its size and in its effect, so the royal power [*regnum*] derives the splendor of its dignity from the pontifical authority.[119]

Comforted by the unquestioned practice of analogical thinking in which metaphors were said to be based on a "similitude of proportion" (in this case, though, as Dante will criticize, the term "power" was arbitrarily assimilated to "light"), the analogy stirred the awe of very truth. We have noted that the analogy had also gained wider currency through the effect of Innocent III's decretal, *Solitæ benignitatis,*[120] addressed to the Byzantine emperor Alexius, one of the first missiles hurled in the papacy's ever-growing claims, and one which, for example, that scholar who was a leading member of the Aristotelian-Thomistic group in Florence before Dante's exile, Fra Remigio de' Girolami of Santa Maria Novella, cites verbatim in his treatise *Contra falsos ecclesie professores,* of circa 1305.[121]

As we might expect, the extremist "Hostiensis" had relied heavily upon the concreteness and causality of the analogy: in his long gloss on *Per venerabilem* (*"Qui filii sint legitimi"*) in his *Summa aurea*, he asserted that "[t]he Moon receives brightness from the Sun, not the Sun from the Moon . . . so the royal power receives its authority from the priestly . . . thus the Sun illuminates the world through the Moon when it cannot do so itself."[122] With an unconscious absurdity arousing the mockery of his later opponents, the venerable cardinal of Ostia then adduces Ptolemy's *Almagest* to prove with mathematical precision the superior brightness of the sun: the pope's power he calculates is thus "seven thousand, six hundred and forty-four and one half times greater than royal authority"![123] Ergo, he concludes, "The emperor holds his empire from the Roman Church and can be said to be its subaltern or vicar, by the person of Charlemagne who transferred the empire from the Greeks to the Germans. And the pope confirms him, and anoints him, and crowns him, or reproves him and deposes him, as is clear from the [bull] *On election* [*Venerabilem*]."[124] From his insistence we sense the genuine pleasure with which Henry of Susa contemplated this relay of power, increased, we might add, by the knowledge that, as the cardinal bishop of Ostia, it was within the office of those bearing the title of his see to consecrate the popes.[125]

Among the Florentine Dominicans whom the poet surely knew personally, Fra Remigio de' Girolami remarked that Hostiensis's observations had become part of the *Glossa* on the *Decretals* and had taken the prelate's comparison between the sizes of the sun and moon so seriously that he too expanded on it as if it were scientific fact: "The sun is three times larger than the moon at present, that is *by the magnitude of* its width, nobility, and *its authority* according to the saints and philosophers; according to this magnitude, the principality of the Church is without doubt greater than any other earthly principality. According to Alfagranum, the sun is one hundred and sixty-seven and a fraction times bigger the earth, as also the moon is thirty-nine and a fraction of the size of the earth, and Ptolemy in his *Almagest* V accepts the proportion of eighteen."[126] We have the impression that Dante appears to be above the astronomic absurdities of the hierocrats, yet not only had he once indulged in similar excogitations himself,[127] but he was also intimately aware of the sheer power of the "two lights" analogy in canonist circles; as we shall see, his response to such indulgence will prove quite subtle.

The ever-increasing veneration given the analogy can be measured best among its cowed opponents: for all of his egotism and his strife with the popes of his time, even Emperor Frederick II of Hohenstaufen had never questioned the novel simile that implied a "dimmer" status for his own authority. In 1239 he wrote that the papacy and the empire were like the sun and moon, for "the greater communicates its brightness to the lesser." But he went on to insist, appropriately, that the sun should follow celestial order and stay out of the moon's lower orbit.[128]

Boniface VIII had more recently given the analogy its most intimidatingly political reiteration. That pope's solemn *Allegacio*, pronounced in consistory to affirm Albert of Hapsburg as emperor on April 30, 1303, affirmed that the moon was not only inferior, but actually powerless without the sun:

God made two great lights, that the greater light might preside over the day and the lesser light might preside over the night. These two lights God were made literally according to Genesis. And nonetheless, spiritually understood, he made the aforesaid lights, namely the sun, that is the ecclesiastical power, and the moon, which is the temporal and imperial, that it might direct the universe. And *just as the moon has no light, except for that which it receives from the sun, so the terrestrial power only has what it receives from the ecclesiastical power* [my emphasis].[129]

This bull, directed at imperial power, and cited later by Pope Clement V in his *Romani principes*, boded an even more comprehensive threat than Boniface's *Unam Sanctam*, directed merely at the French king.[130] Its claims aroused the poet's stern objection (*Mon.* 3:4:11): as Maccarrone has shown, Dante's purposefully redundant passage in *Monarchia* 3:4:2 echoes and responds to the kind of obdurate and repetitive wording used by Boniface and his legal advisers:[131]

In the first place they assert according to the text of Genesis that God made two great lights, a greater light and a lesser light, so that the one might preside over the day and the other might preside over the night; they are wont to interpret these as meaning allegorically the two governing powers: to wit, the spiritual and the temporal. From this they argue that, just as the moon, which is the lesser light, has no light except that which it receives from the sun, in the same way temporal power has no authority except that which it receives from the spiritual power.

The poet attempts first to topple the analogy with the charge, one then much in vogue, of unjustified biblical exegesis.[132] Citing St. Augustine's *The City of God* 16:2 and *On Christian Doctrine* 1:36–37 on acceptable interpretation, he complains of the error of those who wrench the meaning of the inspired writer of Genesis and thus of the Holy Spirit to a sense never intended.[133] He denounces the analogy's soundness on the grounds of chronological order, for the ruling powers are actually "accidents" or qualities of man: the offices of the two guides of mankind were founded far later than the "great lights" to which they are compared, and were necessitated to correct man's later Fall into "the infirmity of sin."[134] God had created the sun and the moon on the fourth day of Creation two days before mankind on the sixth (Gn 1:14–19; 26–27, 31). Citing for his procedure Aristotle's *On Sophistry* 18 [176b29] that "the refutation of an argument is the exposure of error," he rejects as false and inconceivable the assumption that God would create the "accidents," that is, man's sinfulness and its two curative powers, before the substantive subject, man (*Mon.* 3:4:12–15). Demonstrating his forensic powers in logic, he shows that his opponents commit the logical "fallacy of accident" (*fallacia accidentis*).

Dante knew, however, that hierocrats had formulated their claims in a very specific manner, as, for example, did James of Viterbo: "Temporal power preexists in the spiritual power as an inferior capacity does in a superior, and as *that which is cause* [*pre-exists*] *in its cause* . . . whoever is under the temporal power is therefore also under the spiritual." And later, "The Supreme Pontiff . . . is also superior in dignity *and causality* to every temporal power, it can therefore be rightly concluded that *in the Supreme Pontiff there pre-exists fullness of pontifical and royal power.*"[135] Thus, in the second part of his argument, the poet must destroy the analogy in a different way by confuting the assumed *causal relationship* between the sets of objects compared. Unfortunately, however, he has, therefore, perforce, to readmit the hated analogy with a mere modification (just as he had already obliquely conceded it at *Mon.* 1:11:5). Accepting the current scientific hypothesis of the moon's glow during eclipses, he argues that the sun is neither the *cause* of the moon's being, nor the *cause* of its light (for the decretalists, its *"virtus,"* "power"), for God created the moon with "a little light of its own" (*Mon.* 3:4:18).[136] Like the moon, the temporal power derives its being and power directly from God but, as Dante not only concedes but expresses as his central thesis of the two powers' cooperation, it receives *an increase in its ability to function* from the grace of the pope's solar blessing. He thereby reiterates more weakly the eclipse metaphor he had used imaginatively in his *Epistola 5, To the Princes of Italy,* of September–October 1310, heralding Henry VII's coronation: there the "splendor of the lesser luminary" of the empire would continue to shine even if and when papal light was insufficient, as in an eclipse.[137] The awkwardness of the whole controversy, confusing analogy in cause and analogy in reasoning, becomes even more out of focus when we realize that Dante's own "scientific" arguments concerning eclipses are actually aimed at rebutting such fantastic technicalities as Hostiensis's and Remigio's taken from Alfagranus and Ptolemy's *Almagest*.

Tilting at a shibboleth that for over a century had exceeded all bounds of common sense, the poet hoped that a last defense against such illogic might be logic itself and wielded this as his ultimate weapon: finally, at the end of the chapter in *Monarchia* 3:4:21–22, he points to the obvious fault in the hierocrats' syllogism. They are guilty of slipping in a fourth term: "The argument is in error as to its form, because the predicate in the conclusion is not the term of the major premise. . . . While in the term of the major premise they posit 'light,' in the predicate of the conclusion they posit 'authority,' but these are two different things both in their subject and their meaning." Yet even while claiming victory, Dante has permitted, ironically, the lame curial platitude of the "two great lights" to reassert itself.[138] Despite his conclusion that there are two goals *("duo fines")* of both an earthly and a heavenly bliss late in book 3:16:10, he fails to reiterate anywhere in this treatise his own powerful metaphor of *Purgatorio* 16:107–109, based on official imperial imagery, in which *both* powers figure as suns:[139]

> soleva Roma, che il buon mondo feo,
> due soli aver, che l'una e l'altra strada
> facean vedere, e del mondo e di Dio.

Rome, which made the world good, used to have *two suns* that showed both the one way and the other, that of the world and that of God. (My translation)

Amid all the intensity of the controversy, the hierocrats never openly recognized that their grandiose analogy was, in fact, contrary to all orthodox biblical metaphor on the sun and moon that had obtained until the end of the twelfth century. Doctrinal exegesis on the miriad *"luna"* verses in the Bible did indeed spring from the passage describing the creation of the "great lights" in Genesis 1:16, but the Church Fathers and great Doctors had, instead, produced a convention that the decretalists were, understandably, to blanket in total silence: St. Ambrose's seminal exegesis in *Hexæmeron* 4:8 had very early established that in receiving her light from Christ, the Sun of Justice, the *Church* itself was, instead, and most emphatically, the *moon:*

*Fittingly is the moon compared to the Church,* who has shone over the entire world and . . . illuminates the darkness of this world. . . . This is the real *moon* which, from the perpetual light of her own brother, has acquired the light of immortality and grace. *Not from her own light does the Church gleam,* but from the light of Christ. From the Sun of Justice has her brilliance been obtained, so that it is said: "It is now no longer I that live, but Christ lives in me" [Gal 2:20]. (My emphases) [140]

The number of examples attested in the theologians thereafter is too vast to cite adequately so that a few capital instances must suffice. St. Augustine, naturally, follows Ambrose in his *Expositions on the Psalms* where, on Psalm 8:4 (on the verse, "For I will behold thy heavens, the works of thy fingers: the moon and the stars which thou hast founded"), he shows how perfectly suitable it is for the moon to signify the Church.[141] Again in *Epistola* 55:6, Augustine glosses the moon in the same way: "The Church, as yet constituted in that mortality of the flesh, is referred to in the Scriptures by the name of the moon,"[142] Exegetes thereafter echo this unwaveringly. Isidore of Seville, Peter Damian, Honorius Augustodunensis, Peter Lombard, Hildegard of Bingen, and Alain de Lille[143] agree with a legion of other notables: with Prosper of Aquitaine in his exposition of Psalm 120:6 (ca. 390–463),[144] Saint Gaudentius in his sermons on Exodus (ca. fourth–fifth centuries), Saint Eucherius on Psalm 103:19 in *Spiritual Intelligence* (d. ca. 449), Saint Maximus of Turin in his homilies (d. 408/423), Saint Bruno the Carthusian in his *Exposition on the Psalms* (ca. 1032–1101), and Rupert of Deutz in his treatise *On Divine Office* (ca. 1075–1129 or 1130).[145] Garnier de Rochefort, in the *Allegory in Holy Scriptures,* a work that enjoyed much success under its false ascription to Rabanus Maurus, repeats the maxim: "The moon is the Church, as in the Psalms (71 [Vulg. 72:5, 7])."[146] In short, unlike the decretalists of Dante's time, the theologians had unanimously concurred in the same, humbler, spiritual significance: *"Luna est ecclesia."*[147]

It is astonishing, therefore, that at this point Dante with his extreme erudition does not cite the Fathers or Doctors of the Church, the *Glossa ordinaria,* or even his contemporary, John Quidort of Paris, the famous theologian-publicist of Philip IV, with whose *On Royal and Papal Power* he was so amply acquainted. To assess Dante's omission (or his purposeful and respectful conservative reticence?) in adducing this powerful ancient exegesis of *"luna"* against his adversaries, it is worthwhile to transcribe John of Paris's convincing rebuttal at length:

This particular mystical interpretation [of the two great lights] *is not that found among the saints;* their reading tended in the opposite direction. Isidore says in the *Gloss on Genesis* that *"the sun" is to be understood as "kingdom" and "the moon" as "priesthood."* Hence he says: "The splendor of the sun represents the excellence of the kingdom, and people obedient to their king; the splendor of the moon is as a representation of the synagogue; the stars are the princes, and all things are rooted in the stability of the kingdom as in a firm foundation."[148]

Royalists and imperialists well knew that the sun was the temporal authority and that the moon was the priestly power. After Innocent III's acceptance of its reverse interpretation in his letters of 1198, through the thirteenth and fourteenth centuries the canon lawyers of the papacy, many of whom were also prelates and theologians of superior rank, in their zeal for the Church to prevail, persisted in ignoring the earlier univocal gloss.

Just as he had railed against the decretals as the source of clerical venality in *Epistle 8, To the Italian Cardinals,* so Dante would repeat his denunciation in *Paradiso* 9:133–35. *"Per questo l'Evangelio e i dottor magni / son derelitti, e solo ai Decretali / si studia, sì che pare a' lor vivagni"* (For this the Gospel and *the great Doctors are deserted,* and only the Decretals are studied as may be seen by their marginal glosses).[149] But unfortunately, the lawyers' influence was so great that even the poet was himself to forget *"i dottor magni"* and succumb to the decretalist spell in the *Monarchia.* He gives his primary attention to the limited, causative argument, seeming content to label the papalists' chronology absurd—for, as we have seen him argue, how could the cure for man's Fall into sin be symbolized by a sun and moon, which God created on the fourth day, while man, whom he did not create until the sixth day, had not yet even suffered temptation? "For that physician would indeed be a fool who, before a man's birth, prepared him a plaster for an abcess yet to come" (*Mon.* 3:4:15).

But the poet's facile jest will merely leave an opening for Guido Vernani's vitriol. The friar charges that the poet has forgotten God's foreknowledge; and, to color his diversion, the friar, for a second time in his censure, taxes his dead opponent with delirium and raving (*Ref.* 3:3), freely exploiting Dante's readmittance of the analogy of the "two great lights" back into the argument (*Ref.* 3:3, 6). Thus, just as Dante has reproved the decretalists for false scriptural interpretation, so the friar, also following that convention, quotes the pseudo-Dionysius charging that "this type of theologizing ... is not an adducing of proof" (*Ref.* 3:2); he then proceeds in typical curialist vein to demonstrate that Dante's argument from chronology cannot apply. Providence, after all, is above and beyond linear time: thus the typology of the two governing powers as two great lights *must have abided and shall abide* as an idea in the mind of God *ab eterno.* Nor is a physician necessarily a fool who prepares medicine when he foresees disease, for Christ's sacrifice as a cure for sin was foreseen, as in Apocalypse 13:8, after all, "from the beginning of the world." Vernani then proceeds to pile on yet another typology—that of the sacrifice and death of Abel, both prefigurations of Christ's immolation and death—as the solid proof that Christ had been sacrificed mystically from the beginning of the world and that both Adam and Abel's actions testified to their belief in Christ's Coming. Thus the friar's attack succeeds not only in avoiding altogether the theologians' awkward gloss of *"luna est Ecclesia,"* but also in holding the shroud firmly over the canon lawyers' embarrassed silence.

In *Monarchia* 3:5, Dante goes on to dismantle the second papalist error. The decretalists adduce the seniority of Jacob's third son Levi, the founder of the priestly tribe of Levites, over Judah, the younger fourth son, founder of kingship among the Jews (Gn 29:34–35), in order to prove the superiority of the spiritual power over the temporal. The poet counters, that the birth order of Jacob's sons is inapplicable: in fact, the papal syllogism equates, untenably, the term "birth" with the term "authority."[150] It is clear that many who are younger hold positions of power over those who are older. His opponents commit once again the elementary error of using four terms instead of three in their syllogism.[151] Demonstrating his sophisticated knowledge of logic, he shows further that the decretalists also commit the fallacy of taking "a non-cause as a cause" *(fallacia secundum non causum ut causam).*[152]

Vernani must pass over the whole of chapter 5 in one line: "About the argument taken from Levi and Judah, I will not concern myself," for the friar recognizes that Dante's logical rebuttals concerning the errors of noncause and fourth term are professionally incontrovertible. Far from really being of no interest, however, Vernani knew very well that Dante's "argument . . . from Levi and Judah" was actually a barely veiled attack on the prevailing catchphrase for the College of Cardinals, a term given currency, especially in Innocent III's ever-controversial and central *Per venerabilem,* "the priests of the Levitical race . . . our brothers who, according to Levitical law, act as coadjutors in the discharge of the priestly office," whose head was the pope as heir of St. Peter.[153]

In *Monarchia* 3:6, one which seems to have special bearing on the *Si fratrum* controversy, Dante challenges his opponents' third proof: in maintaining that the pope has the power to grant and take away temporal power, they are wrong to assert the precedent of Samuel (1 Kgs[1Sm] 8:11–31; 10:1; 15:23), who raised Saul to the throne and then deposed him, for Samuel did not act as "vicar of God" as does the pontiff. His argument demonstrates that the anachronistic correspondence between Samuel and the pope (asserted by such papal defenders as Giles of Rome, Henry of Cremona, and even the moderate Tolomeo of Lucca) is illusory.[154] To the contrary, like a hammer in the hands of a smith, Samuel acted only according to the direct decision made by God and the limited power of an ad hoc nuncio, unable to take independent action, unlike a "vicar," having final authority and full discretionary powers equal to the one he represents.[155]

Dante's objection here, however, despite that he freely grants the pope's vicariate of Christ, appears to wound Vernani's personal pride to the quick. The friar had, as he himself reminds us, used that very analogy from 1 Kings in his own treatise *De potestate summi pontificis*, in which he had depended so much on his fellow hierocrats and in which he had given, of course, a conclusion contrary to Dante's: kings gain their power from God only indirectly granted through the priesthood.[156] He once again accuses Dante of twisting the sense of Scripture. The infamous confusion of the titles of *"vicar"* and *"nuncio"* in current diplomacy affords the friar a certain license in obfuscating Dante's terms,[157] but Vernani again skews the argument to his own satisfaction by the legerdemain of shifting his metaphors from diplomatic to judicial: "It does not follow that, if Samuel sought God's counsel and will, it was because Samuel was only his nuncio and not his vicar, for he was God's ordinary judge in spiritual and temporal things until late in his old age" (*Ref.* 3:31). Oblivious to the unintended absurdity of ascribing such bureaucratic niceties to the Almighty, Vernani also blithely presupposes that such curial offices were current in ancient biblical times.[158]

With the three Old Testament analogies concluded, for the fourth case in *Monarchia* 3:7, Dante turns to the faulty decretalist analogies from the New. The hierocrats err when they equate the authority of Christ—who possessed both spiritual and temporal authority, shown in the figure of his acceptance of the Magis' gift of frankincense and gold (Mt 2:11)—with that of the pope. Echoing Tolomeo da Lucca's *On the Government of Rulers*, and perhaps the anti-curial *Enquiry into the Power of the Pope*, he rejects the assertion of coequality of Christ with his vicar as untenable, for a vicar never enjoys the same power as he who sends him forth, "for no one who is made vicar either divine or human can be equal to the principal authority, and this is quite obvious" (*Mon.* 3:7:4).[159] Friar Guido makes no comment, for, tacitly, he must allow, as he does in his dedication of the *Refutation* to Graziolo, that Dante here has spoken one of his "occasional truths."[160]

The next two papal arguments, which Dante attacks in Chapters 8 and 9, were among the more traditional, persistent, and problematic, and Dante demonstrates his considerable courage and expertise in dialectic in assailing and clarifying them. Historians know them today under their symbolic names, "the keys of binding and loosing" and the "two swords": that is, the questions of St. Peter as "keeper of the keys of heaven" (*Mon.* 8:9)[161] and his possession of the "two swords of spiritual and temporal authority."[162]

St. Bernard of Clairvaux popularized the nomenclature of the "two swords" tenet in his treatise of advice called *On Consideration* (4:7), addressed to his former Cistercian pupil who had become Pope Eugene III (1145–1153). Bernard's interpretation of Luke 22:38 proved to be one of the most solid papalist buttresses in the controversy and played a shaping role in establishing the doctrines of both the "key" and "sword" images.

Both swords [Lk 22:38], that is, the spiritual and the material, *are of the Church* [*uterque ergo ecclesiæ, spiritualis scilicet gladius et temporalis*]; however, the latter is to be drawn *for* the Church and the former *by* the Church. The spiritual sword should be drawn by the hand of the priest; the material sword by the hand of the knight, but clearly at the bidding of the priest and at the command of the emperor [my emphases].[163]

As the great scholar-churchmen Alfons Stickler and Michele Maccarrone have demonstrated, the hierocrats interpreted the passage, taking the genitive case *"ecclesiæ"* ("*of* the Church") to mean not merely that the pope was *concerned* with affairs of earthly and heavenly import, but that he actually *possessed* both swords—that the temporal and spiritual authorities themselves "*belong* to the Church."[164] Especially, Innocent III had claimed this was so in his decretal *Solitæ benignitatis*, to be followed by Innocent IV in his letter *Eger cui lenia* of 1246.[165] Boniface VIII's notaries were to reiterate it in *Unam Sanctam*.[166] The decretalists freely interpreted the words of Christ to Peter in Matthew 16:19 "whatsoever [Vulgate, *"quodcumque"*] thou shalt bind . . . whatsoever thou shalt loose" to signify Christ's endowing the first of the Apostles with a limitless prerogative to abolish or impose binding laws and decrees in the temporal sphere. Thus, nothing at all was exempted from papal jurisdiction on any occasion in which the popes decided to use their privilege.[167] They comfortably adduced Origen's gloss, incorporated into the biblical *Interlinear Gloss* (in the *Glossa ordinaria*) and also available to all in Aquinas's *Catena aurea super Evangelia*, asserting that Peter judged as if God were judging through Peter's power.[168] But, as the first words of Justinian's *Digest* declared, the emperor also "governed under the authority of God that empire delivered to us by Heavenly Majesty." Imperialists besides the poet had objected to the decretalists' metamorphosis of dualism into a usurping papal monism.[169]

Without naming his opponents, Dante boldly asserts the contrary: the extension and limit of meaning of Christ's term "whatsoever" pertains not to unbounded dominion but only to those things restricted within Peter's office. Christ was referring only to the Apostle's role as keeper of the keys in spiritual affairs (*Mon.* 3:8:1–2).[170] The decretalists commit the "logical fallacy of false distribution" of their term (i.e., the definition and application of the word to mean "all" affairs)."[171] On the contrary, "The universal term that is included in 'whatsoever' is confined within its extension of meaning by the office of the keys of the kingdom of heaven." Were "whatsoever" to signify limitless power, then Peter and his successors, the popes, would be able to perform even forbidden or impossible acts such as divorcing a wife from a man and marrying her to someone else while her husband were still living, or forgiving the sins of those still unrepentant.[172] Even in the realm of the spirit, Peter's successors were obviously not omnipotent.

Vernani does not refute Dante directly, for he may have been aware that some of his more careful and conservative fellow Dominicans (such as Tolomeo da Lucca), had admitted such limitations to papal power in practically the same terms;[173] the friar thus chooses to skew his remarks, avoiding questions of direct temporal dominion and concentrating on the distasteful claim (even ceded by some royal and imperial defenders) that the pope had temporal jurisdictional powers because of his control over obduracy in sin.[174] Here the friar echoes the curial response hammered upon, among others, by Innocent III, Giles of Rome, James of Viterbo, Hervæus Natalis, and Agostino d'Ancona: since the successor of Peter can bind and loose (Mt 16:19), condemn or absolve of sin all the "sheep," the faithful of Christ, he can therefore chastise the emperor as one of that flock.[175] And this will include excommunication and deposition should he prove incorrigible. In the case of laws made by the emperor's decision, they not only may be nullified by different customs, but are also void if they are inconsistent with canon law. While Dante's argument again shows thoughtful originality, Vernani merely rehashes the customary argument from his contending camp.

Dante, for his sixth biblical argument (*Mon.* 3:9), centers on the question of the false interpretation of Peter's words to Christ: "here are two swords, " in a way that implied that the Apostle and his successors possessed both temporal and spiritual powers. The decretalists accepted St. Bernard of Clairvaux's interpretation that when Christ ordered Peter to sheathe his sword (Jn 18:11) he meant that—despite the pope's assumed full possession of both swords—the execution of temporal authority was beneath the dignity of the papal office and would therefore be wielded on its behalf by the temporal power *under mandate* from the Church: it is cogent here to cite Bernard's words, which were to fuel both sides of the issue, in fuller context:

In this finery you are the successor not of Peter but of Constantine. . . . You are the heir of the Shepherd and even if you are arrayed in purple and gold, there is no reason for you to abhor your pastoral duties. . . . "You instruct me to feed dragons and scorpions, not sheep," you reply. Therefore, I say attack them all the more, but with the word, not the sword. Why should you try to usurp the sword anew which you were once commanded to sheathe? Nevertheless, the person who denies that the sword is yours seems to me not to listen to the Lord when he says, "Sheathe your sword." . . . Both swords, that is, the spiritual and the material, belong to [or "are matters of"] the Church [*ecclesiæ*]; however, the latter is to be drawn *for* the Church, and the former *by* the Church. The spiritual sword should be drawn by the hand of the priest; the material sword by the hand of the knight, but clearly at the bidding of the priest and at the command of the emperor.[176]

St. Thomas Aquinas had adapted this statement in his *Commentary on the Sentences*, as Dante was aware: "The Church has also the temporal sword at its command: because at its command it must be unsheathed, as Bernard said." Boniface VIII's decretalists exploited the hierocratic interpretation of the doctrine in the bull *Unam Sanctam*, and Vernani was to embrace those doctrines to the letter in his own commentary on that decretal.[177]

Dante also knew, however, that no accepted teaching by the Saints of the Church had given any such mystical or political construction to Luke 22:38 to allow the swords to be interpreted as the temporal and spiritual powers, and he boldly sets out a differing explanation following the literal and historical sense of the verse. It was not Christ at all but the hasty, sometimes confused, and simple-mannered Peter who spoke of swords. In his ensuing disquisition, listing many examples of the childlike, unreflective brashness of St. Peter, the poet gives a veiled humbling of the canonists' flattery of the Apostle's primacy expounded so boldly, for example, by James of Viterbo.[178] In conclusion, Dante argues that, in context, the Savior's words, "He that hath not, let him sell his coat and buy a sword [Lk 22:36]," and "I came not to send peace, but the sword [Mt 10:34]," meant not Peter's swords alone but the numerous *metaphorical* swords that the disciples needed to spread the faith. Thus the "two swords" signify not realms of authority at all, but, theologically, the "works and deeds" of the Apostles.[179] Dante had read and absorbed John of Paris' *On Royal and Papal Power* where King Philip's publicist had concluded trenchantly, citing the incontrovertible authority of Paul's Letter to the Ephesians 6:17: "And take unto you the helmet of salvation, and *the sword of the spirit—which is the word of God*" *(Gladium spiritus quod est verbum Dei).*[180] Vernani's silence about this point is most revealing, for here again he could quote no counterauthority. In fact, although he had aired his knowledge of the Church's claims to possess both swords in his commentary on *Unam Sanctam,*[181] in the *Reprobatio* he never once inscribes the term *"gladius."*

Dante begins the two historical issues of chapter 10 first with an attack on the Donation of Constantine, whose bitter harvest he so fervently lamented in each of the three canticles of the *Commedia.*[182] Although Dante was unaware that the charter on which it was based was an eighth- or ninth-century forgery from somewhat before or after the coronation of Charlemagne—for only in 1440 did Lorenzo Valla definitively expose the document as a fraud—the poet opposed it on principle.[183] According to the *Constitutum Constantini,* perennially accepted as authentic, although not always as authoritative, by both imperial and papal lawyers of the time, the converted first Christian emperor, Constantine the Great, in gratitude to Pope Silvester for curing his leprosy, and before moving his capital to Constantinople, had supposedly ceded to the pontiff "our imperial palace of the Lateran . . . also the City of Rome and all the provinces, districts and cities of Italy and the Western regions, relinquishing them to the authority of himself and his successors as pontiffs by a definite imperial grant. We have decided that this should be laid down by this our divine, holy and lawfully framed decree and we grant it on a permanent legal basis to the Holy Roman Church."[184] The late medieval popes thus asserted that they were lawfully princes of that part of the Western dominion ruled before by the Roman emperors and were free to appoint rulers for it. Ironically, early attackers of the popes' position had made the self-undermining charge that since the empire had been founded on force, the papacy had therefore in turn acquired territory wrested illegally. Some canonists responded by stating that the sheer antiquity of possession accorded legality and that history had obliterated any certainty about how lands had been acquired; indeed, many territories had been obtained rightfully by gifts or legacy. Imperial writers counterclaimed, in Vergilian fashion, that the Roman Empire had sprung from the centuries of discernment and skill of its rulers. Ironically, on the other side, even canonist scholars, such as Antonio de Butrio, concluded in terms that were in concord with the central argument of the third book of the *Monarchia* "that if there were any doubt, we must presume that the Romans acquired their possessions justly."[185] Dante surely believed that he was righteously backing such Roman legitimacy celebrated in the *Æneid*, asserted by imperialists and ceded even as a weak argument by the high papalists themselves.[186]

Dante thus tackles the second historical problem in *Monarchia* 3:10 by arguing that Constantine had no justification in ceding part of his territory because his office, by its very definition, included the governance of the world entire since human right and law requires an undivided empire. Constantine could not both be emperor and diminish his realm at the same time (3:10:9), for that would be self-negating. Behind Dante's reasoning, is the "Augustus because he augments" topos of the glossators which others, such as John of Paris and Tolomeo da Lucca before him, had adduced. The etymology of "Augustus" derived from *"augesco,"* "increase," according to Isidore's *Etymologies* 9:3: *"semper Augustus . . . ut augeat,"* "always Augustus . . . that he may augment."[187] *Nomina sunt consequentia rerum:* thus any reduction of the empire was quite literally a contradiction in terms. The poet therefore logically goes on to argue that if each successive emperor were to shear off a piece of the realm, the empire, being finite, would eventually be annihilated. Yet not only was the giver and the giving wrong and inappropriate: the Church was also unfit to receive the gift, since Christ, in Matthew 10:9, had forbidden it to own temporal goods. The Church, in sum, could only act as the distributor to the poor of a patrimony endowed upon it by the emperor, provided that his main true dominion remained intact.

In his rejoinder, Vernani resorts to more deprecation and strikes a sour note of puerility in his rhetorical question: "First, I ask of this fellow: whose empire was it at that time?" (Ref. 3:48). Again his posturing depends closely upon Hostiensis's commentary on the *Per venerabilem.* There Henry of Susa had charged that if anyone were to maintain that Constantine had not the right to grant the Donation, he would be falsely implying that the people had not the right to transfer their authority to the prince.[188] After all, Vernani can thus bravely continue, the Roman people had indeed entrusted Constantine with the empire, and should that not be enough, Constantine, the Roman people, the Senate, and the governors could have given it to the Church. And besides, the emperor and the people only gave away what they held unjustly, since by forsaking God they had forfeited their right of ownership anyway through idolatry. The friar takes refuge in the strict decretalist position that the Donation was actually a redress or amends, that is, a restitution, of property illegally seized. Indeed, in the *Refutation*, Friar Guido instead treads so servilely in the steps of Giles of Rome (3:52) that he even fails to verify his clinching second-hand authority—the nonexistent quotation from Augustine's *Confessions* that "whatsoever exists because of the true God is possessed unjustly once he is forsaken"—a phrase that Giles had invented to shore up his arguments in the *De ecclesiastica potestate.*[189]

At this point too Vernani pretends to rely directly on the authority of Innocent III's decretal *Venerabilem fratrem* (*On Election; Decretales* 1.6.34),[190] of March 1202 in which the pope declares that he has the power to examine the imperial candidate before consecration lest the elector-princes be "not only in disaccord but even if they are in accord, conspiring together to elect a sacrilegious, excommunicated person, a tyrant, imbecile, heretic or pagan." That papal letter, however, actually mentions nothing at all about papal authority to demand the support of temporal arms to further the Church's spiritual ends, nor to the emperor's being a "defender of the Church against heretics and schismatics." That the emperor did wield such power at the behest of the papacy was indeed the commonplace opinion among the canonists and decretalists, but it is not mentioned there, and Friar Guido yet again points to the wrong text.[191] Significantly, it is Henry of Susa who cites this detail in his consideration of the bull *Per venerabilem*, and we may be quite sure that "Hostiensis" is again Vernani's real, secondhand, hierocratic source.[192] The friar's argument on the appropriateness of ecclesiastical possession of worldly goods likewise parrots the interpretations given by other decretalists, and, once again, most particularly, the overzealous Giles of Rome. Unlike Dante, Guido Vernani has also the comfort of Church's recent debates (1321–1323) against the doctrine of apostolic poverty (formulated in St. Francis's *Rule* of 1223), of John XXII's bulls, *Cum inter nonnullus* of 1323 and *Quia quorundun mentes* of 1324, and, especially, of the confuting treatise of the Dominican Hervæus Natalis.[193]

Dante's chapter 11:1–2 of book 3 deals only glancingly with the major topic of the *translatio imperii* by which the pope had withdrawn the empire from the Greeks in the East and bestowed it, by coronation, upon Charlemagne (the "Germans") in the West.[194] According to some decretalists, upon this event hung the proof that the pope "possessed both swords" of temporal and spiritual power and could create and depose the emperor. In fact, there were numerous, oft-cited examples of depositions on both sides of the issue. The poet, following his practice of seeming to keep his treatise above the mere contingencies of the fray, avoids wrangling about which power could depose the other—for that is the egregious assumption of *Si fratrum*—and merely labels such action generally as a usurpation of right.

For his part, Vernani is again silent on the matter and he misses a golden opportunity to mock Dante's errors of historical fact, for it was Pope Leo III, not, as Dante says, Hadrian I, who had crowned Charlemagne emperor on that famous Christmas Day in a.d. 800. The poet is repeating Tolomeo da Lucca's error in *De regimine principum* 3:10:8: "Charlemagne, whom Pope Hadrian constituted as emperor,"[195] and since Tolomeo's completion of the treatise often went under the blanket authorship of Thomas Aquinas, Tolomeo's error concerning the coronation seemed authoritative. The empress Irene (797–802), not, as Dante says, Michael (811–813), was reigning in the year of Charlemagne's coronation. The errors, of course, do not alter Dante's point. Vernani, as well, perhaps willing to accept any authority when Church power is bolstered, fails to catch Dante's factual blunders.

Traditionally, in Scholastic theological disputations, arguments from reason came last.[196] Thus, in chapter 12, Dante deals finally with the canonists' ninth argument, based upon the Aristotelian, almost centripetal, principle that all things that fall within a given genus can be reduced to a single term that is the measure or substantial form of all others within that genus: the *reductio omnium ad unum* (*Metaphysics* 10:1:1052b18). For men, this must be reduction to one man—and, according to the *Nicomachean Ethics* 3:12, to the most excellent man as standard measure and ideal of all others. The hieratic conception exalted the pope, with his redefined title of "Vicar of Christ," to this supreme degree among all mankind. Awkwardly for Dante, even the Franciscan minister general, St. Bonaventure, for example, in his *Commentaria in decretales*, commenting upon the words *"plenitudo potestatis,"* had lent it the weight of his considerable authority: "Where there is reduction to the supreme among all men, that one is the Vicar of Christ, the Supreme Pontiff."[197]

In the face of the canonical and theological power of this cliché, Dante thus shows enormous courage and logical acumen in countering that, as men, pope and emperor must be reduced to uniformity, and, thus, that their fortuitous attributes must be stripped and ignored. To be emperor or pope is to hold an incidental position and is not the same as to be a man; the rule must apply to all men irrespective of their attributes or social position. A man is a man by substantial form, but he is a father or a master in charge of others by the category of relationship. Thus a man may be pope and spiritual father to his spiritual sons by the incidental form of the papacy, a relationship, in Aristotelian terms, "accidental," to his human substance. In the same way, a man may be emperor and master of his subordinates by his imperial authority. Thus, contrary to the papal claim, the genus of man is not reducible to the pope: for "to be a pope" is not contained within the definition of "to be a man."[198] The hierocrats' argument commits the logical "fallacy of accident" as described by Peter of Spain in his *Summulæ logicales*.[199] In addition, Dante points out, neither may the accidental relational categories of fatherhood and of mastery be reduced one to the other, but only to the single principle of authority who is God.[200]

Dante's own reading of St. Bernard's *On Consideration* 2:17–18 (as we have seen, a text central for contenders of both sides of the issue) emboldened him in this chapter: the poet deflects back on his curial opponents, in fact, his own Aristotelian reworking of the persuasions culled from Bernard's counsel to Pope Eugenius III:

I told you earlier that when you consider the nature by which you are a man, for *you were born a man*. Now when you ask who you are, the response will be your title, which is Bishop. *This is what you have been made, not what you were born*. Which of these seems to you to pertain more directly to your essence, what you have been made or what you were born? Is it not what you were born? *Therefore I advise you especially to consider what you especially are: what you were born, namely, man. . . . Were you born wearing this mitre?*[201] [my emphasis].

As Abbot Bernard brings the person of his former pupil to humility by separating his being and essence from the accident of his papal office, so Dante, in purely orthodox Catholic fashion, divides the personal moral rectitude of all such occupants from the excellence of their incidental, sacramental incumbency. With this Dante has dealt with all the faulty reasonings of his opponents and now turns to his own arguments.

In *Monarchia* 3:13, Dante proves, with a detailed syllogism supported by precedents, that, since the empire existed historically and exercised complete authority before the Church was founded by Christ, the Church cannot therefore be the source of temporal authority. After passing over chapters 11 and 12 without mention, Vernani replies (Ref. 3:69–77) to this argument with the slippery device, common in decretalist arguments, of altering his definition of the Church whenever he deems it necessary.[202] First, he counters that the Church had been established even from the fall of the wicked angels and man, thereby equating the Church with the City of God, the past, present and future blessed; since the earthly city of the future damned and City of God had been commingled since Cain and Abel, the Church thus predates the empire. In his second definition he identifies the Church with the multiplication of members of the Body of Christ after his death, and then, finally, agrees with Dante's argument concerning the setting up of the Church as a sacerdotal institution, adducing Christ's commission of Peter from Matthew 16:18. To combat the empire's seniority he repeats the argument he had made in the *De potestate summi pontificis* (chs. 4 and 14) that there was, after all, no real empire before the Church, for the emperors, in sum, were merely tyrants. Agreeing with Giles of Rome that all temporal power was illegitimate and unjust unless blessed by the Church or its Old Testament prefigurations, he confutes the objection of the empire's priority in linear time: "[To the] fifth objection: that the empire existed first before the priesthood. I say that this is false, for among the pagans there never was a true king or emperor, but all were the worst tyrants; among the people of God, then, first there existed the priesthood, as has been said."[203] Thus he leaves aside the problematic Augustinian assertion that even tyrants were God-imposed; and in this he differs even from his fellow hierocrat James of Viterbo, who had given due consideration to Romans 13:1, that "[t]he powers that be are ordained by God."[204]

In *Monarchia* 3:14, Dante proceeds with an inquiry into the origins of the papacy's claim to bestow temporal authority upon the emperor. Insofar as the definition of the Church is concerned, Dante makes it clear here that as the temporal body of believers it corresponds neither to all mankind, nor to the sacerdotal institution. In Aristotelian logic, nothing can produce an effect if it does not already possess that effect itself; but no source for such ecclesiastical authority can be identified, for the Church itself derived no worldly sovereignty from God, either via natural or divine law. Self-evidently, it could not have received it from itself, nor did it did gain such power from the empire (as Dante's inquiry into Constantine's Donation has proved); nor did the Church obtain it from the consensus or majority of all mankind, for those of Asia, Africa, and most of Europe even now reject the Church's authority. In fact, as the poet goes on to assert in chapter 15, temporal authority is against the very nature of the Church, and gives it a final definition that would be most difficult to rebut: that its nature and form is the model of the life of Christ. Dante there adduces the main biblical quotations most embarrassing to the Church's involvement in worldly affairs. As Christ renounced the world, so must the Church also in its exemplary actions, sealed as it is with his imprint. Once more, on the arguments of these two chapters, Vernani is silent.

Having now proved the negative, refutational part of his thesis—that the empire's power *does not derive* through the medium of the Church—in chapter 16, Dante arrives at his final, ostensive, and positive proof that the empire's power *does indeed derive* directly from God. Taking up again the seeming interpolation of chapter 2, he now seizes the opportunity to give a series of corollaries to Uguccione de Pisa's dualist doctrine, basing his reasonings upon man's dual nature, his corruptible mortal body, and his incorruptible eternal soul. While Uguccione had dealt with the duality of origins of earthly power, Dante now supplements the position with the duality of ends. The efficient cause of man is that he is generated naturally mortal and corruptible, yet his soul is created by God, immortal. And since every nature is destined toward its own final goal as toward a final cause, Providence has therefore set two consecutive ends for man: the blessedness of this life signified by the earthly paradise and the blessedness of eternity. These man reaches by two complementary means: the first through philosophical teachings and the activation of the acquired moral and intellectual virtues, the second through Holy Scripture, spiritual writings, and the exercise of the infused theological virtues of faith hope and charity (3:16:8). These dual goals require dual mutually aiding guides: the emperor through philosophy; the pope through revelation (3:16:10). On earth, the path to Aristotelian happiness is one with that trodden onward to eternal bliss.[205]

In his peroration the poet reaches the heights of rhetorical and philosophical persuasiveness: he returns again to his central themes of freedom and peace, both effected by the emperor—who stills the excesses of man's cupidity to allow the full exercise of human speculation and action, and whom God alone chooses directly through the electors as his divine spokesmen.[206] The poet's last paragraph describes a vision of cooperation with the fatherly spiritual power lending the grace of its blessings to the reverent temporal power so that it may more effectively shed its light upon the world.

After Dante's wonderful vision of unity, when we return to the final paragraphs of the *Refutation*, we are struck by Vernani's fastidious, factional categorizing. Coming to his final rebuttal of Chapter 16 he protests that "that fellow [*ille homo*] should not have distinguished a dual blessedness on account of our duplex nature—to wit, the corruptible and incorruptible—because neither virtue nor blessedness may be properly found in our corruptible part" (*Ref.* 3:88). His views on the one final goal of man he had already expressed in chapter 5 of his treatise *De potestate summi pontifices*.[207] Properly, man's acquired virtues belong to the upper soul, to the will and the intellect—man's spiritual, eternal part; the lower parts, the sensitive and vegetative parts of the soul that die with the body, acquire no virtue. The friar, however, ignores the teaching that St. Thomas Aquinas (his fellow Dominican canonized only six years earlier) set forth with all due tempering in the *Summa Theologiæ* I, q. 23, a. 1: that man's beatitude was, indeed, twofold *(duplex)*, and the body was *in some way* necessary for man's earthly happiness:

*The end toward which created things are directed by God is twofold;* one which exceeds the proportion and faculty of created nature; and this end is eternal life, which consists in the vision of God and which is above the nature of every creature. *The other end is proportionate to created nature, and a created being can attain to this end by its own natural powers* [my emphases].[208]

In *Summa theologiæ* I-II, q. 4, a. 5, St. Thomas repeats:

*It must be said that happiness is twofold:* the one is imperfect and is had in this life; the other is perfect and consists in the vision of God. Now it is evident that the body is necessary for the happiness of this life. *For the happiness of this life consists in an operation of the intellect, either speculative or practical.* And the operation of the intellect in this life cannot be without a phantasm, which is only in a bodily organ, as was shown in the First Part [q. 84, a. 6, 7]. Consequently *that happiness* [*beatitudo*] *which can be had in this life, depends* in some way [*quodammodo*], *on the body* [my emphasis].[209]

Though the soul can be happy without the body in the afterlife, the body is ultimately necessary for the perfection of man's beatitude *upon this earth*, even if that necessity is unclear to human intellect. St. Thomas adds:

It must be understood that something may belong to a thing's perfection in two ways. First, as constituting the essence thereof: thus the soul is necessary for man's perfection. Secondly, *as necessary for the perfection of a thing since it belongs to its well-being:* thus, beauty of the body and swiftness of wit belong to man's perfection. Therefore though the body does not belong in the first way to the perfection of human happiness, yet it does in the second way.[210]

For Dante, as for Thomas, the well-being of this life consists in the exercise of the highest human faculties by which he specifies as the *operatio proprie virtutis*, "the exercise of one's virtue"; the blessedness of the eternal life consists in the *fruitio divini aspectus*, "the enjoyment of the sight of God."

Although the poet must place his emphasis on the first stage of an Aristotelian earthly happiness for polemical reasons in the *Monarchia*, he nevertheless follows the lead of St. Thomas Aquinas and others before him who had orthodoxly treated the blessedness of this life as ultimately ancillary to eternal blessedness: earthly existence, as partisans of all loyalties agreed, could only give happiness *"quodammodo."*[211] And Dante reiterates this important cautionary word in the universally accepted formulas in the last lines of his treatise. The poet, forced to wander and seek his shelter in strangers' lands, had always recognized, and perhaps, no one ever more clearly, the far greater importance of eternal blessedness and he makes its attainment the ineffable object and culmination of the last canticle of his *Commedia* dedicated to the very friend and patron on whose behalf the *Monarchia* was written.

Though the logic that underlies Dante's strategy in the treatise is forensic, political, and corrective, we are yet left at its end with a glow of hopeful and charitable optimism. Most probably girded historically and spiritually with the cord of a Franciscan tertiary,[212] Dante here records, in his waning exiled years, his simple, optimistic Christian conviction, that, despite the salt bread of implacable earthly tribulation, he viewed life on earth as blest, naturally, directly and sacramentally, by a loving, omnipotent God.

At the end of the *Refutation* Vernani instead returns in self-reference to chapter 10 of his treatise *De potestate summi pontificis*;[213] clearly with the *Si fratrum* controversy in mind, he concludes on the dispiriting note of Samuel's removal of Saul, whose very kingship represented the Jews' rejection of the rule of God. We cannot help but contrast the peaceful ending of the *Monarchia*, enjoining the mutual cooperation of the earthly and the spiritual powers to Vernani's closing allusion to Saul's violent deposition, so vivid to later readers mindful of the dramatizations of Vittorio Alfieri and Robert Browning. Fra Guido's abrupt fall into silence might have been intended to imply, with a mannered *sprezzatura*, that he had triumphed, and that no more was necessary. But that is not the sense he leaves upon the reader.

Despite the static and conservative view of Holy Roman Imperial society that the *Monarchia* upholds, fortune and fame were to give Dante's treatise the last word while Vernani's censure lay foiled in the archives. The poet's arguments in book 3 are cogent and responsible according to the rules of Aristotelian logic and well within the norms of medieval dialectic and rhetoric; his reworking of St. Bernard's exhortation to papal humility is well founded; his temporal chronology is impeccable; his exhortation for the Church to remodel itself on Christ is unexceptionable, and his extrapolations from St. Thomas are far from radical or unreasonable. His errors in historical fact pass unnoticed by his opponent.

Particularly in his last book, Vernani's dogged obsessions, his show of high-handed self-complacency, his purblind self-righteousness, his adamant *parti-pris*, and his determination to show no quarter betray ulterior motives and ultimate frustration. Perhaps to nudge approval from his superiors, either real or socially imagined, he resorts overmuch to humorless mockery. Even though the friar apparently kept his own copy of the *Refutation* with him in his cell at San Cataldo in Rimini until his death (which occurred, most probably, during the Black Death of 1348; his autograph is the manuscript now in the British Library), he left his treatise, in fact, unpolished and unadorned, bereft of limned capital letters, petering out flaccidly without summation and allowing many chapters of Dante's most persuasive reasonings to go unanswered.[214]

# TRANSLATIONS
# OF THE TEXTS

# MONARCHIA

## BOOK I

### Chapter 1

{1} For all men whom a Higher Nature[1] has sealed with a love of truth,[2] this must be seen to be the utmost concern: just as they have been enriched by the efforts of those who came before, they must in the same way strive for those who will come after them so that posterity will have means of being enriched by their efforts. {2} For there is no doubt that anyone is remiss in his duty, who, nourished by teachings on public life,[3] neglects to bring some contribution to the public good[4]: such a man is certainly not that "tree which is planted near the running waters, which shall bring forth its fruit, in due season,"[5] but is rather a pernicious maelstrom that eternally swallows and never returns what is engulfed. {3} Accordingly, having often pondered these things to myself, so as not to be one day found guilty of having buried my talent,[6] I desire not only to bloom but also to bear fruit for the public good and to reveal truths never essayed by others. {4} For what fruit would a man bear if he demonstrated some theorem of Euclid all over again? Or if he strove to explain again Aristotle's explanations of happiness?[7] Or if he took it upon himself again to defend Cicero's defense of old age? None, certainly: his tedious and superfluous screed would instead produce irritation.

{5} And since, among other obscure and useful truths, the knowledge of temporal monarchy is most useful and especially obscure—and since there is no quick monetary gain in it, no one has ever attempted it[8]—it is my aim to pry it from its hiding place so that not only may my vigils be useful to the world but that, to my glory, I may also be the first to win the palm of so great a prize.[9]

{6} Certainly I am setting out on an arduous task, and one beyond my strength, yet I do not trust so much in my own powers as in the light of that Giver "who giveth to all men abundantly, and upbraideth not."[10]

## Chapter 2

{1} Therefore, surely, we must first see what it is that we call "temporal monarchy"—what it is generally like, so to speak, and its scope.[11] {2} Temporal monarchy, then, which they call "empire," is the one single principality placed over all men in time, or among and over those things that are measured by time. {3} Indeed three principal problems are to be investigated in its regard: first, there is some doubt and question whether it is necessary for the well-being of the world; second, whether the Roman people appropriated the office of monarchy to itself *de jure;* third, whether the authority of monarchy depends directly upon God or on some other minister or vicar of God.[12]

{4} But since every truth that is not a principle is demonstrated by the truth of some principle, it is necessary in any inquiry whatsoever to have knowledge of the principle to which one can refer analytically[13] in order to verify all propositions that are assumed thereafter. And since the present treatise is an inquiry of this kind, it is obvious that we have, first of all, to examine thoroughly the principle upon whose strength may be founded those things that come hereafter.

{5} We must, therefore, be aware that there are certain things such as mathematics, natural science, and divinity about which, since they in no way lie in our power, we can merely speculate and yet do nothing. There are, of course, other things upon which, since they do lie in our power, we can not only speculate but also have an effect; and in these cases action is not subordinated to speculation, but speculation to action, since in such cases action is the goal.

{6} Since, then, the present matter concerns politics, or rather the source and principle of all just politics, and since all things that concern politics fall within our power, it is clear, to start with, that the present material is not organized with regard to speculation, but rather with regard to action.[14] {7} Again, since in things pertaining to action, the principle and cause of all is the final end[15] (because it is that end goal that first moves the agent), it follows that the entire raison d'être of those things existing for an end is to be deduced from the end itself. For there is one way to cut wood to build a house and another way to build a ship.

{8} Thus, if there is any that is a universal end for the community of all mankind, this end will be the principle that will fully clarify all those things that we will have to prove below. It is indeed idiotic to think that there is one end for this, or that, community, but that there is no single end for them altogether.

## Chapter 3

{1} Now we must see what the end of the whole of human community is; and having seen this, more than half our task will be complete, as the Philosopher affirms in his *Ethics*.[16] {2} And in proof of what we are seeking, it must be pointed out that just as there is a certain end for which nature produces the thumb, and another end, distinct from that, for which she produces the whole hand, and yet another, different from both, for which she produces the arm, and another, different from all these, for which she produces the whole man; likewise, there is one end to which eternal God orders an individual man and another to which he orders the family as a whole, one the neighborhood, another the city, another the kingdom,[17] and, finally, the supreme end to which he, by his art (which is nature), draws all of mankind into existence.[18] And this end is the one we want to establish here as a guiding principle of our inquiry. {3} On this account one must be aware first that "God and nature do nothing in vain," but that everything that comes into being is made for a particular function. Indeed, the essence of anything created is not its final end in the intention of the Creator, insofar as he creates it; rather, it is made for the proper functioning of its essence; wherefore it follows that the proper function is not for the sake of its essence, but rather that its essence is made for the sake of its function.[19] {4} Ergo, there is a particular function proper to all mankind to which the aggregate of humanity in its great multitude[20] is ordered; a function, indeed, to which neither a single man, nor a family, nor a neighborhood, nor a city, nor a particular kingdom can achieve. What this function may be will be clear once the ultimate potentiality of all humanity becomes apparent.

{5} Therefore, I affirm that no power in which several beings of different species participate is the highest potentiality of any of them. Since, inasmuch as that which is the highest is that which constitutes the species, it would follow that one and the same essence would be specific to several species, and this is impossible. {6} Ergo, the highest power in man is not mere existence taken by itself, since, so understood, even the elements would share in it; nor can we say that it exists in being a compound, since this is already found in minerals; nor is it in being animate, since this is also in plants; nor is it in apprehension, since brute animals also participate in this. It exists rather in apprehension by means of the possible intellect,[21] which certainly belongs solely to man and to nothing else superior or inferior to him. {7} For although there are other beings that share intellect, nonetheless, theirs is not a *possible intellect* like that of mankind, since such beings are a certain intellectual species and nothing else, and their existence is nothing else but the intellection of what they are; and this intellection is a ceaseless act, for otherwise they would not be eternal.[22] It is, therefore, obvious that the highest potentiality of mankind itself is its intellectual potentiality or power.

{8} And since this potentiality cannot be completely brought into action all together[23] through one individual man or by any of the particular communities defined above, it is necessary that there be a multitude[24] among mankind through which this whole potentiality can be actuated—just as it is necessary that there be a multitude[25] of generated things so that all the potentiality of primal matter may always be found actuated,[26] otherwise we would have to posit a separate potentiality, and this is impossible {9} (and Averroës agrees with this opinion in his *Commentary* on the books of *The Soul*).[27]

The intellectual potentiality, then, of which I am speaking, does not concern only the universal forms or species, but also, through a certain extension, particular forms. Wherefore it is usually said that a speculative intellect becomes, by extension, practical, its end being both to act and to make—by which I mean through the actions that are regulated by political prudence and through productions that are regulated by art.[28] {10} These things are all ancillary to speculation as to its highest end to which Primal Goodness draws mankind into existence. Whence that statement in the *Politics* now becomes clear, that is, that those who are strong in intellect naturally have dominion over others.[29]

## Chapter 4

{1} We have now made sufficiently clear, then, that the function proper to mankind taken in its totality is always[30] to effect the whole potentiality of the possible intellect, first in speculation and then, second, on this account, by its extension, in action.

{2} And since, inasmuch as what is in the part is in the whole, to the individual man it happens that "by sitting and resting he may acquire perfection in prudence and wisdom,"[31] it is obvious that in quietude, or in the tranquillity of peace, mankind is able to attend without hindrance or difficulty to its own proper functioning, which is a functioning almost divine, as it is said: "Thou hast made him a little lower than the angels."[32] Accordingly, it is clear that universal peace is the most important of all things that are ordained for our beatitude.[33] {3} For this the voice from on high announced to the shepherds not riches, nor pleasures, nor honors, not long life, health, strength, nor beauty, but peace; for the heavenly host sang "Glory to God on high and on earth peace to men of good will."[34] {4} Because of this, "Peace be with you"[35] was always the salutation of the Salvation of man; for it was fitting that the supreme Savior utter the supreme salutation. Indeed his disciples decided to preserve this usage, including Paul in his salutations, as is clear to everyone. {5} From what we have said, then, it is obvious what the better, or rather, the best way is by which mankind may achieve its proper functioning. And consequently we have seen the quickest way to arrive at that to which all our actions are ordered as to a final end, that is, universal peace, which we must take as a principle for all the arguments that are to follow.[36] {6} This was necessary, as I said, as a measuring point established in advance whereby, as by the light of clearest truth, whatever we are to prove may be settled.

## Chapter 5

{1} Resuming, therefore, what we were saying at the beginning [*Mon.* 1:2:2], there are three principal problems and inquiries to be looked into concerning temporal monarchy, which in common parlance is called "empire." And these problems, as we said before, we intend now to examine on the basis of the established principle, following the order we indicated earlier.

{2} Therefore, the first question is this: whether temporal monarchy is necessary for the well-being of the world. This, certainly, can be demonstrated (since no force of reason or authority is opposed) with extremely strong and valid arguments, the first of which we adduce from the authority of the Philosopher in his *Politics*.[37] {3} There, in fact, this venerable authority affirms that when several things are ordered to unity, one of them must rule or govern, whereas the others must be governed or ruled.[38] Indeed, not only the authority of his glorious name, but inductive reasoning[39] as well makes this assertion merit credence.

{4} For if we consider a single individual, we shall see this verified in him, because, while all his faculties are bent on the pursuit of happiness, his intellective faculty itself rules and governs all the rest, otherwise he could not attain happiness. {5} If we consider the single household, whose end is to prepare its members to live well, it must be that one alone, called the *pater familias*, or someone in his stead, rule and govern it according to the Philosopher's dictum: "All households are ruled by the eldest."[40] And it is up to him, as Homer says, to rule over all the rest and impose laws upon them.[41] Whence comes the proverbial curse, "May you have an equal in your home!" {6} If we consider one single neighborhood, whose end is neighborly aid in regard to both persons and property, there must be one individual over the others, either appointed by another, or rising to the top from among them by common consent. Otherwise, that reciprocal aid is not obtained, but, as often occurs when many contend for preeminence, the whole neighborhood goes to total ruin.[42] {7} If, indeed, we consider one single city whose end is a harmonious and satisfying life, governance must be by one alone, and that not only in a just political situation but also in one which is corrupt. For if it should turn out otherwise, not only do you lose the aim of civic life, but the city itself ceases to be what it once was.[43] {8} If, finally, we consider one single kingdom, whose end is the same as the city's, but with greater confidence in its own tranquillity, there must be one sole king who rules and governs; otherwise, not only will those within the realm not pursue their end, but the kingdom itself will also fall into destruction, just as in the famous dictum of infallible truth: "A kingdom divided against itself cannot stand."[44] {9} Therefore, if things stand this way among these entities and in individuals who are ordered to some single goal, what we assumed above is true. Now, it is agreed that the entire human race is ordered to one goal, as has already been demonstrated; therefore, there has to be one individual to rule or reign, and he must be called "monarch" or "emperor." {10} And thus it is clear that for the well-being of the world there must be a monarchy or empire.

## Chapter 6

{1} And as the part is to the whole, so the partial order is to the entire order; the part stands to the whole as to its end goal and supreme good: ergo, the order of the part stands as to the order of the whole; that is, it stands to the whole as to its end and supreme good. From this we can deduce that the good of the partial order does not exceed the good of the entire order, but rather that it is the other way around. {2} Therefore, since a dual order is found in things, to wit, the orderly arrangement of the parts among themselves, and the orderly arrangement of the parts in respect to one single thing that is not a part (such as the order of the parts of an army among themselves and the order of those parts in respect to their leader), the order of the parts in respect to that one single thing is superior insofar as it is the end goal of the others; for the former order exists for the latter order, and not the other way around.

{3} Wherefore if the form of this superior order is found within parts of the human multitude it must be found far more within the multitude itself or in its totality because of the cogency of the syllogism we have set forth, since this order is superior, or rather the form [that is, the essential principle] of the order is superior.[45] But it is found in all parts of the multitude of mankind as has been sufficiently clarified by what we said in the previous chapter: therefore, it must also be found in the totality itself.

{4} And thus all the aforesaid parts below the kingdoms and the kingdoms themselves must be ordered to a single prince or principality, that is, to the monarch or to the monarchy.[46]

## Chapter 7

{1} Furthermore, the total of all humanity forms a whole in relation to its parts, and it forms a part in relation to a whole. For it forms a whole in relation to its particular kingdoms and nations, as we have demonstrated above [Ch. 6]. And it forms a part in relation to the universe as a whole, and this is obvious in and of itself. {2} Therefore, just as the inferior parts of the total of all humanity fittingly correspond to this whole, so this totality is said to correspond fittingly to the whole.[47] Indeed, the parts correspond to the whole fittingly through a single principle, as one can easily gather from what we said above. Thus, this whole as well, simply through a single principle, that is, through a single prince, fittingly corresponds to the whole universe, or rather to the prince of this universe who is God and Monarch.[48] {3} From this it follows that monarchy is necessary to the world for its well-being.

## Chapter 8

{1} And everything is fittingly, rather, excellently ordered that corresponds to the intention of the First Agent who is God; and this is obvious in itself, except to those who deny that divine goodness attains supreme perfection. {2} It is God's intention that all created things bear his divine likeness to the extent that their nature can receive it.[49] On this account it was said: "Let us make man to our image and likeness."[50] Although it may not be said that "to our image" can be predicated of things inferior to man, "to our likeness," however, can be predicated of anything since the whole universe is nothing else but a certain imprint of divine goodness. Therefore, mankind is at its most excellent and best when, insofar as it is in its power, it is like unto God. {3} But the human race most resembles God when it is, as far as possible, one. Indeed the true reason of being one lies only in him; wherefore it is written: "Hear, O Israel, the Lord thy God is one God."[51] {4} But mankind is most one when it is all united in one, a unity that cannot come about except when it is totally subject to a single prince, as is obvious in and of itself. {5} Ergo, mankind most resembles God when it is subject to a single prince, and consequently, thus most follows divine intent—this is what it means to be "at its most excellent and best," as we proved at the beginning of this chapter.[52]

## Chapter 9

{1} Similarly, every son is at his most excellent and best when, insofar as his own nature may permit, he traces the footprints of a perfect father. Mankind is the offspring of heaven, which is perfect in all of its workings. For man and the sun beget man,[53] as it says in the second book of *Lessons on Nature*.[54] Therefore, mankind is at its best when it traces the footprints of heaven insofar as its own nature permits. {2} And since all of heaven is regulated in all its parts, movements, and movers by a single motion, to wit, the Primum Mobile and through a Single Mover, that is, God, as human reason through philosophizing apprehends most clearly, if our syllogism is correct, then mankind is at its best when it is ruled in its movers and motions by a single prince as by a single mover, by a single law as by a single motion. {3} On this account it seems necessary for the well-being of the world that there be a monarchy or a single principality that is called "empire." Boethius yearned for this order when he said:

> O how happy the human race would be,
> if that love which rules the heavens,
> also ruled your souls![55]

## Chapter 10

{1} And wherever there can be conflict there must be judgment. Otherwise there would be imperfection without the means to perfect it, and this is impossible since God and nature are never deficient in what is necessary. {2} Among any two princes of whom one is not in any way subject to the other conflict can arise either because of their own fault or because of the fault of their subjects, as is quite obvious: therefore, between these two there must be some judgment. {3} And since one cannot hold judgment over the other since one is not subject to the other—for equals do not have dominion over equals—there must be a third with wider jurisdiction who within the scope of his bailiwick rules over both of them. {4} And this will either be the monarch or not. If it is, we have achieved what we proposed; if not, this one again will have someone coequal to him beyond the scope of his jurisdiction. Then again a third will be necessary. {5} And thus there will be an infinite progression—an impossibility—or we will have to come to the first and supreme judge by whose judgment all conflicts are settled directly or indirectly: and this will be the monarch or emperor. Therefore, monarchy is necessary for the world. {6} And the Philosopher understood this reasoning when he said: "Things hate to be in disorder; but a plurality of principalities is disorder; ergo, there is but one prince."[56]

## Chapter 11

{1} Furthermore, the world is most excellently ordered when justice is most powerful within it. Wherefore Vergil wishing to praise that age which was seen to be arising in his time sang in his *Bucolics:* "Now the Virgin returns; now return the Saturnian kingdoms."[57] {2} For Justice was called a "virgin," whom they also called "Astrea." The best of times they called "Saturnian kingdoms," which they also named the "Age of Gold." Justice is most powerful only under a monarch. Ergo, for the best ordering of the world a monarchy or empire is required.[58] {3} In clarification of the minor premise, one must be aware that Justice, considered in herself and in her own nature, is a certain rectitude or rule avoiding any deviation to either side, and, that, thus, she accepts nothing more and nothing less, just as does whiteness, considered in the abstract. {4} There are to be sure certain forms of this kind, which although interacting in compounds, consist, in themselves, of a simple and invariable essence, as the Master of the *Six principles* rightly affirms.[59] Nonetheless, such qualities partially accept more or less from those things subject to them with which they are mixed, according to how much more or less of whatever is in opposition to them is admixed in those subjects. {5} Therefore, where there is the least admixture of Justice's opposite in habit and exercise, there Justice reigns supreme.[60] And then, truly, one can say of her what the Philosopher says: "Neither Hesperus nor Lucifer is so admirable." She is, indeed, like Phoebe, in the blush serenity of dawn, contemplating her brother across the diameter of the sky.[61]

{6} In regard to habit, then, Justice sometimes finds opposition in regard to the will. For where the will is not pure of all cupidity, although there be Justice within it, Justice is still not there in the total splendor of her purity: for Justice encounters a subject that is, albeit very slightly, somewhat resistant to her. Because of this, those who try to arouse a judge's passions are rightly repudiated.[62]

{7} In regard to its exercise, Justice finds opposition in regard to power[63]; for since Justice is a virtue directed toward others, how can one function according to it without the power of rendering to each his due? From this it is obvious that the more powerful a just man is, the greater his justice will be in its exercise.

{8} Thus, from what we have set forth, we can argue as follows: when Justice dwells in a subject with the strongest will, and the strongest power, she is most powerful in the world; only a monarch is such a subject; ergo, Justice is most powerful in the world only when she dwells within a monarch. {9} This preparatory syllogism[64] runs through the second figure[65] with an intrinsic negation, and it goes as follows:

All B is A;
only C is A:
ergo, only C is B.

That is:

All B is A;
nothing except C is A:
ergo, nothing except C is B.

{10} And the first premise is evident from what we have explained above; the second is shown as follows, the first part concerning will and the second part concerning power.

{11} To clarify the first part, we must be aware that cupidity is the supreme opposite of justice, as Aristotle affirms in the fifth book of his [*Nicomachean*] *Ethics*.[66] When cupidity is totally removed, there remains nothing contrary to justice. Hence the opinion of the Philosopher that "whatever can be determined by law can in no way be relegated to a judge"[67]—and this because of the fear of cupidity that can easily twist men's minds. Where, then, there is nothing to be desired, cupidity is impossible; for when their objects have been destroyed, the passions cannot exist. {12} But there is nothing for the monarch to desire,[68] for his jurisdiction is bounded only by the ocean.[69] This is not so of other princes whose principalities are bounded by those of others, as, for example, the realm of the King of Castille by that of the King of Aragon. From this it follows that the monarch is the purest subject for justice among mortals.[70]

{13} In addition, just as cupidity clouds the habit of justice to no matter how small an extent, so charity, that is, rightly ordered love, sharpens and brightens it. In him, therefore, in whom rightly ordered love can be found to the greatest degree can justice be found at its most powerful; such a one is the monarch: therefore, only when there is a monarch does justice exist or can exist most powerfully. {14} That rightly ordered love indeed acts as we have said can be deduced as follows: for cupidity despises man's perseity,[71] and seeks other things. Charity, however, despises all other things and seeks God and man and, in consequence, seeks man's good. And since among other human goods the greatest is to live in peace—as we said above [1:4:5]—and since justice most greatly and powerfully fulfills this, charity most greatly strengthens justice: and the more powerful charity is, the more powerful justice will be.

{15} And [the minor premise] that the highest degree of rightly ordered love should be found in the monarch can be made clear as follows: every thing that is loveable is all the more loved the closer it is to the person loving[72]; but men are closer to the monarch than they are to other princes: ergo, they are loved, or should be loved, by him to the greatest degree.[73]

The first premise is clear if we consider the nature of patients and agents; the second becomes clear from the following: because men are only close to other princes to a certain extent, but they are all as a whole close to the monarch.[74] {16} Again, men are close to other princes because of the monarch and not the other way around; thus the care of all men is first and directly the concern of the monarch; the concern of the other princes, however, comes through the monarch, for their concern derives from his supreme care. {17} Moreover, the more universal a cause, the greater is the reason of that cause, for an inferior cause is only a cause through one that is higher, as is clear from the treatise *On Causes.*[75] And the more a cause is a cause, the more it loves its effect since such love follows per se from the cause.

{18} Since, therefore, the monarch is the supreme universal cause among mortals of man's living well (since other princes are princes because of him, as we have said), it follows that he loves the good of mankind in the highest degree. {19} Who, then, except someone who fails to understand what the term "monarch" means, can doubt that the monarch is indeed the most powerful in the exercise of justice—since, if he is monarch, he can have no enemies? {20} We have, therefore, fully clarified the minor premise because the conclusion is certain: to wit, that a monarchy is necessary for the best world order.

## Chapter 12

{1} And mankind is at its best when it is most free. This will be manifest if the principle of liberty is made clear. {2} On this account we must be aware that the first principle of our liberty is free choice of the will—a principle that many have on their lips but few in their brains. For they come even to the point of stating that "free choice" is the "free judgment of the will." And they speak the truth, but they fail to center in on the sense of their words, just as every day our logicians fail to do with certain propositions that are brought in as examples in treatises on logic (for instance, "a triangle has three angles, equal to two right angles").[76] {3} And, therefore, I say that judgment lies amid apprehension and appetite: for, first, a thing is apprehended, then, once apprehended, it is judged good or bad, and, lastly, the person judging either seeks it or avoids it. {4} Therefore, if judgment wholly sways the appetite and is in no way prejudiced by it, it is free. If, in fact, judgment is swayed by being in some way prejudiced by the appetite, it cannot be free because it does not act by itself but is dragged away captive by another. {5} And this is why brute animals cannot have free choice because their judgments are always prejudiced by their appetite. And this is quite clear from the fact that intellectual substances whose wills are immutable, not to speak of disembodied souls who depart from this world in bliss, do not lose free choice of the will because their will is immutable, but retain it supremely and most powerfully.

{6} In view of this it can again become clear that this liberty, or this principle of all our liberty, is the greatest gift to human nature bestowed by God[77]—as I already said in the *Paradiso* of the *Comedy*[78]—because through it here below we become happy as men and through it elsewhere we become happy as gods.[79] {7} For if it is thus, who will there be who would not say that mankind is at its best when it can use this principle to its supreme degree? {8} But when man lives under a monarch he is supremely free. On this account one must be aware that "free" means "existing for its own sake and not for the sake of something else," as it pleases the Philosopher to put it in his *On Being Simply*.[80] For that which is for the sake of something else is necessitated by that for whose sake it exists, as a road is necessitated by its destination. {9} Only under the rule of the monarch does humankind exist for itself and not for the sake of something else, for only then are perverted forms of political order—such as democracies, oligarchies, and tyrannies, which force mankind into slavery[81]—rectified, as is clear to anyone who checks through them all—and only then do kings, aristocrats (who are named "best"), and those with zeal for the people's liberty set the policy.[82] For, since the monarch loves the people in the greatest degree, as we have already shown, he wills all men to be good—an impossibility among those who play at crooked politics. {10} Wherefore the Philosopher in his *Politics* says that in a perverted form of government a good man is a bad citizen; in a righteous form, however, "a good man" and "a good citizen" are interchangeable terms.[83] And such righteous forms of government aim at liberty, that is, for men to live for their own sake—{11} not, to be sure, citizens for consuls, or a people for their king, but the other way around: consuls exist for the sake of citizens and a king for the sake of his people. Since inasmuch as a form of government is not set up for the sake of laws but rather the laws for the sake of government, therefore, those who live under the law are not there for the sake of the lawgiver, but rather the other way around, as it pleases the Philosopher to put it in those writings left to us by him concerning this issue.[84] {12} From this, likewise, it is clear that although a consul or a king may have dominion over others as far as the means are concerned, as far as the end is concerned, they are servants of others, and especially the monarch who must, without any trace of doubt, be considered the servant of all. From this, besides, it can now be made clear that the monarch is necessitated by the very end fixed for him in establishing laws. {13} Ergo, mankind is at its best when it lives under a monarch; from this it follows that a monarchy is necessary for the well-being of the world.

## Chapter 13

{1} Moreover, he who can be[85] best disposed to rule can best dispose others; for, in any action, what an agent primarily intends is to act so as to duplicate its own likeness, either by the necessity of its nature or voluntarily.[86] {2} Whence it happens that every agent, insofar as it is an agent, delights in action. For since everything that exists desires its own being, and since in action the being of the agent is in some way increased, delight necessarily follows because delight is always bound up with the thing desired.[87] {3} Nothing, therefore, acts unless it already possesses those qualities which its patient must evolve: on this account the Philosopher, in his writings on *On Being Simply*, says that everything that is brought from potentiality to realization is done by the agency of some actual being.[88] Otherwise if something were to attempt to act in any other way, it would try in vain. {4} On this account we can refute the error of those who believe they can mold the lives and morals of others by talking of the good but doing evil, forgetting that the hands of Jacob were more persuasive than his words, although the former led to fraud, the latter the truth.[89] Whence the Philosopher says in the *Nicomachean Ethics:* "In questions concerning the passions and actions, words are less convincing than deeds."[90] {5} Hence also a voice from heaven said to the sinner, David: "Why dost thou declare my justice?"[91] As if to say: "You speak in vain, since your words do not match what you are." From this we gather that anyone who wants to dispose others best must be best disposed himself.

{6} But the monarch alone is he who can be best disposed to rule, and this can be made clear as follows: anything is more easily and perfectly disposed to usage and function the less it has in it that is contrary to such disposition; wherefore those come more easily and perfectly to the usage of philosophical truth who have never learned anything than those who have studied for a long time and have been imbued with false opinions. Concerning these Galen says justly: "Such men need twice the time to acquire knowledge."[92] {7} Therefore, since the monarch can have no occasion for cupidity (or, at all events, the least occasion among mortals, as we have demonstrated above [II:II]—something which is not the case with other princes), and cupidity itself is the only corrupter of judgment and impediment to justice, it follows that only the monarch himself can be either wholly or most well disposed to rule, because he can possess judgment and justice to the highest degree among all others. These two qualities are surpassingly fitting for makers and executors of the law, as that most holy king bore witness when he used to implore God for those things befitting a king and the son of a king: "O God," he would say, "Give to the king thy judgment: and to the king's son thy justice."[93] {8} Therefore, what was affirmed in the minor premise [{6} above] was rightly affirmed: that the monarch alone is he who can be the most best disposed to rule: ergo, only the monarch can best dispose others. From this it follows that monarchy is necessary for the optimum disposition of the world.

## Chapter 14

{1} And when something can be done by one, it is better for it be to done by one than by many.[94] This can be clarified in the following way: let A be one agent by which something may be done, and let A and B be several by which the same thing can be performed; therefore, if that same thing that can be done by A and B can be done by A alone, it is useless to bring in B because nothing is accomplished by the adoption of B—since the same thing was accomplished first by A alone. {2} And since all such adoptions are useless and superfluous, and everything superfluous is displeasing to God and nature, and everything displeasing to God and nature is an evil, as is self-evident, it follows that not only is it better for it to be done by one, if that is possible, than for it to be done by many; but that which is done by one is good; that which is done by many, utterly evil.

{3} Moreover, a thing is said to be better the closer it is to what is most excellent; its end is the cause of what is most excellent; but performance by one approaches the end more quickly: Therefore, it is better. And that it reaches its end more quickly can be made clear as follows: let the end be C; let A be performance by a single agent; let A and B be performance by several; it is clear that the distance is longer from A through B to C than A straight to C. {4} But mankind can be ruled by one supreme prince who is the monarch. In this connection, to be sure, it must be noted that when we say, "Mankind can be ruled by one supreme prince," it must not be so construed that the pettiest decisions of every municipality can come directly from him, although even municipal laws sometimes fall short and require rectification, as is clear from the fifth book of the *Nicomachean Ethics* when he recommends *epyikia*.[95] Nations, kingdoms, and cities have different characteristics one from the other, which must be governed by different laws, for the law is the rule guiding our lives. {6} For the Scythians,[96] who live beyond the seventh clime suffering a great inequality of day and night, oppressed by an almost intolerable freezing cold, must be ruled in one way, and in another the Garamanths,[97] who dwell in the equatorial region, always experiencing the equality of the light of day and the darkness of night, unable to cover themselves with clothes because of the excess of the air's raging heat. {7} But it must be construed as follows: that, on the basis of the things all have in common and that pertain to all men, mankind be ruled by one monarch and be guided toward peace by a common rule. In fact, particular princes must receive that rule or law from him just as the practical intellect, in order to arrive at a conclusion for action, receives the major premise from the speculative intellect, and under it assumes its own particular minor premise and draws in its special case the conclusion that concerns the action. {8} And this is not only possible for one prince but necessarily proceeds from one in order that all confusion about universal principles be eliminated. {9} Further, Moses wrote into the Law that he himself had done this: after he had chosen the heads of the tribes of the children of Israel, he left the minor judgments to them and reserved the major and more general decisions for himself alone; the head of each tribe then made use of these general decisions as they applied to the individual tribe.

{10} Therefore, it is better that mankind be ruled by one than by many, and, therefore, by a monarch who is the sole prince. And if it is better it is more acceptable to God, since God always wills what is better. And since between only two things better and best are the same, it follows not only that between rule by one and rule by many the former is more acceptable to God, but rather that it is most acceptable. {11} Whence it follows that mankind is at its best when it is ruled by one. And thus there must be a monarchy for the well-being of the world.

## Chapter 15

{1} Likewise, I affirm that "being," "the one," and "the good" exist in an order following the fifth meaning of the word "priority."[98] "Being," indeed, precedes the "one" by nature; and "the one," to be sure, precedes "the good." Indeed, perfect being is perfect unity, and perfect unity is perfectly good. And the further distant something is from "perfect being," the further it is from "the one," and, consequently, the further it is from "the good." {2} As a result, in every species of things, the best is that which is "one" to the greatest degree, as it pleases the Philosopher to put it in *On Being Simply.*[99] Whence it turns out that "being one" is seen to be the root of "being good," and "being many" is the root of "being evil." Wherefore Pythagoras in his correlations placed "the one" on the side of good, and plurality on the side of evil, as is clear from the first book of the *On Being Simply.*[100] {3} Hence we can see that to sin is nothing else but to despise unity and advance toward plurality, as indeed the Psalmist saw clearly when he said: "By the fruit of their corn, their wine, and oil, they are multiplied."[101] {4} It is agreed, therefore, that everything that is good is good for this reason: because it consists of "one."

And since concord insofar as it is of such a nature is a good, it is obvious that concord consists at its very root of some single unity. {5} Indeed what this root is will be clear to us if we examine concord's nature or definition: concord is actually a uniform movement of several wills. From this definition it is quite apparent that the unity of wills signified by uniform movement is the root of concord, or rather is concord itself. {6} For just as we would say that several clods of earth are "in concord" if they are falling down together toward a center, and likewise several flames if they are all rising up to a circumference[102]—were they to do this voluntarily—likewise we say that several men are "in concord" if they are moving voluntarily all together toward one single object that is formally in their wills, just as a single shared quality is formally in the clods of dirt, namely, heaviness, and in the flames, namely, lightness. {7} For the power of willing is a certain potentiality, but the species of good it apprehends is its form. This form, then, just as other forms—such as the soul, number, and other forms subject to being composite—is a single unity and becomes multiple through the multiplicity of the material receiving it.[103]

{8} Having given these premises so as to clarify the proposition that we must maintain for our thesis, we may now argue the case as follows: all concord depends upon a unity that is within wills; mankind at its best forms a certain concord, for just as one man at his best forms a certain concord as far as his soul and body are concerned (and similarly a household, a city, and a kingdom), in the same way does all of humanity: ergo, mankind at its best depends upon the unity of wills.

{9} But this cannot be so unless there be one single will, master and guide of all others in unity, for the will of mortals needs direction because of the alluring delights of youth, as the Philosopher teaches in the last book of the *Nicomachean Ethics.*[104] Nor can there be such a single will unless there be one prince over all, whose will can be the master and guide of all the others. {10} If all the above conclusions are true—and they are—for mankind to be at its best, there must be a monarch in the world and, consequently, there must be a monarchy for the well-being of the world.

## Chapter 16

{1} All the above reasons we have set forth bear witness to one unforgettable event: to wit, the state of mortals which the Son of God either awaited, or decided to bring about himself when he was about to become man for man's salvation. For, if we reflect upon the conditions and the ages of man, from the Fall of our first parents, which was the first wrong turning point of all our aberrations, only under the monarch, Divus Augustus, when a perfect monarchy existed, will we find tranquillity throughout the world.[105] And that mankind lived happily in the tranquillity of universal peace at that time all historians and all illustrious poets and even the scribe of Christ's compassion[106] deigned to bear witness.[107] And finally Paul called that most happy state "the fullness of time" [Gal 4:4].[108] The time and all temporalities were indeed full because no agency of our happiness was without its minister. {3} Yet we can read about the kind of condition the world has been in since that seamless garment first suffered rending by the claw of cupidity—would that we could not still see it![109]

{4} O human kind! By how many tempests and misfortunes, by how many shipwrecks must you be tossed while you, having turned into a beast with many heads,[110] strain in such conflicting directions? {5} You are sick in both intellects,[111] as you are in your affective part; you do not cure your higher intellect with invincible arguments, nor your lower with the face of experience, nor your affections with the sweetness of divine persuasions when it is breathed into you by the trumpet of the Holy Spirit: "Behold how good and how pleasant it is for brethren to dwell together in unity."[112]

## BOOK 2

### Chapter 1

{1} "Why have the Gentiles raged, and the people devised vain things? The kings of the earth stood up, and the princes met together, against the Lord, and against his Christ. Let us break their bonds asunder; and let us cast away their yoke from us."[113]

{2} Just as we are generally amazed at some strange effect because we cannot see its cause, and when we do learn the cause we look down with a certain derision upon others who are left marveling, so I indeed once used to puzzle how the Roman people had been, without resistence at all, appointed to rule over the whole globe of the earth. Since I was considering it only superficially, I judged that they had obtained this not *de jure* but merely by force of arms.[114]

{3} But when I fixed the eyes of my mind to its innermost part, I came to understand by the most compelling signs that divine providence had accomplished it, and, as my wonder waned, a certain derisive scorn overcame me as I observed how the Gentiles raged against the preeminence of the Roman people when I saw the people devising vain things (as I used to do); and I grieved above all that kings and princes agreed on one thing only: on defying their Lord and his anointed, the Roman prince. {4} As a result, with some derision and not without a certain grief, I can take up for that glorious people and for Cæsar, the cry of him who cried out for the Prince of Heaven: "Why have the Gentiles raged, and the people devised vain things? The kings of the earth stood up, and the princes met together, against the Lord, and against his Christ." {5} But since natural love cannot suffer derision to last for long, for—like the summer sun, which, upon rising, scatters the morning clouds and shines out radiantly—it dismisses scorn and prefers to pour forth the light of correction; to break the chain of ignorance of such kings and princes and to show forth human kind free of their yoke, I shall cheer myself along with the most Holy Prophet whom I imitate in repeating the following words, to wit: "Let us break their bonds asunder: and let us cast away their yoke from us."[115]

{6} These two things, anyway, will be fulfilled when I have completed the second part of my present plan and when I have shown the truth of the question at hand. For by showing that the Roman Empire did exist *de jure*, not only will the cloud of ignorance be washed from the eyes of kings and princes— who, usurping the tiller of public affairs, mendaciously attribute that very crime to the Roman people—but all mortals will also know that they are free from the yoke of such usurpers.

{7} Indeed the truth of the question can be made clear not only by the light of human reason but even by the divine radiance of authority: when these two concur as one, heaven and earth have to agree together. {8} Therefore, sustained by my faith confessed above [1:1:6], and supported in advance by the testimony of reason and authority, I enter upon the solution to the second question.

## Chapter 2

{1} After having inquired sufficiently into the truth of the first problem insofar as the matter may permit, it now remains to inquire into the truth of the second: this is whether the Roman people assumed for themselves the dignity of empire *de jure*. In fact, the starting point of this inquiry is to discern the main truth to which, as to their own first principle, the reasons of our present inquiry may be referred.

{2} It must be understood that just as art has three steps—that is, in the mind of the artisan, in his tool, or in the material shaped by his art—we can also consider nature as having three steps: nature, in fact, is in the mind of the First Mover who is God; then in heaven as in the tool; and by this means the likeness of eternal goodness is spread forth into changeable matter. {3} And when the artisan is perfect and his tool is in perfect condition, should there happen to be any flaw in the form of the art, it must be imputed to the material alone; likewise, since God achieves highest perfection, and his tool (that is, the heavens) cannot suffer any defect in its condign perfection (as is clear from our philosophical studies on the heavens),[116] it must be that whatever fault remains in things here below is a fault on the part of the subject material contrary to the intention of God the Creator and of the heavens. And whatever good there is in things here below cannot come from the material itself but can only exist in potentiality since it comes initially from the artisan who is God and, second, from the heavens, which are the tools of divine art commonly called "nature."

{4} From what we have said, it is now clear that right,[117] being a good, exists initially in the mind of God; and since everything that is in the mind of God is God (according to the dictum that "whatever was made in him was life [Jn 1:3–4]").[118] and God most especially wills himself, it follows that right, insofar as it is within him, is willed by God. And since in God the will and the thing willed are the same,[119] it follows further that divine will is right itself. {5} And, proceeding, from this it follows that right, in things here below, is nothing but a likeness of divine will. Whence it is that whatever is not consonant with divine will cannot itself be right and whatever is consonant with divine will is right itself. {6} For this reason to ask whether a thing was done *de jure* is exactly the same as asking—notwithstanding the change of wording—whether it was done according to God's will. We may therefore make the assumption that whatever God wills in human society is true and genuine right.

{7} Furthermore, we must recall, as the Philosopher teaches in the first book of the [*Nicomachean*] *Ethics*, that certainty cannot be sought in the same way in every matter but rather according as the nature of the subject permits.[120] Therefore the arguments will proceed satisfactorily under the principle that we have discovered if we examine the right of that glorious people through manifest signs and the authority of sages.[121] {8} Indeed, the will of God is in itself invisible, but the invisible things of God "are clearly seen, being understood by the things that are made."[122] For although the seal is hidden, its wax impress bears clear evidence of it no matter how much it is concealed. Nor should we wonder that divine will is to be sought through signs, since not even human will can be discerned outside the person willing except through signs.

## Chapter 3

{1} On this question I therefore declare that the Roman people received the office of monarch—that is called "empire"—over all mortals not by usurpation, but *de jure*.

{2} This may, in fact, first be proved as follows: it is fitting that the most noble people be preferred before all others; the Roman people were the most noble; ergo, it is fitting that they be preferred before all others. {3} We can prove the major premise logically in this way: now, since honor is the reward of virtue, and all preferment is an honor, all preferment is the reward of virtue. Yet it is established that men are ennobled by the merit of virtue, to wit, either by their own virtue or by that of their ancestors. {4} As the Philosopher says in his *Politics*, "Nobility is virtue and ancient riches"[123]; and according to Juvenal: "Nobility of mind is the one and only virtue."[124] These differing[125] opinions yield two kinds of nobility: that is to say, one's own and that of one's ancestors. Therefore by reason of this cause is the reward of preferment fitting to those who are noble. {5} And since rewards must be commensurate with merits, in accordance with the Gospel: "With what measure you mete, it shall be measured to you again."[126] It is fitting that he who is most noble be especially preeminent.

{6} The minor premise,[127] indeed, is argued persuasively by the testimony of the ancients, for our divine poet, Vergil, throughout the whole *Æneid* bears witness unto eternal memory that the most glorious king, Æneas, was the father of the Roman people. This, Titus Livy, the eminent scribe of Roman feats, corroborates in the first part of his volume whose exordium resumes the history from the capture of Troy.[128] {7} To be sure, I cannot set forth what an invincible and most pious father and of what great nobility that man was, considering not only his own virtue but that of his ancestors, and that of his wives, both of whose nobility flowed together through him by hereditary right—but "I shall trace the main footprints of the events."[129]

{8} Insofar as his own nobility is concerned, we must hear our Poet in supplication as he first introduces this man from Ilion:

Our king was Æneas: no man more righteous than he in piety, or greater in war and arms.[130]

{9} And let us hear him in book six when he speaks of the dead Misenus who had been Hector's subaltern in war, and who after Hector's death had devoted himself to the service of Æneas; the same Misenus of whom he says, "followed no meaner standard,"[131] making a comparison between Æneas and Hector whom Homer glorifies above all (to which comparison the Philosopher alludes in those parts of the *Ethics,* where he describes conduct we ought to avoid).[132] {10} Indeed, as far as hereditary nobility is concerned, we find that all three parts of the globe had ennobled him through both his ancestors and his wives: for example, Asia through his closest forebears, such as Assaracus and the others who ruled Phrygia, a region of Asia; whence our Poet says in his third book:

After it pleased the gods above to overthrow the might of Asia and Priam's guiltless race.[133]

{11} Europe, indeed, through his most ancient ancestor, namely, Dardanus; Africa too through his most ancient ancestress, to wit, Electra, born of King Atlantis of great renown. Our Poet bears testimony of both in his eighth book where Æneas speaks as follows to Evander:

Dardanus, first father and founder of Ilium's city, born (as the Greeks recount) of Atlantean Electra, came to the Teucrians; mightiest Atlas, who on his shoulders sustains the heavenly spheres, begat Electra.[134]

{12} Moreover, that Dardanus drew his origin from Europe our Seer[135] celebrates in his third book:

There is a place the Greeks call Hesperia, an ancient land, mighty in arms and in richness of the soil. There dwelt Oenotrians; now the rumor is that a younger race has dubbed it, from their leader's name, Italy. This is our abiding home; whence Dardanus sprang.[136]

{13} That Atlas did indeed hail from Africa the mountain there bearing his name attests; the one that Orosius says is in Africa, in his description of the world: "Its farthest boundary is Mount Atlas and the islands which people call Fortunate."[137] "Its" means Africa, since that was what he was talking about.

{14} Likewise I also find that he was ennobled through marriage. For his first wife, Creusa, daughter of Priam, was from Asia, as may be gathered from what we said above. And that she was his wife our Poet testifies in his third book where Andromache questions Æneas, Ascanius's father, about his son as follows:

What of the boy Ascanius? Lives and breathes he yet? Whom Creusa bore to you in smouldering Troy?[138]

{15} Dido was the second, queen and mother of the Carthaginians in Africa, and that she was his wife our same author celebrates in his fourth book; for he says of Dido:

No more does Dido dream of a furtive love: she calls it marriage and with that name veils her sin![139]

{16} Lavinia was the third, mother of the Albans and the Romans, daughter and heir alike of King Latinus, if our Poet's testimony in his last book is true, where he introduces the defeated Turnus who begs Æneas thus in supplication:

Victor thou art; and as one vanquished, the Ausonians have seen me stretch forth my palms: Lavinia is thine for wife.[140]

{17} This last wife hailed from Italy, the noblest region of Europe.

Therefore, with these facts pointed out in proof of the minor premise, who is not sufficiently persuaded that the father of the Roman people and consequently the Roman people itself was the noblest beneath the heavens? Or from whom will divine predestination in that double[141] confluence of blood into one man from all parts of the earth still be hidden?

## Chapter 4

Moreover, whatever is aided in its fulfillment by the approval of miracles is done by the will of God and is consequently done *de jure.* And that this is true is clear because, as Thomas says in his third book *Against the Gentiles,*[142] a miracle is that which is "done by divine power apart from the order generally followed in things." Wherefore he proves that the working of miracles belongs to God alone;[143] this is corroborated by the authority of Moses: when it came to the gnats, the Pharaoh's magicians artfully using natural principles failed and said: "This is the finger of God"[144] {3} If, then, a miracle is the direct working of the First Cause without the cooperation of secondary agents—as Thomas himself demonstrates fully in the book we cited—when there is a portent favoring something, it is wickedness to say that the thing favored by the miracle is not foreseen by God as something pleasing to him. {4} Therefore the pious thing to do is to concede the contrary: the Roman Empire was aided in coming to perfection by the approval of miracles; ergo, it was willed by God, and, consequently, it existed and exists *de jure.*

{5} That God did, indeed, portend his will in working miracles to bring the Roman Empire to perfection is proved by the testimony of illustrious authors. Certainly, as Livy attests in the first part of his book, during the reign of Numa Pompilius, second king of the Romans, as he was sacrificing in accordance with the rite of the pagans, a shield tumbled from the sky upon God's chosen city.[145] {6} Lucan recalls this miracle in the ninth book of the *Pharsalia,* where he describes the incredible force of the south wind that Libya suffered, in these words:

In this way those shields, which chosen young patricians bear on their napes, surely fell before Numa as he performed sacrifice: the South wind or the North had robbed the bearers of those bucklers which now are ours.[146]

{7} And when the Gauls, relying on the dark of night after capturing the rest of the city, furtively climbed up the Capitol, which was all that remained before the total destruction of the Roman name, Livy and many illustrious writers agree[147] in testifying that a goose, not seen there before, cackled to warn that the Gauls were at hand and awoke the guards to defend the Capitol. {8} This event was remembered by our Poet when he described the shield of Æneas in the eighth book; he sings as follows:

At the top, before the temple, stood Manlius, warder of the Tarpeian rock, and held the lofty Capitol; the palace was rough, just built with the thatch of Romulus. And here the silver goose, fluttering through the gilded colonnades, cried out that the Gauls were on the threshold.[148]

{9} And when Rome's nobility, hard-pressed by Hannibal, fell to such a low point that there remained nothing to complete final annihilation of all that was Roman save the assault of the Carthaginians upon the city, Livy recounts, among other events in the *Punic War*, that the victors could not follow up their victory because a sudden, relentless hailstorm threw them into confusion.[149]

{10} And was not Cloelia's crossing miraculous, when during Porsenna's siege, a woman and a prisoner, she broke her chains and swam across the Tiber, succored by the wondrous aid of God, as nearly all those who transcribe the affairs of Rome memorialize to her glory?[150] {11} It was truly meet that he, who foresaw everything from eternity in the beauty of his order, should work exactly in this way—he who, become visible, should work miracles on behalf of those things that are invisible, and, when invisible, should work them on behalf of those things which are visible.[151]

## Chapter 5

{1} Further, anyone who is attentive to the common good directs his thoughts to the goal of right. And that this must be the consequence can be shown in this manner: right is a real and personal relation between man and man, which, when observed, preserves human society, and which, when corrupted, corrupts it[152]—for the description in the *Digests* does not state the essence of right, but describes it by teaching its usage.[153]

{2} Therefore, if our definition well comprises the "what" and the "why" of right, and if the end of any society is the common good of its members,[154] it must be that the end of all right is the common good. And right is impossible if it does not aim at the common good. On this account Tully properly states in *First Rhetoric*[155] that "the laws must always be interpreted for the public good." {3} For if the laws are not directed for the good of those who live under the laws, they are laws in name only, but they cannot be laws in substance. Indeed laws must bind men together for their common benefit. Because of this, Seneca, in his book *On the Four Virtues*, justly calls the law "the bond of human society."[156] {4} It is therefore obvious that anyone who attends to the common good directs his thoughts to the goal of right. If the Romans attended to the common good, therefore, it will be true to say that they directed their thoughts to the goal of right. {5} That in subjugating the earth's globe the Roman people attended to the aforesaid good is declared, moreover, by their deeds—in which they dispelled all cupidity, which is always harmful to the common good—for by their delight in universal peace and liberty, that holy, pious, and glorious people are seen to have neglected their own best interests to look after those of the public for the welfare[157] of mankind. Hence rightly has it been written: "The Roman Empire was born in the font of piety."[158]

{6} But since nothing concerning the intentions of any agent in its free choice can be understood outwardly except through external signs, and because statements must be examined according to our subject matter (as we have already said [2:2:7]), we will have sufficient evidence on this point if we can show the indubitable signs of the motives of the Roman people both in their public assemblies and as private individuals. {7} Concerning their public assemblies, then, by which men are seen to be in some way bound to the common good, the sole authority of Cicero in his second book *On Duties* is sufficient: "As long," he says, "as the empire of the republic was maintained by benefits and not by oppression, wars were waged either on behalf of its allies or to maintain its power, and the consequences of these wars were either mild or necessary; the Senate was a haven and refuge for kings, peoples, and nations. Moreover, both our magistrates and our generals strove above all for praise in defending provinces and allies with equity and loyalty; and thus, rather than a 'dominion' our government could have been called a 'protector' of the world."[159] The words of Cicero.

{8} Let me continue briefly concerning private individuals.[160] Must they not be said to have been attentive to the common good, those who, by sweat, poverty, exile, deprivation of their children, loss of limbs, and even by the sacrifice of their lives, strove to increase the public good? {9} Did not the famous Cincinnatus leave us a holy example, when he was taken from the plough and made dictator, of voluntarily putting aside his official dignity at the termination of his charge (as Livy recounts),[161] and after his victory, after his triumph, and after restoring the scepter of command to the consuls, of willingly returning to the plough handle to sweat behind the oxen? {10} It was surely in his praise and mindful of this benefit that Cicero, in his books on *The Goal of All Good*, said while disputing Epicurus: "Even so did our ancestors bring the great Cincinnatus from the plough to be dictator."[162] {11} And did not Fabricius give us a lofty example of how to resist avarice? For though he was poor, out of that loyalty which bound him to the republic, he scoffed at the offer of a great weight of gold, and, spurning it, in a torrent of fitting words, scorned and refused it. The memory of that deed was confirmed by our Poet in his sixth book, as he sang: "Fabricius powerful in poverty."[163] {12} Was not Camillus a memorable example in preferring laws above his own interests? Who according to Livy, although condemned to exile after he had liberated his besieged homeland, also restored to Rome her spoils, and although the whole populace clamored for his return, left the sacred city and did not return to it until he was brought a permit of repatriation on the authority of the Senate. This great-souled hero the Poet commends in his sixth book, saying: "Camillus bringing home the standards."[164]

{13} Did not the first Brutus teach us to place the liberty of our homeland before our sons and all others, as Livy says, when as consul he sentenced his own sons to death for conspiring with the enemy? His glory is renewed by our Poet in his sixth book as he celebrates him: "For fair liberty's sake, the father calls to their doom his sons who stir up new wars."[165]

{14} What did Mucius not convince us to dare for our homeland when he attacked unwary Porsenna, and then, with the same countenance as if he were watching an enemy being tortured, watched his hand—that hand still his own that had missed its aim—burn up in the fire! Even Livy is filled with wonder as he bears witness to it.[166]

{15} There now approach[167] those most holy victims, the Decii, who laid down their lives devoted to the salvation of the republic, as Livy recounts glorifying them, not as they deserve, but as best he can.[168] And there comes forth that inexpressible sacrifice of that sternest of supporters of true liberty, Marcus Cato.[169] The former showed no horror for the shadows of death for their homeland's sake; the latter, so as to kindle the love of liberty in the world, showed how great freedom is and chose to die a free man rather than to remain alive without freedom.

{16} The renown of all these still glows in the words of Tully from those passages of the *On the Goal of All Good* where he says this about the Decii:

When Publius Decius, the first of his family to be consul, made an offering of himself: spurring on his horse, he went charging into the midst of the host of the Latins, was he thinking of personal pleasure, when he should take it and where? For since he knew death was imminent, he sought death with more ardor than Epicurus believes pleasure is to be sought. Because, if his exploit had not been rightly praised, it would not have been imitated by his son in his fourth consulship, and the son of this son would not also have fallen in a battle in which he commanded as consul during the war with Pyrrhus as the third in his line to give himself as victim for the republic.[170]

{17} And, of course, in his *On Duties* he said of Cato:

Did not Marcus Cato find himself in one predicament and were not the others in another who surrendered to Cæsar in Africa? And yet, perhaps, if they had taken their own lives they would have been blamed since their lives were less austere and their characters more easygoing. But Cato had been endowed by nature with an unbelievable austerity and he himself strengthened it by ceaseless constancy, and since he remained firm in his purpose, in his case it was better that he die than to look upon the face of a tyrant [1:31].[171]

{18} Thus two things have been clarified: the first of which is that anyone who attends to the common good directs his thoughts to the goal of right; the second, that the Roman people in their subjugation of the earth attended to the public good.

{19} We now present our argument in support of our proposal in the following manner: anyone who attends to the goal of right proceeds with right. The Roman people in subjugating the earth attended to the goal of right, as was clearly proven above in this chapter: ergo, the Roman people in subjugating the earth's globe did so by right, and consequently the Roman people assumed the dignity of empire *de jure*.

{20} So that our conclusion may be inferred from all the premises we have established, we must clarify what we mean by "that anyone who attends to the end goal of right proceeds with right on his side." For proof of this, we must remember that everything exists for some end, otherwise it would be useless— and this is impossible, as we said earlier. {21} And inasmuch as everything has its own end, every end has its proper object of which it is the end. Whence it is impossible that any two things, properly speaking, insofar as they are two, be directed toward the same end. Otherwise the same erroneous conclusion would follow, that is, that one or the other would be useless. Therefore, since there is a certain end for right, as we have already made clear, having postulated that end, we must postulate right itself as a proper and inherent effect of right. And since in all consequences it is impossible to have an antecedent without its consequent—such as "man" without "animal," as is made clear by affirming and negating the proposition—it is impossible to seek the end goal of right without right since everything stands to its end as a consequent to its antecedent: for it is impossible to attain the good conditioning of one's limbs without health.[172] {23} On this account it is absolutely clear that someone who directs his thoughts to the end goal of right must be directing his thoughts by the right. The example that is usually elicited from the words of the Philosopher, where he treats of "*eubulia,*" is not valid. The Philosopher says, in fact: "It is possible to attain a sound conclusion by a false syllogism, to arrive at it by the wrong means when the middle term is false."[173]

{24} For if from false premises we in some way conclude the truth, it occurs by accident insofar as that truth is brought in by what the words refer to, for, certainly, the truth itself never follows from falsehoods, yet words signifying truth can indeed follow from words signifying falsehoods. {25} So it is with our actions: for although a thief may help a pauper with stolen goods, this cannot be called "almsgiving," yet it is the kind of act, which, had it been performed with his own property, would have had the form of almsgiving. {26} It is the same with the end of right: for if anything were to be obtained as the end of right itself without right means, then that end of right obtained—which is the common good—would be like the example of almsgiving derived from ill-gotten gains. And thus, since in the proposition we spoke of the end goal of right as it really exists and not merely as it appears, the objection is null and void. Therefore the point of our inquiry is quite clear.

## Chapter 6

{1} And that which nature has ordained is preserved *de jure*. For nature in her providence does not lag behind man in his, since if she did, the effect would outdo the cause in goodness, and this is impossible. {2} But we see that in the establishment of organized groups not only is the mutual order among the members considered by the person establishing them but also their power in exercising their offices. This means considering the limits of right within the organized group or within the mutual order; certainly no right extends beyond power. Therefore, nature in her ordinances does not fail to provide for this. {3} It is obvious, therefore, that nature orders things in respect to their capacities, and this respect is the foundation of right that nature invests in things. It follows from this that the natural order among things may not be preserved without right, for the foundation of right is inseparably bound to that order: it is therefore necessary that order be preserved *de jure.*

{4} The Roman people were ordained by nature to rule. And this may be shown as follows: just as someone who directed his attention only to the final form and really cared nothing for the means by which he arrived at that form would fall short of perfection in his art, so nature, were she to direct her attention only to the universal form of divine likeness in the universe, would neglect the means. But nature falls short of no perfection since she is the work of divine intelligence; Therefore, she directs her attention to all means by which she may come to the completion of her intention. {5} Since, therefore, there exists an end for mankind and some necessary means of reaching nature's universal end goal, nature must direct her attention to this. Thus the Philosopher indeed proves in the second book of the *Lessons on Nature* that nature always acts in accordance with an end.[174] {6} And because nature cannot arrive at this end through one single man, since there are many operations necessary for it that require a multitude to perform them, it is necessary for nature to produce a multitude of men ordained for her diverse operations. To this, in addition to the influences of the higher regions, the powers and properties of the lower regions contribute a great deal. {7} As a result we see not only that certain individual men but even some nations are born suited to govern and certain others to be subjects and to serve, as the Philosopher affirms in his writings on *Politics.*[175] And as he says himself, it is not only expedient for such men to be governed but it is just, even if they must be coerced into it.

{8} If this is the situation, there is no doubt that nature disposed a people and a place in the world for universal rule; otherwise she would have failed, and this is impossible. What place that was and what people these might have been is sufficiently obvious from what we have said above [2:2:1, 2:5:19] and from what we have to say below: that place was Rome and its citizens, or rather, its people. {9} Our Poet touched quite subtly upon this in his sixth book as he introduces Anchises prophesying Æneas as father of the Romans:

Others, I doubt not, shall beat out the breathing bronze with softer lines; shall from marble draw forth the features of life; shall plead their causes better; with the rod shall trace the paths of heaven and tell the rising of the stars; remember thou, O Roman, to rule the nations with thy sway—these shall be thine arts—to crown Peace with Law, to spare the humbled, and tame in war the proud![176]

{10} Indeed he subtly touches on the disposition of the place in his fourth book as he introduces Jove speaking to Mercury about Æneas in this way:

Not such as this did his lovely mother promise him to us, nor for this twice rescue him from Grecian arms; but he was to rule over Italy, a land teeming with empire and clamorous with war.[177]

{11} Therefore we have given sufficient proof that the Roman people were ordained to rule by nature; ergo, the Roman people attained empire *de jure* in subjugating the earth for themselves.

## Chapter 7

{1} Also, to track down the truth of the problem properly one must be aware that divine judgment in human affairs is sometimes revealed and sometimes hidden from man; {2} and it can be revealed in two ways, namely, by reason and by faith. For there are certain judgments of God which human reason can arrive at on its own two feet,[178] such as, for example, that man should endanger himself for the salvation of his homeland; for if the part must endanger itself for the safety of the whole, and since man is, as it were, a part of his community, as the Philosopher makes clear in his *Politics*,[179] a man must put himself in danger for his native land, as a lesser good for a greater good. {3} Whence the Philosopher in his *Nicomachean Ethics* says: "It is enjoyable to work for the good of a single person, but it is better and more divine to work for a people or a community."[180] And this is the judgment of God, otherwise human reason in its rectitude would not follow the intention of nature, and this is impossible.

{4} Although there are certain judgments of God that human reason cannot reach by its own powers, it is nevertheless raised to them by the aid of faith in those things that are told us in Holy Scriptures, such as in the following instance: that no one, no matter how perfect in moral and intellectual virtues both in habits and in actions, can be saved without faith, even though he might never have heard anything about Christ.[181] {5} For human reason by itself cannot grasp how this may be just, but it can grasp it when aided by faith. Indeed in Hebrews it is written: "Without faith it is impossible to please God."[182] And in Leviticus: "Any man whosoever of the house of Israel if he kill an ox, or a sheep, or a goat in the camp, or without the camp, and offer is not made at the door of the tabernacle an oblation to the Lord, shall be guilty of blood."[183] {6} The door of the tabernacle figures Christ who is the Door of the Eternal Conclave, as we can deduce from the Gospel[184]; the killing of animals signifies human actions.

{7} Hidden, however, is that judgment of God that human reason cannot reach either by the law of nature or the law of Scripture but only at times by special grace. This may come about in several ways: sometimes by simple revelation, other times by revelation in a decisive test.

{8} It may come about by simple revelation in two ways: either spontaneously from God, or through prayerful supplication. The spontaneous act of God can come about in two ways, either directly, or by sign: directly, as in the revelation of Samuel's judgment against Saul,[185] or by sign, as in the revelation through a sign to Pharaoh that God had decided to free the children of Israel. Those knew the way of prayerful supplication who said in the second book of Paralipomenon [20:12]: "But as we know not what to do, this alone we have left: we can only turn our eyes to thee."[186]

{9} A decisive test can come about in two ways: by lot, or by contest (that is, *certamine*, since *certare*, meaning "to contèst," is derived from *certum facere*, "to make certain").[187] Indeed, the judgment of God is sometimes revealed to men by lot as is clear in Matthias's being a replacement in the Acts of the Apostles.[188] The judgment of God is disclosed to man through a contest in two ways: either through a clash of strength, as occurs in a duel between champions,[189] who can also be called "combatants," or through a competition of many striving to outdo each other to reach some finish line, such as occurs in a contest among athletic contestants running for a prize.[190] {10} The first of these ways was figured among the pagans by the struggle of Hercules and Antæus that Lucan records in the fourth book of the *Pharsalia*,[191] and Ovid in the ninth book of his *Metamorphoses*.[192] The second was figured among the pagans by Atalanta and Hippomene in the tenth book of the *Metamorphoses*.[193] {11} Likewise we must not neglect the fact that in these two forms of contest there are the following conditions: that in the first the contestants may clasp each other without unfairness, as with combatants, but not in the other.[194] Certainly athletes running for a prize must not foul one another, although our Poet is seen to feel otherwise in his fifth book where he has the prize given to Euryalus. In this regard Tully does better in prohibiting this fouling in the third book of his *On Duties*,[195] agreeing with the opinion of Chrysippus he says: "Chrysippus wisely here as in many matters, declares that 'he who runs in the stadium must strive and struggle with all his might to win; but he should never trip his competitor.'"[196]

{13} Having made these distinctions in this chapter, we can learn from them two arguments that lend sway to our assumption: to wit, the first from the outcome of a contest among athletes, and the second from the outcome of a contest among champions. Let me then continue with these in the chapters immediately following.

## Chapter 8

{1} That people, therefore, who prevailed over all other athletic contestants for world empire, prevailed through divine judgment. For since God cares more about intervening in a universal dispute than in a particular one, and since in certain particular disputes we seek divine judgment through athletic contestants (as the trite proverb says: "To him whom God concedes the winner, let Peter give his blessing"), there is no doubt but that God's judgment was followed by the superior strength of athletic contestants struggling for world empire. {2} The Roman people prevailed over all other athletic contestants for world empire: and this will be obvious—if we consider the athletic contestants—and provided we consider the prize or the goal. The prize or goal was dominion over all mortals. This, then, is what we call "empire." But this was attained by none but the Roman people; they were not only the first, but indeed, the only ones to reach the goal of the contest, as will immediately become clear. {3} For truly Ninus, the king of the Assyrians, was the first among mortals to strive eagerly for this prize. Although he, together with his queen consort, Semiramis, tried for ninety or more years to gain world empire by arms, and subjugated all of Asia, as Orosius reports, the western parts of the earth, however, never became subject to them.[197] Ovid records them both in his fourth book where he tells about Pyramus:

The city which Semiramis is said to have girded with walls of brick.[198]

And further on:

They were to meet at Ninus' tomb and hide in the shadow.[199]

{5} The second to aspire to this prize was Vesozes, king of Egypt, and although he shook the south and north of Asia, as Orosius records,[200] he never occupied half of the world; instead, barely half way between the other athletic contestants and the finish line, he was turned aside from his foolhardy enterprise by the Scythians. {6} Then Cyrus, king of the Persians, made his try: after destroying Babylonia and transferring the empire to Persia, but before he could even make any attempt on the western regions, succumbing to Thamyris, queen of the Scythians, he surrendered both his life and his ambition.[201] {7} To be sure, after these came Xerxes, the son of Darius and king of Persia: he attacked the world with a such a huge multitude of people and with such might, that he managed to build a bridge across the strait that divides Asia from Europe between Sestos and Abydos.[202] Lucan records this admirable feat in the second book of his *Pharsalia* where he sings:

Such, by the report of fame, was the road built over the seas by proud Xerxes.[203]

But, at last, he was ingloriously driven back from his enterprise and never reached the prize.

{8} Besides, and later than these, Alexander, king of Macedonia came closest of all to the palm of monarchy at the time he forewarned the Romans to surrender through his legates; before the Roman response, and in sight of Egypt, he fell almost in midcourse, as Livy relates.[204] {9} Lucan gives testimony of his tomb there as he inveighs against Ptolemy the king of Egypt in his eighth book saying:

Last scion of the line of Lagus, doomed and degenerate king, who must surrender your crown to your incestuous sister, though you preserve the Macedonian in a consecrated vault.[205]

{10} "O the depth of the riches of the wisdom and of the knowledge of God"[206]—who will not be astounded before Thee? For as Alexander strove to trip up his fellow Roman contestant in the race, Thou snatched him from the contest lest his temerity push on further.

{11} But that Rome won the palm of so great a prize is proved by the testimony of many. Truly our Poet says in his first book:

Hence, certainly, sometime, as the years rolled on, the Romans were to arise; from them, even from Teucer's restored line, should come rulers, to hold the sea and all land beneath their sway.[207]

{12} And Lucan in his first book:

Divided by the sword was the kingdom, and the fortune of the mighty people who possessed sea and land of the whole earth, could not allow two such peoples.[208]

{13} And Boethius in his second book discussing the prince of the Romans says the following:

Yet with his scepter he ruled the peoples whom Phoebus sees as he plunges his rays beneath the waves and as he rises from the farthest east; the peoples whom the freezing Wain oppresses and those whom violent south wind scorches with his burning breath that bakes the torrid sands.[209]

{14} Luke, that scribe of Christ who spoke the truth in all things, affords the same testimony in the part of his account that states: "There went out a decree from Cæsar Augustus, that the whole world should be enrolled."[210] From these words we can clearly comprehend that at that time the universal jurisdiction of the world belonged to the Romans. {15} From all this it is obvious that the Roman people prevailed over all other athletic contestants for world empire. Ergo, they prevailed by divine judgment, and consequently held it by divine judgment—which means they held it *de jure.*

## Chapter 9

{1} And what is acquired by duel is acquired *de jure.*[211] For wherever human judgment falls short either because it is wrapped in the shadows of ignorance or because it does not have the aid of a judge, to preserve justice we must have recourse to Him who loved her so much that He died to provide for her wants with His own blood, whence the Psalm says: "For the Lord is just, and hath loved justice."[212] {2} Now this comes about when, through free assent of the parties, not from hate, but from love of justice,[213] in a mutual clash of the powers of both the mind and the body, we seek divine judgment. This "clash," precisely because originally it was invented for single combat, we call a "duel."[214] {3} But we must always be careful: for just as in matters of war everything must first be tried through the decision of a contest and only lastly must battle be joined (as Tully and Vegetius concur in their teaching, the former in his *On Duties,*[215] the latter in *On Military Affairs*[216]), and just as in medical cures everything must be tried before we have to have final recourse to steel and fire, in the same way we may only have final recourse to this remedy, driven to it by a certain necessity of justice, when we have first inquired into all others for a judgment in the conflict.

{4} Two rules, then, appear essential for a duel: we have already dealt with the first; the other we touched on above, to wit, that through neither hate nor love, but only out of zeal for justice through common assent may the fighters, or champions, enter the arena. Therefore Tully spoke well in touching on this matter: indeed he stated: "But wars waged for the crown of empire should be waged less bitterly."[217] {5} But if the essential rules of dueling are respected (for otherwise it would not be a duel), have those—who have gathered together from the necessity of justice and by common assent—not gathered together because of their zeal for justice in the name of God? {6} And if so, is God not "in the midst of them," as he himself promised us in the Gospel?[218] And if God is present, is it not wickedness to suppose that justice could miscarry—justice, whom he loves so much, as we noted above [2:9:1]? And if justice cannot fail to win in a duel, is not that which is acquired by duel acquired *de jure?* {7} Of this truth even the pagans were aware whenever they sought judgment from fortune in a duel, before they knew the trumpet call of the Gospels. {8} Whence the illustrious Pyrrhus—noble by both the blood and the morals of the Æacidæ[219]—gave this response when the Roman legates had been sent to him to ransom the prisoners: "I seek not gold and you shall pay me no price, being not warmongers, but men of war. Let each decide his fate with steel, and not with gold. Whether it be you or I that Hera wills to reign, or what chance may bring to each, let us try by valor. Those whose valor the fortune of war has spared, their liberty will I too spare. Take them as my gift."[220] Here Pyrrhus called Fortune "Hera," that very cause we name, more correctly and righteously, "divine providence."[221] {9} Therefore let the champions beware that price be not their motive, for then it would be labeled not a duel but a marketplace where blood and justice are up for sale.[222] Nor could we believe that God is here as umpire but rather that Ancient Enemy who had instigated the conflict.[223] {10} If they want to be champions and not bloodmongers of justice, as they enter the enemy's arena let them keep Pyrrhus before their eyes, who, while in contest for the empire, spurned gold as we have told. {11} If some one were to invoke some saw about an ill-matching of strength against the truth we have revealed, let us refute this objection by the example of David's victory over Goliath.[224] And if the heathens need another example, let them refute this objection by the victory of Hercules over Antæus.[225] It is absolute nonsense to imagine that the strength of a champion supported by God could turn out to be inadequate.

{12} It is now quite clear that what is acquired by duel is acquired *de jure*.[226] But the Roman people acquired empire by duel, and this is proved through witnesses worthy of credence. In setting this forth it will not only turn out to be unambiguous but will also show that any matter from the beginning of the Roman Empire calling for arbitration used to be settled by duel. {13} For from the very first, the quarrel turned on the question of the settlement of Æneas, who was the first father of this people; at the end, given the opposition of Turnus, king of the Rutulians, both kings agreed to fight single-handedly between themselves in order to find out what God's pleasure was, as is celebrated at the end of the *Æneid*.[227] {14} As the last book of our poet bears witness, in this combat the clemency of the winner, Æneas, was so great that, had he not glimpsed the belt that Turnus had stripped from Pallas after he killed him, he would, as victor, have granted both life and peace to his conquered enemy. {15} When two peoples had burgeoned forth from the same Trojan root in Italy, to wit, the Romans[228] and the Albans, and they had long struggled with each other over the eagle ensign, the other Trojan household gods, and the honor of rule, so as to find out what the judgment of the case might be, they at last, through the mutual assent of both parties, fought it out before the eyes of the expectant kings and peoples of both factions with the three Horatii brothers on one side and the same number of Curatii brothers on the other. When three champions of the Albans and two of the Romans had been slain, the palm of victory was ceded to the Romans under King Hostilius.[229] This Livy has diligently described in the first part of his work, and Orosius also bears witness to it.[230] {16} Livy narrates how they next fought for empire with their neighbors, the Sabines and the Samnites, observing all the laws of war and using the form of a duel, although a multitude took part in the contest. In this struggle with the Samnites, however, Fortune nearly repented, so to speak, of what she had begun. {17} And this Lucan takes as an example in his second book as follows:

How many slain encumbered the Colline Gate on that day when the capital of the world and the government of mankind was nearly transferred to a different seat, and the Samnites hoped to inflict on Rome a more serious wound than by the Caudine Forks![231]

{18} After the strife among the Italians had been settled and they had not yet contested with the Greeks and the Carthaginians to reveal any divine decision (both of them had set their sights on empire), they did indeed fight for a decision with multitudes of soldiers to win the glory of the empire, Fabricius for the Romans and Pyrrhus for the Greeks; and Rome won. When Scipio for the Italians, and Hannibal for the Africans waged a war in the form of a duel, the Africans succumbed to the Italians, as Livy and other[232] writers of Roman history strove to bear witness.

{19} Who, now, has a mind so obtuse that he cannot see that that glorious people gained the crown of the earth by right of duel? Indeed, a Roman could say what the Apostle said to Timothy: "There is laid up for me the crown of justice"[233]—"Laid up," that is, in the eternal providence of God. {20} Let the presumptuous jurists now see how far beneath that watchtower of reason they stand from which the human mind surveys these principles and let them be silent and content in rendering judgment and counsel according to the intent of the law.[234]

{21} And now it is clear that the Roman people acquired their empire by duel; ergo, they acquired it *de jure*—and this is the main proposition of this book.

## Chapter 10

{1} So far we have demonstrated our thesis by way of reasons that rest chiefly upon rational principles, but from now on we must prove it by the principles of the Christian faith. Especially[235] those who call themselves zealots of the Christian faith have raged, and devised vain things against Roman sovereignty; they show no pity for the poor of Christ, for these not only are defrauded of the revenues of the churches, but even their very patrimonies are stolen daily, and the Church is impoverished; all the while they make a pretense of justice but refuse to recognize the dispenser of justice.[236] {2} Nor indeed can such impoverishment of the Church come about without the verdict of God, for the poor are not aided by the Church's assets, which are their patrimony, nor are those assets held with any gratitude toward the empire who offers it. {3} Let them go back where they came from![237] For they came righteously but they return in iniquity, since they were given in righteousness but possessed in wickedness. What is that to such shepherds? What is it to them if the wealth of the Church vanishes as long as the properties of their relatives are increased? But perhaps it is better to proceed with our thesis and in pious silence await the help of our Savior.

{4} I therefore affirm that if the Roman Empire did not exist *de jure*, then Christ by his birth approved something unjust; the consequent is false; ergo, the contradictory of the antecedent is true.[238] For contradictory propositions can be understood mutually from each other since they have diametrically opposed meanings.[239] {5} There is no need to demonstrate the falsity of the consequent to the faithful, for anyone who is a believer will concede that it is false[240]; and if he does not concede it, he is no believer; and if he is no believer this reasoning does not apply to him.

{6} I demonstrate the consequence as follows: whoever honors any edict by choice, approves by his actions that it is just; and since actions speak louder than words (as the Philosopher likes to put it in the last book of his *Nico-machean Ethics*[241]), he convinces us more than if he were to approve it by words. But as his scribe, Luke,[242] bears witness, it was Christ's will to be born of his Virgin Mother under an edict promulgated by Roman authority so that he, the Son of God, made man, would be enrolled as a man in that unique census of the human race; and this means that he honored the edict. {7} And perhaps it is more devout to believe that this edict went forth through Cæsar by divine will so that Christ, who had been expected amid the society of mortals through so many ages, might himself be enrolled among mortals. {8} Therefore, by his action, Christ approved the justice of that edict of Augustus who was exercising the authority of the Romans. And since the just issuing of an edict follows from jurisdiction, it must be that whoever approves an edict as just also has approved the jurisdiction. If it did not exist *de jure*, the jurisdiction was unjust.

{9} And we must note[243] that the argument based on denying the conse-quent,[244] although it holds up in its form by virtue of a certain common logi-cal procedure,[245] nevertheless, shows its force when reduced to a second figure [that is, to an impossible conclusion], just as the argument based on the affir-mation of the antecedent[246] shows its force in the first figure.[247] {10} The re-duction is made as follows:

> Every injustice is approved unjustly;
> Christ did not approve unjustly;
> ergo, He did not approve an injustice.

By proceeding from the assumption of the antecedent [the argument is re-duced to an impossible conclusion] as follows:

> Every injustice is approved unjustly;
> Christ approved an injustice;
> ergo, He approved unjustly.[248]

## Chapter 11

{1} And if the Roman Empire did not exist *de jure*, Adam's sin was not pun-ished in Christ; but this is, of course, false; therefore, the contradictory of the antecedent premise is true. {2} The falsity of the consequent can be proved as follows: since we are indeed all sinners because of the sin of Adam, as the Apostle says, "As by one man sin entered into this world, and by sin death; and so death passed upon all men, in whom all have sinned."[249] If satisfaction had not been made for that sin by the death of Christ, we would still be "by nature children of wrath,"[250] that is, by our corrupted nature. {3} But this is not true inasmuch as the Apostle writes to the Ephesians speaking of God the Father "who hath predestined us unto the adoption of children through Jesus Christ unto himself: according to the purpose of his will: unto the praise and the glory of his grace, in which he hath graced us in his beloved son. In whom we have redemption through his blood, the remission of sins, according to the riches of his glory, which hath superabounded in us."[251] And inasmuch as Christ himself, suffering in himself the punishment, says in the Gospel of John, "It is consummated."[252] For where all is consummated, nothing remains to be done. {4} On account of this consequence,[253] we may properly understand that "punishment" is not simply "the penalty upon him who commits a wrong," but "the penalty upon him who commits a wrong imposed by one having the jurisdiction to punish." Wherefore unless the penalty is imposed by an ordinary judge[254] it is not to be called a "punishment" but an "injustice." For this reason that man said to Moses: "Who hath appointed thee . . . judge over us?"[255] {5} Therefore, if Christ had not suffered under an ordinary judge that penalty would not have been a punishment. And a judge ordinary could only have been one who had jurisdiction over all mankind inasmuch as the whole of the human race was punished in the flesh of Christ,[256] the bearer (as the Prophet says)[257] or sufferer[258] of our sorrows. And Tiberius Cæsar, whose vicar was Pilate, would not have had jurisdiction over all mankind if the Roman Empire had not existed *de jure*. {6} Whence it came about that Herod— though he was as ignorant of what he did as Caiaphas was when the latter spoke the truth about the heavenly decree—remanded Christ to Pilate for judgment, as Luke recounts in his Gospel.[259] Herod was not in fact a deputy to Tiberius under the ensign of the eagle or the ensign of the Senate but a king appointed by him over a particular kingdom and he ruled under the ensign of the kingdom in his charge. {7} Therefore let those who pretend to be sons of the Church desist from reproaching the Roman Empire given that Christ the Bridegroom thus sanctioned it both at the beginning and at the end of his militant life. And I believe that I have now made it perfectly clear that the Roman people assumed the empire of the world *de jure*.

{8} O happy people! Thou, o glorious Ausonia![260] Would that he who weakened your empire had never been born, or else that he had never been misled by his own pious intent![261]

## BOOK 3

### Chapter 1

{1} "He hath shut up the mouths of lions, and they have not hurt me: forasmuch as before him justice hath been found in me."[262] At the beginning of this work we proposed an inquiry, as far as the subject permitted, into three problems of which the first two, I believe, have been fully treated in the preceding books. {2} Now indeed the third remains to be dealt with; the truth of this problem, however, cannot emerge without bringing shame to some and will perhaps be the cause of some resentment against me.

{3} Since, however, Truth, from her immutable throne, pleads, and Solomon as well, beginning his harvest of Proverbs,[263] teaches (by his own promise to do as he teaches) that we must "meditate truth" and "hate wickedness," and since that teacher of morals, the Philosopher,[264] exhorts us to destroy all self-interest for the sake of truth (trusting in the words of Daniel, which we cited, where he affirmed that divine power is the shield of the defenders of truth), girding on the breastplate of faith as Paul admonishes,[265] with the heat of those coals that one of the Seraphim took from the celestial altar to touch the lips of Isaiah [6:6–7], I shall now enter this gymnasium,[266] and, with help of him whose arm freed us from the powers of darkness[267] by his own blood, I shall, while the world looks on, hurl the wicked and the liar from the wrestling ring.[268] {4} What shall I fear, when the Spirit coeternal with the Father and the Son says through the mouth of David: "The just shall be in everlasting remembrance: he shall not fear the evil hearing."[269]

{5} The present question, which we will have to discuss, centers upon "the two great lights," namely, the Roman pontiff and the Roman prince.[270] And it inquires whether the authority of the Roman monarch, who is *de jure* the monarch of the world as we proved in the second book, depends directly upon God or upon some[271] vicar or minister of God who, I know, is the successor to Peter and is truly bearer of the keys of the kingdom of heaven.[272]

### Chapter 2

{1} Just as we have done in the preceding books, to examine this problem we must adopt some principle upon whose strength we can make arguments to unveil the truth.[273] For unless we pre-establish some principle, what good does it do to exert ourselves, even to tell the truth, given that this principle is the sole root from which we can derive the middle terms[274] of the argument?

{2} Let us, therefore, take this incontrovertible truth as a point of departure: to wit, "that God does not will anything that is repugnant to the intention of nature." For if this were not true, its contradictory would not be false, which is "that God is not unwilling regarding anything that is repugnant to the intention of nature." {3} And if this is not false, neither are those things which follow from it, because it is impossible in a necessary deduction that the consequence of a premise that is not false, be false.[275] {4} But from the concept "not to be unwilling" there follows by necessity one of two of the following: either "to be willing" or "not to will at all." Just as, indeed, from "not to hate" there follows either "to love" or "not to love." For "not to love" does not mean "to hate," neither does "not to will" mean "to will not to," as is obvious. But if those things are not false, this will not be false either: "God wills what he does not will"—a proposition that could have no higher degree of falsity.[276] {5} On the other hand, that which was stated is true I clarify as follows: it is manifest that God wills the end goal of nature, otherwise he would move the heavens in vain. And this simply cannot be asserted. If God were to will the impediment of this end he would also will the end goal of this impediment, otherwise his willing would once again be in vain. And since the purpose of an impediment intends that the thing impeded not come into being, it would follow that God wills there to be no end goal to nature—and we have said that he does indeed will such an end. {6} For if God were not to will the impediment of this end, insofar as he were not to use his will at all, it would follow from his not willing that he cared nothing whether the impediment existed or not. But he who does not care about an impediment, does not care about the thing that may be impeded, and consequently does not have that thing within his faculty of volition, and what one does not have within one's faculty of volition one does not will. {7} For this reason, if the end goal of nature can be impeded—and it can—it follows of necessity that God does not will the end goal of nature, and thus there follows what we said before, namely, that God wills that which He does not will. Most absolutely true, therefore, is that principle from whose contradictory there follow such absurdities.[277]

## Chapter 3

{1} At the threshold of this [third] problem, we must note that the truth of the first question had to be made clear more to remove ignorance than to avoid conflict, but that of the second question was concerned almost equally with ignorance and conflict. Indeed we are ignorant of many things about which we do not enter into conflict. {2} For the geometrician does not know how to square the circle, but he does not get into an argument over it.[278] The theologian does not know how many angels exist, but he does not get into a quarrel about it. The Egyptian certainly knows nothing of the civilization of the Scythians, but on this account does not get into a squabble about their civilization.[279] {3} But the truth of this third question has so much contention surrounding it that, while in other matters, ignorance is usually the cause of strife, so in this, strife is rather the cause of ignorance. {4} For this often happens even to men who fly ahead of their wills in the contemplation of reason, that, when biased by their emotions, they abandon the light of reason and, dragged along like blind men by passion, they stubbornly deny their blindness. {5} Whence it very frequently comes about not only that falsehood battens up its defenses, but that many, straying beyond their bounds, invade the turf of others where they understand nothing and are in turn understood by none, thus provoking some to wrath, others to disgust, and many to derision.

{6} Consequently, three kinds of men especially struggle against the truth that we are seeking. {7} In fact the Supreme Pontiff, the Vicar of Our Lord Jesus Christ, and Peter's successor (to whom we owe not what is due to Christ but what is due to Peter)[280] is driven perhaps through zeal for the keys[281]— not to speak of other shepherds[282] of Christian flocks, and others who, I believe, are moved solely through the zeal of Mother Church—perhaps through zeal, as I said, and not through pride—to oppose the truth that I am about to demonstrate. {8} There are certain others, to be sure (whose stubborn greed extinguishes the light of truth, and who profess themselves sons of the Church,[283] although they proceed from their father the devil[284]), not only launch an attack on this question, but in abhorrence even of the mere name of the most holy principate, would shamelessly deny the principles of the preceding question and of this one. {9} There is also a third category whom they call decretalists, who are ignorant and unskilled in any knowledge of theology and philosophy,[285] basing their whole cause upon their decretals (which I truly consider to be worthy of veneration)[286] and placing their hopes (I believe) in the supremacy of these decretals, denigrate the empire. {10} And no wonder, since once I heard a certain member of this group state and impudently maintain that the "traditions" of the Church were the foundation of the faith.[287] May those truly banish that wickedness from the opinion of mortals who, before any Church traditions, believed in Christ, the Son of God—

either to come, to be at hand, or to have already suffered—and in faith hoped, and in hope, burned with charity, and so burning (the world has no doubt) are made coheirs with him![288]

{11} And so that these decretalists may be totally ousted[289] from this gymnasium, it must be pointed out that there is a Scripture before the Church, one with the Church, and one after the Church.[290] {12} Certainly predating the Church are the Old and the New Testaments, which "he hath commanded as his covenant forever," as the Prophet says.[291] For this is what the Church says addressing her Bridegroom: "Draw me after thee."[292] {13} Concurrent with the Church are to be revered those great Councils in which no believer doubts Christ's presence—for we have Christ's own statement to His disciples as He was about to ascend into heaven: "Behold I am with you all days, even to the consummation of the world," as Matthew bears witness.[293] There are also the Scriptures of the Doctors,[294] of Augustine and others; anyone who doubts that they were aided by the Holy Spirit either has not seen their fruit at all, or if he has seen it, has not tasted it.

{14} Postdating the Church surely are those traditions that are called "decretals," which, while they are worthy of veneration for their apostolic authority, are still to be assigned, with absolutely no doubt, to a place lower than the fundamental Scriptures inasmuch as Christ chided the priests for doing the opposite. {15} For when they had questioned him: "Why do thy disciples transgress the traditions of the ancients?"[295]—since they neglected to wash their hands—Christ answered them, as Matthew bears witness: "Why do you also transgress the commandment of God for your tradition?"[296] With this he clearly meant that tradition was to be given a lower place. {16} For if the traditions of the Church postdate the Church, as we have explained, authority must not come to the Church from its traditions but to the traditions from the Church. Thus[297] those who hold only to traditions, as was said, are to be ousted from this gymnasium;[298] it is necessary for anyone hunting for this truth to proceed by investigating the source of ecclesiastical authority.

{17} Having thus ousted those preceding we must oust those others who bedecked with crow feathers[299] make an ostentatious display of themselves as white sheep in the flock of the Lord. These, the sons of iniquity, who, so that they may perpetrate their shameful crimes, prostitute their mother, expel their brothers, and then refuse to submit to a judge.[300] For why should we try to argue against these men since, mired as they are in their greed, they would not understand first principles?

{18} Wherefore there remains only the dispute with those who, led by some zeal on behalf of Mother Church, are ignorant of that very truth we are seeking. Relying on that reverence[301] that a pious son owes a father, that a pious son owes a mother, pious toward Christ, pious toward the Church, pious toward her Shepherd, pious toward anyone who professes the Christian faith, in this book I begin the contest with them for the salvation of truth.[302]

## Chapter 4

{1} Those against whom the whole following disputation will be aimed are motivated by several different arguments in their assertion that the authority of the empire depends on the authority of the Church, as an inferior artisan depends on the architect.[303] These, indeed, they draw from Holy Scripture and from certain acts of both the Supreme Pontiff and of the emperor himself. In fact, they strive to have some token of proof from reason. {2} In the first place[304] they assert according to the text of Genesis that God created two great lights,[305] a greater light and a lesser light, so that the one might preside over the day and the other might preside over the night; they are wont to interpret these as meaning allegorically the two governing powers: to wit, the spiritual and the temporal.[306] {3} From this they argue that, just as the moon, which is the lesser light, has no light except that which it receives from the sun, in the same way the temporal realm has no authority except that which it receives from the spiritual power.[307]

{4} In order to refute this and other arguments of theirs, we must point out that, as the Philosopher likes to put it in his writings *On Sophistical Refutations:* "The refutation of an argument is the exposure of error."[308] And when a mistake can be found both in the matter and in the form of an argument, it can result in a twofold error: namely, either by assuming what is false, or erring in syllogizing. With these two errors the Philosopher reproaches Parmenides and Melissus saying: "Because they assume false premises and syllogize illogically."[309] And here I take the term "false" in the widest sense even to mean "untenable," which in matters concerning probability is the same as being false.

{5} If, indeed, the error is in the form, the conclusion must be destroyed by anyone who wants to rebut it, by showing that the form of the syllogism has not been observed; if, however, the error is in the matter, it is either because something totally false has been assumed or because of something relatively false. If it is totally false, then it is to be refuted by destroying the assumption; if relatively false, it must be done by making distinctions.[310]

{6} With this in view, for a better proof to rebut this problem and of those that will follow, we must point out that, as far as the mystical sense is concerned, errors can occur in two ways: either because we are seeking it where it does not exist, or we are comprehending it in a way in which it is not to be understood. {7} As far as the first way is concerned, Augustine says in his *City of God:* "Of course[311] one must not assume that all events narrated are symbolic, but those that lack such significance are interwoven in the interest of such as do possess it. It is only the ploughshare that furrows the earth, but to enable it to do this you must have the other parts of the plough also."[312] {8} As far as the second is concerned, in *On Christian Doctrine,*[313] he says, speaking of someone understanding something in Scripture differently from what the writer means,[314] that "he is deceived in the same way as a man who wanders off the path by mistake and rambles in a circle to the same place toward which the road leads." And he adds: "He must be shown that . . . his habit of wandering forces him to take a a sidetrack and go astray."[315] {9} He then indicates the reason why one is to be wary in scriptural exegesis, stating: "Faith will stagger if the authority of the Divine Scriptures wavers."[316] {10} I say, however, that if anyone, after he has been diligently corrected, does such things out of ignorance, we must pardon him, just as we must pardon someone who might be frightened by a lion in the clouds.[317] If, though, anyone does such things deliberately, we must treat anyone who errs in that way no differently than we would treat tyrants who do not follow public laws for the common welfare but strive to twist them to their own benefit.

{11} Oh, what utter outrage, even if committed merely in one's dreams, to abuse the intention of the eternal Spirit![318] This is, to be sure, not a sin against Moses, against David, against Job, against Matthew, or against Paul, but against the Holy Spirit who speaks through them. For although the scribes of the divine word may be many, there is still only one God who dictates, who has deigned to set forth his good pleasure to us through the pens of many.[319]

{12} After these preliminary considerations, therefore, regarding what was said above, I now give my rebuttal of that assertion they made claiming that those two lights convey figuratively the two governing powers: in fact, in this statement lies the whole force of their argument. That their interpretation is quite untenable, however, can be shown in two ways. {13} First, since, inasmuch as such governing powers are accidental attributes[320] of man himself, God would seem to have followed a perverted order of things in first producing accidents before the subject to which they belong. And to say this of God is absurd. For those two lights were produced on the fourth day and man on the sixth, as is obvious from the literal sense.[321] {14} Second, since these governing powers guide man toward certain ends, as will be made clear below, if man had remained in the state of innocence in which God created him, he would not have needed such guides. Therefore, such governing powers are remedies for the infirmity of sin.

{15} Therefore, since man was not only not a sinner on the fourth day, but simply did not even exist, it would have been useless to produce those remedies. And this is contrary to divine goodness. For that physician would indeed be a fool who, before a man's birth, prepared him a plaster for an abcess yet to come.[322] {16} It is wrong to say, therefore, that God created these two governing powers on the fourth day, and, consequently, what my opponents are fabricating could not have been Moses' intention.[323]

{17} Even if we patiently allow this falsehood, we can also rebut this argument by making a distinction: for indeed a rebuttal through making a distinction is gentler to one's adversary for he does not appear such an utter liar as destroying his conclusion makes him seem. Therefore, I affirm that although the moon does not have abundant light except inasfar as it receives it from the sun, it does not follow on that account that the moon itself depends upon the sun. {18} Accordingly, we must be aware that the existence of the moon is one thing, its power is another, and its function is yet another. As far as its existence is concerned, in no way does the moon depend upon the sun; nor does it depend upon it as far as its power is concerned; nor, to put it simply, does it do so as far as its function is concerned, because its movement derives from its own mover, and its influence from its own rays. It has, in fact, a little light of its own, as is shown during its eclipse.[324] {19} But as far as its better and more efficacious functioning is concerned, it receives something from the sun, that is, an abundance of light, and by the reception of this light it can function more powerfully. {20} Therefore, I affirm likewise that the temporal realm[325] does not receive its being from the spiritual; neither, to put it simply, does it receive its power, that is, its authority, nor even its functioning from it. But it does indeed receive from the spiritual the wherewithal to function with greater efficacy through the light of grace that in heaven as on earth the benediction of the Supreme Pontiff infuses into it.[326]

{21} Thus the argument is in error as to its form, because the predicate in the conclusion is not the term of the major premise, as is obvious: indeed it goes as follows: the moon receives light from the sun, which is the spiritual power; the temporal power is the moon; ergo, the temporal power receives its authority from the spiritual power. {22} While in the term of the major premise they posit "light," in the predicate of the conclusion they posit "authority," but these are two different things both in their subject and their meaning, as we have seen.[327]

## Chapter 5

{1} They also take their argument from Moses' text, saying that the figure of these two governing powers sprang from the loins of Jacob, that is, Levi and Judah.[328] The first of whom was the forebear of the priests; the second, of temporal power. Whence from this they argue as follows: as Levi stands to Judah, the Church stands to the empire; Levi preceded Judah by birth, as is evident from the letter of the text; ergo, the Church precedes the empire in authority. {2} And this point is really easy to refute: for when they say that Levi and Judah, sons of Jacob, figure these governing powers, I will in the same way rebut it by destroying the premise. But let us concede it. {3} For when they infer from their argument, "Just as Levi preceded by his birth, so the Church precedes in authority," I assert in the same way that the predicate of the conclusion is one thing and the term of the major premise another.[329] For "authority" is quite different from "birth," both in subject and in meaning.[330] On this account the error is formal. And it follows a process like this:

A precedes B concerning C;
D is to E as A is to B:
ergo, D precedes E concerning F.

However, F and C are different. {4} And if they object saying that F is a consequent of C, that is authority from birth, and that one can replace the antecedent with the consequent (as "animal" with "man"), I insist that this is false. For there are many elders who not only do not come first in authority but are even preceded by their juniors, as is obvious where bishops are temporally younger than their archpriests. {5} And thus their counterstatement is seen to be in error because it takes "a noncause as a cause."[331]

## Chapter 6

{1} Moreover, from the text of the first book of Kings[332] they take the creation and deposition of Saul and say that Saul was enthroned as king and cast down from his throne by Samuel who, by God's command, functioned as His vicar as the letter of the text makes clear.[333] {2} And from this they argue that just as that vicar of God had the authority of giving and taking away temporal governance and of transferring it to another, so now, the vicar of God, that is, the head of the universal Church, has the authority of giving and taking away and even of transferring the scepter of temporal power. From this it would follow without doubt that the authority of the empire would be dependent as they say.[334] {3} And to this we must respond by rebutting their assumption that Samuel was the vicar of God. For he did this not as a vicar but as a special ad hoc legate, or a nuncio, bearing the express commandment of God. This is evident because he performed and conveyed only whatever God said.

{4} Wherefore we must be aware that it is one thing to be a vicar and another to be a nuncio or a minister[335]; just as it is one thing to be a teacher and another an interpreter.[336] {5} For a vicar is one to whom jurisdiction is entrusted with legislative or with judgmental power; and therefore within the scope of the jurisdiction entrusted to him with the said legislative and judgmental power he can take action concerning those things of which his lord is entirely unaware. A nuncio, on the other hand, insofar as he is a mere nuncio, cannot do so; but just as a hammer functions only through the strength of the smith,[337] likewise does the nuncio only act according to the judgment of the one who sends him. {6} It does not follow, therefore, if God did this through his nuncio, Samuel, that the vicar of God may also do it. God has done, does, and will do many things through his angels that the vicar of God, Peter's successor, may not do. {7} Whence their argument proceeds from "the whole to the part" and in the affirmative goes as follows: "Man can see and hear; ergo, the eye can see and hear." But this does not hold. The negative, however, would hold as follows: "Man cannot fly: ergo, neither can the arms of man fly." And in the same way as follows: "God through his nuncio (according to the opinion of Agathon)[338] cannot make undone deeds that have been done." Ergo, his vicar cannot do so either.

## Chapter 7

{1} They also take the gift of the Magi from the literal sense of Matthew [2:11], saying that Christ received gold and frankincense to signify that he alone was lord and ruler of things spiritual and temporal. And from this they infer that the vicar of Christ is the lord and ruler of the same things and consequently has authority over both. {2} In responding to this, I confess belief both in the literal and figurative sense of Matthew, but I confute what they presume to infer from it. In fact, they syllogize as follows: "God is the Lord of things temporal and spiritual; the Supreme Pontiff is the vicar of God: ergo, he is lord of things temporal and spiritual." {3} And indeed both premises are true, but the middle term changes and is argued with four terms by which the form of the syllogism is not preserved, as is clear from the *On the Syllogism Simply.*[339] For "God," who is the subject of the major premise, is different from "the vicar of God," who forms the predicate in the minor premise.

{4} And if anyone might object that God's vicar is His equivalent, his objection is worthless for no one who is made vicar either divine or human can be equal to the principal authority, and this is quite obvious. {5} For we know that the successor to Peter, to say the least, is not equal to divine authority in the workings of nature: he could not, after all, make earth rise up, or fire fall[340] through the office entrusted to him! {6} Nor is it possible either that all things could be entrusted to him by God, since God could in no way entrust him with the power of creating, or, likewise, of baptizing, as can be clearly proved, despite the fact that the Master [Peter Lombard] affirmed the opposite in his fourth book.[341] {7} We also know that a man's vicar is not his equal, insofar as he is his vicar, since no one can give what is not his own. Princely authority does not belong to the prince, except for his use, since no prince can grant any authority to himself; he can, indeed, accept or renounce it, but he cannot create it, because the creation of a prince does not depend upon the prince. {8} Since this is so, it is obvious that no prince can appoint a vicar for himself who is equal to him in all things. Therefore their objection has no force.

## Chapter 8

{1} They also take from the text of the same Gospel what Christ says to Peter: "And whatsoever thou shalt bind upon earth, it shall be bound also in heaven: and whatsoever thou shalt loose on earth, it shall be loosed also in heaven"[342]; a statement that was made also to all the apostles. They cite the same thing from the text of Matthew,[343] and likewise from John.[344] {2} Upon this they make their case that Peter's successor can, by God's concession, both bind and loose all things. And from this they infer that he can loose the laws and decrees of the empire and make binding laws and decrees as if he were a temporal power. Were this the case, what they assert would make sense.

{3} But we must answer this by making a distinction in the major premise of the syllogism they are using: their syllogism therefore runs as follows:

Peter could loose and bind all things;
Peter's successor can do whatever Peter could do;
ergo, Peter's successor can loose and bind all things.

From this they infer that Peter's successor can loose and bind the authority and decrees of the empire. {4} I concede the minor premise; but I surely do not concede the major premise without making a distinction. I therefore affirm that this universal term "all things," which is implied in "whatsoever," never extends beyond the range of the term's extension.[345] {5} For if I say, "every animal runs," "every" extends to all beings comprised under the genus of animal; if, on the other hand, I say, "every man runs," then the universal term extends only to those beings supposed by the term "man"; and when I say "every grammarian," the range of extension is even more limited.[346]

{6} As a result we must always keep the range of extension[347] of the universal term in mind, and thus we will easily see just how far its range extends, knowing the nature and scope of the term so extended. {7} Whence when one says, "whatsoever thou shalt bind," if that "whatsoever" were to be taken in its absolute sense, then what my opponents say would be true—and not only could Peter do what they say, but he could even loose a wife from her husband and bind her to another while her first husband was still alive—something which he cannot do at all. He could even absolve me even though I might be impenitent of my sins—something that not even God could do.[348] {8} Therefore, since this is the case, it is obvious that that extension is not to be taken in its absolute sense, but relative to something. What that something may involve, however, is quite clear when we consider what was granted to Peter—for the range of extension is limited to this concession. {9} Christ, after all, says to Peter: "I will give to thee the keys of the kingdom of heaven,"[349] that is, "I will make thee gatekeeper of the kingdom of heaven." To which he then adds, "and whatsoever," which means "all things," that is, "all things relative to that office thou shalt be able to loose and bind." {10} And thus the universal term that is included in "whatsoever" is confined within its range of extension by the office of the keys of the kingdom of heaven; and by taking the term thus, that proposition is true; taken in an absolute, it is not, as is obvious. {11} And, therefore, I affirm that although Peter's successor may have the power to loose and bind according to the requirements of the office entrusted to Peter, nonetheless it does not follow on this account that he may have the power to loose or bind imperial decrees or laws[350] as my opponents were asserting, unless it be shown further that it is relative to the office of the keys. The contrary of this shall be proved below [Chapter 14].

## Chapter 9

{1} They take also the text of Luke, where Peter addresses Christ and says: "Behold here are two swords,"[351] and they assert that by those two swords are meant the two governing powers we spoke of; for these, Peter said, were there where he was, that is, upon his person. From this they argue that those two governing powers, insofar as their authority is concerned, rest upon Peter's successor.[352] {2} And to this we must reply by rejecting the figurative sense upon which they base their argument. For they claim that those two swords that Peter indicated figure the two aforesaid powers.[353] This must be completely denied, both because that response would not have accorded with Christ's intention and because Peter, who was of hasty character, used to reply only with regard to the outward appearance of things.

{3} The fact that his answer surely went counter to Christ's intention will not long be hidden if we think about the words that came before and the reason for those words. Thus we must take into account that he said this on the day of the Last Supper, whence Luke a little before, begins as follows: "And the day of the unleavened bread came, on which it was necessary that the paschal lamb should be killed."[354] At this supper Christ had in fact spoken of his impending passion for which he had to separate himself from his disciples. {4} We must likewise keep in mind that when these words came to be spoken all twelve disciples were together. Whence just a little after those words we cited, Luke says: "And when the hour was come, he sat down, and the twelve apostles with him."[355] {5} And whereupon, as the conversation continued, he came to these words: "When I sent you forth without purse, and scrip, and shoes, did you want for anything? But they said: Nothing. Then he said unto them: But now he that hath a purse, let him take it, and likewise a scrip; and he that hath not, let him sell his coat, and buy a sword."[356] {6} In this the intention of Christ is quite clear; for he did not say, "buy or procure two swords," but, rather, twelve, inasmuch as he was speaking to twelve apostles—"He that hath not, let him buy"—so that each of them would have one. {7} And he spoke this also while warning them of the approaching persecution and imminent contempt that would befall them, as if he were saying: "As long as I was with you, you were received; now you shall be chased out. Therefore, you must provide for yourselves in time of need even those things that I formerly forbade you to own." {8} Accordingly, if Peter's response to these words were made with the intent they ascribe to it, it would not then have anything to do with Christ's meaning. And Christ would have chided him for it as he did so often when Peter would answer without thinking. Here, however, he did not do so, but acquiesced, saying to him: "It is enough,"[357] as if to say, "I say this out of necessity, but if they cannot have one each, two swords may suffice."

{9} And that Peter habitually spoke with regard only to outward appearance his hasty and unreflective impulsiveness proves; not only did the sincerity of his faith impel him to this, but (I believe) the purity and simplicity of his nature. All the scribes of Christ attest to this impulsiveness of his. {10} Matthew,[358] indeed, writes that when Jesus asked his disciples: "But whom do you say that I am?"[359] Before all the others, Peter replied, "Thou art Christ, the Son of the living God."[360] He also writes that when Christ said to his disciples that he had to go to Jerusalem and suffer many things, Peter took him aside and began to rebuke him saying, "Lord, be it far from thee, this shall not be unto thee."[361] Christ, turning, reproved him and said: "Go behind me Satan."[362] {11} Likewise he writes that on the Mount of Transfiguration, before Christ, Moses, and Elias, and the two sons of Zebedee, Peter said: "Lord, it is good for us to be here: if thou wilt, let us make here three tabernacles, one for thee, and one for Moses, and one for Elias."[363] {12} He also writes that when the disciples were in a boat at night and Christ was walking upon the water, Peter said: "Lord, if it be thou, bid me come to thee upon the waters."[364] {13} He also writes that when Christ predicted the scandal to his disciples, Peter answered: "Although all shall be scandalized in thee, I will never be scandalized."[365] And further on: "Though I should die with thee, I will not deny thee."[366] {14} And Mark also bears witness to this[367]; Luke, on the other hand, writes that, somewhat earlier than the words we cited, Peter also said to Christ concerning the swords: "Lord, I am ready to go with thee, both into prison, and to death."[368] {15} Moreover, John reports of him that, when Christ wanted to wash his feet, he said: "Lord, dost thou wash my feet?"[369] And further on: "Thou shalt never wash my feet."[370] {16} He says further on that he struck the priest's servant with his sword,[371] an account given by all four.[372] John also says that when he came to the tomb, he went in directly, seeing the other disciple hesitating at the door.[373] Yet again he recounts that when Christ stood on the shore after his Resurrection, "When Peter heard that it was the Lord, he girt his coat about him (for he was naked) and cast himself into the sea."[374] Lastly he says that, when Peter saw John, he said to Jesus: "Lord, and what shall this man do?"[375]

{17} It is truly a delight to have recounted one by one these episodes concerning our Archimandrite[376] in praise of his innocence, for by them one can easily grasp that when he was speaking of the two swords he was answering Christ with simple-hearted intent. {18} But if the words of Christ and Peter are to be taken figuratively, they ought not be taken to the extreme my opponents say they should be drawn to, but should be taken in the sense of that sword of which Matthew writes as follows: "Do not think that I came to send peace upon earth: I came not to send peace, but the sword. For I came to set a man at variance against his father . . . ,"[377] and so on. {19} This indeed came to pass both by word and deed. As a result Luke told Theophilus of those things "which Jesus began to do and teach."[378] Such was the sword that Christ enjoined them to buy, about which Peter also replied in the same passage that there were already two: they were prepared for the words and deeds by which they would fulfill what Christ said He had come to do by the sword, as we have said.[379]

## Chapter 10

{1} Certain of them affirm, furthermore, that the Emperor Constantine, cured of leprosy by the intercession of Sylvester who was Supreme Pontiff at that time, donated the seat of the empire, that is, Rome, to the Church together with many other imperial privileges.[380] {2} From this they argue that no one from that time on could assume those privileges unless he received them from the Church to whom, they say, such privileges belong; and it would indeed follow from this that one authority depends upon the other, as they would have it.

{3} Having set forth and rebutted the arguments that seemed to have their roots in Divine Scripture, it remains now to set forth and rebut those which have their roots in human deeds and human reason. The first of these, to which we have already alluded, they syllogize as follows: "Those things that are of the Church, no man can have *de jure* except from the Church (and this we concede!); the Roman governing power belongs to the Church; ergo, no one may possess it *de jure* except from the Church." They prove the minor premise by that which we have touched on above concerning Constantine. {4} Ergo, I reject that minor premise; and as for their proof, I assert that it is null and void because Constantine could not transfer the dignity of empire, nor could the Church accept it. {5} And if they stubbornly insist, what I say can be demonstrated as follows: no one is permitted to do anything by means of the office entrusted to him that is contrary to that office—for if that were the case, one and the same thing would be contrary to itself, and this is impossible. It is, however, contrary to the office entrusted to the emperor to split the empire, inasmuch as his office is to hold mankind subject to a single will in choosing and refusing, as can be easily understood from the first book of this treatise.[381] Therefore , the emperor is not permitted to split the empire. {6} If therefore some dignities had been alienated from the empire by Constantine—as they affirm—and ceded to the power of the Church, that seamless garment would have been rent that not even those who pierced Christ, the true God, with a lance would have dared to rend.

{7} Besides, just as the Church has its foundation, so does the empire. For the Church's foundation is Christ, as the Apostle says in Corinthians: "For other foundation no man can lay, but that which is laid; which is Christ Jesus."[382] He himself is the rock upon which the Church is built. The empire's foundation is human right.

{8} I merely affirm that, just as the Church is not permitted to go against its own foundation, but must always lean upon it according to the text of the Canticle of Canticles: "Who is this that cometh up from the desert, flowing with delights, leaning upon her beloved?"[383]—in the same way it is not permitted to the empire to do anything against human right. But it would be against human right if the very empire were to destroy itself: therefore, the empire is not permitted to destroy itself. {9} Since, then, to split the empire would be to destroy it, given that the empire consists of the unity of universal monarchy, it is obvious that it is not permitted to anyone functioning as imperial authority to split the empire. That to split the empire is indeed contrary to human right is clear from what we have said above.[384]

{10} Furthermore, every jurisdiction comes prior to its judge; for the judge is appointed to the jurisdiction, and not the other way around; but the empire is a jurisdiction comprising all temporal jurisdiction in its scope; therefore, it came prior to its judge who is the emperor, because the emperor is appointed to it, and not vice versa. From this it is clear that the emperor does not have the power to change it, insofar as he is emperor, inasmuch as he receives from it what he is. {11} I merely assert the following: either he was an emperor when they say he endowed the Church, or he was not. If he was not, it is plain that he had no power to confer anything that belonged to the empire; if he was, since such an endowment would be a diminution of his jurisdiction, insofar as he was the emperor, he did not have the power to do it. {12} Furthermore, if one emperor could split off some small portion from the jurisdiction of the empire, by the same reasoning, so could another. And inasmuch as temporal jurisdiction is finite, and every finite object may be consumed by finite subtractions, it follows that the primary jurisdiction could be annihilated. And this is irrational.

{13} Moreover, since he who confers is in the position of an agent and he upon whom something is conferred is in the position of a patient (as the Philosopher likes to put it in the fourth book of the *Ethics*),[385] in order for a donation to be lawful not only is the fitness of him who confers it required but even that of him upon whom something is conferred: "It seems indeed that the action of agents subsists in the patient fit to receive it."[386] {14} But the Church was totally unfit to receive temporal goods by an express command forbidding it, as we read as follows in Matthew: "Do not possess gold, nor silver, nor money in your purses: nor scrip for your journey,"[387] and so on. For, although in Luke[388] we have a relaxation of the command as far as certain things are concerned, after that prohibition I have, however, been unable to discover that the Church had the license to possess gold and silver. {15} That being the case, if the Church had no power to receive, even given that Constantine might have been able to do it on his own, his action, notwithstanding, was impossible on account of the unfitness of the patient. It is clear, therefore, that neither did the Church have the power to receive it by way of possession, nor did he have the power to confer it by way of transferral. {16} The emperor could, however, delegate into the guardianship of the Church a patrimony or other holdings as long as his superior dominion, whose unity does not allow division, remained undisturbed. {17} The vicar of God could also receive it, not as a possessor, but as a dispenser of fruits to the poor of Christ on behalf of the Church—as we know the Apostles did.[389]

## Chapter 11

{1} They say, furthermore, that Pope Hadrian called upon Charlemagne to defend him and the Church against the outrages of the Langobards during the time of their king Desiderius[390]; and that Charles received the authority of the empire from him despite the fact that Michael was emperor in Constantinople.[391] {2} On this account they affirm that all those who were Roman emperors after him are themselves also defenders of the Church and must be called upon by the Church; from this there would also follow that dependency they wish to establish.[392] {3} And to refute this argument, I declare that what they say is meaningless, for the usurpation of a right certainly does not constitute a right. For if this were the case, one could demonstrate in the same way that the authority of the Church has depended on the emperor from the time that the Emperor Otto restored Leo as pope and deposed Benedict to lead him off into exile in Saxony.[393]

## Chapter 12

{1} Their argument from reason[394] proceeds in the following way: they assume as their own the principle from the tenth book of the *First Philosophy*,[395] saying: all things of a single genus can be reduced to one that is the standard measure of all those that are within that genus; all men are of one genus; ergo, they must be reduced to one as to a standard measure of them all. {2} And since the supreme high priest and the emperor are men, if that conclusion is true, they must be reduced to one single man. And since the pope is not to be reduced to another, it remains for the emperor and all other men to be reduced to the pope, as to their standard measure and rule. On this account too there follows the very thing that they wish to establish.

{3} To rebut such reasoning I affirm that when they say, "Those things belonging to the same genus must be reduced to one entity of that genus, which is the standard measure of that genus," they speak the truth! Likewise they speak the truth when they say that all men are of one genus; and they are right again when they conclude by inferring from these premises that all men must be reduced to one single standard measure of their genus. But, when from this conclusion they draw their inference concerning the pope and the emperor, they fall into the fallacy of "accidental attributes."[396]

{4} To make this clear, we must keep in mind that it is one thing to be a man and another to be a pope. And likewise, it is one thing to be a man and another to be an emperor, just as it is one thing to be a man and another to be a father or a master.

{5} For man is what he is on account of his substantial form because of which he is classified in a species and genus and because of which he is placed in the category of a substance. A father, however, is such by an accidental form that consists in a relationship by which he is classified in a certain species and genus and is placed in the category of "*ad aliquid*," that is, "as being for a certain function regarding something else," or in the category of relationship. Otherwise, inasmuch as no accidental form can subsist per se apart from the foundation of a substance underlying it, everything would be reduced to the category of substance: but this is false. {6} Therefore, since the pope and the emperor are what they are through certain relationships, namely, because of their papacy and their emperorship, one of whose relationships fall under the scope of paternity[397] and the other's under the scope of dominion, it is clear that the pope and the emperor, insofar as they are such, must be classified in the category of relationship, and consequently must be reduced to something that is within that genus.

{7} I therefore declare that there is one standard measure to which they must be reduced insofar as they are men, and another to which they must be reduced insofar as they are pope and emperor. For, insofar as they are men, they must be reduced to the supreme man—whoever that may be—who is the standard measure of all the others, and their "idea,"[398] so to speak, that is, to him who is supremely one in his own genus, as we may gather from the end of the *Ethics.*[399] {8} Insofar as they are terms implying relationship, as is obvious, they must be reduced either one to the other (if one is subordinate to the other), or they share in the same species through the nature of their relationship, or else they must be reduced to some third to which they may be reduced as to their common denominator. {9} But it cannot be said that one is subordinate to the other, because, if that were the case, one would be predicated of the other; and this is false, for we do not say, "the emperor is the pope," nor do we say the reverse.[400] Nor can we say that they share the same species, since the basis for being pope, as such, and the basis for being emperor are quite different. Ergo, they are to be reduced to something else in which they have their unity.

{10} On this account we must keep in mind that a relationship stands to a relationship as one related thing stands to another. If, therefore, the papacy and the emperorship, insofar as they are relationships of superior position,[401] are to be reduced to a nexus of superior positions from which the two relationships derive together with their differentiating characteristics, the pope and the emperor, as two related things, must be reduced to some single thing in which the same relationship of superior positions may still be found without the other differentiating attributes.

{11} And this unity will either be God himself, in whom all relationships are universally united, or it will be some substance inferior to God in which the relationship of superior positions may be particularized descending from a simple relationship through a difference in superior positions.[402] {12} And thus it is clear that the pope and the emperor, insofar as they are men, must be reduced to one thing, but insofar as they are pope and emperor, they must be reduced to something else.

And thus their argument from reason is cleared up.

## Chapter 13

{1} Having explained and refuted those errors upon which those who say that the authority of the Roman Prince depends upon the Roman Pontiff lean most heavily, we must go back and show the truth of the third question that we proposed to examine at the beginning. That truth will certainly become fully clear if, following the principle of enquiry that I have established, I manage to demonstrate that the aforementioned authority depends directly on the culmination of all being, which is God. {2} And this will be shown, either if the Church's authority over it be set aside (given that the quarrel does not concern any other authority), or if it may be proved by ostensive demonstration that it depends directly upon God.[403]

{3} Now, that the authority of the Church is not the cause of imperial authority is proved as follows: if while something does not exist or is not exercising power, something else is enjoying its full power, the first cannot be the cause of the power of the second. But when the Church did not exist or was not operating, the empire did enjoy its full power. Ergo, the Church is not the cause of the empire's power, nor, consequently, of its authority, because its power and authority are the same thing.[404] {4} Let the Church be A; the empire B; the authority or power of the empire C. If A does not exist, and C is in B, it is impossible for A to be the cause by which C is in B, since it is impossible for the effect to precede the cause of its existence. Moreover, if A is not in operation, and C is in B, by necessity A is not the cause by which C is in B, since for the production of an effect it is necessary that the cause be already in operation, especially an efficient cause[405] about which we are concerned here.

{5} The major premise of this demonstration is made clear from its terms. Christ and his Church confirm the minor: Christ by his birth and death, as we said above; his Church inasmuch as Paul says to Festus in Acts:[406] "I stand at Cæsar's judgment seat, where I ought to be judged." And likewise when the angel of God said to Paul a little after: "Fear not, Paul, thou must be brought before Cæsar."[407] And again, further on, Paul says to the Jews dwelling in Italy: "But the Jews contradicting it, I was constrained to appeal unto Cæsar; not that I had any thing to accuse my nation of"[408] "but so that I might rescue my soul from death."[409] {6} But if at that time Cæsar had not already had authority to judge in temporal matters, Christ would not have approved it, nor would the angel have pronounced those words, nor would he, who said, "[I] desire to be dissolved and to be with Christ,"[410] have appealed to a judge with no jurisdiction. {7} Likewise, if Constantine had not had the authority, those imperial goods that he entrusted to the guardianship of the Church, he could not have entrusted *de jure*, and thus the Church would have profited from that donation unjustly, whereas God wills that offerings are to be spotless, according to the text of Leviticus: "Every oblation that is offered to the Lord shall be made without leaven."[411] {8} That precept, indeed, although it seems directed toward those making offerings, is, nevertheless, consequently made to those who accept. For it is foolish to believe that God would want something that he prohibits giving to be accepted, since there is also, in the same text of Leviticus, the precept: "Do not defile your souls, nor touch ought thereof, lest you be unclean."[412] {9} But to say that the Church would so abuse the patrimony entrusted to it would be quite absurd:[413] ergo, the proposition from which it followed was false.

## Chapter 14

{1} Let me go further: if the Church had the power to bestow authority upon the Roman prince, it either would have received it from God, or from itself, or from some emperor, or from the assent of all mortals, or, at all events, from those in the majority[414] among them: there is no other chink through which this power could have trickled down to the Church. But the Church had it from none of these: ergo, it did not have the aforesaid power. {2} That it indeed did not have it from any of these can be shown as follows: for if it had received it from God, this came about either through divine or natural law, for whatever is received from nature is received from God, but not, of course, the other way around. {3} But it was not through natural law since nature does not impose any law except for her own results, given that God cannot be deficient when he brings something into being without secondary agents. Therefore, since the Church is not an effect of nature but of God who said, "Upon this rock I will build my Church,"[415] and in another place, "I have finished the work which thou gavest me to do,"[416] it is clear that nature could not have given it the law.

{4} But neither was it through divine law, for all divine law is contained in the bosom of the two Testaments, in which, truly, I cannot find that care or concern of temporal things was entrusted to the priesthood, ancient or modern. {5} I find, rather, that the ancient priests were made aloof from that by commandment, as is clear from those words that God said to Moses; and modern priests by those words that Christ said to his disciples.[417] It is surely not possible that this care would have been taken from them if the authority of temporal power had derived from the priesthood since, at least, some solicitude would have goaded them concerning provision of its authorization—and from this a continual vigilance lest the person so authorized should wander from the path of righteousness. {6} That, on the contrary, the Church did not receive this power from itself is readily obvious. There is nothing that can give what it does not have. Hence, anything that produces something must be such in actuality as that which it intends to produce, as we find written in the treatise *On Being Simply*.[418] But it is patently obvious that if the Church gave itself that power, it did not have it to give in the first place, and thus it gave itself[419] something it did not have—and this is impossible. {7} That it certainly did not get it from any emperor is clear enough from what we showed above. And who could doubt that it did not get it either from the assent of all men or from the majority of them—since not only would all Asians and Africans but even the greater part of the inhabitants of Europe shudder at the thought? It is really tiresome to adduce proofs for things so obvious.[420]

## Chapter 15

{1} Similarly, whatever is contrary to the nature of a thing is not to be numbered amongst its powers, since the powers of each thing follow from its nature for the attainment of its end goal; but the power of conferring authority on the realm of our mortality is against the nature of the Church: ergo, it is not numbered among its powers. {2} In support of the minor premise, we must remember that the nature of the Church is the form of the Church, for although "nature" may refer to matter and form, nevertheless, it is above all the form that is meant, as is shown in the *Lessons on Nature*.[421] {3} The form of the Church is, however, nothing else but the life of Christ, which is contained both in his sayings and in his deeds; for his life was the ideal and model of the Church militant, and especially for his shepherds and above all for his supreme Shepherd whose duty it is to feed his lambs and sheep.[422] {4} Whence, in bequeathing the form of his life in John,[423] he himself said: "I have given you an example that as I have done to you, so you do also," and in particular he said to Peter, after he had entrusted the office of shepherd to him, as we read in the same Gospel, "Peter, follow me."[424] {5} But Christ, in the presence of Pilate, refused a kingdom such as this:[425] "My kingdom is not of this world. If my kingdom were of this world, my servants would certainly strive that I should not be delivered to the Jews: but now my kingdom is not from hence."[426] {6} This is not to be understood as if Christ, who is God, were not the Lord of this kingdom—since the Psalmist says, "For the sea is his and he made it: and his hands formed the dry land"[427]—but because, as an example to the Church, he had no concern for this kingdom.[428] {7} It is as if a gold seal were to speak of itself saying: "I am not a standard measure for any genus of beings." This statement certainly makes no sense insofar as it consists of gold, since gold *is* the measure of the genus of metals, but it does insofar as it consists in a certain seal that can be received by impression.[429]

{8} It is the formal principle of the Church, therefore, to speak and think the same thing; to speak and think in opposing ways is contrary to its form, as is evident, or contrary to its nature, which is the same thing. {9} From this we can gather that the power of conferring authority to the kingdom on earth is contrary to the nature of the Church. Indeed, the contradiction between thinking and speaking follows from the contradiction that is in the thing spoken or in the thing thought, just as the true and the false in speech come from the existence or nonexistence of the thing discussed, as the doctrine of the *Categories* teaches us.[430] {10} Therefore, by means of the aforementioned arguments—by "reduction to the absurd"[431]—we have proved satisfactorily that the authority of the empire does not depend on the Church in any way.

## Chapter 16

{1} Although we have shown in the preceding chapter by "reduction to the absurd" that the authority of the empire is not derived from the authority of the Supreme Pontiff, it has not, however, been positively proved, except by inferred consequence, that it depends directly upon God. The inferred consequence, indeed, is that, if it does not depend upon the vicar of God, it must depend upon God. {2} And, therefore, for a perfect determination of our proposition, we must prove by ostensive demonstration[432] that the emperor, or world monarch, holds his office directly from the Prince of the universe who is God.

{3} To understand this we must remember that man alone among beings holds the mean between things corruptible and incorruptible; therefore he is rightly compared by philosophers to the horizon that is the midway between the two hemispheres.[433] {4} For man, if he is considered according to both his essential parts, that is, his body and his soul, he is corruptible; if he is considered only according to one, namely, the soul, he is incorruptible. Thus, in the second book of *On the Soul,* the Philosopher justly speaks of this part insofar as it is incorruptible, when he says: "And to this alone, since it is perpetual, is it given to separate itself from the corruptible."[434]

{5} Therefore, if man is some kind of mean between corruptible and incorruptible beings, since every mean has the essence of both extremes, man must necessarily impart something of both natures.[435] {6} And since every nature is ordained to its own final goal, it follows that man's goal is twofold; and since he alone among all beings participates in the corruptible and the incorruptible, so he alone among all beings is ordained to two final goals, one of which is his goal insofar as he is corruptible, the other insofar as he is incorruptible.

{7} Therefore, ineffable Providence has set before man two goals to attain: that is, the blessedness of this life, which consists in the functioning of his own powers and is figured by the earthly paradise,[436] and the blessedness of eternal life that consists in the enjoyment of God's countenance to which man's powers can ascend only by the aid of divine light; and this blessedness is made intelligible by the celestial paradise. {8} To these beatitudes, indeed, as to different conclusions, we must arrive by different means. For we come to the first through philosophical teachings provided we follow them by acting according to the moral and intellectual virtues[437]; to the second, on the other hand, we arrive through spiritual teachings that transcend human reason, provided we follow them by acting according to the theological virtues, namely, faith, hope, and charity. {9} These conclusions and means have thus been vouchsafed to us: the former made known to us wholly by the philosophers through human reason; the latter by the Holy Spirit, who, through the Prophets and holy writers,[438] through Jesus Christ, the Son of God coeternal with him, and through his disciples, has revealed to us the supernatural truth necessary for us. Human cupidity, however, would cast these aside unless men, like horses, wandering astray in their bestiality, were held in check on their path "by bit and bridle."[439] {10} On this account it was necessary for man to have a dual guide for his dual end: namely, the Supreme Pontiff who would lead mankind to eternal life according to those things that have been revealed, and the emperor, who would direct mankind to temporal felicity according to philosophical teachings.

{11} And since to this port either none, or very few could arrive—and these with excessive difficulty—unless the waves of seductive cupidity be stilled so that mankind may rest free in the tranquillity of peace, this is the aim to which the guardian of this globe, who is called the Roman Prince, must especially strive so that we may live free and in peace on this little threshing-floor of mortals.[440] {12} And since the disposition of this world follows the disposition inherent in the circling of the heavens, in order that useful teachings of liberty and peace appropriate to time and place be applied, it is necessary that this guardian be provided by him who contemplates the total disposition of the heavens all at once. This, however, is he alone who preordained that disposition so that by this means he in his providence might link everything according to his plans. {13} If this is so, God alone elects, he alone confirms, since he has no superior. From this we may gather further that neither those who are nowadays, nor others who may in any way have been called "electors," should be given that name.[441] They should be called, rather, "heralds of divine providence." {14} Whence it has happened that sometimes those to whom the honor of heralding has been granted fall into disagreement, either because all, or certain among them, are so beclouded by the fog of cupidity that they do not discern the face of divine dispensation.[442] {15} Therefore, it is thus obvious that the temporal authority of the monarch descends to him from the Fount of universal authority without intermediary. Indeed, this Fount, at one in the fortress of its very simplicity, flows out into many streams from its plentiful goodness.[443]

{16} And now I believe I have, all in all, reached the goal I set for myself, since I have pried out the kernel of truth[444] of the problem under investigation: whether the office of monarch was necessary for the well-being of the world, and whether the Roman people appropriated the empire *de jure*, not to speak of the last problem, whether the authority of the monarch depended directly upon God or upon someone else.

{17} The truth of the last, of course, must not be understood so strictly that the Roman prince is not in a certain sense under the Roman pontiff, since the happiness of this mortal life is in some way ordered toward eternal happiness. {18} Therefore, let Cæsar show Peter that reverence[445] that a firstborn son should show his father,[446] so that, illuminated by the light of paternal grace,[447] he may enlighten the globe of the earth more powerfully, for he presides over it solely by way of him who is the ruler of all things temporal and spiritual.

# HERE BEGINS THE TREATISE OF
# FRIAR GUIDO VERNANI OF THE ORDER
# OF PREACHERS, CONCERNING
## *The Refutation of the Monarchia*
# COMPOSED BY DANTE[1]

### (DEDICATION)

{1} To Graziolo de' Bambaglioli,[2] greetings from Fra Guido Vernani of Rimini, of the Order of Preachers, to his most beloved son and chancellor of the noble Commune of Bologna, that he may so pass through earthly goods that he may not lose those eternal.

{2} Just as it often occurs that a vessel, holding in its bowl food or drink poisonous and deadly to our corporeal and transitory life, flaunts[3] outside on its convex surface, such a false and counterfeit beauty that it may deceive not only the ignorant and slothful but even the diligent,[4] so, likewise, we experience and come to know that more frequent vicissitudes and more serious dangers befall us in spiritual matters. {3} To be sure, the liar and father of pernicious lies possesses his own vessels,[5] which, tarted up on the outside with spurious colors and deceitful figures of truth and honesty, contain a poison more deadly and pestilential to that very degree that the rational soul (illumined by the life of Divine Grace, from which he fell—he who, falling through pride did not stand in the truth)[6] is known to transcend the corruptible flesh.[7]

{4} Among the devil's other vessels, there was, indeed, a certain individual[8] who wrote many fantastic things in poetry, a palaverous sophist,[9] pleasing many through his eloquence with its hollow words; one who, using his poetical phantasms and fictions[10] and, in the words of Philosophy as she consoled Boethius,[11] bringing whores onto the stage with their sweet, siren songs, fraudulently seduces not only sick minds, but even zealous ones, to the destruction of salutary truth.[12]

{5} Though, to be sure, I pass over the other works of this fellow in disgust, there remains, however, a certain screed[13] of his that he chose to call *Monarchia*, and which I have decided to investigate, since in this work he proceeded in a specious, yet somewhat methodical, fashion, all the while mixing many lies with occasional truths. {6} He there inscribed many falsehoods along with his own whimsical reasonings, so that—using the words of the most excellent doctor Augustine—"I scoff with confidence, scrutinize with care, and with clear reasoning demolish."[14]

{7} I therefore send this[15] to you, my most beloved son, so that your intellect (by nature brilliant, by divine grace perspicacious, avid for truth, zealous in its own fragrance and in those things that must be sought after diligently— insofar as the Republic's concerns entrusted to you permit) may both[16] choose and value the useful, spew forth the false, prune the superfluous, and shun the useless and harmful.

## (BOOK I)

{1} That screed is divided into three principal parts[17]; in the first of which our fellow strains to prove that, for the good of the whole world, a monarchy is required: that is, one sole prince and one sole principality. {2} Yet however much truth this idea may hold,[18] his substantiation leads to many errors. {3} In fact, he goes on as follows: different parts have different ends, and ends that differ from the final goal of the whole. For example, there is one end for the eye, that is to say, to see colors and distinguish their gradations, and there is another end for the ear, that is, to recognize sounds; thus, these ends differ from the final goal of the individual man, of whom these parts are natural faculties. {4} Nonetheless he does not clarify what the ultimate end of the individual man may be,[19] yet he says that, just as the end of a part of a man is different from the end of the man as a whole, likewise, the end of one single man is unlike and different from the end of mankind as a whole, despite the

fact that one single man is a mere part of the entire multitude [*Mon.* 1:3].[20] {5}
That this is clearly false, however, is proven by authority, reason, and example.

{6} For Aristotle, in his *Politics* 7, in the chapter "Whether happiness be
. . ." clearly states that the happiness of one man is the same as the happiness
of the entire city; and he asserts that all men are unanimous in this opinion.
{7} Indeed, those who say that an individual man is happy on account of his
wealth, also say that his city is happy if it be rich. {8} Likewise, those who say
that a tyrant is happy on account of his dominion, will say that his city, having dominion over many others, is also happy[21]; and if they say that an individual is happy by reason of his virtue, they will also say that his city is happy
because of its virtue. {9} Ergo, there is not one end for the individual and another for the human race as a whole. {10} The blessed Augustine says the
same thing in *The City of God* 1:15, where he speaks as follows: "For the blessedness of a community and of an individual flow from the same source; for a
community is nothing else than a harmonious collection of individuals."

{11} From this it is obvious that, since blessedness is the final goal, there is
not one final goal for the individual and another for the human race as a
whole.[22] {12} To prove this, one must be aware that God, Creator of all, who
made all things according to his eternal wisdom, "ordered all things in measure, and number, and weight," as it says in Wisdom 11:21. The blessed Augustine declares the same in his exegesis, [*The Literal Meaning*] of *Genesis* [4:3]: "Measure places a limit on everything; number gives everything form; and weight
draws each thing to a state of repose and stability."[23]

{13} Ergo, just as anything is characterized by having a limit and terminal
goal according to its species (on account of which definition of a thing is
called its "terminus"), in the same way, everything tends toward a certain end
and terminus in which to find rest and repose; now, this tendency in corporeal things is called weight. {14} Whence, weight in earth and earthly bodies
drags everything downward, while lightness draws fire upward. {15} This tendency in spirits, however, is love, as Augustine states in *The City of God* 11:28:
"For the specific gravity of bodies is, as it were, their love, whether they are
carried downward by their weight, or upward by their levity. For the body is
borne by its gravity, as the spirit by love, wherever it is borne." {16} Indeed,
just as all heavy things are naturally moved by their weight toward the center,
there thus cannot be one center for all heavy things and another center for one
single heavy thing, just as there is not one goal for one single man and another for the human race as a whole.

{17} Thus, all men in general and each one of them in particular desire one single, final goal, which is blessedness. {18} Blessedness, moreover, which is the terminus of the rational appetite, is none other than the vision and enjoyment of highest Truth and highest Goodness, and for this reason the human heart cannot rest in any created thing. {19} Wherefore Augustine in his *Confessions* 1[:1], addresses God as follows: "Oh Lord, you made us for yourself and our heart will grow restless, until it reposes in you." And thus in Book 4:12, he says: "Return, sinners, to your own heart and cling to him who made you, stand in him and you shall stand fast; rest in him and you shall find peace. . . . There is no peace where you seek it. Seek what you seek, but it is not there where you are seeking. You seek the blessed life in the realm of death; such a life is not there. How can you find the blessed life where there is no life at all?" {20} These words clearly state that blessedness cannot be had in this mortal life, and the blessed Thomas Aquinas lucidly and clearly proves the same in his *Summa against the Pagans*, Book 3[:48].[24] {21} And if anyone were to say that political blessedness, which consists in the practice of moral virtues, is possible in this life, let him hear Augustine in *The City of God* 19[:4], where he says that no one is competent to explain all the miseries of this world among which blessedness cannot exist. {22} And he says later [19:4] that, in this life, moral virtue wages perpetual war against vice. As long as we are amid this warfare, therefore, let us avoid calling ourselves blessed.

{23} The argument, however, concerning the differences among parts has no validity at all, because the parts of the individual are different from one another in kind, such as the hand from the foot and the eye from the ear. An individual man, however, does not differ in this way from other men. {24} Therefore the final goal of one individual man does not differ from the final goal of another man, nor from the final goal of the whole human race. {25} Whence it is clear that this man has shamefully erred through the fallacy of his equivocation, because the relation of the integral parts, such as the eye and the hand, in respect to the man as a whole, is not the same as the relation of substantial parts, such as Peter and Paul, in respect to the whole human race. {26} It must, though, be kept in mind that the difference in blessedness between different men, such as Peter's blessedness and that of Paul, exists only in degree—but not in kind, and not in its object, which is the highest good for all men.[25]

{27} The second error is found in his statements in the same chapter [*Mon.* 1:3]: that among the intellectual substances that we call angels, existence and intellect are one, so that, unless the angels use their intellects continuously, they could not exist eternally. {28} This statement, however, is an intolerable error philosophically speaking. {29} For according to natural philosophy, heavenly bodies are eternal, and yet they make no use of intellect; and the human soul is also eternal, and yet it does not always make use of its intellect. {30} Ergo, it is a false conclusion to say that a substance that does not always makes use of intellect cannot be eternal. {31} It is most special and proper that in God alone, who is pure act, God is his own action; wherefore, he alone is at once his intellect and his will. {32} But, because all this has little to do with our purpose, I therefore do not insist on refuting that error at greater length.

{33} The third is the worst kind of error. He actually says in the same chapter and the following [*Mon.* 1:3–4], that the possible intellect cannot be actualized, that is, it cannot be perfected, except through the whole human race, just as the potentiality of prime matter cannot be brought totally to actuality and perfection, except through the multitude of natural things. {34} And for this he adduces the authority of Averroës, who says as much in his *Commentary* on Book 3 of *On the Soul;* and he affirms that this is the end and perfection not of one individual man, but of all mankind lumped together.[26] {35} By such a statement it clearly follows that there is one single intellect for all mankind; but to say and hear such a thing is to commit the flagrant error of its author and inventor, Averroës, to whom he refers. {36} First, it is an error as far as natural philosophy is concerned, which states in *On the Soul* 2[:2], that the soul is that by which we live, feel and think. {37} Therefore, it is necessary that our soul be intellective, that is to say, that it have a power by which we may understand. {38} And in *On the Soul,* Book 3[:4], it says that the intellect by which the soul knows and thinks is part of the soul, that is to say, one of the powers of the soul. {39} Ergo, the possible intellect is not a separate substance, neither is it one and the same in all mankind. {40} The error also goes against moral philosophy, which states in the *Ethics,* Book 6,[27] that knowledge, wisdom, intellect, prudence, and art[28] are virtues of the individual man; this would not be so if our intellect were a certain separate substance, because these powers are found within the intellect as in a subject. Similarly, it says in the *Ethics,* Book 9,[29] that man is principally intellect. {41} The error also goes against *The First Philosophy,* which states in Book 12[:3],[30] that there was no corporeal form before the body; but, once the flesh meets with corruption, something of it may remain: not indeed the whole form, but the soul; not the whole soul, but the intellect. {42} Here Aristotle clearly says[31] that the intellect, that is to say the intellective soul, is the form of the body and that it remains after the body meets corruption, and is separated from it. {43} But I have already said enough about this in my own *On the Soul*, Book 3, and many a treatise has been written against this error by other learned men.[32]

{44} However much of the conclusion of Part 1 may be granted, namely, that it is beneficial for the world to have one single monarch, still, a foolish love of his own opinion obscured his wits and our writer was unable to discover who the true monarch was.[33] {45} For according to Aristotle in his *Politics*, Book 3, a monarch must excel and exceed the whole multitude of his subjects in virtue, and he ought to be compared to all his subjects, just as the whole is compared to its parts.[34]

{46} The monarch of all mankind must therefore outdo the whole human race in moral virtues and prudence. It was, however, never possible to find a man so righteous. {47} Wherefore, according to this philosophical reasoning, only our Lord Jesus Christ—and no other—was the true monarch. {48} This doctrine is more fully and more perfectly set forth in our treatise *On Papal Power*, chapter 4.[35] {49} For, since all men are considered, by the necessity of salvation, as the faithful of Christ, because, as the Apostle says in Hebrews 11:6: "Without faith it is impossible to please God," he alone must hold and, indeed, holds supremely the dignity and power of monarchy. {50} For he alone is the one who established the law and precept of peace by which the universal republic is founded, ruled, and defended in its best possible state, as Augustine bears witness in his *Epistle to Volusianus*, where he says that in Christ's law "[t]here dwells the salvation of a praiseworthy commonwealth. Because the best possible city may not be either founded or guarded without the foundations and bonds of faith and steadfast harmony, as men love the universal, absolute, and most truthful goodness which is God, and, in turn, they love each other most sincerely in him, for they love each other on account of him and cannot conceal from him how much they love each other."[36] {51} And what is said about the city, by the same reasoning, applies to the community of all mankind. {52} Monarchy would therefore be optimum, if the whole human race kept the laws and the precepts of peace according to the teaching of the Gospel of our Lord Jesus Christ. {53} And whatever is correctly affirmed on this matter in this fellow's treatise fits our Catholic and philosophical way of thinking consistently; for this, to be sure, is for the benefit of the world: it is thus that the whole human race may spend its life in the true tranquillity of peace, and thus the whole might be ordered as one, and, especially, be one; then all things would be moved by the one. {54} Thus there would be no strife, and if at some time any were to spring up, it would be easily quieted through the law given by the one. {55} At that time justice would stand pure and unblemished in one monarch. {56} Thus, the human race would be most perfectly free, because, if the Son of God were to free man, he would be truly free. {57} Then he would have a monarch most perfectly disposed to reign, since he would be mighty in words and deeds before God and all people. {58} Thus, all things would come about in orderly sequence through the one. {59} Thus, the wills of all men would meet in the one, ruled by the one. Indeed, according to the Gospel of John,[37] this true monarch prayed for, and procured, all this, that all men might be one. {60} Wherefore, it must be understood, as Augustine says in *On the Trinity*, 4:9, that all men may not be one so much through nature, but so that they might be one through the same charity aspiring toward the same blessedness and most harmonious will with one spirit kindled, as it were, by the fire of charity. {61} Thus, in brief and in sum, none of the reasonings that the writer puts forth in the first part of his treatise, although they have a certain appearance of truth, can or could in truth ever be found in any other monarch except the Lord Jesus Christ.

{62} But, because Christ himself departed from men's sight, and ascended in the flesh to heaven, lest his body, which is the Church, might remain without head, he left on earth his universal vicar, that is, the Apostle Peter, and whosoever becomes his legitimate successor, to be the true and legitimate monarch in Christ's place,[38] whom all men are charged to obey as they are the Lord Jesus Christ, just as Cyril, a doctor of the Greeks says expressly; and this the blessed Thomas of Aquinas adduces in the book he wrote *Against the Errors of the Greeks*.[39] {63} Ergo, the prince of the world is the supreme pontiff of the Christians, the universal vicar of Jesus Christ, in whom, if all men obeyed according to the law of the Gospels handed down by Christ, there would exist the most perfect monarchy in the world. {64} Never was there in the world any true monarch except for him, as I have clearly proved by reasoning and authority in my treatise *On Papal Power*[40]; and that no other power is necessary among men I have clearly demonstrated in the same place.

{65} In a certain chapter [*Mon.* 1:9], moreover, the fellow attempts to argue for the unity of monarchy on absurd grounds, saying that a son is at his best when he follows in the footsteps of a perfect father. {66} Indeed the true proposition goes as the Apostle says [Eph 5:1]: "Be ye therefore followers of God, as most dear children." God is rightly called "father of men," whom he made in his image and likeness. {67} But what this man assumes, that mankind is the offspring of the heavens, is absurdly and even ignorantly asserted. {68} And the argument of the *Physics*, Book 2, which he adduces [*Mon.* 1:9:1]—that man and the sun beget man—must be understood only in respect to the flesh.[41] {69} For according to the proof of true doctors, the rational soul is not brought forth from the potentiality of matter through transmutation, nor is it by transference, but comes from God most high through creation. {70} For this reason in the book, *On Church Dogma*, chapter 15,[42] it says that, once the body is formed, the soul is created and infused into it; the souls of brute animals, however, have their origin with the body and die with it. {71} And for this reason, the generation of other animals, rather than the generation of man, must be attributed to the heavens. {72} And that is why the heavens should be called "father of dogs and pigs" rather than of man, although both statements are made absurdly and outrageously, because, if we are to speak naturally and aptly, the words "fatherhood" and "filiation" may not be used properly, except in reference to those things that are united by likeness of species.[43]

{73} And let what we have said suffice concerning those things that pertain to the first part.

## (BOOK 2)

{1} We next look at the second part of the treatise in which this fellow sets forth some bombastic rhetoric in which he promises something beyond the powers of his smug ignorance. {2} He intends and promises to prove that the Roman people acquired imperial authority *de jure* and not by usurpation; and he strives to prove it through seven arguments.

{3} This is the gist of the first of them [*Mon.* 2:3]: it is just that the noblest of nations govern over all the others; the Roman people was the noblest because it was born of Æneas and of the noblest of mothers, as the poets attest; ergo, it should govern over all.

{4} To this, one must reply that that true nobility, which is worthy to rule, is that which derives from excellence of virtue and prudence, as may be understood from what is said above, and this is true nobility, as Aristotle states in the first book of his *Politics*.[44] {5} By the mere mention of this kind of nobility is his minor premise—to wit, that the Roman people is the noblest—made simply false; and this is proven in several ways.

{6} First, because that people lay in the perpetual whoredom of the idolatrous worship of the foulest demons—and even more so than any other recorded nation, as Valerius makes clear in Book 2, chapter 1 [of his *Memorable Deeds and Sayings*], where, among other things, he states as follows: "It must be concluded that our city has never turned her eyes from the most scrupulous observance of ceremonies," that is to say, from the worship of demons.[45] {7} And Paul the Apostle, writing to the Romans [1:21–23], speaks thus: "[They] became vain in their thoughts, and their foolish heart was darkened. For professing themselves to be wise, they became fools. And they changed the glory of the incorruptible God into the likeness of the image of a corruptible man, and of birds, and of four-footed beasts, and of creeping things."[46] {8} And then, after having listed nearly all the kinds of sin by which the Roman people had been polluted, he concludes: "They who do such things, are worthy of death (Romans 1[:32])." {9} Wherefore, according to Augustine, they were citizens of the city of the devil. And, in *The City of God* 1:1 [Preface], he speaks of them as follows: "This, which is God's prerogative, the inflated ambition of a proud spirit also affects, and dearly loves that this be said in his praise, to 'Show pity to the humbled soul and crush the sons of pride' [*Æn.* 6:854]. . . . even though nations serve it, the lust for ruling rules the earthly city." {10} The blessed Bernard likewise, speaking of the Romans, states the following in his book [*On Consideration* 4:2] to Pope Eugenius: "What shall I say about the Roman people? . . . What has been so well known to the ages than their impudence? A nation unaccustomed to peace, and accustomed to tumult; a rough and intractable tribe . . . incapable of submission, except when resistance is pointless."[47] {11} And so below: The Romans, irreverent toward God, disrespectful toward holy things; quarrelsome among themselves, envious of their neighbors, discourteous to strangers. Loving no one, no one loves them. . . . Disloyal to superiors, insupportable to inferiors; shameless in demanding, inflexible in denying; ungrateful in receiving . . . fawning in flattery, biting in slander."[48] {12} And the blessed Jerome, in his *Commentary on Isaiah* [1:8], says: "The ancient records, both Latin and Greek, attest that there was no one more avaricious than the Roman people."[49] {13} Behold the noble nation that should rule the others *de jure!* {14} Surely, if it is a question of the nobility of a nation, far nobler were the Jewish people, whose nobility descended unbroken from the Patriarch Noah, who was lord of all the earth by the authority and will of God almighty, and in as much as they had noble and unblemished progenitors, to wit, Abraham, Isaac, Jacob and the twelve Patriarchs who followed; this was, then, the chosen people of God most high. {15} Concerning this people, Deuteronomy, 26:17 says the following: "Thou hast chosen the Lord this day to be thy God. . . . And the Lord hath chosen thee this day, to be his peculiar people . . . and to keep all his commandments. And to make you higher than all nations." {16} But if this did not come about, their own sins were the cause.

{17} Secondly, the writer argues as follows: whatever is done by the will of God is done justly; the Romans acquired imperial power through the will of God: ergo, they did it justly. The major premise is clear.

{18} The minor one he proves as follows: in respect to the Romans' holding imperial power, many miracles were observed [*Mon.* 2:4]. {19} First, when Numa Pompilius was king of the Romans, in accordance with heathen custom—of course, while he was sacrificing to the demons!—a buckler fell from the sky upon Rome. {20} Another time, when nearly all Rome had already been overrun except for the Capitol, a goose woke the Capitol guards and told them that the enemy was at hand. {21} And, when Hannibal pressed the Romans so hard that there remained nothing to complete their final extermination save the enemy's assault on the city, a sudden, relentless hailstorm forestalled his victory.

{22} We must reply to this argument by making a distinction. {23} In fact our theologians (in *Sentent.* 1)[50] distinguish among the many modes of God's will. {24} For there is "a will of God in antecedence" by which he wills all men to be saved, as the Apostle says in 1 Timothy 2[:3–4], but this is not always fulfilled. {25} There is another "will of God in consequence" by which he wills Peter and Paul to be saved, and this is always fulfilled. {26} His will is also distinguished in another way, because there is a will known as "the will of God's good pleasure [Eph 1:9]," and whatever is done in accordance with this will is done justly. {27} Further, there is a certain will, which is called "the will of sign," and this, in turn, is multiform: to wit, precept, prohibition, permission, counsel, and operation.

{28} And, whatever is done under these latter forms of God's will is done justly, except for that which is done under the will of permission. {29} For he who does what God prescribes and counsels, and avoids what God forbids, acts justly; but he who does what God permits does not always act justly. {30} For God suffers a man to steal and commit other sins, but, nonetheless, he who steals and commits adultery does not act justly. {31} Therefore it does not follow that, if God suffered the Romans to vanquish and conquer other peoples, the Romans subjugated them justly on this account. {32} For God has justly suffered sinful men to be subject to the power of demons; yet, the devil has always enmeshed them with injustice.

{33} But that God willed the Romans to rule by the "will of His good pleasure" our writer tries to prove by miracles—a proof that is more to be mocked than refuted. {34} To satisfy the ignorant, however, let us first state that it was a simple task for the demons to bear off a mere buckler (that is, a shield) from somewhere else, raise it into the air, and let it fall upon Rome.[51]

{35} The tale of the goose is even sillier because this goose was either a real, living creature or a fantastic one. {36} If it was a real goose, a creature extremely alert by nature, and if it was sleeping, it awakened and cackled at the slightest noise; therefore the tale is not to be regarded as miraculous but ridiculous. {37} Concerning this, the blessed Augustine speaks derisively as follows in *The City of God* 2[:22]: "For then the whole city was in the hands of the enemy, save only the Capitoline Hill, and this too, was about to be taken, were it not that the geese at any rate were awake while the gods slept. Hence the Romans sank almost to the level of the Egyptians, who worship beasts and birds, when the goose was honored in annual ceremonies."[52] {38} If, on the other hand, the goose was a phantasm, it was easy for the demons not only to shape it but also to speak through it, in just the way the devil spoke to our first parents through the serpent.

{39} The things that he says about the hailstorm really cannot be considered a miracle at all because, first of all, it could have occurred by chance, just as it could also have come about by chance that, as I might be taking a stroll, a hailstorm could blow up quite naturally and suddenly turn into a downpour. {40} It could also be that the event had been arranged by demons, since they can gather together the natural elements with which they are so well acquainted and suddenly produce hail and rain with no difficulty whenever and in whatever quantity God allows, as we read in Exodus [7:11] concerning the Pharaoh's magicians; and the blessed Augustine says the same thing in *On the Trinity* 3:6 and 7.[53] {41} Concerning the maiden Cloelia, in Book 3, chapter 2, Valerius reports that "at nightfall she escaped the guards and, mounting a horse, swiftly crossed the river."[54] {42} There does not seem anything miraculous in this at all.

{43} In the third case [*Mon.* 2:5], he argues as follows: a people who strive for the good of the commonwealth ought to hold sway over all others; the Romans were such a people; ergo, and so on. {44} This argument fails first in its major premise: for it can happen that any two nations—or even three or four—may strive at once for the common good. {45} There would be no reasons, therefore, to indicate why one nation should assume rule over another.

{46} His minor premise, which says that the Roman people was attentive to the good of the commonwealth, is also simply false: first, because according to what Augustine says in the *Epistle to Volusianus*,[55] the "good of the commonwealth" is the true God and his true worship, the very adversary of whom was the Roman people, not only in and of itself, but also in all the nations where they encouraged and enforced the worship of idols; secondly, because the good of the commonwealth is the true blessedness that must quiet human desire, otherwise it would not be the final goal. {47} The Romans, however, set their "blessedness" on worldly glory, which, since it is vain and fickle, can in no way quiet human desire. Whence, the blessed Augustine says in *The City of God* 5[:12]: "As the Romans, greedy of praises, immolated victims to the demons, they became prodigal in lavishing money and very ardently esteemed great glory, by which they wanted to live, and for which they did not hesitate to die. Every other desire they repressed by that single passion. At length their country itself, because it seemed inglorious to serve, but glorious to rule and govern, they first earnestly desired to be free, and then to be mistress."[56] {48} It is, therefore, perfectly obvious that the Roman people did not strive for the true good of the commonwealth. No, indeed. {49} It was "ambition" that "possessed all the rewards of virtues" among them, as Cato says, according to Augustine in *The City of God* 5:12.[57] {50} For this reason, they could not rule other nations justly. {51} Who, indeed, but a madman dares to say that such a people could govern men justly—a nation, which, turning away from the true God, was entirely subject to demons? {52} And they served these very demons thinking that in this way they would obtain power and glory from other men. {53} Wherefore Valerius in Book 1, chapter 1, states the following: "The empire doubted not about serving religion, since it was believed that they would hold control over the future of human affairs, if they properly and constantly served the divine powers."[58] {54} These divine powers, whom they sedulously served as if they were gods, they nonetheless called "the powers of demons"!

{55} In the fourth place [*Mon.* 2:6], our writer argues as follows: it seems that nature does not fail to provide whatever is necessary; but so that the whole human race might attain its final goal, it was necessary for nature to provide one place and one people to rule all the others and bring peace to the world. {56} That place, indeed, was Rome, and her people were provided by nature for the aforesaid purpose.

{57} We must counter this argument by pointing out that however much the will of man is naturally inclined to blessedness, the attainment of blessedness, however, and other things by which men arrive at happiness are not to be found in them by nature, as Aristotle proves in his *Ethics*, Book 2.[59] {58} For all our deeds by which virtues are generated within us, are voluntary and not natural acts. {59} And it is in our power to be both good and evil, as Aristotle says in his *Ethics*, Book 3,[60] in the chapter "On Voluntary Action." {59} Therefore, this is not in nature's power. {60} And besides, the ordering of the entire human race to desire and attain blessedness is the work of God and not that of nature or of any single nation. {70} Thus in Proverbs 8:15, God says: "By me kings reign, and lawgivers decree just things." {71} And in Daniel 4:14, it says: "Know that the Most High ruleth in the kingdom of men; and to whomsoever he shall wish shall he deliver it."[61]

{72} Also, the blessed Augustine affirms in *The City of God* 5:1, that "the cause of the Roman Empire's greatness is not fortuitous," as if resulting from no determined reason; "neither was it fated," that is, as if it came from a certain order of necessary and natural causes, "but it is directly by divine providence that human kingdoms are established."[62] {73} And Aristotle says in his *Politics* 7[63] that a city must not be overpopulated, because such a multitude cannot be well governed by laws, but only by divine power, which encompasses, regulates, and guides the whole universe.

{74} And if any natural disposition is to be sought in any part of the world, it is more probably in the land of the Greeks, and to be sure, among the Greeks themselves, as Aristotle says expressly in his *Politics*, Book 7.[64]

{75} I myself believe, on the contrary, that far more rightly[65] should the Jewish people have ruled the nations rather than the Romans, both because of their location on earth, which is in the midst of our inhabitable hemisphere,[66] and because of their religion, since they cherished the one true God, Creator and Ruler of Heaven and earth. Concerning these people, it says as follows in Deuteronomy [4:6–8]: "Behold a wise and understanding people, a great nation. Neither is there any other nation so great, that hath gods so nigh them, as our God is present to all our petitions. For what other nation is there so renowned that hath ceremonies, and just judgments, and a universal law, which I set forth this day before your eyes?" {76} It is also absolutely extraordinary how this "nature," which was supposed to care for the Roman Empire for sake of the blessedness of the human race, took so long in doing so. {77} For from the creation of the world up to the founding of the city, 4,484 years passed. {78} Indeed, from the founding of the city up to Christ's birth, another 715 years went by, and only then did Cæsar Augustus hold the monarchy in peace; before him, no one was ever able to maintain it. {79} Furthermore, before the Lord Jesus Christ had been born into the world, the republic of the Romans had become utterly foul and dissolute, as the blessed Augustine affirms on the testimony of Sallust, in *The City of God* 2:17 and 18.[67] {80} He says, in fact, to use his own words, that before the Advent of Christ, the Roman republic had been made utterly base and dissolute through lust, covetousness, and vile, barbarous customs. How was it then to rule others, when it had become so disgusting and profligate? {81} Even Cæsar Augustus himself, as we find in the chronicles, was, quite apart from his idolatry, a gross libertine. For it was his habit to lie abed every day amid twelve girls and catamites. {82} Shame, therefore, on the partisans of that baneful doctrine, who, like the blind following the blind, are led astray by this from the light of truth to fall into the depths! {83} And spurning their error, let them return to the right path by which they may find true blessedness.

{84} The fifth case [*Mon.* 2:9], he argues as follows: those things that are acquired in war are acquired justly[68]; the Romans acquired the empire in war; ergo, they acquired it justly. {85} He gives proof of his major premise: inasmuch as divine judgment is made manifest by war, whatever is acquired by it is said to be acquired justly. {86} Even at first glance this reasoning is seen to be immoral in anyone's view, even in that of uncouth peasants, because many wage unjust wars through which, even if they win, they acquire nothing justly. {87} Ergo, this fellow ought to have distinguished between just and unjust wars and to have given proof that the Romans always waged just wars. {88} For if he intends to prove that divine judgment manifests itself in war,[69] it follows that no victory is unjust; and given this, although the Roman republic was very often exhausted and nearly annihilated by war, as their own historians and others have recorded, all was done justly. {89} And had their own rebels been justly victorious, the Romans themselves would have been justly conquered and would have justly become slaves of others. {90} Futhermore, according to the blessed Augustine, in his book *Against Faustus* [22:74],[70] there are five crimes in war which are legally punishable: to wit, "a craving to harm, cruelty in revenge, unappeased and implacable rancor, savageness in rebellion, lust for domination, and such like." {91} All these, and many more, are truly and justly punishable in the case of the wars of the Romans. {92} In addition, as the blessed Isidore says, according to the law of nature, there is one liberty for all men,[71] and the *Decretals* have it thus in Distinction 1, chapter [7], "The Law of Nature."[72] {93} Ergo, the Romans, in their desire to subjugate other nations, acted against the law of nature.

{94} In the sixth place [*Mon.* 2:10], he says that Christ approved of Cæsar's empire when he chose to be born under that edict of which Luke [2:1] says: "There went out a decree from Cæsar Augustus, that the whole world should be enrolled."

{95} According to this reasoning, it follows that the devil acted justly in tempting Christ, Judas in betraying him, the Jews by their tongues in crucifying him, the soldiers in scourging him, and Pilate in condemning him to death. {96} For Christ decided to place himself under the power of all these people, "He was offered because it was his own will" [Is 53:7]. {97} Despite all that, he did not condone their wickedness. {98} Ergo, he did not approve of that edict, since two vices, of course, avarice and vainglory, drove Cæsar to proclaim it.

{99} In the seventh place [*Mon.* 2:11], he states his case as follows: if the Roman Empire did not exist *de jure*, Adam's sin was not punished in Christ. This, however, is false. {100} He tries to prove the conclusion of his major premise thus: no sin may be punished except by the sentence of a judge, for if someone deserving of punishment suffers through a private individual, it cannot be said that that person was duly punished, but that he suffered injustice; ergo, Pilate, who put Christ to death by the authority of the Roman emperor, was a judge *de jure* [*Mon.* 2:11:2–3].

{101} Here the wretch[73] reached the heights of his delirium: as he raised his mouth to heaven, his tongue lolled along the ground. {102} Who ever made such a disgraceful error as to say that the punishment due for original sin lay in the power of any earthly judge? {103} Otherwise, any earthly judge could summarily punish a newborn child with death because corporal death, for such a sin is deservedly inflicted upon men by divine ordinance, as the Apostle says to the Hebrews 9[:27]: "It is appointed unto men once to die." {104} Adam's sin, however, forasmuch as it persists in the human race, is nought but original sin. {105} No human lawgiver ever ordained anything about this in his laws, nor did the heathen even know of this sin, nor did Pilate sit in judgment upon Christ on this account. {106} But for this reason: that there might be full satisfaction for that sin to God on behalf of all mankind, it was sufficient that Christ, very God and true man, for the preservation of justice, be obedient to God the Father "unto death, even to the death on the cross" [Phil 2:8]. {107} This the blessed Anselm proves more than sufficiently in the first book of his *Why God Was Made Man* [1:9].[74] {108} Christ had, moreover, always observed this obedience, and he would have still observed it, even if he had been condemned to death by anyone other than a judge. {109} For if two or more private individuals compelled a Christian to deny Christ, and this man persisted in the confession of his faith and met death steadfastly at their hands, he would truly be declared a martyr by the Church and would be crowned by Christ as a martyr in heaven. {110} Thus, if the Lord Jesus Christ, who neither committed personal sin nor contracted original sin, and because of this, ought not to have been put to death for this through anyone other than a judge for the preservation of righteousness (which he was bound had to observe out of obedience), a death by which he honored and glorified God the Father, would he have redeemed all men, and expiated the sin of all mankind? {111} For that obedience, that life that he voluntarily offered to his Father in obedience, and that death that he suffered for his Father's honor found such pleasing acceptance in the godhead that God accounted himself fully satisfied for the iniquity of all mankind. {112} And for this reason all those who believe in Christ and are configured to his death through baptism, according to the Catholic faith [Rom 6:4–5; Phil 3:10], are believed to have satisfied God. {113} Or it might be better to say that Christ gave satisfaction for all men, as the blessed Anselm proves and declares in the second book of his *Why God Was Made Man* [2]:13 and in those following.[75] {114} And that which is said above in the aforementioned useless argument—that, if Pilate had not been judge *de jure*, Christ's death would not have been the penalty for sin—is false, as has already been demonstrated. {115} And that which is tacitly or covertly implied, that in as much as he was a judge his actions were not an injustice, is utterly false, because the supreme injustice was inflicted upon Christ. {114} Wherefore, Augustine in his book *On True Religion*, chapter 29, speaking of Christ's condemnation by Pilate, says: "What greater injustice than that a just and innocent man be condemned?"[76]

{115} That useless and ludicrous argument was not worthy of the present response, but I have recorded it for the benefit of my readers.


## (BOOK 3)

{1} In the third part of his treatise, this fellow strives first to rebut some reasons that have been adduced for the ascertainment of truth [*Mon.* 3:4]; and as far as the first two arguments are concerned, I affirm and concede that they are not necessarily conclusive. {2} For to say that the two great lights signify two governing powers constitutes a mystical or metaphorical exposition; this type of theologizing, however, is not an adducing of proof, as the blessed Dionysius says in his book *On Mystic Theology* [1:1].[77] {3} The fellow, however, does seem to rave on a good deal in rebutting this argument. {4} Indeed, he proceeds as follows: these two governing powers are accidents [*Mon.* 3:4:13]; ergo, they were not instituted before the creation of man, otherwise the accident would have existed when the subject did not; for the lights were created on the fourth day, while man was indeed created on the sixth.

{5} But one must say in reply to this that these two governing powers did precede the creation and multiplying of mankind according to divine providence in which all things have their being before they are created. {6} They preceded, rather, through these two lights as in a figure, according to what the Apostle says in 1 Corinthians 10:11: "Now all these things happened to them in a figure." {7} By the same reasoning, he says in 1 Corinthians 10:4, "And the rock was Christ," and the two sons of Abraham, that is, Isaac and Ishmael, "are the two testaments," Galatians 4:24. {8} Ergo, these two governing powers were figured in the two lights, even though they had not been instituted among men.

{9} Further on he says that they had been instituted because of the infirmity of sin [*Mon.* 3:4]; ergo, they could not have been instituted before sin. {10} But in reply to this, it can be said that even if sin did not exist there was nonetheless a disposition for it in mankind just as there was and is among the angels, in whom there neither was nor is any sin.

{11} Moreover, the example concerning the doctor and the patient that this fellow adduces is rather to be declared for our side of the argument, for a physician who foresees a future illness is no fool if he prepares medicine for it. {12} Wherefore, concerning this medicine of ours, that is, Christ's passion, Apocalypse 13:8 says that "all who adored the beast, are not written in the Book of the Lamb, which was slain from the beginning of the world."[78] {13} Here the *Glossa* says that this lamb was slain either according to divine providence, about which we have already spoken, or by way of a figure, for the sacrifice of Abel was a figure of the true sacrifice of Jesus Christ, and the very death of Abel was also a figure of Christ's own,[79] as Augustine says in *The City of God*, Book 20, chapter 8.[80] {14} Whence it can be said that Christ had been put to death from the beginning of the world, not in his own person but in a figure, or even that in the faith of Adam himself, Abel, and of the other faithful who believed that this Jesus Christ was to come and suffer death—he whom we firmly believe has already come, has died, and has risen from the dead for the salvation of mankind.

{15} About the argument taken from Levi and Judah [*Mon.* 3:5], I will not concern myself.

{16} The third argument [*Mon.* 3:6] was taken from 1 Kings, chapter 8, which I also used in our treatise *On Papal Power* because Samuel, who was a priest, set up Saul as king and deposed him.[81] To this, that fellow responds by saying that Samuel did this not as the vicar of God but as his nuncio. {17} Ergo, it does not follow that if a nuncio could do it, a vicar can as well. {18} It ought to have been enough for that fellow to pervert philosophy and he should have left Scripture unharmed in its true sense. {19} For according to the blessed Jerome, "The most iniquitous kind of teaching is to pervert the sense and twist the Scripture to its contrary meaning."[82] {20} This is what the fellow did when he said that the priest, Samuel, in setting up the king was God's nuncio, and that he did not do it by priestly authority. But from the very text of the Book of Kings this statement is at once revealed as false. {21} Indeed, 1 Kings 8:1 says: "And it came to pass when Samuel was old, that he appointed his sons to be judges over Israel," to wit, one in Bethlehem, and the other in Beersheba, as the *Glossa* there says.[83] {21} Observe that by the authority he possessed as ordinary judge, and not as some odd nuncio of God, he gave his sons authority and power in temporal things. {22} And it there follows in the same chapter [1 Kgs 8:3–5] that "his sons . . . turned aside after lucre, and took bribes, and perverted judgment. Then all the ancients of Israel being assembled, came to Samuel . . . and they said to him: Behold thou art old, and thy sons walk not in thy ways. Make us a king, to judge us, as all nations have." {23} These ancients therefore knew that Samuel possessed the power of bestowing upon them a leader in temporal things, otherwise so many wise men would not have demanded this of him. {24} But, because this was a novel and great thing and required the establishment of a new law, Samuel, therefore, consulted the Lord on this matter, whose vicar he was among the people. {25} Indeed, any wise and virtuous lawgiver ought to act thus; wherefore, in his book *On True Religion*, chapter 56, Augustine says: "The founder of temporal laws, if he is a good and wise man, consults eternal law, which no living soul is given to judge, so that according to its immutable rules, he may determine what should be commanded or forbidden in temporal things."[84] {26} Likewise, this fellow seems to say that a nuncio is not a vicar, and that a vicar is not a nuncio—an assertion, however, that is found to be false. {27} For the Apostles were nuncios sent by the Lord Jesus Christ, as he himself says in John [20:21]: "As the Father hath sent me, I also send you." {28} And yet they were ordinary judges, whose place bishops hold today in the Church, as Gratian's *Decretals*, Part 1, Distinction 21: "In the New Testament ..." has it.[85] {29} Thus, these legates of his are nuncios sent by him, and yet, they act as ordinaries and with the power of him who sent them. {30} On this account Christ used to say to his Apostles: "He that heareth you, heareth me; and he that despiseth you, despiseth me" [Lk 10:16]. {31} Ergo, it does not follow that, if Samuel sought God's counsel and will, it was because Samuel was only his nuncio and not his vicar, for he was God's ordinary judge in spiritual and temporal things until late in his old age, as is clear from the aforementioned Book of Kings.

{32} In the same way he says [*Mon.* 3:8] that the words of Christ "whatsoever thou shalt loose on earth" [Mt 16:19], and so on, may not be understood except in reference to those things subjected to the power of the keys; wherefore he adds that the pope cannot abolish the laws and decrees of the emperors.

{33} To this it is obvious that we must respond that the power of the keys follows priestly orders, and it is conferred at the same time as those orders upon the priest that he may use it in the tribunal of conscience in absolving the contrite sinner who confesses his sins, and in binding him to a satisfactory penance for them. {34} And this power was equally conferred upon Peter and the other apostles when, in John 20:22–23, Christ said to all of them: "Receive ye the Holy Ghost. Whose sins you shall forgive, they are forgiven them," and so on. {35} There is another power of jurisdiction, by which an ecclesiastical judge, acting in the outward tribunal, binds in the bond of excommunication and also absolves from it, or binds by condemnation and absolves the innocent by proclamation. {36} Moreover, Peter received this power from Christ together with the whole Church without any distinction, as in John 21:17, where it says: "Feed my sheep." {37} Here the *Glossa* says: "To feed His sheep is to comfort the believers in Christ (lest they be wanting in faith), to provide the subjects with earthly sustenance, if necessary, to apply examples of virtue through preaching the word, to withstand adversaries, and to discipline errant subjects."[86] {37} From this it is obvious that Christ gave Peter and Peter's successors the power of judicial discipline over all his sheep.[87] {38} Ergo, the pope may chastise the emperor, who is one among Christ's sheep. {39} Thus it is also determined by the councils that every Christian man is his subject and is to be disciplined by him. {40} And if he is incorrigible, not only is he to be excommunicated, but also to be deposed from every office and deprived of all dignity, because the power of the keys thus covers not only spiritual things but also temporal ones in both tribunals, hidden or outward, according to the transgression. {41} Whence the Church of God expels with justice not only heretics, but also schismatics and the contumacious altogether, deprives them of their goods, remands them up to the custody of collectors, and, except for capital punishment, may impose any penalty upon all those aforesaid.

{42} Indeed, to his statements about the laws and decrees of emperors, I reply that the emperor's law is derived from natural justice, either by way of necessary conclusion (in which case it cannot be abolished unless natural justice, which no man may ever abolish, is itself annulled), or it is derived by way of decision, and this type of justice certainly has no effect before it is instituted but is binding once it is established by a prince, and it may be changed and annulled either through contrary practice or through a certain rational cause.[88] {43} And even if, through a certain insight, the pope were to establish a decretal contrary to such justice, the papal statute holds sway, because the law says that the emperor's legislation is not to spurn consistency with sacred canons, as the *Corpus authenticorum* says.[89]

{44} Further on [*Mon.* 3:10] this fellow says that Emperor Constantine did not have the power to give up, as he did, Rome and other parts belonging to the empire. {45} This he proves as follows: no one is permitted to do through the office conferred upon him anything that is contrary to that office. {46} But it is against the conferred office of emperor to split the empire. {47} Had that donation made by Constantine been valid, the empire would have been left divided; indeed it could even have been annihilated, for just as he gave up one part, in the same way, he could have given up another, and another, and all the rest.

{48} First, I ask of this fellow: whose was the empire at that time? {49} He would reply, I believe, because of other things he said, that it belonged to the Roman people. {50} Ergo, the empire was entrusted to Constantine by the Roman people. {51} And if Constantine alone could not give it up, he himself, however, along with the whole people, the whole senate, and with all the provincial governors and all those to whom the empire belonged, did give it to the Church, and he had the power to give what he gave with justice, or, rather, he renounced those things that he possessed unjustly. {52} Indeed, according to the blessed Augustine, in his *Confessions*, whatsoever exists because of the true God is possessed unjustly once he is forsaken.[90] {53} Thus, the emperor himself, together with all the people, forsook the true God; and all that was due to the faith, all that was due to the worship of God, and all that they owed to the true God, they offered to the demons.

{54} To be sure, whatsoever he retained for himself the supreme pontiff, the Vicar of Jesus Christ, conceded to him so that the emperor himself might be the advocate and defender of the Church against heretics and schismatics, as it is said in the *Decretals*, Extra: Concerning Election: "Venerabilem."[91] {55} Nor would the empire either have been divided or annihilated as a result, since it would have remained whole and united under the vicar general of Jesus Christ, as is quite clear from what is said above.

{56} For, certainly, when he says that the Church cannot hold earthly possessions and did not have the power to accept them [*Mon.* 3:10], he speaks in ignorance, failing to understand either what he says or what he affirms. {57} For when Christ charged the apostles with the duty of preaching, he said to them: "Do not possess gold, nor silver, nor money in your purses" [Mt 10:9]. {58} And this he admonished them lest they preach for temporal goods. {59} Wherefore he prescribed: "Freely have you received, freely give" [Mt 10:8]. {60} And he immediately added the precept above. {61} I am therefore amazed that that presumptuous person failed to keep in mind that which holy martyrs, confessors, and especially the holy doctors, Augustine, Ambrose, and Gregory, held, maintained and increased the earthly wealth of their churches. {62} Nor would they have done this either against God or against conscience. {63} Whence, Prosper, in his book *On the Contemplative Life*,[92] says that the blessed Paulinus bequeathed his enormous property to the poor; but, once he was made bishop, did not disdain the wherewithal of the Church but distributed it most faithfully. {64} In doing this, he well demonstrated that one must disdain one's own property for the sake of one's own perfection and, thus, be able to possess the resources of the Church, which are truly common possessions without any impediment to one's perfection. {65} In the same way, Saint Hilarius, bishop of Arles, "not only possessed the goods that the Church held at that time, but also increased them by accepting numerous inheritances from the faithful. And thus if men, who were unambiguously well learned both in secular and divine Scriptures and had bequeathed their all, had known that the properties of the Church should be contemned, they ought never have accepted them." These things are found written in the *Decre-*

*tals*, 12 Question, 1 Expedit.[93] {66} On the same question, Augustine says likewise: "The Lord had a purse to hold the offerings of the faithful, which he used to distribute for the needs of his own and for other indigents. At that time he first distributed the established form of church property, so that we might understand that he taught us not to dwell upon the needs of the morrow; it was not for this purpose that the Saints should keep no wealth, but lest God be served on account of these offerings or lest justice be deserted on account of the fear of poverty."[94] {67} Therefore shame upon him who said that the Church of God may not hold earthly possessions!

{68} Further on [*Mon.* 3:13], he argues as follows: when there was as yet no Church, the empire existed, enjoyed its own power, and was confirmed by Christ's birth and by his death. Ergo, the empire does not depend upon the Church, because something prior cannot depend upon something that comes later. {69} As evidence for this argument, it must be known that we can speak of the Church in two ways, either concerning the institution or concerning its multiplication and manifestation. {70} In the first way, the Church of God is the same as the *City of God*; now the city of the devil may be also called a "church," as it is said in the Psalm [25:5]: "I have hated the church of the malignant."[95] {71} After the sin of demons and mankind, these two cities were always commingled in this world, and progressed apace, as Augustine says in *The City of God*, Book 11, chapter 1, and Book 18, chapter 1.[96] {72} These two cities came into existence at the beginning of the human race, that is, with Cain and Abel. Once the latter had died, Seth succeeded to his place instead. {73} And from then until now these two cities have progressed apace in this world, "though, until the revelation of the New Testament, the City of God ran its course not in light but in shadow," as Augustine says in *The City of God*, Book 18, chap. 1.[97] {74} And if we may speak of the Church of God in this way, the Roman Empire at no time existed nor had any power when the Church did not exist, because the Church has always existed.[98]

{75} In another way we may speak of the Church in respect to the time of the manifestation of the faith and of the multiplication of the faithful on this earthly sphere. {76} For the Church thus began with Christ and his apostles, as Christ said unto the blessed Peter who truly confessed his faith: "Upon this rock I will build my Church" [Mt 16:18]. {77} Thus there was no real empire before the Church; rather, all those who were called emperors were the worst of tyrants, as was fully stated above, and in our treatise *On Papal Power*.[99]

{78} Finally [*Mon.* 3:16], the fellow states the following: since man is of a dual nature, that is, corruptible and incorruptible, in the same way, he has a dual end. {79} One, which he attains through moral virtues acquired by human effort, is temporal happiness; the other, which he attains through the virtues infused by God (that is, faith, hope, and charity), is the blessedness of eternal life. {80} And to these two ends man is ordered directly by God: for his temporal happiness, man requires the emperor; for his eternal blessedness, he requires the supreme pontiff. Ergo, just as these ends are directly ordained by God, so likewise are those two princes, such that one does not depend upon the other.

{81} In refuting this argument, one must be fully aware that all that there is in man, except for his intellective part (on whose account he is made in the image of God), is wholly common both to us and to the beasts. {82} And by nature all else, save the vegetative power, which is common to us, to the plants, and to the trees, must be wholly subject to the power of the mind, and must obey it in all things. {83} The latter, in fact, on account of its imperfection, cannot participate in reason, and, therefore, neither happiness nor virtue may be found in it.

{84} In truth no virtue is acquired by the operation of the other powers of the soul, unless it is supplied by something superior to these powers, that is, by the intellect and the will, to which belongs the ordering of all things. {85} Thus, however, moral virtues are acquired, because by doing just deeds, men become just, and, by doing strenuous deeds, men become strong (as Aristotle says in his *Ethics* 2),[100] just as by frequent harp playing men become good harpists. {86} This virtue, so acquired, therefore, is not proper to the inferior powers that belong to that corruptible nature common both to us and to the beasts, for those powers are mere instruments of the will and reason, just as the art of harp playing is found neither in the hand nor in the harp but in the mind of the harpist (unless, perhaps, we may sometimes want to call a certain fine characteristic of the instrument inappropriately a "virtue"). {87} Ergo, according to full and proper reason, moral virtues are found in the will. {88} Ergo, that fellow should therefore not have distinguished a dual blessedness on account of our duplex nature—to wit, the corruptible and incorruptible—because neither virtue nor blessedness may be properly found in our corruptible part.

{89} He likewise affirms that man is ordered by God to these two ends [*Mon.* 3:16:5–10]. {89} To this I rejoin that man is not ordered by God to temporal blessedness as to an ultimate end because such blessedness was never able to limit or sate his appetite; but, even philosophically speaking, the operation of such virtues is ordered toward contemplative happiness, so that, to wit, through virtues man in his wisdom may contemplate eternal things more peacefully and freely, once his passions are calmed. {90} And, therefore, even Socrates was of the opinion that man should be urged to purify his life with good morals, so that the mind, delivered from the oppressing weight of lusts, might raise itself to eternal things with native vigor, as Augustine says in *The City of God*, Book 8, chapter 3.[101] {91} Ergo, man is ordered toward eternal happiness as his ultimate end; in order to attain this he ought to turn and direct all his natural, moral, and voluntary goods.

{92} The fellow also arrives at a false conclusion when he states that, if some things come directly from God, one thing does not depend upon another [*Mon.* 3:15]: for the soul and the body both come directly from God, and yet, the body depends upon the soul, for, once the soul departs, the body immediately expires and rots away, as Aristotle says in his *On the Soul*, Book 1.[102] {93} And many other instances are furnished in our afore-named treatise.[103] {94} Moreover, concerning those two powers, that is, the spiritual and the temporal, I stated in that treatise [*On Papal Power*] and now affirm, that, among the people of God, God himself ordained the temporal power through the power of his priests, and, as it was there proven at length, I do not press the case here.

{95} And I add that when the people of Israel begged Samuel to give them a king, it is seen that, according to the text of the Holy Scripture, that plea was displeasing to God. Wherefore the Lord said unto Samuel: "They have not rejected thee, but me, that I should not reign over them."[104] {96} It is seen that this was said to this end: that the law of God fully sufficed to rule that nation, of whose law the priest Samuel was minister, and according to this law he judged the people, for in those times God reigned indeed. {97} Wherefore when the people begged for a change in government, God deemed himself contemned and forsaken by them. {98} And despite the fact that he had set Saul up as king through the ministry of his priest, once he had enquired into Saul's sins, he cast Saul from his kingdom by means of this same Samuel.[105]

[EXPLICIT]
Here ends the treatise of Friar Guido Vernani of Rimini of the Order of Preachers on the
*Refutation of the False Monarchia Composed by Dante.*

# POPE JOHN XXII'S BULL,

## *Si fratrum*

### *A Warning Lest Anyone Dare to Assume the Title of Imperial Vicar When the Empire Is Left Vacant*[1]

{1} If we desire to preserve the rights of our Brothers and fellow Bishops, and our own, and the rights of any person whatsoever, to be inviolate and free from any danger of abridgment, and if we apply most freely our careful concern to this—more vigorously, indeed, for the conservation of the rights and honors of Our Bride the Roman Church—we are obliged to discharge the functions of the apostolic provision according to the obligation of our office imposed upon us, lest in our times these rights may suffer the violation of usurpation or incur the harm of any kind of disparagement.

{2} It has been brought fully to our notice and to that of our Brothers via widespread report, that, notwithstanding the fact that it has been upheld *de jure*, unbrokenly, and without interruption through the ages, that when the empire is left vacant (as it is thus now recognized to have been left vacant through the death of the late Henry, emperor of the Romans), since in this matter it is impossible to have recourse to secular judgment, the jurisdiction, government, and disposition[2] of the aforesaid empire devolve to the Supreme Pontiff—to whom, in the person of the Blessed Peter, God Himself committed the rights both of the Earthly and the Heavenly Empire, and this jurisdiction itself during the said vacancy of the empire is known to be exercised either by God himself, by another, or by others, as long as the empire can be remembered, {3} in spite of this, in parts of Italy, several of those of the highest level of power and dignity, unlawfully doing their utmost to cause harm to us and to our Mother, the Holy Roman Church, and to abridge honor and right, have presumed in their daring temerity, after the emperor's death and without seeking or obtaining our permission or that of the Apostolic See, to retain for themselves the title of vicar or of some other office that they used to hold in certain lands, territories and areas, from the emperor himself by personal appointment when he was alive; {4} and, several [have presumed] again to assume something which they did not hold, or had not held before, or to resume what they had held after dismissal; they have not so far feared to abuse this or those titles, and, not shrinking from being involved in various crimes and not dreading to offend Divine Majesty, under the pretext of this or those titles, they are known to be perpetrating and to have perpetrated many actions which have clearly redounded to our harm and that of the aforesaid Church.

{5} Inasmuch, therefore, as this error, which is meeting with no resistance, is spreading widely and is seen to be approved by those who are abandoning the Bosom [of the Church] who offers no resistance to their wicked efforts, since we wish in this case to protect our own rights and honors and those of Our Bride the Church, and to oppose at once the evils and scandals that have so far arisen from the retention, assumption, or resumption of such titles, and those which might perilously arise in their wake hereafter, and since we desire also to resist and remedy the perils to the soul posed by such retention, assumption, and resumption of such titles and from their abuses, {6} as we have set forth, by the authority of those present, we warn under penalty of excommunication all those singly and severally of whatever rank of preeminent dignity or status they may be—even if they glitter with patriarchal or whatever other superior or pontifical or royal dignity, or other whatsoever—who, after the empire is left vacant, and without our permission or that of the aforesaid See, have retained, have assumed, or have resumed and retain—and who, assume or resume, perchance, as imposters—the title of such vicariate or whatever other office, wherever, and, under cloak of such entitlement, have abused, are abusing, or even might abuse any power and jurisdiction whatsoever or its public or private exercise, {7} so that, as for the rest, they may also utterly abstain and totally desist from such entitlements or the assumption, resumption, and retention of the aforesaid titles, and also from the use of the power and from the exercise of the aforesaid; we moreover restrain under the aforesaid penalty all patriarchs and prelates, singly and severally, and others of higher and lower rank, and kings, cities, communities, societies, captains, *podestàs*,[3] rectors, counts, viscounts, barons, and all others of whatsoever rank or status of dignity they may be, from receiving or granting audiences to those who retain such aforesaid titles in the said empire, as we have set forth, {8} or those who assume or resume any title under such entitlement or claim, and [we restrain them from receiving or granting audiences to] their procurators, commissioners, judges, or their lieutenants, under any farfetched excuse whatever, and from either abetting or serving any vicars or vicar or officials of the empire, or from performing or permitting by such abetment or service, or in any way, or from lending aid, counsel, or favor to such person or persons in these matters.

{9} Furthermore, against all patriarchs, singly and severally, all prelates, both of high and low rank, kings and others, who retain, assume, or resume by reason of the aforesaid entitlement, as we have set forth, and exercise by any pretext whatever offices, powers, or jurisdictions, {10} and against those who receive them as vicars or officials of the empire or their commissioners as such, and against those who abet or obey them as such, or those who lend them counsel, aid, or favor in this matter, we promulgate from our Brothers in public council sentences of the interdict of excommunication against such individuals and against their territories, their lands, and against any community, society, city, or village—{11} unless within the space of two months to be counted from the present, dated from this day, they shall completely recover their senses, or shall show that they possess a license from the Apostolic See for this matter. {12} There shall be, nonetheless, graver proceedings against these, spiritually and temporally, according as their disobedience might require and the nature of their deed might sanction; and we shall see this carried out.

{13} And lest anyone seize the opportunity of abetting such a person, all those, singly and severally, who are held bound by an oath of fidelity to those retaining, assuming or resuming the title of such a vicariate, we hold firmly absolved from such an oath as far as this matter is concerned by the Plenitude of Our Power through our Apostolic Authority, lest such individuals might abet or serve vicars or officials of the empire in any way.

{14} And concerning all covenants, obligations, pledges, and pacts entered into by any one whatsoever in any way involving this, protected in any way by oath or force whatever, we totally dissolve, we void by our powers, we invalidate, and from whatever event they may issue, we revoke. And we sever all such and other oaths whatsoever sworn by anyone at all concerning these matters, and any which could be injurious to our aforementioned rights and those of the aforesaid Church, especially, since an oath must not be a bond of iniquity.

{15} As for the rest, so that these proceedings of ours may be brought to the common notice of all, we shall have papers and parchments containing the same proceedings hung or affixed to the doors or lintels of the Church of Avignon that shall publish these same proceedings as if by its loud proclamation and open[4] judicial investigation—in order that in this way all those whom, singly and severally, these proceedings concern and may concern, may not hereafter claim any excuse that such proceedings failed to reach them, or that they might be ignorant of the same, since by this means they are unlikely to remain unknown or hidden to them, in that they are clearly made public to all.

{16} Given at Avignon at the Episcopal Residence, the second kalends of April in the first year.[5]

# Notes

1. All the extant MSS and the *editio princeps* attest to the title *Monarchia*, or *Liber Monarchiæ*. The form "De Monarchia" is an editorial invention. Dante makes clear what he means by "monarch" in 1:5:9: "Now, it is agreed that the entire human race is ordered to one goal, as has already been demonstrated; ergo, there has to be one individual to rule or reign, and he must be called 'monarch' or 'emperor.'" And in ch. 2:1 he gives his definition of temporal monarchy, "which is called empire," as "the one single principality placed over all men in time, or among and over those things that are measured by time." Dante transferred from Can Grande's Verona to Ravenna sometime in 1318; I believe it is most probable that the *Mon.* saw completion at the court of Guido Novello, and for several months it may have siphoned off energy from the poet's final touches to the *Paradiso*. N. Zingarelli dated the treatise between 1317 and 1318 in "La vita, i tempi e le opere di Dante," *Storia letteraria d'Italia* 3 (1931): 679–710. All recent editors—Imbach and Flüeler, Pizzica, Shaw, and Kay—have followed Pier Giorgio Ricci's determination of 1318 in his 1965 edition. In 1976, Michele Maccarrone, in his "Papato e impero nella *Monarchia*," *Nuove letture dantesche* 8 (1976): 332, also ceded to Ricci's assignment. Presenting no new research, and merely asserting old claims, Carlo Dolcini's dating of the *Monarchia* close to Henry VII's coronation was wholly unconvincing. He simply asserted that "Dante's confession belongs to a single period: 1312–1313" ("Dante Alighieri e la *Monarchia*," in *Crisi di poteri e politologia in crisi da Sinibaldo Fieschi a Guglielmo d'Ockham* [Bologna: Pàtron, 1988], p. 428). Failing to understand the concept of the "two last ends of man" outlined in St. Thomas Aquinas and in Dante's treatise, and merely dismissing the proofs in the MS tradition, J. F. Took likewise retreats to an earlier dating in *Dante: Lyric Poet and Philosopher: An Introduction to the Minor Works* (Oxford, U.K.: Clarendon Press, 1990), pp. 149–151. Maurizio Palma di Cesnola argues unpersuasively for a return to 1314 in his *Semiotica dantesca: profetismo e diacronica* (Ravenna: Longo, 1995), pp. 100–103. Among many recent writers, Stephen Bemrose, in *A New Life of Dante* (Exeter, U.K.: University of Exeter Press, 2000), p. 199, concurs with the 1318 date, but, as with many, the historian's closer association of the treatise with Henry VII's earlier invasion of Italy for coronation still persists; see p. xx, et passim. On the date of composition, see also Friedrich Schneider, "Neue Deutungen und Datierungen [Die Entwicklung des

jungen Dante zu seiner künstlerischen und wissenschaftlichen Reife (B. Nardi); Zur Entstehungszeit der *Monarchia* (M. Maccarrone, B. Nardi, P. R[G.]. Ricci u. a.)]," *Deutsches Dante-Jahrbuch* 36–37 (1958): 158–219; Emilia Mongiello, "Sulla datazione della *Monarchia* di Dante," *Le parole e le idee: Rivista internazionale di varia cultura* 11, nos. 43–44 (1969 [1971]): 290–324; Giovanni Di Giannatale, "Per una prospettiva della *Monarchia* di Dante: Appunti e problemi," *Ævum* 52, no. 2 (1978): 218–227, esp. 226; and Giorgio Padoan, *"Alia utilia reipublice,'* la composizione della *Monarchia* di Dante," *Letture classensi* 28 (1999): 7–27 (cited henceforth as "La composizione della *Monarchia*").

2. After Emperor Henry VII's death in 1313, in his famous bull *Pastoralis cura,* Clement V had extended the doctrine evolved by Innocent IV and Hostiensis, *"vacante imperio papa est verus imperator"* (when the empire is vacant, the pope is true emperor), to again assert the superiority of the papacy over the empire by claiming the right to appoint imperial vicars in times of such vacancy. He then nominated Robert III, "the Wise," of Naples as imperial vicar of Italy. In the election of 1314, during the vacancy of the papacy, six months after the death of Pope Clement V, Ludwig IV of Bavaria was one of two candidates ambiguously elected and crowned king of the Germans. After threats of a schism in the Church, Jacques de Duèse or Deuse of Cahors was elected Pope John XXII on August 7, 1316, and consecrated on September 5; he reasserted his own possession of imperial power almost as the first gesture of his papacy. John, who reigned till 1334, and his successors, Benedict XII and Clement VI, refused to recognize Ludwig under any circumstances. The emperor, who, despite all opposition, declared his own election legitimate and sufficient to make him emperor again at the Diet of Frankfurt in 1338, died in 1347. The split election of Ludwig as king of the Romans became, as we will see, the cause célèbre of the first half of the fourteenth century—it appears as such in *Mon.* 3:16. The identity and rights of the German electors were to be formally set by Charles IV's Golden Bull of 1356 to prevent a repetition of the 1314 débâcle. See Guillaume Mollat, *The Popes at Avignon, 1305–1387,* trans. Janet Love (London/Edinburgh/Paris/New York: Thomas Nelson, 1963), pp. 96–98, 206; and Luigi Salvatorelli, *L'Italia communale dal secolo XI alla metà del secolo XIV,* Storia d'Italia 4 (Milan: Mondadori, 1940), p. 792.

3. Decretals, bulls, or papal letters and decrees on various subjects were referred to by the first words of the text. See below, pp. 198–202, for the English translation of the celebrated decree *Si fratrum,* entitled also *In nostra et fratrum,* issued on March 31, 1317, with the rubric *"Monitio quod vacante imperio nemo vicarii imperatoris nomen assumat."* By this letter John formally announced that the imperial throne was empty and claimed his right to administer it. See the critical edition by Jacqueline Tarrant, ed., *Extravagantes Iohannis XXII,* Monumenta Iuris Canonici, Series B: Corpus Collectionum, vol. 6. (Vatican City: Biblioteca Apostolica Vaticana, 1983), pp. 156–162; see also the version in *Extravagantes Iohannis XXII,* Titulus V (*CIC,* 2:1211–1212). On the theory that led up to *Si fratrum,* see Michael Wilks's careful, informative, and entertaining chapter "Papa est verus imperator," in *The Problem of Sovereignty in the Later Middle Ages: The Papal Monarchy with Augustinus Triumphus and the Publicists* (Cam-

bridge, U.K.: Cambridge University Press, 1963), pp. 254–287. Carlo Dolcini carefully evaluates the contributions of the Carlyles, Wilks, Firpo, Ullmann, E. H. Kantorowicz, Charles T. Davis, and others, and gives an exhaustive bibliography of the historiography in the "Prolegomeni" to his *Crisi di poteri* (1988), pp. 9–117. The anonymous *Summa parisiensis* (here C. 2, q. 6) is edited by T. P. McLaughlin (Toronto: Pontifical Institute of Mediæval Studies, 1952), p. 108. Friedrich Baethgen describes John XXII's interference in imperial matters in "Der Anspruch des Papsttums auf das Reichsvikariat: Untersuchung zur Theorie und Praxis der *potestas indirecta in temporalibus*," *Zeitschrift der Savigny-Stiftung für Rechtsgeschichte, Kanonistische Abteilung X*, vol. 41, pt. 3 (Weimar: Hermann Böhlaus Nachfolger, 1920), pp. 168–286, esp. pp. 247–263, and in his important "Die Entstehungszeit von Dantes Monarchia," in *Sitzungsberichte der Bayerische Akademie der Wissenschaften, Philosophisch-historische Klasse* (Munich: Jahrgang, 1966), 5:30–34. Mollat recounts the exploitation John XXII made of his declaration of the empire's vacancy and his use of *Si fratrum*, in *The Popes at Avignon*, p. 80, et passim. P. G. Ricci asserted in 1967 that "[t]he *Monarchia* was considered, rather, as a providential demonstration that the imperial vicars were legitimately such because they had been named by a legitimate sovereign [Henry VII]. In this sense, the *Monarchia*, woven from arguments that were prevalently philosophical and theological, integrated what the other treatises, composed by experts in law, were striving to show by another route, within the confines of civil and canon law" ("La *Monarchia* dantesca e l'idea dell'Impero nella sua realtà giuridica e politica al tempo di Dante," in *Il processo di Dante [Celebrato il 16 aprile 1966 nella Basilica di S. Francesco in Arezzo]*, ed. Dante Ricci [Florence: Edizioni Arnaud, 1967], pp. 67–71, my translation, here, p. 70). Ruedi Imbach (in "Einleitung: Dante und die Philosophie," in *Monarchia: Lateinisch-Deutsch Studienausgabe*, ed. Ruedi Imbach and Christoph Flüeler [Stuttgart: Philipp Reclam, 1989], p. 24) also ascribes the genesis of the *Mon.* to Pope John XXII's attempt to deprive Can Grande of his imperial vicarship. See also Richard Kay's "Introduction" to his edition of the *Mon.*, pp. xxvi–xxviii; and Joan M. Ferrante's chapter "Political Theory and Controversy," in *The Political Vision of the "Divine Comedy"* (Princeton, N.J.: Princeton University Press, 1984), pp. 3–43. According to Arrigo Solmi, Can Grande is vicar of the emperor as the emperor too is vicar of Christ: we can wonder (in desperation) whether the DXV of *Purg.* 33:43, "*un cinquecento diece e cinque*," could indeed be interpreted as "I.D.X.V. = I[mperator] D[omini] C[hristi] V[icarius]"; see Arrigo Solmi, *Il pensiero politico di Dante* (Florence: La voce, 1922), p. 98.

4. John XXII, welding the sword to his crosier, appointed King Robert, "the Wise," who was a feudal vassal of the Church, as imperial vicar. See Giorgio Padoan, "Il Vicariato Cesareo dello Scaligero: Per la datazione dell'*Epistola a Cangrande*," *Lettere italiane* 50, no. 2 (1998): 161–175, esp. pp. 164–166, and "La composizione della *Monarchia*," pp. 7–27. By swearing fealty to Ludwig's rival, Frederick of Austria, Can Grande independently obtained a renewal of his vicariate on March 16, 1317, two weeks before the promulgation of *Si fratrum*. He continued to use the titles "sacri Imperii Vicarius" and "Vicarius per sacrum Imperium" in official documents and all political affairs. The reconfirmation is

206 / Notes to Chapter 1

found in *MGH, Constitutiones*, vol. 6, pt. 1, p. 339; cited by Padoan, p. 166. Can Grande della Scala of Verona was, however, to die as vice-emperor to Ludwig and prince of the empire on July 22, 1329.

5. On April 6, 1318, John XXII had declared the expiration of Can Grande's office, had warned him of excommunication, and had ordered him to present himself in Avignon; Can Grande was by then head of the Ghibelline league. The excommunication was repeated on June 18, 1320, for his having maintained his title; Can Grande's break with Frederick of Austria also became public knowledge in May–June 1320 (Padoan, "Il Vicariato Cesareo," pp. 167–168, 171, 174). On Guelphs and Ghibellines, see John Koenig's entry in the *Dictionary of the Middle Ages*, ed. Joseph P. Strayer (New York: Charles Scribner's Sons, 1989), 6:6–7, with useful bibliography. On Cardinal Bertrand du Poujet, see Giovanni Tabacco, *La casa di Francia nell'azione politica di Papa Giovanni XXII*, Istituto Storico per il Medio Evo, Studi storici, nos. 1–4 (Rome: Istituto Storico per il Medio Evo, 1953), pp. 192, 200, 206, 271, 283–287, et passim.

6. Dante speaks long of their friendship and describes himself as having "vigor of intellect and reason" in common with the great leader in *Epistola* 10 (13), the *Letter to Can Grande*, para. 2, et passim; see *Dantis Alagherii Epistolæ: The Letters of Dante*, 2nd ed., ed. Paget Toynbee, rev. Colin Hardie (Oxford, U.K.: Clarendon Press, 1966), pp. 169, 197; and *Epistole*, ed. Arsenio Frugoni and Giorgio Brugnoli, in Dante Alighieri, *Opere minori* (Milan/Naples: Riccardo Ricciardi, 1979), 2:604–605.

7. Dante had witnessed the punishment of heretics and tells us in *Purg.* 27:17–18 that he knew firsthand the smell of roasting human flesh. Niccolò Ottokar publishes the original order for the heretical Farinata degli Uberti's posthumous public cremation (see *Inf.* 9–10) in Florence in 1283: his bones and those of his wife, Adaleta, were to be "exhumed and burned in public view," as the accustomed sentence ran, "if they could be distinguished from those of the faithful." All his chattel and property were forfeit. See "Intorno a Farinata e alla sua famiglia," *Archivio storico italiano* 2 (1919): 159–163; rpt. in *Studi comunali e fiorentini* (Florence: La Nuova Italia, 1948), esp. p. 118.

8. Nevio Matteini, *Il più antico oppositore politico di Dante: Guido Vernani da Rimini: Testo Critico del "De Reprobatione Monarchiæ,"* Il Pensiero medievale collana di Storia della Filosofia, ser. 1, vol. 6 (Padua: CEDAM-Casa Editrice Dott. Antonio Milani, 1958).

## NOTES TO CHAPTER 1: TIARA AND SCEPTER

1. In the Proem to his political-theological tract *On Royal and Papal Power*, John Quidort of Paris had complained in 1302 of "the opinion of *certain modern thinkers* . . . that the lord Pope, inasmuch as he stands in the place of Christ on earth, has dominion, cognizance and jurisdiction over the temporal goods of princes and barons." See *Tractatus de potestate regia et papale*, ed. J. Leclerq, in *L'ecclésiologie du XIIIe siècle* (Paris: J. Vrin, 1942), p. 174, ll. 4–8; or see Arthur P. Monahan's translation, *On Royal and Papal Power: A Translation, with Introduction,*

*of the De Postestate Regia et papali of John of Paris,* The Records of Civilization: Sources and Studies 90 (New York/London: Columbia University Press, 1974), p. 2 , whose version follows the original faithfully at this point. Watt's version, *On Royal and Papal Power,* trans. with intro. by J. A. Watt. (Toronto: Pontifical Institute of Mediæval Studies, 1971), is, unfortunately, not literal at this point (p. 71). Also see James Heft, *John XXII and Papal Teaching Authority,* Texts and Studies in Religion 27 (Lewiston/Queenston/ Lampeter: Edwin Mellen Press, 1986).

2. The excessively Gelasian *Authenticum* (as Vernani recognized, and cited it in his *Ref.* 3:43) was the part of civil-criminal law that appeared most concessive to Church laws. Walter Ullmann cites the text and describes the effects of *Authenticum, Collatio* I, titulus 6, *Præfatio:* "They proceed from one and the same principle and adorn human life." And again, "Indeed the greatest gifts of God among men conferred by his supreme mercy: the priestly and imperial powers [*sacerdotium et imperium*], the former administered by divine, the latter presided over by human agency" (in *The Medieval Idea of Law as Represented by Lucas de Penna: A Study in Fourteenth-Century Legal Scholarship,* intro. by Harold Dexter Hazeltine [London: Methuen, 1946; New York: Barnes & Noble, 1969], pp. 172–173, n. 2; my translation). Cf. *Novellæ* 83, 1, in *Corpus Iuris Civilis,* ed. Rudolf Schoell and Wilhelm Kroll (Berlin: Weidmann, 1899), 3:410. Dante can hardly be accused of being a dreaming idealist: as the papacy radically waned in its effective political power as the century proceeded, fourteenth-century civil jurists in the generation after the poet, such as Bartolomeo da Capua and Luca da Penna (b. ca. 1320), not going to the extremes of Marsiglio of Padua, insisted on a radical dualism and reaffirmed the independence of rulers from the pope: "God himself deputized the governance of human affairs"; "The powers [of the monarch] do not depend upon the pope" (pp. 170–173). On the opposite, utopian idea in Dante and its influence, see Christoph Miething, "Politeia und Utopia: Zur Epistemologie der literarischen Utopie," *Germanisch-Romanische Monatschrift* 37, no. 3 (1987): 247–263. See also Pier Giorgio Ricci, "L'ultima fase del pensiero politico di Dante e Cangrande vicario imperiale," in *Dante e la cultura veneta: Atti del Convegno di Studi organizzato dalla Fondazione "Giorgio Cini" in collaborazione con l'Istituto universitario di Venezia, l'Università di Padova, il Centro scaligero di Studi Danteschi, e i Comuni di Venezia, Padova, Verona. Venezia, Padova, Verona, 30 marzo–5 aprile 1966* (Florence: Olschki, 1966), pp. 367–371.

3. Walter Ullmann ascertained that the learned and careful head of the Augustinian order (after 1292), Giles of Rome, passed over Pope Nicholas I's idea of separation in total silence in his *De ecclesiatica potestate* of 1302, supporting more Gregorian and Bonifacian theories. Ullmann noted that Henry of Cremona, writing his *De potestate papæ* to correct those who denied that the pope had jurisdiction in all the world in temporal matters, also spurned Nicholas's niceties; according to Henry, that pope had spoken merely rhetorically and out of "humility of mind" *(causa humilitatis hoc dicit).* This is an extraordinary assertion on Henry's part, given that pope's notoriously autocratic personality. See *The Medieval Idea of Law,* p. 171, n. 3; see also R. W. Carlyle and A. J. Carlyle, *Mediæval Political Theory in the*

*West*, 6 vols. (Edinburgh, U.K.: William Blackwood, 1903–1936; rpt. 1950), here, 5:398–399. William of Ockham, like most of the imperialist Franciscans involved with disputes with John XXII, was aware that Nicolas I had asserted in his bull *Cum ad verum* 96 that "[s]ince the [world] has come to the truth, no longer has the emperor seized for himself the rights of the pontificate, nor has the pontiff usurped the name of emperor. For the same mediator between God and men, the man Jesus Christ, distinguished the duties of both powers by their own acts and distinct offices" (*Opus nonaginta dierum*, cap. 93; *The Work of Ninety Days*, in *A Letter to the Friars Minor and Other Writings*, ed. Arthur Stephen McGrade and John Kilcullen, trans. John Kilcullen [Cambridge, U.K.: Cambridge University Press, 1995], p. 93). Remigio de' Girolami refers not to Nicholas I, but more likely, as Monsignor Tamburini indicates, to Nicholas II, in the hierocratic version he gives of St. Peter's commissioning in *Contra falsos professores ecclesie*, ed. Filippo Tamburini, preface by Charles T. Davis (Rome: Libreria Editrice della Pontificia Università Lateranense, 1981), p. 70.

4. *Quellen zur Geschichte des papsttums und des römsichen Katholozismus*, ed. Carl Mirbt, 5th ed. (Tübingen: Mohr, 1934), pp. 197–198. Walter Ullmann traces the Melchisedech tradition in "Frederick II's Opponent, Innocent IV, as Melchisedek," *Atti del Convegno internazionale di Studi Federiciani* (Dicembre 1950), Palermo, 1952; rpt. in *Law and Jurisdiction in the Middle Ages*, ed. George Garnett (London: Variorum Reprints, 1988), essay 5, pp. 53–81, esp. p. 55.

5. *"Eius vicarius qui est sacerdos in æternum secundum ordinem Melchisedech, constitutus a Deo iudex vivorum et mortuorum"* ("His Vicar, who is priest through eternity according to the order of Melchisedech, constituted by God, judge of the living and the dead"); see *Per venerabilem*, in *Decretales* 4:17:13, *CIC*, ed. Richter and Friedberg, 2:716. "Melchisedech" signifies *"rex iustitiæ,"* "king of justice." On the royalty of Christ and the pope, see F. Quarta, "Regalità di Cristo e del Papa in Innocenzo III," *Angelicum* 19 (1942): 227–288; Jean Leclerq, *Jean de Paris et l'ecclésiologie du XIIIe siècle* (Paris: J. Vrin, 1942), esp. 45–48, and *L'idée de la royauté du Christ au moyen âge* (Paris: Éditions du Cerf, 1959); and G. Martini, *"Regale sacerdotium,"Archivio della Società Romana di Storia Patria* 4 (1938): 1–166. See also Carlyle and Carlyle, 1:184–185; Michele Maccarrone, *Chiesa e stato nella dottrina politica di papa Innocenzo III* (Rome: Facultas Theologica Pontificii Athenæi Lateranensis, 1940), p. 48; and Marguerite Boulet-Sautel, "Encore sur la Bulle *Per venerabilem,"* in *Collecteana Stephan Kuttner* 3, in *Studia Gratiana* 13 (1967): 371–382. The Melchisedech imagery of king and priest (from Gn 14:18; Ps 109:4 [110:4]; Heb 5:6, 5:10, 6:20, 7:1, 7:10, 7:11,7:15, and 7:17) gained universal currency through the *Glossa Ordinaria* and through the popularity of such writings as Peter Lombard's *Collectanea* (*PL* 192:448) and Peter Comestor's *Historia scholastica* (*PL* 198:1094). Most important, St. Bernard used the comparison of the king-priests' position to the papal office in his book of advice *De consideratione* 2:15 ("in orders you are Melchisedech"), dedicated to Pope Eugenius III (*PL* 182: 751); see *Five Books on Consideration*, trans. John D. Anderson and Elizabeth T. Keenan, Cistercian Fathers Series 37 (Kalamazoo, Mich.: Cistercian Publications, 1976), p. 66. Innocent III adopted it together with Mt 16:18 to broaden his claims in *Per venerabilem;* cf. his letter to the bishop of Fermo: "Because the Roman pontiff . . . in the

order of Melchisedech, . . . not only holds the supreme power in spiritual affairs, but in fact even in temporal affairs he holds great power from the same lord" (*PL* 215:767); and his sermon for St. Silvester's Day (*PL* 217:481). Canonists stressed Mt 16:18, *"Tibi dabo claves regni cælorum"* (I give you the keys of the heaven) because it stressed the singular gift to Peter, but into, and beyond, the reign of John XXII, they generally ignored the passages in Mt 18:18 that gave jurisdiction to all the Apostles. The Melchisedech formula is found in the excoriating encyclical letter drafted for Innocent IV, *Eger cui lenia* (sometimes entitled "Eger cui levia" with no change of meaning), of 1245–1246; see the study and documents in Brian Tierney, *The Crisis of Church and State 1050–1300, with Selected Documents* (Englewood Cliffs, N.J.: Prentice-Hall, 1964; rpt. Toronto/Buffalo/London: University of Toronto Press/Medieval Academy of America, 1988, 1992), pp. 136–138, translated text, pp.147–149; also see Peter Herde, "Ein Pamphlet der päpstlichen Kurie gegen Kaiser Friedrich II. von 1245/46 [*Eger cui lenia*]," *Deutsches Archiv für Erforschung des Mittelalters* 23 (1967): 468–538; and Carlo Dolcini, *"Eger cui lenia* (1245/46): Innocenzo IV, Tolomeo da Lucca e Guglielmo d'Ockham," *Rivista di Soria della Chiesa in Italia* 29 (1975): 127–148, rpt. in his *Crisi di poteri,* pp. 119–146. According to the hierocrats, the (so-called) Donation of Constantine, whatever it also entailed, had only been Constantine's *recognition* of Christ's kingly powers, obviously including all those temporal, conferred on Peter "after the order of Melchesidech"; cf. Innocent III's *Epistle* 103, in *Innocentii III PP, Registorum Lib. XVI, Epistula CXXXI* (*PL* 216:923), and his sermon on the Feast of St. Silvester, *Sermo VII In Festo D. Silvestris* (*PL* 217:4810). See Brian Tierney, "The Continuity of Papal Political Theory in the Thirteenth Century," *Mediæval Studies* 27 (1965): 241–242. Closer to Dante's circle, Tolomeo da Lucca, the communal-republican high papalist, saw the Church itself as a monarchy *(monarchia)*—the most perfect form of government—and a kingdom *(regnum),* and he absorbs St. Thomas Aquinas's statement that Christ is "not priest alone but also king"; the pope is now *"vicarius Christi"* in his stead; see Tolomeo's completion of St. Thomas's treatise *De regimine principum ad regem Cypri* (esp. 1:15:9–10), translated as *On the Government of Rulers: De regimine principum: Ptolemy of Lucca with Portions Attributed to Thomas Aquinas,* by James M. Blythe (Philadelphia: University of Pennsylvania Press, 1997), esp. p. 100; Blythe's comments on Tolomeo's use of the term "regal" are especially valuable (pp. 28–29). Cf. Giles of Rome, *De ecclesiastica potestate* 3:5–8 (*On Ecclesiastical Power: The "De Ecclesiastica Potestate" of Ægidius Romanus,* trans. with intro. and notes by Robert W. Dyson [Woodbridge, Suffolk, U.K.: Boydell Press, 1986], pp. 11, 14, 17, 148–149, 164), who is followed by James of Viterbo, *On Christian Government (De regimine christiano),* ed., trans., and intro. by R. W. Dyson (Woodbridge, Suffolk, U.K.: Boydell Press, 1995), pp. 62, 118–119. Tolomeo, in his *Determinatio compendiosa (Short Determination),* cites the forged *Constitum Constantini* to the effect that, after Constantine moved east, the pope and the cardinals took the place of the consuls and senate; see the *Determinatio compendiosa de iurisdictione imperii* 29–31, ed. Marius Krammer (Hannover/Leipzig: Hahn, 1909), pp. 59–64; and G. Martini, "Regale sacerdotium," *Archivio della reale Deputazione romana di Soria patria,* n.s., 4, no. 6 (1938): 1–166. Also see W. H. V. Reade, "Political Theory to ca. 1300," *Cambridge Medieval History* (Cambridge, U.K.: Cambridge University Press, 1929), 6:629–632; and Otto Gierke, *Political Theories of the Middle Ages*, trans. with an intro. by Frederic William Maitland (Cambridge, U.K : Cambridge University Press, 1900), pp. 106–107. See Wilks's informative *"Vicarius Christi,"* in *The Problem of Sovereignty*, pp. 331–410. Michele Maccarrone dealt with the question extensively in his studies; see esp. *Vicarius Christi: Storia del titolo papale*, Lateranum, n.s., 18, nos. 1–4 (Rome: Facultas Theologica Pontificii Athenæi Lateranensis, 1952).

6. Maccarrone saw Dante's position as akin to that of Siger of Brabant, who "syllogized invidious truths" (*Par.* 10:136–138); see "Papato e impero nella *Monarchia*," *Nuove letture dantesche* 8 (1976): 261.

7. See Aldo Vallone, *Antidantismo politico nel XIV secolo: Primi contributi* (Naples: Liguori, 1973), and his *Antidantismo politico e dantismo letterario* (Rome: Bonacci, 1988).

8. As we might expect, Dante's citations of Christ's protestations were much the concern of nineteenth-century liberal scholars. See Francesco Lanzani, *La Monarchia di Dante: Studi storici* (Milan: Tipografia del Pio Istituto di Patronato, 1864), pp. 149–155, 157–186. In *Mon.* 3:15, Dante affirms that the Church should conform in every way to the life of Christ—especially imitating his lack of temporal possessions. Naturally, the anonymous supporters of the French monarchy had wielded such biblical citations; see *Antequam essent clerici (Before There Were Clerics)* and *Quæstio in utramque partem (For and Against Pontifical Power)*, in *Three Royalist Tracts, 1296–1302*, trans. R. W. Dyson (Bristol, U.K.: University of Durham/Thoemmes Press, 1999), pp. 4–5, 52–53. Dante deals with Christ's lack of concern for the earthly kingdom in *Mon.* 3:15:6. In his *On Royal and Papal Power*, Jean Quidort of Paris insisted that Christ, as God, as man-God, and as man, could only have exercised temporal authority over temporal goods and the state as man; and this he did *not* do; ergo, since he did not exercise this power himself, he could not have transferred it to his successors. In his Proem, to prove Christ's separation from the worldly, John also lists Mt 6:19, 24, 26, 34; Lk 14:33; Acts 3:6; and 1 Tm. 6:8, 9 (ed. J. Leclerq, in *L'ecclésiologie du XIIIe siècle*, in *L'église et l'état au Moyen Age* [Paris: J. Vrin, 1942], 5:173, 190–192; trans. Watt, p. 70; and trans. Monahan, pp. xxxi–xxxiii, 2, 30–33). Dante's fellow Florentine, the hierocratic Fra Remigio Girolami, orator and lector at Santa Maria Novella from ca. 1273 to ca. 1319, lists interpretations of Christ's saying "My kingdom is not of this world" (*Contra falsos ecclesie professores* 27, ed. Tamburini, pp. 62–63). It is clear that Dante believed that the Church should be purely spiritual and above any earthly entanglement; Jesus' outright rejection of earthly power often met, and still meets in all Christianity's separate manifestations, East, West, reform, and Protestant, with blurring obfuscation, if not refutation. Maccarrone, for example, gave his personal synopsis of St. Thomas Aquinas's view in the *De regimine principum* (*On Kingship, On Princely Government*, or *On the Rule of Princes*): "[T]he submission of kings to the pope is implicit also in the temporal field, because it is identified with that of Jesus Christ, who was the true earthly king; however, he did not wield any exercise of temporal power, since the two powers remained distinct" (*"Potestas directa et poetestas indirecta* nei teolo-

gi del XII e XIII secolo," in *Sacerdozio e regno da Gregorio VII a Bonifacio VIII: Studi presentati alla sezione storica del congresso della Pontificia Università Gregoriana, 13–17 ottobre 1953. Miscellanea Historiæ Ponteficiæ* 18 (Rome: Pontifia Universita Gregoriana, 1954), p. 40; see also "Papato e impero," p. 302). Bruno Nardi, in *Dal Convivio alla Commedia (sei saggi danteschi)*, con premesso alla ristampa di Ovidio Capitani (Istituto Storico Italiano per il Medio Evo: Nuovi Studi Storici 18 [Rome: Nella sede dell'Istituto, 1992]), pp. 278–280, gives differing, if often exuberantly expressed, views.

9. Cf. the passages cited by the anonymous monarchist writer of *Quæstio de potestate papæ (Rex pacificus) / An Enquiry into the Power of the Pope*, ed. and trans. R. W. Dyson, Texts and Studies in Religion 83 (Lewiston/Queenston/Lampeter: Edwin Mellen Press, 1999), pp. 14, 68. The otherwise hierocratic, yet inconsistent, Fra Remigio de' Girolami cites a series of passages against the popes' temporal power in his digression on papal politics in the *Contra professores*, esp. ch. 19, p. 48, but also see pp. 62–63; the section on the dignity of the Church is found on pp. 18–48. Just as when considering any canonist involved in dialectic, we must be careful to distinguish exactly where Remigio is simply restating *notabilia* or *argumenta*, i.e., opinions not his own, or rendering his own, personal conclusion. While these two are always easily distinguishable, e.g., in Aquinas, Remigio has not come down to us so neatly organized. With Fra Guido Vernani, as we will see, whatever the extreme curial, hierocratic opinion, it will always be his own.

10. See H. A. Drake, *Constantine and the Bishops: The Politics of Intolerance*, Ancient Society and History (Baltimore/London: Johns Hopkins University Press, 2000).

11. See the documents in *Church and State through the Centuries*, ed. Sidney Z. Ehler and John B. Morrall (Westminster, Md.: Newman Press, 1954), pp. 4–9.

12. Pope Gelasius, however, stated that Jesus Christ had reunited in himself the two powers temporal and spiritual (in the order of Melchisedech), confused and mixed in the Old Testament, *so as to divide them* in the New. Some papalist writers after ca. 1250 began to make, rhetorically, no distinction between the powers of Christ and those of the Roman pontiff, considered his vicar on earth. Cf. Maccarone, *"Potestas directa,"* p. 44.

13. *Decretum, dist. XCVI, 10, "Duo sunt" (CIC*, 1:340); trans. in Tierney, *Crisis*, pp. 13–14. See Carlyle and Carlyle, 1:184–193; and Aloysius P. Ziegler, "Pope Gelasius I and His Teaching on the Relation of Church and State," *Catholic Historical Review* 27 (1942): 412–437. S. E. Donlon puts it in a way meaningful for our understanding of Dante: "If the occasion demanded a frank statement of the autonomy of the episcopate in deciding the doctrine and the discipline of the Church, an independence for which the Church had been struggling since the days of Constantine . . . it did not suggest to Gelasius that a 'distinction' of powers should evolve into a 'separation' of powers" ("Gelasian Letter," *New Catholic Encyclopedia*, 6:315).

14. We must here distinguish "decretists" from "decretalists." Those who made commentaries upon Gratian's original collection of four thousand patristic texts, conciliar decrees, and papal letters of the mid-twelfth century (ca. 1140–1150), entitled the *Concordantia*

*discordantium Canonum* and known as the *Decreta* or *Decretum Gratiani*, are called "decretists." The "decretalists" are the theocratic commentators upon collections of (especially, but not exclusively) pontifical letters containing a *decretum*, rescript, or decision of a date later than Gratian's *Decretum*. Eventually some of these decretal collections received official recognition and also form part of what is now known as the *Corpus iuris canonici*. See Tierney's useful notes in *Crisis*, pp. 116–119, 150–153. See Dante's scolding of the decretalists in *Par.* 9:134–135.

15. A vivid example in artistic depiction of kingship given directly by Christ is the famous coronation of Roger II of Sicily in a mosaic in the Church of the Martorana in Palermo, founded in 1143: Roger is shown standing while a larger figure of Christ with cruciform nimbus presses the crown upon the king's head with his right hand. All law (the emperor was *"lex animata"*) in any sense, of course, was divine, insofar as "the powers that be are ordained of God." See the imperial texts cited by W. Ullmann, in *Medieval Papalism: The Political Theories of the Medieval Canonists*, The Maitland Memorial Lectures Delivered in the University of Cambridge in Lent Term 1948 (London: Methuen, 1949), pp. 138–9, and in Tierney, *Crisis*, p. 15. Also see *Novella* VI, in *Novellæ*, in *Corpus iuris civilis* 3:35–36; *The Digest of Justinian*, ed. Theodor Mommsen with Paul Kreuger, original texts with an English trans. by Alan Watson, 4 vols. (Philadelphia: University of Pennsylvania Press, 1985), here, vol. 1, esp. pp. xlvi, lvi, et passim. On the divinity of human law, see *Dist.* 8, cap. 1: *". . . iura humana per imperatores et reges sæculi Deus distribuit generi humano"* (God distributed human laws through the emperor and kings of the earth to humankind), and *Dig.* 1:2:2: *". . . omnis lex inventum et munus deorum est . . ."* (all law is a device and function of the gods); see Brian Tierney, "'Sola scriptura' and the Canonists," in *Collecteana Stephan Kuttner*, ed. J. Forchielli and Alfons M. Stickler, in *Studia Gratiana* 11 (1967): 351, n. 6.

16. Involvement in direct power over temporals worried St. Bernard of Clairvaux and the later hierocrats. James of Viterbo writing ca. 1303 cites Bernard: "The Blessed Bernard in his book *On Consideration* [1:6], expounding that saying of the Apostle: 'Set them to judge who are at least esteemed [most despised] in the Church' [1 Cor 6:4], admonishes Pope Eugenius that he should not entangle himself in secular affairs unless for a good cause. He speaks as follows: 'According to the Apostle, then you, apostolic man that you are, usurp to yourself a mean and unworthy office [if you undertake to judge temporal things]. Hence it is that, instructing a bishop, the Apostle says: "No soldier of God entangleth himself in the affairs of this life" [2 Tm 2:4]. . . . Your power, therefore, is over cases of sin, not over possessions'" (*De regimine christiano* 8; *On Christian Government*, trans. Dyson, p. 117). For the original, see St. Bernard, *De consideratione* 1:7 (*PL* 182:735); *On Consideration*, trans. Anderson and Kennan, p. 35. Dante's reading of that work led him to choose St. Bernard as the pilgrim's last guide in *Par.* For William of Ockham, who formulated the extreme Franciscan theory of temporal power in the fourteenth century, the temporal was that which Christ refused, i.e., the Roman Empire; quite unlike Dante, Ockham thus cleaved closely to an Augustinian, pessimistic understanding of earthly power even while

vehemently differentiating it from the pope's. See, e.g., his statement in *On the Power of Emperors and Popes*, trans. and ed. Annabel S. Brett (Bristol, U.K.: University of Durham/ Thoemmes Press, 1998), esp. "Introduction," p. 21.

17. *Concordantia discordantium canonum* or *Decreta* or *Decretum Gratiani* became the first part of the body of canon law; see text in *CIC.*, vol. 1; Alphonse van Hove, *Prolegomena*, in *Commentarium Lovaniense in Codicem Iuris Canonici*, vol. 1, tom. 1 (Mechlin/Rome: H. Dessain, 1928), esp. pp. 338–348. For Gratian, see Stephan Kuttner, "The Father of the Science of Canon Law," *Jurist* 1 (1948): 2–19. Still useful is Charles Homer Haskins's "The Revival of Jurisprudence," in his *Renaissance of the Twelfth Century* (Cambridge, Mass.: Harvard University Press, 1927; rpt. Cleveland/New York: World Publishing, 1968), esp. pp. 214–217. For relations between Roman and canon law in the late Middle Ages, see Pierre Legendre's thesis, *La pénétration du droit romain dans le droit canonique classique de Gratien à Innocent IV, 1140–1254* (Paris: Imprimerie Jouve, 1964).

18. See C. Francisco Bertelloni, "'Constitutum Constantini' y 'Romgedanke': La donacion constantiniana en el pensmiento de tres defensores del derecho imperial de Roma: Dante, Marsilio de Padua y Guillermo de Ockham," *Patristica et Mediævalia* 3 (1882): 21–46 [first part]; *Patristica et Mediævalia* 4–5 (1984): 67–99 [second part].

19. Maccarrone, "*Potestas directa*," pp. 28–29.

20. Canon lawyers well recognized the political and spiritual uselessness of the Donation. Giles of Rome mainly avoids discussing the Donation because of the possible accusation that the popes owed their power to a secular monarch; James of Viterbo claims briefly that Constantine could not have given it, since it was not his to give (an argument that may have inspired Dante to different ends), but comes eventually to say that Constantine *merely confirmed* in civil law what the pope already owned by divine or natural law and as priest and king in the order of Melchisedech; see his *De regimine christiano (On Christian Government)*, trans. Dyson, pp. xxv, 119, 153. Tolomeo da Lucca adopts the same position in his high-papalist *Determinatio compendiosa (Short Determination)*, ed. Krammer, p. 21.

21. The hierocrats made much of this passage; see Tolomeo da Lucca, *Determinatio compendiosa (Short Determination)*, ed. Krammer, p. 16.

22. *Decretales* 1:33:6, *Solitæ Benignitatis (PL* 216:1185) of 1201; trans. Tierney, *Crisis*, p. 133. The power was broadened in April 1204 by *Novit ille* by the "*ratione peccati*" doctrine that theoretically had no limitations; the decretal can now be found in the monumental Austrian edition, *Die Register Innocenz' III.*, 7:7. *Pontifikatsjahr, 1204/1205, Texte und Indices*, ed. Andrea Sommerlechner and Herwig Weigl, with Christoph Egger and Rainer Murauer, *Publicationen des Historischen Instituts beim Österreichischen Kulturinstitut in Rom*, II. Abt., 1. Reihe (Vienna: Österreichische Akademie der Wissenschaften, 1997), p. 43. See *Mon.* 3:8:3–11, on the breadth of meaning of "whatsoever."

23. See "The Sermon of Innocent the Third, Preached at His Own Consecration," in C. H. C. Pirie-Gordon, *Innocent the Great: An Essay on His Life and Times* (London/New York: Longmans, 1907), pp. 220–229. St. Benedict, ca. 540, reaffirming earlier monastic rules,

had asserted that even the elected abbot of a monastery held the place of Christ and was to be called "lord" ("*dominus*") and "father" (*abbas* ["*abbot*"]) out of honor and love of Christ; see *The Rule of St. Benedict*, ch. 63, ed. Timothy Fry (New York: Vintage Books, 1981), p. 60. See W. Ullmann's chapter "The Pope and Natural Law," in *Medieval Papalism*, esp. pp. 50–56. Unfortunately, Tierney translates but a snippet in *Crisis*, pp. 131–132.

24. Kenneth Pennington, *The Prince and the Law, 1200–1600: Sovereignty and Rights in the Western Legal Tradition* (Berkeley/Los Angeles: University of California Press, 1993), p. 46.

25. Innocent III proclaimed the "*ratione peccati*" doctrine in his decretal *Novit ille*, asserting his right to settle differences between King John of England and the French king, Philip-Augustus (*Decretales* 2:1:13; *CIC*, 2:243–44; Tierney, *Crisis*, pp. 134–135); Hostiensis expanded it in his commentary on *Per venerabilem*. Innocent III's novel claims to interfere in the temporal affairs of the empire were three in number: primarily, as we have noted, "by reason of sin," secondly, when the imperial throne was vacant ("*vacante imperio*"), and, thirdly, by reason of heresy. The claim to earthly power *because of spiritual care over sinful souls* was based on, but ultimately violated, the spirit of St. Bernard's warnings concerning humility to Pope Eugenius III in the *De consideratione* 1:7: "Clearly your power is over sin and not property, since it is because of sin that you have received the keys of the heavenly kingdom, to exclude sinners, not possessors" (*On Consideration*, trans. Anderson and Kennan, p. 36). See also Joan Ferrante's comments, in *The Political Vision of the "Divine Comedy*," pp. 23–24.

26. Dante's contemporaries remained acutely aware of these plenary claims and were sorely offended by them. As the anonymous royalist author of the *Disputatio inter Clericum et Militem* put it during the Boniface–Philip IV controversy in 1302: "By reason of sin, therefore, the pope ought to judge capital offences. But this is clearly not so. Therefore your argument is blown away by the light of reason" (*A Debate between a Clerk and a Knight*, trans. Dyson, pp. 20–21). See also Kenneth Pennington, *Pope and Bishops: The Papal Monarchy in the Twelfth and Thirteenth Centuries* (Philadelphia: University of Pennsylvania Press, 1984).

27. *Decretales* 2:1:13; *CIC*, 2:243–244; Tierney, *Crisis*, pp. 134–135. R. W. Dyson discusses *Novit ille* usefully in his "Introduction" to James of Viterbo, *On Christian Government*, p. viii, n. 11.

28. Legend has it that Thomas of Tolentino, later popularly invoked as a plague saint, met martyrdom at Tana in India in 1321, though there may have been some confusion with the Genoese enclave Tana at the mouth of the Don River. Clement V was to create the diocese of Cambaliensem, Peking, in 1307.

29. Maria Picchio Simonelli, "L'inquisizione a Dante: alcune osservazioni," *Dante Studies* 97 (1979): 129–149; rpt. *Dante Studies* 118 (2000): 303–321, here, p. 304.

30. See "King John Lackland's Infeodation to Innocent III, May 15, 1213," in William Stubbs, ed., *Select Charters and Other Illustrations of English Constitutional History from the Earliest Times*, 8th ed., rev. by Henry William Carlos Davis (Oxford, U.K.: Clarendon Press, 1905), p. 276; trans. in *The Church and State*, ed. Ehler and Morrall, pp. 73–76.

31. Almost astonishingly, and in the reverse spirit of the biblical meaning of the "trib-

ute money," papal lawyers construed Mt 22:20–21 as an example of Christ's royal authority and as a basis for the pope's control over coinage; the pontiff, as Christ's Vicar, thus had
the power to render the authority of coinage to a sovereign. Rote imitation of the action
usurped, in exact inversion, the content and spirit of Christ's example of obedience, submission, and disinterest. Cf. the views, perhaps of St. Thomas Aquinas, given by Tolomeo
da Lucca in *On the Government of Rulers*, trans. Blythe, pp. 132–136.

32. On the events of Innocent's reign, see S. C. Ferruolo, "Innocent III, Pope
(1160/1161–16 July 1216)," in *Dictionary of the Middle Ages*, 6:464–465; Helena Tillmann, *Pope
Innocent III*, trans. Walter Sax, Europe in the Middle Ages 12 (Amsterdam/New York/Ox-
ford, U.K.: North Holland Publishing Company, 1980); Colin Morris, *The Papal Monarchy:
The Western Church from 1050 to 1250* (Oxford, U.K.: Clarendon Press, 1989), esp. ch. 3, "The
Pontificate of Innocent III (1198–1216)," pp. 417–447, and Morris's thorough bibliographies; Maccarrone, *Chiesa e stato nella dottrina di papa Innocenzo III* (1940), *Studi su Innocenzo III*
(1972), and his posthumous *Nuovi studi su Innocenzo III*, ed. Roberto Lambertini, intro. by
Ovidio Capitani, Nuovi Studi Storici 25 (Rome: nella sede dell'Istituto [Storico Italiano
per il Medio Evo], Palazzo Borromini, 1995)—esp. useful is ch. 6, "Innocenzo III e la feu-
dalità: 'Non ratione feudi, sed ratione peccati,'" pp. 209–269; and Christopher R. Cheney,
*Pope Innocent III and England* (Stuttgart: Anton Hiersemann, 1976). Useful English translations of documents are found in C. H. C. Pirie-Gordon's otherwise quite unreadable *Innocent the Great: An Essay on His Life and Times* (London/New York: Longmans, 1907).

33. "*Venerabilem fratrem [nostrum Salzburgensem]*," [Duci Caringiæ] *Decretales* 1:6:34; *CIC*, 2:80
(on imperial elections); a partial translation of the *Venerabilem fratrem* is found in *The Church
and State*, ed. Ehler and Morrall, pp. 71–72; and in Tierney, *Crisis*, p. 133. Guido Vernani
concludes in his *De potestate summi pontificis* 7: "The Supreme Pontiff has the power to force
the emperor to obey, to punish him if disobedient, and depose him if obdurate" (F.
Guidonis Vernani Ariminensis Ordinis Prædicatorum, *De potestate summi pontificis et De reprobatione Monarchiæ compositæ a Dante Aligerio florentino tractatus duo nunc primum in lucem editi*
[Bononiæ: apud Thomam Coli, ex Typographia S. Thomæ Aquinatis, 1746], p. 69). We
must observe that, through the centuries, references to Innocent's bull *Venerabilem fratrem*
concerning election of the emperor are conflated and confused with references and glosses on his even more famous *Per venerabilem* (*Decretales* 4:17:13; *CIC*, 2:714–716) addressed to
the Count of Montpellier concerning the legitimizing of children and asserting the
Melchisedech doctrine; this occurs so frequently because of the influence of Hostiensis's
commentary "Qui filii sint legitimi" in his *Summa aurea* that conflates the doctrines of the
two bulls (see Carlyle and Carlyle, 5:324–334).

34. The exception was the unworldly hermit Pietro da Morrone, who became Pope Celestine V at the age of eighty. He reigned only five and a half months from July 5, 1294, to
his abdication on December 13, 1294; he was canonized as St. Peter Morrone under
Clement V in 1313, but now is commonly called St. Peter Celestine. Celestine, however, is
probably he whom Dante had earlier consigned to *Inf.* 3:59–60 to suffer among the pusil-

lanimous as *"colui / che fece per viltà il gran rifiuto."* The *"pastores"* (shepherds) of whom Dante speaks with some sarcasm in *Mon.* 3:3:7 are the bishops of the Church, the majority of whom were canon lawyers; see Michele Maccarrone, "Teologia e diritto canonico nella *Monarchia* III, 3," *Rivista di Storia della Chiesa* 5 (1951): 7–42, here, p. 12.

35. Some clear definitions are in order. On *"dualitas,"* see Wilks, *The Problem of Sovereignty,* pp. 74–81. In 1965, Brian Tierney warned against the "abuse of the current jargon words 'dualistic' and 'hierocratic'" (expressed in his "The Continuity of Papal Political Theory," p. 229). Even Innocent III's and Innocent IV's monist politics, for example, had been termed by some as "dualistic"—both Michele Maccarrone and Mochi Onory had been particularly guilty of such obfuscation (cf., e.g., *"Potestas directa,"* pp. 29–31, and the last half of *Fonti canonistiche*; see also Brian Tierney, "Some Recent Works on the Political Theories of the Medieval Canonists," *Traditio* 10 [1954]: 594–625, esp. pp. 605–606). Tierney's irritation was understandable, but the learned terms are hardly jargon, and I have used them as shorthand to express my own working axioms. "Dualists," or rather "dual originists," were those who believed in two separate, parallel powers bifurcating straight from God—i.e., those who affirmed the direct origin of the empire from God (such as Uguccione da Pisa), regardless of their tempering of that idea *after* supporting its direct, divine origin. "Hierocrats," "high papalists," or "monists" were those, particularly the decretalists against whom Dante argues in *Mon.* 3:3, who insisted that power descended in series only from the papacy—that only the pope had both the temporal and the spiritual power directly from the deity, that, no matter how much leeway they allowed the empire, all imperial power derived secondhand from the pontiff. For hierocratic monists, ultimately, the pope was the true emperor or monarch, both as the source of power and the incumbent in that power, whenever he took it upon himself, unilaterally, to declare the imperial throne vacant—the position asserted in John XXII's *Si fratrum.* Some modern historians have erroneously posited a thirteenth- and fourteenth-century high-papalist "dualism" simply because some certain writers acknowledge the mere existence of two powers, derived, indifferently, by series or parallel; Dante's supporter, the jurist Bartolo da Sassoferrato, however, could see the difference sharply: "Dante debated . . . *whether the Emperor depends upon the Church,* and he held that he did not; but *because of this,* after his death, he was almost condemned for heresy" (my emphasis). Still useful are the essays by Olindo Guerrini and Corrado Ricci in *Studi e polemiche dantesche* (Bologna: Nicola Zanichelli, 1853), esp. pp. 81–82. Gelasius's letter of protest that his papal power was being depreciated first came to be interpreted as meaning that the Church was a partner in the power system; it later suggested ever greater theocratic claims through daring insistence that the Church was, in fact, the senior partner. Gelasius, however, recorded no theory about any origins. Dante is, of course, a "dualist" or, better, a "dual originist" in my use of the term; however, as is evident, especially in *Mon.* 3:16, he works, sometimes distressingly, within the viscous stranglehold of what the Gelasian fabric had become, as did Uguccione da Pisa. James Muldoon's *Empire and Order: The Concept of Empire, 800–1800* (New York: St. Martin's Press, 1999) has useful summaries for the general reader.

36. See Wolfgang Peter Müller, "Huguccio, Twelfth-Century Canonist and Author of the *Summa decretorum* (Ph.D. diss., Syracuse University, 1991; Ann Arbor, Mich.: University Microfilms, 1992), and *Huguccio: The Life, Works, and Thought of a Twelfth-Century Jurist* (Washington, D.C.: The Catholic University of America Press, 1994), esp. p. 9. Also see Giuseppe Cremascoli, "Uguccione da Pisa: Saggio bibliografico," *Ævum* 42 (1968): 123–168; Kenneth Pennington, "Huguccio," in *Dictionary of the Middle Ages*, 6: 327–328 (Pennington, unfortunately, does not discuss Uguccione's dualism); G. Schizzerotto, "Uguccione de Pisa," in *Enciclopedia dantesca*, 5:800–802; and James A. Brundage, *Medieval Canon Law* (London/New York: Longman, 1995), pp. 215–216. We must observe that just as there is no incontrovertible documentation to prove that Dante actually studied under Remigio de' Girolami and Tolomeo da Lucca at Santa Maria Novella (a most likely assumption), we similarly do not know whether Lotario de' Segni had actually been Uguccione's pupil (a most doubtful probability). We must note that both outstanding pupils defied their presumed masters.

37. Kenneth Pennington, in his early articles ("The Legal Education of Pope Innocent III," *Bulletin of Medieval Canon Law* 4 [1974]: 70–77, and "Pope Innocent III's Views on Church and State: A Gloss to *Per Venerabilem*," in *Law, Church and Society: Essays in Honor of Stephan Kuttner*, ed. Kenneth Pennington and Robert Somerville [Philadelphia: University of Pennsylvania Press, 1977], pp. 49–68; both reprinted in Pennington's collected essays, *Popes, Canonists and Texts, 1150–1550* [Aldershot, U.K.: Variorum/Ashgate Publishing, 1993], essay 1, pp. 1–10, and essay 4, pp. 1–25), showed, noting that positive evidence is fairly slim, that Lotario de' Segni was not actually Uguccione's pupil in legal studies. Indeed, it is abundantly clear that Lotario consistently demonstrated a substantially different spirit and attitude toward the papacy from Uguccione: Uguccione *is* a dual originist in my sense of the term; Innocent III most decidedly *is not*. That Lotario, as reigning pontiff, may not have acted autonomously as his own legal adviser or amanuensis in drawing up his own incredibly powerful papal decrees does not remove the pope's total responsibility for their effects. I must mention that Antonio Martina deals only with Uguccione's *Magnæ derivationes* in "Uguccione nel proemio della *Monarchia* di Dante," *L'Alighieri* 13, no. 1 (1972): 69–74, not with the theoretical positions of Uguccione the canonist.

38. The doctrine, mainly the result of the codification and acquiescence of Henry IV in his struggles with Gregory VII, had been a withdrawal from the traditional position in which the emperor had held the superior position now claimed by the popes; see Wilks, *The Problem of Sovereignty*, pp. 78–79, et passim. Many canonists asserted similar claims, particularly concerning the deposition of the emperor. See Uguccione's comments and original Latin texts in Gætano Catalano's most useful *Impero, regni e sacerdozio nel pensiero di Uguccio da Pisa* (Milan: Giuffrè, 1959), p. 36, n. 74. Uguccione followed Rom 13:1, "There is no power but from God: and those that are, are ordained of God." For the Florentines Remigio and Dante, both followers in their own singular ways of St. Thomas Aquinas (*ST* I-II, q. 90, a. 3), God's ordaining of order did not invalidate the natural character of the state; the duty of the ruler (either the people as a whole or a public person in whom it was vest-

ed) came in the realm of rights, laws, and duties willed by nature, guaranteeing the order, harmony, and tranquillity among citizens. See Wilks's instructive and witty comments on *dualitas* in *The Problem of Sovereignty*, pp. 74–81, et passim; and Alfons Stickler, "Der Schwerterbegriff bei Huguccio," *Ephemerides iuris canonici* 3 (1937): 201–242, esp. pp. 213–215. Stickler claimed in two important articles, "Magistri Gratiani sententia de potestate ecclesiæ in statum," *Apollinaris* 21 (1948): 36–111, and "Imperator vicarius Papæ," *Mitteilungen des Institut für Österreichische Geschichtsforschung* 62 (1954): 165–212, that Gratian had earlier asserted that the temporal power was not dependent on the spiritual power either by divine or human law. The issue is impossible to decide given that the jurist's whole effort was to make obviously discordant canons agree; the issue emphatically does not merely concern Gelasianism, i.e., the conceded existence of two powers, but rather what relation those two powers bear to each other hierarchically.

39. Richard de Mores or Morins, a canon regular at Merton Priory and later prior of Dunstable in England after 1202, who had studied both at Paris and Bologna wrote, *"Videtur nobis securior via eorum qui dicunt quod imperator a solo deo habet potestatem. . . ."* (They have the surer path, it seems to us, who say that the emperor has his power only from God). This is cited as "uncompromisingly dualistic and . . . hardly [to] be distinguished from later antipapalistic views" by W. Ullmann, in his *Medieval Papalism*, p. 213; but the attribution to de Mores is questioned by Christopher R. Cheney, in *Pope Innocent III and England*, Päpste und Papsttum, Band 9 (Stuttgart: Anton Hiersemann, 1976), pp. 17–18. In 1202, the English decretalist Alanus made a famous gloss on Uguccione's *Distinctio* 96, cap. 6, to be echoed often, especially in *Unam sanctam:* "Today Innocent [III] has by right the material sword. . . . If the emperor were not subject to the pope in temporalities, he could not sin against the Church in temporalities. Again the Church is one body and so it shall have only one head or it will be a monster." The English Church, jealous of its privileges, had recently come forth from the struggles between Thomas Becket and Henry II. The statement became a topos of the hierocrats. See Alfons M. Stickler, "Alanus Anglicus als Verteidiger des monarchischen Papsttums," *Salesianum* 21 (1959): 361–363; and trans. Tierney, *Crisis*, p. 123.

40. *"Hinc aperte colligitur quod utraque potestas, scilicet apostolica et imperialis, instituta sit a deo et quod neutra pendeat ex altera et quod imperator gladium non habeat ab apostolico. . . . Ego autem credo, quod imperator potestatem gladii et dignitatem imperialem habet non ab apostolico, sed a principus per electionem et populo . . . ante enim fuit imperator quam papa, ante imperium quam papatus"* (my emphasis). See Uguccione da Pisa, *Summa decretorum*, Distinctio 96, cap. 6; Catalano gives the full Latin text of the chapter in *Impero, Regni e Sacerdozio*, pp. 64–68, here, pp. 65–66. Unfortunately, Uguccione's *Summa decretorum* has, as yet, to be published in its entirety. See also trans. Tierney, *Crisis*, pp. 122–123; W. Ullmann, *Medieval Papalism*, pp. 142–151, 167 (note that Ullmann badly misquotes the text); Michele Maccarrone, *Chiesa e stato nella dottrina politica di papa Innocenzo III*, pp. 69–70, 76; and Müller, *Huguccio*, p. 9. Uguccione da Pisa does not refer to Justinian authority but only to Gratian. Uguccione's views, however, repeat the the-

ory of diarchy expressed in imperial documents, especially after the humiliation of Emperor Henry IV before Pope Gregory VII at Canossa; see Ullmann's *Medieval Papalism*, p. 151, and his *Growth of Papal Government*, pp. 404–405. The Blessed Henry of Susa's immense *Summa aurea super titulis Decretalium (Summa copiosa, Summa titulorum decretalium*, or *Summa Hostiensis)*, his "Golden Summa," survives in two versions, is available in many early printings, and can be easily consulted in two modern reprints: the edition entitled *Summa una* (Lyons, 1537; rprt. Darmstadt: Scientia Aalen, 1962), and another entitled *Summa aurea* (Venice, 1574; rprt. Turin: Bottega d'Erasmo, 1963). In his commentary on the bull *Per venerabilem (Decretales* 4:17:13), he rejects Uguccione—referred to only by the abbreviation "H" ("Huguccio") in the manuscripts (*Summa una*, ff. 215$^r$–216$^v$; *Summa aurea*, cols. 1385–1387). See Sergio Mochi Onory, in *Fonti canonistiche dell'idea moderna dello stato (Imperium spirituale— iurisdictio divisa—sovranità)*, Pubblicazioni dell'Università Cattolica del Sacro Cuore, n.s., 38 (Milan: Società Editrice "Vita e Pensiero," 1951), pp. 152, 163–164; and Maccarrone, "La dottrina politica di Uguccione," in *Chiesa e stato*, pp. 68–78, and "Nuovi studi su Innocenzo III," *"Potestas directa*,*"* and "Papato e impero," in *Rivista di storia della Chiesa in Italia* 9 (1958): 40–46, 27–47, and 259–332, respectively.

41. For many of Uguccione's Latin texts, see Gætano Catalano, *Impero, regni e sacerdozio nel pensiero di Uguccio da Pisa;* here, for *Distinctio* 96, cap. 6, p. 66.

42. Maccarrone, *Chiesa e stato*, p. 78. According to Uguccione, the emperor does not receive his power from the pope, and may consider himself emperor after his election, insofar as his dignity is concerned; however, the pope must examine, consent to, and consecrate the emperor; it is left unclear what might ensue if these three things were not carried out. Uguccione wrote: "I believe that he is emperor by election of the people and of the princes, although he may not be so called before he receives the crown from the pope: he is king before he is crowned: the sacramental mark is imprinted at his royal unction" (S. Mochi Onory, *Fonti canonistiche*, pp. 150–151). Thus it might appear that for Uguccione the emperor's power is in some way *not complete* until coronation and unction. The possibilities for interpretation of the emperor's power after he derives it from God through election are left ambiguous, but are thus, ultimately, *in some way* under the pope. Dante in *Mon.* 3:16 leaves a similar ambiguity. It is clear that Uguccione considered the "sword of temporal power" to be a distinct, divinely ordained reality, not merely a metaphor of coercion possessed and delegated *causaliter* by the Church, a concept that would argue against the papal theory put forth by Alfons Stickler in his many erudite articles on the "two swords" question.

43. For Uguccione, the pope is greater in spiritual affairs, has jurisdiction in spiritual matters over the emperor, and in such matters can bind and condemn; the emperor, however, is not in the same way greater than the pope in his temporal affairs, since he has no jurisdiction or superiority at all over the pope *("nullam enim iurisdictionem vel prelationem habet imperator super papam")*, but only greater power in matters that are merely temporal. See S. Mochi Onory, *Fonti canonistiche*, p. 154; also see the corrections to both Maccarrone and

Mochi Onory in Tierney, "Some Recent Works," pp. 603–604, rpt. in *Church Law and Constitutional Thought in the Middle Ages* (London: Variorum Reprints, 1979), essay 1, same pagination.

44. "But by whom is the sentence pronounced? By the lord pope before whom he was convicted or by his princes if the Roman pontiff has approved this" (Uguccione, *Distinctio* 96, cap. 6; Catalano, *Imperio, regia e sacerdozio*, pp. 64–68). Catalano (p. 43) suggests that such power derived not necessarily from any feudal pact—although we know that that was the case in many instances—but from a natural order of jurisdiction, or of public law, *ratione defectus justitiæ*, in the absence of any other superior. Cf. Maccarrone, *Chiesa e stato*, pp. 75, 77; and Mochi Onory, *Fonti canonistische*, p. 152. Even the ardent Marsiglio of Padua was to give lip service to the superiority of spiritual power, although he held it unnecessary in earthly government.

45. Maccarrone, *Chiesa e stato*, pp. 74–75.

46. Catalano, *Impero, regia e sacerdozio*, pp. 39, 43.

47. Bruno Nardi reiterated in his many, now classic, studies that he saw the author of the *Mon.* as deeply Averroistic—though not accepting of Averroës's doctrines against the immortality of the soul—and as heralding Marsiglio of Padua's *Defensor pacis*. He tended to concur with Giovanni Gentile's view of Dante more as a rebel than as a Catholic reformer. Nardi, as some of us have had the privilege of witnessing in person, often liked to overstate his case not only in print but in public forums. The *Mon.*, he held, represented the first act of rebellion against Scholastic transcendence. It appears clear to the present writer, however, given the historical circumstances surrounding Dante's treatise, that Dante is concerned to be as conservative and orthodox as he can manage in his confutation of those close to the curia. His spiritual aim was to cure the internecine conflicts in Italy stirred up by John XXII, whose novel exaggerations had erupted in this crisis of temporal power.

48. Dante's last paragraph may be compared to Uguccione's ultimate statement: "The pope is in fact superior to the emperor and stands above him" (cited in Maccarrone, *Chiesa e stato*, p. 75). On the question of the pope's benediction and unction of the emperor, see below. Dante knew that St. Paul clearly affirmed in Heb 7:7 that "[t]he inferior is blessed by the superior." And he knew that Hugh of St. Victor had cited the verse to prove the pope's superiority, as we noted above. Hebrews also bears most of the hallowed verses on Melchisedech concerning Christ as king and priest. We must further note, in passing, in order to complete the understanding of Uguccione da Pisa as a central *auctor* for Dante, that the poet also made extensive use of Uguccione's dictionary, the *Magnæ derivationes*, throughout his works; cf. *Conv.* 4:6:5, 4:24:1. However, W. Müller has recently brought into question whether the authorship of the *Summa decretorum* and the *Derivationes* ascribed to "Huguccio" was actually based on anything more than a coincidence of name; see Müller's ch. 1, "Canonist, Bishop, Grammarian?," in *Huguccio*, pp. 21–66.

49. *Contra falsos ecclesie professores*, ed. Tamburini, pp. 54–56. See Lorenzo Minio-Paluello,

"Remigio Girolami's *De bono communi:* Florence at the Time of Dante's Banishment and the Philosopher's Answer to the Crisis," *Italian Studies* 11 (1956): 56–71. Dante agrees with Remigio's early opinions of the pope's lack of authority in the temporal sphere (see note 50, below)—one that Remigio was to abandon. Cf. Dante's *Epistola* 5, esp. 5:5:17 (ed. Toynbee, pp. 53–54, 60). Also see Charles T. Davis, "The Florentine *Studia* and Dante's 'Library,'" in *"The Divine Comedy" and the Encyclopedia of Arts and Sciences,* ed. Giuseppe di Scipio and Aldo Scaglione (Amsterdam: J. Benjamins, 1988), pp. 339–366. Joan Ferrante makes a brief comparison between Dante's experiences and concepts with some of Remigio's in *The Political Vision of the "Divine Comedy,"* pp. 16–17. Dante's works, and especially the *Mon.,* have been mainly studied in relation to Uguccione's dictionary, the *Magnæ derivationes,* but Uguccione's ample juristic-legal presence in Dante has not been sufficiently studied, nor have the pertinent original documents, such as Uguccione's own *Summa decretorum,* appeared in complete modern editions. On the semantic presence of the *Derivationes* in the first paragraphs of the *Mon.,* see Martina's "Uguccione nel proemio della *Monarchia,*" pp. 69–74. A useful annotated bibliography on Uguccione is given in Cremascoli's "Uguccione da Pisa: Saggio bibliografico," pp. 123–168. For the question of whether Uguccione was the author of both the *Derivationes* and the *Summa,* see Müller, *Huguccio,* pp. 21–66.

50. In the *Contra falsos ecclesie professors 19,* Remigio himself had concluded in an earlier, youthful judgment, "Therefore temporals, insofar as they are temporals, are *not* subject to the authority of the pope principally and directly [*principaliter et directe*]" (ed. Tamburini, p. 48; my emphasis), and he avers, in a passage echoed by Dante, "Huguccio [Uguccione] said that the pope has his power from God only in regard to spirituals; the emperor indeed has his power from God only inasfar as temporals are concerned, nor is he subject to the pope in them; there was an empire before there was an apostolate," and goes on to cite sources from Gratian and the *Gloss on the Decretals* for the opinion (pp. 54–55). Remigio was later to change his public stance radically. Martin Grabmann assumed wrongly that a Dominican *studium generale* at Santa Maria Novella was already open in the 1290s for laymen such as Dante to hear lectures ("Die Wege von Thomas von Aquin zu Dante," *Deutsches Dante-Jahrbuch* 9 [1925]: 1–35, and *Mittelalterliches Geistesleben* [Munich: Heber, 1926], 1:361–369). While we know that a school existed there as early as 1231, however, it was only assigned as a *studium theologiæ* by the Roman Provincial Chapter in 1281. By 1288, it was already far larger and more important than the schools of Rome and Naples, but only after 1307 could it have officially become a *studium generale.* This means that when Dante attended it, after Beatrice's death (June 8, 1290), Santa Maria Novella was still under the Roman Province. There Remigio taught only theology, for no courses in philosophy were offered; nonetheless, it is clear that Aristotle's *Nic. Ethics,* and probably other Aristotelian works, were referred to in the lectures on Peter Lombard's *Sentences,* the central theological textbook. In such Dominican *studia,* laymen could attend the courses on theology and be present at the weekly disputations. The sundry ecclesiastical prohibitions against the laity's attendance in philosophy courses where they were offered to the religious in *studia generalia,* such as in

the Neapolitan Chapter of 1278 "that lectors may not admit secular persons to philosophical lectures," however, most probably reflect laymen's persistent presence and reveal that such restrictions were mostly observed in the breach. See Charles T. Davis, "An Early Political Theorist: Fra Remigio de' Girolami," *Proceedings of the American Philosophical Society* 104, no. 6 (1960): 662–676; "Education in Dante's Florence," *Speculum* 40 (1965): 415–435; and "The Florentine *Studia* and Dante's 'Library,'" in *"The Divine Comedy" and the Encyclopedia of Arts and Sciences,* ed. Giuseppe di Scipio and Aldo Scaglione (Amsterdam: J. Benjamins,1988), pp. 339–366. Also see Marvin B. Becker, "Dante and His Literary Contemporaries as Political Men," *Speculum* 41 (1966): 665–680.

51. In *Contra falsos ecclesie professores,* Remigio makes a typical canonist list of citations pro and contra the breadth of papal power over the jurisdiction of temporal rulers, including not only those arguing *ratione delicti* [*ratione peccati*], "by reason of crime [or sin]," (ed. Tamburini, pp. 47, 71), but also (among many others) those adamantly affirming Innocent III's supreme power over the whole world ("*per totum orbem aliqualiter*"), and absolutely over all and everything ("*super omnes et omnia aliqualiter*") (ed. Tamburini, pp. 67, 68). See also Charles T. Davis, "An Early Political Theorist," p. 673.

52. *The Letters of Dante,* ed. Toynbee, pp. 53–54, 60.

53. On the question of the last paragraph of the *Mon.* and the important and cautionary "*quodammodo,*" see Anthony K. Cassell, "The Exiled Dante's Hope for Reconciliation: *Monarchia* 3:16:16–18," *Annali d'Italianistica* 20 (2002): 425–449.

54. *Quæstio in utramque partem,* in *Three Royalist Tracts,* trans. Dyson, pp. 46–47.

55. John of Paris, *De potestate* 10; *On Royal and Papal Power,* ed. Watt, pp. 115, 124. The *Antequam essent clerici,* the *Disputatio inter clericum et militem,* and the *Quæstio in untramque partem* are translated by Dyson in *Three Royalist Tracts.* The *Quæstio in utramque partem,* written by an anonymous theologian, also expresses the Uguccionian dualism in support of the French Crown (Robert Dyson's excellent edition, with a welcome translation, now replaces that of Melchior Goldast, *Monarchia Sancti Romani Imperii* [Frankfort: Hoffmann, 1614], 2:96–107). This treatise was once, oddly and erroneously, attributed to Giles of Rome. Raoul de Presles made a French translation in ca. 1331. The *Quæstio de potestate papæ (An Enquiry into the Power of the Pope),* also titled *Rex pacificus* (1302), was written probably by a master at the University of Paris; see also this edition by Dyson, Texts and Studies in Religion 83 (Lewiston/Queenston/Lampeter: Edwin Mellen Press, 1999). Consult also P. Dupuy, ed., *Histoire du differend d'entre le Pape Boniface et Philippes le Bel Roy de France* (Tucson, Ariz.: Audax Press, 1963): 663–683; and Carlo Cipolla, "Il trattato *De Monarchia* di Dante Alighieri e l'opuscolo *De potestæ regia e papalis* di Giovanni di Parigi," *Memorie dell'Accademia di Torino,* ser. 2 (42): 325–419. That Dante wrote the *Mon.* in 1318 solves Cipolla's quandary about whether Dante derived some of his ideas from John of Paris, or John from Dante.

56. Even the indignant monarchist author of the *Quæstio de potestate papæ (Rex pacificus)* granted this: "If dignity is the point at issue, then priestly authority is greater in dignity than royal power or any other secular power, just as spirit is greater in dignity than body" (trans. Dyson, pp. 41, 91).

57. *"Si quis diceret dominum Imperatorem non esse dominum et monarcham totius orbis, esset hæreticus, quia dicerat contra determinationem Ecclesiæ, contra textu sancti Evangelii, dum dicit* Exivit edictum a Cæsare Augusto, ut describeret universus orbis, *ut habes Lucas II[:1]"* (If anyone should say that our lord emperor is not lord and monarch of the whole globe, he is a heretic, for he speaks against the decision of the Church, against the text of Holy Gospel, where it says that *"There went out a decree from Cæsar Augustus, that the whole world should be enrolled,"* as Luke has it in Chapter 2:1). Bartolo (the pupil of Cino da Pistoia, a jurist and friend to Dante) was replying to such extremists as the anonymous commentator on *Clericos laicos*, that even to discuss the limits of papal power was itself heresy (text in Richard Scholz, *Die Publizistik zur Zeit Philipps des Schönen und Bonifaz'VIII: Ein Beitrag zur Gschichte der politischen Anschauungen des Mitelalters*, Kirchenrechtlicher Abhandlungen, ed. Ulrich Stutz [Stuttgart: Ferdinand Enke, 1903], pp. 471–484; also in Carlyle and Carlyle, 5:397, n. 3); Bartolo was himself often quoted as an authority thereafter; the jurist gives us valuable information on Dante and knew his works intimately. E. H. Kantorowicz cites Bartolo's text in *The King's Two Bodies* (Princeton, N.J.: Princeton University Press, 1957); rpt. with preface by William Chester Jordan (1997), p. 466, n. 42; see also the text in Ullmann, "The Development of the Medieval Idea of Sovereignty," *English Historical Review* 46 (1949): 5, now found in the collection of Ullmann's articles, *Law and Jurisdiction in the Middle Ages*, ed. George Garnett (London: Variorum Reprints, 1988), essay 7, with original pagination. The controversy was slow to die. Panormitanus, in his *Commentarium* on *Decretales* 2:1:13, writing some hundred years after Dante, declared that "to posit two equal vicars on earth is heretical" (cited in Ullmann, *Medieval Papalism*, p. 140). Also see Cecil N. Sidney Woolf, *Bartolus of Sassoferrato: His Position in the History of Medieval Political Thought* (Cambridge, U.K.: Cambridge University Press, 1913).

58. Marsiglio of Padua, in Alan Gewirth, *Marsilius of Padua*, Records of Civilization (New York: Columbia University Press, 1956), 2:7; rpt. as Marsilius of Padua, *Defender of Peace: The Defensor Pacis*, trans. and intro. Alan Gewirth (New York: Harper & Row, 1956; rpt. 1965, 1967), p. 7.

59. Vernani, *De potestate summi pontificis*, pp. 73–77.

60. See Egidio Spiritale's text in Richard Scholz, *Unbekannte kirchenpolitische Streitschriften aus der Zeit Ludwigs des Bayern (1327–1354)*, 2 vols. (Rome: Loescher, 1911–1914), here, 2:111. Also see Wilks, *The Problem of Sovereignty*, pp. 306, 548. Although Maccarrone (*"Potestas directa,"* pp. 29–31) tries in vain to make a case for Innocent III's close dependence on Uguccione's dualism, he cites no passage anywhere in Innocent's letters where the radical *origin* of the empire from God is acknowledged. An anonymous papalist pamphleteer commenting on *Clericos laicos*, probably Henry of Cremona, tried to deny the Gelasian principle of two powers, for the pope held both authorities as *"vicarius Dei"* (see Scholz, *Die Publizistik*, pp. 471–484; also see Carlyle and Carlyle, 5:395–397). It is notable that Egidio Spiritale's death coincided with the resolution of the question at the first Diet of Frankfurt: in 1338, when the emperor's council declared that imperial authority derived immediately from God, not from the pope, and with the decree of the second Diet that Ludwig

IV rightfully enjoyed imperial rank and power without the pope's consent. The decrees became the material bases for the Golden Bull of 1356.

61. *De Sacramentis* 2:2:4 (*PL* 176, cols. 417–418); Hugh of Saint Victor, *On the Sacraments of the Christian Faith*, trans. Roy J. Deferrari (Cambridge, Mass.: Mediæval Academy of America, 1951), p. 256. Maccarrone points out that, despite the later interpretations by hierocrats, this passage does not strictly say that *direct power* over temporalities resides *originally* in the papacy (*"Potestas directa,"* pp. 29–31). See Remigio de' Girolami, *Contra falsos ecclesie professores* 19, ed. Tamburini, p. 48.

62. M. Maccarrone, *"Potestas directa,"* pp. 37–38.

63. For Henry of Susa's immense "Golden Summa," *Summa aurea super titulis Decretalium (Summa copiosa, Summa titulorum decretalium,* or *Summa Hostiensis),* see note 40, above; see also *Lectura in quinque libros Decretalium* (called the *Apparatus*), Venice, 1581; and James A. Brundage, *Medieval Canon Law* (London/New York: Longman, 1995), esp. pp. 101–103, 163–164, 214. After being raised to the bishopric of Sisteron, England, in 1244, in 1250 Henry had been made bishop of Embrun (see Richard Kay, "Hostiensis and Some Embrun Provincial Councils," *Traditio* 20 [1964]: 503–513). Hostiensis's original Latin text from the *Lectura* 1:15:1 is cited in John A. Watt, *The Theory of Papal Monarchy in the Thirteenth Century: The Contribution of the Canonists* (London: Burns & Oates, 1965), pp. 57–58. Dante denounced "Ostiense" and the Machiavellian Innocent IV in *Epistola* 8:7 (ed. Toynbee, pp. 135, 145) much as he censured the Italian cardinals for their devotion to decretals; he remembered that St. Thomas Aquinas also had the virtue and courage to criticize both Hostiensis and Innocent IV in the *ST* II-II, q. 88, a. 2; consult St. Thomas Aquinas, *Summa theologica*, ed. Ottawa Institute of Medieval Studies, 4 vols. (Ottawa: Impensis Studii Generalis Ordinis Prædicatorum, 1941–1944), and St. Thomas Aquinas, *Summa theologica*, trans. Fathers of the English Dominican Province, 3 vols. (New York: Benziger Brothers, 1947–1948). Also see Maccarrone, "Teologia e diritto," pp. 21–22. Carlyle and Carlyle (5:324–334) give a convenient printing of Hostiensis's commentary on *Per venerabilem* from his *Summa aurea* and a synopsis of his theories. Friar Guido Vernani slavishly follows Hostiensis's views on the "keys" and the Donation of Constantine in the *Ref.* 3:32–43, 44–55.

64. See Watt, *Theory of Papal Monarchy*, pp. 39–41, 57–58, 127. See Brian Tierney, "'Tria quippe Distinguit Iudicia . . .': A Note on Innocent III's Decretal *Per Venerabilem*," *Speculum* 37 (1962): 48–59. See also Watt's "Hostiensis on *Per Venerabilem:* The Role of the College of Cardinals," in *Authority and Power: Studies in Medieval Law and Government Presented to Walter Ullmann on His Seventieth Birthday*, ed. Brian Tierney and Peter Linehan (Cambridge, U.K.: Cambridge University Press, 1980), pp. 99–113.

65. In documents, Giles of Rome is referred to variously as Ægidius (Egedius) Colonna, or Egidio Romano.

66. In *Con.* 4:24:9, Dante mentions the first part of "Egidius the Hermit's" (Giles of Rome's) Aristotelian-Thomistic *On the Rule of Princes* in the same breath as Cicero's *De officiis* and Vergil's *De senectute*; see *De regimine principum libri III*, ed. Girolamo Samaritano

(Rome: Zannetti, 1607; rpt. Darmstadt: Scientia Aalen, 1967); Ewart Lewis, *Medieval Political Ideas* (New York: Knopf, 1954), p. 253; Charles F. Briggs, *Giles of Rome's "De regimine principum": Reading and Writing Politics at Court and University, c. 1275–c.1525* (Cambridge, U.K.: Cambridge University Press, 1999), p. 18; and Vallone, *Antidantismo politico*, p. 52.

67. *On Ecclesiastical Power*, trans. Dyson, p. 8. As Dante does in the *Mon.*, Giles of Rome divides his treatise into three books, but for diametrically opposite reasons. In the first he demonstrates that the pope is supreme judge of all temporal and spiritual matters, since he holds both the temporal and the spiritual swords; in the second he refutes the assertion that the Church is forbidden to own any earthly goods since the pope has jurisdiction over all that may be possessed; in the third he follows St. Bernard's tempering of papal authority of any excess severity that could hinder the autonomy of the temporal power, yet he concludes by affirming the limitless plenitude of papal power. In his earlier treatise, *De regimine principum* (there is no modern edition), completed before 1285, dedicated to Philip the Fair, Giles had not dealt with the ecclesiastical origin of the state at all, but had distinguished three natural modes of temporal government's generation. See the text in Scholz, *Die Publizistik*, pp. 32–129.

68. James of Viterbo, in *De regimine Christiano (On Christian Government)* 5, declares: "[The pope] is the universal judge who judges all the faithful of whatever condition, dignity and station, and who can himself be judged by no one; rather, as the voice of the Apostle declares: 'He that judgeth me is the Lord'" (*On Christian Government*, ch. 5, trans. Dyson, p. 86). In ch. 8, James affirms, even against St. Bernard's cited strictures, that although worldly affairs be unworthy, "In cases of necessary need, however, [the spiritual power] can and must involve itself directly with temporal matters" (p. 117).

69. See a translation of the text in *The Church and State*, ed. Ehler and Morrall, pp. 90–92; and in *Readings in Church History*, ed. Colman J. Barry (Westminster, Md.: Newman Press, 1960), 1:465–467.

70. J. A. Watt, "Introduction" to John of Paris, *Royal and Papal Power*, p. 29. For the royal reaction to *Unam sanctam*, see Sophia Menache, "A Propaganda Campaign in the Reign of Philip the Fair, 1302–1303," *French History* 4 (1990): 427–454; and William J. Courtney, "Between Pope and King: The Parisian Letters of Adhesion of 1303," *Speculum* 17, no. 3 (1996): 577–605.

71. Vernani, *De potestate summi pontificis*, ch. 6, pp. 64–66.

72. Cf., e.g., Marsiglio of Padua's complaints in *Defensor pacis* 1:19:11 (trans. Gewirth, p. 95).

73. F. Guidonis Vernani Ariminensis Ordinis Prædicatorum, *De potestate summi pontificis et De reprobatione Monarchiæ compositæ a Dante Aligerio florentino tractatus duo nunc primum in lucem editi* (Bologna,1746, apud Thomam Coli, ex Typographia S. Thomæ Aquinatis); the text of the commentary is edited by Martin Grabmann as "Kommentar des Guido Vernani von Rimini O.P. zur Bulle *Unam Sanctam*," in his monograph *Studien uber den Einfluss der aristotelischen Philosophie auf die mittelalterlichen Theorien über das Verhältnis von Kirche und Staat* (in *Sitzungsberichte*

*der bayerischen Akademie der Wissenschaften,* Philosophisch-historische Abteilung [Jahrgang 1934], Heft 2), pp. 144–157.

74. Charles T. Davis cites two fundamental later sermons by Remigio, the first perhaps from July 7, 1305, to commemorate Benedict XI's death, and the second in honor of the death of Clement V on April 20, 1314. In the first, Remigio rejects any Uguccionian dualism by stating that all crowned heads depend on the papal crown as subjects to the pope. Not only is the pope empowered to depose kings by reason of sin, but, he affirms, elaborating on Hostiensis, "The pope crowns the emperor and deposes emperors and kings and institutes them when he sees fit [*quando hoc iudicat oportunum*]." In the second, he recants both his *De bono pacis,* where he had affirmed the temporal goal of human peace in the commune as supreme, and his *Contra falsos ecclesie professores,* by totally accepting the extreme hierocratic position: now the pope is placed above all men, possesses all things (like Dante's emperor), and has the cure of all matters in both *temporalia* and *spiritualia.* He echoes Innocent III's famous coronation speech asserting that the pope is king of kings and emperor of emperors. Christ had ordained him his vicar fully in all things, possessing the kingdom of David and the empire of Octavian. See Charles T. Davis's informative "Preface" to Tamburini's edition of *Contra falsos ecclesie professores,* pp. xvii–xviii, and nn. 37–39.

75. Notably James of Viterbo's chameleon concept of the membership of the Church parallels, while contrasting with, Dante's secular, but equally nebulous use of the *"multitudo"* of man constituting the subjects of the fulfilled empire in *Mon.* 1:3:4–9 and 2:6:5–6. See James of Viterbo, *De regimine christiano* 1:1; *On Christian Government,* trans. Dyson, esp. pp. 4–10; on regal appointments, p. 122.

76. Wilks, *The Problem of Sovereignty,* p. 6. Salvatorelli dates the *Summa de potestate ecclesiastica,* also entitled the *Summa de potestate papæ,* at 1320 (*L'Italia comunale,* p. 794). Cf. Vernani, *De potestate summi pontificis,* p. 69.

77. Cf. Agostino Trionfi's *Summa de potestate ecclesiastica,* cited by Aldo Vallone, in "Il pensiero politico di Dante dinanzi ad A. Trionfi e a G. Vernani da Rimini," in *Atti del Convegno Internazionale di Studi Danteschi a cura del Comune di Ravenna and Società Dantesca Italiana, Ravenna, 10–12 settembre 1971* (Ravenna: Longo, 1979), pp. 174–201, here, pp. 181, 183. See Augustinus Triumphus, *Tractatus brevis de duplici potestate prelatorum et laicorum,* in Scholz, *Die Publizistik,* p. 500.

78. See the exhaustive study by Wilks, *The Problem of Papal Sovereignty.*

79. In *Inf.* 19:53, Nicholas III, among the simonists, grimly and comically mistakes the pilgrim, Dante, for Boniface VIII. The latter is cursed by Guido da Montefeltro for his fraudulent counsel in *Inf.* 27:70. The reference to Boniface in *Purg.* 20:87 shows outrage in a different sense, for it separates in an orthodox manner the person of Boniface from the see he occupied; Dante demonstrates his deep respect for the office of pope and his title as "Vicar of Christ," as he has Hugh Capet foretell: *"veggio in Alagna intrar lo fiordaliso, / e nel vicario suo Cristo esser catto. / Veggiolo un'altra volta esser deriso; / veggio rinovellar l'aceto e'l fiele, / e tra vivi ladroni esser anciso"* (I see the fleur-de-lis enter Anagni, and, in His Vicar, Christ made

captive. I see Him mocked a second time; and I see renewed the vinegar and gall, and I see Him slain among living thieves). In *Par.* 30:148, however, Boniface is *"quel d'Alagna,"* "him of Anagni," and the butt of Beatrice's last vituperation of earthly cupidity. A republican, a high papalist, and prior of Santa Maria Novella in Florence, Tolomeo da Lucca, was, like most of the European public, shocked at the notorious absolution of Guillaume de Nogaret from the crime, for which the French Crown paid one hundred thousand florins to Clement V's treasury; see his *Secunda vita Clementis V (Vitæ paparum Avenionensium hoc est pontificum romanorum . . . ab anno Christ 1305 usque ad annum 1394*, ed. Etienne Baluze, new ed. Guillaume Mollat (Paris: Letouzey et Ané, 1914–1928), 4 vols; here, 1:39. Also see Sophia Menache, *Clement V,* Cambridge Studies in Medieval Life and Thought 36 (Cambridge, U.K.: Cambridge University Press, 1998), p. 196.

80. Philip had arrested a French bishop as a traitor; upon Boniface's complaint, Philip released the bishop but failed to apologize and make amends. Boniface then called a council of French prelates to hear the king's crimes and propose reform. The council's decision and censure was promulgated in *Ausculta fili* of December 5, 1301, in which Boniface claimed he was acting for the welfare of France and its good government but forcefully asserted his superiority over kings, and especially over Philip.

81. Pope Stephen VI (VII), 896–897, had ordered his predecessor, Pope Formosus, exhumed, and had tried his corpse arrayed in full papal regalia during the shameful "Cadaver Synod"; Sergius III reinstated the acts of that synod. The Church condemned the notorious precedent as sheer sacrilege but the usage persisted. Mollat records a later farce (*The Popes at Avignon,* p. 217): on February 19, 1329, Ludwig IV's wretched antipope, Nicholas V, tried John XXII as a heretic, substituting a bedecked dummy in Pisa's cathedral. He had it stripped of all its dignities and handed to the secular arm for incineration.

82. See Giles of Rome's treatise on papal abdication composed on Boniface's behalf: *De renunciatione pape,* ed. John R. Eastman, Texts and Studies in Religion 52 (Lewiston/ Queenston/Lampeter: Edwin Mellen Press, 1992).

83. Between these dates, 113 of the total 134 cardinals elevated were Frenchmen.

84. See Menache, *Clement V:* on his election, pp. 13–23; on the move to Avignon, pp. 23–30.

85. King Robert was a vassal of the papacy by his title of "Duke of Provence"— wherein now sat the Papacy.

86. The Franciscans, according to the bull *Exiit qui seminat* (1279) of Nicholas III (1277–1280), were not allowed to own property or have property rights but had only the "simple use of fact" of property owned by the Holy See; Nicholas banned any future discussion of the issue. The Spirituals, the followers of Peter John Olivi, placed the doctrine of absolute poverty as the rule of the gospel above any power of the pope to change it. On March 26, 1322, John XXII promulgated the bull *Cum inter nonnullos,* followed by *Quia nonnumquam* of November 12, 1323, condemning the doctrine that Christ and his Apostles possessed no property individually or communally.

87. See J. G. Sikes's edition of Hervæus Natalis, *Liber de paupertate Christi et apostolorum*, in *Archives d'histoire doctrinale et littéraire du moyen âge*, 12–13 (1937–1938 [publ. 1938]), esp. p. 214; the careful study, notes, and translation of the *The Poverty of Christ and the Apostles (Liber de paupertate Christi et apostolorum)*, by John D. Jones (Toronto: Pontifical Institute of Mediæval Studies, 1999), with extensive bibliography, esp. pp. 149–155; Salvatorelli, *L'Italia Comunale*, pp. 793–794; and Decima L. Douie, *The Nature and Effect of the Heresy of the Fraticelli* (Manchester, U.K.: University of Manchester Press, 1932), p. 20. See also the studies by Heft, *John XXII and Papal Teaching*; and by Mollat, *The Popes at Avignon*, pp. 16–17.

88. Innocent III, *Decretales* 2:2:10, *"Licet ex suscepto"*; *CIC*, 2:250–251; trans. Tierney, *Crisis*, pp. 153–154. Henry of Susa (Hostiensis) affirms it in his *Summa aurea* 4 (*Summa una*, f. 216; *Summa aurea*, col. 1387–1388).

89. James of Viterbo, *De regimine christiano* 8 (*On Christian Government*, trans. Dyson, pp. 119–220). Augustinus Triumphus, *Summa* 38:1:224, 40:1 ad 2:230, text cited in Wilks, *The Problem of Papal Sovereignty*, pp. 254–255. Vallone, "Il pensiero politico," pp. 174–201.

90. *"Quod nullus tunc nomen vicarii imperatoris vel alterius cuiuscunque officii retineat, assumat vel resumat...."* (*Extravagantes*, Titulus V, cap. 1 of John XXII in *CIC*, 2:1211–1212). See the translation of *Si fratrum* at the end of this volume. See Baethgen, "Der Anspruch des Papsttums auf das Reichvikariat," pp. 168–286, esp. 247–263; Baethgen later accepted the obvious authenticity of the *"sicut ... dixi"* sentence as archetypal along with Ricci's later dating, but did not see the *Mon.* as a reaction to contemporary events (cf. his "Die Entstehungzeit von Dantes *Monarchia*," pp. 30–32). Later John XXII probably accepted, or even helped spread, the rumor that Ludwig of Bavaria had had himself crowned at his first coronation by the now elderly Sciarra Colonna—guilty of the notorious assault and battery upon Pope Boniface—in Rome in 1328; John declared Ludwig a heretic in 1324.

91. Raoul Manselli, "Cangrande e il mondo ghibellino nell'Italia settentrionale alla venuta di Arrigo VII," in *Dante e la cultura veneta. Atti del Convegno di Studi organizzato dalla Fondazione "Giorgio Cini" in collaborazione con l'Istituto universitario di Venezia, l'Università di Padova, il Centro scaligero di Studi Danteschi, e i Comuni di Venezia, Padova, Verona. Venezia, Padova, Verona, 30 marzo–5 aprile 1966* (Florence: Olschki, 1966), pp. 39–49.

92. P. G. Ricci, *Il processo di Dante*, p. 70; Padoan, "Il Vicariato Cesareo," pp. 167–168.

93. Karl Hampe, "Die Abfassung der *Monarchia* in Dantes letzten Lebensjahren," *Deutsches Dante-Jahrbuch* 17 (1935): 58–74; Wilks, *The Problem of Papal Sovereignty*, pp. 254–255; *Mon.*, ed. Kay, p. xxix. For the *Si fratrum*, see Tarrant, ed., *Extravagantes Iohannis XXII*, pp. 156–162; and Mollat, *The Popes at Avignon*, p. 81.

94. Padoan, in "Il Vicariato Cesareo," p. 171, gives the date of the change as June 18, 1320.Lisetta Ciaccio, *Il Cardinale Legato Bertrando del Poggetto in Bologna (1327–1334)* (Bologna: Nicola Zanichelli, 1905), p. 13; in her still-useful volume, unfortunately lacking any list of contents or index, Ciaccio gave an exaggeratedly congratulatory view of the cardinal legate's ruthless despotism; she published the texts of the official documents in her appendix.

95. My emphasis. *"Magnifico atque victorioso domino domino* [sic] *Cani Grandi de la Scala sacratissimi Cesarei Principatus Principatus in urbe Verona et civitate Vicentie Vicario generali"* (*Epistola* 10 [13], ed. P. Toynbee, rev. C. Hardie, pp. 165–166, 195; ed. Brugnoli, pp. 598–599). The challenges to the genuineness of the letter have been put to rest by Robert Hollander's meticulous examination in *Dante's Epistle to Cangrande* (Ann Arbor: University of Michigan Press, 1993). Hollander, citing Giuliani, points to the parallel in the tribute to Can Grande in *Par.* 17:85: "Le sue *magnificenze* conosciute." Can Grande would suffer ignominious defeat at Padua on August 26, 1320, an event recorded by Albertino Mussato (see Padoan, "Il Vicariato Cesareo," p. 161, n. 1), setting the *ante quem* for dating the letter. The glowing tribute to Can Grande in *Par.* 17 would be published with the rest of the *Commedia* by Dante's sons in 1322. On the difficult question of the Veltro and DXV identification with the Veronese leader, see Anthony K. Cassell, *Lectura Dantis Americana: Inferno I* (Philadelphia: University of Pennsylvania Press, 1989), pp. 94–113.

96. Padoan noted that Dante's reference to his patron at the end of the *Questio* was "a polemical affirmation of the title of imperial vicar which Can Grande, with Matteo Visconti and Passerino Bonaccolsi, had no intention of renouncing, despite the pressure of Pope John XXII and the consequent excommunication" (*De situ et forma aque et terre*, ed. Giorgio Padoan [Florence: Le Monnier, 1968], p. 41). Also see *Questio de aqua et terra*, ed. Francesco Mazzoni, *Dante Alighieri-Opere Minori* (Milan/Naples: Ricciardi, 1979), pp. 772, 877–878). Giorgio Padoan, in *Introduzione a Dante*, 2nd ed. (Florence: Sansoni, 1981), p. 112, and in "Il Vicariato Cesareo," p. 161, cites the armistice with Padua and Treviso as the basis of Dante's use of *"invicto,"* "unconquered," in the dedication (p. 170). Giuseppe Mazzotta speaks of a "break" with Can Grande, but he must mean simply the change of abode ("Life of Dante," in *The Cambridge Companion to Dante*, ed. Rachel Jacoff [Cambridge, U.K.: Cambridge University Press, 1993], pp. 1–13). As attractive as the environs and imperial history of Ravenna were to him, Dante's loyalty to the Veronese leader remained firm until the end.

## NOTES TO CHAPTER 2: DANTE IN THE EYE OF THE STORM

1. See Chapter 1, n. 1, above.

2. Critics have generally remarked on the placidity of the style. The contrast with the poet's vehemence and preoccupation in his letters is considerable; cf. *Epistolæ* 5, 7, and 8, in *Dantis Alagherii Epistolæ: The Letters of Dante*, ed. Toynbee, rev. Hardie, pp. 42–120; *Epistole*, ed. Frugoni and Brugnoli, pp. 540–573. In *Par.* 30:133–138, Dante gives ardent tribute to the servant-monarch Henry VII, paramount in kingly righteousness, reserving for him a throne of justice and a crown of mercy in the center of the Celestial Rose: *"E'n quel gran seggio a che tu li occhi tieni / per la corona che già v'è su posta, / prima che tu a queste nozze ceni / sederà l'alma (che fia giù agosta) / de l'alto Arrigo, ch'a drizzare Italia / verrà in prima che ella sia disposta"* (And in the great chair whereon you fix your eyes because of the crown that already is set

above it, before you sup at these nuptials shall sit the soul, which on earth will be imperial, of the lofty Henry, who will come to set Italy straight before she is ready). See H. Theodore Silverstein, "The Throne of the Emperor Henry in Dante's Paradise and the Medieval Conception of Christian Kingship," *Harvard Theological Review* 32 (1939): 115–129. Vinay observed: "The idea of the *Monarchia* matured in the thoughtful calm that came after the prophetic anguish of the *Epistole*." Dante only gives the most general censure, e.g., of prelates who abscond with church revenues to enrich their families (*Mon.* 2:10:1). George Holmes notes that the *Mon.* "contains no reference to contemporary events," but disregards Ricci and the MS evidence concerning the date of composition ("*Monarchia* and Dante's Attitude toward the Popes," in *Dante and Governance*, ed. John Woodhouse [Oxford, U.K.: Clarendon Press, 1997], pp. 46–57). See also L. Sebastio, "Il 'philosophus' e la 'Monarchia' in Dante: Per una funzione sociale del sapiente," *Italianistica* 10 (1981): 323–347. But Dante's strategy of ignoring contemporary events (except for the reference to his own progress on the *Par.* and the split in the imperial election; see below, n. 3) and the tempering of his style has led to a misinterpretation of the poet's fierce involvement in his subject, for he raises high his prophet's fist. Friedrich Baethgen, e.g., believed, wrongly, as it turns out that "Dante's *Monarchy* is not a piece written for a special occasion with which the Poet interferes in a contemporary conflict or contemporary polemic" (*Die Entstehungszeit von Dantes Monarchia, in Sizungsberichte der Bayerische Akademie der Wissenschaften, Philosophisch-historische Klasse*, Heft 5 [Munich: Jahrgang, 1966], p. 31; cf. N. Zingarelli, *La vita*, pp. 679–710). Allen Mandelbaum strikes a different chord: for him the *Mon.* is "a passionate pamphlet"; see his "Introduction" to *Lectura Dantis* [*Californiana*]: *Inferno*, ed. Allen Mandelbaum, Anthony Oldcorn, and Charles Ross (Berkeley/Los Angeles/London: University of California Press, 1998), p. 7; but Mandelbaum unfortunately neglects the latest scholarship on the dating.

3. The clause at *Mon.* 3:16:14—"it has happened that sometimes those to whom the honor of heralding has been granted fall into disagreement"—clearly points to the notorious difficulties experienced by Ludwig of Bavaria *after* the disputed election of 1314 that was to culminate in the grand solution of the Golden Bull in 1356. Earlier, the electors' choice of Henry of Luxembourg had been unanimous, and approved with blessings, at least at first, by Pope Clement V—events all out of tune with the protests of the *Mon.*

4. Kenneth Pennington, "Henry VII and Robert of Naples," in *Das Publikum politischer Theorie im 14. Jahrhundert*, ed. Jürgen Miethke, with Arnold Bühler, Schriften des Historisches Kolleg, Kolloquien 21 (Munich: R. Oldenbourg, 1992), pp. 81–92.

5. Karl Hampe, "Die Abfassung der *Monarchia* in Dantes letzten Lebensjahren," *Deutsches Dante-Jahrbuch*, n.s., 17, no. 8 (1935): 58–74, here, pp. 65–66.

6. See Walter Ullmann, "The Development of the Medieval Idea of Sovereignty," *English Historical Review* 46 (1949): 1–33, here, p. 5; rpt. in *Law and Jurisdiction in the Middle Ages*, ed. George Garnett (London: Variorum Reprints, 1988), selection 7, same pagination. Cino da Pistoia, the poet and imperialist lawyer, agreed with Dante: "Temporally all peoples

and all kings are under the empire, as they are spiritually under the pope" (Maria Monti Gennaro, *Cino da Pistoja giurista* [Città di Castello: "Il Solco" Casa Editrice, 1924], p. 176).

7. Such as in the treatise of the Austrian abbot of Admont, Engelbert, in his *De ortu et fine Romani imperii*, outlining the real state of affairs at the time of Henry VII's descent into Italy for coronation (see W. Ullmann, "The Development of the Medieval Idea of Sovereignty," p. 2).

8. As if to palliate the deeply held animosity that the imperial-papal quarrels aroused, decretalist writings, in the wake of St. Thomas Aquinas, are most often characterized by dispassion (e.g., Agostino d'Ancona's [Augustinus Triumphus's] style in his enormous *Summa de potestate ecclesiastica* completed in 1326, five years after Dante's death, is rigidly impersonal). Vernani makes the exception to this contemporary convention in his rhetoric of the *Ref.*—but not in his earlier canonistic works—with his censurous aim of arousing future polemics: the *Mon.* had, by 1328, become caught up in the atmosphere of dispute of the papacy against Marsiglio of Padua's *Defensor pacis*. Ettore Paratore gives a useful bibliography on the poet's style and authors whom he read in "Il latino di Dante," *Cultura e Scuola* 4 (1965): 94–124; rpt. in *Dante nella critica d'oggi: Risultati e prospettive*, ed. Umberto Bosco (Florence: Le Monnier, 1965), with the same pagination.

9. *Nic. Ethics* 1:3:5–8:1094b; trans. H. Rackham, LCL, pp. 8–9. St. Thomas Aquinas, *Commentary on the Nicomachean Ethics*, trans. C. I. Litzinger, Library of Living Catholic Thought, 2 vols. (Chicago: Henry Regnery, 1964), here, 1:17.

10. "I have found nothing more fitting even for your exalted station than the sublime Cantica of the *Commedia*, which is adorned with the title *Paradiso;* this then, dedicated to yourself, with the present letter to serve as its superscription, I inscribe, dedicate, and, in fine, entrust to you." (*Epistolæ* 10 [13], para. 3, in *Dantis Alagherii Epistolæ: The Letters of Dante*, ed. Toynbee, rev. Hardie, pp. 170, 197; *Epistole*, ed. Frugoni and Brugnoli, pp. 602). Francesco Mazzoni settles on a dating of the letter between sometime in 1315 and December 1317, centering on 1316, while, more persuasively, Giorgio Padoan notes that Dante had dedicated the *entire* unpublished *Par.* ("canticam ... illam ... vobis offero") to his former benefactor and would assign the *Letter* ("by way of an introduction to the presented work"; para. 4) to the more likely date of the second half of 1319 or August 1320 ("Il Vicariato Cesareo," p. 174). Thus the *Letter* and the *Mon.* would be perfectly contemporary. See Mazzoni's many admirable studies: "Per l'epistola a Cangrande," *Studi dedicati a Angelo Monteverdi* (Modena: STEM, 1959), pp. 3–21, rpt. in *Contributi di filologia dantesca* (Florence: Sansoni, 1966); "Le *Epistole* di Dante," in *Comitato Nazionale per le Celebrazioni del VII Centenario della Nascita Di Dante, Conferenze Aretine, 1965* (Arezzo: Accademia Petrarca-Bibbiena, Società Dantesca Casentinese, 1966), pp. 47–100; "L'edizione delle opere latine minori," in *Atti del Convegno Internazionale di Studi Danteschi a cura del Comune di Ravenna and Società Dantesca Italiana, Ravenna, 10–12 settembre 1971* (Ravenna: Longo, 1979), pp. 129–143, 159–166; and "Bruno Nardi dantista," *L'Alighieri* 23 (1982): 8–28, rpt in Bruno Nardi, *"Lecturæ" e altri studi danteschi*, ed. Rudy Abardo (Florence: Casa Editre Le Lettere, 1990), pp. 3–21. See the convincing points of

verbal comparison made by Mazzoni in "L'Epistola a Cangrande," *Rendiconti della Accademia Nazionale dei Lincei.* Classe di Scienze morali, storiche e filologiche, ser. 8, vol. 10 (1955): 157–198, esp. 177; see also Padoan in "La composizione," pp. 15–16, 24–25, et passim. Hollander discusses parallels with the letter, the *Par.*, and the *Mon.* in his *Dante's Epistle to Cangrande*, pp. 11–12, 21–22, 44–49, 52–53, 80–81, 91.

11. On Dante's struggle for an authoritative voice, see Albert Russell Ascoli, "The Unfinished Author: Dante's Rhetoric of Authority in *Convivio* and *De vulgari eloquentia*," in *The Cambridge Companion to Dante*, ed. Rachel Jacoff (Cambridge, U.K.: Cambridge University Press, 1993), pp. 45–66. See also E. Gorra's useful comments in "Dante e Clemente V," *Giornale storico della letteratura italiana* 69 (1917): 193–216.

12. On the influence of Brunetto Latini, his *Rettorica*, and the his use of Pier della Vigna's chancery letters, see Charles T. Davis, *Dante's Italy*, pp. 179–180.

13. *wrestling ring: "palestra."* As his vivid rhetoric proves, Dante knew that the term designated a public place for training or exercise, especially in wrestling; the word παλαίστρα derives from Greek παλαίειν "to wrestle" (cf. also his use of the word in *Epistola* 8, To the Italian Cardinals, ed. Toynbee, pp. 142, 147). The poet's rhetoric has a humanist strategy: these two first, conspicuous, transliterated Greek terms, "gymnasium" and "palæstra," not only carry further the metaphor of Rome's achievement of preeminence through athletic contest, but in this medieval debate-come-wrestling-match, the "auctor," Dante himself, becomes one with the ancient Roman athletes, both wrestler and champions with sword and shield.

14. Cf., e.g., the blasting quote from Dn 6:22 at the beginning of book 3, the weariness and sarcasm expressed in *Mon.* 3:3:17: against the Guelph partisans ("who bedecked with crow feathers make an ostentatious display of themselves. . . . These, the sons of iniquity, who . . . prostitute their mother [Church], expel their brothers, and then refuse to submit to a judge . . . mired as they are in their greed, they would not understand first principles"), and the poet's irritation at 3:7:4. Most helpful on Dante's letters is Lino Pertile's article "Dante Looks Forward and Back: Political Allegory in the Epistles," *Dante Studies* 115 (1997): 1–17.

15. In his *Fundamenta militantis ecclesiæ* of July 18, 1278, Pope Nicholas III ascribed the glory of present Rome to the martyred saints Peter and Paul, calling the city, *"Gens sancta, populus electus, civitas sacerdotalis et regia"*; Charles T. Davis recounts Nicholas's use of republican tactics to strengthen his hold on Rome in "Ptolemy of Lucca and Pope Nicholas III," *Speculum* 50 (1975): 422–423. Dante also describes the Romans as "that holy, pious, and glorious people" in *Mon.* 2:5:5. Eugenio Dupré Theseider calls Nicholas III's *Fundamenta* the "Magna Carta" of relations between the papacy and the Roman people (*Roma dal comune di popolo alla signoria pontificia* [1252–1377] [Bologna: Licinio Cappelli, 1952], p. 211). See also Charles T. Davis, *Dante and the Idea of Rome* (Oxford, U.K.: Clarendon Press, 1957), p. 20. Davis concluded that Boniface VIII's Jubilee of 1300, which Dante had also hailed, "sealed the historical predominance of the *civitas sacerdotalis et regia* [priestly and royal city] over the

other aspects of the medieval idea of Rome" (p. 22; see also p. 35). Vernani attacks Dante for failing to mention the Jews as the Chosen People and, ironically, neglects to mention this revisionist, conciliatory, and more positive view held by the Church concerning Rome and the Romans.

16. The "earthly city," signifies, in Augustinian terms, the damned—those cursed and lost in the hereafter and the future damned who are still living on earth. It is not to be identified with the earthly realm or state where, daily and indistinguishably, the future blessed and the future damned dwell together; see St. Augustine, *De civitate Dei* 14:28, 19:6 and 13. On St. Augustine's ideas on the lack of progress in human history and his concomitant refutation of the cyclical theories of both pagan philosophers and Origen, see Theodore E. Mommsen, "St. Augustine and the Christian Idea of Progress: The Background of *The City of God*," in *Medieval and Renaissance Studies*, ed. Eugene F. Rice Jr. (Ithaca, N.Y.: Cornell University Press, 1959), pp. 265–298. Still useful is Herbert A. Deane's *The Political and Social Ideas of St. Augustine* (New York/London: Columbia University Press, 1963).

17. Aristotle, *Nic. Ethics* 1130b: "Perhaps to be a good man is not the same as to be a good citizen in any state" (text in St. Thomas Aquinas, *Commentary on the Nic. Ethics*, trans. Litzinger, 1:3940; and in *Nicomachean Ethics*, in *The Complete Works of Aristotle: The Revised Oxford Translation*, ed. Jonathan Barnes, Bollingen Series 71, 2 vols. [Princeton, N.J.: Princeton University Press, 1984], 2:1747).

18. Aristotle, *Pol.* 1:1:9:1252a: "It is clear that the city-state is a natural growth, and that man is, by nature, a political animal" (trans. R. Rackham, LCL, pp. 8–9; trans. Barnes, 2:1986). William of Moerbeke had rendered the *Pol.* into Latin in the 1260s; see St. Thomas Aquinas's *In libros Politicorum Aristotelis Expositio*, ed. R. M. Spiazzi (Turin/Rome: Marietti, 1951), *Textus Aristotelis*, p. 5; Thomas's *Lectio* 1, no. 34, p. 11.

19. Aristotle, *Metaph.* 194b16–195b30, 983a24–b1, 1013a24–b28; consult also St. Thomas Aquinas's *Commentary on Aristotle's Metaphysics: S. Thomæ Aquinatis, In duodecim Libros Metaphysicorum Aristotelis Expositio*, ed. M. R. Cathala and R. M. Spiazzi (Turin/Rome: Marietti, 1964), ad loc.; Paul E. Sigmund, "Law and Politics," in *The Cambridge Companion to Aquinas*, ed. Norman Kretzmann and Eleonore Stump (Cambridge, U.K.: Cambridge University Press, 1993), pp. 217–231; and A. Toscano, "Dante: Il discorso aristotelico nella *Monarchia*," *Forum Italicum* 15, nos. 2–3 (1981): 139–152.

20. Tolomeo da Lucca, in his completion of St. Thomas Aquinas's treatise *De regimine principum ad regem Cypri* (beyond book 2:10:4), states: "It is natural for human beings to be social and political animals, living in a multitude, as natural necessity requires" (*On the Government of Rulers*, trans. Blythe, p. 61); according to Aquinas, the republic, or the "polity," was the natural Edenic state—as it was for Tolomeo (p. 124). See also J. D. Dawson's translation of Thomas's *On Princely Government*, in *Aquinas: Selected Political Writings*, ed. A. P. D'Entrèves (Oxford, U.K.: Blackwell, 1948), p. 3. See Oscar J. Brown, *Natural Rectitude and Divine Law in Aquinas*, Studies and Texts 55 (Toronto: Pontifical Institute of Mediaeval Studies, 1981), pp.

22–23. St. Thomas's description of man as not only a "political animal," as Aristotle had described him, but also as a "social" creature, was in common use at the theological *studium* in Santa Maria Novella. See Charles T. Davis, "Remigio de' Girolami and Dante: A Comparison of Their Conceptions of Peace," *Studi danteschi* 36 (1959): 105–136, esp. 106–107, and "Roman Patriotism and Republican Propaganda: Ptolemy of Lucca and Pope Nicholas III," *Speculum* 50 (1975): 411–433. Also see Maria Consiglia De Matteis, *La "Teologia politica comunale" di Remigio de' Girolami* (Bologna: Pàtron, 1977); R. A. Markus, "Two Conceptions of Political Authority: Augustine, *De civitate Dei* XIX 14–15, and Some Thirteenth-Century Interpretations," *Journal of Theological Studies* [Oxford, Clarendon Press], n.s. 15, pt. 1 (April 1965): 68–100; and Charles T. Davis, "Education in Dante's Florence," in *Dante's Italy and Other Essays* (Philadelphia: University of Pennsylvania Press, 1984), pp. 137–165.

21. Augustine's retelling of the pirate tale, revealing that kingdoms were nothing but robberies on a vast scale, was of especial use to some extreme papalist writers (although, as we shall see, Tolomeo da Lucca was a great exception). In his *On Ecclesiastical Power* [1:5;5], dedicated to Boniface VIII, ca. 1301–1302, the Augustinian hermit Giles of Rome (Egidio Romano) used it to charge the illegitimacy of any heathen or profane rule: "Any royal power not instituted through the priesthood was either not rightful, in that it was more robbery than power" (trans. Dyson, p. 11). Still most useful for an examination of St. Augustine's thought and influence is Henri-Xavier Arquillière's *L'Augustinisme politique: Essai sur la formation des théories politiques du Moyen-Age* (Paris: J. Vrin, 1934).

22. "The truth of valid inference [from historical events] was not instituted by men; rather it was observed by men and set down that they might learn and teach it. For it is perpetually instituted by God in the reasonable order of things [*ipsa tamen veritas conexionum non instituta, sed animadversa est ab hominibus et notata, ut eam possint discere vel docere. Nam est in rerum ratione perpetua et divinitus instituta*]. Thus the person who narrates the order of events in time does not compose that order himself. . . . In the same way, he who says, 'When a consequent is false, it is necessary that the antecedent upon which it is based be false also,' speaks very truly; but he does not arrange matters so they are this way. Rather he simply points out an existing truth" (*De doctrina christiana* 2:32[:121]; *On Christian Doctrine*, trans. D. W. Robertson (Indianapolis/New York: Bobbs-Merrill, 1958), p. 68. As Charles T. Davis has put it, "For Dante, later revelation did not contradict but only deepened the earlier conception of the Roman destiny" (*Dante and the Idea of Rome*, p. 76).

23. *Dantis Alagherii Epistolæ*, ed. P. Toynbee, pp. 128 and 143. With the late Charles T. Davis we can concur that "[Dante] did not merely value the ancient city for itself; he used it as an exemplum which could compel humility, rather than arrogance." As Dante believed, "Christ came, and Peter established the see of Rome, not to interrupt the tradition, but to fulfil it" (*Dante and the Idea of Rome*, p. 32).

24. See the bibliography by Earline J. Ashworth, in *The Tradition of Medieval Logic and Speculative Grammar from Anselm to the End of the Seventeenth Century: A Bibliography from 1836 Onwards*, Subsidia Medievalia 9 (Toronto: Pontifical Institute of Mediaeval Studies, 1978).

25. See Kenelm Foster, *Petrarch: Poet and Humanist,* Writers of Italy Series 9 (Edinburgh, U.K.: Edinburgh University Press, 1985), p. 152.

26. Immanuel Kant, *Critique of Pure Reason,* trans. Norman Kemp Smith (London: Macmillan, 1929), p. 17.

27. See Henry B. Veatch, *Aristotle: A Contemporary Appreciation* (Bloomington/London: Indiana University Press, 1974), p. 163.

28. The humanist Lorenzo Valla demonstrated the purely rhetorical value of dialectic logic in his *Dialecticæ disputationes* of 1439. See P. Osmund Lewry, "Dialectic," in *Dictionary of the Middle Ages,* 4:168–171; Eleonore Stump, "Dialectic," in *The Seven Liberal Arts in the Middle Ages,* ed. David L. Wagner (Bloomington: Indiana University Press, 1983), pp. 125–146; Donald A. White, *Medieval History: A Source Book* (Homewood, Ill.: Dorsey Press, 1965), p. 518; and Elizabeth Marilyn Mozzillo-Howell, "Dialectic and the *Convivio,*" *Italian Culture* 9 (1991): 29–41.

29. See Aristotle's own claim for this in *De sophisticis elenchis* 34:184b1–4; in *Aristoteles Latinus* 4:1–3, ed. Bernardus G. Dod (Leiden: E. J. Brill; Brussels: Desclée de Brouwer, 1975), p. 108.

30. *Averroës' Middle Commentaries on Aristotle's Categories and De Interpretatione,* trans., notes, and intro. by Charles E. Butterworth (Princeton, N.J.: Princton University Press, 1983).

31. Porphyry the Phoenician, *Isagoge,* trans., intro., and notes by Edward W. Warren (Toronto: Pontifical Institute of Mediæval Studies, 1975).

32. After Boccaccio's assertions in his *Trattatello* (ed. Pier Giorgio Ricci, in *Tutte le opere di Giovanni Boccaccio,* vol. 3, ed. Vittore Branca [Milan: Mondadori, 1974] in the first redaction, para. 25, 75, 123, pp. 443–444, 455, 467–468: in the the second redaction, para. 20, 56, 76, pp. 501, 509, 413), some scholars still contend that Dante spent some of his exiled years, 1306–1307 in Paris, and even at Oxford; the Parisians claim he actually frequented the lectures of Siger de Brabant, hearing the master syllogize "invidious truths" in the "Street of Straw," "Rue de Fouarre," and identify it today with that sign posted as "Rue Dante." See Dorothy Sayers, in Dante Alighieri, *The Divine Comedy: Paradiso,* trans. D. Sayers (New York: Penguin Books, 1973), p. 370; and Pearl Kibre, "Dante and the Universities of Paris and Oxford," in *"The Divine Comedy" and the Encyclopedia of Arts and Sciences,* ed. Giuseppe Di Scipio and Aldo Scaglione (Amsterdam/Philadelphia: John Benjamins, 1988), pp. 367–371. Except for Boccaccio's, the evidence is slim.

33. See E. L. Fortin, *Dissidence et philosophie au Moyen Age* (Montreal: Bellarmin; Paris: J. Vrin, 1981), esp. pp. 69–70, with extensive, useful references in the notes. See also D. H. Salman, "Jean de la Rochelle et les débuts de l'averroïsme latin," *Archives d'histoire doctrinale et littéraire du Moyen Age* 22–23 (1947–1948): 133–144.

34. Lists of errors had been made at Paris and Oxford in 1240, 1270, 1277, and 1284. Many works were written against reading Aristotle and his Arabic and Jewish commentators uncritically: among them, St. Albertus Magnus, *De unitate intellectus contra Averroistas,* ed. Alfons Hufnagel, in Albert the Great, *Opera omnia* (Monasterii Westfalorum in Ædibus

Aschendorff, 1975), vol. 17, pt. 1, pp. 1–30; St. Bonaventure, *De decem præceptis*, in *S. Bonaventuræ Opera Omnia* (Florence: Quaracchi, 1882–1902), 5:514, and *De donis spiritus sancti*, 5:496–498; St. Thomas Aquinas, *On the Truth of the Catholic Faith: Summa contra gentiles*, trans. Anton C. Pegis, Vernon J. Bourke, and Charles J. O'Neil, 4 vols. (Garden City, N.Y.: Doubleday, 1955–1957), and *On There Being Only One Intellect, Against the Averroists* of 1270, trans. Ralph McInerny (Weast Lafayette, Ind.: Purdue University Press, 1993), especially McInerny's "Introduction," pp. 1–13. Giles of Rome's (Egidio Romano) *Errores philosophorum Averrois, Avicenna, Algezelis, Alkindi, Rabbi Moysis* is available in the original and English translation in *Errors of the Philosophers*, ed. Joseph Koch, trans. John O Riedl (Milwaukee, Wis.: Marquette University Press, 1944). See also Ignatius Brady, "Questions at Paris, c. 1260–1270," *Archivum Franciscanum historicum* 61 (1968): 434–461, and "Background to the Condemnation of 1270: Master William of Baglione, O.F.M.," *Franciscan Studies* 30 (1970): 6–48; and Fernand Van Steenberghen, *Thomas Aquinas and Radical Aristoteliansim* (Washington, D.C.: The Catholic University of America Press, 1980). The bibliography on Averroism is vast; see Bruno Nardi, *Saggi di filosofia dantesca* (Milan: Società Anonima Editrice Dante Alighieri, 1930; 2nd ed., Florence: La Nuova Italia, 1967), esp. pp. 239–306; and Michael E. Marmura, "Rushd, Ibn (Averroës)," in *Dictionary of the Middle Ages*, 10:571–575.

35. *Conv.* 2:12:7. Contemporaneous with the theological *studium* at Santa Maria Novella in Florence, like the Franciscans at Santa Croce, the Augustinians at Santo Spirito had a *studium* also as early as 1287, and perhaps as early as 1274, but as yet little has been learned of the school's possessions and teaching practice. Peter John Olivi (Pierre Jean Olieu, or Petrus Iohannis Olivi), the leader of the Franciscan Spirituals, had left his two-year tenure as principal lector at the *studium* of Santa Croce for a position at Montpellier in 1289. Olivi attacked the papal claim to universal power with sarcasm and irony (e.g., in his *Quodlibeta, Quæstio* 18; see Maccarrone, *Terzo libro*, pp. 6–9). While we can hazard that Olivi's direct influence upon the poet would have been at the most from public sermons and reading, the friar's adherents and successors at the convent also keenly followed Olivi's tenets (see Charles T. Davis, "The Florentine *Studia* and Dante's 'Library,'" pp. 340–341).

36. See Davis, "The Florentine *Studia* and Dante's 'Library,'" esp. pp. 419, 423, 424, 430–431, for lists of authors, manuscripts, and didactic methods; also see Mineo-Paluello, "Remigio Girolami's *De bono communi*," pp. 56–71.

37. Dante compares veiled Mercury to dialectic in the tradition of John of Salisbury's *Metalogicon* 4:29, et passim; see *The Metalogicon of John of Salisbury: A Twelfth-Century Defense of the Verbal and Logical Arts of the Trivium*, trans. Daniel D. McGarry [Berkeley/Los Angeles: University of California Press, 1962], p. 246, et passim): "The heaven of Mercury may be compared to dialectic on account of two properties, because Mercury is the smallest star in the heavens, for the length of its diameter is no more than 232 miles, according to Alfraganus, who asserts that it is one twenty-eighth the diameter of the earth, which is 6,500 miles; the second property is that it pursues its course more veiled by the rays of the sun than any other star. These two properties are found in dialectic too, for dialectic is a more

compact body of knowledge than any other science, being set out in its entirety in a text more veiled than any other science in that it proceeds by more subtle and hypothetical arguments than any other science" (*Conv.* 2:13:12; trans. Ryan, p. 68). As to Dante's method here, probably based on lucubrations of Remigio de' Girolami, we can compare the poet's reticence and ultimate acceptance and revision of the "two lights" analogy with the empire and the papacy that we examine in Chapter 3.

38. See *Tractatus, Called Afterwards Summule logicales*, ed. L. M. de Rijk, Philosophical Texts and Studies 22 (Assen: Van Gorcum, 1972), and *The "Summulæ logicales" of Peter of Spain*, ed. and trans. Joseph P. Mullally, Publications in Medieval Studies 8 (South Bend, Ind.: University of Notre Dame Press, 1945). Dante records his early attitude toward dialectic in *Conv.* 2:13:11–12, where he metaphorically stresses its rhetorical power by comparing the discipline to Mercury and compares it to the diminutive planet by reason of its size ("a more compact body of knowledge than any other science"; see n. 37, above), and by reason of its subtle, veiled methods. On such traditional imagery, see John of Salisbury, who cites Martianus Capella's *Metalogicon*; see *The Metalogicon*, trans. Daniel D. Garry, pp. 79, 94, 245–246.

39. Esp. the ch. "De sillogismo" in Peter of Spain, *Summule logicales, Tractatus* IV, 2, in ed. de Rijk, pp. 43–44.

40. On Agostino d'Ancona, see P. B. Ministeri, "De Augustini de Ancona O. E. S. A. (†1328) vita et operibus," *Analecta Augustiniana* 22 (1951–1952): 154, 163–166. Also see the monograph by Wilks, *The Problem of Sovereignty*; William D. McCready, "The Problem of the Empire in Augustinus Triumphus and Late Medieval Papal Hierocratic Theory," *Traditio* 30 (1974): 325–349, and "Papalists and Anti-papalists: Aspects of the Church-State Controversy in the Later Middle Ages," *Viator* 6 (1975): 241–273; and Lawrence Gushee, "Augustinus Triumphus," *Dictionary of the Middle Ages*, 2:1. The partisan surname "Triumphus" does not appear until the sixteenth century.

41. For the process, see George Hayward Joyce, *Principles of Logic* (London/New York: Longmans, Green, 1908; rpt. 3rd ed., 1949), p. 255; and Elizabeth Mozzillo-Howell's useful comments in "Dante's Art of Reason: A Study of Medieval Logic and Semantics in the *Monarchy*" (Ph.D. diss., Harvard University, 1998; Ann Arbor, Mich.: UMI, 1998), pp. 97–98.

42. See the essay and bibliography listed on the "DXV" prophecy in Cassell, "Il Veltro," in *Lectura Dantis Americana: Inferno 1* (Philadelphia: University of Pennsylvania Press, 1989), pp. 100, 176, et passim.

43. On the *"vulneratio naturæ"* and Dante's use of it in *Inf.* 1, see John Freccero, "Dante's Firm Foot and the Journey without a Guide," *Harvard Theological Review* 51 (1960): 3–14; Cassell, *Lectura Dantis Americana: Inferno 1*, pp. 33–36, 155; and Bruno Nardi, *Saggi di filosofia dantesca*, p. 380.

44. Curiously, the repeated wars against imperial and monarchical dictatorships in the twentieth century drove certain readers into seeing the autocratic *Mon.* as a precursor for

the organization of the United Nations; Herbert Schneider's loose paraphrase of the *Mon.* entitled *On World Government* with Dino Bigongiari's desultory preface in the Library of Liberal Arts series (1949) is a prime example, as is Donald Nicholl's British version of 1954. Useful are: Antonio De Angelis, *Il Concetto d'imperium e la communità sopranazionale in Dante* (Milan: Giuffrè, 1965); Katharina Comoth, *"Pax universalis:* Philosophie und Politik in Dantes *Monarchia,"* in *Soziale Ordnung im Selbstverständnis des Mittelalters, Akten des VI Internaz. Kongress für Mittelaltische Philosophie der Société internationale pour l'étude de la philosophie mediévale. Bonn 29 August–3 September 1977,* ed. J. P. Beckmann et al., 2 vols. (Berlin/New York: De Gruyter, 1981), vol. 2, ed. Albert Zimmermann, pp. 341–350; and J. J. Ledesma Uribe, "El Orden internacional en la *Monarquia* de Dante," *Juridica* 12 (1980): 375–403.

45. A valid categorical syllogism must have exactly three terms, each of which must occur twice and in precisely the same sense; otherwise the syllogism is said to commit the fallacy of four terms; if a term is used with more than one sense it also commits the fallacy of equivocation. In *Prior Analytics* 1:25:41b36:1, Aristotle lays out the fundamental rule that "every demonstration will proceed through three terms and no more." (Dante quotes the *Prior Analytics* under the title *De sillogismo simpliciter.*) See *Analytica priora, translatio Boethii* 1:25, in *Aristoteles latinus,* ed. Lorenzo Mineo-Paluello (Bruges/Paris: Desclée de Brouwer, 1962), p. 54. Peter of Spain (Pope John XXI) affirms that "[e]very syllogism consists of three terms and two propositions" in his "De sillogismis," *Summulæ logicales, Tractatus* IV, 2 (ed. de Rijk, pp. 43–44), and also see "De sillogismo," *Tractatus* V, 8 (ed. de Rijk, pp. 48–49). Cf. Cicero, *De inventione,* in *Cicero,* trans. H. M. Hubbell, LCL, 2:101–110. But Dante himself commits this error, as in *Mon.* 1:11:2.

46. Dante only labels it as such in the third—textbook—case, 3:7:3.

47. Dante's concept of noncause is actually based not on logical procedure but on the rhetorical *post hoc, propter hoc* fallacy outlined in Aristotle's *Rhetoric* 1401b30 (trans. Barnes, 2:2234–2235). See also Mozzillo-Howell, "Dante's Art of Reason," pp. 222–225. Vernani does not interest himself in this argument.

48. Filippo Villani's story, that Dante died suddenly, probably from malaria, because he had been ill received by the Venetians, and, refused permission to return safely by sea, was thus forced to take the circuitous journey back along the malarial coast is probably mere anti-Venetian, Black Party propaganda; see Giorgio Petrocchi, "Commiato del Poeta," in *Vita di Dante* (Bari: Laterza, 1984), pp. 221–222. At some point, perhaps after 1328, both because of such threats as those of du Poujet, and because of the unceasing Florentine demands for the poet's body, the Franciscans of San Pier Maggiore (now the Church of San Francesco) in Ravenna apparently were forced to hide Dante's mortal remains. Again, in 1677, the Franciscan Antonio Santi removed the poet's bones from his mausoleum, bricking them up within the protective church walls for their later, fortuitous, and quite remarkable rediscovery just in time for the centenary year, 1865. The poet's remains were then finally interred in the nearby eighteenth-century tomb that had long stood empty.

49. See Ciaccio, *Beltrando del Pogetto*, p. 12, text, and n. 2; Mollat, *The Popes at Avignon*, pp. 83–84. On John XXII and later theories of absolutism, see E. H. Kantorowicz, "Mysteries of State: An Absolutist Concept and Its Late Medieval Origins," in *Selected Studies by Ernst H. Kantorowicz* (Locust Valley, N.Y.: J. J. Augustin, 1965), pp. 381–398.

50. *The Liber Augustalis; or, Constitutions of Melfi Promulgated by the Emperor Frederick II for the Kingdom of Sicily in 1231*, trans. James M. Powell (Syracuse, N.Y.: Syracuse University Press, 1971), p. 9.

51. The archbishops of Mainz claimed the right to crown the German kings, but had gained the habit of always siding with the papacy against the empire—e.g., Archbishop Siegfried (d. 1249) crowned two kings who were papal rivals to Frederick II, and these actions are proudly celebrated on Siegfried's tomb. On Ludwig's coronation, see Henry Stephen Lucas, "The Low Countries and the Disputed Imperial Election of 1314," *Speculum* 21 (1946): 72–114, esp. "The Coronation of the Rivals," pp. 106–109. Ludwig repeatedly implored Archbishop Henry to come to him, but in vain (Lucas, p. 108).

52. See Mollat, *The Popes at Avignon*, pp. 96–98, and esp. p. 206; Luigi Salvatorelli, *L'Italia communale dal secolo XI alla metà del secolo XIV*, Storia d'Italia 4 (Milan: Mondadori, 1940), p. 792; Carl Müller, *Der Kampf Ludwigs des Baiern mit der römischen Curie: Ein Breitrag zur kirchlichen Geschichte des 14. Jahrhunderts*, 2 vols. (Tübingen: H. Laupp, 1879–1880); and H. S. Offler, "Empire and Papacy: The Last Struggle," *Transaction of the Royal Historical Society* 5, no. 6 (1956): 21–47.

53. See "Iohannis XXII. Papæ Primus processus contra Ludewicum Regem," in *MGH Constitutiones*, ed. J. Schwalm, vol. 5, no. 792, p. 617; and Offler, "Empire and Papacy: The Last Struggle," pp. 23–24.

54. Salvatorelli, *L'Italia comunale*, p. 792. See Ludwig's own account in his letter of 1326 to the duke of Brabant, in *MGH Constitutiones*, vol. 6, no. 241, p. 158.

55. Giovanni Villani, *Cronica* 9:157 (Florence, 1823; rpt. Rome: Multigrafica Editrice, 1980), 4:147–148.

56. Mollat, *The Popes at Avignon*, p. 206.

57. Before his difficult coronation in Rome, Emperor Henry VII had conferred, for a certain large monetary consideration, the title "imperial vicar" upon Alboino and Can Grande of Verona for life on March 7, 1311. After dallying with Frederick of Austria for over two years for the reconfirmation of his privilege or even a lifetime vicariate from Frederick, in 1320 Can Grande reverted to the original formulas of vicarship granted by Henry. The wily Lord of Verona reentered the pope's graces when du Poujet again revoked Henry's appointments and at the same time accepted their reconferral under the authority of the papal curia. Exactly a year after Dante's death, in September 1322, Ludwig captured and imprisoned his rival Frederick (then in alliance with the papacy), and Can Grande at last joined the victor. Ludwig reconfirmed Henry's appointment of Can Grande on June 18, 1323. See Padoan, "Il Vicariato Cesareo," pp. 166, 172, and "La composizione della *Monarchia*," pp. 7–27.

58. Giovanni Villani, *Cronica* 10:20; 5:27; the original documents are collected in Eugenio Dupré Theseider, "L'incoronazioni di Enrico VII e di Lodovico il Bavaro; Decisione di Rhens," in *L'Idea imperiale di Roma nella tradizione del medioevo* (Milan: Istituto per gli Studi di Politica Internazionale, 1942), pp. 230–254, here, p. 238. Also see Mollat, *The Popes at Avignon*, p. 208.

59. G. Villani, *Cronica* 10:55; 5:69–70.

60. G. Villani, *Cronica* 10:55; 5:69–70. See Eugenio Dupré Dupré Theseider, "L'incoronazione imperiale e le reazioni curiali," in *Roma dal comune di popolo alla signoria pontificia (1252–1377)* (Bologna: Licinio Cappelli, 1952), pp. 464–473. On the so-called Roman theory of the empire, by which, without the participation of the Roman Church, the emperor could be legitimately created by the Roman people, see Offler, "Empire and Papacy: The Last Struggle," p. 35.

61. On October 23, 1327, the day John XXII declared Ludwig a heretic, he also condemned Marsiglio's *Defensor pacis*, which promoted the theories of a lay state and the superiority of general councils over the papacy. See Mollat, *The Popes at Avignon*, p. 210. On Marsiglio of Padua, see Alan Gewirth, *Marsilius of Padua*, Records of Civilization (New York: Columbia University Press, 1956), 1:20–23, 302; vol. 2 was rpt. as Marsilius of Padua, *Defender of Peace: The Defensor Pacis*, trans. and intro. by Alan Gewirth (New York: Harper & Row, 1956; rpt. 1967), p. xix. See Gewirth's "John of Jandun and the *Defensor pacis*," *Speculum* 23 (1948): 267–72, where he proves Marsiglio to be the sole author of the work in 1324. The anathematized *Defensor pacis* was first published in 1522 and placed on the first *Index librorum prohibitorum*.

62. Mollat, *The Popes at Avignon*, p. 210.

63. On the dual coronation, see Mollat, *The Popes at Avignon*, p. 212; on the schism so caused, see pp. 213–219. Ludwig tardily affirmed that his election was legitimate and sufficient in 1338. See Geoffrey Barraclough, *The Origins Of Modern Germany* (Oxford, U.K.: Blackwell: 1952), pp. 309–312. See also Harald Zimmermann, *Papstabsetzungen des Mittelalters* (Graz/ Vienna/Cologne: Hermann Böhlaus Nachf., 1968), pp. 223–224.

64. Giovanni Orsini had been appointed to relieve and aid Cardinal Poujet in central Italy on April 17, 1326. See Mollat, *The Popes at Avignon*, p. 99; Salvatorelli, *L'Italia comunale*, pp. 804–808, 864; Baethgen, "Der Anspruch des Papsttums auf das Reichsvikariat," pp. 168–268; and Douie, *The Heresy of the Fraticelli*.

65. Mollat, *The Popes at Avignon*, p. 218.

66. Notably, the first Italian printing of the *Mon.* in the Venice 1740 edition (whose title page reads falsely, "Coloniæ Allobrogum Apud Henr. Albert. Gosse & Soc. MDCCXL") gives the incipit as *"Dantis Aligherii Florentini 'MONARCHI' Scripta temporibus 'LUDOVICI BAVARI'"* (Dante Alighieri, Florentine, *Monarchia*, written *in the time of Ludwig the Bavarian"*; my emphasis). Incidently, the publisher, Zatta, republished it in 1757, 1758, 1760, and 1768 with Venice given as the place.

67. The two redactions can be found in Ricci's edition in vol. 3 of *Tutte le opere di Gio-*

*vanni Boccaccio*, ed. Vittore Branca (Milan: Mondadori, 1974): the first redaction on pp. 417–496; the second on pp. 497–538.

68. Boccaccio, *Trattatello*, first redaction, para. 196, pp. 487–488.

69. *"Fu il detto libro, sedente Iovanni papa XXII, da messer Beltrando cardinal del Poggetto, allora per la Chiesa di Roma legato in Lombardia, dannato sì come contenente cose eretiche, e per lui proibito fu che studiare alcun non dovesse"* (Boccaccio, *Trattatello*, second redaction, para. 134, p. 530). In 1335 the convent of Santa Maria Novella, the Provincial Chapter of the Dominican Order, forbade the reading of the *Commedia*, although scant heed was paid to the prohibition; see Maccarrone, "Dante e i teologi," p. 24. Also see Manlio Pastore Stocchi, *"Monarchia:* Testo e cronologia," *Cultura e Scuola* 4, nos. 13–13 (1965): 714–721; whole volume, with same pagination, rpt. as *Dante nella critica d'oggi: risultati e prospettive*, ed. Umberto Bosco (Florence: Le Monnier, 1965), pp. 8–9. Nevio Matteini's *Il più antico oppositore politico di Dante: Guido Vernani da Rimini: Testo critico del "De Reprobatione Monarchia,"* Il Pensiero medievale collana di Storia della Filosofia, ser. 1, vol. 6 (Padua: CEDAM, 1958), now a half-century old, presents the latest edition of Vernani's *Ref.* Derivative from Matteini is Edoardo Fumagalli's "I condizionamenti del mondo ecclesiastico esemplificato attraverso Guido Vernani," in *Lectura Dantis mystica: Il Poema Sacro alla luce delle conquiste psicologiche odierne*, Atti della Settimana Dantesca 28 luglio–3 agosto 1968 (Florence: Leo S. Olschki, 1969): 286–300, here, p. 290.

70. Boccaccio, *Trattatello*, first redaction, para. 197, ed. Ricci, p. 488; second redaction, para. 134, p. 510.

71. Olindo Guerrini and Corrado Ricci, *Studi e polemiche dantesche* (Bologna: Nicola Zanichelli, 1853), pp. 186, 191; Boccacio, *Trattatello*, second redaction on p. 530. Any participation by Graziolo de' Bambaglioli in this condemnation must be rejected. See also Rossi, "Tre dictamina," p. 90, and "Nota biografica," in Graziolo de' Bambaglioli, *Commento all'Inferno di Dante*, ed. Luca Carlo Rossi (Pisa: Scuola Normale di Pisa, 1998), p. xxxvi.

72. *"Disputavit* [Dantes] *tres questiones; quarum una fuit*, an Imperator dependeat ab Ecclesia, *et tenuit quod non: sed post mortem suam, quasi, propter hoc fuit damnatus de hæresi"* (emphasis added). Cited first by O. Guerrini in *Studi e polemiche dantesche*, pp. 81–2; see also Cecil N. Sidney Woolf, *Bartolus of Sassoferrato* (Cambridge, U.K.: Cambridge University Press, 1913), p. 91; Maccarrone, "Dante e i teologi," pp. 20–28; and Fulvio Crosara, "Dante e Bartolo da Sassoferrato: Politica e diritto nell'Italia del Trecento," in *Bartolo da Sassoferrato: Studi e documenti per il VI centenario*, Università degli Studi di Perugia (Milan: Giuffrè, 1962), 2:105–198, esp. 145–165. Consult the useful pages on Bartolo in Kenneth Pennington, *The Prince and the Law, 1200–1600: Sovereignty and Rights in the Western Legal Tradition* (Berkeley/Los Angeles/Oxford, U.K.: University of California Press, 1993), pp. 196–101.

73. See the Latin text cited in Carlyle and Carlyle, 5:397, n. 3.

74. See Gianfranco Folena, "La tradizione delle opere di Dante," in *Atti del Congresso Internazionale di Studi Danteschi* (Florence: Sansoni, 1965), 1:1–78, here pp. 4, 29; and Vallone, *Antidantism politico*, p. 80.

75. See Maria Picchio Simonelli, "L'inquisizione e Dante: Alcune osservazioni," *Dante*

*Studies* 97 (1979): 129–149, here, pp. 134–135 and 142; rpt. in *Dante Studies* 118 (2000): 303–321, here, p. 308.

76. Simonelli, "L'inquisizione e Dante," p. 309. See *Summa una* (Lyons, 1537; rpt. 1962), f. 299ʳ.

77. *"ad prædicandum non admittitur aliquis, quamvis dicat se vidisse Deum in somniis"*; (*Summa una* f. 239ʳ; cited by Simonelli, "L'inquisizione e Dante," pp. 309, 319).

78. See the ch. "De sortilegis et divinis et invocatoribus demonum," taken from an anonymous manual of the thirteenth century called *Practica officii Inquisitionis heretice pravitatis*, as Mollat indicates, in Bernard Gui, *Manuel de l'inquisiteur*, édité et traduit par G[uillaume] Mollat avec la collaboration de G. Drioux, Classiques de l'Histoire de France au Moyen Âge 8–9, 2 vols. (Paris: Champion, 1926; rpt. New York: AMS, 1980), here 1:20–22. The inquisitor is told to inquire *"quid sciunt aut sciverunt . . . de animabus perditis seu dampnatis . . . de statu animarum defunctorum . . . de prenentiationibus futurorum eventuum. . . ."*; cited also by Simonelli, "L'inquisizione e Dante," pp. 312, 320.

79. See also Raoul Manselli, "Dante e l'*ecclesia spiritualis*,'" in *Dante e Roma: Atti del Convegno di Studi a cura della "Casa di Dante," sotto gli auspici del Comune di Roma, in collaborazione con l'Istituto di Studi Romani, Roma, 8–9–10 aprile 1965* (Florence: Le Monnier, 1965), pp. 115–135.

80. See Maccarrone, "Dante e i teologi," p. 21; and Ricci, "L'ultima fase del pensiero politico di Dante," p. 370.

81. See, e.g., the reactions of contemporaries in the letters collected in *Babylon on the Rhone: A Translation of Letters by Dante, Petrarch, and Catherine of Siena on the Avignon Papacy*, ed. and trans. Robert Coogan (Madrid/Potomac, Md.: José Porrúa Turanzas, 1983).

82. Among others, William of Ockham found John XXII's bulls "heretical, erroneous, silly, ridiculous, fantastic, insane, and defamatory." See *The Work of Ninety Days*, in *A Letter to the Friars Minor and Other Writings*, p. 3; the editors' "Introduction" is especially useful.

83. The six sermons, some reconstructed from secondary citations, are edited by Marc Dykmans in *Les sermons de Jean XXII sur la vision béatifique, texte précedé d'une introduction et suivi d'une chronologie de la controverse avec la liste des écrits pour et contre le pape*, Miscellanea historiæ pontificiæ 34 (Rome: Presses de l'Université grégorienne, 1973). William of Ockham lists John's errors in *A Letter to the Friars Minor:* "After the constitution *Quia vir reprobus*, he preached and taught many assertions contrary to truths he is obliged to believe explicitly. . . . The third is that the souls of the saints in heaven do not see God and will not see him before the day of general judgment. The fourth is that the souls of the reprobate are not and will not be in Hell before the day of general judgment. The fifth is that the demons are not punished and will not be punished until the day of general judgment. . . . Because of the errors and heresies written above and countless others, I withdraw from the obedience of the pseudo-pope and all who support him to the prejudice of the orthodox faith" (p. 12). Even after the 1333 Paris condemnation of the first four sermons, John persisted in asserting in his last sermon on May 4, 1334: *"Anima et angelus non erunt in regno cælorum et paradiso ante generalem hominum resurrectionum"* (The soul and the angel shall not

be in the Kingdom of Heaven and Paradise before the general resurrection of men; ed. Dykmans, p. 160). See also Verlaque, *Jean XXII*, pp. 214–216; D. L. Douie, "John XXII, Pope," *New Catholic Encyclopedia*, 7:1015, and *The Heresy of the Fraticelli*, p. 192; and the entry on John XXII, unfortunately without listed sources, in Richard P. McBrien, *Lives of the Popes: The Pontiffs from St. Peter to John Paul II* (New York: HarperCollins, 2000), pp. 237–238.

84. In his letter "Contra Iohannem XII," William of Ockham asserted that John's deathbed repentance made when of unsound mind, *"quando non erat bene conpos sui,"* was a fraud, *"ficta fuit"* (in Scholz, *Unbekannte kirchenpolitische Streitschrifien*, 2:398–399). An anonymous pamphlet (cited by Douie, in *The Heresy of the Fraticelli*, pp. 193–195) declared, *"Reprobatio revocationis quam fecit dominus Iohannis in morte quodam non valuit"* (The recantation of refutation that Lord John made at the time of death is worthless).

85. See the interesting remarks on the *Mon.*'s practical scope and effect by P. G. Ricci, in "La *Monarchia* dantesca e l'idea dell'Impero nella sua realtà giuridica e politica al tempo di Dante," in *Il processo di Dante*, pp. 70–71.

86. Vallone, "Il pensiero politico," pp. 174–201.

87. Pennington, *The Prince and the Law*, pp. 113–117.

88. William of Ockham's anti-papal works are numerous; among the most important is his most impersonal work, the *Dialogus*, written during the papacy of John XXII (*A Dialogue*, excerpts trans. by J. Kilcullen, in A. S. McGrade and J. Kilcullen, *William of Ockham: A Letter to the Friars Minor and Other Writings* (Cambridge, U.K.: Cambridge University Press, 1995). He also outlined his major opposition to that pontiff in his *Compendium errorum papæ*. In order to distinguish himself from the theories of Marsiglio of Padua, accursed of the papacy (see Gewirth's "Introduction" to the *Defensor pacis*, p. xix), and especially from Marsiglio's anathematized *Defensor pacis*, William composed the *De potestate papæ et cleri*. Marsiglio wrote his *Defensor minor* in reply (ed. C. Kenneth Brampton [Birmingham, U.K.: Cornish Brothers, 1922]). To Leopold of Babenburg's *De iure regni et imperii*, William of Ockham responded with the *Octo quæstionum decisiones super potestatem summi pontificis* (*Eight Questions on the Power of the Pope*, excerpts trans. by J. Kilcullen, in A. S. McGrade and J. Kilcullen, *William of Ockham*). He presented the clearest statement of his political views in 1334–ca. 1337 in the *Breviloquium de principatu tyrannico* (trans. J. Kilcullen, in *William of Ockham, A Short Treatise on Tyrannical Government* [Cambridge, U.K.: Cambridge University Press, 1992]). In 1338–1339 he drafted *An princeps pro suo succursu, scilicet guerræ, possit recipere bona ecclesiarum, etiam invito papa*, a defense of Edward III's right, in opposition to the pope, to levy subsidies against the English clergy to help in the war against the French. In his last work, *De pontificum et imperatorum potestate*, written in 1347 during the pontificate of Benedict XIII, Ockham railed against what he called the *"ecclesia avionica"*—what was to become known as the "Babylonish Captivity"—and condemned John XXII as a heretic (see *On the Power of Emperors and Popes*, trans. Brett, esp. chs. 27 and 28, pp. 137–172). See Cesare Vasoli, "La pace nel pensiero filosofico e teologico-politico da Dante a Okham," in *La Pace nel pensiero, nella politica, negli ideali del Trecento* (Rimini: L'Accademia tudertina, 1975): 29–43, and "Papato e

Impero nel tardo Medioevo: Dante, Marsilio, Ockham," in *Storia delle idee politiche, economiche e sociali*, ed. L. Firpo (Turin: UTET, 1985), vol. 2:2, pp. 543–649.

89. See P.G. Ricci's "Introduzione" to his edition of the *Mon.* (1965), pp. 4–5.

90. On this question, see the careful study by Maria Picchio Simonelli, *Lectura Dantis Americana: Inferno III* (Philadelphia: University of Pennsylvania Press, 1993), passim.

91. *Petri Allegherii super Dantis ipsius genitoris Comoediam Commentarium, nunc primum in lucem editum*, ed. Vincenzo Nannucci (Florence: G. Piatti, 1845); *Il "Commentarium" di Pietro Alighieri nelle redazioni ashburnhamiana e ottoboniana*, ed. R. della Vedova and M. T. Silvotti, intro. by Egidio Guidubaldi (Florence: L.S. Olschki, 1978).

92. See Maccarrone, "Dante e i teologi," p. 20, for his description of the MS.

93. P.G. Ricci, "Introduzione," to the *Mon.*, pp. 7–8.

94. See the facsimile edition by Friedrich Schneider, *Die Monarchia Dantes aus der Berliner Handschrift Cod. Lat. Folio 437* (Weimar: Hermann Böhlaus Nachfolger, 1930).

95. Folena, "La tradizione," p. 30.

96. "We should not wonder that so often manuscript copies escaped the dogged research of Dantologists of the nineteenth century. Copied in a Gothic script rich in abbreviations, the entire treatise occupies but a few pages and could easily be hidden amid other writings; need we say that, not rarely, it escaped in manuscripts preserved anonymously or anepigraphically" (Ricci, "Introduzione," to the *Mon.*, pp. 5–6, n. 6).

97. See the edition and introduction by Pier Giorgio Ricci, "Il Commento di Cola da Rienzo alla *Monarchi* di Dante," *Studi medievali*, ser. 3, 6, no. 2 (1965): 665–708.

98. "For the *princeps* we have to wait, nonetheless, until the second half of the Cinquecento in Lutheran [*sic*] territory," writes Ricci, in his "Introduzione," p. 6. The *Index librorum prohibitorum* would be first instituted during the Council of Trent in 1557 and published by the Holy Office by order of Pope Paul IV in 1559; the *Mon.* was placed on it in 1564. Lists of books (and sometimes of their authors) condemned to the flames and whose reading was punishable by excommunication had, however, had already appeared centuries before: e.g., Arius's *Thalia* had been condemned at the Council of Nicea in 325, and the works of Origen at the Oecumenical Council of 553. More recently there had been procedures against the English Franciscan scientist Roger Bacon, along with the condemnations of Pietro d'Abano and, frightening for Vernani, of his fellow *lector* in Bologna, Cecco d'Ascoli.

99. Ricci, "Introduzione," to the *Mon.*, p. 19, n. 2. On John Foxe, see Paget Toynbee, *A Dictionary of Proper Names and Notable Matters in the Works of Dante*, rev. Charles S. Singleton (Oxford, U.K.: Oxford University Press, 1968), pp. 238–239; "Introduction," ed. Kay, p. xxvi, n. 82.

100. Ricci, "Introduzione," to the *Mon.*, pp. 19–20, n. 2; Folena, "La tradizione," p. 30.

101. Ricci, "Introduzione," to the *Mon.*, pp. 20–21, n. 3.

102. Ricci, "Introduzione," to the *Mon.*, pp. 3–4, n. 1; Maccarrone, "Dante e i teologi," p. 28.

103. This is the subject of a meticulous examination by Prudence Shaw, published as "Il Volgarizzamento inedito della *Monarchia*," *Studi danteschi* 47 (1970): 59–224. Kay attributes the actual work of translation to its copyist, Bernardo di Filippo del Nero. Shaw notes to the contrary, however, that del Nero knew no Latin, and, because of the obvious weakness of the anonymous Italian version, it was del Nero himself and Antonio Tuccio Manetti who had encouraged Ficino to undertake another (pp. 115–116). See also Ricci, "Introduzione," to the *Mon.*, pp. 25–26.

104. See Pier Giorgio Ricci, "Donazione di Costantino," *Enciclopedia dantesca*, 2:569–570; Francesco Tateo, "Marsiglio Ficino," *Enciclopedia dantesca*, 2:853–854; Kay, "Introduction," to the *Mon.*, p. xxxiii, n. 67.

105. John Van Engen, "The Donation of Constantine," *Dictionary of the Middle Ages*, 4: 257–259.

106. Ricci, "Introduzione," to the *Mon.*, p. 25.

107. "The manuscript tradition, then, is meager. . . . Only six copies were known in 1844, but nine in 1874, fifteen in 1921, and today, nineteen"; Ricci, "Introduzione," to the *Mon.*, p. 5. Ricci describes the eighteen MSS that he actually employed on pp. 7–19.

108. Prudence Shaw, "Il codice uppsalense della *Monarchia*," *Studi danteschi* 46 (1969): 293–331.

109. Ciaccio, *Beltrando del Pogetto*, p. 38.

110. Mollat, *The Popes at Avignon*, p. 100.

111. Ciaccio, *Beltrando del Pogetto*, pp. 31–76, here, esp. 43; Mollat, *The Popes at Avignon*, pp. 99–101.

112. Giovanni Villani, *Cronica* 10:198; 5:250–251; Ciaccio, *Beltrando del Pogetto*, pp. 128–129. The bestowal of the title, which betokened in public opinion and among chroniclers arbitrary papal interference, had precedent: notably, Boniface VIII's scheming nomination of Charles of Valois as peacemaker in Tuscany and as count of Romagna had led to a devastation of Florence worse than any caused by earlier strife between Guelphs and Ghibellines—and especially to Dante's exile and condemnation as a White Guelph.

113. Giovanni Villani, *Cronica* 10:197; 5:249.

114. Historians have recognized that amid the complicated negotiations during John of Bohemia's intervention in Lombardy (1331–1333), there was a scheme in which John was to obtain his dominions from the king of France, who was also to submit to the pope's suzereignty (see Hilary Seton Offler, "Empire and Papacy: The Last Struggle," *Transaction of the Royal Historical Society*, ser. 5, no. 6 (1956): 21–47, here, p. 27). On Bambaglioli's Guelph motivations, see the *Dictamen super adventu regis Boemie in Lombardiam*, in Luca Carlo Rossi, "Tre dictamina inediti di Graziolo Bambaglioli con una nota biografica," *Italia medievale e umanistica* 31 (1988): 81–125, here, pp. 91–92, 100–104.

115. Ciaccio, *Beltrando del Pogetto*, pp. 148–150; Mollat, *The Popes at Avignon*, pp. 103–106, 109.

116. Petrarca, *Familiares* 12:6, from February 1, 1352, is somewhat conciliatory: "While I am writing this letter to you the Cardinal of Ostia is on the verge of death. By the time

you read this, he will have expired; in my opinion he will surrender to a death that will be ripe for him and for nature, but unfortunate for the state" (Francesco Petrarca, *Letters on Familiar Matters: Rerum familiarium libri IX–XVI*, trans. Aldo S. Bernardo [Baltimore/London: Johns Hopkins University Press, 1982], p. 150). See, however, his wonderfully libellous *Liber sine nomine* 17; *Petrarch's Book without a Name*, trans. Norman P. Zacour (Toronto: Pontifical Institute of Mediæval Studies, 1973), p. 102.

117. See Fumagalli, "I condizionamenti," pp. 286–300.

118. Vernani intimates strongly but never specifies any heretical doctrine in the *Mon.*, as he might had the condemnation already been pronounced by the cardinal legate. See also Maccarrone, "Dante e i teologi," p. 24, where Maccarrone misleadingly supposes a "close rapport" between Poujet and the Dominican friar, but supplies no documentation for such a collaboration. In *Il processo di Dante (Celebrato il 16 aprile 1966 nella Basilica di S. Francesco in Arezzo)*, ed. Dante Ricci [Florence: Edizioni Arnaud, 1967]), p. 64, however, Maccarrone acutely affirmed that "[i]f Vernani had written under the Cardinal's orders he would have to have taken aim principally, if not exclusively, at the third book of Dante's *Monarchia*, and used arguments to show that it was filled with heresies. Instead he avails himself of philosophical arguments to condemn him and accuses him of *errors*."

119. "Generally it was said in public that he was his son, and in many ways he was just like him"; Giovanni Villani, *Cronica* 11:6; 6: 44; Petrarca, *Liber sine nomine* 17; *Petrarch's Book without a Name*, p. 102. Pious scholars denying the bastardy have missed the point. Far from being a scandalous liability, the supposition of the pope's paternity, true or false, only *increased* the clever and capable Bertrand's princely reputation and power, just as the merits of Cesare and Lucrezia Borgia were similarly overvalued two centuries later. Without attending to the substantial political ramifications of the rumors, Lisetta Ciaccio, for example, primly rejects John XXII's paternity out of hand and gives no further historical testimony; see *Bertrando del Pogetto*, p. 11. Guillaume Mollat, while less prudishly ruffled, is also doubtful; see his *The Popes at Avignon*, p. 84, and his entry, "Bertrand du Poujet," in the *Dictionnaire d'histoire et de géographie écclésiastiques* (Paris: Librairie Letouzey, 1935), vol. 8, col. 1068–1074. Also see Salvatorelli, *L'Italia comunale*, pp. 787–789; Ludovico Frati, "La contesa fra Matteo Visconti ed il papa Giovanni XXII secondo i documenti dell'archivio vaticano," *Archivio Storico Lombardo* 15 (1888): 241–258; and G. Biscaro, "Le relazioni dei Visconti di Milano con la chiesa," *Archivio storico lombardo* 46 (1919): 84–229.

120. Vernani was an excellent conversationalist and enjoyed many intimacies with the famous. On February 23, 1317, Vernani was in Treviso to draw up a will for Tolberto da Camino, count of Ceneda, for whom the friar acted as father confessor; Tolberto had lost his wife, Gaia, whom Dante mentions in *Purg.* 16:140 and had married Samaritana Malatesta, daughter of Ferrantino da Rimini in 1314 (Matteini, "La vita," in *Il più antico oppositore*, pp. 11–12). On October 11 of that year the friar was at the Provincial Synod in Bologna, where as Filippo da Ferrara recounts in his *Liber de introductione loquendi*, Vernani's remarkable tabletalk included hierocratic parables and repartee with Archbishop Rinaldo of Mi-

lan. Matteini reproduces the conversation on p. 13. Filippo's (so far unpublished) book extolling Vernani was written on ecclesiastical orders as a manual of everyday conversation
for preachers. Despite Vernani's apparently great social presence, he never reached social
prominence, a factor, perhaps, that caused the bitterness he so often indulges. In sum, we
gather the image of a rather overbearing *esprit borné*. Käppeli calls Vernani *"eine hervorrragende
Persönlichkeit"* (a conspicuous personality) in his edition of the *Ref.* in "Der Dantegegner
Guido Vernani O.P. von Rimini," *Quellen und Forschungen aus italienischen Archiven und Bibliotheken
heausgeben von Deutschen Historischen Institut in Rom* 28 (Rome:1938), p. 108. See also Matteini,
"La vita," p. 16; and Fumagalli's derivative "I condizionamenti," p. 287.

121. A. Vallone in his *Antidantismo politico* lists and describes many of the refutations that
we need not repeat here. Unfortunately, his discussion is entirely devoid of dates and
chronology so that the development and progress of the controversies are impossible to
follow.

122. See Cecco d'Ascoli [Francesco Stabili], *L'Acerba*, ed. Achille Crespi (Ascoli Piceno:
Giuseppe Cesari, 1927); and Francesco Filippini, "Cecco d'Ascoli a Bologna," *Studi e memorie per la storia dell'Università di Bologna* 10 (1930): 8–9. For St. Antonino, see R. Piccini's brief
"Introduction" to his edition of Vernani's *Reprobatio*, under a nom de plume, entitled *Contro Dante (Contra Dantem): Fr Guidonis Vernani Tractatus De Reprobatione "Monarchiæ" compositæ a
Dante Aligherio Florentino*, rarissimo opuscolo del secolo XIV per la prima volta tradotto in
italiano e ripubblicato da Jarro (R. Piccini) (Florence/Rome/Milan: Bemporad, 1906), p.
vi. Ficino's translation of the *Mon.* comes from Antonino's period of polemics. On the
censures, see also Vallone, "Il pensiero politico," pp. 174–201.

123. See Bruno Nardi, "La *'Monarchia'* e frate Guglielmo da Cremona," in *Nel mondo di
Dante* (Rome: Edizioni di "Storia e Letteratura," 1944), pp. 174–191, 195. Also see Gugliemi
Centueri da Cremona, *Trattato "De iure Monarchiæ,"* ed. Cesare Cenci, preface by Gino Barbieri (Verona: Palazzo Giuliari, 1967); and Vallone, *Antidantismo politico*, p. 135. Guglielmo's
treatise, written in 1400, deals philosophically and theologically with major issues of the
1300s: the broad questions of the relation of empire and papacy, of monarchies vs. re-
publics, communal and private good, and the poverty of Christ and the Apostles. See
Johannes Falkenberg, O.P., *De monarchia mundi*, ed. W. Seńko, in *Materiały do historii filozofii
średniowiecznej w Polsce* 20, Polska Akademia Nauk (Breslau: Zaklad Narodowy im. Ossolinskich, 1975), n.s. 9 (1975). See also the *Mon.*, ed. Imbach and Flüeler, p. 357. Kay, in his "Introduction" (p. xxxii) to his edition correctly observes the fact that Guglielmo da
Sarzano's *Tractatatus de poetestate summi pontefice* is not a refutation of the *Mon.*, and that Vallone's contention (in *Antidantismo politico*, pp. 29–61) that Augustinus d'Ancona wrote his
immense *Summa de potestate ecclesiastica* of 1326 to censure Dante's treatise is likewise invalid;
Padoan had been similarly unconvinced (see "La composizione," p. 9).

124. As the notice in the 1746 publication of the *De potestate* and the *Reprobatio* states, and
as Matteini has confirmed in his introduction to his edition of Vernani's treatise, Dominican histories and bibliographies are completely silent on Vernani: *"Ad Vernanum nostrum quod*

*attinet, altum omnino de illo silentium apud omnes Historicos et Bibliographos Ordinis Prædicatorum"* (Matteini, *Il più antico oppositore,* p. 7; *De potestate . . . et De reprobatione,* p. 5). Vernani was never "chancellor" either of the University of Bologna or any institution, as Giuseppe Ferrari strangely reports (*Gli scrittori politici italiani* [Milan: Monanni, 1929], p. 64), somehow confusing the title of the dedicatee of the *Refutation* with the author (did Ferrari *read* Vernani?). See Matteini, *Il più antico oppositore,* pp. 7–18. On Cecco, see the documentation of Rossi, "Nota biografica," pp. xxiv–xxxv; and Francesco Filippini, "Cecco d'Ascoli a Bologna," *Studi e momorie per la storia dell'Università di Bologna* 10 (1930), esp. pp. 8–9. The polymath Cecco had been engaged to teach medicine and philosophy; we know from a letter to Graziolo de' Bambaglioli that he also penned the treatise on logic, *Logica di Aristotile,* a manuscript later consulted in the Montefeltro library in Urbino by Pico della Mirandola. See P. G. Ricci, "Vernani, Guido," *Enciclopedia dantesca,* 5:986.

125. In addition to his fame as poet, philosopher, astronomer, astrologer, occultist, and magus—his *Acerba* comprises almost all the known science of his times. Before his fall from grace, Cecco had once enjoyed a high reputation as a popular physician; the aged Pope John XXII had especially wanted him to come to Avignon as his personal doctor. Fumagalli supposes that it was envy of Dante's superior knowledge of astronomy that drew Cecco to attack him ("I condizionamenti," pp. 288–289).

126. See the documents, letters, and sermons noted in Käppeli, "Der Dantegegner," pp. 118–123, and details of mentions and minutia from Vernani's life supplied by Matteini in his "Introduzione" to the *Ref.* in *Il più antico oppositore,* p. 127

127. See Vernani's text edited from the Cod. JX51 by Martin Grabmann as "Kommentar des Guido Vernani von Rimini O.P. zur Bulle *Unam Sanctam*," in his monograph, *Studien über den Einfluss der aristotelischen Philosophie auf die mittelalterlichen Theorien über das Verhältnis von Kirche und Staat* (in *Sitzungsberichte der bayerischen Akademie der Wissenschaften,* Philosophisch-historische Abteilung, [Jahrgang 1934], Heft 2), pp. 144–157.

128. On recent citations of Vernani's works, see J. De Raedemaeker, "Informations concernant quelques commentaires du *De Anima*," *Bulletin de Philosophie Médiévale édité par la Société Internationale pour l'Etude de la Philosophie Médiévale* [S.I.E.P.M.], 8–9 (1966–1967): 102–104; C. J. Lohr, "Medieval Latin Aristotle Commentaries, Authors G–I," *Traditio* 24 (1968): 191–192; R. Macken, "Un apport important e l'ecdotique des manuscrits à pièces. A propos de l'édition léonin du Commentaire de Thomas d'Aquin sur la Politique d'Aristote et sa Tabula Libri Ethicorum," *Scriptorium* 27, no. 2 (1973): 319–327; Thomas Käppeli, *Scriptores Ordinis Prædicatorum Medii Ævi. II, G–I (Romæ ad S. Sabinæ 1975),* pp. 76–78; Carlo Dolcini, "Guido Vernani e Dante. Note sul testo del *De reprobatione Monarchie*," in his *Crisi di poteri,* pp. 439–452; also see his corrections to Käppeli's edition of the *Ref.* in "Der Dantegegner," p. 439, n. 4.

129. Vernani copied the *Reprobatio* into B.L. Codex Add. 35325, continuing with his *De potestate,* in his expert, notarial hand, using massed abbreviations, and leaving blank spaces for large capital letters; however, he never engaged a limner to insert them—proof of his

later poverty, his later distaste, or both. A different, smaller, hand has noted on f. 9ᵛ: *"Explicit tratactatus de reprobatione false monarchie."* Vernani never dignifies Dante's *scriptum* itself with the name *"tractatus."* The initial page of the London MS has been scraped and bears abraded holes. As is indicated in the added, modern, initial pages of the manuscript, the British Museum purchased it at a Sotheby's sale, lot 125, June 5–10, 1899, and catalogued it in 1900.

130. Käppeli ('Der Dantegegner," p. 114), cites the folio numbers of Vernani's treatise in the Classense MS incorrectly, and Matteini blindly follows his error (*Il più antico oppositore*, p. 27, n. 37); the *Ref.* is actually found on f. 65ʳ (col. 2) to f. 69ᵛ (col. 2). Carlo Dolcini recounts the vicissitudes of Vernani's autograph, the British Library MS, in "Guido Vernani e Dante," in his *Crisi di poteri*, pp. 441–443.

131. F. P. M. Domaneschio, *De rebus coenobii cremonensis ordinis prædicatorum, deque illustribus, qui ex eo prodiere viris commentarius* (Cremona: Petri Richini, 1767), pp. 363–398. According to Domaneschio, Thomas Richinius, O.P., was himself the editor of the 1746 edition; on p. 382 we find the notation: *"Edit. Primum Romæ apud Peccarinios anno 1741. Tum Bononiæ apud Thomam Colli anno 1746."* See Matteini, p. 27. See also Fumagalli, "I condizionamenti," p. 287.

132. F. Guidonis Vernani Ariminensis Ordinis Prædicatorum, *De potestate summi pontificis et De reprobatione Monarchiæ compositæ a Dante Aligerio florentino tractatus duo nunc primum in lucem editi* (Bononiæ, 1746, apud Thomam Coli, ex Typographia S. Thomæ Aquinatis); M. Grabmann, *Studien über den Einfluss der aristelischen Philosophie*, pp. 144–157; *Contro Dante (Contra Dantem): Fr Guidonis Vernani Tractatus De Reprobatione "Monarchiæ" compositæ a Dante Aligherio Florentino*, rarissimo opuscolo del secolo XIV per la prima volta tradotto in italiano e ripubblicato da Jarro (R.Piccini) (Florence/Rome/Milan: Bemporad, 1906); Thomas Käppeli, "Der Dantegegner Guido Vernani O.P. von Rimini," in *Quellen und Forschungen aus italienischen Archiven und Bibliotheken heausgeben vom Deutschen Historischen Institut in Rom* 28 (Rome: 1938), pp. 107–146; Antero Meozzi, "I trattati politici di Guido Vernani e Dante Alighieri," *Giornale dantesco* (1930): 18–30. Matteini gives a complete description of the MMS of all of Vernani's works on pp. 19–22.

133. We know neither Graziolo's date of birth nor his date of death. See L. C. Rossi, "Preface" to Graziolo's *Commento*, pp. xxix, xxxix.

134. See L. C. Rossi's "Nota biografica," in his edition of Graziolo's *Commento*, p. xxix. Alessandro Torri recorded much information in his edition of the *Ottimo commento della Divina Commedia* (Pisa: N. Capurro, 1827–29), 1:121–125; see also the older editions, *Il Commento più antico [del Bambaglioli] e la versione latina dell'Inferno di Dante dal codice di Sandaniele del Friuli*, by Antonio Fiammazzo (Udine: Doretti, 1892), p. vi, and *Il Commento dantesco di Graziolo de' Bambaglioli dal "Colombino" di Siviglia con altri codici raffrontato*, ed. Antonio Fiammazzo (Savona: Bertolotto, 1915), pp. x, xxiv, n. 4. For Dante's early reception in central Italy, see Giovanni Livi, *Dante: Suoi primi cultori, sua gente in Bologna con documenti inediti facsimili e illustrazioni figurate* (Bologna: Licinio Cappelli, Editore, 1918), and *Dante e Bologna. Nuovi Studi e*

*documenti* (Bologna: Licinio Cappelli, 1921), esp. pp. 34–36. In 1375 a *cattedra dantesca* was set up by the Bolognese Commune in imitation of that instituted by Boccaccio in Florence in 1373 (Livi, *Dante e Bologna*, p. 54). Also see Lodovico Frati, "Notizie biografiche di rimatori italiani dei secoli XIII e XIV: vii, Graziolo Bambaglioli," *Giornale Storico della letterature italiana* 17 (1891): 367–380; Tommaso Casini, "Intorno a Graziolo Bambaglioli," *Archiginnasio* 11 (1916): 146–170; and Emilio Orioli, *La cancelleria pepolesca: Atti e formule* (Bologna: Stabilimento Poligrafo Emiliano, 1910).

135. See Tommaso Casini, "Intorno a Graziolo Bambaglioli," *Archginnasio* 11 (1916): 148–149; and L. C. Rossi, "Nota biografica," in his edition of Graziolo de' Bambaglioli's *Commento all'Inferno di Dante*, p. xxxi.

136. *"continuus et solicitus cancellarius"*; Frati, *Notizie*, pp. 372, 378–379; Rossi, "Nota biografica," p. xxxi.

137. Casini, "Intorno a Graziolo Bambaglioli," pp. 149–150.

138. Graziolo's *Commentary* is internally dated at 1324 in the gloss on *Inf.* 21:112–114: "hodie MCCCXXIIII" (pp. 149–150). See also the earlier editions: *Il Commento più antico [del Bambaglioli] e la versione latina dell'Inferno di Dante dal codice di Sandaniele del Friuli*, ed. Antonio Fiammazzo (Udine: Doretti, 1892); and *Il Commento dantesco di Graziolo de' Bambaglioli dal "Colombino" di Siviglia con altri codici raffrontato*, ed. Antonio Fiammazzo (Savona: Bertolotto, 1915).

139. Jacopo Alighieri, *Chiose all'Inferno*, ed. Saverio Bellomo, Medioevo e Umanesimo 75 (Padua: Antenore, 1990).

140. After suffering banishment with eight other members of his family and fifteen hundred other Guelphs from Bologna in 1334, Graziolo found a position as vicar to Manfred, count of Sarriano, who had been appointed *capitano* of the city of Naples by King Robert III. Graziolo was there to write his *Trattato delle volgari sentenze sopra le virtu morali* and to dedicate it to Bertrando del Balzo, King Robert's brother-in-law and the captain of the army of Guelph Florence. In order to prevent confiscation of his goods, Bambaglioli had to report his whereabouts to the Bolognese authorities. See the documents printed by Ludovico Frati, in "Graziolo Bambaglioli esiliato a Napoli," *Giornale dantesco* 1 (1894): 212–216.

141. On the "Officio spiarum comunis Bononiæ pro Sancta Romana" (Office of Spies of the Commune of Bologna for the Holy Roman Church), see the documents printed in Casini, "Intorno a Graziolo Bambaglioli," p. 155, esp. n. 2. Guelph Florence also had a similar secret office for military espionage; it was not an institution peculiar to Cardinal Bertrand du Poujet's dictatorship in Bologna. See also Giovanni Livi, *Dante: Suoi primi cultori*, p. 103.

142. See the Latin text edited by Martin Grabmann in *Studien über den Einfluss der aristotelischen Philosophie auf die mittelalterlichen Theorien*, pp. 144–157.

143. The list and the point is Simonelli's, in "L'inquisizione," p. 308; rpt., p. 34.

144. Francesco Petrarca is one of our best professional witnesses; the exclusive poet of

Vaucluse feigned to find the tawdry illiteracy of Dante Alighieri's ubiquitous admirers repulsive (*Familiares* 21:15; *Seniles* 5:2). Yet Dante's phenomenal popularity drove Petrarca's ambition to eclipse him in becoming *the* popular European poet of his time (boasting, or regretting, *"al popol tutto / favola fui gran tempo"*), and especially to scheming his own coronation as laureate on the Roman Capitoline Hill in 1341. See Kenelm Foster, *Petrarch: Poet and Humanist*, Writers of Italy Series (Edinburgh, U.K.: University of Edinburgh Press, 1984), p. 41; *Petrarch's Lyric Poems*, trans. and ed. Robert M. Durling (Cambridge, Mass.: Harvard University Press, 1976), here, *Canzoniere* 1, p. 37.

## NOTES TO CHAPTER 3: THE 'MONARCHIA' AND VERNANI'S CENSURES

1. "It is my aim to pry [temporal monarchy] from its hiding place" (1:1). "It is necessary in any inquiry whatever to have knowledge of the principle to which one can refer analytically . . ." (1:2). ". . . things which . . . do lie in our power, we can speculate . . . [and] also have an effect." "Politics fall within our power . . ." (1:2).

2. See Herbert A. Davidson, "Averroës on the Material Intellect," *Viator* 17 (1986): 91–137.

3. With the promotion of peace as the end of civil government, Dante cites a cliché of medieval political theory—one that later will be overturned by Machiavelli. The poet's stress on the willing use of reason by citizens for the unified peace and good of the commonwealth has, as we will see, much in common with Remigio de' Girolami's concepts of an association of a community's intellective power expressed in the *De bono pacis* of 1304 and the *De bono communi* of 1305 (see Maria Consiglia De Matteis, "Il *De bono communi* di Remigio de' Girolami [†1319]," in *Annali dell'Università degli Studi di Lecce*, Facoltà di lettere e filosofia e di magistero 3 [1965–1967]: 11–88), rather than with some Averroistic union of all mankind's intellects into a world soul. See Charles T. Davis, "Remigio de' Girolami and Dante," pp. 110, 116, 126–127.

4. That the good of the community would be achieved through the integration of the individual intellects of the body politic became a commonplace theme of Florentine civic theory.

5. Cf. the diction parallels, e.g., in John XXII's *Quia quorundam mentes*, Pt. 1; see the text in James Heft, *John XXII and Papal Teaching Authority*, Texts and Studies in Religion 27 (Lewiston/Queenston: Edwin Mellen Press, 1986), pp. 32–34, Latin text, p. 233. See the critical edition in J. Tarrant, ed. *Extravagantes Johannis XXII*, here, pp. 257–258.

6. On Averroës's error, see Patrick Boyde, *Dante: Philomythes and Philosopher: Man in the Cosmos* (Cambridge, U.K.: Cambridge University Press, 1981), pp. 276–279, 377; and Maccarrone, "Dante e i teologi," p. 24. Vernani accuses Dante of error, never of heresy.

7. See the commentary and edition by De Matteis, "Il *De bono communi* di Remigio de' Girolami," pp. 11–88, esp. pp. 20–21. Remigio's Latin treatise *De bono pacis* has been edited

by Davis, in "Remigio de' Girolami and Dante," pp. 123–136, esp. 129; see esp. Davis's comments, pp. 113–114.

8. Cf. *Mon.* 1:5:3–4.

9. Cf. Davis, "Remigio de' Girolami and Dante," passim, but esp. p. 110.

10. Vernani facilely ignores Dante's statements in *Mon.* 1:2:6 that the aim of the treatise is practical action on earth. Clearly, according to Christian theology, all men seek God and the end goal of eternal beatitude; even sin is a perverse seeking for God. As the *Commedia* vividly describes, in practice, however, some men seek lesser goods and actually end pertinaciously in damnation. Vernani only deals with the ideal as it suits him.

11. See *Ref.*, ed. Matteini, p. 43. Vernani's argument is hollow since he omits any definition of "qualitative."

12. In *De anima* 3:5:430a:10–25; *The Complete Works of Aristotle: The Revised Oxford Translation*, ed. Jonathan Barnes, Bollingen Series 71, 2 vols. (Princeton, N.J.: Princeton University Press, 1984), here, 2:683–684. Aristotle discusses the differentiation between "passive" (or "possible") and "active" intellects. The passive, like matter and potentiality, can become all things, while the active acts upon the passive to make it operate. For Aristotle, passive intellect and passive thought is perishable, while the active is "separable, impassible, unmixed . . . immortal and eternal" (p. 684). See the *Textus Aristotelis*, familiar to Dante, in Sancti Thomæ Aquinatis, *In Aristotelis librum De Anima commentarium*, ed. Angelo M. Pirotta (Turin: Marietti, 1959), pp. 171, 173. Averroës, Siger of Brabant, and John of Jandun extrapolated from this that, because matter was the principle of numerical multiplicity, the active intellect, being an immaterial "nature" or "form," could not receive such multiplicity: thus they concluded that there was a single active intellect for all mankind. As St. Thomas had realized, such a view would destroy not only individual personality but the free choice of the will; see *Against the Averroists*, trans. McInerny, pp. 18–19, 34–35, 74–75. See also St. Thomas's central arguments in *Summa contra gentiles* 2:76: "That the agent intellect is not a separate substance, but part of the soul" (trans. and intro. by James F. Anderson, in *On the Truth of the Catholic Faith: Summa contra gentiles*, ed. and trans. Anton C. Pegis, Vernon J. Bourke, Charles J. O'Neil, 5 vols. [Garden City, N.Y.: Doubleday, 1955–1957], 2:239–245). The heresy is clearly antithetical to all Dante's principles and conclusions throughout his works; most especially, as I note, it would obviously have made the *Commedia* inconceivable.

13. In the *Par.* the poet pursues the forced analogy of the reception of light in causing dark and light moon spots with the amount of beatitude enjoyed by the blessed. The poet has Beatrice explain how light suffuses the pearl-like, diaphanous moon inside more brightly or dimly because of the difference in quality, not quantity or denseness (*Par.* 2:146) of the moon's different parts; she warns of the limitations of human philosophy for "reason's wings are short" for comprehension of the phenomenon. The difference is parallel to the soul's being more observably present in some parts of the body than in others because of the *quality* of the body's members (*Par.* 2:133–141). Light informs the moon qualitatively as the soul informs the body. Thus, analogously, the differences of beatitude

shine more or less through the Empyrean as the blessed experience a hierarchical difference in receiving the glory of God to the fullness of each of their quantitative capacities.
As Sapegno points out, "The theory of rarity and density is therefore *insufficient* to explain, philosophically, a diversity that is *not only quantitative* in kind, *but also qualitative*" (my
emphases). For this and the question of moon spots, Dante's precedents, and a basic,
scholarly commentary, see C. S. Singleton, *Paradiso: 2 Commentary*, pp. 50–53.

14. I disagree with Matteini's contention that Dante would only have been correct had
he held to a quantitative difference in the two goals (introduction to *Il più antico oppositore*,
p. 42). See also Nardi, *Saggi di filosofia dantesca*, pp. 9–13; and Enrico Proto, "La dottrina
dantesca delle macchie lunari," in *Scritti varii di erudizione e dicritica in onore di Rodolfo Renier*
(Turin: Fratelli Bocca Editori, 1912), esp. pp. 201–204.

15. "The worst kind of error," *"error pessimus"* (*Ref.* 1:33). See Grabmann, *Studien über den
Einfluss der aristotelischen Philosophie*, pp. 83–99. See *Averrois Cordubensis Commentarium Magnum in
Aristotelis De Anima librum tertium*, in *Commentarium magnum in Aristotelis De anima libros III*, ed.
F. Stuart Crawford, Corpus commentariorum Averrois in Aristotelem, Latin, vol. 6:1, Me-
dieval Academy of America Publication no. 59 (Cambridge, Mass.: Mediæval Academy of
America, 1953), esp. pp. 406–407 and 491.

16. The poet was most surely acquainted with the arguments of St. Thomas's *De unitate
intellectus contra Averroistas* that we mentioned above. See Fortin, *Dissidence et philosophie*, esp.
"La philosophie politique dans le monde chrétien," pp. 51–72. Also see René Gauthier,
"Notes sur les debuts (1225–1240) du premier 'Averroisme,'" *Revue des sciences philosophiques et
theologiques* 66, no. 1 (1982): 321–373; and Boyde, *Dante Philomythes*, pp. 276–279, 377.

17. In practice, a human individual would be no different from a member of any other
species that would fail to attain its perfection; see Nardi, "Di un'aspra critica di fra Guido
Vernani a Dante," *Alighieri: Rassegna bibliografica dantesca* 6 (1965): 42–47, rpt. *Saggi e note di critica dantesca*, pp. 377–385, here p. 379. Nardi cites Aristotle, *De anima* 2:4:415–426.

18. Cf. St. Augustine, *Confessions* 3:8 (text and trans. William Watts [1631]; LCL [Cam-
bridge, Mass.: Harvard University Press; London: William Heinemann, 1912; rpt. 1946]).
"For there is faultiness and deficiency in every part that does not fit in with the whole, of
which it is a part" (trans. Rex Warner, *Confessions* [New York: New Amrican Library of
World Literature], p. 63).

19. Nardi, *Saggi e note*, p. 379.

20. Noted by Maria Sampoli Simonelli in her review, "G. Marcovaldo, *Aspetti dello spirito di Dante*," in *Studi danteschi* 33 (1955), fasc. 1, pp. 239–240; Matteini, *Il più antico oppositore*, p.
50.

21. See the *Textus Aristotelis, Metaph.* 5:13:1020a10–15, and Lectio 15, no. 978, in St. Thomas
Aquinas, *In Metaph. Exp.*, ed. Cathala and Spiazzi, pp. 260–261. See also note in *Mon.* ed.
Kay, p. 19. Edward Williamson sets up a radical, straw argument and attributes it to
Dante, and then proceeds to censure the poet: "[I]n every one of these views [of Clement
of Alexandria, Origen, John of Damascus, and St. Thomas Aquinas] there is the basic as-

sumption that the truths of philosophy and religion are the same and are directed to the same end. What the Fathers are really talking about is two kinds of faith, that which is bolstered by reasoning and that which exists *per se*, and the notion *that a Christian might lead a life of reason independent of faith* would be wholly foreign to their thought. But this unprecedented idea is precisely what Dante is specifying" ("De Beatitudine Huius Vite," *Annual Report of the Dante Society of America* 76 [1958]; rpt. *Dante Studies* 118 [2000]: 119–120; my emphases). Dante *never* defines such a "life independent of faith," for that leads to damnation, not beatitude; Dantean man is under the guidance of both distinct powers, temporal and spiritual. The dramatization that the poet gives in Purgatory reveals that the baptized, faithful Wayfarer can enter the Garden of Eden atop the mountain and go beyond; but at Beatrice's appearance the Wayfarer realizes that the pagan rebel to God's law and the faith, Virgilio, has disappeared (*Purg.* 30:49–51)—we surmise, to return, once his divinely directed but nonecclesiatical mission is completed, to his place in Limbo, in Hell.

22. *ST* I-II, q. 4, a. 5. On the concept of *"ius naturale"* and *"universitas,"* see Gierke, *Political Theories of the Middle Ages*, trans. Maitland, esp. pp. 75–87, and notes; P. Michaud-Quantin, *Universitas: Expressions du Mouvement communautaire dans le moyen-âge latin* (Paris: Vrin, 1970); and J. Ferrante, *The Political Vision of the "Divine Comedy,"* pp. 12–13. For the state as having, metaphorically, a life of its own and as a multitude of individual intellects, see E. Lewis, *Medieval Political Ideas*, pp. 199–206. This is the concept, accepted and common in Aristotelian thought, and as outlined in the *Mon.*, that Vernani taxes with the charge of Averroism.

23. "If we speak of the happiness of this life, the happy man needs friends as the Philosopher says (*Nic. Ethics* 9:9) . . . for the purpose of good operation, viz, that he may do good to them . . . for in order that man may do well, whether in the works of the active life, or in those of the contemplative life, he needs the fellowship of friends" (*ST* I-II, q. 4, a. 8).

24. St. Thomas Aquinas, *ST* I-II, q. 90, a. 2.

25. *De bono communi*, ed. De Matteis, pp. 24, 65. See also Charles T. Davis, "An Early Political Theorist," p. 668.

26. *De bono communi*, ed. De Matteis, p. 71.

27. This is decidedly *not* man's attainment of the earthly paradise "through his own devices" nor "a purely intellectual perfection and philosophic self-redemption," as E. H. Kantorowicz oddly claims in *The King's Two Bodies*, pp. 469–471. Dante would shrink at such Pelagian heresy. The poet dramatizes the error of such a proud and preposterous notion of autonomy in the failed initial climb of *Inf.* 1:1–64. When Dante's Wayfarer finally reaches the Earthly Paradise in *Purg.* 27–28, he has been led there by a chain of God's grace (*Inf.* 2) and by obedience and surrender to the fact that the journey, as Virgilio is made to say, "is willed there above where will and power are one" (*Inf.* 3:95, 5:23, 7:11). Virgilio represents, as all critics agree, at least in some major sense, the God-ordained empire (*Inf.* 2:16–24) and its philosophical teachings; these, also, are direct expressions of God's will and ordaining.

28. *Epistola* 8, ed. Toynbee, pp. 142, 147. Cf. the hierocrat, Augustinus Triumphus, who, at one moment in his *Summa*, writes expansively that "[a]ll the faithful, both lay and clerics are members of the Church," and, immediately, must nicely straiten his view to signify the Church as an institution: "The Pope presides over the contemplative and active men of the Church, since he presides over the shepherds and the sheep, religious and clerics, the lettered and the lay" (Wilks, *The Problem of Sovereignty*, p. 19, n. 1).

29. Vernani himself argued the doctrinal imagery of the Church as one body in his commentary on *Unam sanctam;* see his text, edited by Grabmann, in *Studien über den Einfluss der aristotelischen Philosophie*, pp. 144–145.

30. On the question of lost original justice, the gaining of personal justice, and the dramatization in the *Purg.*, see the classic study by Charles S. Singleton, "Virgo or Justice," in *Journey to Beatrice* (Cambridge, Mass.: Harvard University Press, 1958), pp. 184–203.

31. Cf. Davis, "Remigio de' Girolami and Dante," p. 115. See Wilks's chapters in Part 2, "The Universal Society," of *The Problem of Sovereignty*, pp. 15–150.

32. Fritz Kern, in *Humana Civilitas (Staat, Kirche, und Kultur): Eine Dante-Untersuchung*, Mittelalterliche Studien 1:1 (Leipzig: Koehler, 1913), pp. 7–50, oddly agrees with Vernani.

33. E. H. Kantorowicz, "Man-Centered Kingship: Dante," in *The King's Two Bodies*, pp. 451–495. Kantorowicz is not clear on the ambivalent senses of *humanitas* and *humana civilitas*, and, as we have noted, his eccentric Pelagian views obfuscate much of his explanation.

34. See Michele Barbi, "Nuovi problemi della critica dantesca, VI: L'ideale politico-religioso di Dante," *Studi danteschi* 23 (1938): 68; Matteini, *Il più antico oppositore*, pp. 48–49.

35. Bruno Nardi, *Dante e la cultura medievale. Nuovi saggi di filosofia dantesca*, p. x; Matteini, *Il più antico oppositore*, p. 49; Barbi, "Nuovi problemi," p. 68.

36. Matteini, *Il più antico oppositore*, p. 50.

37. The poet does not cite the Arab philosopher as a source or authority here at all, but, as Maria Sampoli Simonelli notes ("G. Marcovaldo, *Aspetti dello spirito di Dante*," pp. 239–240; Matteini, p. 50), he merely observes, in an offhand aside or afterthought, that Averroës would be in concord with his immediately preceding point *that potentiality could have no separate existence*. It seems most likely that Dante is citing from memory.

38. Etienne Gilson, *Dante the Philosopher*, trans. David Moore (Sheed & Ward, 1949); rpt. with same pagination with the title *Dante and Philosophy* (New York: Harper & Row, 1963), p. 179. On the *"imitatio sacerdotii"* phenomenon of medieval politics, see Percy E. Schramm, "Sacerdotium und Regnung im Austausch ihrer Vorrechts: Eine Skizze der Entwicklung zur Beleuchtung des 'Dictatus papæ' Gregors VII," *Studi Gregoriani* 2 (1947): 403–457, and Kantorowicz, *The King's Two Bodies*. The intermimicry on the part of sacred and lay governances was a continuous and mutual reciprocation through the centuries. See the remarks of the high papalist James of Viterbo on the likeness of governmental unity to God in *De regimine Christiana (On Christian Government)* 2:1 (trans. Dyson, p. 42). Also see J. Ferrante, *The Political Vision of the "Divine Comedy,"* pp. 12–13.

39. Notably, Tolomeo da Lucca avoided such symmetry; see James M. Blythe, *Ideal Gov-*

*ernment and the Mixed Constitution* (Princeton, N.J.: Princeton University Press, 1992), p. 117.

40. See Thomas Hobbes, *Leviathan*, ed. M. Oakeshott (Oxford, U.K.: Blackwell, 1946), p. 457. Cf. Watt, *The Theory of Papal Monarchy*, pp. 78–79: "In the whole history of the Roman Church as a composite juridical entity, the model of the structure of the Roman Empire has always been a powerful conditioning feature."

41. Lucius Cæcilius Firmianus Lactantius (ca. A.D. 240–ca. 320). See Lactantius's *Istitutiones divinæ (PL* 6:111–1016); *Divine Institutions*, trans. Mary Francis McDonald, The Fathers of the Church 49 (Washington, D.C.: The Catholic University of America Press, 1964).

42. *Divine Institutions*, trans. McDonald., p. 22.

43. *Divine Institutions*, trans. McDonald, p. 23.

44. Hugh of Fleury cites the pseudo-Augustinian phrase on the soveriegn-deity likeness in his *Tractatus de regia postestate et sacerdotali dignitate*, written in the early years of the twelfth century and dedicated to Henry I of England (Carlyle and Carlyle, 3:98, 11; see also 1:149, 179, 215). Likewise, John of Salisbury asserts that "[t]he Prince is a certain image of the divinity"; see *Policraticus* 8:17:778a, ed. M. F. Markland (New York: Ungar, 1979), p. 138. St. Thomas Aquinas expresses the same idea in his *De regimine principum* 1.9.72; *On Princely Government*, in *Selected Philosophical Writings*, trans. J. G. Dawson, ed. d'Entrèves, p. 51: "[A] king's singular likeness to God . . . a thing is dearer to God the closer it comes to imitating Him." See Eschmann's note on the tradition in St. Thomas Aquinas, *On Kingship*, trans. Gerald B. Phelan, rev. with intro. and notes by I. T. Eschmann, O.P. (Toronto: Pontifical Institute of Mediaeval Studies, 1949; rpt. 1989), p. 41, n. 6. Cf. St. Thomas Aquinas's *Summa contra gentiles* III, q. 76–77 and *ST* II-I, q. 91, a. 1 and 3. See also Gierke, *Political Theories of the Middle Age*, trans. Maitland, pp. 30–31. The twinned persona of the sovereign after the image of Christ as Man and God is the subject of Kantorowicz's classic *The King's Two Bodies*.

45. *De regimine principum (On the Rule of Princes)*, trans. J. G. Dawson, in *Aquinas: Selected Political Writings*, ed. d'Entrèves, pp. 50–51; see also the version in Tolomeo da Lucca's *On the Government of Rulers* 1:10:5, trans. Blythe, p. 86.

46. See Boyde's comments on the rule of one in *Dante: Philomythes*, pp. 219–220.

47. See the useful gathering of texts on the emperor as *"vicarius Dei,"* "vicar of God," in Jean Rivière, *Le problème de l'Eglise et de l'état au temps de Philippe le Bel*, Spicilegium Sacrum Lovaniense, Etudes et Documents 8 (Louvain/Paris: Université de Louvain, 1926), pp. 435–440. Dante obviously would not go on to say that this monarch is Jesus Christ; cf. Matteini, *Il più antico oppositore*, p. 50. Since Vernani wrote the *De potestate*, solidly supporting the temporal authority of the pope, and especially in the light of his virulent arguments in ch. 4, it is natural that he would adduce this most powerful argument to twist Dante's meaning to one unintended. See also Michele Maccarrone, *Vicarius Christi: Storia del titolo papale*, Lateranum, n.s., 18, nos. 1–4.(Rome: Facultas Theologica Pontificii Athenæi Lateranensis, 1952), esp. pp. 78–84.

48. Davis, "An Early Florentine Political Theorist," p. 666, and n. 38.

49. For arguments from authority, see "De loco ab auctoritate," in Peter of Spain, *Summulæ logicales*, Tractatus V, 36 (ed. de Rijk, pp. 75–76); on the enthymeme *(entimema)*, see Tractatus V, 3 (ed. de Rijk, pp. 56–57), and "The Aristotelian Enthymeme," in George Hayward Joyce, *Principles of Logic* (London/New York: Longmans, Green, 1908; rpt. 3rd ed., 1949), pp. 253–255. See esp. *Mon.* 2:5:6.

50. *Nic. Ethics* 1:3:4:1094b, trans. H. Rackham, LCL (Cambridge, Mass./London: Harvard University Press, 1926, rprt. 1994), pp. 8–9; St. Thomas Aquinas, *Commentary on the Nic. Ethics*, trans. Litzinger, 1:16. The end or good sought depended upon the discipline involved; ibid., pp. 45–46.

51. *Nic. Ethics* 1:3:2:1094b, trans. Rackham, pp. 6–7; St. Thomas Aquinas, *Commentary on the Nic. Ethics*, trans. Litzinger, 1:18–19.

52. On contemporary understanding of the derivation of "dialectic" from the Greek, see *Logica modernorum*, ed. L. M. de Rijk, pp. 104–105.

53. "If justice be removed, then what are kingdoms but great robber bands? For what are robber bands but little kingdoms?" (*The City of God* 4:4; trans. adapted from Green, LCL, 2:16–17). St. Augustine learned the anecdote from Cicero, *De republica* 3. Interestingly, the Dominican friar Tolomeo da Lucca, a hierocrat, but also a supporter of the republican, "political," commune-form of government, gives an opposite, positive interpretation of the pirate tale in *De regimine principum: On the Government of Princes* 3:5:4 (trans. Blythe, pp. 158–159).

54. Prv 8:15; St. Augustine, *The City of God* 5:19.

55. St. Augustine also had stated that the Romans owed their empire not to the gods but to the one true God: "Without any doubt kingdoms are set up by divine providence" (*The City of God* 5:1, trans. Grreen, LCL, 2:134–135). In *The City of God* 5:12, St. Augustine assured that his censure of idolatry would not overshadow his message of God's providence: "I would not have anyone, after I had convinced him that the Roman Empire was not extended and preserved because the gods were worshiped, go on to ascribe Roman success to fate of some sort or other, rather than to the overruling will of God most high" (trans. Green, LCL, 2:190–191). We might note that a similar question of God's use of Roman paganism in his foreordaining is taken up by Dante in the *Divina Commedia:* there Virgilio is *both* the bearer of Divine Grace in intercession as well as the empire's representative.

56. These signs will not merely be the miraculous events of Roman history, but, as revealed at *Mon.* 2:11:6, also the words of Caiaphas's prophecy of God's will in Jn 11:49–50, and Christ's own acknowledgment of Pilate's jurisdiction in Jn 19:10–11. See P. G. Ricci, "L'ultima fase del pensiero politico di Dante e Cangrande vicario imperiale," in *Dante e la cultura veneta*, pp. 367–371; and Cesare Vasoli, "Filosofia e politica in Dante tra *Convivio* e *Monarchia*," *Letture classensi* 9–10 (1982): 11–37.

57. R. A. Marcus, "Two Conceptions of Political Authority: Augustine's *De civitate Dei*, XIX, 14–15, and Some Thirteenth Century Interpretations," *Journal of Theological Studies*, n.s., 16 (1965): 68–100. Dante actually deals with this concept of the correction of sin only

briefly in *Mon.* 3:4:14, since if he elaborated upon it he would weaken the positive Aristotelian and Thomistic arguments that form the bulk of his treatise.

58. Dante here is, of course, at his most illogical. P. Shaw, however, convincingly shows the numerological care he takes in the second, central book of the *Mon.*, with its two introductory chapters, seven chapters of argumentation and two concluding (2-3-1-3-2), thus giving, in her count, the overall pattern of the chapters in the whole treatise as 16-11-16 or, more engagingly, 16-2-3-1-3-2-16. See the "Introduction" to her ed., pp. xxvi–xxvii.

59. Dante cites from memory. Aristotle had actually said "*a good birth* is wealth plus virtue going back to one's forbears." Moerbeke, in the widely distributed first Latin translation, used by both Dante and St. Thomas Aquinas, had rendered "good birth" as "*ingenuitas,*" not "*nobilitas*": "Ingenuitas *enim est virtus et divitiæ antiquæ*" (being well-born is virtue and ancient riches); see *Pol.* 4:7:1294a22–23, ed. Raymundi and Spiazzi, *In politicorum*, Lectio VII, *Textus Aristotelis* 470, p. 211; *The Politics*, trans. T. A. Sinclair, rev. Trevor J. Saunders (London/New York: Penguin Books, 1992), p. 260. H. Rackham (*Pol.* 4:6:294a22–23) translates the passage ambiguously as "nobility means ancient worth and virtue"; see *Aristotle in Twenty Three Volumes*, LCL (Cambridge, Mass./London: Harvard University Press, 1932, rpt., 1990), 21:319. Dante substitutes "good birth" with St. Thomas's "*nobilitas.*"

60. Charles T. Davis has shown that Brunetto here follows the text of Gulielmus Peraldus in the *Summa virtutum ac vitiorum* (Venice 1571) 1:10, p. 32; see "Brunetto Latini and Dante," in *Dante's Italy*, pp. 180–184); also see my notes to *Mon.* 2:3:2 below.

61. R. A. Marcus believed that "Ptolemy of Lucca was the herald of a comfortable obliviousness to a profound cleavage in the tradition of Christian political thought" ("Two Conceptions of Political Authority," pp. 96–97). Blythe disagrees: "Ptolemy never openly admits any conflict between Augustine and Aristotle, but 'comfortable obliviousness' is hardly the way to describe Ptolemy's wriggling. . . . [His conflict with Thomas] is one of Ptolemy's most original contributions" (*Ideal Government*, p. 99). Dante similarly avoids any open admission of the conflict in his confession of a change of mind—a philosophical rejection of the Latin Father St. Augustine—concerning the legitimacy of the empire.

62. See the *De potestate* 4, in Vernani, *De potestate summi pontificis et De reprobatione Monarchiæ compositæ a Dante Aligerio florentino tractatus duo* [1746]), pp. 56–60: "*Quod in Infidelibus nunquam fuit vera Respublica, nec aliquis verus Imperator*"; cf. *Ref.* 1:48.

63. Vernani, *De potestate summi pontificis*, ch. 4, pp. 56–58.

64. Giles of Rome (Ægidius Romanus), *De ecclesiastica potestate* 2:11:1; *On Ecclesiastical Power*, trans. Dyson, p. 91.

65. St. Augustine, e.g., uses the negative wording of the old Latin version of Prv 8:15 in *The City of God* 5:19: "By me kings reign, and tyrants possess the land," while the Vulgate states *positively* (in the Douay-Rheims rendering): "By me kings reign, and lawgivers decree just things."

66. See the text of Innocent IV's letter *On Decretals* 3:34:8 in trans. Tierney, *Crisis*, p. 155.

67. Vernani here closely follows Giles of Rome, *On Ecclesiastical Power* 2:11, "That Unbelievers Are All Unworthy of Any Possession of Lordship or Power" (ed. Dyson, pp. 91–95). St. Thomas Aquinas had warned that unbelievers are forbidden *to seek or acquire* dominion over believers, and speaks only of the legitimacy of *authority already in force*, recognizing that all power came from God. Further, the right of dominion in whatever case can "be justly done away with by the sentence or ordination of the Church who has the authority of God." And, as he continues with this thorny problem, Aquinas admits, "This the Church does sometimes, and sometimes not." Vernani omits all cautions and centers in, as usual, secondhand, on St. Thomas's statement of justification for ouster, "since unbelievers in virtue of their unbelief deserve to forfeit their power over the faithful who are converted into the children of God." But St. Thomas had then cited laissez-faire exceptions in regard to the Jews and Moslem rulers not under Christian power. The whole question is found in his response, *ST* II-II, q. 10, a. 10. Maccarrone concludes, quoting the *De regimine principum* 1:14, that St. Thomas "accepted the principles of *potestas directa* [of the papacy], although he did not develop them in his ecclesiological doctrine, and concerning the state" (*"Potestas directa,"* p. 40). We must note, however, that St. Thomas is only speaking in that passage of the *priesthood* of *all believers*, not that of the pope, in the spiritual realm— but, granted, a priesthood that, obviously, would be under the pontiff. In the *De regimine principum*, St. Thomas is more emphatic about authority in the spiritual kingdom; concerning the glory of heaven and the enjoyment of God, he writes: "All the faithful in Christ, being members of Him, become thus, priests and kings. The ministry of this kingdom [of which Christ is king] is entrusted not to the rulers of this earth but to priests, so that temporal affairs may remain distinct from those spiritual: and in particular, it is delegated to the High Priest, the successor of Peter and Vicar of Christ, the Roman Pontiff; to whom all kings in Christendom should be subject, as to the Lord Jesus Christ Himself. For those who are concerned with the subordinate ends of life must be subject to him who is concerned with the supreme end and be directed by his command" (trans. Dawson, in *Aquinas: Selected Political Writings*, ed. D'Entrèves, pp. 76–77; see also the version recorded by Tolomeo da Lucca in *On the Government of Rulers* 1:15:10, trans. Blythe, p. 100).

68. St. Augustine instead harshly criticizes Numa's failure to bring peace in *The City of God* 3:9–10.

69. *De potestate summi pontificis*, pp. 60–64

70. My emphases. See *Ref.* 2:35–38. Cf. Livy, *Ab urbe condita* 5:37ff. See St. Augustine, *The City of God* 2:22: "Really now, where was this crowd of gods when, long before the ancient morals had decayed, Rome was taken and burned by the Gauls? Were they present then, perhaps but asleep? For then the whole city was in the hands of the enemy, save only the Capitoline Hill, and this too, was about to be taken, were it not that the geese at any rate were awake while the gods slept" (trans. McCracken, 1:228–229). In 3:8, Augustine returns to it sarcastically: "Perhaps [the pagan gods] were at Ilium when Rome itself was captured

and burned by the Gauls? Having the sharpest hearing and the greatest celerity, they returned at once when the geese cackled, in order to protect at least the Capitoline Hill, which had been spared. Yet the warning came too late for them to return in time to defend anything else" (trans. McCracken, 1:288–289). Vernani conflates the two references and quite misses Augustine's irony by lamely transferring the gods' sharpness of hearing to the geese.

71. Though demons appear eighty-one times in the New Testament, there was no theological unanimity as to the real existence of wicked spirits who tempted mankind and created disturbances in the cosmos; it was taken for granted that God did not create them. Notably, where they did meet acceptance, as in St. Bonaventure, Albert the Great, and in St. Thomas Aquinas (*ST* I, q. 12, a. 2), they work independently of heavenly bodies, condensing precipitation in the dark, cloudy regions of the atmosphere (see Eph 2:2), just as Vernani argues with the divine ordination of Hannibal's defeat by the hailstorm, and as Dante has his character, Buonconte da Montefeltro, recount the end of his body in *Purg.* 5:109–129. Dante is on the stronger ground: we recognize that the torments of Buonconte's body are not only personifications of the actual stormy meteorological conditions during the Battle of Campaldino as recounted in the chroniclers, but are also poetic metaphors for Buonconte's historical mistreatment by his enemies. Vernani does the opposite, reducing all to the letter, literalizing the demons, and erecting them into a kind of superstitious, Manichaean force, opposing that of God. On Buonconte, see Dante Alighieri, *La Divina Commedia* con i commenti di Tommaso Casini-Silvio Adrasto Barbi e di Attilio Momigliano, *Purgatorio* (Florence: Sansoni, 1977), ad loc.; L. J. Elmer, "Demons, Theology of," *New Catholic Encyclopedia*, 4:752–756; and M. A. Glutz, "Demonology," *New Catholic Encyclopedia*, 4:756–757.

72. *The City of God* 5:18; trans. Green, LCL: for Brutus, 2:218–219, 2:224–225; Camillus, 2:226–229; Mucius, 2:228–229, Decii, 2:230–231; Quintius Cincinnatus, 2:234–235; Fabricius, 2:234–235. For those mentioned by Remigio and Tolomeo in St. Augustine's chapter, Torquatus, 2:226–227; Marcus Regulus, 2: 232–233; Valerius, 2: 232–235.

73. Tolomeo da Lucca cites St. Augustine on Brutus to the opposite effect; see *De regimine* 3:5:5, 3:16:1; *On the Government of Rulers*, trans. Blythe, pp. 159, 193.

74. *The City of God* 1:23, trans. McCracken, pp. 100–103.

75. St. Thomas's treatise is commonly entitled *De regimine principum*. See *On Princely Government*, trans. Dawson, ed. D'Entrèves, pp. 2–83. Also see Tolomeo da Lucca, *On the Government of Rulers: De regimine principum, with Portions Attributed to Thomas Aquinas*, trans. Blythe. Although Blythe holds that the concepts of kingship in books 1 to 2:4 of the *De regimine principum* are compatible with the views on monarchy outlined in the *Summa theologiæ*, he doubts that St. Thomas definitely penned them; see his "Introduction," to *On the Government of Rulers*, p. 5, and his chapter on "Ptolemy of Lucca," in *Ideal Government and Mixed Constitution in the Middle Ages* (Princeton, N.J.: Princeton University Press, 1992), pp. 92–115, esp. p. 92. It is hard to tell when or whether Dante knew or believed the work was by St.

Thomas or Tolomeo; in any event, the poet felt very secure in adapting such Aristotelian modifications to St. Augustine's censures.

76. See the text of the *Short Determination* in *Determinatio compendiosa de iurisdictione imperii,* edited by Krammer. Ironically, as a good Dominican, Tolomeo entered the debate on the nature and extent of papal power giving all primary authority in this world to the pope. See the useful "Introduction," by Blythe, to *On the Government of Rulers,* esp. pp. 7–8. H. Theodore Silverstein, in "On the Genesis of *De Monarchia,* II, v," *Speculum* 13 (1938): 326–349, gives a tentative discussion of passages that Dante imitates; Silverstein, however, confuses and conflates the different parts of *On the Government of Rulers* written by St. Thomas and by Tolomeo. Silverstein's study has been corrected by Charles T. Davis in "Ptolemy of Lucca and the Roman Republic," *Proceedings of the American Philosophic Society* 118 (1974): 30–50, and in "Roman Patriotism and Republican Propaganda: Ptolemy of Lucca and Pope Nicholas III," *Speculum* 50 (1975): 411–433. See also Carlyle and Carlyle, 5:74; and Walter Ullmann, *Law and Politics in the Middle Ages: An Introduction to the Sources of Medieval Political Law* (Ithaca, N.Y.: Cornell University Press, 1975), p. 274.

77. *"Deus illis inspiravit ad bene regendum"; De regimine principum* 3:4; *On the Government of Rulers,* ed. and trans. Blythe, 153–154. See Silverstein, "On the Genesis," p. 328. Also see Tolomeo's favorable comments on the ancient Romans in his *Determinatio compendiosa (Short Determinations),* ed. Krammer, pp. 45–46; and on the modern Romans, pp. 46–47.

78. See Davis, "Ptolemy of Lucca," pp. 30–50, and "Roman Patriotism and Republican Propaganda," pp. 411–433; and Blythe, *On the Government of Rulers,* "Introduction," p. 34.

79. Davis, "Ptolemy of Lucca," p. 33.

80. Tolomeo names five heroes from *The City of God* 5:18 in his *Determinatio compendiosa* 21: Brutus, Torquatus, Curtius, Regulus, and Fabricius, and he adds Curius (ed. Krammer, p. 43); in the *De regimine principum* he includes all these, adding Scipio and Marcus Marcellus (3:4:5 and 3:5:5; *On the Government of Rulers,* trans. Blythe, pp. 155–159). Remigio de' Girolami in the *De bono communi* gives six, all from Augustine's chapter: Lucius Valerius, Quintus Concinnatus, Fabricius, Curtius, Torquatus, and Regulus; he adds Cato. Tolomeo da Lucca quotes Cato's words many times in admiration in the *Determinatio compendiosa;* in the *De regimine,* he uses Cato's suicide to cap his own list of heroism for the common good, after Mucius's fiery torture, Fabricius's poverty, Rutilius's exile, Regulus's torments, and Socrates' poison (*De regimine* 4:18:3; *On the Government of Rulers,* trans. Blythe, pp. 260–261). See Silverstein's "On the Genesis," p. 328, and more especially, Davis's corrective discussion and comparative lists in "Ptolemy of Lucca," pp. 35–36; see also Davis's "An Early Florentine Political Theorist," p. 666. The three writers' lists do not match and are most probably derived from a common point of view, and as we shall note, possibly from personal discussions, rather than merely from a common text; Dante's later monarchic-imperialist view in the *Mon.* differs from the Guelph, republican, communal government stress of both Tolomeo and Remigio de' Girolami. See also David Thompson, "Dante's Virtuous Romans," *Dante Studies* 96 (1978): 145–162.

81. *Conv.* 2:12:7. In addition to Tolomeo da Lucca and Remigio, members included the preacher Giordano da Pisa, the traveler and diarist Riccoldo da Montecroce, and the translator of Sallust Bartolomeo da San Concordio. Charles T. Davis describes the erudite company gathered there in his "Prefazione" to Filippo Tamburini's edition of Remigio dei Girolami's *Contra falsos ecclesie professores*, pp. iii–iv. See also the partial monograph edition of the *Contra falsos ecclesie professores*, ed. Emilio Panella, in *Per lo studio di Fra Remigio dei Girolami (†1319): Contra falsos ecclesie professores cc. 5–37*, VII Centenario della Fondazione di S. Maria Novella in Firenze (1279–1979), vol. 1, Memorie Domenicane, n.s., 10 (Pistoia: Memorie Domenicane, 1919).

82. "Three Tuscan contemporaries, Ptolemy, Remigio, and Dante, were the first medieval writers to meet Augustine on his own ground and stand his moral on its head" (Davis, "Ptolemy of Lucca," p. 34). See the study and edition by De Matteis, "Il *De bono communi* di Remigio de' Girolami," pp. 11–88, and esp. pp. 56–61. See also Remigio's companion treatise, *De bono pacis*, edited by Davis in "Remigio de' Girolami and Dante," pp. 105–136; Davis examines historians' conflicting views, including those of Martin Grabmann, Michele Maccarrone, Bruno Nardi, and Jean Leclerq. On Remigio's position on the temporal power of the pope; see esp. the text of the treatise, pp. 123–136. Also see L. Mineo-Paluello, "Remigio Girolami's *De bono communi*," *Italian Studies* 11 (1956): 79–92.

83. Remigio cites six examples from Augustine's chapter—and then, like Dante, adds Cato (*De bono communi*, ed. De Matteis, pp. 56–58).

84. Silverstein, "On the Genesis," pp. 326–329. Tolomeo theoretically separates the republican and imperial forms of government but, just as Dante does, selects examples from one or the other as he sees fit: "Now that I have covered these things, I must compare imperial lordship to political [i.e., republican] and regal lordship because it overlaps with both, as is apparent from what I have said" (*De regimine* 3:20; *On the Government of Rulers*, trans. Blythe, pp. 204–205).

85. *Ref.* 2:50.

86. Biblically, by tradition, and as most *mappamundi* had displayed since ca. 1250, Jerusalem was the center of the northern hemisphere of land, that is, the center of the earth, to be the place of Christ's Redemption; cf. Ez 5:5: "Thus saith the Lord God: This is Jerusalem, I have set her in the midst of the nations, and the countries round about her," and Ps 73[74]:12: "He hath wrought salvation in the midst of the earth."

87. This wide, but minor, tradition was to be taken up and amended most influentially two and a half centuries later by the Calvinistic literalist James Ussher (1581–1656), archbishop of Armargh, who blithely established that the world had been created on a bright Thursday morning, October 23, at precisely 9 A.M. in 4004 B.C.—a date still found emblazoned on many a sectarian portal.

88. It is noteworthy that Friar Guido fails to reiterate this "empire as Johnny-come-lately" argument later in his rebuttal of *Mon.* 3:12–15 (*Ref.* 3:68–77) concerning the Church's priority in time.

89. A commonplace of Roman poetry; we recall Horace's famous *"Dulce e decorum est pro patria mori"* (It is sweet and fitting to die for one's country). Remigio da Girolami had exaggerated the concept by insisting, rhetorically, that a citizen should prefer to damn his very soul rather than damage the common good: extreme measures were needed to overcome Florentine partisan fratricide; see *De bono communi*, p. 80. Dante deals with the sinful pretense of self-sacrifice in his narrative of Pier della Vigna's *apologia pro vita sua* and suicide in *Inf.* 13.

90. Cf. *Par.* 19:70–72.

91. Dante apparently did not realize, or else ignores, that duels had been forbidden by the Roman curia and by the legendary Pepo, founder of Bolognese law studies; in fact, most jurists doubted that the judgment of God would be shown in the outcome of duels. Hermann Kantorowicz, late professor of law at Freiburg, Kiel, and Cambridge, gives valuable documentation in *"De pugna:* La letteratura langobardistica sul duello giudiziario," in the collected essays *Rechtshistorische Schriften,* ed. H. Coing and G. Immel, Freiburger Rechts- und Staatswissenschaftliche Abhandlungen 30 (Karlsruhe: C. F. Müller, 1970), pp. 255–271. Also see Henry Charles Lea, *The Duel and the Oath* (Philadelphia: University of Pennsylvania Press, 1974); Giovanni Diurni, "Duello," *Enciclopedia dantesca,* 2:605–607; Piero Fiorelli, "Sul senso del diritto nella *Monarchia," Letture classensi* 16 (1987): 79–97, esp. pp. 94–95; and Frederick H. Russell, *The Just War in the Middle Ages* (Cambridge, U.K.: Cambridge University Press, 1975), pp. 243, 259–261, 277. The majority of theologians censured professional duelists, although some very few saw a limited value in them. St. Augustine expresses outrage in *The City of God* 3:14; St. Thomas deals with the concept of just war and the licit use of arms by authorities in *ST* II-II, q. 40, 64, and 83, where he carefully follows Augustine. Innocent III's Fourth Lateran Council (that met on November 4, 1215) prohibited the clergy from participating in ordeals or any judicial proceedings involving the spilling of blood (in Canon 18); see S. C. Ferruolo, "Innocent III, Pope (1160/1161–16 July 1216)," *Dictionary of the Middle Ages,* 6:465. Despite prohibitions, duels continued in popular practice and were common in the Italy of Dante's time. We must note, besides, that Dante's chiastic order reverses the plan from his initial introduction to the treatment of these arguments; it is typical of the Italian inversion of the "former . . . latter" sequential order common in English. Cf. the order of the final syllogistic figures in *Mon.* 2:10:10.

92. *The City of God* 5:22; trans. Green, LCL, 2:252–253. See the well-researched treatment of Cicero's and St. Augustine's theories of just war in Russell, *The Just War.*

93. Dyson's translation here of *The City of God* 3:14 is most accurate: "Did it matter that they furnished an ungodly spectacle [*impium spectaculum*] both to those then alive and, for as long as their fame is handed down, to their posterity also?" (p. 112); see also trans. McCracken, 1:316–317.

94. *PL* 214:1106; *PL* 216:502.

95. H. Kantorowicz, *"De pugna,"* p. 270

96. See H. Kantorowicz, *"De pugna,"* esp. pp. 270–271; and Fiorelli, "Il senso del diritto nella *Monarchia,"* pp. 92–95. Ancient Lombard—Langobardic—law, which approved of duel by a battle-wager of *"campiones,"* applied in Pavia, Piacenza, Milan, and Mantua, as well as in southern Italy; Frederick I of Hohenstaufen had approved it in certain cases in the *Libri feudorum*. Not unrelated to his support of duels is Dante's acceptance, even favoring, of vendetta. Cf. his regret in *Inf.* 29 for having failed to avenge the death of his kinsman Geri del Bello.

97. The poet ultimately presents altogether an unconvincingly positive view of such blood contests, and, disturbed, historians and editors present differing views on Dante's theoretical grounds. Charles T. Davis, in "Dante, Machiavelli, and Rome," saw it as based on the "judgment by battle" in Germanic history and literature (*Dante Studies* 106 [1988]: 43–60, here, pp. 53–56); without reference to Davis, P. Shaw substantially agrees (ed. *Mon.* [1995], p. 84). Kay (*Mon.*, ed., p. 165) ultimately denies that Dante bases his concept on Burgundian and Germanic sources and holds convincingly that it derives from the Bible (David and Goliath), Virgil (Æneas and Turnus), and Livy (Horatii and Curiatii). See Kurt Georg Cram, *Judicium belli: Zum Rechtscharakter des Krieges im deutschen Mittelalter* (Münster/Cologne: Böhlau, 1955); Russell, *The Just War*; T. A. Sandquist, "Inquest, English," in *Dictionary of the Middle Ages*, 6:481–482; Charles M. Radding, "Ordeals," *Dictionary of the Middle Ages*, 9:259–260; and H. Kantorowicz, *"De pugna,"* pp. 255–271.

98. St. Augustine distinguished between the motives of false virtue of pagan emperors, whose highest good was human glory (the ammunition for Vernani's counterattack) achieved through treachery and deceit, and the virtue of the Christian emperors who followed Constantine. In examining the "true happiness of Christian emperors," Augustine concludes that "we call them happy if they rule justly," while pagan emperors were driven only by earthly glory (*The City of God* 5:24; trans. Green, LCL, 2:260–263). Following the then-established topos, Tolomeo of Lucca asserted that the emperors, after the transfer to Constantinople, were obedient and reverent to the Roman Church as their subjection to four Church councils showed (*De regimine principum* 3:17; *On the Government of Rulers*, ed. and trans. Blythe, pp. 198–199).

99. See "De equipollentis cathegoricarum: . . . Lex contradictoriarum," in Peter of Spain, *Summulæ logicales*, Tractatus 1, 14 (ed. de Rijk, p. 7). P. Shaw gives a clear explanation of the procedure encapsuled in the traditional example "if X is a man, then necessarily, by definition, X is an animal" in "Some Proposed Emendations to the Text of Dante's *Monarchia,"* *Italian Studies* 50 (1995): 3–4. She points out that "the logical implication works only in one direction." We must clarify that Dante is trying to apply Aristotle's rule that a false consequent cannot follow from a true antecedent, while a true consequent may follow from a false antecedent: and, most important, from true premises nothing can follow except the true; see *Prior Analytics* 2:2–4, in *The Complete Works of Aristotle*, 1:84–92; "De syllogismus ex falsis," in *Analytica priora*, in *Aristoteles Latinus*, 3:1–4, *Translatio Boethii recensio Florentina (partim recensio Carnutensis)*, ed. L. Minio-Paluello (Bruges/Paris: Desclée de Brouwer,

1962), pp. 94–99. Since nothing can be truer for Dante than Christ's redemption, only the truth may follow from it; for him, falsity is therefore impossible. Dante succeeds in making his reasoning appear procedurally valid; Vernani will assail its application but not its formal validity, nor, as we will see, ultimately, can he rebut its soundness—based on Jn 19:10–11 where, of course, Christ affirms that Pilate's power over him is in fact derived from God.

100. *Rhetoric* 1:1:1354a15–19; *The Complete Works of Aristotle*, 2:2152.

101. It is difficult, as Vernani shows, to complete the midterms, the assumed and omitted series of logical inferences, of Dante's enthymeme. See Ettore Carruccio, "La logica nel pensiero di Dante," *Physis* 8, no. 3 (1966): 233–246, here, 238–240; also see Mozzillo-Howell, "Dante's Art of Reason," pp. 121–140;

102. *The City of God*, trans. Green, LCL, 2:190–191.

103. Nardi gives a just critique of Vernani's *"stupidità"* on this point in "Di un'aspra critica," *Saggi e note di critica dantesca*, pp. 377–385. We must note that Dante does affirm the Augustinian position of the state as "a remedy for the infirmity of sin" in *Conv.* 4:5:3–8 and, briefly, in *Mon.* 3:4:14, although in the latter case it weakens his main thesis of the positivity of the empire. However, Dante views it in what we could describe as a most Thomistic manner: the Redemption perfects the natural *pax romana* after the perfect natural condition under a monarch first had been met. *Gratia perficit naturam.*

104. *"Quæ major injuiria quam justum innocentemque damnari"*; *De vera relione* 16 (*PL* 34:135).

105. Cf. *Par.* 7:47:48: *"Però d'un atto uscir cose diverse: / ch'a Dio e a' Giudei piacque una morte; / per lei tremò la terra e'l ciel s'aperse"*; and *Epistola* 5:10; ed. Toynbee, pp. 57, 62.

106. Cf. Nardi, "Di un'aspra critica," p. 383; Lino Pertile, "Dante Looks Forward and Back: Political Allegory in the Epistles," *Dante Studies* 115 (1997): 1–17, esp. p. 10. We must note that Remigio de' Girolami would also have disagreed sharply with Vernani's construction, as he cites Caiaphas's very prophecy in *De bono communi* (pp. 53–54) as the *supreme* example of dying for freedom and the common welfare: in fact, Remigio adds that (the then-well-famed and sainted) Thomas Becket had died for justice in the same way *in imitatione Christi* (*De bono communi*, p. 60), as one who "would rather die than see the liberty of the Church infringed." Innocent III a century before, having spent eight months at Becket's shrine (with his young fellow student in Paris, Stephen Langton, whom he would later nominate as the archbishop of Canterbury), had taken the legend of the martyred Becket as his Christlike spiritual model.

107. For *"exemplum"* (meaning "analogy" or "similitude") as a serious proof of an inference (or consequent), see Joyce, *Principles of Logic*, pp. 259, 358 and 286. Peter of Spain, in *Summulæ logicales*, Tractatus V, 3, writes: *"Exemplum* [analogy] occurs, when by means of one particular, another particular is proved on account of a similarity [*simile*] found within it" (ed. de Rijk, p. 58). In the last century, Sigmund Freud (let his example suffice) based his method on such pre-Renaissance thought; for him, as, *mutatis mutandis* for Dante, trained analogizing led to scientific knowledge. Social-scientific criticism of Freud's thought rou-

tinely points to this theory as its corroding flaw. Since all language is analogical, however, it is risky to pursue such criticism without great circumspection.

108. The Church of Rome called the Guelphs "sons of the Church": *"Guelphos, quos sancta romana ecclesia filios nominavit."* See Scholz, *Die Publizistik*, p. 460; and Maccarrone, "Teologia e diritto," p. 14. Padoan identifies, particularly, the Angevin king Robert the Wise of Naples, vassal and vicar of the Church, as the one with most to gain ("La composizione," p. 11).

109. The habit of mind, more typical in Italian speakers, and especially in medieval Italian thought, of dealing with "former" and "latter" in a reverse (chiastic) order from the typical Anglo-Saxon custom, probably also accounts for the reversal of the second and first figures of the syllogism in *Mon.* 2:10:10. The fourteenth-century Italian reader would logically expect it.

110. See Tierney, "'Sola scriptura' and the Canonists," pp. 346–364. See below, my editorial notes to *Mon.* 3:3: 11–14.

111. The monarchist writer of the *Disputatio* has the cleric declare: "I call 'law' [*ius*] the decrees of the fathers and the statutes of the Roman pontiffs." The knight replies, "Their statutes may be 'laws' for you, but they certainly are not for us. For no one can make statutes in respect of those things over which he clearly has no lordship" (trans. adapted from Dyson, pp. 12–13; for the recent bulls, pp. 14–15; see Dyson's informative "Introduction," pp. xix–xx). Scholz, in *Die Publizistik*, publishes an additional MS page ascribed to the treatise that employs the term "ecclesiastical traditions" (p. 485); Dyson does not include it.

112. Emphases added. For Dante, Hostiensis's statement commenting on *Per venerabilem* in the *Commentaria in quartum librum decretalium* (Venice, 1581), f. 39, was clearly most irritating: *"In omnibus dissentionibus magis est credendum legi canonicæ quam dictis sanctorum vel magistrorum inter se in multis descrepantibus, quia pape et non alii data est talium interpretatio dubiorum."* Hostiensis was reflecting the same sort of statements as those in the *Summa antiquitate et tempore: "in obscuris scripturis et maxime circa articulos fidei maioris auctoritatis esset interpretatio papæ quam Augustini"* (in obscure writings [or obscure Scriptures], and above all concerning articles of faith, the pope's interpretation is of greater authority than that of Augustine). Unsurprisingly, Dante's "insolent decretalist" quotes Hostiensis himself; for a discussion of the question of this "protervo decretalista," see Maccarrone, "Teologia e diritto canonico," pp. 24–31. See Brian Tierney's well-researched but surprisingly overapologetic argument in "'Sola scriptura' and the Canonists," pp. 346–364, esp. 357; rpt. as essay 9 in his collected essays, *Church Law and Constitutional Thought in the Middle Ages*. See also Francesco Torraca, "A proposito d'un luogo della Monarchia (III, iii, 9–10)," *Atti della R. Accademia di archeologia, lettere e belle arti di Napoli* n.s. 8 (1924): 149–163. Dante's inclusive view of the degrees of authoritative texts contrasts with the extremes of John Wycliffe (ca. 1330–1384), for whom the eternal "exemplar" of the Christian religion, Holy Scriptures, was the *sole* criterion of doctrine. See more recently Aldo Vallone, "A proposito di Monarchia III, iii, 10." *Dante Studies* 113 (1995): 167–173.

113. Maccarrone, "Teologia e diritto," p. 21, nn. 65–66.

114. Maccarrone, "Teologia e diritto," p. 24.

115. Obsessed with nepotism, that pope, buried headfirst like a treacherous assassin in the third *bolgia* of Hell's eighth circle, kicks his flaming feet as he impatiently awaits the arrival of Boniface VIII and Clement V who will squeeze him further down the depths of his "baptismal" hole in a grim, hellish satire of apostolic succession. The wayfarer hurls at him the taunting question: "Ah now tell me: how much treasure did Our Lord demand from Saint Peter, before he gave the keys into his keeping?" (*"Deh or mi dì: quanto tesoro volle / nostro Segnore in prima da san Pietro / ch'ei ponesse le chiavi in sua balìa?"*; *Inf.* 19:90–93).

116. E.g., The *Glossa ordinaria* to the Bible nowhere makes reference to the spiritual and temporal powers as an exegesis of the "two great lights"; consistently in all glosses, the moon is instead the Church, while the sun symbolizes Christ.

117. Vittorio Russo gives a useful synopsis of the "two great lights" problem in *Impero e stato di diritto: Studio su "Monarchia" ed "Epistole" politiche di Dante*, Memorie dell'Istituto Italiano per gli Studi Filosofici 18 (Naples: Bibliopolis, 1987), pp. 64–66.

118. This letter did not enter official decretals.

119. *"Sicut universititatis conditor Deus duo magna luminaria in firmamento coeli constituit, luminare majus, ut præesset diei, et luminare minus, ut nocti præesset; sic ad firmamentum universalis Ecclesiæ, quæ coeli nomine concupatur, duas magnas instituit dignitates: majorem, quæ quasi diebus animabus præesset et minorem, quæ quasi noctibus præesset corporibus: quæ sunt pontificalis auctoritas et regalis potestas"* (*Epist.* CCCCI [*PL* 214: 377]); see the translation in *Church and State through the Centuries*, ed. and trans. Sidney Z. Ehler and John B. Morrall (Westminster, Md.: Newman Press, 1954), p. 73; rpt. in Roland Bainton, *The Medieval Church* (Princeton, N.J.: Van Nostrand, 1962), pp. 137–138. Archbishop Baldwin of Canterbury, in his *Second Tractate*, had already applied the all-encompassing "firmament-sky" image to the Church, the sun to the spiritual authority, and the *"regnum"* (royal power) to the moon before 1188 (*PL* 204:416; see also the translation in Baldwin of Ford, *Spiritual Tractates*, trans. David N. Bell [Kalamazoo, Mich.: Cistercian Publications, 1986], 1:70). The humble Premonstratarian Adam of Dryburgh had used the same novel exegesis in his *Sermo* 30, again certainly before 1188, the year he entered the first English charterhouse (*PL* 198: 274–275). Adam died on March 20, 1212; on his life, see James Bulloch, *Adam of Dryburgh* (London: S.P.C.K., 1958). In these southern English examples coming in the wake of Thomas Becket's murder and dating a decade before Innocent III's use, the temporal power is thus relegated to the status of an inferior planet within the Church-firmament—which also holds as its own, of course, the brighter planet of the sun.

120. *"Solitæ Benignitatis," Decretales Gregorii* IX (Lib. 1, Tit. XXXIII, cap. 6, *CIC*, 2:196–198; here, col. 198); also in *PL* 216:1185. On arguments by "exemplum," or analogy, see Ralph M. McInerny's *The Logic of Analogy: An Interpretation of St. Thomas* (The Hague: Martinus Nijhoff, 1961), esp. pp. 144–152; and Giovanni Di Giannatale, "Alcune note a *Mon.* III, 4, 18, 20–21 e ad *Ep.* V, 30: Considerazioni sull'argomento della 'illuminatio' in Dante," *Ævum* 52,

no. 2 (1978): 317–321. Without knowing the simile's derivation, Othmar Hageneder affirmed: "The simile of the sun and the moon as the relationship between the *sacerdotium* and *regnum* was expounded for the first time and in the most detailed manner by Innocent III in his letter of October 1198 . . . to Acerbo Falseroni, Consul of Florence. . . ." ("Das Sonne-Mond-Gleichnis bei Innocenz III: Versuch einer teilweisen Neuinterpretation," *Mitteilengen des Instituts fur Österreichische Geschichtsforschung* [Vienna, Böhlaus] 65 [1957]: 340–368, here p. 340). Ernst H. Kantorowicz examined the Byzantine imagery in his "Dante's 'Two Suns'" (in *Semitic and Oriental Studies Presented to William Popper*, University of California Publications in Semitic Philology 11 [Berkeley/Los Angeles, 1951], pp. 217–231; rpt. *Selected Studies by Ernst H. Kantorowicz* [Locust Valley, N.Y.: J. J. Augustin, 1965], pp. 325–338); Kantorowicz simply assumed that the "dangerous image's" influence had somehow existed in the West sometime "ever since the age of Gregory VII [1073–1085]" (p. 327). Stewart Farnell assumes that the image was "old and well-established" but gives no background (*The Political Ideas of the "Divine Comedy": An Introduction* [Lanham/New York/London: University Press of America, 1985], p. 64). M. Maccarrone was simply wrong when he asserted that examples of the sun and moon as analogies respectively to the spiritual and temporal governances dated back to the fourth century ("Terzo libro," p. 33). John A. Scott believed he saw in Cardinal Umberto di Silva Candida's railing against the imperial use of a "sun" image ca. 1050 a first instance of the analogy (*Libri III adversus simoniacos* in *MGH, Libelli de Lite*, 1:225), but Umberto's protest in fact makes no use at all of the all-encompassing "firmament" imagery that Innocent III made famous (In "Una contraddizione scientifica nell'opera dantesca: I *due soli* del *Purgatorio XVI 107*," in *Dante e la scienza*, ed. Patrick Boyde and Vittorio Russo [Ravenna: Longo, 1995], pp. 149–155). As we note, the earliest theological exegeses of the Fathers of the Church on Gn 1:16 and the myriad other references to "*luna*" in the Bible, as well as the hundreds of references in the eight hundred years or so thereafter, consistently run counter to this later tendentious hierocratic interpretation of the Church as the sun. For the origin of the "two lights" topos, see Anthony K. Cassell, "'*Luna est Ecclesia*': Dante and the 'Two Great Lights,'" *Dante Studies* 119 (2001): 1–26.

121. *Contra falsos ecclesie professores*, ed. Tamburini, p. 51. Tolomeo da Lucca never mentions Gn 1:14 nor the high-papalist sun-moon cliché in the *De regimine*.

122. The dark of the moon and the eclipse of the sun continued to be warring metaphors in the controversy. According to Hostiensis, "*Luna accipit claritate a Sole, non Sol a luna, sic regalis potestas recipit auctoritatem a sacerdotali . . . sicut et Sol illuminat mundum per Luna quando per se non potest . . .*" (*Summa una* [Lyons, 1537; rpt. Darmstadt: Scientia Aalen, 1962], ff. 215ʳ–216ᵛ, here 215ᵛ, col. 2; *Summa aurea* [Venice, 1574; rpt. Turin: Bottega d'Erasmo, 1963], cols. 1385–87, here 1385). See Jean Rivière, *Le problème de l'Eglise*, pp. 56–57; and Tierney, "'Tria Quippe . . . ,'" pp. 48–59. Hostiensis uses the "two great lights analogy" to contradict Uguccione (whom he cites conventionally as "H"): he affirms that the use of the temporal sword must be received from the pope, even though the power over temporalities may come only from God.

123. Hostiensis, *Summa una*, 215$^v$, col. 2; *Summa aurea*, col. 1385. See the anonymous French monarchist's sarcastic comments in *Quæstio de potestate papæ (Rex Pacificus): An Enquiry into the Power of the Pope*, ed. and trans. Dyson, pp. 42, 92: "The attempt by Hostiensis [to prove that pontifical authority is greater in dignity than royal power] . . . is unnecessary, though elegant."

124. "*Imperator ab ecclesia Romana imperium tenet et potest dici officialis eius seu vicarius ab ecclesia Romana, in persona magnifici Caroli, qui a Græcis transtulit imperium in Germanos. Et Papa ipsum confirmat, et inungit, et coronat, vel reprobat, et deponit, ut patet* de ele. Venerabilem." Here Vernani is citing the *Venerabilem fratrem* verbatim (see *Decretales* 1:6:34, *CIC*, 2:80; *The Church and State*, ed. Ehler and Morrall, pp. 71–72; Tierney, *Crisis*, p. 133).

125. The anonymous author of the *Quæstio de potestate papæ (Rex Pacificus): An Enquiry into the Power of the Pope* notably uses the consecration to rebut the theory of the pope's authority over the emperor: "Some say that just as the Cardinal of Ostia consecrates the Pope and yet after the consecration has no spiritual jurisdiction over the pope, so the pope confirms and even crowns the emperor, yet does not have any temporal jurisdiction over him after the confirmation and coronation" (ed. and trans. Dyson, pp. 51, 100).

126. "How the Church Is Greater in Authority, as It Is Proved from Figural Statements in the Old Testament," *Contra falsos ecclesie professores*, ed. Tamburini, pp. 18–20. Remigio shows the analogy's tremendous power as he grants in a later passage that the sun and the moon image is a mere symbol, not a substantiation—and then immediately affirms again what he has just ceded: "It must be said generally that persuasive proof cannot be obtained from any figurative statement since symbolic theology is not accepted as logically proving the truth of something [*argumentativa*], as Dionysius says in his *Letter to Titus*. Nevertheless, it must be said that without doubt the moon receives light from the sun; and all the same, it principally presides over the night and thus it is said to signify fleshly things; this is not fitting for the sun. *Thus for us the figure is to the point*" (pp. 67–68). Though Remigio, having studied in Paris, was also a *magister* in sacred theology, and was, in his earlier years, more temperate than other hierocrats, he too completely ignores the traditional exegesis in the early Church Fathers that the moon in Gn figures the Church. Cf. also Davis's thumbnail evaluations of Remigio's theories in "An Early Florentine Political Theorist," p. 674, n. 90.

127. Dante had himself excogitated similar far-fetched mathematical analogies with the planets and the liberal arts in *Conv.* 2:13, probably in imitation of John of Salisbury's *Metalogicon*. See Chapter 2, n. 37, above.

128. Frederick II's text is found in J.-L.-A. Huillard-Bréholles, ed., *Historia Diplomatica Friderici Secundi* (Paris: Henri Plon, 1857), vol. 5, pt. 1, p. 348. On July 26, 1310, Clement V also employed the image in his letter *Divinæ Sapientiæ* to Henry VII of Luxembourg, approving Henry's election: "The unfathomable wisdom of the Most High, in so disposing earthly things after the model of heavenly things and in so causing the waters to flow from the mountain heights that, by the fruit of His works, the world here below might

prosperously be ordered, just as He appointed in the firmament of the heavens two chief lights to enlighten the world by turns, so on earth He made especial and supreme provision in the form of the priesthood and of the Empire, for the full direction and governance of things spiritual and mundane" (*MGH, Legum sectio IV, Constitutiones*, no. 298, vol. 4, pp. 261–263, here p. 261. On September 1, 1310, Clement issued a second letter, *Exultet in Gloria*, repeating the "two great lights" image, calling upon all Christians to receive and honor Henry. See Henry's missives, no. 391, ibid., p. 340, no. 393, pp. 343–346 and no. 454, pp. 395–398.

129. The Latin text of the *Allegacio* is given in Michele Maccarrone, "Il terzo libro della *Monarchia.*" *Studi Danteschi* 33 (1955): 5–142, here p. 34.

130. Maccarrone, "Il terzo libro," p. 33

131. Maccarrone, "Il terzo libro," pp. 34–35. Nardi, rather twisting the import of Maccarrone's arguments (which seeks to show the tradition of the "two great lights" image), does not view Dante's words (as Maccarrone does) as a *direct* refutation of Boniface's *Allegacio* (*Dal Convivio alla Commedia*, pp. 186–188). Dante, in all events, is directly refuting the papal analogy, whose wording was common and widespread.

132. St. Thomas Aquinas's critique of exegesis as the basis of doctrine had soured some thinkers toward this form of proof; see Ceslas Spicq, *Esquisse d'une histoire de l'exégèse latine au Moyen Âge* (Paris: J. Vrin, 1944), pp. 273–288; Beryl Smalley, *The Study of the Bible in the Middle Ages*, 2nd ed. (South Bend, Ind.: University of Notre Dame Press, 1964), pp. 300–301; Maccarrone, "Il terzo libro," p. 36. Cf. *Conv.* 2:1:2–3; and *Par.* 26:40–41, 29:41. See also Giacomo Poletto, *La Santa Scrittura nelle opere e nel pensiero di Dante Alighieri* (Siena: Tipografia Pontificio S. Bernardino, 1909), p. 276. In attacking the analogy of the two great lights, Dante faced a widely accepted circle of metaphors that involved also the symbolism of the sublunary *sæculum*, the world and all temporal objects, the immanent orb of flux and change bounded by the inmost celestial sphere (or heaven) of the moon in the Ptolemaic system. The innermost circumference of the circle of the moon was Aristotle's dividing point between earthly and celestial physics. The moon, which waxed and waned, although celestial, still symbolized temporal inconstancy, and its circuit enclosed the flux of immanent things. Cf. *Inf.* 2:77–78 "*ogne contento / di quel ciel c'ha minor li cerchi sui.*"

133. Dante, like Vernani, knew that St. Augustine and the Pseudo-Dionysius the Areopagite had established the principle of methodology in doctrine: that the mystical or allegorical interpretation of Scripture was insufficient to establish any proposition, for proof had to come from a nonmystical and nonallegorical source; see St. Augustine, *Letter to Vicentius, Epistola* 93:8 (*PL* 33:334); Vernani depends on Pseudo-Dionysius, *De mystica theologia* 1:1 (*PG* 3: 997–1000) and *Epistula* 9:1 (*PG* 3:1103). Remigio de' Girolami gives the same caution when adducing both authorities in *Contra falsos ecclesie professores* (ed. Tamburini, pp. 67–68).

134. Only in *Mon.* 3:4:14 does Dante briefly make such concession to Augustinian negativism concerning earthly governance, for it undermines the positive, Aristotelian

bent of his whole position concerning the emperor's rule leading to worldly happiness.

135. James of Viterbo, *De regimine christiano* 8:1, 9:1; *On Christian Government*, trans. Dyson, pp. 112–114, 128.

136. See Joyce, *Principles of Logic*, p. 260. It is unnecessary to repeat Dante's criticism of the hierocratic reasoning from the two luminaries: that it depends on recognizing the similitude of proportion of the effect of *light* between the planets and of the effect of *power* between the two authorities (exaggerated to "splendor, quality, size and power"), much as the term "fire" is predicated of God. The might of the simile of the "two great lights" lay also and especially in the fact that the sun was accepted as the analogical cause of all generable things; thus, the similitude affirmed the Church as cause in a more universal sense. In causality, the agent and its effect are in some way similar (the sun and the moon are both planets; their causal relation must equate with that of the empire and the papacy, which are both powers upon the earth). Dante cites from Aristotle *Nic. Ethics* 4:1, in another context, in *Mon.* 3:10:13: "It seems indeed that the action of agents subsists in the patient fit to receive it." There must be a similitude of cause to effect, agent and patient. The effect from the agent upon the patient receiving can, as Aristotle says in *Metaph.* 8, nn. 1444–6, be, first, either *totaliter univoco*, totally univocal (as fire generates fire, man generates man); second, *partim ex univoco*, as with the artisan who builds a house (the form in his mind is the same as the form he effects, although their forms of existence differ); or, third, *partim ex æquivoco*, as when a medecine produces heat for the health of a patient without heat's being present in the drug. The relationship of God to his creatures is entirely nonunivocal, or, rather, equivocal, for God is being in itself and creatures are beings by participation; God is thus said to be the *analogous* cause of creatures (see "The Analogical Cause," in McInerny's *The Logic of Analogy*, pp. 126–135). Thinking by analogical cause and logic by *exemplum* were identical. Ironically, when Dante asserts that the moon in some way already has light, he is thus actually working *within* this system to *preserve* the simile of lights and powers—even if the sun does not *cause* the moon, but merely *increases* the light of that planet, as he argues in *Mon.* 3:16:17.

137. See the text of *Epistola 5*, where the light of the empire glows brightly in the case of a *shortcoming* of the priestly power: "Clement, the present successor of Peter, illumines with the light of the Apostolic benediction . . . where the spiritual ray suffices not, there the splendor of the lesser luminary [splendor minoris luminaris] may lend its light" (*Letters of Dante*, ed. Toynbee, 2nd ed. by C. Hardie, pp, 58 and 62). In *Epistola 8*, Rome is left bereft and widowed of both lights, *"Nunc utroque lumine destitutam,"* pp. 137 and 146. But see Took, *Dante: Lyric Poet and Philosopher*, p. 148.

138. Dante had praised justice in the empire in *Mon.* 1:11:5: " 'Neither Hesperus nor Lucifer is so admirable.' She is, indeed, like Phoebe, in the blush serenity of dawn, contemplating her brother across the diameter of the sky." Hesperus and Lucifer both signify the planet Venus. The quotation is from Aristotle's *Nic. Ethics* 5:1 [:1129b:28–29]. But Dante goes on to substitute Phoebe, the moon, for the evening and morning star, Venus—ironi-

cally, there too accepting the moon's decretalist identification with the empire. Cf. "the children of Latona" image, the sun and moon, in *Par.* 29:1–9.

139. Even Boniface VIII in the *Allegacio* had been "disposed to welcome the emperor [Albert] like the sun, since this king of the Romans [was] about to be promoted to emperor who is the sun insofar as the monarch of all must illumine all with his light and defend the spiritual power in as much as he ha[d] been given and 'sent by him for the punishment of evildoers, and for the praise of the good' [1:2:14]." But in the context, Albert shines in Boniface's eyes only as the temporal vassal-defender of the Church, and not as an independent authority. See Nardi, *Dal Convivio alla Commedia*, p. 187. Dante surely based his image of the two suns on Is 30:26, "And the light of the moon shall be as the light of the sun." And perhaps on the conventions of Byzantine imagery such as E. H. Kantorowicz examined in "Dante's Two Suns," pp. 217–231; see above, n. 9.

140. St. Ambrose, *Hexæmeron* 4:8:32[:78] (*PL* 14:203–206); *Hexameron, Paradise, Cain and Abel*, trans. John J. Savage (New York: Fathers of the Church, 1961), p. 156.

141. St. Augustine, *Enarratio in Psalmum* 8:9 (*PL* 36:112); *Expositions on the Book of Psalms*, in *The Nicene and Post-Nicene Fathers*, 8:30.

142. St. Augustine, *Epistola* 55:6 (*PL* 33:209); *Letters*, Vol. 1: *Letters 1–82*, trans. Sister Wilfred Parsons, The Fathers of the Church 12 (New York: Fathers of the Church, 1951), p. 268.

143. All the Bible exegetes hark back to the early Fathers' identification of the moon as the Church: *"luna est ecclesia."* See Isidore of Seville, *In Genesim 2*, in *Quæstiones in veteres testamentum* (*PL* 83: 213). Peter Lombard (ca. 1100–1160), in his *Commentaria in Psalmos*, cites St. Augustine's explanation of "the sun shall not smite thee by day" of Ps 121: *"Vers. 6.: 'Per diem sol non uret te, neque luna per noctem.'* [Aug.] *Deus est sol; dies, sapientia Dei, luna, Ecclesia"* (*PL* 191:1140). Honorius Augustodunensis, in *Expositio in Cantica canticorum* repeats: *"Samson quod dicitur 'sol,' est Christus sol justitiæ, qui pro sponsa Ecclesia...."* (Samson who is called "sun," is Christ the Sun of Justice; for the bride, the Church) (*PL* 172: 355). The moon shines because she is the Blessed Virgin, or the Church, who is clothed by the Sun, who is Christ (Rv 12:1), as Hildegard of Bingen (1098–1179) reiterates in her *Liber divinorum operum simplicis hominis* (*PL* 197:1012). In her *Explanatio symboli S. Athanasii*, she declares: *"Ecclesia ordinata est, ut luna cum stellis in firmamento constituta est"* (The Church is instituted as the moon is constituted with the stars in the firmament) (*PL* 197:1068–1069). Alain de Lille (Alanus de Insulis, d. 1203), in the *Distinctiones dictionum theologicalium*, writes: *"Ecclesia, quæ superni luminis splendore protegitur, quasi sole vestitur"* ("The Church, which is protected by the light of the supernal light, is, as it were, clothed by the sun) (*PL* 210:842). Petrus Damianus, in *Collectanea in Vetus Testamentum*, writes: *"'Sol justitiæ Christus.' Luna autem primo sancta universalis Ecclesia"* ("The Sun of Justice, Christ." First the moon is the Holy Universal Church) (*PL* 145:1048). Rupert of Deutz, in *De Trinitate et operibus ejus*, asks: *"Et quæ luna, nisi præsens Ecclesia, quæ ... minus lucet quandiu peregrinatur in ista vita?"* (And what is the moon but the present Church which ... glows less as long as it is a pilgrim in this life?) (*PL* 167:508). Also see Rupert's *De Divinis Officiis* 10 (*PL* 170:273).

144. Prosper of Aquitaine, *Psalmorum expositio: Psal. CXX, esp. V. 6* (*PL* 51:365); Prosper's gloss on Ps120:6 cites St. Augustine, as does the *Glossa ordinaria*, "Aug. Luna ecclesia," at this point (*Biblia Latina cum Glossa Ordinaria (Biblia cum Glossa)* Facsimile Reprint of the *Editio Princeps* Adolph Rusch of Strassburg 1480/81, in 4 vols; here vol. 2, p. 623, col. 2).

145. See St. Gaudentius, *Sermo III De Exodi Lectione terti* (*PL* 20:861); St. Eucherius, *Liber formularum spiritalis intelligentiæ*, Cap. II, *De supernis creaturis* (*PL* 50:739), on Ps 103:19; the *Glossa ordinaria*, on Ps 103:19, gives the interlinear gloss *"ecclesiam"* for *"lunam"* (*Biblia cum Glossa*, vol. 2, p. 587, cols 1 and 2); St. Maximus of Turin, *Homily 101, De eodem argumento II* [*scil. De defectione lunæ*] (*PL* 57:488); and St. Bruno the Carthusian, *Expositio in Psalmun XI* (*PL* 152:665), and *Expositio in Psalmun LXXI* (*PL* 152:992).

146. Garnier de Rochefort, *Allegoriæ in Universam Sacram Scripturam* (*PL* 112:991).

147. Isidore of Seville, *In Genesim 2* (*PL* 88:813). John of Paris goes on, as does Dante, wearily to concede the "great lights" simile, but John instead, mindful of analogical causality, and the moon's (that is the *regnum*'s) independence, asserts not that the moon has light of its own, but that the moon is *not similar* to the sun (thus, we quietly understand that there can be no cause or causation, since there is nothing to transmit!), but has "a virtue proper to itself, *given to it by God, which it does not receive from the sun*, by which it can cause cold and wet, *the very opposite* of what the sun causes" (*De potestate regia et papale* 14:4; *On Royal and Papal Power*, trans. Watt, pp. 165–166; my emphasis).

148. John of Paris, *De potestate regia et papali* 14:4; translation adapted from *On Royal and Papal Power*, trans. J. A. Watt, pp.165–66, and trans. A. P. Monahan, pp. 72–73.

149. "Your Gregory lies among the cobwebs; Ambrose lies forgotten in the cupboards of the clergy, and Augustine along with him; and Dionysius, Damascenus, and Bede; and they cry up instead I know not what *Speculum*, and Innocent, and him of Ostia. And why not? The former sought after God as their end and highest good; the latter get for themselves riches and benefices" (*Epistola* 8, ed. Toynbee, pp. 134–135, 145).

150. Dante followed more than common sense: St. Benedict had set down in his *Rule* (ch. 63), e.g., that "absolutely nowhere shall age automatically determine rank." On "the fallacy of four terms" (*quaternio terminorum*), censured also in *Mon.* 3:5:3 and 3:7:3, see above, pp. 32–33.

151. See also *Mon.* 3:7:3.

152. See "De fallacia secundum non causam ut causam," in Peter of Spain, *Summulæ logicales*, Tractatus VII, 164–1870 (ed. de Rijk, pp.173–176); however, Dante appeals more to rhetoric than to formal logic here.

153. For the phrase in *Per venerabilem*, see *CIC*, 2:716; partial trans. in Tierney, *Crisis*, here, p. 137. Dante is being fittingly circumspect toward the institution of the Church; his arguments here still show a respectful reticence. We can compare his originality to the argument he had read in John of Paris, who had used a different tack in dealing with historical precedence. John denied that the Old-Testament "tribe of Levi" were true priests, and argued that they were merely prefigurations; even Melchisedech was only figuratively priest

and king; there was no priesthood before Christ, who made *all* the faithful priests (*On Royal and Papal Power* 4, trans. Watt, pp. 89–90). See also Watt's "Hostiensis on *Per Venerabilem*," pp. 99–113. Vinay believed that Vernani was scorning Dante for the poet's lack of knowledge of the publicists; Vinay himself, oddly, takes Vernani's side and impatiently dismisses Dante's whole chapter as reducible "to an idle repetition, which, indeed, could not interest anyone" (*Mon.*, ed. Vinay, pp. 221–222, n. 2).

154. Giles of Rome, *De ecclesiastica potestate* 1:5:5–6, 2:5:3–4; *On Ecclesiastical Power*, trans. Dyson, pp. 10–11. 50. Henry of Cremona gives a plethora of antagonistic biblical quotations in his *De potestate papæ* (in *Publizistik*, ed. Scholz, p. 464). See Tolomeo of Lucca's ch. 4, *"Probatur hoc idem ex regibus antiquis, quod sola electio non sufficiat ad administrationem imperii"* (In which it is proven by the kings of old that mere election does not suffice for the administration of the empire). See also *Determinatio compendiosa*, ed. M. Krammer, pp. 9–11. See also *Mon.*, ed. Vinay, p. 226, n. 2; and Maccarrone, *Vicarius Christi*, pp. 168–169.

155. See Maccarrone, *Vicarius Christi*, pp. 169–173.

156. Vernani, *De potestate summi pontificis* (*On the Power of the Supreme Pontiff*), ch. 10, pp. 74–75.

157. Dante carefully chooses the word *"nuntius,"* for he knew that the term had been used in the Vulgate for the prophet Ahias in 3 Kgs [1 Sm] 14:6, and that it had precise legal precedents. See Maccarrone, *Vicarius Christi*, p. 170.

158. The anonymous defender of the autonomy of the French throne, the author of *Quæstio de potestate papæ (Rex pacificus)* (*An Enquiry into the Power of the Pope*) argues, contrary to the decretalists, that the pope is *not* the ordinary judge of the whole Church in temporal matters, any more than any bishop would be in his diocese (ed. and trans. Dyson, pp. 16, 70). Both Matteini (ed. *Rep.*, p. 112) and Kay (ed. *Mon.*, p. 238), have noted Vernani's absurdity; however, Vernani is basically following high-papalist claims; see the many examples of the hierocratic commonplace of the pope as *iudex ordinarius*, below, n. 175. In 1316, Pope John XXII had asserted the immemorial antiquity of Church assumptions in his bull *Si fratrum;* see translated text at the end of this volume.

159. *De regimine principum* 3:10:10; *On the Government of Rulers*, ed. and trans. Blythe, pp. 177; *Quæstio de potestate papæ (Rex pacificus): An Enquiry into the Power of the Pope*, ed. and trans. Dyson, pp. 18–19, 72–73.

160. Concerning the lesser powers of the pope as Vicar of Christ, see Tolomeo da Lucca, *De regimine principum* 3:10; *On the Government of Rulers*, ed. and trans. Blythe, pp. 177.

161. "Thou art Peter. . . . And I will give you the keys of the kingdom of heaven. And whatsoever thou shalt bind upon earth, it shall be bound also in heaven; and whatsoever thou shalt loose on earth, it shall be loosed also in heaven" (Mt 16:19).

162. W. Ullmann believed that Henry IV was the first to use the "two swords" doctrine and the first to use the term *"dualitas,"* denying the title and mediatory role of the pope as "Vicar of Christ," and accusing him of usurping both kingship and priesthood (*Growth of Papal Government*, pp. 345–346). Whatever its origin, St. Bernard of Clairvaux's use of it in

his *On Consideration* played, perhaps, the greatest part in its divulgation on both sides of the issue. See Joseph Lecler, "L'argument des deux glaives (Luc XXII, 38) dans les contro-verses politiques du Moyen Age: Ses origines et son développement," *Recherches de Science Re-ligieuse* 21 (1931): 299–339, and "L'argument des deux glaives (Luc XXII, 38): Critique et dé-clin (XIVᵉ–XVIᵉ siècle)," *Recherches de Science Religieuse* 22 (1932): 151–177. Also see Alfons M. Stickler, "De potestate gladii materialis ecclesiæ secundum 'Quæstiones Bambergenses' ineditas," *Salesianum* 6 (1944): 113–140; "Der Schwerterbegriff bei Huguccio," *Ephemerides Iuris Canonici* III (1947): 1–44; "Il 'gladius' nel registro di Gregorio VII," *Studi Gregoriani* 3 (1948): 88–103; and "Il 'gladius' negli atti dei concilii e dei RR. Pontefici sino a Graziano e Bernardo di Clairvaux," *Salesianum* 13 (1951): 414–445. Other useful studies include B. Jacqueline, "Le pouvoir pontificale selon saint Bernard: L'argument des deux glaives," *L'année canonique* 2 (1953): 197–201; H. Hoffmann, "Die beiden Schwerter im hohen Mitte-lalter," *Deutsches Archiv* 20 (1964): 78–114; and B. Tierney, "The Continuity of Papal Politi-cal Theory," pp. 227–228, esp. n. 1.

163. *De consideratione* (*PL* 182: 776); *On Consideration*, trans. Anderson and Kennan, p. 118.

164. Stickler, "Il 'gladius' negli atti dei concilii," p. 443; Maccarrone, *"Potestas directa,"* pp. 31–32.

165. Innocent III, *Solitæ benignitatis*, no. 74 (*PL* 216, col. 1185); *Decretales Gregorii IX*, Lib. I, 33, 6, *Solitæ benignitatis; CIC*, 2:196–198; partial trans. in Tierney, *Crisis*, p. 133. See also *On Kingship*, trans. Gerald B. Phelan, "Introduction," p. xix; and Maccarrone, *"Potestas directa,"* pp. 31–32.

166. The commission of the keys, from Mt 16:19, was the chief basis for the pope's ju-risdiction. *Unam sanctam* reads: "This authority [*scil.* of the spiritual power to judge the temporal power] although granted to man and exercised by man, is not human but divine, being given to Peter by the voice of God and confirmed to him and to his successors in him, the rock whom the Lord acknowledged when he said to Peter, 'Whatsoever thou shalt bind etc.' Whoever, therefore resists this power ordained of God resists the ordi-nance of God" (trans. Tierney, *Crisis*, p. 189). See Watt's "Introduction" to John of Paris' *Royal and Papal Power*, p. 29. The anonymous defender of Philip the Fair's autonomy, the writer of the *Quæstio de potestate papæ (Rex pacificus) (Enquiry into the Power of the Pope)*, roundly rebuts Hostiensis's commentary on *Per venerabilem*, together with both Alanus Anglicus and Tancred, whom Hostiensis cites as holding that the emperor receives the temporal sword from the Church; see ed. and trans. Dyson, pp. 21–23. After St. Bernard's *De consideratione* 3:1 (*PL* 182:758), as we would expect, the repetitions of the hierocratic exegesis of Jn 21:15–17 and Mt 16:18–19 as Peter's commissioning are legion; see, e.g., Augustinus Triumphus, *Summa*, q. 20:4, 5 (cf. Wilks, *The Problem of Sovereignty*, pp. 322, 419, 498, 535); James of Viter-bo, *De regimine christiano* 2:5; *On Christian Government*, trans. Dyson, pp.82–96; and Tolomeo da Lucca, *On the Government of Rulers: De regimine principum* 3:10, trans. Blythe, pp. 173–177. Remigio de' Girolami gives a hierocratic version in *Contra falsos professores ecclesie*, ed. Tam-burini, p. 70. For the views of Remigio di Girolami's successor as teacher of theology and

personal tutor to Clement V at the papal court after 1306, those of the extremist Guillaume de Pierre in his treatise on Church power, see *The Theory of Papal Monarchy in the Fourteenth Century: Guillaume de Pierre Godin, Tractatus de causa immediata ecclesiastice potestatis*, ed. W. D. McCready, Studies and Texts 56 (Toronto: Pontifical Institute of Mediaeval Studies, 1982), Prolegomena, pp. 22–23, and *Tractatus* 2, pp. 991–1006, 1064–1079, 1098–118, 6:212–218; A: 170–173, 639–671. These texts are central for understanding Vernani's discussion of St. Peter in the *Ref.*, book 3.

167. Emphatic is the wording of Innocent's *Solitæ benignitatis:* "We need hardly mention, since they are so well known, the words that Christ spoke to Peter and through Peter to his successors, 'Whatsover you bind upon earth, etc.' [Mt 16:19], excepting nothing when he said, 'Whatsoever'" (trans. Tierney, *Crisis*, p. 133). Cf. the text of Innocent IV's famous encyclical letter from the first council of Lyons, written to defend the deposition of Frederick II (Tierney, *Crisis*, p. 147). See Ullmann, *Medieval Papalism*, pp. 178, 186–188.

168. *Catena aurea* 16:19 [St. Matthew, vol. 2] (Oxford/London: Parker, 1874), vol. 2, pt. 2, pp. 586–587. James of Viterbo cites it in his *On Christian Government* 2:5: "He is not giving them only to Peter . . . but . . . to his successors . . . : it is added in the Gloss, 'See how great a power has the Rock upon whom the Church is built, that his judgments may indeed stand as firmly as though God were judging through him'" (trans. Dyson, pp. 91–92).

169. Kantorowicz, *The King's Two Bodies*, p. 456.

170. William of Ockham, who later labels Innocent III's interpretation that Christ had excepted nothing from the power of Peter as "false, and dangerous" (*Short Discourse* 2:2, ed. McGrade, pp. 20–21), will parallel Dante's reasoning here.

171. See "De distributionibus," in Peter of Spain, *Summulæ logicales*, Tractatus XII, ed. de Rijk, pp. 209–232, esp. pp. 209–212.

172. Cf. Boniface's "forgiving" of Guido da Montefeltro in *Inf.* 27.

173. Tolomeo da Lucca had written "*The power of Peter and his successors is not equal to that of Christ*, on the contrary, Christ's power totally transcends Peter's. For example, Christ could save someone without baptism. . . . Christ could change the form and matter of sacraments, [all of which] neither Peter nor his successors could do" (*De regimine principum* 3:10; *On the Government of Rulers*, ed. and trans. Blythe, pp. 177, my emphases). Although he appears to have been ignorant of Tolomeo's contributions, it is, of course, possible that Vernani may even have taken the whole of *De regimine* as being the work of St. Thomas and had chosen to ignore it.

174. See the useful remarks, particularly regarding depositions of rulers, by Watt in his "Introduction" to John of Paris, *On Royal and Papal Power*, pp. 47–53.

175. Every crime is sin; every matter is subject to papal jurisdiction: the pope is *iudex ordinarius*. Hierocrats glowingly reflect on the pope's ability to act in any matter whatsoever "*ratione peccati*" or "*ratione delicti*," although in their legions of references to this power they usually mention, in passing, that its use was merely occasional. See Innocent III's bull *Novit*

*ille* (Tierney, *Crisis,* pp. 134–135). Giles of Rome, in *De ecclesiastica potestate (On Ecclesiastical Power)* 3:6 insists: "Why, although the Church may rebuke every Christian for every criminal sin, and so may exercise a temporal jurisdiction" (trans. Dyson, p. 172). James of Viterbo, in *De regimine christiano (On Christian Government)* 2:4 notes: "The prelates of the Church ... are indeed also kings, because they are spiritual judges in matters of sin and in spiritual cases" (trans. Dyson, p. 75). Concerning the pope, Tolomeo da Lucca states in *De regimine principum* 9, "*ipse est iudex omnium,*" and even maintains the pope's right, as judge of all and monarch, to tax all of Christendom and have any town or city destroyed for the conservation of his realm (3:19:2); see Blythe's useful editorial comments on Tolomeo's concepts of government and sin, in *On the Government of Rulers,* p. 42. Cf. also, in Remigio's *Contra falsos ecclesie professores,* the citations on *ratione delicti (ratione peccati)* (ed. Tamburini, pp. 47, 71), with those affirming Innocent III's supreme power over the whole globe entire ("*per totum orbem aliqualiter*"), over all and everything altogether ("*super omnes et omnia aliqualiter*") (ed. Tamburini, pp. 67, 68); and see C. T. Davis, "An Early Political Theorist," p. 673. Cf. the citations and comments on the concept in Wilks, *The Problem of Sovereignty,* pp. 264, 315–316, including Durandus de Porciano, the anonymous *Somnium viridari,* Ugolinus de Celle, and Hervæus Natalis; the latter insists, "The Pope is the immediate judge of final appeal in anything concerning the Church, in whatsoever matter, the ordinary judge in whatsoever case ... the Pope is the immediate judge of final appeal of everything concerning the Church, and in every case." See the Latin text in Wilks, p. 264. William of Ockham (cf. Wilks, p. 316) describes the limitless power of the pontiff in *De imperatorum et pontificum potestate* of 1347, but he also censures the usurpation of the papacy in a manner that Dante would not dare (see *On the Power of Emperors and Popes,* trans. Brett, esp. pp. 137–172). In his commentary on *Unam sanctam,* Guido Vernani affirms unequivocally that "every king and every man who can sin is subject to the pope" (Grabmann, "Kommentar des Guido Vernani von Rimini," p. 154). The occasion of Can Grande's alleged sin of disobedience and contumacy sits at the heart of Dante's defense in the *Mon.*

176. *De consideratione* 4:6–7 (*PL* 182:776); *On Consideration,* trans. Anderson and Kennan, pp. 117–118.

177. *Comment. In Sententiis (Commentary on the Sentences)* 4:D:37. See Watt, *The Theory of Papal Power,* p. 91; and John of Paris, *On Royal and Papal Poer,* trans. Watt, p. 30.

178. Dante corrects hierocratic practice by listing all the weaknesses and foibles of the Apostle: James of Viterbo, e.g., totally ignores Peter's many errors, his truancy, and his denial of Christ in his long exegesis on St. Peter as "head and prince of the Apostles," and his primacy over all earthly princes in ch. 5 of the *De regimine christiano (On Christian Government),* ed. and trans. Dyson, pp. 91–95.

179. Dante's view here is parallel to that of John of Paris, his earlier contemporary in the attack on papal temporal power, who in *On Royal and Papal Power* 12 wrote: "Six powers were granted to the Apostles and disciples of the Lord and so therefore to their successors. ... [the second is] the power of administering the sacraments and especially the

sacrament of penance, which is the power of the keys or of spiritual jurisdiction in the sphere of conscience. . . . *This power in the spiritual forum was promised to Peter, as Matthew says, 'I will give you the keys' etc'"* (my emphasis). Unlike Marsiglio of Padua, Dante never denies that Christ had commanded Peter to be superior to the other Apostles, and often affirms Petrine succession, but, like John of Paris and Marsiglio of Padua, Dante denies that the pope enjoys a worldly plenitude of power.

180. The poet knew that even St. Bernard of Clairvaux, although a supporter of the pope's *plenitudo potestatis*, had maintained in his advice to Pope Eugenius that temporal affairs were beneath a pope's consideration: "Clearly your power is over sin and not property, since it is because of sin that you have received the keys of the heavenly kingdom. . . . Why do you invade someone else's territory? Why do you put your sickle to someone else's harvest? Not because you are unworthy, but because it is unworthy for you. . . ." Bernard had gone on to assert simply, "Dominion is forbidden for Apostles," and, citing Jesus's saying to Peter in Jn 18:11, had warned Eugenius, his former ward: "Why should you try to usurp the sword anew which you were once commanded to sheathe?" (*De consideratione* 2:10, 4:7 (*PL* 182: 750, 776; *On Consideration*, trans. Anderson and Kennan, pp. 59, 117–118). Also see John of Paris, *On Royal and Papal Power* 18 (trans. Watt, pp. 26, 30, 196–197). As we note, St. Bernard was cited by writers on both sides; cf. Marsiglio of Padua, *Defensor pacis* 2: 24:8, et passim (trans. Gewirth, here, p. 324). A check of St. Thomas Aquinas's *Legenda aurea*, ad loc., and of some of the earlier major medieval spiritual dictionaries renders no such interpretation of the sword: cf. *"gladius"* in the pseudo-Rabanus Maurus's *Allegoriæ in Universam Sacram Scripturam* (*PL* 112:940–942).

181. "No one doubts that the spiritual sword is in the power of the Church." The text of Vernani's commentary and his arguments on the two swords is found in Grabmann, "Kommentar des Guido Vernani," pp. 151–153, esp. 152.

182. *Inf.* 19:115–7; *Purg.* 32:124–129; *Par.* 20:55–60.33.

183. See Christopher B. Coleman, ed. and trans., *The Treatise of Lorenzo Valla on the Donation of Constantine* (New Haven, Conn.: Yale University Press, 1922); Bruno Nardi, "La 'donatio Constantini' e Dante," in *Nel mondo di Dante*, pp. 109–59; Domenico Maffei, *La donazione di Costantino nei giuristi medievali* (Milan: A. Giuffrè, 1964); Antonio Pagliaro, "Ahi Costantin . . . ," in *Ulisse: Ricerche semantiche sulla Divina Commedia* (Messina/Florence: D'Anna, 1966), 1:253–291; Horst Fuhrmann, "Konstantinische Schenkung," *Lexikon des Mittelalters*, vol. 5, cols. 1386–1387; and G. Gonnet, "La donazione di Costantino in Dante e presso gli eretici medievali," in *Dante nel pensiero e nella esegesi dei secoli XIV e XV, Atti del III Congrsso Nazionale di Studi Danteschi* (Convegno di Studi realizzato dal Comune di Melfi in collaborazione con la Biblioteca Provinciale di Potenza e il Seminario di Studi Danteschi di Terra di Lavoro), Melfi, 27 settembre–2 ottobre 1970, ed. A. and P. Borraro (Florence: Olschki, 1975), pp. 325–337. On ecclesiastical poverty, see Felice Tocco, *La questione della povertà nel secolo XIV* (Naples: Francesco Perella, 1910); Ernst Benz, *Ecclesia spiritualis. Kirchenidee und Geschichtstheologie der franziskanischen Reformation* (Stuttgart: W. Kohlhammer, 1934); Raoul Manselli, "Dante

e l'*ecclesia spiritualis*," in *Dante e Roma: Atti del Convegno di Studi* a cura della "Casa di Dante" (Florence: Felice Le Monnier, 1965) pp. 115–135; and Vallone, "Dante, A. Trionfi, G. Vernani," p. 193.

184. See the translation in *Church and State through the Centuries*, ed. Ehler and Morrall, pp. 16–22.

185. "Nor is there anything to oppose the Church's holding possessions and territories or other areas that had been occupied by violence, and thus unlawfully by the Roman emperors, for we must therefore presume if there is any doubt, that they acquired them justly [*ideo præsumere debemus in dubio, quod juste quæsiverunt*]" (Antonius de Butrio, *Commentaria*, in V *Libros Decretalium* [Venice, 1578], III, xxxiv, 8, fol. 151, no. 8; text printed in Ullmann, *Medieval Papalism*, p. 133, n. 1). Other later papalists claimed, more prudently, that Constantine had done nothing but return possessions that the papacy had already held by right from God. See next note.

186. I.e., Constantine's gift was only an act of submission, reverence, and veneration toward the origin of his imperial power, a recognition of the center of divine and human law; cf. James of Viterbo, *De regimine christiano (On Christian Government)*, trans. Dyson, pp. xxv, 119, 153.

187. "*Augustus quia auget.*" Cf. John of Paris: "The emperor is called 'aug-ustus' because it is his continual task to 'aug-ment' the Empire, not to diminish it" (*On Royal and Papal Power*, trans. Watt, ch. 21, p. 222). Tolomeo of Lucca (with whom Dante agrees so often, even though Tolomeo was a Guelph) writes: "Octavian was called '*Augustus*,' as Isidore also wrote, because he *augmented* the republic" (*De regimine principum* 3:12:3; *On the Government of Rulers*, ed. and trans. Blythe, pp. 183). See also Fulvio Crosara, "Dante e Bartolo da Sassoferrato," pp. 130–131, 146.

188. Hostiensis, *Summa una*, ff. 215ᵛ–216ᵛ; as *Summa aurea*, cols. 1385–1392; the text is reprinted in Carlyle and Carlyle, pp. 326–328.

189. Giles of Rome writes: "That unbelievers are all unworthy of any possession, lordship or power" (*De ecclesiastica potestate* 2:11:1; *On Ecclesiastical Power*, trans, Dyson, p. 91). Giles feigns to cite "wicked men do not even possess themselves," alleging bk. 6 of the *Confessions*, where no such statement occurs; indeed, there is nothing in the *Confessions* to this effect (*De ecclesiastica potestate* 2:11:7; *On Ecclesiastical Power*, trans. Dyson, pp. 93 and 237). Giles may be distorting ideas on man's general curiosity and vanity, and the pride of philosophers such as St. Augustine expresses, for example, in the passage of the *Confessions* 10:8 that Petrarch was to find so riveting: "*Men* go abroad to admire high mountains . . . and *forsake themselves* [*se relinquunt*]." The constant inaccuracies that mar Vernani's work are to be expected in a fourteenth-century scholar, but as a notary and lector, his hasty carelessness still contrasts unfavorably with the accuracy of his fellow Dominicans, especially with Tolomeo da Lucca and Remigio de' Girolami (see Davis' comments on Remigio's care, in "An Early Florentine Political Theorist," p. 665). Dante, of course, in all his works habitually cites sources secondhand, as we have seen, often getting them spectacularly wrong.

190. Innocent III's decretal *Venerabilem fratrem* (On elections) *Decretales* 1:6:34, *CIC*, 2:79–82, here, col. 80. See Tierney, "Tria quippe Distinguit Iudicia . . . ," pp. 48–59. See also Vernani's *De potestate summi pontificis* 10, pp. 76–77, "de election" (C. *Venerabilem*, Lib. 1, *Decr. Tit.* 6. 34), where the friar adduces that decretal for the pope's power of instituting and transferring the empire.

191. By 1300 the hierocrats had succeeded in reinterpreting the concept of the emperor's coercive military power from that of arms-*for*-the-Church at the pontiff's request for discipline and defense (the real sense of the *gladius*) into an arm-*of*-the-Church. John XXII in *Si fratrum* assumed that, since he was true emperor, the military imperial vicars of north-central Italy were doubly his to appoint and claim. Alfons Stickler in "Imperator vicarius Papæ," *Mitteilungen des österreichischen Institut für Geschichtsforschungen* 62 (1954): 165–212, deals with the emperor's power in protecting the Church from heretical and infidel attack; see also Kantorowicz, *The King's Two Bodies*, p. 456. See next note.

192. The *Per venerabilem (Liber extra: Qui filii sunt legitimi: "Per venerabilem")*, and not the *Venerabilem fratrem*, was the document appealed to for the pope's occasional temporal jurisdiction via the civil arm. Alvarus Pelagius, for instance, would be adamant on the manner in which the papacy wielded its "sword": "The Church can demand from the secular power and its subjects any help, be it by arms or otherwise, for the furtherance of the ecclesiastical common weal" (cited in Ullmann, *Medieval Papalism*, pp. 93–94). In his *Summa*, Stephen de Tournay asserted that secular rulers had only been established to suppress schismatics and heretics. Cf. Giles of Rome, *De ecclesiastica potestate* 3:4:2–17; 3:7:6; *On Ecclesiastical Power*, trans. Dyson, pp. 157–171, 177, et passim; and Ullmann, *Medieval Papalism*, p. 151, and *Growth of Papal Government*, pp. 404–405. Henry of Susa, Hostiensis, in his commentary on the bull *Per venerabilem* (*Decretales* 4:17:13), cites Uguccione but ultimately refutes him; see *Summa una*, ff. 215$^r$–216$^v$, and *Summa aurea*, cols. 1385–87. Tierney gives a partial translation of *Per venerabilem* in *Crisis*, pp. 136–138. In 1347 William of Ockham would insist on the limits of papal power despite the *Per venerabilem*; he charged that "[t]he Avignonese Church [*ecclesia avinionica*] injures the Roman Empire in claiming that it derives from the pope" (*On the Power of Emperors and Popes* 19, trans. Brett, pp. 117–118).

193. Hervæus Natalis, *The Poverty of Christ*, trans. Jones pp. 1–8. Hervæus died in 1323. With his condemnatory bull *Quia nonnumquam* of March 26, 1322, John XXII, not bound by the precedent of his predecessors, abrogated Nicholas III's *Exiit qui seminat*, which had legitimated Franciscan poverty. On the question, see William of Ockham's responses in his *The Work of Ninety Days*, *Dialogues*, and the *Eight Questions on the Power of the Pope*, conveniently translated in *William of Ockham: A Letter to the Friars Minor and Other Writings*, ed. McGrade and Kilcullen; see especially the editors' useful "Introduction."

194. William of Ockham also chose not to refute the *translatio imperii* doctrine in his works and preferred, like Dante, to consider the different origins of temporal and spiritual power; in this both authors positions contrast sharply with Marsiglio of Padua's virulent attacks.

195. *On the Government of Rulers*, trans. Blythe, p. 175.

196. Maccarrone, "Il terzo libro," p. 92.

197. *"Ubi est reductio ad summum in genere hominum. Eiusmodi est Christus vicarius, pontifex summus"*; St. Bonaventure, *Commentaria in decretales* (Venezia, 1581), III, f. 193 AB; cited by Maccarrone, *"Potestas directa,"* pp. 41–42.

198. Maccarrone and Nardi note other texts that correspond to the argument that Dante is opposing: that all human beings are reducible to the pope. See Maccarrone, *Vicarius Christi*, pp. 135–136, and "Il terzo libro," pp. 93–94; and Nardi, *Dal Convivio alla Commedia*, p. 263. See also Kay, *Mon.* ed, ad loc.

199. See "De accidente," in Peter of Spain, *Summulæ logicales*, Tractatus VII, 102–105, ed. de Rijk, pp. 146–148. We must note that, further, the fallacy of absolute or qualified statement *(fallacia a dicto simpliciter ad dictum secundum quid)* is committed here: in the decretalist reduction, the predicate of best-as-pope is falsely affirmed *secundum quid:* i.e., by merely *being pope*, a man is the best man. See "De fallacia secundum quid et simpliciter," in Peter of Spain, *Summulæ logicales*, Tractatus VII, 120–130, ed. de Rijk, pp. 157–161; and Joyce, *Principles of Logic*, pp. 275–276.

200. A clear explanation of this principle is given by Gilson, in *Dante and Philosophy*, pp. 188–191.

201. *De consideratione* 2:17–18 *(PL* 182:752*)*; *On Consideration*, trans. Anderson and Kennan, pp. 69–70.

202. Pelagius Alvarus uses the same ploy in his *Collirium* against a list of heresies that he confutes: "Another heresy which holds that there were emperors and kings, especially ancient ones, before the Church; this is false and erroneous. For the Church existed before kingdoms and empires as is proved as follows: the Church is understood as the body of the faithful. Which is called the mystic body of Christ . . . this is the Holy Mother Church which the Psalmist says is the Church of the Holy [*ecclesia sanctorum*]; it began with the first man created in innocence" (ed. Scholz, in *Unbekannte kirchenpolitische Streitschriften*, 2:504). Cf., e.g., James of Viterbo: "That the Church may be called a kingdom is made clear by 1 Corinthians XV . . . the kingdom of Christ is said to be the whole creation, and the Church in another . . . the faithful themselves . . . the Church may rightly be called these three names . . . the ecclesiastical community . . . many congregations" (*On Christian Government* 1:1, ed. R. W. Dyson, pp. 4–10, esp. 7–8).

203. *De potestate summi pontificis* 14, pp. 58, 85).

204. James of Viterbo, e.g., hesitates to say that all temporal power is unjust and illegitimate, finding "a middle way, which seems more reasonable"; he arrives at a Thomistic solution: faith and grace perfect the natural origin of power (*De regimine christiano* 8; *On Christian Government*, trans. Dyson, pp. 102–103; see also Dyson's discussion in the "Introduction," esp. p. xxiii).

205. See the illuminating pages on the two goals penned by Patrick Boyde, in *Dante: Philomythes and Philosopher: Man in the Cosmos* (Cambridge, U.K.: Cambridge University Press, 1981), pp. 293–294.

206. Here Dante is in total disagreement with Tolomeo da Lucca (and other hiero-

crats), who warns all believing princes to beware, for their election is only a concession from the Holy See; see his *Determinatio compendiosa*, ed. Krammer, p. 73, and n. 1. I disagree with Edward Williamson, who contends that Dante's earthly happiness is independent of the heavenly: Dante does indeed subordinate the earthly to the spiritual (see "De Beatitudine Huius Vitæ," *Annual Report of the Dante Society of America* 76 [1958]: 1–22; rpt in *Dante Studies* 118 [2000]: 109–127).

207. *De potestate summi pontificis* 5, pp. 67–68.

208. St. Thomas speaks in the context of man's end and destiny, and God's predestination: [Responsio . . . .]: *"Finis autem ad quem res creatæ ordinantur a Deo, est duplex. Unus, qui excedit proportionem naturæ creatæ et facultatem; et hic finis est vita æterna, quæ in divina visione consistit; quæ est supra naturam cujuslibet creaturæ, ut supra habitum est. Alius autem finis est naturæ creatæ proportionatus, quem scilicet res creata potest attingere secundum virtutem suæ naturæ"* (*Summa theologiæ*, Vol. 5: *God's Will and Providence* Ia, 19–26 [New York: Blackfriars/McGraw-Hill; London: Eyre & Spottiswoode, 1967], pp. 108–109).

209. St. Thomas discusses the conditions of twofold beatitude: *"Responsio: Dicendum quod duplex est beatitudo, una imperfecta, quæ habetur in hac vita, et alia perfecta, quæ in Dei visione consistit. Manifestum est autem quod ad beatitudinem hujus vitæ de necessitate requiritur corpus. Est enim beatitudo hujus vitæ operatio intellectus, vel specualtivi vel practici. Operatio autem intellectus in hac vita non potest esse sine phantasmate, quod non est nisi in organo corporeo, ut in Primo habitum est. Et sic beatitudo quæ in hac vita haberi potest, dependet quodammodo ex corpora"* (*Summa theologiæ*, Vol.16: *Purpose and Happiness* Ia2æ, 1–5 [New York: Blackfriars/McGraw-Hill; London: Eyre & Spottiswoode, 1969], pp. 100–103). See Vinay's discussion, *Interpretazione della Monarchia*, Lectura Dantis Scaligera (Florence: Le Monnier, 1962), pp. 18–22.

210. *"Sed sciendum quod ad perfectionem alicjus rei dupliciter aliquid pertinet. Uno modo, ad constituendam essentiam rei; sicut anima requiritur ad perfectionem hominis. Alio modo requiritur ad perfectionem rei quod pertinet ad bene esse ejus: sicut pulchritudo corporis et velocitas ingenii pertinet ad perfectionem hominis. Quamvis ergo corporis primo modo ad perfectionem beatitudinis humanæ non pertineat, pertinet tamen secundo modo"* (*Summa theologiæ*, Vol. 16: *Purpose and Happiness* Ia2æ, 1–5 [[New York: Blackfriars/McGraw-Hill; London: Eyre & Spottiswoode, 1969], pp. 102–105).

211. St. Thomas cautiously averred, *"Et sic* beatitudo quæ in hac vita *haberi potest, dependet* quodammodo *ex corpora"* (And, thus, that *happiness*, which can be had *in this life*, depends *in some way* on the body; my emphasis). The relation between spiritual and temporal cannot be exactly determined. We must note, concerning Dante's use of *"quodammodo"* (in a certain sense) and accompanied by the expressions "not . . . so strictly" and "in a certain sense" in *Mon.* 3:16:17, that such imprecision or qualified *akribeia* in ethical judgments is typical in the language of Aristotle himself (cf. *Nic. Ethics* 1:3:2:2; see also St. Thomas Aquinas, *Summa theologiæ*, Vol.16: *Purpose and Happiness* Ia2ae, 1–5:103). In the *Nic. Ethics* 1:3, Aristotle states that his assertions should be taken as valid "for the most part," for there are no universal ethical judgments. See Jonathan Barnes's "Introduction" to *The Ethics of Aristotle*, trans. J. A. K. Thomson, rev. Hugh Tredennick, intro and bibliography by

Jonathan Barnes (London/New York: Penguin Books, 1976), pp. 20–23. Vernani does not address the conventional *"quodammodo"* attenuation in Dante's text, as we note; it would have weakened his attack. For the friar from Rimini, the emperor and all civil and temporal life *were* under the *direct and full* control of the pope, not *"in some certain way"*! And for him earthly life was less than ancillary. On the qualifications that Dante makes to the relationship of the pope and the emperor in Dante's final paragraphs of the *Mon.*, see Bortolo Martinelli, "Sul 'quodammodo' di *Monarchia* III, 15, 17," in *Miscellanea in onore di Vittore Branca*, Biblioteca dell'Archivum Romanicum, ser. 1, Storia-Letteratura-Paleografia 178–182 (Florence: Olschki, 1983), 1:193–214. On the question of the pope's blessing, the reverence of the emperor in *Mon.* 3:16:17, and Dante's relative conservatism in his view of the two power's reciprocity, see Anthony K. Cassell, "The Exiled Dante's Hope for Reconciliation: *Monarchia* 3:16:16–18," *Annali d'Italianistica* 20 (2002):425–449.

212. Cf., e.g., *Inf.* 16:106–111. The papal curia, of course, never brought an official charge of heterodoxy against Dante.

213. *De potestate summi pontificis* 10, pp. 74–76.

214. See Matteini's "Introduzione" to *Il più antico oppositore;* for conjectures on Vernani's death, p. 17; on the manuscript, p. 22. See Dolcini's remarks on the vicissitudes of the *Ref.*, in *Crisi di poteri*, pp. 439–444.

## NOTES TO DANTE'S 'MONARCHIA'

1. *Higher Nature:* God impresses on man a desire to know. Immediately with such authoritative terminology, Dante demonstrates his familiarity with a formula common in the study of law (cf. Uguccione da Pisa's *"summa natura"*). For the juristic use of the phrase, "Nature, that is, God," and for *"ius divinum,"* "divine law," as a synonym for *"ius naturale,"* "natural law," the immutable rules of morality, see Brian Tierney, *"Natura id est Deus:* A Case of Juristic Pantheism?," *Journal of the History of Ideas* 24, no. 3 (1963): 307–322. The Scholastics accepted the juristic concept of *"natura naturans,"* derived from Averroës, the great commentator on Aristotle: it signified the "nature that is the Supreme Cause of everything that occurs *according to* nature," i.e., God. Cf. *Mon.* 2:2:2: "Nature, in fact, is in the mind of the first mover who is God." And 2:2:3: "Whatever good there is in things here below . . . comes initially from the artisan who is God and, secondly, from the heavens, which are the tools of divine art commonly called 'nature.'" In *Purg.* 16:79, Dante speaks of God as *"miglior natura,"* "a better nature" (cf. also *Par.* 10:28 and *Par.* 13:79). On the stability of the unmoved Empyrean's influence in directing all to natural ends, see St. Thomas Aquinas Aquinas, *ST* I, q. 66, a. 3, ad. 2.

2. As in the opening the *Conv.*, Dante here echoes the famous axiom at the beginning of Aristotle's *Metaph.* 1:1: *"Omnes homines natura scire desiderant,"* "All men desire to know," but he limits the quest from "all men" here to those who love truth. See the *Textus Aristotelis* in St. Thomas Aquinas, *In duodecim Libros Metaphysicorum Aristotelis Expositio*, ed. Cathala and

Spiazzi, p. 5; cf. *Conv.* 3:3:11: through his angelic, or rational nature, "Man has a love for truth and virtue." (Dante will cite the *Metaphysics* under the titles *On Being Simply* and *First Philosophy.*) The axiom was popular in Florence; on Remigio de' Girolami's use, see Charles T. Davis, "An Early Political Theorist," pp. 662–676, esp. p. 663, and n. 14.

3. Dante calques these opening passages of the *Mon.* closely on Aristotle's *Nic. Ethics* 10:9:1181a, where the philosopher made a similar complaint and urged similar involvement in teaching posterity as he set about examining three major questions on the ideal state: "Certainly in other practical sciences persons, like doctors and painters, who teach technique seem to be the very ones who put it into operation, that being left to those who are engaged in politics. These seem to perform their public activities more from a kind of habit and experience than from intellectual discernment. Apparently they do not produce anything either in speeches or in writing about matters of this kind; although it might be more to their credit . . . surely they could leave nothing better to their countries; nor could they choose anything more acceptable . . . than the ability to make others statesmen. . . . *Those who would wish a knowledge of politics must have [in addition] practice. But the sophists who profess to teach political science seem to be a long way from teaching it. . . . Since our predecessors have left the subject of legislation uninvestigated, perhaps it will be much better for us to attempt to treat this and the forms of government in general. . . .* [W]e will begin to inquire what is the ideal state, how it ought to be organized and what laws and customs it should follow" (my emphasis). The version of the text is found in St. Thomas Aquinas, *Commentary on the Nic. Ethics*, trans. Litzinger, 2:937–938. Vernani recognizes the claim and pounces on the term "sophist" to hurl at Dante, the commonplace disparagement that church hierocrats used for anyone arguing against their position. The insult is poignant, given Dante's real, courageous experience in political life and his life-long exile from Florence.

4. Dante here sets the authoritative rhetoric of his temporal duty as a loyal Roman citizen intending the common good; above all, he identifies himself with the ancient champions of Rome in this debate with "modern" assailants of the empire; in book 3, he will couch the historical struggle and his participation in contemporary dialogue in terms of an athletic contest and a blood duel.

5. This beautiful and eloquent opening passage extolling the fruitful virtues and duties of the senior statesman is central for our understanding of the role Dante believed he played in the politics of the time and in the eyes of posterity. The poet uses passages from the Old and New Testaments to contrast his own ideals with those of his delinquent contemporaries. Two allusions here especially illuminate the sterile and sear punishments of the politicians Pier della Vigna, Brunetto Latini, and the sodomites damned in the *Inf.* 13, 15 and 16. First, see Ps 1:3: "They who have not walked in the counsel of the wicked . . . are like trees planted by streams of water, bearing fruit fruit in due season . . . ," and Jer 17:5–10: "Blessed are those who trust in the Lord. . . . They shall be like a tree planted by water, sending out its roots by the stream." Second, see Mt 7.16–19: "By their fruits ye shall know them. Do men gather grapes of thorns, or figs of thistles? Even so every good

tree bringeth forth good fruit, and the evil tree bringeth forth evil fruit. A good tree cannot bring forth evil fruit, neither can an evil tree bring forth good fruit." Piero's sterile soul-become-thornbush and the sterility of the burning plain that rejects "every tree [*pianta*] from its bed" embody the extreme failing of their true duty to man and God.

6. Mt 25:14–30

7. Ironically, of course, happiness, seen as a Christian twofold beatitude, *will be* the topic of the *Mon.*, including a pivotal extrapolation from St. Thomas Aquinas on the "blessedness of this life" (*Mon.* 3:16:7).

8. Frequently in his work Dante censures the prostitution of knowledge for profit, especially by churchmen, instead of its use for the common good. In *Conv.* 1:9:2–3, he affirms that his own vernacular commentary will be of service; in *Conv.* 3:11:10 he contrasts philosophers with "lawyers, doctors and almost all religious" who are intent on using knowledge for gain. Cf. *Inf.* 7:46–48; *Purg.* 16:100–102, 32:103. On the popes' and prelates' fixation on decretals for lucre, see *Par.* 9:127–138, 11:1–11.

9. *the palm of so great a prize: "palmum tanti bravii."* The word *"bravium,"* derived from Greek, is late Latin, from the Vulgate Bible; see 1 Cor 9:24: *"Nescitis quod hii qui in stadio currunt omnes quidem currunt sed unus accipit bravium"* (Know you not that they run in the race; all run indeed, but one receiveth the prize?). Not only the term but the concept expressed by St. Paul here influences Dante's choice of vocabulary—one that he melds with the classical idea of a champion fighting for a cause. "Bravium" appears again six times in the second book of the *Mon.*, at 2:7:9, and at 2:8:2, 3, 5, 7, and 11; and see 2:8:8 ("palm of monarchy"). Dante's is not an idle boast of originality, for Aristotle does not mention "universal empire," let alone discuss the powers of an emperor.

10. Jm 1:5.

11. *"what it is generally like, so to speak, and its scope": "typo ut dicam et secundum intentionem."* In the other occurrences of the term *"intentio"* in the *Mon.*, Dante uses it to signify some variant sense of "intent," "intention," or "purpose," as I understand it here. The poet refers to the purpose or end goal of the empire in the last sentences of this chapter and in the chapter following. Nardi has argued—unnecessarily and awkwardly, I believe—that the term "intentio" here would signify an appearance or image, a phenomenon, or a representation in the mind, as in "intentional psychology"; cf. *Purg.* 18:22–23. See Nardi, *Nel mondo*, pp. 93–96; *Mon.*, ed. Nardi, ad loc., p. 284), and T. Gregory, "Intenzione," *Enciclopedia dantesca*, 3:480–482. On this epistemological sense of "intentio," see note 103, below.

12. Here Dante sets forth the subjects of each of the three books of the treatise. The high-papalist Giles of Rome (ca. 1247–1316), in his *De ecclesiastica potestate* 5:5:7 of ca. 1301–1302, e.g., had put the opposite case firmly: "For if we give diligent attention to whence royal power has come and to whence it has been instituted, it follows that, *since it has been instituted through the priesthood*, royal power must be subject to priestly power, and especially to the power of the Supreme Priest" (*On Ecclesiastical Power*, trans. Dyson, p. 12, my emphasis). The Dominican friar and student of St. Thomas Aquinas Tolomeo of Lucca

encapsulates Aristotle's views on legitimacy of rule in the *Nic. Ethics* as follows: "Aristotle
. . . posits three things about a legitimate king: first, he principally intends the good of his
subjects; second, he is found to be sufficient in himself and to excel superabundantly in all
good qualities, not burdening his subjects; and third, he undertakes the care of his subjects so that they may function well, just as shepherds act toward their sheep" (*De regimine
principum* 3:11:2; *On the Government of Rulers*, trans. Blythe, p. 178). Cf. *Nic. Ethics* 8:10:1160b:1–7
and 11:1161a: 11–15; see the translation of Moerbeke's Latin text in St. Thomas Aquinas,
*Commentary on the Nic. Ethics*, trans. Litzinger, 2:750–751, 756–757.

13. *analytically: "analetice,"* i.e., by a deductive argument. In an analytic proposition the
predicate is already contained in the definition of the subject. Dante will try to show that
anything affirmed or denied about the government of a single world ruler will be attributes resulting necessarily from the nature of the subject. Aristotle maintained that in order to develop a body of knowledge on a topic, i.e., a *scientia* for the Scholastics, one had
to have premises both necessary and valid, whose inferences were valid. See Stump, "Dialectic," p. 130.

14. In the *Epistle to Can Grande*, Dante calls himself a "poet of rectitude" and insists that
the *Commedia* too is aimed at moral action: it is *"doctrinalis,"* "didactic" (*Epistola* 10:6, ed.
Toynbee, rev. Hardie, pp. 172, 198).

15. *end:* I have rendered the term *"finis"* as "end," "goal," or "end goal" throughout.

16. Aristotle, *Nic. Ethics* 1:7:1098b:6–7; see St. Thomas Aquinas's *Commentary on the Nic.
Ethics*, trans. Litzinger, 1:45–46. For Dante and his contemporaries Aristotle was "the master of those who know" (*Inf.* 4:131).

17. On the definition of the household, see St. Thomas Aquinas, *In libros Politicorum
Aristotelis Expositio* 1:1 (*Pol.* 1:2:1252b:12; for the definition of the clan-village identified with a
"neighborhood," called *vicus* in the medieval Latin translation, see 1252b:16; for the definition of the city, see 1252b:27). Dante's fellow Florentine Remigio de' Girolami uses a similar Aristotelian metaphor of the foot and the body in his *De bono pacis*, ed. Charles T.
Davis, in "Remigio de' Girolami and Dante," p. 129.

18. According to the doctrine of "final causes" (the goal toward which all things tend),
God created everything for a final purpose planned before creation, rather than creating a
purpose for things after their creation. A similar argument dealing with the extension of
governance from the family to the monarchy is found in St. Thomas Aquinas's *On Princely
Government* 1.1.14 (trans. Dawson, ed. d'Entrèves, pp. 73–79); see his text also in Tolomeo
da Lucca, *On the Government of Princes* 1:15, trans. Blythe, pp. 97–101.

19. *"God and nature do nothing in vain": "Deus et natura nil otiosum facit."* From Aristotle, *De cælo*
1:4; 271a33; see text in St. Thomas Aquinas, *In Aristotelis libros de cælo et mundo, De generatione et
corruptione, Meteorologicorum expositio*, ed. R. M. Spiazzi (Turin: Marietti, 1952), p. 38: *"Deus
autem et natura nihil frustra faciunt"* (God and nature create nothing that does not fulfill a purpose). See below, *Mon.* 1:10. Cf. St. Thomas Aquinas, *"Ociosum sit quod non pertingit ad finem ad
quem est"* (That thing is futile which does not attain the end for which it is designed); see

*De unitate intellectus contra Averroistas (Against the Averroists)* 2:115; also see *Mon.* 2:2:2–3. Dante employs St. Thomas Aquinas's word, *"otiosum,"* instead of William of Moerbeke's rendering, *"frustra,"* in the *De cælo et mundo.*

20. *multitude:* Note that in this first usage, Dante might imply *the whole of mankind as a universal totality;* we can only puzzle whether he meant across time and space, but this will clearly *not* be the case in his second use immediately below. The poet foresees a final *period* of rebirth of the ancient era of the *pax Romana "sotto 'l buono Augusto"*—one that clearly does not exist in his present.

21. *possible intellect:* The highest part of the intellect; it has possibilities, potentialities, and capabilities beyond what it may presently be putting into effect. Also known as the "passive intellect." The Averroist view (expounded, among others by the Swede Boethius of Dacia and by Siger of Brabant in his *Commentary on Aristotle's Third Book On the Soul*) that the possible intellect is an eternal entity existing separately from the individual, and that this single, separate intellect is common to all humans, came under attack in 1270 by St. Thomas Aquinas, among others (Saint Bonaventure, Albertus Magnus, Giles of Rome). See *Against the Averroists,* ed. and trans. Ralph McInerny, pp. 8, 10, 34–37; and William A. Wallace, "The Philosophical Setting of Medieval Science," in *Science in the Middle Ages,* ed. David C. Lindberg (Chicago/London: University of Chicago Press, 1978), pp. 104–105.

22. Vernani will censure this passage as an "intolerable error"; see *Ref.* 1:27. In his *Pol.* 7, Aristotle says that the individual and the whole body politic have the same end. Dante holds that the potentiality of all mankind cannot be realized in a single individual fully; he does not deny a common end for the individual man and mankind; practically, howeverer, there are *also* lesser, subordinate goals in addition to, and leading to, the supreme end; cf. *Mon.* 1:2:8.

23. *all together:* "simul."

24. *multitude:* In this second use of the term Dante has restricted the multitude to whatever number of humanity should be living at a hypothetical period in the future; here it clearly does *not* include all men born from the Sixth Day of Creation until the Last Judgment; he intends the contemporary multitude of human beings on earth at that time at which peace and freedom under one monarch will occur. Cf. his *Letter to the Italian Cardinals (Epistola 8),* ed. Toynbee, pp. 142 and 147: *"tota civitate* peregrinante in terris," "the whole body politic *in pilgrimage on earth"* (my emphasis). He speaks of "particular forms" here in the *Mon.,* and is far from adopting any heretical idea of the unity of all human intellect from the beginning and through eternity (such as in the monopsychism defended by Averroës); his reference to the Arab philosopher in the next paragraph simply indicates, in an afterthought, Averroës' concord with some elements of his own argumentation.

25. *multitude of generated things so that all the potentiality of primal matter may always be found actuated:* In this third use of the word "multitude," Dante includes all matter beneath the sphere of the moon whose total material content would remain constant at any point in time. The poet's analogy is, obviously, quite inexact and ambiguous: it leaves his argument open

to Vernani's merciless accusations. The limited "multitude" of individual human beings alive at one particular future point, or at any era in history, is obviously not identical and consistent with this "multitude": the souls and identities on earth "change" because they succeed one another. Matter, in the sublunar world, on the contrary, is constant in quantity but has no permanent identity, unlike human souls. See *Mon.* 2:9:6 below.

26. Cf. Remigio de' Girolami's similar disquisition (following St. Thomas Aquinas) on man as a cooperating, social animal: "Man naturally bond together and make a city or other community for the sake of their common benefit in order to remedy the defect of human life which one individual cannot heal" (*De bono communi*, ed. Matteis, pp. 33–34, 71).

27. It is clear that Dante means *that to "posit a separate potentiality"* is impossible; i.e., it is the idea *that pure potentiality can have its own existence* that Averroës would reject. The Arab philosopher would thus agree with Dante's argument. The idea of a separate world soul does not enter the context. See above, pp. 55–60.

28. *by art:* Latin *ars*, Aristotle's τέχνη On the strict difference between, first, doing or acting morally (a speculative act measured by virtue that remains in the subject) and, second, the skill in making or production (an act that passes into outward matter and shapes it), see *Nic. Ethics* 1139a:26–30, 1140a:6–23 and *De anima* 3:2:433a:14; see also St. Thomas Aquinas, *In Aristotelis Librum de anima commentarium*, ed. Pirotta, pp. 193, and *Commentary on the Nic. Ethics*, trans. Litzinger, 2:543–545, 550–553.

29. *those who are strong in intellect naturally have dominion over others:* Aristotle discusses the requirements and natural abilities necessary for governing in *Pol* 1:1–2:1252a:1–31. Dante classifies himself along with his patron, Can Grande, as having the "vigor of intellect and reason" as the basis for their friendship in *Epistola* 10 (13), the *Letter to Can Grande*, para. 2 (ed. P. Toynbee, rev. C. Hardie, pp. 169, 197; ed. Brugnoli, pp. 604–605). We have noted elsewhere that there is some question whether Dante knew Aristotle's *Pol.* at firsthand; Giles of Rome's *De regimine principum* and St. Thomas Aquinas's commentary on the *Pol.* and *Metaph.* appear to have been Dante's major sources. The poet's citations do not specify the *Pol.'s* book numbers and are unlike his more specific references to the *Nic. Ethics* and other works. Enrico Berti, however, insists that some references to the *Pol.* are direct (*Enciclopedia dantesca*, 4:585–587). It is possible, after all, that Dante may simply have had only intermittent and undependable access to the work, depending otherwise on memory and notes. Kay believes that Dante is here citing at secondhand from *Auctoritates Aristotelis* (ed. *Mon.*, ad loc.).

30. *always: "semper."* The ideal of actuating this potential (the function and goal of the human race *always* to put this into action) is *always* there, but it is a perfection that will only be effected or realized historically at some point in the future, as it had been in the fullness of time in the Augustan past, with a limited number of human beings—that is in a "multitude *among* mankind" (*multitudinem in humano genere*). Cf. the foretaste of the Earthly Paradise in *Purg.*, where Dante's Wayfarer attains only to *personal justice*, not to universal *original justice*, for *all* men fell in Adam (see Charles S. Singleton, *Journey to Beatrice* [Cambridge, Mass. Harvard University Press, 1958], esp. "Justification," pp. 57–71); original jus-

tice was lost by all mankind at the Fall forever, as was the immortality of the flesh; not all souls shall be among the blest in Heaven. Dante's Wayfarer is led back to this transposed Eden atop Purgatory, indeed, through a chain of heavenly grace in the person of his guide-messenger Virgilio (*Inf.* 2:49–74), who "crowns and miters" Dante's Wayfarer over himself (*Purg.* 27:142), as an earthly monarch was crowned and mitered (kings ranking temporally as bishops). Virgilio is not only the messenger of a particular heavenly intercession, but because he was born *"sotto 'l buono Augusto,"* he is the representative of the Roman Empire ordained by God's grace (*Inf.* 1:71, 2:10–21), and the flawed spokesman of human wisdom and philosophy, with all its limitations dramatized in the episodes of the first canticle of the *Commedia*.

31. *by sitting and resting . . . acquire perfection in prudence and wisdom:* Aristotle, "For the condition of understanding or knowing results from the soul coming to a state of stillness out of the turbulence natural to it." (*Physics* 7:3:247b–248a; *The Physics*, Books 5–8, trans. Wicksteed and Cornford, LCL, 5:236–239; Barnes, 1:414). Dante echoes the words of Moerbeke's translation, *"In quietare enim et residere anima sciens fit et prudens."* See St. Thomas Aquinas, *In octo libros Physicorum Aristoteleis expoistio,* ed. P. M. Maggiòlo (Turin: Marietti, 1954), p. 473; St. Thomas Aquinas, Lectio VII, n. 925, pp. 475–476. Cf. the ironic words of the "lazy" Bellacqua in *Purg.* 4:97–139:

32. Ps 8:6 [8:5]; Heb 2:7.

33. *universal peace . . . ordained for our beatitude:* St. Thomas Aquinas too takes peace as the axiomatic basis of human society in *De regimine principum* 1:2 (trans. Dawson, ed. D'Entrèves, pp. 10–13; see St. Thomas Aquinas's text transcribed verbatim in Tolomeo da Lucca, *On the Government of Rulers* 1:3, trans. Blythe, pp. 65–66).

34. Lk 2:13–14.

35. Lk 24:36; Jn 20:21, 26.

36. Cf. the similar exaltation of peace as the common good of the human multitude in Remigio de' Girolami's *De bono communi,* ed. Matteis, pp. 33, 53.

37. *extremely strong and valid arguments . . . from . . . authority:* The medieval commonplace procedure of argument from authority, *ab auctoritate,* to give plausibility to an inference, derives not from Aristotle, but from Cicero's *Topica* 4:24: "Extrinsic arguments depend principally on authority" (*Cicero: De Inventione, De Optime genere oratorium, Topica,* trans. H. M. Hubbell, LCL, pp. 396–397). See Stump, "Dialectic," pp. 126–135. Dante here makes a mature reprise of the inductive case upon the authority of Aristotle that he had outlined in the *Conv.* 4:1–7; 8–12 and ch. 5 as a whole all anticipate *Mon.* books 1 and 2. Dante places this argument from authority from that earlier work here first in the series of eleven reasons (10 + 1), realizing that it was less logically solid but more persuasive rhetorically. He knew Peter of Spain had taught that while such reasoning might be more convincing and clear, argument from authority carried, however, *less* force and effectiveness in debate than the more "perfect and complete" syllogism (*Summulæ logicales,* Tractatus VII, 3, ed. de Rijk, p. 90).

38. Cf. *Conv.* 4:4:5: "The Philosopher says in the *Politics:* in a plurality directed to one end, one member must direct and rule, and all the others must be ruled and directed." Aristotle in the *Pol.* 1:2:1254a:29–31 states: "In every composite thing, where a plurality of parts, whether continuous or discrete, is combined to make a single common whole, there is always found a ruling and a subject factor" (trans. H. Rackham, LCL, p. 18–19; cf. Barnes, 2:1990). But Dante's wording follows more closely St. Thomas Aquinas's arguments on a plurality ordered to a single goal in the Proemium of *In Metaph. Exp.*, ed. Cathala and Spiazzi, p. 1.

39. *inductive reasoning:* In *Summulæ logicales*, Tractatus V, 10–20, Peter of Spain explains that *"inductio,"* inductive reasoning, is the second of the four species of argumentation, preceded by syllogism (deduction), and followed by enthymeme and exemplum (simile or analogy), in order of strength: "Inductive reasoning proceeds from the particular to the universal" (ed. de Rijk, p. 56). Peter makes it clearer in his "Treatise on Insolubles," in the *Tractatus Syncategorematum* (ed. and trans Joseph P. Mullally and Roland Houde [Milwaukee, Wis.: Marquette University Press, 1964], pp. 154–155): from the particular statements "Socrates runs; Plato runs; Cicero runs," and adding "and so forth," we induce the universal "ergo, all men run." In the *Mon.* Dante covers the gamut from the individual to the ultimate extension of the meaning of the term "man" to prove his induction: as reason rules in one man, and as one person must rule the family, the neighborhood, the city, and the kingdom, therefore among all mankind—all, as in the subcategories, ordered to one goal—one ruler must rule.

40. "Every household is under the rule of its eldest member": *Omnis enim domus regitur a senissimo* (*Pol.* 1252b:20; "Every family is ruled by the eldest," trans. Barnes, 2:1987); see also *Pol.* 1:7:1255b:19: "The rule of a household is a monarchy; for every house is under one head." Dante may have learned this through Moerbeke's translation and St Thomas Aquinas's commentary (St. Thomas Aquinas, *In libros Politicorum Aristotelis expositio*, Lectio 1:15, ed. Spiazzi, pp. 5, 11). The poet had understood from Aristotelian thought, perhaps through secondary sources, that the family function was to supply its members' *physical* needs: "The family is the association established by nature for the supply of men's everyday wants" (trans. Barnes, 2:1987; orig. and trans. H. Rackham, LCL, pp. 4–5; Spiazzi, p. 5) for the continuance of the species and security; however, as a Christian, Dante here corrects pagan philosophy by turning the stress to man's spiritual needs; he thus subtly emends Aristotle, much as he often rectifies Vergil-Virgilio's heathen perspective in the *Divine Comedy*. Remigio de' Girolami (who might have been Dante's real source from conversations, sermons, or lectures) affirmed similar ideas on the life of virtue and the self-sufficiency of the body politic in his *De bono pacis*, ed. Charles T. Davis, in "Remigio de' Girolami and Dante," pp. 110, 128–129.

41. Dante knew no Greek and was only acquainted with the poetry of Homer at secondhand; this quote from *Odyssey* 9 appears in Aristotle's *Pol.* 1:2, but as we have noted, we cannot ascertain whether Dante was acquainted firsthand with William of Moerbeke's

translation, although he shows familiarity with St. Thomas Aquinas's commentary on that work.

42. St. Thomas Aquinas, in his *De regimine principum*, gives his own version of Aristotle: "It is natural for human beings to be social and political animals, living in a multitude, as natural necessity requires. . . . It is therefore necessary for humans to live in a multitude, so that one might help another" (*De regimine principum* 1:1, trans. Dawson, ed. D'Entrèves, pp. 2–3; see Thomas's text also in Tolomeo da Lucca's *On the Government of Rulers* 1:1:3–4, trans. Blythe, p. 61).

43. The community must fulfill a common end under a single leader or else it ceases to exist; the influence of Remigio de' Girolami's ideas as expressed in the *De bono communi* is evident here (ed. De Matteis, p. 39).

44. Lk 11:17; Mt. 12:25.

45. Dante's syllogism is complicated but clear. He contrasts the relation *among* the parts to the relation *between* those parts and their leader, and considers the latter (by which he means the position of the emperor toward his subjects) a relationship superior to the former. The relation of the ruler to the ruled is parallel to the Deity's ordering of Creation. Cf. *Conv.* 4:4:4–5.

46. Dante's contemporary John of Paris (ca. 1250–1254–1306), contending for Philip the Fair and the particular kingdom of France, ca. 1302–1303, argues *against* the empire: "It is true that a multitude will readily disagree in any single issue and so a regal constitution is better than an aristocratic one. . . . Yet *it is better that many should rule in many kingdoms than one alone should rule the whole world*" (*On Royal and Papal Power* 23, trans. J. A. Watt, p. 227; my emphasis). See, however, John's support of monarchy, n. 52, below.

47. I here follow Ricci's reading of *"dicitur,"* "it is said to," in preference to Nardi's defense of other earlier editors' *"debet,"* "must"; similarly, in the next sentence, I read *"enim,"* "for," "indeed," instead of *"eius,"* "its". I must note that Nardi's posthumous edition is absurdly confusing to use, since Ricci's 1965 version is reprinted as the *texte de base*, while Nardi's argumentative and, at times, rather capricious readings are given only in the footnotes. P. Shaw, "Sul testo," pp. 205–206, also follows Ricci's reading.

48. Vernani will (purposefully?) miss Dante's clear statement here on God as monarch of the universe; see *Ref.* 1:64.

49. On man's thirst for God and God's turning all into an image of himself, cf. Remigio de' Girolami, *De bono communi*, ed. Matteis, pp. 33, 64.

50. Gn 1:26.

51. Mk 12:29, 12:32; Dt 6:4.

52. John of Paris, arguing for the French monarchy in *On Royal and Papal Power*, expresses the belief: "Government of a community is more effective when conducted by one man according to virtue, than when exercised by many or few virtuous men" (ch. 1., ed. and trans. Watt, p. 78).

53. *"man and the sun generate man"*: *"generat enim homo hominem et sol."* From Aristotle, *Physics*

2:2:194b:13: "Man is begotten by man and by the sun as well" (Barnes, 1:332). In St. Thomas Aquinas's *In octo libros Physicorum Aristotelis*, Moerbeke's version reads *"homo enim hominem generat* ex materia *et sol"* (ed. Maggiòlo, pp. 86, 88). St. Thomas Aquinas also omits the words *"ex materia"* in *De anima* 3:3:427a25, lectio 4, no. 619: *"homo enim generat hominem et sol"* (*Sancti Thomæ Aquinatis In Aristoteleis Librum. De Anima*, ed. Pirotta, p. 154). But in the treatise *De unitate intellectus contra Averroistas (Against the Averroists)* 2:30, St. Thomas Aquinas cites it fully in one place: *"Homo enim hominem generat ex materia, et sol"* (ed. and trans. McInerny, pp. 48–49); and abridged in another: *"homo generatur ab homine et a sole"* (Man is generated by man and by the sun) (ed. and trans. McInerny, pp. 82–83). Cornford translates Aristotle's passage as: "In Nature man generates man; but the process presupposes and takes place in natural material already organized by the solar heat" (*Physics* 2:4:194b:14–15, LCL, pp. 126–127). On Vernani's attack on this point, see the end of his censure of *Mon.* 1, in *Ref.* 1:72 and note.

54. *Lessons on Nature: "De Naturali auditu."* Dante also uses the title *De simpliciter ente (On Being Simply)* for the *Physics*—a work of natural history that deals fundamentally with all things that "become," generate, move, or change. See Francis M. Cornford's very useful "General Introduction" to the edition of the *Physics*, in Aristotle's works, LCL, 4:xv–xx.

55. *Cons. Phil.* 2:8.

56. *"Things hate to be in disorder; but a plurality of principalities is disorder; ergo, there is but one prince":* See Aristotle, *Metaph.* 12:10:1076a:5; cf. Barnes, 2:1700. See Moerbeke's Latin text in St. Thomas Aquinas, *In Metaph. Exp.*, ed. Cathala and Spiazzi, p. 611. Dante, ironically, could not know that Aristotle was actually citing Homer's *Iliad* 2:204: "The rule of many is not good; let there be one ruler." He thus did not know that the citation in context was quite wrong for his argument in the *Mon.:* in Homer the guileful Ulysses, countermanding Agamemnon's orders and stealing his scepter, was seizing sole, arbitrary command, regaining control of his men "by Zeus the Son of Cronos of the Crooked Ways," in order to destroy the city of Troy, Rome's predecessor. Amusingly, although Petrarch should have known better, since he boasts of his direct knowledge of the *Iliad* via Leontius Pilatus's translation, he falls into the same error in "On His Own Ignorance and That of Many Others"; his source was probably Dante (see the English version in the *Renaissance Philosophy of Man*, ed. and trans. Ernst Cassirer, Paul Oskar Kristeller, and John Herman Randall Jr. [Chicago/London: University of Chicago Press, 1948], pp. 47–133, here p. 77).

57. Vergil, *Eclogue* 4:6. Lactantius had taken the line, as indeed the whole of the *Eclogue*, as a pagan prophecy of Christ-to-come, and Emperor Constantine, followed by St Augustine, also accepted it as such; St. Jerome disapproved, but the tradition of Vergil as prophet held through the Middle Ages. See Domenico Comparetti, *Vergil in the Middle Ages*, trans. E. F. M. Benecke (London: Swan Sonnenschein; New York: Macmillan, 1895), pp. 96–103. In the fiction of the *Divina Commedia*, Virgilio's tragedy is to have ignored his own prophecy of *Christus venturus*. Dante clearly interprets the *Eclogue* as purely a pagan allegory of justice. We can compare the irony of Statius's conversion in *Purg.* 22:64–73, where Dante par-

aphrases Vergil's verses from *Eclogue* 4:5–7. See Domenico Consoli, "Virgilio," *Enciclopedia dantesca*, 5:1031; Ettore Paratore, "Stazio," *Enciclopedia dantesca*, 5:419–425.

58. Dante's syllogism is incorrect in form, betraying the *quaternio terminorum*, the fallacy of four terms: he substitutes the term "monarch" in the first premise by "monarchy" in the consequent. A high papalist such as Vernani could just as easily have inserted "papacy."

59. This is Dante's only reference to a current, widespread, and commonplace passage from "the Master of the Six Principles," an anonymous twelfth-century writer of an extant but incomplete commentary on Aristotle's *Categories* entitled *Liber sex principiorum*. The author was, occasionally, wrongly identified as Gilbert de la Porrée (Gilbertus Porretanus), bishop of Poitiers (1070–1154). The work had been attributed sporadically, before 1230, to Aristotle himself as a completion of his *Metaph*. See Lorenzo Mineo-Paluello, "Magister sex principiorum," *Studi medievali* 3, no. 6 (1965): 123–51; *Liber sex principiorum* 1:5, ed. Lorenzo Mineo-Paluello and Bernard G. Dod, in *Aristoteles Latinus* (Bruges/Paris: Desclée de Brouwer, 1966), 1:6–7, *Categoriarum supplementa*, pp. 33–59, here pp. 35–36. See also *Mon.*, ed. Nardi, ad loc. Forms that are intrinsically definitive and supreme (e.g., rectitude and whiteness), may only be found more or less present, imperfectly, in different subjects.

60. Aristotle, *Nic. Ethics* 5:1:1129a:27–32–1129b:1 (Barnes, 2: 782). On justice as the foremost virtue, see St. Thomas Aquinas, *ST* II-II, q. 58, a. 12.

61. *Hesperus nor Lucifer:* Both signify the planet Venus. The whole quotation from Aristotle's *Nic. Ethics* 5:1:1129b:28–29, as it appeared for St. Thomas Aquinas and Dante, reads: "For this reason justice seems to be the most excellent among the virtues. Hence we have the proverb: 'neither the evening star nor morning star is so wonderful'" (Barnes, 2:1783; see the version in St. Thomas's *Commentary on the Nic. Ethics*, trans. Litzinger, p. 388). Notably, Dante substitutes Phoebe, the moon, for Venus, the evening and morning star, thus ironically accepting the decretalist identification of the moon with the justice of the empire. We must also reinterpret the significance of the question of the "balance," the balance of the two powers at a perfect time of spring at the vernal equinox in the apparently mere chronological image of "the children of Latona," the sun and moon, in *Par.* 29:1–9.

62. Cf. *Conv.* 1:4:8.

63. Paragraphs 6 and 7 dealing with the habit and practice of justice recall the "golden bough" formula spoken in various versions by Virgilio at several points through Hell, *"vuolsi così colà dove si puote ciò che si vuole"* (It is willed there above where will and power are one; *Inf.* 3:95). The contrast lies between man's conflict of flesh and spirit and God's perfection, where will is power; only a most powerful, moral monarch will reflect this on earth.

64. *preparatory syllogism:* Literally "prosyllogism," a syllogism that demonstrates the premise of another syllogism. See Chapter 2, above. See Aristotle, *Prior Analytics* 1:25:42b:4–10, 1:28:44a:1–35 (Barnes, 1:67, 1:70); *Aristoteles latinus: Analytica Priora translatio Boethii (Recensiones duæ)*, ed. Lorenzo Minio-Paluello (Bruges/Paris: Desclée de Brouwer,

1962), p. 62 (the other version has a lacuna, p. 235). The main syllogistic argument of the chapter, stated in para. 1, is: [Major premise] "The world is most excellently ordered when justice is most powerful within it. . . . [Minor premise] Justice is most powerful only under a monarch. [Conclusion] Ergo, for the best [most excellent] ordering of the world a monarchy or empire is required" (*Mon.* 1:11:2). The conclusion of the "preparatory syllogism," or "prosyllogism," which proves the minor premise, serves as the premise for that main syllogism, i.e., for the main thrust of this chapter. The "intrinsic negation," i.e., its implicit negation "nothing except" [= "no non . . ."] in the second figure is founded on the syncategorematic term "only" in the first (i.e., exclusively, or "only in C," and not in anything else). We can reconstrue it thus for clarity:

> All B is A: [the most powerful justice is always found *in/under* the strongest will];
> only C is A: [only *in/under* the monarch is found the strongest will];
> ergo, only C is B [the most powerful justice is only found *in/under* the monarch: i.e.,
> "Justice is at its most powerful only under a monarch"].

and:

> All B is A: [the most powerful justice is always found *in/under* the strongest will];
> Nothing except C is A: [*in/under* nothing except the monarch is the strongest will] (or
> "no non-C is A");
> ergo, nothing except C is B [therefore, *in/under* nothing except under the monarch is
> found the most powerful justice] (or "no non-C is B").

See Mozzillo-Howell, who points out Dante's irregularities, explains the poet's use of syncategorematic terms, and discusses the problem of identifying the mood of this syllogism (*camestres*) with its intrinsic negation ("Dante's Art of Reason," pp. 98–108).

65. Concerning the "second figure" that always concludes negatively, see "De secunda figura," in Peter of Spain, *Summulæ logicales*, Tractatus IV, 7, ed. De Rijk, p. 48. While trying to adhere to the standards of the professional logician, Dante is carefully aiding his nonprofessional reader (Can Grande and his advisers would be the first of those intended): thus he lavishes more than the usual simplifications.

66. *cupidity is the supreme opposite of justice:* the unjust man is covetous. See *Nic. Ethics* 5:1:1129a:32–b10, 5:2:1130a:16–32. See text in St. Thomas Aquinas's *Commentary on the Nic. Ethics*, trans. Litzinger, 1:382–383.

67. Aristotle, *Rhetoric* 1:1:1354b:2–13: "The judge should be allowed to decide as few things as possible" (Barnes, 2:2152).

68. Cf. *Conv.* 4:4:3–4.

69. Concerning the limits of the empire, see *Conv.* 4:4:8–12, where Dante cites the *Æn.* 1:25, 296.

70. Dante argues from a notably Franciscan perspective. The Spirituals among the Minor Friars believed that they imitated the perfection of Christ and the Apostles in their

renunciation of dominion over possessions, for, traditionally, the highest human perfection was said to consist in the greatest removal of solicitude for temporal things. Dante neatly modifies their currently embattled arguments for total poverty to his own good use: the Monarch, having dominion, right, ownership, and use of *all* goods, would therefore enjoy an identical removal of solicitude in pursuing and holding them; he would thus enjoy the highest perfection. For the question of Pope John XXII's condemnation of poverty as heresy and for arguments from both sides of the issue, see J. G. Sikes's "Introduction" to his edition of Hervæus Natalis, *Liber de paupertate Christi et apostolorum;* and John D. Jones's careful study of, notes for, and translation of *The Poverty of Christ and the Apostles* (Toronto: Pontifical Institute of Mediæval Studies, 1999), with extensive bibliography, pp. 149–155. Hervæus's work, probably written ca. 1321–1323, came too late for Dante, but Hervæus reports the preceding and ongoing burning arguments. See Heft, *John XXII and Papal Teaching Authority;* and Decima L. Douie's classic study, *The Nature and Effect of the Heresy of the Fraticelli.* John XXII's ruthless ideology met a storm of opposition; for example, among many other prelates, Cardinal Vitale, bishop of Albano, was to defend the doctrine of the poverty of Christ thus: "[Christ] showed Himself to be the exemplar of the highest perfection of the perfect by retaining for himself no ownership of or dominion over anything" (Appendix, Jones, p. 121). Dante had already set his monarch up as the perfect complement.

71. *man's perseity:* Man's "perseity" is his innate goal of the right ordering and function of the soul toward which he is led by the emperor who guards man from concupiscence, the Aristotelian opposite of this justice: compare Aristotle's equation of the equity and right order of the soul and state with justice in *Nic. Ehtics* 5:11 (1138a 1–38; 1138b 1–15; Barnes, 2:1796–1797). Dante had read that Seneca, as summarized by Martin of Braga, asked, "[w]hat is justice if not our own makeup?" (see *Mon.* 2:5:3, and n. 156 below). As Dante has already stated, man is created not for his mere existence (*Mon.* 1:3:5) but by and for the final cause of his perfect functioning: i.e., the use of his intellect in justice, peace, and tranquility as the first of the *"duo fines."* According to Aristotle, man's function is the activity of his soul according to reason, in acting equitably and to the best of his ability following his rational powers (*Nic. Ethics* 1:7, 1098a 5–10; Barnes 2:1735; text in Thomas's *Commentary,* trans. Litzinger, p. 52); concupiscence leads man astray to follow the baser instincts and desires of the senses. Personal justice is the goal of Dante's Earthly Paradise here and in the *Commedia.* Dante writes *"perseitas,"* an abstract noun coined by philosopher-theologians ca. 1300 (self-evidently!) from *"per se"*; it does not occur earlier, for example, even in St. Thomas Aquinas (d. 1274). Scholars have set up an unnecessarily dubious and fanciful history of disagreement on Dante's meaning at this point. Nardi, (cf. ed. *Mon.,* ad loc.), followed by Pizzica, sees *"perseitas"* as that, which taken by itself, makes life something desirable and deficient in nothing: that is, the ultimate of man's desire, bliss or happiness, the beatitude that can only be from God, the *bonum per se.* For Vinay, it is the "essence of man." P. Shaw translates it as "the intrinsic nature of man"; Richard Kay as "that which is

specifically good for man." For Saint Augustine, God, the Efficient and Final Cause, made man for himself and man's hearts shall not rest until they rest in him (*Confessions* 1:1). Dante, seeing no conflict between the earthly and spiritual goals, indeed conflates these pagan and Christian formulas in para. 7 below.

72. On love for those closest, cf. Remigio de' Girolami, *De bono communi*, ed. Matteis, pp. 33, 65.

73. The emperor has the task of giving universal laws, local princes the task of adapting them to local conditions; thus local princes and their subjects only have relations with their close neighbors, not with all men. The universal laws of the empire, however, apply to all directly. Dante is, of course, being rhetorically overingenious, intending that the difficulty of his argument will increase its sense of authority; one could, after all, in a similar manner, make the case for the pope's temporal ascendancy, as Vernani realized. In fact, Dante is in general agreement here with Remigio de' Girolami and Tolomeo da Lucca, both of whom supported local communal government under the papacy. See the following note.

74. The argument is obscure unless we take note that Dante is about to cite the *Liber de causis*, whose first proposition is that "[e]very primary cause infuses its effect more powerfully than does a universal second cause." By analogy, the emperor is the earthly source and cause of men's righteous living; not all men would be close to a secondary prince of a different subject state, yet all men, regardless of subject state, have a direct relation to the single supreme monarch. See *Mon.* 1:14:4–7.

75. This anonymous work, long attributed to Aristotle, was translated by Gerardo da Cremona by May 18, 1268. See Adriaan Pattin, "*Le Liber de causis*. Édition établie à l'aide de 90 manuscrits avec introduction et notes," *Tijdschrift voor Filosofie* 28 (1966): 90–203; Anon, *The Book of Causes*, trans. Dennis J. Brand, 2nd ed. (Milwaukee, Wis.: Marquette University Press, 1984); and St. Thomas Aquinas, *Commentary of the Book of Causes (Super librum De causis expositio)*, trans. Vincent A. Guagliardo, Charles R. Hess, and Richard C. Taylor, Thomas Aquinas in Translation (Washington, D.C.: The Catholic University of America Press, 1996), esp. p. ix, for dating. Also see Nardi, *Saggi di filosofia dantesca*, pp. 88–89; and Attilio Mellone, "*Liber de Causis*," *Enciclopedia dantesca*, 2:327–329.

76. The point is that such cryptic formulas are opaque to a reader in need of context and explanation. Though not verbatim, similar shorthand references to the triangle are found in Aristotle, such as in *Metaph.* 9:9:1051a:21–34 (Barnes, 2:1660). See S. Thomæ Aquinatis, *In Metaph. Exp.*, ed. Cathala and Spiazzi, Lectio X, 1889–1890, pp. 354–354; and "*De fallaciis*," in Peter of Spain, *Summulæ logicales*, Tractatus VII, 109, 111 (ed. de Rijk, pp. 150–151). See also Kay, ed. *Mon.*, pp. 64–65.

77. On freedom of the will, cf. one of Dante's favorite authors, Richard of St. Victor, *De statu interioris hominis post lapsum* 1:3 and 14 (*PL* 196:1118–1119 and 1126–1127), and *De eruditione hominis interioris* 1:30 (*PL* 196:1280–1282).

78. *as I already said in the Paradiso of the Comedy: "sicut in Paradiso Comedie iam dixi."* As we not-

ed above, this phrase appears in all manuscripts of the *Mon.*, and is not an alien, scribal interpolation. It is not printed in the *editio princeps* (although a blank space is left in the text, perhaps for hand-transcription by the reader) because the publisher, G. B. Pasquali, based the authorship, either by ruse (to escape the *Index librorum prohibitorum*), or by simple error, on the falsehood that the *Mon.* had been written by a philosopher friend and contemporary of Angelo Poliziano. The passage thereafter closely follows Beatrice's words in *Par.* 5:19–24: "*Lo maggior don che Dio per sua larghezza / fesse creando, e a la sua bontate / più conformato, e quel ch'e' più apprezza, / fu de la volontà la libertate; / di che le creature intelligenti / e tutte e sole, fuoro e son dotate*" (The greatest gift that God in His bounty bestowed in creating, and the most conformed to His own goodness and that which He most prizes, was the freedom of the will, with which the creatures that have intelligence, they all, and they alone, were and are endowed). See also Francesco Mazzoni, "Teoresi e prassi in Dante Politico," in *Monarchia, Epistole politiche*, con un saggio introduttivo di Francesco Mazzoni (Turin: Edizioni RAI Radiotelevisione Italiana, 1966), pp. lx–lxi. Most important, Dante here begins to voice the doctrine of a twofold beatitude of man, advancing on that suggested by St. Thomas Aquinas concerning the "beatitude of this life"; see *Mon.* 3:16:7 ff., and Chapter 3, pp. 104–6.

79. *"happy as gods":* Dante self-consciously adopts the term "gods," meaning "the blessed," from the Psalms and St. Thomas Aquinas; in *ST* I, q. 13, a. 9, Aquinas explains how such a term as "god" can be "communicated," or fittingly used "by way of similitude, so that those are called gods who share in divinity by likeness, according to the text, 'I have said, You are gods [*ego dixi dii estis*]' [Ps 81:6]." In *Par.* 5:123, Beatrice convinces the Wayfarer to speak and trust in the blessed "as gods," "*come a dii.*" Dante knows that the initial whiff of paganism will force the reader into speculation about the term's Christian context; here, as usual, he forces the reader to pause and interpret. Cf. his use of "*divus Augustus,*" below (*Mon.* 1:16:1, n. 105).

80. *"free" means "existing for its own sake and not for the sake of something else":* The text of the *Metaph.* states: "For just as we call a man free who exists for himself and not for another, so we pursue this [Metaphysics] the only free science, for it alone exists for itself" (*Metaph.* 1.2:982b:25–29; Barnes, 2: 1554–1555). Dante cites the Moerbeke translation verbatim; see S. Thomæ Aquinatis, *In Metaph. Exp.*, ed. Cathala and Spiazzi, pp. 17–18. Although he does not always demonstrate a firsthand acquaintance with Aristotle's *Pol.*, the poet had a rote knowledge of both the *Metaph.* and the *Nic. Ethics.*

81. St. Thomas Aquinas expressed the same commonplace preference for monarchy: "Just government is more beneficial in so far as it proceeds from greater unity; and monarchy is better than aristocracy, which in turn is better than polity" (*De regimine principum* 2. 3. 23; *On Princely Government*, in *Selected Writings*, trans. Dawson, ed. D'Entrèves, pp. 14–15; Tolomeo da Lucca, *On the Government of Rulers* 1:4:2, trans. Blythe, p. 67). Notably, Dante does not specify what forms of government he would favor *under* the world monarchy in the various realms and provinces subordinate to it, although he does affirm region-

al differences (*Mon.* 1:14:6). Tolomeo da Lucca absorbed St. Thomas Aquinas's first books of the *De regimine* verbatim into his own *De regimine*, but the prior of Santa Maria Novella preferred the local system of the communes, which he names *"politia"* (polity), after Aristotle, and which we can understand as a benevolent republic where the commune's welfare is the prime objective. As for world monarchy, however, Tolomeo ardently believed that the pope was the absolute monarch, "the fount of law and, ultimately, the master of the world" (Davis, "Ptolemy of Lucca," p. 49), although he certainly did not see the pope's power as equal to Christ's (*De regimine principum* 3:10; *On the Government of Rulers*, trans. Blythe, p. 177). Remigio Girolami was inconsistent, for early in his career he did not see the pope as a universal monarch directly governing spiritual and temporal affairs; and while he believed "secular power was derived from the ecclesiastical," he denied that Christ had bequeathed all his temporal power to his vicar, St. Peter, as the decretalists insisted: "[T]he pope cannot be said to be simply the vicar of Christ, in as much as he does not have the whole of Christ's dominion" (*Contra falsos professores ecclesie*, ed. Tamburini, p. 66). See also Davis's generalizations on Remigio, unfortunately without references to specific texts, in "Ptolemy of Lucca," p. 45. Antonio Sarubbi, *Chiesa e stato comunale nel pensiero di Remigio de' Girolami*, Nobiltà dello Spirito 18 (Naples: Morano, 1971), gives a useful summary. Later in his public sermons Remigio, reflecting increasing Guelph bias in Florence, expressed firm support of the papal universal monarchy. On the six modes of government, Dante's follower Bartolo da Sassoferrato cites and refutes Giles of Rome in his papalist treatise *Tractatus de regimine civitatis*, concluding, *"Monarchia vero, seu unius regis regimen, est optimum"* (Indeed, monarchy, that is the government of one king, is the best). See the full text in Diego Quaglioni, "Per una edizione critica e un commento moderno del *Tractatus de regimine civitatis* di Bartolo da Sassoferrato," *Il pensiero politico: Rivista di Storia, delle Idee Politiche e Sociali* 9, no. 1 (1976): 70–93, esp. pp. 74–78, 80.

82. *set the policy: "politizant."* Nardi (ed., ad loc.) argues for a neutral meaning of the verb, suggesting the addition of a *"bene"* or *"recte"* to the text to make "set policy well" (see also *Nel mondo di Dante*, pp. 104–106). The verb, *"politizo,"* apparently coined by William of Moerbeke for his translation of Aristotle's *Pol.*, means "to rule or govern in the public interest." It is possible that Dante discovered the neologism from a reading of Moerbeke's version, but many scholars, such as Alan H. Gilbert's and Lorenzo Mineo-Paluello, believe that the poet had no firsthand knowledge of the *Pol.* (Gilbert, "Had Dante Read the *Politics* of Aristotle?," *PMLA* 43 [1928]: 602–613; Mineo-Paluello, "Remigio Girolami's *De bono communi*: Florence at the Time of Dante's Banishment and the Philosopher's Answer to the Crisis," *Italian Studies* 11 [1956]: 56–71). While I believe that we cannot completely discount a desultory, quondam consultation of the *Pol.* by the poet (would he have been so often duplicitous in his citations?), St. Thomas Aquinas and probably Remigio were Dante's true source for the usage.

83. *in a perverted form of government a good man is a bad citizen; in a righteous form, however, "a good man" and "a good citizen" are interchangeable terms:* This is not a direct quotation from Aristotle;

cf., however, the philosopher's views on tyrants and oligarchies in *Pol.* 3:4–5:1276b:6–1278b:5 (Barnes, 2: 2025–2029). St. Thomas Aquinas, like Dante, preferring the government of one just monarch over that of many or few under any form, interpreted Aristotle's censure of tyrants in just this way in the *De regimine* 1:3:26: "Such [tyrannical] oppression does not weigh merely upon the material good of the subjects, but their spiritual welfare is also impeded. . . . Few virtuous men are found under tyrants" (*Aquinas: Selected Political Writings*, ed. and trans. J. G. Dawson, ed. A. P. D'Entrèves, p. 161–19; see the version in Tolomeo da Lucca, *On the Government of Rulers* 1:4:6, trans. Blythe, p. 69).

84. *a form of government is not set up for the sake of laws but rather the laws for the sake of government:* Again, this is not a direct quotation. In *Pol.* 4:1:1289a:13–15, Aristotle wrote: "The laws are and ought to be framed with a view to the constitution, not the constitution to the laws" (Barnes, 2: 2046; ed. and trans. H. Rackham, LCL, pp. 280–281; see *Mon.*, ed. Ricci, ad loc.). Vinay in his edition (ad loc.) noted that the concept of the ruler as servant for the public weal had become a Scholastic topos.

85. *can be:* Vinay, followed by Kay (eds., ad loc.), notes the significance of the repetition "can be" (*potest*), stressing the *potential* perfection in execution of the monarchy. Dante throughout his argument is mindful of the difference between the ideal fulfilling of an office and the limited capacities of the incumbent (a principle of both canon and civil law). Vernani will sunder Dante's impossible ideal from the reality of human failing. He will argue that since only Christ could be virtuous enough for the monarchy of this world, ergo, the pope, his vicar, must be the true monarch. See below, *Ref* . 1:62–64. Vernani, of course, carefully omits any consideration that the pope also is a human incumbent and not the ideal.

86. Dante here, as in *Conv.* 3:14:2–6, cites the Scholastic commonplace: "When [natural agents'] power descends into objects passive to their influence, they draw those objects into similarity with themselves to the greatest extent of which they are capable" (trans. Ryan, pp. 112–113). Cf. ed. Vasoli, and ed. Kay, *Mon.*, ad loc.

87. Cf. Aristotle *Metaph.* 12:7:1072a:38–1072b:30 (trans. H. Tredennick, pp. 144–151; cf. Barnes, 2: 694–1695); cf. St. Thomas Aquinas, *In Metaph. Exp.*, ed. Cathala and Spiazzi, p. 593; and, on the influence, power, and joy of virtue, see *Nic. Ethics* 10:7; and St. Thomas Aquinas's *Commentary on the Nic. Ethics*, trans. Litzinger, 2:859–861. Vinay (*Mon.*, ed., ad loc.) followed by Kay, cites St. Thomas Aquinas, *ST* I-II, q. 31, a. 1.

88. "The actually existent is always generated from the potentially existent by something which is actually existent" (*Metaph.* 9:8:1049b:24–26; trans. Tredennick, LCL, pp. 456–457; cf. Barnes, 2:1658). See St. Thomas Aquinas, *In Metaph. Exp.*, ed. Cathala and Spiazzi, p. 443. Cf. *Mon.*, ed. Nardi, p. 350; *Mon.*, ed. Kay, pp. 71–72. Dante applies the concept to the Church in *Mon.* 3:14:6: "There is nothing that can give what it does not have."

89. Gn 27:1–45. Dante is obviously enjoying the chiasm of the double reversal in this passage.

90. Aristotle, *Nic. Ethics* 10:1:1172a:34–35 (Barnes, 2:1853). See the text in St. Thomas

Aquinas's *Commentary on the Nic. Ethics*, trans. Litzinger, 2:860, 862. Dante will repeat this in *Mon.* 2:10:6.

91. Ps 49[50]:16.

92. Dante is not citing his source firsthand; in the *De propriorum animi cuiuslibet affectuum dignotione et curatione* 10, Galen says that untrained minds grasp twice as much in a given time (ed. Wilko De Boer, Corpus Medicorum Græcorum, vol. 5, no. 4, pt. 1, sect. 1 [Leipzig and Berlin: Teubner, 1937], p. 37); the text was identified by Witte, ed. *Mon.* ad loc., and see also the editions of Nardi and Kay, ad loc. John of Salisbury cites a variant of the topos in the *Metalogicon* 2:8, citing it from Quintilian's *Institutio oratoria* 2:3: 3–4; see *The Metalogicon*, trans. D. D. McGarry, pp. 87–88.

93. Ps 71:2.

94. St. Thomas Aquinas emphasizes the same necessity of the singleness of the ruler throughout his *On the Government of Rulers* 2.2: "That which is itself a unity can more easily produce unity than that which is a plurality . . . government by one person is more likely to be successful than government by many. . . . So it is better for one to rule rather than many who must first reach agreement" (see *Selected Political Writings*, trans. Dawson, ed. D'Entrèves, pp. 10–11; cf. Tolomeo da Lucca, *On the Government of Rulers* 1:3:1–5, trans. Blythe, pp. 65–67).

95. *epyikia:* See *Nic. Ethics* 5:10:1137a:31–1138a:2 (Barnes, 2:1794). Dante does not use the Latin translation *æquitas* but prefers this more impressive transliteration from the Greek ἐπιείκεια. There was no systematic method for transliteration. The Grosseteste-Moerbeke text used in St. Thomas Aquinas's *Commentary on the Nic. Ethics* transliterates it as *epiichia* and *epiyichia;* Dante follows Aquinas; see trans. Litzinger, 1:464–466. The word signifies "equity," "the equitable thing," i.e., acting equitably according to fairness, decency, and seemliness in actions toward others; it is a species of justice whether dictated by legislation or without it. Cf. Dante's other transliterated Greek terms, *eubulia*, 2:5:23; *gignasium*, 3:1:3; *palestra*, 3:1:4; [*h*]*agiographos*, 3:16:9.

96. Dante had learned of the Scythians of the Caucusus from St. Albertus Magnus, who says they live in the seventh clime, in the northern quarter of the northern hemisphere. See Albertus Magnus, *De natura loci* 1:9, 3:3, ed. Paul Hossfeld, pp. 15–17, 37. Also see Fernando Salsano, "Sciti," *Enciclopedia dantesca*, 5:81; and Giovanni Buti and Renzo Bertagni, "Clima," *Enciclopedia dantesca*, 2:43.

97. *the Garamanths of Africa:* In *Conv.* 3:5:12, Dante situates the Garamanths in the first, hottest climate; Lucan places the "naked Garamanths . . . beneath the sign of Cancer," rather than at the equator (*Phars.* 4:333–334, 679; 9:369, 460, 512). See Albertus Magnus, *De natura loci* 3:8, ed. Paul Hossfeld, in *Opera omnia*, vol. 5, pt. 2 (Monasterii Westfalorum in Ædibus Aschendorff, 1980), pp. 42–43; and Clara Kraus, "*Garamanthi,*" in *Enciclopedia dantesca*, 3:96.

98. *priority:* In the *Categories*, Aristotle uses the whole twelfth chapter to define five meanings of the word "prior"; the last use (*Categories* 14b:11–13; Barnes, 1:22), concerning

existence, is applied to "those things, the being of each of which implies that of the other; that which is in any way the cause may reasonably be said to be by nature 'prior' to the effect." See Peter of Spain's synopsis of the five meanings in "De prius," *Summulæ logicales*, Tractatus III, 3:30, ed. de Rijk, p. 40. Dante cites the concept in the *Conv.* 3:2:7: "The primary category is being, and prior to that there is simply nothing."

99. *the best is that which is "one" to the greatest degree, as it pleases the Philosopher to put it in* On Being Simply: *On Being Simply* and *First Philosophy* are Dante's titles for Aristotle's *Metaphysics*. The concept is solidly Aristotelian, but Dante's exact reference has not been identified; Ricci suggests *Metaph.* 5:16:1021b:30 (see trans. in Tredennick, LCL, pp. 266–269).

100. *Pythagoras in his correlations placed "the one" on the side of good, and plurality on the side of evil:* In *Metaph.* 1:5:985b:24–25, and 986a:24–30, as well as in other passages, Aristotle actually speaks not of Pythagoras himself but of "the so-called Pythagoreans" who reduce all to ten pairs of contraries (Barnes, 2:1559; trans. Tredennick, LCL, pp. 30–34, the ten contraries, p. 35). On being and unity, see *Metaph.* 10:2:1053b:20–28, 1054a:9–13. See also St. Thomas Aquinas, *In Metaph. Exp,.* ed. Cathala and Spiazzi, pp. 37–39. On "*Plurality,*" P. Shaw, ed., ad loc., reads "*plura,*" while Kay, ed., ad loc., reads "*plurale.*"

101. Ps 4:8[7].

102. For Aristotle, each element seeks to return to its natural place: water and earth fall toward the center, air rises, and fire seeks the circle of fire just beneath the orbit of the moon; see *De cælo* 4:1–4:307b:28–312a:21; *On the Heavens*, Barnes, 1:502–50. Dante states much the same in *Conv.* 3:3:2–6, and uses the concept in *Quæstio de acqua e terra* 16:34, *Purg.* 18:28–30, and *Par.* 1:115–117.8:28.

103. *the power of willing is a certain potentiality . . . this form . . . becomes multiple:* In Scholastic epistemology, all knowledge must come through sense perception, with the senses taking from an object an image *(intentio)*; the appetite then turns toward it in pleasure *(love)* or away in aversion *(fear, anger, pride)*. The intellect, once informed by the appearance, form, or shape *(species)* of the thing, forms within itself an "intention" of the thing understood; the deliberative faculty of the will is only a potentiality; in order to be actualized, the will must have this "intention" as a goal to choose and fix on (i.e., for the will to "*intend*" it). Cf. St. Thomas Aquinas, *Summa contra gentiles* 1:53; *Purg.*, 18:19–45; and Singleton's notes in *Purg.: 2. Commentary*, pp. 411–423. The object perceived, though single, becomes multiplied in the number of men's minds perceiving it, with each forming its own "intention."

104. Aristotle, of course, makes no such mention of a universal ruler who is "master and guide of all the others," and is somewhat uncertain that virtue can actually be exhorted by precept or extorted by fear and laws. Dante is extrapolating from certain passages from the last book of the *Nic. Ethics* to make them conform to his own theories. After stating that virtue cannot be taught, since the power to follow it "is not contained in any paternal precept nor in anyone who is not a ruler or person in authority," Aristotle, however, continues with the statement that "public laws and customs have the same place in the state as paternal precepts have in families." For the philosopher, tutelage is best if person-

alized, but he adds that "a thing will be done with the greatest care if a doctor or trainer ... knows *in a universal way what is common to all men* or to a particular class" (*Nic. Ethics* 10:9:1179b:32–1180a 5; Barnes, 2:1864; see also the version in St. Thomas Aquinas's *Commentary on the Nic. Ethics*, trans. Litzinger, 2:926–935; my emphasis). Dante's thinking here is most influenced by the analogy of the monarch's power-over-the-state to the soul-over-the-body; in *Conv.* 4:9:10, he writes, "One may describe the emperor in figurative language as rider of the human will" (trans. Ryan, p. 144). The popular topos concerning kingship, e.g., appears in St. Thomas Aquinas's *De regimine principum* 1:12 (in *Aquinas: Selected Political Writings*, trans. Dawson, ed. d'Entrèves, pp. 66–67); it is transcribed by Tolomeo da Lucca in *On the Government of Rulers* 1:14, trans. Blythe, pp. 95–97.

105. *Divus Augustus:* Dante adopts the term *"divus"* (see n. 79, above) both humanistically and as a Christian; the term stresses for him the reflected image and will of the one God (cf. *Mon.* 2:6:4: "the universal form of divine likeness") just as Lactantius expresses it in the *Divine Institutes;* the pagan term emphasizes that God had ordained Augustus's rule as the age of the *pax romana,* Pauline "fullness," and Sapientia's "quiet silence" (Wisdom 18:14). See pp. 27, 58, 65, above, and note 107, below.

106. *all illustrious poets and even the scribe of Christ's compassion:* The scribe is Luke (2:1, 14), here meekly placed as if on par with the pagan poets, especially Vergil (who, Dante as an erudite man of his time believed, or feigned in his poetry to believe) sang of the return of the Golden Age and the coming of Christ in his *Eclogue* 4, but then ignored his own prophecy; see n. 57, above, and n. 108, below. Cf. the touching meeting of Statius and Virgilio in *Purg.* 21–22, where Luke is named as recorder of Christ (21:7 ff.). As Statius there makes clear (22:70ff.) in citing the *Eclogue,* Virgilio is indeed a *vates,* a seer and prophet, predicting what "the messengers of the eternal kingdom" had heralded. *Purg.* 22 ends as a voice from the Tree in the circle of gluttony compares the first Age of Gold with St. John the Baptist's humble frugality. The "teste David cum Sibylla" of the *Dies iræ* bore witness to the traditional consonance of Christian and pagan revelation later illustrated most famously in Michelangelo's frescoed ceiling of the Sistine Chapel.

107. Dissenting voices had already been heard among the defenders of the French monarchy who argued that France had never been under the domination of the emperor historically after Charlemagne had divided his realm equally among his sons. Cf. also John of Paris's contentions—diametrically opposed by Dante—that *"it is better that many should rule in many kingdoms* than one alone should rule the whole world. This is made clear from the fact that *the world was never as peaceful in the time of the emperors* as it was beforehand and afterwards" (*On Royal and Papal Power,* ch. 21, trans. Watt, p. 227, my emphases). Dante argues, without mentioning particular adversaries—here notably against John of Paris with whom he was in general agreement on so many points—but also against the whole tradition that followed Augustine and his *The City of God.*

108. Extrapolating from St. Paul in Gal. 4:4, the idea of "tranquillity throughout the world" under a Roman emperor became commonplace. P. Shaw (ed. *Mon.,* ad loc.) notes

the influence of Paulus Orosius's view in which the first monarch, Augustus, brought peace for the birth of Christ. Such expressions were legion. E.g., Otto of Friesing believed that Rome had been given sovereignty over the world and that the earth had been given a new peace through that city so that the work of the Apostles might be made easier; see Tillmann, *Pope Innocent III*, p. 322. The Franciscans were particularly celebrative of Christ's coming in the "quiet silence" (Wis 18:14) of the reign of Augustus; Dante may have been moved more directly by current Franciscan views such as those of St. Bonaventure in the *Arbor vitæ* 1: 3–4 as he contemplates Gal 4:4: "Under the reign of Cæsar Augustus, the *quiet silence* . . . of universal peace had brought such calm to an age which had previously been sorely distressed that through his decree a census of the whole world could be taken" (*Tree of Life*, in *Bonaventure*, trans. Ewert Cousins [New York: Paulist Press, 1978], pp. 127–8, my emphasis). See, below, *Mon.* 2:10:6; and *Epistle to Henry VII*, April 7, 1311, ed. and trans. Toynbee, pp. 92–3, 102.

109. *seamless garment:* cf. Jn 19:23. For Dante, the Donation of Constantine had rent the unity of the empire symbolized by Christ's seamless garment; he uses the image purposely to correct its application to the Church's unity in the bull *Unam sanctam* (see *CIC*, 2:1245; *Church and State through the Centuries*, ed. Ehler and Morrall, p. 91). See also P. de Lapparent, "L'oeuvre politique de François de Meyronnes et ses rapports avec celle de Dante," *Archives d'histoire doctrinale et littéraire du Moyen Age* 15–17 (1940–1942): 126–151.

110. Dante is correcting the hierocrats' "monster with two heads" image used by the drafter of the bull *Unam sanctam*. The image recalls the dragon with seven crowned heads in Rv 12:3 and 17:9; Kay (ed., ad loc.) points to the image of the people of Rome as a wild beast with "many heads" in Horace's *Epistula* 1:1:76, and "one hundred heads" in *Carmina* 2:13:34; Dante employs it as the hydra-that-must-be-decapitated in his *Epistola* 7:6:21, addressed to the Italian cities that opposed Henry VII (ed. Brugnoli, in *Opere minori*, 2:568–569).

111. *"both intellects":* I.e., both the "higher intellect," the speculative (theoretical or contemplative) intellect as it seeks knowledge for the sake of knowledge, and the "lower intellect," the active (operative or practical) intelligence or reason, used in functioning, acting, or doing, which puts its knowledge to use. Such terms for the "parts" of the intellect are purely heuristic and not ontological in Christian philosophy, for although in order to teach Scholastics distinguished the intellect as "part" of the soul, the intellect, like the soul, is one theologically. Christian thinkers, especially after the condemnations of Aristotelianism by Bishop Etienne Tempier in Paris in 1270, and on March 7, 1277, thus accommodated and altered Avicenna's (980–1037) heretical position, adapted by Averroës, in which there was but one *"intellectus agens,"* or active intellect, each individual possessed his own mortal *"intellectus possibilis,"* or passive intellect, wherewith to have his own thoughts; in Christianity each eternal individual soul possessed both functions, but all men bare the "wounding of nature," the hindering wounds of concupiscence and ignorance, from the Fall. We note, especially, that Vernani, having the same understanding, makes no quibble

here. Politics concerns the functioning of the civil multitude, of public or civic virtue in *using right reason* in acting equitably for the good (cf. *Mon.* 1:3:9, 1:14:7). See n. 21, above.

112. Ps 132 [133]:1.

113. Ps 2:1–3.

114. Dante had already expressed his new attitude in the *Conv.* 4:4:8–12; sometime earlier, obviously, he had agreed with St. Augustine who had seen the Roman Empire as unjust. The change of mind marks Dante's conversion to the positive view of the state that he had learned from studying Aristotle and the Aristotelians in the 1290s. It is noteworthy in the following paragraphs how Dante speaks of the ancient Roman Empire ideally in the *present tense*; he hopes that, as it was in the fullness of time in the era of the *Pax Romana* of Divus Augustus at Christ's birth, so it shall be again in some future period under a just world monarch. See Maria Consiglia De Matteis, "Il mito dell'impero romano in Dante: a proposito di *Monarchia* II, i," *Letture classensi* 9–10 (1982): 347–356; and Vasoli, "Filosofia e politica in Dante tra *Convivio* e *Monarchia*," *Letture classensi* 9–10 (1982):11–37. Bartolo da Sassoferrato reiterated Dante's ideas of the universal peace of the empire *"sotto il buon Augusto."* See Crosara, "Dante e Bartolo da Sassoferrato," p. 140.

115. Ps 2:3.

116. Cf. *Mon.* 2:2:3 below, and *Inf.* 11:99–100, *"natura lo suo corso prende / dal divino intelletto e da sua arte"* (Nature takes her course from divine intellect and from its art). Nardi (ed., ad loc.) sees the passage as a precise reference to Aristotle's *De cælo*, while Ricci views it as generic. I agree with Ricci: Dante is pursuing the metaphors of his *"natura naturans—natura naturata"* concept begun in *Mon.* 1:1:1. See also P. Shaw, "Sul testo," pp. 200–201.

117. *right: "ius."* The Latin term means "right" or "law"; Dante uses it here in the sense of "prerogative," and elsewhere in the general sense of "jurisprudence" (as in the French *"droit"*). The word implies something different from *"lex,"* which signifies a particular ordinance or single law, or a body of laws. See Fiorelli, "Sul senso del diritto nella *Monarchia*," pp. 79–97.

118. *"whatever was made in Him was life": "quod facta est in ipso vita erat"* (Vulgate, Jn 1:3–4). The A.V. reads: "All things were made through him, and without him was not anything made that was made. In him was life. . . ." Dante cites from the Vulgate in conflating verses 3 and 4.

119. Cf. *Inf.* 3:95.

120. Aristotle, *Nic. Ethics* 1:3:1094b:23–25, and 1:7:1098a:25–28 (Barnes, 2:1730, 1735–1736). Aristotle insisted that an educated man understood that the amount of certainty or exactness in a proof, and the end and the good derived from it, depended upon the discipline or subject involved.

121. *examine . . . through manifest signs and the authority of sages:* The arguments from "authorities" here are from poets and historians who, through their judgment (*a rei iudicio*) from events in history, saw and recorded such "manifest signs" of the will of God. Dante is appealing to Augustine's concept of "the truth of valid inference" (*veritas conexionum*) from events put into history by God: "The truth of valid inference was not instituted by men;

rather it was observed by men and set down that they might learn and teach. For it is perpetually instituted by God in the reasonable order of things. Thus the person who narrates the order of events in time does not compose that order himself" (*De doctrina christiana* 2:32 [50]; *On Christian Doctrine*, trans. Robertson, p. 68). In Scholastic logic, syllogisms based on premises that were merely probable could only yield probable conclusions. See "De loco ab auctoritate," in Peter of Spain, *Summulæ logicales*, Tractatus V, 36, ed. de Rijk, pp. 75–76, where Peter of Spain cites the maxim "Every expert is to be believed in his field of knowledge." See also *Mon.*, ed. Imbach and Flüeler (1989), p. 293; and ed. Kay, ad loc.

122. Rom 1:20.

123. Aristotle, *Pol.* 4:8:1294a:21–22 (Barnes, 2: 2054). For Dante's early views, see *Conv.* 4:3:6–7, 4:3:14–15, 4:20–21; *Vita nuova* 20 (ed. Contini, *Poeti del Duecento*, pp. 460–64). Moerbeke's translation of *Pol.* 4:8:1294a:20 reads: *"Ingenuitas enim est virtus et divitiæ antiquæ"* (Being well-born is virtue and ancient riches) (*In libros Politicorum Aristotelis expositio*, ed. Spiazzi, *Lectio* VII, *Textus Arist.* 470, pp. 211, n. 612, p. 213). Here in the *Mon.* Dante follows not the text of the *Pol.* (once again he gives no book number reference for it), but the commentary of St. Thomas Aquinas in *In libros Politicorum Aristotelis expositio* (ed. Spiazzi, Lectio VII, no 612, p. 213): "Nobility is a type of virtue, that is, an inclination to virtue descending from parents to children, and to parents from others who came before, and thus in a way to antiquity." Kay (ed., ad loc.) notes that Dante adopts Aquinas's term *"nobilitas"* instead of Moerbeke's *"ingenuitas."* See Busnelli-Vandelli's and Vasoli's extensive notes to *Conv.* 4:3:14–15, Nardi's commentary to the *Mon.* (ad loc.), and Davis's *Dante's Italy*, pp. 180–186, esp. p. 183, n. 76.

124. *"Nobility of mind is the one and only virtue."* *"Nobilitas animi sola est atque unica virtus."* Dante seems to be citing Juvenal's *Satire* 8:20 from memory, adding the word *"animi"* (of mind) that he had found in the twelfth-century *Moralium dogma philosophorum* compiled by William of Conches (or, perhaps, Walter of Châtillon); see the edition of the *Moralium* by John Holmberg (Uppsala: Holmquist & Wiksells; Paris: H. Champion, 1929), p. 54; see also the ed. in Migne, *PL* 171:1073. Dante cites Juvenal's satire on ancestral pride in *Conv.* 4:29:4; there Dante closely follows Brunetto Latini, *Tresor* 2:114, where Brunetto also cites the *Moralium* as he affirms the idea of virtue's constituting nobility (see *Li livres dou Tresor* 2: 114, ed. F. Carmody [Berkeley/Los Angeles: University of California Press, 1948]); however, Brunetto attributes the "virtue alone" thesis to Horace instead of Juvenal (see Davis, *Dante's Italy*, pp. 180–181).

125. *these differing opinions:* Kay and P. Shaw read *"que due sententie,"* "these two opinions." André Pézard noted the abbreviation notation of a tilde above the "u"—or the "v"—in some manuscripts, and read *"dũe"* as *"que diverse sententie,"* "these *differing* opinions," at this point (*"Monarchia* II iii 4.—*Nobilitas animi sola . . . ,"* in *La Rotta gonna*, 3:258–260). Dante's opinion here does, indeed, *differ* from his earlier anti-Aristotelian position denying inherited nobility.

126. Mt 7:2.

127. *the minor premise:* i.e., that the Roman people were the most noble.

128. Livy, *Ab urbe condita* 1:1:2; all references are to *Livy with an English Translation in Thirteen [Fourteen] Volumes*, trans. B. O. Foster, Frank Gardner Moore, et al., LCL (London: Heinemann; New York: Putnam, 1919–1967). Some scholars doubt whether Dante knew Livy's text firsthand. See A. Martina, "Livio," *Enciclopedia dantesca*, 3:673–677.

129. *Æn.* 1:342: Vergil: *"sed summa sequar* fastigia *rerum"* (but I shall trace the *high points* of the story). Dante, perhaps in the wake of his reading of St. Bonaventure, corrects Vergil, giving his line a Bonaventuran-Christian bent by changing *"fastigia"* to *"vestigia"* ("footprints," "imprints," "traces"). Cf. above, *Mon.* 1:9:1: "Every son is at his most excellent and best when, insofar as his own nature may permit, he *traces the footprints* of a perfect father." As we will see, Vernani purposefully "misses" the delicateness of the poet's central point: the isomorphic relation of the human family with God's unity.

130. *Æn.* 1:544–545. All translations are cited from *Virgil with an English Translation . . . in Two Volumes*, trans. H. Rushton Fairclough, LCL (Cambridge Mass: Harvard University Press; London: William Heinemann, 1967).

131. *Æn.* 6:170.

132. Aristotle, *Nic. Ethics* 7:1:1145a:20–1146b:5 (Barnes, 2:1808–1809). The whole of the seventh book of the *Nic. Ethics* deals with the triple concept of the wrongful actions "vice, incontinence and brutishness," which Dante reinterprets in *Inf.* 11:79–83 as *"le tre disposizion che 'l ciel non vuole, / incontinenza, malizia e la matta / bestialitade"* (the three dispositions, which heaven rejects, incontinence, malice and mad bestiality). Although keeping close to St. Thomas Aquinas's commentary, Dante modified and rearranged the Aritotelian order for the plan of his first canticle of the *Divina Commedia*, correcting Aristotle and following Cicero in holding that *fraus* (fraud), "the sin peculiar to man," was a worse evil than *vis* (force, violence). See Cicero, *De officiis* 1:13; *De Officiis* [*On Duties*], trans. Walter Miller, in *Cicero*, vol. 21, LCL [Cambridge, Mass.: Harvard University Press, 1913; rpt 1997], here pp. 44–45). See St. Thomas Aquinas, *Commentary on the Nic. Ethics*, trans. Litzinger, 2:607), for a translation of Moerbeke's Latin text known to Dante. Whether Dante intended the phrase "mad brutishness" to be the sin of violence or to be the worse sin of treachery, punished in deepest Hell, is still a subject of great debate among Dante scholars.

133. *Æn.* 3:1.

134. *Æn.* 8:134–137.

135. *seer: "vates."* Vergil, mostly because of his *Eclogue* 4, was considered not only a poet but a pagan prophet of Christ. See Comparetti, *Virgil in the Middle Ages*, esp. pp. 96–103.

136. *Æn.* 3:163–167.

137. The legendary Fortunate Isles of the Western Ocean are identified today as the Canaries. Paulus Orosius, *The Seven Books of History against the Pagans* 1:2, reads: "The boundaries of Africa toward the west are the same as those of Europe. . . . The farthest boundaries are the Atlas Range and the islands which people call Fortunatæ" (trans. Roy J. Deferrari [Washington, D.C.: The Catholic University of America Press, 1964), p. 8).

138. *Æn.* 3:339–340.

139. *Æn.* 4:171–172.

140. *Æn.* 12:936–937.

141. *double: "duplici"* is attested by the MSS; i.e., the nobility flowing (1) from his wives and (2) from his ancestors. I agree with Ricci, P. Shaw, and Kay in rejecting Rostagno's emendation to *"triplici."*

142. St. Thomas Aquinas, *Summa contra gentiles* 3:101.

143. God alone works miracles. See Ps 135:4; cf. St. Thomas Aquinas, *Summa contra gentiles* 3:102.

144. *gnats: "sciniphes."* See Ex 8:16–19. From Hebrew, *"cinnin."* The Vulgate and the Douay-Reims read *"ciniphs."* The A.V. reads "lice," the R.S.V. "gnats."

145. *as Livy attests in the first part of his book:* Actually, Livy, in *Ab urbe condita* 1:20:4, only mentions Numa's gift of these shields to the Salian priests without saying that the original one had fallen from heaven; but in the fifth book, 54:7, he clarifies it somewhat, "the Capitol . . . [w]here the shields . . . were sent down from heaven." Cf. Ovid, *Fasti* 3:259–398; Vergil, *Æn.* 8:663–665; *Mon.*, ed Nardi, p. 384; *Mon.*, ed. Kay, ad loc.

146. *Pharsalia* 9:477–480; all translations of the *Pharsalia* are cited or adapted from *Lucan with an English Translation*, trans. J. D. Duff, LCL (Cambridge, Mass.: Harvard University Press; London: William Heinemann, 1977).

147. *writers agree in testifying that a goose . . . cackled:* On the contrary, writers disagree amusingly. Livy is at variance with Dante's text, for the Roman historian has a flock of geese (*Ab urbe condita* 5:47:4), while the poet Vergil records but one goose, as Dante records in *Conv.* 4:5:18 and here. But the poet knew that St. Augustine, first, in *The City of God* 2:22, had the invading Gauls thwarted by *geese* on the Capitoline while the gods slept and left the rest of Rome to destruction; and then, in *The City of God* 3:8, has the cackle of a single goose sound the alarm. In Paulus Orosius's Christian *Against the Pagans* 2:19, the Gauls succeed in their siege in the absence of any poultry at all. Kay (*Mon.* ed., ad loc.) lists other possible sources. See Vernani, *Ref.* 2:35–38, below.

148. *Æn.* 8:652–656.

149. The tale of Hannibal and the hailstorm is found in Livy, *Ab urba condita* 26:11:1–3; and in Paulus Orosius, *Historia adversus paganos* 4:17 (*Against the Pagans*, trans. Deferrari, pp. 155–156).

150. For Cloelia, see *Ab urbe condita* 2:13:6–11; Livy says that "Cleolia's feat was greater than those of Cocles and Mucius," and that Porsenna was so impressed that he "protected the brave girl." Most important, Paulus Orosius praises Cloelia's "admirable daring in crossing the river" (*Historia adversus paganos* 2:5; *Against the Pagans*, trans Deferrari, p. 50). Vernani will see fit to scoff despite such precedents, but he was probably quite familiar with the unremarkable width of the modern Tiber when not in flood.

151. Dante is speaking of the Incarnation as developed especially by Anselm of Canterbury in his *Cur Deus homo* (*Why God Became Man*). The typical symmetrical, hysteron-

proteron, chiastic, or reverse mirror-image way of medieval formulation is clearly in evidence here. Before the unseen Creator became visible in the incarnate Christ, he worked miracles in the visible world governed by the earthly empire; when God became man in his Son, Christ, he worked miracles in the invisible order represented now by the Church.

152. This stirring formulation is the personal belief of the poet. Fiorelli notes Dante's use of this word *"realis,"* to mean "real" ("substantial," "actual," "an actual thing"), a neologism (apparently one seldom attested before Galileo) deriving from *"re,"* "thing" (as opposed to *"realis"* in the sense of "regal," "royal," deriving from *"rex"*); see Fiorelli's "Sul senso del diritto nella *Monarchia,"* pp. 84–86.

153. Justinian, *Digest or Pandects: De iustitia et iure (Of Justice and Law)* 1:1: "A law student at the outset of his studies ought first to know the derivation of the word *jus*. Its derivation is from *justitia*. For . . . the law is the art of goodness and fairness. . . . we cultivate the virtue of justice and claim awareness of what is good and fair, discriminating between fair and unfair, distinguishing lawful from unlawful, aiming to make men good not only through fear of penalties but also indeed under allurement of rewards, and affecting a philosophy which . . . is genuine, not a sham" (Latin and English text in *The Digest of Justinian*, ed. Theodore Mommsen and Paul Kreuger, trans. Alan Watson [Philadephia: University of Pennsylvania Press, 1985], vol. 1, pp. 1ʳ–1ᵛ). Cf. *Conv.* 1:10:3, 4:9:1–3.

154. Cf. the praise of the common good in Remigio de' Girolami, *De bono com.*, ed. De Matteis, pp. 33, 61, 64.

155. *First Rhetoric: De inventione* 1:38:68; trans. Hubbell, LCL, *Cicero*, 2:112–113.

156. *Seneca, in . . . On the Four Virtues:* "What is justice but a silent agreement of nature invented for the aid of many? And *what is justice if not our own makeup*, and yet at the same time a divine law and the bond of human society (my emphasis)." Dante follows Isidore of Seville in this attribution of the *Formula vitæ honestæ de quatuor virtutibus (PL* 72:27) to Seneca, however, the short essay on the four cardinal virtues, most probably a summary of a lost work by Seneca, is actually by Martin of Braga who became bishop of Dumio in 556 and who penned it shortly after his accession as Metropolitan of Braga in Galitia, Spain in 570. See *Rules for an Honest Life*, trans. Claude W. Barlow, in *Martin of Braga, Paschasius of Dumium, Leander of Seville*, in *Iberian Fathers* 1, Fathers of the Church 62 (Washington, D.C.: The Catholic University of America Press, 1969), pp. 87–97, here, p. 94. For Dante, justice is man's "perseity"; see *Mon.* 1:11:14, and n. 71 above.

157. *welfare:* Dante plays on the meanings of the Latin word *"salus"* meaning, for him, not only health or well-being, but religious salvation. Dante's argument for the threefold effort of the Romans, the public good *(bonum rei publice)*, the common good of society's members *(commune sociorum bonum)*, and the welfare of all mankind *(salus humani generis)*, are nearly identical to those brought to bear by Tolomeo da Lucca in his *De regimine principum*, esp. bk. 3, chs. 5, 6, and 7 *(On the Government of Rulers*, ed. Blythe, pp. 157–166). See also Silverstein, "On the Genesis of *De Monarchia* II, 5," pp. 328–329.

158. *piety:* Dante puns on the term *"pietas"* meaning both "pity" and "piety" as he did in *Inf.* 1: 21, *"pieta,"* and in *Epistle* 5:3:7. Jacopo da Varagine uses the phrase in the *Legenda aurea*,

in recounting Emperor Constantine's refusal to obey his doctors' absurd prescription to bathe in the blood of three thousand infants to cure his leprosy. Paget Toynbee allies the concept to "pius Æneas" (*Dante Studies and Researches* [London: Methuen, 1902], pp. 297–298). Also see J. Balogh, "Romanum Imperium de Fonte nascitur pietatis," *Deutsches Dante-Jahrbuch* 10 (1928): pp 202–205; and Silverstein, "On the Genesis of *De Monarchia* II, v.," esp. p. 331.

159. *De officiis* 2:8:26–27; *De Officiis (On Duties)*, trans. Miller, pp. 194–195.

160. As we have discussed, all the following Roman examples are taken from St. Augustine's *The City of God* 5:18 and from Anchises' heroic account of Rome in the *Æn.* 6:756–853. See above, pp. 70–74.

161. On Quinctius Cincinnatus, see Livy, *Ab urbe condita* 3:26–29; St. Augustine, *The City of God* 5:18; cf. trans. Green, LCL, 2:234–235. Tolomeo da Lucca cites Cincinnatus in the *De regimine* 3: 20:1; *On the Government of Rulers*, ed. Blythe, p. 205.

162. Cicero, *De finibus* 2:4:12: cf. *De finibus bonorum et Malorum*, trans. Rackam, LCL (Cambridge, Mass.: Harvard University Press, 1914; rpt, 1994), 17:90–91.

163. *Fabricius:* Charles T. Davis says that "Augustine, plus Lucan and Seneca are . . . sufficient to account for all the elements in Dante's references to Fabricius in the *Convivio* and the *Monarchia*" ("Ptolemy of Lucca," p. 37). On Lucan's *Pharsalia*, see P. Toynbee, *A Dictionary of Proper Names and Notable Matters in the Works of Dante*, rev. Charles S. Singleton (Oxford, U.K.: Oxford University Press, 1968), p. 399. See Seneca, *Epistulæ morales*, 3 vols., ed. R. M. Gummere, LCL (London/Cambridge, Mass.: Harvard University Press, 1953), Letter 120, 6, 3; vol. 3, p. 382. But also see *Æn.* 6:843–844; Valerius Maximus, *Memorable Deeds and Sayings* (Valerii Maximi, *Factorum et dictorum memorabilium: Libri Novem*, ed. Carolus [Karl] Kempf, 2nd ed. [Stuttgart: Teubner, 1966]), 4:3:6; and Tolomeo da Lucca on Fabricius, *De regimine* 2: 8:3, 3:4:5; 3:14:4, 3:20:1, 4:15:4–5, and 4:17:3, *On the Government of Princes*, ed. Blythe, pp. 121, 156, 190, 205, 256–257, and 260–261. Fabricius also appears in Tolomeo's *Determinatio compendiosa*, ed. Krammer, p. 43.

164. *Camillus:* See Livy, *Ab urbe condita* 6:8; and *Æn.* 6:825. Tolomeo da Lucca mentions Camillus's devotion to Rome in a different context; see *De regimine* 2:10:2 (*On the Government of Rulers*, ed. Blythe, p. 126). Camillus also appears in *Conv.* 4:5:15.

165. Lucius Junius Brutus, the nephew of Tarquinius Superbus, who organized the uprising to oust the Tarquins and free Rome, became one of the first two Roman consuls; Livy recounts that he put his own two sons to death for plotting to reinstate the Tarquin kings (*Æn.* 6:820–821; Livy, *Ab urbe condita* 2:3, 2:5; St. Augustine, *The City of God* 5:18, trans. Green, LCL, 2:224–227). St. Augustine uses Brutus as an example to Christians of the extremes that pagan honor can be taken as opposed to the easy yoke of Christ, and a lesson to the foolish who might believe that they can merit eternal glory. Tolomeo da Lucca cites St. Augustine on Brutus, but draws opposing moral, in *De regimine* 3:5:5; 3:16:1; *On the Government of Rulers*, ed. Blythe, pp. 159, 193. Brutus appears also in Tolomeo's *Determinatio compendiosa*, ed. Krammer, p. 43.

166. *Mucius:* Livy recounts the legend that Gaius Mucius Scævola had failed to kill

Porsenna and had slain his secretary instead; brought before Porsenna, Mucius thrust and held his left hand into the fire "as if his spirit were unconscious of sensation." The impressionable Porsenna was moved by his fortitude and made peace (*Ab urbe condita* 2:12–13). Kay (ed., ad loc.) points to Florus's *Epitoma* 1:4:5–6 as Dante's real source; however, St. Augustine retells Livy's story quite adequately in *The City of God* 5:18 (trans. Green, LCL, pp. 2:228–229). Tolomeo cites Mucius positively as an example of military fortitude in *De regimine* 4:17:3; *On the Government of Rulers*, ed. Blythe, p. 260.

167. Dante conceives his list of illustrious heroes as a triumphal procession. His "invention" of the triumphal form (beginning at *Purg.* 29:15) was to be imitated by Boccaccio in the *Amorosa visione* and by Petrarch in the *Trionfi*.

168. *the Decii:* Three generations of Decii, each bearing the same name, had each, successively (in 343, 295, 279 B.C.), fulfilled his vow to die while killing his enemies in battle; See Livy, *Ab urbe condita* 8:9; 10:28. St. Augustine, again, uses the Decii's vainglorious bravery to urge imitation of the humble willingness of Christian martyrs (*The City of God* 5:18; trans. Green, LCL, pp. 2:230–231). Dante refers to the Decii in *Conv.* 4:5:14 and in *Par.* 6:47–48.

169. *Marcus Cato:* See n. 171.

170. *Publius Decius . . . for the republic:* Dante adapts Cicero, *De finibus* 2:19. Cf. trans. H. Rackam, LCL, pp. 17:90–91.

171. On Marcus Porcius Cato, the Younger, called Uticensis, see Cicero, *De officiis* 1:31 (*On Duties*, trans. Miller, LCL, 21:114–115). Dante mentions Cato in the same context in *Conv.*, esp. 4:5:16 (also at 3:5:12, 4:6:10, 4:27:3, and 4:28:13–19). In *Purg.* 1 and 2, Dante makes Cato the guardian of that realm of the afterlife. St. Augustine, however, had written of Cato somewhat derisively in *The City of God* 1:23–24 (also 5:12 and 19:4), stressing the pagan nature of his ethics, suicide, and worship; his negative interpretation is the basis for Vernani's rebuttal of *Mon.* 2:5. The Dominican prior of Santa Maria Novella, Tolomeo da Lucca, cites Cato's words many times in admiration in both the *Determinatio compendiosa* and the *De regimine*, and, most important, names him as a supreme example of Aristotelian fortitude in dying for the public good, culminating the list of Mucius's fiery torture, Fabricius's poverty, Rutilius's exile, Regulus's torments, and Socrates' poison (*De regimine* 4:18:3, *On the Government of Rulers*, ed. Blythe, pp. 260–261).

172. Dante here gives his explanation and use of conditional arguments (as opposed to syllogisms) that he will employ later in chapters 10 and 11 (see esp. n. 126, below). Here he refers in explanation to the classical textbook example as it appears in "De fallacia secundum consequens: De consequentia," in Peter of Spain's *Summulæ logicales*, Tractatus VII, 153, ed. de Rijk, p. 169. The logical inference derives from the fact that the condition of the consequent is already implied in the antecedent and the reasoning can only move in one direction: if X is a man, then necessarily X is an animal. The only other logical implication can be had by negation: if X is not a animal, then X is not a man, for to say either "if X is an animal, then X is a man" or "if X is not a man, then X is not an animal" is to speak an absurdity. Prudence Shaw gives a lucid explanation in "Some Proposed Emenda-

tions to the Text of Dante's *Monarchia*," *Italian Studies* 50 (1995): 1–8; also see Mozzillo-Howell's dissertation, "Dante's Art of Reason: A Study of Medieval Logic and Semantics in the *Monarchy*," esp. p. 5, et passim. See n. 331, below.

173. *eubulia:* Aristotle, *Nic. Ethics* 6:9:1142b:22–24 (Barnes, 2:1804). Again Dante prefers using the transliteration from the Greek, εὐβουλία. By *euboulia* Aristotle had meant "excellence in deliberation," the capacity, habit, and virtue of giving the prudence or correctness of one's deliberations and understanding in good counsel. See the version and discussion in St. Thomas Aquinas, *Commentary on the Nic. Ethics,* trans. Litzinger, 2:579–580; Thomas uses the Greek transliteration as he devotes the whole of *Lectio* 8 to the concept. Dante has Ulysses and Guido da Montefeltro violate the principle of *euboulia* in *Inf.* 26 and 27.

174. Aristotle's *Lessons on Nature* are his *Physics*. Dante refers here to *Physics* 2:3:194a:16–195a:1: "We must proceed to consider causes . . . men do not know a thing until they have grasped the 'why' of it . . . that . . . is called a cause . . . in the sense of an end or the for the sake of which a thing is done" (cf. Barnes, 1: 332–333). Aristotle is explaining final causes, or teleology, that which "pulls from the front," as it were, causing something as a goal that must be reached. See text and commentary in St. Thomas Aquinas, *In Metaph. Aristotelis Exp.,* ed. Cathala and Spiazzi, pp. 86, 87–88: *"Natura autem finis est et cuius causa fit"* (Nature is the end goal, or that-for-the-sake-of-which).

175. *certain individual men but even some nations are born suited to govern and certain others to be subject and to serve:* Aristotle, *Pol.* 1:5:1254a:21–24: "For that some should rule and others be ruled is a thing not only necessary but expedient; from the hour of their birth, come are marked out for subjection, other for rule" (Barnes, 2:1990). Again the statement is a Scholastic topos. See the *Textus Aristotelis* in St. Thomas Aquinas's *In libros Politicorum Aristotelis expositio,* ed. Spiazzi, pp. 14, 17. See also *Pol.* 1:5:1255a:1–2, 1:5:1255b:5–9.

176. *Æn.* 6:847–853.

177. *Æn.* 4:227–230.

178. *human reason can arrive at on its own two feet:* The "feet of the soul" was a topos of theology, in which the soul and mind were given metaphorical feet; usually the left foot signified the senses or the lower soul (or sometimes the will), and the right, the upper soul or the intellect. Here, however, Dante means the theoretical and the practical intellects (cf. *Mon.* 1:3:9, 1:14:7, and 1:16:5). For Dante's use of the topos in *Inf.* 1, see John Freccero, "The Firm Foot on a Journey without a Guide," in *Dante: The Poetics of Conversion,* ed. Rachel Jacoff (Cambridge, Mass.: Harvard University Press, 1986), pp. 29–54; rpt. from "Dante's Firm Foot and the Journey without a Guide," *Harvard Theological Review* 52, no. 3 (1959): 245–281.

179. Each individual, when separate, is not sufficient; see Aristotle, *Pol.* 1:2:1253a:25–29 (Barnes, 2:1988); and the *Textus Aristotelis* 21, in St. Thomas Aquinas's *In libros Politicorum Aristotelis expositio,* ed. Spiazzi, p. 6.

180. Aristotle, *Nic. Ethics* 1:2:1094b:9–11 (Barnes, 2:1730); see St. Thomas Aquinas, *Com-*

*mentary on the Nic. Ethics*, trans. Litzinger, 1:12. Remigio de' Girolami cites the same passage in the same vein in his exaltation of the common good; see *De bono communi*, ed. De Matteis, pp. 33, 64.

181. Dante deals with the question of the salvation of those who could not have heard of Christ in *Par.* 19:32, 67–90, and resolves it by showing that the pagans Ripheus and Trajan achieved salvation. Dante had pondered deeply upon St. Thomas Aquinas's questions: "That it is reasonable to hold a man responsible if he does not turn toward God, even though he cannot do this without grace" (*Summa contra gentiles* 3:159); also see "Whether unbelief is a sin," *ST* II-II, q. 10, a. 1).

182. Heb 11:6.

183. Lv 17:3–4.

184. Jn 10:9.

185. *Saul:* Vernani will take this relatively insignificant point and turn it against Dante in the conclusion of the *Ref.* 3:95–98.

186. Paralipomenon 20:12 [2 Chr 20:12]

187. *"contest": "certare": "'certare'* etinam ab eo quod est *'certum facere.'"* Vinay and Pizzica (eds., ad loc.) point to the *Magnæ derivationes* where Uguccione da Pisa indicates that *"certamen"* derives from *"cerno,"* "to decide" or "discern." See also Kay (ed., ad loc.).

188. Acts 1:23–26.

189. *champions:* Dante uses the Latin term *"pugiles"* here (2:7:9), and in 2:7:13, 2:9:9, 2:9:11, and 2:9:15. It is clear that he does not mean, narrowly, champions who fight with their fists.

190. *athletic contestants running for the prize:* The image is based on 1 Cor 9:24: "Know you not that they run in the race, all run indeed, but one receiveth the prize? So run that you might obtain." Cf. *Mon.* 1:1:5. Dante implies a parallel between the spiritual race for salvation, A.D., and the temporal race for dominion and justice, B.C. The passage is revealing of Dante's irony in *Inf.* 15:122, where the tragic, damned, sodomitic politician Brunetto Latini is last seen as if the winner in a naked race for the *"drappo verde,"* the victor's *"palio"/"pallium,"* or "green mantle."

191. *Phars.* 4:609–661.

192. *Metamorphoses* 9:183–184.

193. *Metamorphoses* 10:560–590.

194. Cf. *Inf.* 16:19–45, where, ironically, the Florentine sodomites who were great but ultimately failed politicians appear in Hell as wrestlers, "champions naked and oiled." Cf. Dante's manifesto of the stateman's duty in *Mon.* 1:1.

195. *On Duties: De officiis* 3:10, 42.

196. *Æn.* 5:286–361. At the games in honor of Æneas's father, Anchises, Nisus enabled his friend Euryalus to win a race by slipping on blood-soaked turf and throwing himself in Salius's path. Salius receives a consolation prize to soothe his anger, as do all the contestants, for Dante is not telling us the whole truth: this was not a contest to settle any dispute.

197. Paulus Orosius, *Historia adversus paganos* 1:4 (*Against the Pagans*, trans. Deferrari, pp. 21–23). Dante uses Semiramis, "*che libito fè licito in sua legge*," "who made lust lawful in her law," as an example of the destructiveness of *lussuria-luxuria* in *Inf.* 5:56.

198. *Metamorphoses* 4:58.

199. *Metamorphoses* 4:88.

200. Orosius, *Adversus paganos* 1:14 (trans. Deferrari, pp. 34–35).

201. Orosius, *Adversus paganos* 2:6–7 (trans. Deferrari, pp. 52–55). After ambushing Cyrus, to avenge her son, Thamyris beheaded the Persian king and had his head placed in a leather bag filled with blood; Dante alludes to the gory tale as one of the examples of pride in *Purg.* 12:55–57.

202. Cf. *Purg.* 28:71.

203. *Phars.* 2:672–673.

204. *Ab urbe condita* 9:16:19–18:6. Again Dante seems to be stretching the point or misremembering. Livy describes no contest between Alexander and the Romans at this point; he, in fact, specifies that Alexander had *not* turned his arms against Europe! Further, in the later passage the historian rejects the slander that the Romans "would have been unable to withstand the majesty of Alexander's name," and avers, "I think they had not so much as heard of him." Such solecisms have made editors doubt that Dante could have been citing the *Ab urbe condita* at firsthand.

205. *Phars.* 8:692–694.

206. Rom 11:33.

207. *Æn.* 1:234–236.

208. *Phars.* 1:109–111.

209. *De cons. Phil.* 2, metr. 6.

210. Lk 2:1.

211. *what is acquired by duel is acquired de jure:* This is the first proposition of Dante's syllogism in *barbara* mood, that will continue at *Mon.* 2:9:20: "The Roman people acquired their empire by duel; ergo, they acquired it *de jure.*" See Carruccio, "La logica nel pensiero di Dante," p. 236.

212. Ps 10:8.

213. With Prudence Shaw ("Sul testo della *Monarchia*," p. 192), I read "*non odio, sed amore*," as attested in the whole MSS tradition, rejecting Rostagno's proposed emendation, "*non odio, non amore, sed solo zelo*" (not through hatred, not through love, but solely through zeal), accepted by both Ricci and Nardi in their editions. Dante was fully aware that "zeal" actually had a derogatory implication because of St. Paul's use in Rom 10:2, a New Testament hapax legomenon.

214. *duel:* "*duellum*," the proper term for a Roman judicial contest between two fighters. See Giovanni Diurni, "Duello," *Enciclopedia dantesca*, 2:605–607. We may note that Dante nowhere uses the medieval Latin "*ordalium*," meaning "trial by ordeal," deriving from Germanic practice; cf. modern German "*Urteil*," "judgment."

215. *De officiis* 1:12, 38. By the term "*disceptatio*" Dante does not imply any modern notion

of "peaceful conflict resolution" or "arbitration," but rather the outcome of lesser conflicts by a legal blood duel, lest more serious collective battle be joined and more serious consequences ensue. Contrary to Vinay's interpretation (p. 168, nn. 3, 4, and 5.), Dante is not here speaking of using reason to bring pacific remedies to conflict. (The duel of Æneas and Turnus that ends the *Æn.* is a major example. We might also compare its reflection in Ariosto's numerous ironic and comic duels or jousts to "prove" the superiority, innocence, or guilt of characters in the *Orlando Furioso*, for example.) Dante's citation of Cicero bears this out; in the *De officiis* 1:12:38, bellicosity is attenuated but very much at the core. Cicero argues as follows for justice in war: "Those wars which have glory for their end must be carried on with less bitterness. For we contend, for example, with a fellow citizen in one way, if he is a personal enemy, in another, if he is a rival: with the rival it is a struggle for office and position; with the enemy for life and honor" (LCL, trans., pp. 40–41). "Every expedient must be thought of previously, tried out in advance." See Vegetius, *De re militari: Epitome of Military Science* 3:9, para. 1 (trans. N. P. Milner, Translated Texts for Historians 16 [Liverpool, U.K.: Liverpool University Press, 1993], pp. 80–82). Dante most likely learned of Vegetius from the twenty-three references to the *De re militari* that Giles of Rome makes in the *De regimine principum;* Giles wrote his earlier treatise on kingship for the young Philip of France before the careful scholar suffered the break with the French king and all the anti-papal consequences following Boniface VIII's death. On Giles's authors, see Charles F. Briggs, *Giles of Rome's De regimine principum: Reading and Writing Politics at Court and University, c. 1275–c. 1525* (Cambridge, U.K.: Cambridge University Press, 1999), p.11.

216. *De re militari* 3:9.

217. *De officiis* 1:11, 34.

218. Cf. Mt 18:20: "For where there are two or three are gathered together in my name, there I am in the midst of them." The passage is cited also in the Prayer of St. Chrysostom. Dante is on the thinnest ground here, for, obviously, the Romans, ignorant of God, could not intentionally foregather in his name for heavenly justice. Meditations and considerations of Roman ignorance and the rebellious Virgilio's disregard of his own presumed prediction of Christ in *Eclogue* 4 form the basis of the Roman poet's tragic portrait in the *Divina Commedia:* "That God you did not know" (*Inf.* 1:131). On the question of the prohibition of blood duels in both civil and canon law, see Chapter 3, above, pp. 76–77, and notes.

219. *Æacidæ:* the descendants of Æacus. Æacus, the son of Zeus and Ægina, was a man of such virtue and piety that after death he became a judge of the dead. Pyrrhus claimed to be descended from him. Dante learned of Æacus from Ovid's *Metamorphoses* 7:507–660; cf. *Conv.* 4:27, 17–20. See Edward Moore, *Studies in Dante*, First Series (Oxford, U.K.: Clarendon Press, 1896), p. 219. It becomes ever more evident why Dante, having earlier in the *Conv.* rejected the concept that noble birth played a part in virtue, would so eagerly have embraced it in the *Mon.* (see n. 124, above).

220. *De officiis* 1:12, 38.

221. Cf. Dante's description of Fortune in *Inf.* 7:73–96.

222. I reject Nardi's arbitrary reading of *"iniustitie"* (p. 420, n. 9). Ricci, in conformity with the manuscripts, reads *"iustitie,"* here and in the sentence below. Cf. P. Shaw, "Sul testo," pp. 200–204.

223. Dante was fully aware that the Fathers and Doctors of the Church had often viewed the struggle between God and Satan as just such a legal duel; Dante is probably recalling the tradition that led St. Anselm of Canterbury (*Cur Deus homo* 1:7) to argue that Satan had gained possession of lordship over sinners unjustly and by unjust motives; see C. W. Marx, *The Devil's Rights and the Redemption in the Literature of Medieval England* (Woodbridge, Suffolk, U.K./Rochester, N.Y.: Boydell & Brewer, 1995), pp. 17–19.

224. 1 Kng 17:4–51 (1 Sm 17:4–51).

225. Cf. *Phars.* 4:593–653. David was unequal to Goliath, but still justice overcame; Hercules and Antæus were perfectly matched so that any charge of inequality of the combatants as a reason for injustice is also groundless: God's will always prevailed.

226. See Vernani, *Ref.* 2:84–93.

227. *Æn.* 12:693–942.

228. Nardi reads *"romanus videlicet populus et albanus"* (to wit, the Roman people and the Albans); I here follow Ricci, who omits *"populus."* Cf. P. Shaw, "Sul testo," p. 206.

229. Dante fails to reveal St. Augustine's vehement deploring of the combat duel of the Horatii and the Curatii, in *The City of God* 3:14, as a cruel and impious spectacle and a tragic waste of life: "Rome, conquered on that occasion by this lust [for mastery] was triumphant over Alba; and gave the name of glory to the memory of her crime.... Away with these deceptive cloaks and fraudulent whitewashings! ... Gladiators also fight, and they also are victorious" (trans. McCracken, LCL, 1:111).

230. The contest of the Horatii and the Curatii is found in Livy, *Ab urbe condita* 1:24–26. Only one king was present: the Alban king had just died and the elected dictator, Mettius, represented them at the contest. See Paulus Orosius, *Historia adversus paganos* 2:4; *Against the Pagans,* trans. Deferrari, pp. 48–49. Orosius, mindful of Augustine's diatribes against the ungodly gore (see note 229, above), does not elaborate on the duel, simply mentioning "the brief conflict of the triplets." Here, Dante is most lawyerlike in bending his sources.

231. *Phars.* 2:135–138.

232. Ricci here reads *"alii"*; P. Shaw (ad loc.), reads *"omnes."*

233. 2 Tm 4:8.

234. *presumptuous jurists . . . far beneath that watch-tower:* Dante does not refer merely to the decretalists here: the "jurists" include both civil and ecclesiastical lawyers. As we have noted, most jurists doubted that the judgment of God would be shown in the outcome of duels. Maccarone believes that Dante is even censuring Cino da Pistoia at this point; see "Papato e impero," p. 303, and n. 3. On the "watchtower" (*"specula"*) image, see Boethius, *De*

*consolatio philosophiæ* 4:6; and Dante *Epistole* 7:23 (*To the Emperor Henry VII*; ed. Frugoni and Brugnoli, p. 570) and 11:2 (*To the Italian Cardinals*, ed. Frugoni and Brugnoli, p. 580).

235. *So far . . . Especially: "Usque . . . Maxime."* I here follow Ricci's edition that was the first to divide the beginning of chapter 10 at the words *"usque adhuc"* rather than at *"maxime."* Imbach and Flüeler, P. Shaw, Pizzica, and Kay have all adopted Ricci's emendation. The chapter division is not derived from the MSS.

236. The usurpation of the emperor's privileges, most recently by John XXII and his bull *Si fratrum.*

237. *Let them go back where they came from!:* Ricci preferred *"redeunt unde venerunt"* (they return whence they came), believing that the reading *"redeant unde venerunt"* (let them [the assets of the Church] return whence they came) derived only from Ficino's translation. The subjunctive *"redeant,"* however, makes the only logical sense. Nardi argues warmly and convincingly for it in *Saggi e note*, pp. 408–416, and in his ed., pp. 426–427, ad loc.—although, bafflingly, the accompanying text above his note prints *"redeunt"* from Ricci (!). P. Shaw also accepts *"redeant"*; see "Sul testo," pp. 207–208, and her ed., ad loc.

238. Dante begins to use conditional arguments as opposed to syllogisms. In their editions, Imbach and Flüeler, P. Shaw, and Kay cite (ad loc.) the rule given by Peter of Spain in the "De fallacia secundum consequens" ("On Fallacy According to the Consequent") in the *Summulæ logicales*, Tractatus VII, 153; ed. de Rijk, p. 169: "A *consequentia econtraria* occurs when the opposite of the antecedent follows from the opposite of the consequent. For example, 'if a man is an animal; ergo if it is not-animal, it is not-man.'" Dante's proposition is introduced as an enthymeme; this is the governing fact in Vernani's attempt at rebuttal. See Dante's reference to the classical syllogism of "man as animal" in *Mon.* 2:5:22 p. 138.

239. I.e., the contradictories are "the Roman Empire did exist *de jure*," "the Roman Empire did not exist *de jure*." Dante cleverly follows Peter of Spain in the *Summulæ logicales*, Tractatus V, 31 (ed. De Rijk, p. 73) who sets down the procedural maxim: "If one [of two contradictories] is true, by contradictory of opposites, the remaining one is false, and vice versa." See ed. Nardi and ed. Kay, ad loc. P. Shaw points out that Dante's procedure is complicated by the fact that both his antecedents here are formulated as negative statements, but she intelligently affirms that this has no effect upon the logical *process* involved, for to negate a negative will produce a positive conclusion ("Some Proposed Emendations," p. 4). See also E. Cecchini, "Dante, *Mon.* II, x, 4–10," in *Miscellanea in onore di Vittore Branca*, Biblioteca dell'Archivum Romanicum, ser. 1, 178–182, 5 vols.(Florence: Olschki, 1983), 1:177–184.

240. This is a key passage in which Dante's tacit opposition to St. Augustine's negativity toward the Roman Empire is revealed. The poet's appeal to the "faithful" is not ingenuous.

241. *actions speak louder than words:* This common saw is repeated from *Mon.* 1:13:4; but Aristotle had also said that arguments were less convincing than deeds in *Nic. Ethics*

10:1:1172a:34–35; see St. Thomas Aquinas, *Commentary on the Nic. Ethics*, trans. Litzinger, 2: 860.

242. Lk 2:1.

243. P. Shaw reads *"nota";* I follow *"notandum"* in Ricci's edition.

244. *argument based on denying the consequent:* i.e., *modus tollens.* Ricci, followed by Pizzica, Imbach and Flüeler, and Kay, preferred the reading *"argumentum sumptum ad destructionem consequentis"* (eds., ad loc.), while P. Shaw, whom I follow here, emends the text to *a destructione.*

245. *a certain common logical procedure: "per aliquem locum."* Literally, perhaps, "by means of one of the commonplaces," i.e., by the commonplace procedure of contradictory opposites; see nn. 238 and 239, above.

246. I.e., the antecedent from para. 4: "if the Roman Empire did not exist *de jure"* [i.e, the Roman Empire was unjust], and the false consequent, "then Christ by his Birth approved an injustice." The consequent, "ergo, he approved something unjustly," is outrageously false; therefore, the contradictory of the antecedent is true. P. Shaw emends the reading of the majority of the MSS, suggesting that *"a positione antecedentis"* be replaced by *"a positione consequentis"* ("Some Proposed Emendations," pp. 7–8); she believes that the error dates back to the archetype—an error that some individual scribes noticed and corrected; cf. her ed., ad loc. See also Kay's meticulous arguments to the contrary in his ed., p. 187, n. 27.

247. The "first figure" proves the argument positively; the second negatively. See "the commonplace of contradictory opposites" in nn. 238 and 239, above. "In the second figure there is always a negative conclusion"; see "De secunda figura," in Peter of Spain, *Summulæ logicales,* Tractatus IV, 7–8; ed. de Rijk, p. 48. See P. Shaw, ed., p. 94, n. 9; Kay, ed., pp. 182, 186–187, nn. 26–27; Nardi, ed., ad loc.

248. The unacceptable idea that Christ could have supported a single instance of injustice—even unaware (impossible)—is multiplied exponentially by the horrific conclusion that he could have acted unjustly absolutely *by choice.* Cf. "De reductione per impossibile," in Peter of Spain *Summulæ logicales,* Tractatus IV, 9; ed. de Rijk, p. 49.

249. Rom 5:12.

250. Eph 2:3.

251. Eph 1:5–8.

252. Jn 19:30.

253. *consequence:* Ricci here gives the reading *"propter convenientiam,"* and is followed by Kay (ed., ad loc.). I accept Dino Bigongiari's earlier suggestion of *"propter consequentiam"* as being logically required by the text ("Notes on the Text of Dante," *Romanic Review* 41 [1950]: 5). P. Shaw argues cogently for Bigongiari's emendation in "Some Proposed Emendations," pp. 5–6, noting that it occurs in four MSS, and adopts it in her edition (ad loc.).

254. *ordinary judge: "iudex ordinarius"* was a term of Roman law taken over into current ecclesiastical and common law: it signified a judge who has immediate jurisdiction of his own right and not by special deputation; he bore full responsibility only to himself for his decisions, after which there was no appeal. At the beginning of the thirteenth century the

decretalists had proclaimed the pope "the universal ordinary," whose courts were not merely supreme but also the ordinary tribunals, i.e., taking cases for both their very first and their final hearing from all parts of Christendom. With the coming of the national monarchies, a king came to be proclaimed "ordinary of his kingdom." Watt puts it thus: "An ordinary judge, according to Roman law, was one who exercised his function *suo iure* and not by delegation." And later, "The Roman Church had the right of judging all: from its sentences there was no appeal; no one might judge it; all had the right of appeal to its judgment." The term was synonymous with "plenitude of power" enjoyed by the pope. See Watt's "Papa est iudex ordinarius omnium," in *Theory of Papal Monarchy*, pp. 92–97. Dante's argument of Pilate's full and final divine authority as judge ordinary is completely supported by Jn 19:10–11: "Pilate therefore saith to him: Speakest thou not to me? knowest thou not that I have the power to crucify thee, and I have the power to release thee? Jesus answered: Thou shouldst not have any power against me unless it were given thee from above."

255. Ex. 2:14.

256. For Christ's declaration of the justice of his death and Caiaphas's prophecy of God's will, see above, pp. 81, 149, 257, 265.

257. Is 53:4–5; Heb 12:2.

258. I follow Kay (ed., ad loc.), who noticed that the editions of Rostagno, Ricci, and P. Shaw all oddly omitted the words *"vel substinentis"* (or [in the flesh] of the sufferer) that are found in all the MSS, and restored the phrase.

259. Lk 23:11.

260. *Ausonia:* Italy.

261. On the Donation of Constantine, see above, Chapter 3, pp. 62, 98–100.

262. Dn 6:22.

263. Prv 8:7.

264. Aristotle, *Nic. Ethics* 1:6:1096a:13–15; see text in St. Thomas Aquinas, *Commentary on the Nic. Ethics*, trans. Litzinger, 1:32: "It seems indeed better, and in fact especially obligatory upon philosophers, to sacrifice even the rights of friendship for the sake of truth. . . . we ought to honor truth as sacred above friends."

265. 1 Thes 5:8.

266. *gymnasium: "gignasium."* A place where Greek youths met for—as the etymology implies, naked—exercise and discussion. Note that Dante is again pursuing the terms and metaphors of an athletic contest that have already informed the greater part of his discussion, especially in book 2. Although Dante had no close acquaintance with Greek, it is intriguing and revealing to see how he manipulates his familiarity with transliterated Greek terms (cf. *epyikia,* 1:14:5; *eubulia,* 2:5:23; *palestra,* 3:1:3; [*h*]*agiographos,* 3:16:9) to exalt the authority of his arguments.

267. Col 1:13–14.

268. *wrestling ring: "palestra."* As his vivid rhetoric here proves, Dante knew that the

term designated a public place for training or exercise, especially in wrestling; the word παλαίοτρα derives from from Greek παλαίειν "to wrestle" (cf. his use of the word in *Epistola 8; To the Italian Cardinals*, ed. Toynbee, pp. 142, 147). On these transliterated Greek terms, "gymnasium" and "palæstra," see Chapter 2, note 13 above. See also nn. 95 and 266, above.

269. Ps 111:7.

270. On the image of the "two great lights," see above, pp. 86–90, and Cassell, "'*Luna est ecclesia*': Dante and the Two Great Lights," *Dante Studies* 119 (2001): 1–26.

271. I read *"ab aliquo Dei vicario"* with Ricci and Shaw ("Sul testo," p. 208), rejecting Nardi's reading *"ab alio."*

272. This is the third question or principle from *Mon.* 1:2:3: "Whether the authority of monarchy depends directly upon God or on some other minister or vicar of God." Dante first gives a profession of his belief and his reverence for the hierarchy of the Church, knowing that the question of temporal autonomy could arouse charges of heresy among radical hierocrats. It was thus customary for monarchist and imperialist writers to make such affirmative statements about the papacy. Cf. John of Paris's "Proemium" to his *On Royal and Papal Power:* "I make solemn declaration that in nothing I assert do I purpose anything against faith, good morals or sound doctrine, or against the reverence due to the person or office of pope" (trans. Watt, p. 73). Dante had earlier affirmed that the origins of the Church and the empire were the one and the same, as in his *Epistola* 5:5: God had willed the power of Peter and of Cæsar which "bifurcated from Him as from a single point" (ed. Toynbee, rev. Hardie, pp. 53–54, 60).

273. Dante had set down his principle for book 1 in *Mon.* 1:2:4, and for book 2 in *Mon.* 2:2. Here, in book 3, however, he only begins to affirm it after responding to his opponents in a list of ten objections that take up most of the book (six biblical, three historical, and the tenth, from reason, filling chapters 3–12); cf. *Mon.* 3:13:1: "We must go back and show the truth of the third question that we proposed to discuss at the beginning." His proofs will demonstrate that God's ordaining of the Roman Empire can be seen directly from nature: there was and is no need of any papal mediation.

274. *middle term:* see Chapter 2, "Dante's Forensic Procedure," pp. 27–33. As Peter of Spain states "De sillogismo," in the *Summulæ logicales*, Tractatus IV, 2: *"Medium est terminus bis sumptus ante conclusionem"* (The middle term is assumed twice before the conclusion). Also see Tractatus V, 2 (ed. de Rijk, pp. 43–44; 55–56). I.e., the "middle term" is common to both the major and minor premises and is excluded from the conclusion.

275. Peter of Spain, *Summulæ logicales*, Tractatus VII, 153 (ed. de Rijk, p. 169).

276. Cf. *Mon.* 2:10:4. Dante again proves his proposition by contradictories ("If this were not true, its contradictory would not be false") as outlined by Peter of Spain in *Summulæ logicales*, Tractatus V, 31, and VII, 153 (ed. de Rijk, pp. 73, 169). See the discussion of Aristotle's passages on negations and contradictories from *De interpretatione* and *De sophisticis elenchis* with Boethius's commentaries in L. M. de Rijk, *Logica modernorum*, 1:24–27. Dante's

principle is "that God does not will anything that is repugnant to the intention of nature." He shows that the consequences of the negative can only lead to nonsense, to a *reductio ad impossibilem*. The principle's contradictory is "God is not unwilling regarding anything that is repugnant to the intention of nature." And from this two impossibilities follow either that God wills what is repugnant or that he is indifferent in making a choice against what is repugnant.

277. The end goal of nature, of man's immanent life upon earth, is the full use of his reason for equity and justice. See above, nn. 71 and 156.

278. Aristotle had accepted Antiphon's proof that the circle could not be squared (*Physics* 1.2:185a14–17). In *Conv.* 2:14:27, Dante thus correctly assumes, as modern mathematicians agree, that the procedure is impossible (cf. Vasoli ed., pp. 239–240 and notes), and he concludes his *Par.* 33:133–135 in total ineffability, with this fact as a poetic anacoluthon.

279. Cf. Aristotle: "The Spartans do not take counsel about how the Scythians ought best to live their lives" (*Nic. Ethics* 3:3(5):1112a28; see the text in St. Thomas Aquinas, *Commentary on the Nic. Ethics*, trans. Litzinger, 1:202.

280. Dante here readily concedes the papal title "vicarius Christi," "the Vicar of Christ," an appellation given early to bishops and abbots, used by Leo I (440–461), and one put in great vogue at the beginning of the thirteenth century by Innocent III's official assumption of it in addition to his title *"vicarius Petri,"* "the Vicar of Saint Peter." Dante, knowing that the appellation was also given to the emperors, along with the regal denomination *"vicarius Dei,"* insists, otherwise, that the pontiff is strictly Peter's successor, not Christ's. Cf. *Mon.* 3:6:2. See Maccarrone, *Vicarius Christi*.

281. Cf. St. Paul's censures in Rom 10:2–3. Despite the animosity he expresses openly for the person of the incumbent, Dante shows respectful regard to the pontifical office of John XXII. Clearly, he also means to include, collectively, the previous hierocratic popes, nearly all formerly professors of law and learned canonists, Innocent III, Innocent IV (author of the *Apparatus* censured in the *Letter to the Italian Cardinals* [para. 8]), Nicholas III, Boniface VIII, and Clement V.

282. The "shepherds" are the bishops of the Church. Dante's censure is circumspect. The popes handsomely rewarded most of the important hierocratic decretalists with prelacies: Wilhelmus Durandus (writer of the *Speculum iudiciale* [or *Speculum iuris*] whom Dante obliquely censures in the *Epistola* 8:7, *To the Italian Cardinals*) was bishop of Mende in Languedoc; Cardinal Enrico Bartolomei of Susa was known as the decretalist "Hostiensis" from his archbishopric of Ostia (see above); Egidio Romano was archbishop of Bourges; Giacomo da Viterbo was succcessively archbishop of Benevento and Naples; Enrico da Cremona was bishop of Reggio Emilia; and Matteo d'Acquasparta, author of *De potentia pape ac primatu ecclesie Romane* was bishop of Porto. Philip the Fair's publicist, John of Paris, shows a like respect in regard to the prelates; see *On Royal and Papal Power* 18. See also Maccarrone, "Teologia e diritto canonico," pp. 12–13.

283. Those who call themselves "sons of the Church" are the "the Guelphs whom the Holy Roman Church called its sons" *(Guelphos quos sancta Romana Ecclesia filios nominavit)*, according to Enrico da Cremona (Scholz, *Die Publizistik*, p. 460). Also see Maccarrone, "Teologia e diritto canonico," p. 14.

284. Jn 8:44. Vernani, seeing himself included in this category of the Guelphs as sons of Satan, hurls the insult back at Dante, calling the poet a vessel of the Father of Lies in the "Dedication" to his *Ref.* 3–4.

285. *ignorant and unskilled in any knowledge of theology and philosophy:* Ironically, the criticism would certainly apply to Fra Guido Vernani's lawyerly treatises, which are marred with biblical, theological, and philosophical citations slavishly taken at secondhand from canon-law texts, with many errors in attributions.

286. Those who even presumed to speak in contempt of sacred canons *(contra sacros canones . . . loqui presumunt)* committed blasphemy against the Holy Spirit, according to Gratian; see *Decretum*, Causa 25, qu. 1, cap. v, *Violatores (CIC*, 1:1008).

287. *I heard a certain member of this group state and impudently:* For the evocation of the presence of the "member" amidst this "group," we can compare the *"vidi e conobbi colui"* (I saw and recognized him) of *Inf.* 3:59, most probably identifying Celestine V from among the wretched choir of the *ignavi* (despite the other identifications of Esau and Pontius Pilate given by Dante's son Piero, who was motivated by the desire to protect himself and his father's reputation). Dante inveighed against the decretals as the source of clerical venality in *Par.* 9:133–135. Dante could have actually have heard this "impudent" statement from *any* supporter of the decretals! As we have outlined, it was actually the official theory and practice of canon law. Theoretically, in matters of governance and discipline, canon law was indeed to be preferred over the Fathers; canonists assumed that their laws had already been conceived *within* the doctrines flowing from Holy Scripture, the Councils, and the Fathers. Clearly, however, one could not so neatly distinguish matters of doctrine from matters of discipline: cases of sin and heresy make this abundantly obvious. These are not the apostolic traditions of the Church at its origin but are merely "those [recent] traditions that are called 'decretals'" (see above, p. 85, and Dante's text below, para. 14). For a discussion of the hierarchy of Church texts, see Cassell, "'*Luna est ecclesia*,'" pp. 8–9.

288. Rom 8:16–17.

289. As is clear, Dante definitely does not mean *"excludantur"* in the sense that the decretalists will "be ignored" or "disregarded" as opponents in this metaphorical "wrestling match," as some editors have mistakenly construed the passage; rather, these papalist lawyers are to be the first confuted, "to be ousted," i.e., to be metaphorically *hurled* summarily and unceremoniously, like vanquished professional wrestlers, from the ring, for upon their arguments depend the positions of their superiors.

290. Vinay pointed out *(Mon.*, ed., ad. loc.) that Dante's categories of the importance of Church texts follows that of Gratian listed in *Decretum*, Distinct. 15, ch. 3, *Sancta romana (CIC*, 1:36–41).

291. Ps 110:9.

292. Sg 1:3.

293. Mt 28:20.

294. *"Doctors"*: the Doctors of the Church. For Dante's use of this word, signifying "teachers," see *Mon.* 3:6:4, and n. 336, below. For the canonists, decreta and decretals did in fact stand above the Greek Church Fathers, and at the very last came the Latin Fathers. Guido de Baysio cites Hostiensis's hierarchy of descending authority of scriptures in his *Rosarium ad Distinctiones* 20:3: "For first reference must be made to the Old and New Testaments. Secondly, to the canons of the Apostles and Councils. Thirdly to decreta or decretals of the Roman Pontiffs. Fourth to the writings of the Greek [Fathers]. And lastly to the writings of the Holy Latin Fathers" (Tierney, "Sola Scriptura," p. 359).

295. Mt 15:2.

296. Mt 15:3.

297. *Thus*: reading *"itaque"* with Shaw; Ricci has *"hiique,"* a text that Kay follows in the Latin, but translates as "thus."

298. *gymnasium: gignasio*. See nn. 95, 173, 266, and 268 above.

299. Those dissemblers bedecked with crow feathers are the Guelphs; in Dante's *Epistola* 5:4 (ed. Toynbee, pp. 52, 60), the Guelphs are *"corvuli,"* the "little crows," who usurp the nest of the sons of the imperial eagle.

300. Gregory VII in the *Dictatus papæ* 19, and popes thereafter, claimed to be judged by no one. See *Mon.*, ed. Kay, p. 218, n. 43. It became central to the doctrine of Hugh of St. Victor in the *De Sacramentis* 2:2:4 (*PL* 176:417–418); cf. *On the Sacraments*, trans. Deferrari, p. 256.

301. *reverence: reverentia*. See n. 445 below, and Cassell, "The Exiled Dante's Hope for Reconciliation," pp. 431–433..

302. This centrally important passage on respect and reverence for the papacy, which now begins the last arguments of the third book, connects with the ending of the treatise: the final paragraph of the *Mon.* must not be taken out of context.

303. *"as an inferior artisan depends on the architect"*: Cf. Aristotle, *Metaph* 1:1:981a30–b1; see Moerbeke's version in St. Thomas Aquinas, *In Metaph. Exp.*, ed. Cathala and Spiazzi, p. 5. Vinay notes that the image of the architect and the artisan is common in St. Thomas Aquinas (cf. *Summa contra gentiles* 3:114), and in the Aristotelian-Thomistic tradition; cf., e.g., James of Viterbo, *De regimine christiano* (*On Christian Government*, trans. Dyson, p. 105).

304. Dante, in the tradition of Scholastic disputation, begins enumerating the arguments of his adversaries; of the many he could have mentioned, he chooses only nine, a number very dear to him. St. Thomas Aquinas, e.g., in the *Book of Sentences*, states that one must first proceed with the destruction of one's opponent's errors, arguing by citation of authorities, by reason, and by natural comparisons; see Maccarrone, *Il terzo libro*, pp. 31–32.

305. Gn 1:14–16.

306. On the "two great lights," the sun and moon, see above, pp. 86–90.

307. Pope Boniface VIII's famous *Allegacio*, given on April 3, 1303, had been a most important recent broadcasting of the "two lights" image to signify the subordination of the empire. Clement V refers to the *Allegacio* in his *Romani principes*. We have noted that Dante's text is a close paraphrase of Boniface's document—but the formulas had been widely cited; Dante will later refer to it in *Mon.* 3:6. The document was far more threatening to the imperial position than the famous bull *Unam sanctam*, which was directed only against Philip the Fair of France (see Maccarrone, "Il terzo libro," p. 35).

308. *"The refutation of an argument is the exposure of error"*: Aristotle wrote that "a proper solution is the exposure of a false deduction"; and later, "one solves arguments that are properly deduced by demolishing them, whereas one solves merely apparent arguments by making distinctions" (*De sophisticis elenchis* 18:176b:29–30; Barnes, 1:301). The quote from the Latin versions of *De sophisticis elenchis* here is not exact; see Moerbeke's translation, ed. Bernard G. Dod, in *Aristoteles latinus*, vol. 6, 1–3, p. 96; Boethius's translation, p. 40. Maccarrone has shown that after St. Thomas Aquinas's opposition, theologians were more skeptical of arguments using allegorizing exegesis as proof: only the literal or historical sense was considered valid in this regard ("Il terzo libro," p. 36). Dante thus has precedent for rejecting the allegory or analogy of the sun and moon as he attempts to confute the decretalists by showing the literal impossibility of their interpretation. See *Mon.*, trans. Wicksteed; and Kay, ed., ad loc.

309. Parmenides of Elea (b. ca. 505 B.C.) argued about the beginnings of "what is," and defined whether "what is" can have limits in time; his follower Melissus of Samos, the last member of the Eleatic School, maintained the spatial infinity of the universe. Aristotle refutes these two pre-Socratic philosophers in his *Physics* 1.3:186a:6–7 (*Physics*, trans. Wicksteed and Cornford, in *Aristotle*, LCL, 4:28–29): "Both Parmenides and Melissus argue sophistically, inasmuch as they make unsound assumptions and argue unsoundly from them." Cf. Latin text and commentary, St. Thomas Aquinas, *In Phys. Exp.*, ed. Maggiòlo, pp. 8, 10. Dante sees the question of the beginnings of the Church and the empire as a reflection of that debate, earthly infinity being impossible in Aristotle. The poet's reference, however, gives Vernani the cue for his rebuttal—that the Church was created by the transcending infinity of God, *ab eterno*. See also Giacomo Poletto, *La Santa Scrittura nelle opere di Dante Allighieri* (Siena: Tipografia Pontificio S. Bernardino, 1909), p. 276, n.1.

310. *making distinctions:* A technical term in logic for discovering a difference between the meaning of a term used in a proposition and the meaning in which it must be taken in support of a conclusion.

311. *of course: The City of God* 16:2; Shaw restores *"sane,"* omitted by Ricci, to the citation in the text.

312. St. Augustine, *The City of God* 16:2; trans. Sanford and Green, LCL, 5:14–15. Proofs from mystical theology are not conclusive. As Dante cites St. Augustine on correct scriptural exegesis (*Letter to Vicentius, Epistola* 93:8 [*PL* 33:334]), Vernani will cite Dionysius the Æreopagite (Pseudo-Dionysius), *De mystica theologia* 1:1 (*PG* 3:997–1000) and *Epistula* 9:1

(*PG* 3:1103). See the similar caution, to the opposite end, in John of Paris, *On Royal and Papal Power* 18, trans. Watt, p. 196. Cf. Remigio de' Girolami's warnings in *Contra falsos ecclesie professores*, ed. Tamburini, pp. 67–68.

313. St. Augustine, *De doctrina christiana* 1:36[41]: "Anyone who understands in the Scriptures something other than that intended by them is deceived, although he does not lie"; *On Christian Doctrine*, trans. modified from Robertson, p. 31.

314. I read "*de illo aliud in Scripturia sentire*," with Ricci and Shaw ("Sul testo," p. 208), instead of the emendation of Witte, Nardi, Capitani, Kay, and Imbach, "*illo qui vult aliud in Scripturis sentire*." See Ovidio Capitani, *Chiose minime dantesche*, Il mondo medievale: Studi di storia e storiografia. Sezione di Storia delle istituzioni della spiritualità e delle idee 12 (Bologna: Patron, 1983), pp. 13–23. On scriptural interpretation, see Poletto, *La Santa Scrittura nelle opere di Dante Allighieri*, pp. 274–276.

315. *De doctrina christiana* 1:36[41].

316. *De doctrina christiana* 1:37[41]; *On Christian Doctrine*, trans. modified from Robertson, p. 31.

317. See John A. Scott, "*Monarchia* III, iv, 10: Un leone tra le nuvole," *Miscellanea in onore di Vittore Branca*, 1:185–192.

318. Dante's invective here is echoed in the *Purg.* 29:89–90; Heaven is outraged when Divine Scripture is put aside or twisted.

319. That God is the sole "dictator" of Holy Scripture is an axiom of theology. The parallel in wording here to *Purg.* 24:52–54, is unmistakable: Dante makes a great claim there for the divine inspiration of his own poetry.

320. *accidental attributes:* The word "accident" alone is the technical Aristotelian term for the qualities or attributes of a substance. Material substance was known by such accidents as heat, cold, hardness, color, etc. Accidents also regard relationships, such as that a man may be a father, a son, a merchant, a customer, a subject, a king, a believer, a pope, and so forth. See nn. 396 and 401 below.

321. Gn 1:19, 31.

322. Dante's attempt to ridicule his opponents backfires with Vernani's rebuttal; see above, Chapter 3, p. 92. Dante had argued earlier, following Aristotle, that government was natural to man; St. Thomas Aquinas's doctrine, as included and repeated by Tolomeo da Lucca, also assumed that government would arise among men regardless of chronology, whether before or after the Fall, before or after Christ ("It is natural for human beings to live in the society of many"; "It is necessary that there be something that governs in every multitude"; *De regimine principum* 1:1:3, 1:1:7; *On the Government of Rulers*, trans. Blythe, pp. 61, 63). Consequently, government would *not* be a cure for original sin. By nodding to St. Augustine here, Dante effectively contradicts himself.

323. According to theological teaching, a "typical," typological, allegorical sense of a scriptural passage could not be accepted unless that sense had been the intention and will of the original author. Dante tries to prove that the decretalist allegory of the sun and the moon as human government was not Moses' intention—Moses being the presumed

writer of Genesis. Dante here uses *"intentio"* in the usual sense of English "intent" or "intention."

324. Dante is following currently accepted scientific precedent: that the moon shone of its own accord was also held in the schools of theology. In *Par.* 4: 32, as the Wayfarer and Beatrice enter the substance of the moon itself, it appears as a glowing cloud: *"Parev'a me che nube ne coprisse /* lucida, spessa, solida e pulita." Cf. Godfrey of Saint Victor in the *Fons Philosophiæ* 5:231: "The moon begs not her shine from sun—she does her own lighting" (*The Fountain of Philosophy*, trans. E. A. Synan [Toronto: Pontifical Institute of Mediæval Studies, 1972], p. 47). Dante used the concept ironically accepting the analogy of the moon as the empire in his earlier *Epistola* 5:30. Henry VII's virtue is the lesser light, yet it can shine very well alone indeed when the "sun" of the Church is eclipsed: "the glow of the lesser light may lend its splendor."

325. *earthly realm: "regnum temporale."* "Regimen" ("rule") and *"regnum"* ("realm") could be readily confused in their various abbreviated forms by copyists; given the lack of an autograph or MSS of the first generation, the reading is moot. The rest of the passage encapsules Dante's theories in a nutshell. Indeed, the word *"regnum"* seems to reflect and correct the novel language of *Solitæ*, where the *earthly realm* of the moon not only receives its light from the sun, but is merely one of the satellites, along with the spiritual sun, all circling within the vast firmament of the Church. The first examples of the "two great lights" analogy in ecclesiastical documents before Innocent III's usage in his two early bulls deal with the *"regnum"* of England after the murder of Thomas Becket. I thus read *"regnum"* ("realm") with Ricci and Kay, rather than *"regimen"* ("rule" or "government") with Nardi. See Pézard, *La rotta gonna,* 2:91–93. Shaw prefers *"regimen"* in the Latin text ("Sul testo," pp. 206–207), although she also translates it as "realm" (ed. *Mon.* [1995], pp. 112–113).

326. Here the poet anticipates and prepares for the final passage, *Mon.* 3:16:18. Cf. *Epistola* 5:30 (ed. Toynbee, rev. Hardie, p. 62). Dante insists that the addition of the blessing of the pope increases the efficacy of the emperor's power received directly from God. I reject Nardi's emendation *"quam in celo* Deus *et in terra ..."* ["which in heaven, *God,* and on earth"], which appears in no MS, preferring *"quam in celo et in terra."* The sense seems to reflect God's will as the source of both powers upon heaven and earth as expressed in the Lord's Prayer rather than through hierocratic extrapolations (which Dante would reject) based on Mt 16:18–19: "Thou art Peter.... And I will give you the keys of the kingdom of heaven. And whatsoever thou shalt bind upon earth, it shall be bound also in heaven; and whatsoever thou shalt loose on earth, it shall be loosed also in heaven."

327. Aristotle lays out the fundamental rule that "every demonstration will proceed through three terms and no more," in *Prior Analytics* 1:25:41b:36. "Light" and "authority" are separate terms, thus the syllogism is marred by the common error of four terms. Cf. above, Chapter 2, pp. 32–33.

328. Gn 29:34–35. Dante is actually arguing against Innocent's *Per venerabilem* at the precise passage where the pope refers to the cardinals as "priests of the tribe of Levi," continues with the commissioning of St. Peter (Mt 16:18), and then claims that the pope is

the Vicar of Christ as priest and king in the order of Melchisedech (*Decretales* 4:17:13; *CIC*, 2:716).

329. I read *"maior extremitas"* with Ricci, Nardi, and Shaw ("Sul testo," pp. 209–210). The subject was actually very important to the hierocrats. Cf. the twisted arguments for the precedence of the Levites (together with erroneous biblical quotations) as supreme spiritual and temporal judges in Giles of Rome's *On Ecclesiastical Power* 1:8:10–11; trans. Dyson, pp. 26–27, and notes. Vernani will silently pass over the analogy of the "two swords" and refuse to discuss the arguments concerning Levi.

330. Cf. above, *Mon.* 3:4:22: there "light" and "authority" were two different things, both in their subject and their meaning, as are "birth" and "authority" here. Both syllogisms are defective in form through the mistaken inclusion of a fourth term. See Aristotle, *Prior Analytics* 1:25:41b:36 (*Analytica priora, translatio Boethii* 1:25 in *Aristoteles latinus*, ed. Mineo-Paluello, p. 54). See above, Chapter 2, pp. 86–90.

331. One can infer that if one is man, one is an animal, as a consequent from antecedent; we cannot infer the opposite, as if from the universal term "animal," the particular term "man" would follow, see n. 172 above. For "a noncause as a cause," see "De fallacia secundum non causam ut causam," in Peter of Spain, in *Summulæ logicales*, Tractatus VII (ed. de Rijk, pp.173–176). Rather basing his argument on strictly logical procedure and terminology, in which some extraneous factor might be introduced that does not affect the consequent in any way, Dante's concept of noncause, however, is based on the rhetorical *(post hoc, propter hoc)* fallacy as outlined in Aristotle's *Rhetoric* 2:24:1401b:30–35 (Barnes, 2: 2234–2235). See Mozzillo-Howell, "Dante's Art of Reason," pp. 222–225. Vernani does not interest himself in this argument; see above, Chapter 3, on book 3, pp. 33 and 93.

332. 1 Kng (1 Sm) 8:11–31:13.

333. 1 Kng (1 Sm) 10:1, 15:23.

334. Nardi, ed., accepts Rostagno's emendation of the text as *"dependeret ab Ecclesia"* (would be dependent *on the Church*; pp. 456–457), a reading that appears in Ficino's translation but in no MS and had been first included by Torri. See Ricci, ed., ad. loc., and P. Shaw, "Sul testo," p. 210.

335. Although no consistent contemporary diplomatic terminology can be cited that would fix Dante's distinction, his idea is clear: a vicar is allowed to take the place of or to play the role of the main holder of authority, making broad independent papal or imperial decisions as might a viceroy or one having the power of attorney; the nuncio or minister must not depart from his master's orders, for he is limited in power only to relay the specific message or decisions of the one commissioning him in that specific task. Garret Mattingly (*Renaissance Diplomacy*, 27–29) discusses the lack of clarity among the various terms, as does Donald Queller (*The Office of Ambassador in the Middle Ages* [Princeton, N.J.: Princeton University Press, 1967], pp. 57–59). Dante here makes no distinction even between the *"legatus,"* most often a cardinal (as with Bertrand du Poujet), who in papal termi-

nology was roughly the equivalent of ambassador with discretional power, and the *"nuncio,"* who was merely a spokesman often lower in rank or even a layman: both are merely and purely messengers. Vernani, aware of Dante's firm point and the laxity of fit terms, attempts a rebuttal, removing the argument from its diplomatic to a courtroom analogy, by claiming that Samuel was instead a *"iudex ordinarius"* in canon law—an "ordinary judge," a judge of last resort, who had (like an archbishop or a bishop) of his own right and not by special deputation immediate and final jurisdiction in ecclesiastical cases. In essence, Vernani is weakening his own argument by partially acknowledging Dante's case: the second type, the more powerful vicar, "can take action concerning those things *of which his lord is entirely unaware"* (*Mon.* 3:6:7), indeed, whether those deeds *be righteous or not!*

336. *"sicut aliud est esse doctorem, aliud est esse interpretem":* Perhaps "it is one thing to be Doctor and another to be an exegete." Dante means a "Doctor," or "teacher," of the Church, such as the "Four Doctors" *par excellence,* Gregory the Great, Ambrose, Augustine, and Jerome, and in later times, over thirty other theologians of outstanding merit and saintliness. The "doctor" teaches his own ideas; the exegete or interpreter merely expounds those of others, as might a lector. Cf. *Mon.* 3:3:13 and n. 294 above.

337. *hammer functions . . . through . . . the smith:* The hammer image appears at the end of Aristotle's *De generatione animalium (Generation of Animals)* 5:8:789b:10; see also Nardi, ed., and Kay, ed., ad loc. Giles of Rome uses it in *De ecclesiastica potestate* 2:14:2; *On Ecclesiastical Power,* trans. Dyson, p. 125), and Dante uses it elsewhere, in *Conv.* 1:13:4 and in *Par.* 2:128.

338. "Agathon was right, for God lacks only this—to undo things already done." Aristotle, of course, makes no mention of a nuncio; see *Nic. Ethics* 6:2:1139b:10 (Barnes, 2:1799); St. Thomas Aquinas, *Commentary on the Nic. Ethics,* trans. Litzinger, 2:545, 548.

339. Dante quotes Aristotle's *Prior Analytics* (1:25:41b:36–37; Barnes, 1:66) under the title *De Sillogismo simpliciter.* See Boethius's version in *Analytica priora: Translatio Boethii (recensiones duæ), Translatio Anonyma, Pseudo-Philoponi Aliorumque Scholia, Specimina Translationum Recentiorum,* ed. L. Minio-Paluello, Aristoteles Latinus 3, 1–4 (Bruges/Paris: Desclée de Brouwer, 1962), p. 54; and Peter of Spain, *Summulæ logicales,* Tractatus IV, 2 (ed. de Rijk, p. 43). A valid categorical syllogism must have exactly three terms, each of which must occur twice and in precisely the same sense; otherwise the syllogism is said to commit the fallacy of four terms. This is the only time Dante actually identifies the fallacy since here its form fits the textbook cases. See also *Mon.* 3:4:22 and 3:5:3. See above, Chapter 2, pp. 32–33.

340. See *Conv.* 3:3:2. That fire should *fall* is a reversal for the medieval mind, for fire had a natural love for its own sphere; i.e., in the Aristotelian-Ptolemaic system, it rose to the sphere of fire just inside and just below the sphere in which the moon revolves around the earth. Dante uses the notion to great poetic effect for the unnatural, hellish Rain of Fire upon the blasphemers, sodomites, and usurers in *Inf.* 15 and 16, echoed from the punishment on the Cities of the Plain in Gn 19:24.

341. Peter Lombard, *Liber sententiorum,* 4, dist. 5, cap. 3: "De sacramentis" (Paris: Vivès, 1892), p. 564. According to doctrine, confirmed by St. Augustine, the sacrament of bap-

tism may be performed by any Christian regardless of his faith or worthiness as long as it be in the correct form prescribed by Christ (Jn 3:5; Mt 28:19), with water and in the name of the Trinity. The salvific effects were produced by God independently of the minister. Peter Lombard, however, contrary to accepted teaching, gave unwonted power to the officiant: "God can create something by means of someone, not by means of him as author, but as a minister with whom and in whom He might operate." Kay (ed., note to *Mon.* 3:7:6, ad loc.) notes that in the Quaracchi publication of Peter Lombard, the editors note: *"Hæc magistri sententia communiter non recipitur"* (This interpretation of the Master is not generally accepted) (Petri Lombardi, *Libri IV sententiarum*, Liber III, et IV, tom. 2, 2nd ed. [Ad Claras Aquas [Quaracchi] prope Florentiam ex Typographia Collegii S. Bonaventuræ, 1916], p. 776, n. 4). In his broader argument, Dante closely follows Tolomeo da Lucca, defender of the papal monarchy, who has, nonetheless, similar severe reservations concerning papal power: "The power of Peter and his successors is not equal to that of Christ, on the contrary, Christ's power totally transcends Peter's. For example, *Christ could save someone without baptism.* . . . *Christ could change the form and matter of the sacraments,* [something] *which neither Peter nor his successors could do"* (my emphases); see *De regimine principum* 3:10; *On the Government of Rulers,* trans. Blythe, p. 177.

342. Mt 16:19.

343. Mt 18:18.

344. Jn 20:23.

345. *the range of the term's extension: "ambitum termini distributi,"* literally, "the range of the term distributed." The technical word "distribution," originating in twelfth-century logic, meant that the term was used in its full extension or limit, to include all or every individual of the class designated by the term. The term "cats" in the phrase "At night all cats are gray" is distributed, because it supposedly refers to every cat; in contrast, the same term used in "The cat sat on the mat" is not distributed because it only refers to one cat. I have used the word "extension" throughout to clarify the Medieval Latin term *distributio.* In Tractatus XII, "De distributionibus," Peter of Spain explains: "Distribution is the multiplication of a common term made by a universal [quantifying] sign. Thus when we say 'every man,' through the sign 'every' the term 'man' is distributed to or fuses together of any of the particulars under it" (*Summulæ logicales* 12:1, ed. de Rijk, p. 209; see also *Summulæ logicales,* ed. J. P. Mullally, pp. 62–63). Dante defines and qualifies "whatsoever" (the word that his opponents are misinterpreting) as *"omnes quod,"* "all things *that,*" "everything *that,*" since the words "all" and "every" suggest "distribution," i.e., the extension and the *limit* of meaning.

346. *all grammarians run:* The oddly comic vision of coursing grammarians brings to mind perforce the naked, galloping sodomites in *Inf.* 15 and 16. See André Pézard, *Dante sous la pluie de feu,* Etudes de Philosophie Médiévale 40 (Paris: J. Vrin, 1950), p. 153, n. 1.

347. *extension:* "distribution." See above, n. 345.

348. Rom 7:3. The limit of papal power in such cases was a *topos.* Dante's fellow Floren-

tine Remigio makes similar points. Christ had not bequeathed either all his spiritual or his temporal power to his vicar, St. Peter; the pope could not establish a new article of faith nor ordain a new sacrament, for example; and he could not intervene regularly, but only occasionally, in secular matters, those involving sin or where a higher judgment could not be obtained. See Charles T. Davis, "Ptolemy of Lucca," p. 44. Dante dramatizes the limitation of human judgment in spiritual power in the damnation of Guido da Monte-feltro in *Inf.* 27, as the black cherub snatches his impenitent soul from St. Francis; in *Purg.* 5:64ff., Guido's kinsman, Buonconte da Montefeltro, dies penitent, with the name of Mary upon his lips. An angel of God in turn snatches his soul from a demon.

349. Mt 16:19.

350. John XXII's *Si fratrum* countermanded Henry VII's decree conferring the title "Imperial Vicar" on Can Grande of Verona for life on March 7, 1311.

351. Lk 22:38.

352. Ullmann has traced the principal argument for the Church's possession of the "two swords" in the temporal sphere to the English canonist Alanus (*Medieval Papalism*, pp. 10, 14, 146, esp. p. 151). Closer to the controversies in Dante's time are the arguments put forth by Giles of Rome (ca. 1301–1302) in his *On Ecclesiastical Power:* "[God] has ordained two swords: a material, lest we be impeded by body or with respect to bodily food; and this belongs to the earthly power, whose task it is to defend and protect bodies and the possessions from which a spiritual sword, that is, ecclesiastical and priestly power, lest we be impeded with respect to spiritual food and in those matters that bear upon the good of the soul" (1:7:2; trans. Dyson, p. 19) "These two powers are contained in one and the same person, namely, in the Supreme Pontiff, by reason of a certain excellence" (1:8:1; trans. Dyson, p. 23). The pontiff possesses the material sword "not as user, but as commander" (1:8:2; trans. Dyson, p. 24). Guido Vernani does not employ the imagery of the two swords in the *Ref.* For a full discussion, see above, Chapter 3, pp. 96–98, and n. 379, below.

353. Cf. *Mon.* 3:4:2. Indeed, Boniface VIII's bull *Unam sanctam* of 1302 had set this forth against the kingdom of France and the other "little kingdoms," in no uncertain terms: "In the Church and in her power are, as we learn from the words of the Gospel, *two swords, the spiritual and the temporal . . . both are in the power of the Church,* both the spiritual and the material sword; but the latter is to be exercised on behalf of the Church, the former by the Church, the former by the hand of the priest, the latter by the hands of kings and soldiers but at the bidding and by the forbearance of the priest . . . the temporal power ought to be subject to the spiritual power . . . for as truth itself testifies, it belongs to the spiritual power to institute the earthly power, and, if it be not good, to judge it. Whosoever, therefore, resists this power ordained of God, resists the ordinance of God . . . Furthermore, we declare, state, define, and pronounce that for every human creature to be subject to the Roman pope is altogether necessary for salvation" (*Extravagantes communes* 1:8:1; *CIC*, 2:1245–1246; Carlyle and Carlyle, 5:392–393). Giles of Rome echoes: "The Church possesses both swords" (*On Ecclesiastical Power* 1:8:13, trans. Dyson, p. 24).

354. Lk 22:7, altered.

355. Lk 22:14.

356. Lk 22:35–36.

357. Lk 22:38.

358. Mt 16:15, 16, 21, 22, 23.

359. Mt 16:15.

360. Mt 16:16.

361. Mt16:22.

362. Mt 16: 23.

363. Mt 17:39.

364. Mt 14:28.

365. Mt 26:33–35.

366. Mt 26:35.

367. Mk14:29–31.

368. Mt 22:33.

369. Jn 33:6.

370. Mt 13:8.

371. Jn 18:10–11.

372. *all four:* Mt 26:51–52; Mk 14:47; Lk 22:49–51; Jn 18:10–11.

373. Jn 20:5–6.

374. Jn 21:7.

375. Jn 21:21.

376. *archimandrite:* i.e., "head shepherd." Dante uses the term for St. Francis in *Par.* 11:90–99. See also *Epistola* 11:6 (ed. G. Brugnoli, pp. 586–587).

377. Mt 10:34–35.

378. Acts 1:1.

379. Just as he attempts to rebut the "two lights" analogy, so Dante refuses to accept the hierocrats' analogy of the two swords; we note that Vernani does not discuss or even mention the term. St. Thomas Aquinas cites Chrysostomos to the effect that Christ's referring to the two swords did not signify human, but divine aid (*Catena aurea* [on Luke 22:39–42]; *Catena Aurea: Commentary on the Four Gospels, St Luke* [Oxford/London: James Parker, 1874], 2:719–720). Cf. the Dominican, John of Paris's differing opinion: "The two swords refer to the sword of the word and the sword of impending persecution" (*De eccl. pot.* 18:30; *On Royal and Papal Power*, trans. Watt, p. 197). See Maccarrone "Il terzo libro," p. 70; and Kay, ed., *Mon.*, pp. 260–261.

380. I.e., the Donation of Constantine. See above, pp. 98–100.

381. Cf. Isidore, *Etymologies* 9:3; John of Paris, *On Royal and Papal Power*, ch. 23, trans. Watt, p. 222; and Tolomeo of Lucca, *De regimine principum* 3:12:3; *On the Government of Rulers*, ed. and trans. Blythe, pp. 183. See also Fulvio Crosara, "Dante e Bartolo da Sassoferrato," pp. 130–131, 146.

382. 1 Cor 3:11.

383. Sg 8:5.

384. Dante's argument is a paraphrase of the civilian, imperial argument against the validity of the so-called Donation; if it was admitted that Constantine had the power to give away a small portion of the empire, the whole could gradually be dissipated. Cf. Accursius, *Authenticum, collatio* I, tit. vi, præfatio, cited in Ullmann, *Medieval Papalism*, p. 164, n. 2. For full discussion, see, pp. 4, 43, 62, 98–100, 165, 169, 193, 209, 213, 224, 245, 278.

385. *he who confers is in the position of an agent and he upon whom something is conferred is in the position of a patient:* Aristotle does not actually give such simple, bare definitions; he states that "giving implies doing good and doing what is noble, and taking implies having good done to one and not acting basely" (*Nic. Ethics* 4:1:1120a:14–15; Barnes, 1:1768).

386. The second part of Dante's sentence reflects the preceding Aristotelian notion of *fitness* on the part of both donor and recipient: "Liberality is rather the bestowal of wealth on the *right* persons than the acceptance of wealth from *proper* sources or the refusal of wealth from *improper* sources" (Aristotle, *Nic. Ethics* 4:1:1120a:10–13; my emphasis; text and trans.in Rackham, LCL, pp. 192–193; cf. Barnes, 2:1768. See St. Thomas Aquinas, *Commentary on the Nic. Ethics*, trans. Litzinger, 1:286.

387. Mt 10:9.

388. Lk 22:35–36.

389. My rendering has the more prevalent chapter numbering, familiar to English readers, for example, from the Temple Classics (by P. H. Wicksteed) translation and the Bobbs-Merrill Library of Liberal Arts' liberal paraphrase (by H. W. Schneider). Ricci's and Nardi's editions continue ch. 10 at this point; Witte's 1874 edition numbers this ch. 11 and is followed in this, among many others, by Shaw. Kay prefers the Ricci-Nardi divisions. As P. Shaw notes, it is Dante's use to begin a new chapter with each argument. The devoting of this chapter to a new subject (in this case, the crowning of Charlemagne) and the chiastic pattern of the chapter numbers of the three books, 16–11–16, seems to me more typical of the poet's procedure and desires, as Shaw indicates. The chapter division here appears in the preferred two manuscripts of the α group now identified by Shaw; see her cogent observations in the "Introduction" to her edition, pp. xxxvi–xxxvii, and the arguments she advances for the more usual chapter divisions and a new *stemma* in "The *Stemma Codicum* of Dante's *Monarchia*," *Italian Studies* 51 (1996):19–21.

390. In 773 Pope Hadrian I called on Charlemagne to conquer Lombardy and depose its king, Desiderius, thus freeing the papacy from an enduring threat. One explanation for the confusion of the facts here may be that the canonists had divided the Coronation of Charlemagne in A.D. 800 from the supposed "*Translatio* (Transfer) of the Empire" from the Greeks to the Germans: but they differed in the dating of that "Translatio" before Charles's crowning. Tancred, a decretalist professor at Bologna in the time of Honorius III, for example, placed the transference at 766: Alvarus Pelagius makes it seven years before the coronation, in 794. Ullmann cites Tancred's gloss and Alvarus on the subject, in *Medieval Papalism*, p. 170. See n. 392, below.

391. On Dante's factual errors here, see above, Chapter 3, p. 101.

392. The hierocrats taught that the temporal sword was wielded at the behest of the Church. See above, pp. 96–98. Dante significantly omits direct mention of the so-called Translation of the Empire, whose formulation is probably to be credited to Innocent III, four hundred years after the alleged event. On Christmas Day in the year 800 Charlemagne received the imperial crown from Pope Leo III, thus transferring the empire from the Greeks to the Germans: "The empire was translated by the Church and through the Church from Greece, so that she might be better defended." See the *Deliberatio Domini pape Innocentii super facto imperii de tribus electis,* cap. 29 (*PL* 216:1025). The "translation" appears officially in the decretal *Venerabilem fratrem* concerning the imperial electors: "Wherefore we recognize, as we should, the right and power of those princes to whom it is known to pertain by right and ancient custom to elect a king who is subsequently to be promoted to the dignity of emperor; and particularly so as this right and power has come to them from the Apostolic See, which had transferred the Roman Empire from the Greeks to the Germans in the person of Charlemagne" (*Venerabilem fratrem* [*nostrum Salzburgensem*], *Decretales* 1:6:34; *CIC,* 2:80; *The Church and State through the Centuries,* ed. Ehler and Morrall, p. 72; Tierney, *Crisis,* p. 133.

393. *exile in Saxony:* For Dante, Charlemagne is a true emperor, receiving his power directly from God by election. The hieratic assumption that pontifical blessing is necessary for his temporal power is a usurpation. In fact, after Pope Leo VIII (963–965) had been duly elected with the emperor Otto's support, the Romans contemptuously expelled him and put John XII, his predecessor, in his place. At John's death, in 964, the Romans replaced him with (the antipope) Benedict V. Otto promptly restored Leo, who summoned a Church council in 964 that condemned Benedict as a usurper. Otto, however, intervened to protect Benedict's life and sent him north into merciful exile in Hamburg. Dante is mistaken: the council, not Otto deposed Benedict (see Kay, ed. *Mon.,* p. 277). Dante is following Tolomeo da Lucca's *Short Compendium* (*Determinatio compendiosa,* ed. Krammer, pp. 27–29; Vinay, ed. *Mon.,* ad loc.). On the question of papal benediction at the coronation of the emperor, see Cassell, "The Exiled Dante's Hope for Reconciliation," pp. 436–441

394. Having responded to the decretalist arguments *ab auctoritate,* "from authority," Dante now turns to their arguments *ratione,* "by means of reason or logic." See G. Di Giannatale, "Papa e Imperatore in *Monarchia* III, 12," *Alighieri* 22, no. 2 (1981): 46–60; and Martinelli, "Sul 'quodammodo,'" p. 206.

395. *"all things of a single genus can be reduced to one that is the standard measure. . . .":* *Metaph.* 10:1:1052b:15–30, 10:2:1053a:18–20. See the Latin version in St. Thomas Aquinas, *In Metaph. Exp.,* ed. Cathala and Spiazzi, pp. 461, 464. See above, Chapter 3, pp. 101–2.

396. *"accidental attributes":* "*secundum accidens.*" See n. 320 above, and pp. 33, 89, 155, 166–67, 183 n. 211.

397. *"pope":* "*papa*" means "father." Dante is building the case for his final statement concerning the reverence (not obedience) that the emperor, "like a firstborn son," owes to the pope as father. On the sense of "*reverentia,*" see Cassell, "The Exiled Dante's Hope for Reconciliation," pp. 431–433.

398. Aristotle, *Metaph.* 10:1:1052b:15–30, 10:2:1053a:18–20 (Barnes, 2:1662–1663). Considering the term "idea" used by the Aristotelians of the thirteenth century, St. Thomas Aquinas returns, rather, to the earlier accepted definition from Platonism: "The Greek word 'idea' is in Latin 'forma.' Hence by ideas are understood the forms of things, *existing apart from the things themselves*. Now the form of anything existing apart from the thing itself can be for one of two ends; either to be the type of that which is called the form, or to be the principle of knowledge of that thing" (*ST* I, q. 15, a. 1). Dante says that the human form or idea is determined by intention within the Divine Mind, i.e., an ideal form (*Conv.* 3:6:5). See Nardi, ed., ad loc. Most important, as Vinay points out (ed., ad loc.), since *such ideas are within the mind of God*, thus, the "idea" of man is a *metaphysical* not a *political* concept. On the "reduction to one," see Maccarrone, "Il terzo libro," pp. 91–97. In the *Conv.* 3:6:6, Dante writes that if the human form is not perfect when reproduced in individual beings, it is not the fault of the exemplar but of the material that furnishes that individuality. Only transcendent ideas, Dante says, that are known only to heavenly intelligences have that perfection not found in any immanent, individual example. His philosophical position is that "Man" is a substantial form, and the perfection of man is an "idea" (speaking Platonically) in the mind of God, while "being pope," on the other hand, like "being a judge, a potentate, a postman, or an emperor," is merely an earthly accident, attribute, or quality indicating a relationship among men. By artfully couching his opponents arguments in a syllogism, Dante shows that they commit the logical error termed *"secundum accidens,"* confusing accidental qualities with substances (see above, pp. 33, 89, and 281, and n. 396). The whole discussion reveals the depth of training that the author gained from his formal and independent studies. Nardi and Maccarrone unnccessarily assume that Dante was responding to a very specific and abstruse supporter of pontifical authority, Giovanni Lemoyne (perhaps to be rendered simply as "John the Monk"). This otherwise anonymous papalist compiler of the *Glossa ad Extravagantes* on Boniface VIII's bull *Unam sanctam* first cites the source of this method of argumentation: "According to Proclus [*Elementatio theologica* 1–6, 21], every multitude can be reduced to a single unity. And according to the Philosopher [Aristotle, *Metaph* 10:1], in one single genus whatsoever one can find one that is first and supreme, one which is the measure and norm of all the others contained in that genus. Elsewhere the dyad follows the monad." Giovanni then brainstorms a double conclusion wrenching the concepts from metaphysics into a theory of raw temporal power as he deals with "Punishments and Remission": "Therefore it is necessary that a multitude of men be reduced to one, and among the genus of men there is to be found one first man who may be the supreme one of that genus; of such a kind is the Roman pontiff who is supreme among all men, existing as a measure and ruling standard of all others, to whom all Catholics are fully subject." Nardi (ed., ad loc.), as previously in his *Dal Convivio* (pp. 263–265), points to this citation in the *Glossa ad Extravagantes* 1:5, tit. 9, discovered, yet not cited, by Maccarrone (*Il terzo libro*, esp. pp. 93–94). But such statements had become a topos by Dante's time. St. Bonaventure's statement in his *Commentaria in decretales* ("Where there is reduction to the supreme among all men, that one is the Vicar of Christ, the

Supreme Pontiff" *(Ubi est reductio ad summum in genere hominum. Eiusmodi est Christus vicarius, pontifex summus)*, cited by Maccarrone, *"Potestas directa,"* pp. 41–42), and those of Tolomeo da Lucca and Remigio de' Girolami on this hierocratic assessment that are more probably Dante's main sources—and tacitly recognized obstacles. Dante shrouds the identity of the actual butt of his attack in silence just as Vernani cannot bring himself to speak Dante's name even once in the text of the *Ref.* (despite the fact that the name is given in the *incipit* and the *explicit*); we catch the poet in the same forensic strategy. Dante is surely arguing here most immediately against his fellow Tuscans—against Tolomeo's *Short Compendium (Determinatio compendiosa*, ed. Krammer, pp. 19, 34) and against Remigio de' Girolami, who had also, unspecifically, acquiesced in the principle of *reductio ad unum* in this regard. For Remigio (as Davis indicated in "An Early Florentine Political Theorist," p. 673), the entire body of the Church was one body and therefore had one head—otherwise it would be a monster, as Remigio cites the hierocratic commonplace echoed in *Unam sanctam:* Christ was the true head, but since he was separated from the body by physical absence, in his place is the pope, who is of the same species as the body, and not of divine substance: the pontiff is thus the *unus summus homo* under whom all men are subjects. Misciting St. Bernard's *On Consideration* 3:18, where the pope is said to be over other prelates, Remigio says that just as God is over all angels in heaven, so the pope is over all other men on earth (*Contra falsos professores ecclesie*, ed. Tamburini, esp. pp. 69–70).

399. Editors searched long to identify the exact passage in Aristotle's *Nic. Ethics* to which Dante refers in this last allusion. Vinay, e.g., suggested *Nic. Ethics* 10:4 rather than 10:5 suggested by others; Ricci points to 10:2 and 10:5, but the principle is actually set forth in the *Metaph.* 10:1:1052b:15–30 and 10:2:1053a:18–20 (see nn. 398 and 402 above). St. Thomas Aquinas, in his *Commentary on the Nic. Ethics* 9:4, had used the concept of measuring a genus according to its one supreme "idea" in the context of the relation of friendship: "For that which is the perfect being in any order of reality must be considered a measure in that order, because all other things are judged more or less perfect according as they approach or recede from what is most perfect. Consequently, since virtue is the proper perfection of man and the virtuous man is perfect in the human species, this should be taken as the measure in man's affairs" (trans. Litzinger, 2:804). The poet, however, would have received the principle of the "reduction of genus to the supreme monad" from myriad sources; see Maccarrone, "Il terzo libro," pp. 91–97; and B. Nardi, *Dal Convivio alla Commedia*, pp. 263–272, and his ed., ad loc.

400. Dante is being most subtle in demonstrating this absurdity: the hierocrats did, in fact, claim that "the pope is the true emperor"! See above, pp. 19, 204, 258.

401. *relationships of superior position: "relationes superpositiones."* Again, it may seem that Dante is being tiresomely obvious, but he knew that Peter of Spain, in *Summulæ logicales*, Tractatus III, 18 (ed. de Rijk, p. 34–35), had been equally elementary in explaining that some things may be related as the same and as equals, and others "according to superior position, as lord, double, triple" *(secundum superpositione, ut dominus, duplum, triplum)*, and others "accord-

ing to inferior positions, as servant" *(secundum suppositione, ut servus)*. "The lord is placed over the servant and the father to the son . . . the servant is placed under the lord and the son to the father." See Nardi, *Dal Convivio all Commedia*, p. 271.

402. All things and thus all relationships can be reduced to God (the culmination of all being, of all substances, and of all accidents of relationship), but Dante allows the possibility that such a general commonality between the *papatus* (office and authority of the pope) and the *imperiatus* (office and authority of the emperor) may be found in a substance below God. Kay (ed., ad loc.) believes this angelic substance to be the Heaven of the Sun (the Heaven of the angelic order of Powers, where rulers and popes dwell in the afterlife) and the angelic Powers themselves that regulate those subordinate to them. He points to St. Thomas Aquinas, *ST* I, q. 108, a. 3. Shaw (ad loc.) cites Ricci, ed. pp. 264–265, and Kantorowicz's *The King's Two Bodies*, p. 458.

403. The rest of ch. 13, and the next two chs., 14 and 15, *disprove*, i.e., *give negative proofs* of, the thesis that the Church has authority over the Holy Roman Empire. The last chapter *will give positive*, "ostensive" *proof* or "proof positive." Peter of Spain, in the *Summulæ logicales*, Tractatus 7, 164, says, "There are two kinds of syllogism, that is, the demonstrative [*ostensivus*] syllogism and the syllogism 'ad impossibilem.' The ostensive syllogism is the one that has only one conclusion. The syllogism 'ad impossibilem' occurs when we are led to some impossible conclusion and, because of this, one of the premises that is the cause of the impossibility is destroyed. Hence this syllogism always has two conclusions" (ed. de Rijk, pp. 173–174). See also, Kay, *Mon.* ed., ad loc.

404. These were burning issues that had been much argued. As we noted above, Uguccione had asserted that there had been an emperor before there was a pope, and an empire before there was a papacy. John of Paris insisted that "there was no priesthood before Christ Jesus"; the priesthood of the Old Testament was merely a figure to be fulfilled (*On Royal and Papal Power*, trans. Watt, pp. 90–91). On the other hand, for Hugh of St. Victor, God instituted the priesthood before the empire (*De sacramentis* 2:2:4; trans. Deferrari, p. 256). Giles of Rome had vehemently defended the priority of the Church in his *On Ecclesiastical Power* 1:6:1 (trans. Dyson, pp. 14–18): "Priestly power is prior to royal power, not only in dignity, but also in time." Vernani, as usual, follows Giles, saying that the Church existed potentially as an entity before the temporal power, in his *De potestate summi pontificis* 10, pp. 73–77 and 81, and in the *Ref.* 3:74: "The Roman Empire at no time existed nor had any power when the Church did not exist, because the Church has always existed." Like Giles (1:6:2)., he will also argue the case of Samuel's priestly precedence over Saul (*Ref.* 3:16–31, 95–98).

405. Aristotle had outlined four causes: material, formal, efficient, and final (*Physics* 2:3:194b:15–195a:27; *Metaph.* 5:2:1013a:24–1014a:25; Barnes, 1:332–332, 2:1600–1601). On the erroneous, political, attribution of causes, see Aristotle, *Rhetoric* 2:24:1401b:30–35; and see St. Thomas Aquinas, *In Phys. Exp.*, ed. Maggiòlo, pp. 91–94, and *In Metap. Exp.*, ed. Cathala and Spiazzi, pp. 211–213. Cf. *Conv.* 4:20:10. The efficient cause of something is the force or

agent that does the work or performs the change. Vinay, followed by Kay (eds., ad loc.), notes that Dante's arguments bear a resemblance to St. Thomas Aquinas's proofs that Old Testament sacraments did not confer grace in *ST* III, q. 62, a. 6.

406. Acts 25:10.

407. Acts 27:24.

408. Acts 28:19.

409. Dante, as usual, cites from memory, conflating Jos 2:13: "And deliver our souls from death," and Ps 32:19: "To deliver their souls from death."

410. Phil 1:23.

411. Lv 2:11.

412. Lv 11:43.

413. *absurd: "inconveniens."* I translate the term so as to make it most familiar to the reader. See, below, *Mon.* 3:15:10, where Dante will refer to these arguments as being technically "reduced to the absurd."

414. *those in the majority:* Dante's term, *"prevalentes,"* may mean either "those who had more distinguished power" (i.e., qualitatively; e.g., Vinay translates *"migliori"* as "the best"; ad loc) or "those in the majority," as in a voting majority (i.e., quantitatively; thus, Maccarrone, in "Il terzo libro," p. 106, n. 1). Clearly here *"prevalentes"* signifies "those in the majority," "those who prevail," since below Dante states: "It did not get it either *from the assent of all men."* Dante notes that in his day Asians, Africans, European pagans, and others reject the Church; the Ghibellines reject its temporal authority. Of course, no supporter of the hierocracy of the Church had ever claimed—or would claim—that a *vote* or referendum of all mankind had ever granted temporal authority to the Church (although in this chapter Dante does grant such a democratic origin to the empire). Note the tone of Dante's puckish argument in allowing such a possibility—but it does give him the opportunity to wave a haughty dismissal of his stooping opponents with a flourish of tongue-in-cheek legalese!

415. Mt 16:18.

416. Jn 17:4.

417. In Dt 18:1–2, Moses through God's commandment excludes the priests and the Levites from any part of the inheritance of lands conquered by Israel; they are to be supported materially by a share from the sacrifices of their brethren (cf. *Purg.* 16:130–132); and in Mt 10:9–10, Christ exhorts the disciples, "Do not possess gold, nor silver, nor money in your purses: nor scrip for your journey, nor two coats, nor shoes, nor a staff." Priests thus are released of any burden of care of, for, or over worldly possessions and, as Dante now thinly stretches his point, temporal power.

418. *On Being Simply:* See Aristotle's *Metaph.* 7:7 (Barnes, 2: 1629–1631); and 9:8 (Barnes, 2: 1657–1660; trans. Tredennick, LCL, 1:336–337, 454–457). Cf. *Conv.* 4:10 and *Mon.* 1:13:3.

419. *gave itself: "daret sibi."* Shaw restores *"sibi,"* omitted by Ricci.

420. *tiresome to adduce proofs for things so obvious:* Cf. *Conv.* 4:19: "Those things which are

manifest, that is, obvious, require no proof." Dante is citing the *Glossa Accursiana*; see L. Chiappelli, "Ancora su Dante e il diritto," *Giornale Dantesco* 20 (1912): 205.

421. *"'nature' may refer to matter and form . . . Lessons on Nature"*: i.e., in the *Physics* 2:1:193b6: "The form indeed is nature, rather than the matter" (see Barnes, 1:330; and the Latin text and commentary in St. Thomas Aquinas, *In Phys. Exp.*, ed. Maggiòlo, pp. 78–80). Cf. *Mon.* 1:1.

422. Jn 21:16.

423. Jn 13:15.

424. Jn 21:19.

425. Reading *"huiusmodi,"* attested by most MSS, with Ricci and P. Shaw ("Sul testo," pp. 208–209), rather than the infelicitous *"huius mundi"* supported by Nardi.

426. Jn 18:36.

427. *dry land:* Ps 94:5 (AV 95:5). Dante is, as usual, quoting from memory and replaces the Vulgate's *"siccam"* with *"aridam"*; the sense is the same.

428. On Christ's concern for his kingdom on earth, see Chapter 1, p. 6.

429. The passage is difficult, but its meaning is clear. Christ was both God and man. As Incarnate, *Christ-the-man is the seal that is impressed;* the gold is Christ-as-God Eternal. Christ-as-man did not concern himself with earthly power, although, as God (and unlike his vicar), he possessed all. This Christ-as-man is the form or impression to be imitated by the Church. In other words, man cannot be God (gold), but he can imitate the humble actions of Christ to be Christlike (the impression of the seal). *The example or form of Christ's life should be as a pattern stamped upon the Church.* After his deposition by Innocent IV, we find the emperor Frederick II in his *Letter to the Kings of Christendom* using the analogy of a gold seal on wax for the importance of an example in moral life; see Frederick's text in ed. Tierney, *Crisis*, p. 145. This is probably Dante's source. Also see Kay (ed., ad loc.), who cites Pézard, *"La rotta gonna,"* 2:96–160.

430. *Categories* 12:14b:18–22 (Barnes, 1:22). See Boethius's and William of Moerbeke's versions in *Categoriæ vel Prædicamenta: Translatio Boethii-Editio Composita, Translatio Guillelmi de Moerbeka Lemmata e Simplicii Commentario Decerpta Pseudo-Augustini Paraphrasis Themistiana*, ed. Lorenzo Mineo-Paluello, Aristoteles Latinus 1, 1–5 (Bruges/Paris: Desclée de Brouwer, 1961), pp. 38, 114. Truth or falsity does not come from speech, the signifier, but from the truth or falsity of what is spoken about, the signified. Kay (ed., ad loc.) points to Peter of Spain's *Summulæ logicales*, Tractatus III, 30: "True discourse is not the cause of a thing's being. From what a thing is or is not, however, discourse is said to be true or false" (ed. de Rijk, p. 40).

431. *reduction to the absurd: ducendo "ad inconveniens."* Cf., above, *Mon.* 3:12:9, and notes.

432. *ostensive demonstration:* See above, n. 403. "Ostensive proof" or a "proof positive"; just how persuasive Dante believed this to be can be gathered from the sense of *"ostendere"* and *"ostensivus"* that, when used in a spiritual context, has an epiphanical sense of "to reveal" and "be revelatory."

433. *horizon that is the midway between the two hemispheres:* Dante's direct source for the "horizon" image is St. Thomas Aquinas's chapter on "How an intellectual substance can be the form of the body," in *Summa contra gentiles* 2:68. J. F. Anderson (*On the Truth of the Catholic Faith*, 2:205) translates and emphasizes: "The intellectual soul is said to be on the *horizon* and *confines* of things corporeal and incorporeal, in that it is an incorporeal substance and yet form of a body," and indicates editorially that the *Liber de causis* 2:22, is in turn, Thomas's source. The intellectual soul of man is the lowest of all intellectual substances, beneath that of God and the angelic hosts; thus it is at the point or confine where corporeal substance begins exactly beneath it. See also the useful glosses of Nardi, Imbach-Flüeler, and Kay, ad loc. Friar Guido Vernani, seeing the incontrovertibility of Dante's authority here, will pass over this striking image in silence.

434. *this alone, since it is perpetual, is it given to separate itself from the corruptible:* See *De anima* (*On the Soul*) 2:2:413b:24–29. Moerbeke's Latin version reads: *"De intellectu autem et perspectiva potentia nihil adhuc manifestum est, sed videtur genus alterum animæ esse; et hoc solum contingit, separari, sicut æternum a corruptibili"* (There is no evidence yet about intellect or the power of reflection, but it appears to be a different kind of soul; and this belongs to it alone: to be separated, as eternal from the corruptible). See St. Thomas Aquinas, *In Aristotelis librum De Anima commentarium*, ed. Pirotta, pp. 69–72; Thomas rewords the phrase *"separari . . . sicut perpetuum a corruptibili"*—hence, Dante's use of "perpetual" for Moerbeke's "eternal" (p. 70). Imbach, followed by Kay (*Mon.* eds., ad loc.) notes that Dante mainly models his doctrine of the soul upon St. Thomas Aquinas, but with different emphases. Cf. Nardi, *Dante e la cultura medievale*, pp. 284–308.

435. Dante is employing a poetic trope of food and flavor here that might be rendered more precisely, but, unfortunately, rather too oddly, in English as: "since every mean bears the savor [*sapiat*], [or has the pungency] of both extremes, man must necessarily smack [*sapere*] of both natures."

436. We must recall that Dante's Earthly Paradise atop the purgatorial mountain is not so high as to reach the sphere of the moon; it is located within the *sæculum*. Dante will have his Wayfarer enjoy an *"arra,"* a "figure," or "foretaste" (*Par.* 28:93) of that blessedness within the fiction of the *Commedia*. See the comments of Singleton, in *Journey to Beatrice*, p. 144.

437. Dante's dependence on the thought of Tolomeo da Lucca becomes clear where the prior of Santa Maria Novella cites Aristotle to identify the earthly, common good as per se divine: "Something participates in divine actions to the degree that it is ordained to an excellent end. This describes a kingdom of any community or an association, whether it is regal, a polity [a republic], or of some other condition, since, when one intends an exceptionally noble end, as Aristotle notes. We understand that divine action is in it from the start, and that the common good is especially divine. Perhaps Aristotle states that the common good is especially divine because government takes it origin from the truth." Tolomeo, however, ends with the ruler's leading his subjects to *eternal* beatitude. See *On the Government of Rulers* 3:3:2–4; trans. Blythe, p. 151–152.

438. *"holy writers": "agiographos."* Dante again adopts a Greek transliteration that he found in Uguccione da Pisa's *Magnæ derivationes: "quod est agyographia dictur, id est sancta scriptura."* See Paget Toynbee, *Dante Studies and Researches* (London: Methuen,1902), p. 102. Also see Kay, *Mon.* ed., ad loc. See nn. 95, 493, 268, and 266 above.

439. Ps 31:9: The verse suggested Dante's equestrian metaphors *("freno," "camo")* for the scourging and curbing teachings in circles of Purgatory; cf. *Purg.* 13:40, 14:143.

440. *threshing-floor: "areola ista."* Since the emperor is "lord of the world," Dante means the northern hemisphere, believed to be the only inhabited part of the earth in classical and medieval times. Dante uses the term in Italian in *Par.* 22:151: *"L'aiuola che ci fa tanto feroci"* (the little threshing floor that makes us so ferocious) and in 27:85–86: *"E più mi fora dis-coverto il sito / di questa aiuola . . ."* (more of the space of this little threshing floor would have been disclosed to me). The image is suggested by Mt 3:12 and Lk 3:17; but cf. Vergil, *Georgics* 1:178–181. James of Viterbo used the image in his *De regimine christiano* 1 to signify the Church: "Upon the Church's threshing floor there is grain mixed with chaff, until Christ, the winnower of the threshing floor, shall come and separate the wheat from the chaff" (*On Christian Government*, trans. Dyson, p. 10). Dante puns on the Last-Judgment images of winnowing straw and milling to describe Satan and the frozen damned in deepest Hell in *Inf.* 34. The thickening mixture of metaphors in these paragraphs (equestrian, nautical, winnowing) are a foreshortening of the same variety of images that the poet uses in other various parts of his *Commedia*. Dante assigns the highest place to peace and tranquillity as the means to the full use and right order of the intellect, but does not give it quite the same supreme position endowed upon it by his fellow Florentine Fra Remigio de' Girola-mi, who, shocked by the internecine strife between the White and the Black Guelphs of Florence, subordinates all other human goods to tranquillity at almost any cost in his *De bono pacis*.

441. *"electors":* The six German princes who according to the *Sachsenspiegel* of 1220, codi-fying Saxon law, were the electors of the emperor. They were usually—but not always—the archbishops of Cologne, of Mainz, and of Trier; the count palatine of the Rhine; the duke of Saxony; and the margrave of Brandenburg. Historically, a seventh, the king of Bohemia, was also included in some elections. The identity and rights of the electors were to be formally recognized by Charles IV's Golden Bull of 1356, published especially to prevent a repetition of the double, or rather, split, election of 1314 in which, as we have seen, Ludwig of Bavaria and Frederick the Fair of Austria were left to vie as claimants to be king of the Romans, with Ludwig's reign never recognized by the Holy See. See John B. Freed, "Elections, Royal," *Dictionary of the Middle Ages*, 4:425–429. An English translation of "The Golden Bull of the Emperor Charles IV, 1356 A.D." is found in *Select Historical Documents of the Middle Ages*, trans. Ernest F. Henderson (New York: Bilo & Tannen, 1965), pp. 220–261.

442. Clearly a reference to the perennial, burning issue of the split election of Ludwig of Bavaria and the myriad of troubles it caused after 1314; see pp. 12–13, 14, 34, 39 and n.

441, above, to the translation. On Ludwig's dubious coronations, see Chapter 2, pp. 34, 36–37. The electors' earlier choice of Henry of Luxembourg in 1309 had been, in contrast, unanimous; this fact is important for establishing the later date of composition of Dante's treatise. Since the problem of the contested dual election endured for nearly half of the fourteenth century and was not to be resolved until 1356, long after Dante's death, 1314 can only be used as a *terminus ab quo* of the *Mon.*'s composition, not as its *terminus ad quem* as Maurizio Palma di Cesnola arbitrarily asserts in his *Semiotica dantesca*, p. 103. John XXII's *Si fratrum* of late 1316, or more likely 1317, triggered the strife and eventual official papal Crusade against the Ghibellines.

443. An echo of Boethius, *Consolation of Philosophy* 4, prose 6: "the fortress [*arx*] of its own simplicity." In his *Epistle* 5:5:17, Dante speaks of God as a fount of universal authority, *"a quo, velut a puncto bifurcatur Petri Cesarisque potestas,"* "from whom, as from a point, the power of Cæsar and Peter doth bifurcate" (ed. Toynbee, pp. 53–54, 60).

444. *"pried out":* Cf. *Mon.* 1:1:5.

445. *reverentia:* Like John of Paris, his earlier contemporary, Dante never denigrates the pope's authority in *spiritualia;* cf. *On Royal and Papal Power* 18, trans. Watt, pp. 190–193. Tolomeo da Lucca cites the *Decreta*, apparently from memory: *"Ponuntur autem in dicta distinctione* Decreti *tres comparationes imperatoris ad papam, per quas haberi potest, summum pontificem imperatori preferri et esse superiorem. Dicitur enim ibi sic se habere papam ad ipsum sicut magistratum ad discipulum et sicut patrem ad filium . . ."* (Three comparisons of the emperor to the pope are suggested in the said distinction of the *Decretum* by which the pontiff is to be held privileged and superior: It says that the pope is to him as a master to a pupil and as a father to a son . . .; see *Determinatio compendiosa*, cap. 3, ed. Krammer, p. 8). The reverence of son to father occurs more than once as a pattern in Dante's works. We recall that in the presence of *"la cara immagine paterna,"* Brunetto Latini, on the burning Plain of the Sodomites, the Wayfarer "kept his head bowed as one who walks in reverence" (*Inf.* 15:44–45), and when he suddenly sees Cato, the guardian of Ante-Purgatory, standing next to him, the poet describes the sage as "an old man, alone, worthy of as much reverence as any boy-child owes a father" (*Vidi presso di me un veglio solo, / degno di tanta reverenza in vista, / che più non dee a padre alcun figliuolo"; Purg.* 1:31–33). On the question of the emperor's due *"reverentia,"* see Cassell, "The Exiled Dante's Hope for Reconciliation," pp. 431–433.

446. Cf. *Conv.* 1:12:4–7.

447. I.e., grace from the pope's blessing.

## NOTES TO VERNANI'S 'REFUTATION'

1. The title appears in the Classense manuscript; that on f.1ʳ of Vernani's autograph in the British Library has been scraped clean; there is no *incipit*, f. 2ʳ. My translation follows Matteini's reproduction and emendations of Käppeli's edition, with the corrections and the hazarded variant expansions of the abbreviations, as I have noted, by Carlo Dolcini.

When in doubt about any reading, I have consulted the Classense copy but more especially the British Library autograph, preferring the latter as my *texte de base*. The book numbers
of the Latin *Reprobatio* text are editorial and correspond to Dante's three books; Vernani
makes no break in his autograph. For ease of reference and consistency, I have inserted
phrase and sentence numbers between { } to correspond in sense and subject matter both
to Matteini's and Tarrant's presentation of the Latin sentences and to larger clausal divisions in the *Refutation* and *Si fratrum.*

2. Completed ca. 1324, Graziolo de' Bambaglioli's is the earliest *dated* Latin commentary
on any part of the *Divine Comedy* that has come down to us. Graziolo had staunchly defended many of Dante's ideas against those, such as Cecco d'Ascoli, who had ill used the
poet as the butt of his mockery in *L'Acerba*. Cecco and Vernani were fellow lectors at the
University of Bologna where there was a groundswell of anti-Dantesque sentiment even
before Cardinal-Legate du Poujet's condemnation of the poet in the name of the Bolognese Commune; an early collusion of Cecco and Vernani is not to be dismissed, and it
may be an association that Vernani came to regret after Cecco's notorious condemnation
for heresy. Vernani may have thought to exculpate himself by besmirching Bambaglioli's
"unseemly" admiration for Dante, unaware that Graziolo was deeply entrenched in secret
Guelph political schemes with du Poujet. The exact chronology of Graziolo's composition is uncertain: we cannot tell, for example, whether the gloss concerning Fortuna, by
Bambaglioli on *Inf.* 7, predates or postdates Cecco's attack in *L'Acerba*, vv. 707–774. Cf.
Bambaglioli's *Commento*, ed. Rossi, p. xxvii, 58–67.

3. *flaunts:* Carlo Dolcini ("Guido Vernani e Dante: Note sul testo del *De reprobatione
Monarchiæ*," *Letture Classensi* 9–10 [1982]: 261) reads *"pretendit"*; all published versions of the
*Reprobatio* prefer *"protendit."* Vernani's abbreviation obviously makes any decision arbitrary.

4. Vernani uses Dante's own words in the *Commedia* against him: here the friar is slyly
alluding to Ciampolo's charge against Fra Gomito in Dante's *Inf.* 22:82, labeling him the
*"vasel d'ogni froda"* (vessel of every fraud). Vernani's description of the bowl, however, owes
much to the description of the hypocrites' cloaks in *Inf.* 23: 64–65 *"di fuor dorate son . . . ma
dentro tutte piombo"* (outside they are gilded . . . but within they are all lead). Despite his pro-
fessions of scorn, Friar Guido knows the *Commedia* very well. Cf. Brunetto Latini in the
*Tresor*, 2:54: ". . . a man is called noble on account of his noble and virtuous deeds, and
from this is born originally the nobility of a gentle race, and not from ancestors, for to
have a vulgar heart and high lineage is to be an earthen vessel gilded outside with gold."

5. *liar and father . . . of lies:* Vernani is responding—and going one better—to Dante's
charge that the Guelphs are sons, not of the Church, but of Satan, in *Mon.* 3:3:8. Cf. Jn
8:44: "You are of your father the devil, and the desires of your father you will do. He was
a murderer from the beginning, and he stood not in the truth; because truth is not in him.
When he speaketh a lie, he speaketh of his own: for he is a liar and the father thereof." We
must also note that Vernani's language here and below haughtily echoes that of John
XXII, especially in the decretal *Quia quorundam mentes:* "The father of lies is said to have

blinded the minds of some so much that they have attempted with clear temerity to detract from our constitutions" (trans. Heft, *John XXII and Papal Teaching Authority*, p. 33). The friar also recalls Dante's verses put into the mouth of Catalano in *Inf.* 23:142–144, concerning the demons guarding the previous bolgia of the barrators: *"I' udi' già dire a Bologna / del diavol vizi assai, tra 'quali udi' / ch'elli è bugiardo e padre di menzogna"* (At Bologna once I heard it said that the devil has many vices, among which I heard that he is a liar and the father of lies). The Dominican friar enjoys the malice of lumping the poet together with the denizens of both those "evil ditches" of Lower Hell, knowing that Dante had been exiled precisely on a trumped-up charge of barratry. The reference jabs derisively at Graziolo de' Bambaglioli's devotion to Dante as a writer and at Bambaglioli's commentary on the *Commedia*.

6. *he fell . . . could not stand in the truth:* Cf. Ps 35:13: "The workers of iniquity are fallen, they are cast out, and could not stand." As a seraph in Heaven, Satan-Lucifer had been a pure rational soul, a pure intellectual substance bathing in the light of the divine countenance: cast into Hell for pride (cf. Is 14:13), he seeks to corrupt the rational soul of man.

7. Cf. Giles of Rome in *De potestate ecclesiastica* 1:3:6: "The power of the Supreme Pontiff . . . is as much more exalted and noble than any earthly and secular power as the soul is more excellent and noble than the body and the spiritual life more excellent than the earthly" (*On Ecclesiastical Power*, trans. Dyson, p. 7).

8. Vernani never mentions Dante's name anywhere in the body of the text, referring to him disparagingly in Latin as *"quidam,"* "a certain individual" (as in this passage); *"ille homo"* or *"ille,"* "that fellow"; or *"iste homo,"* perhaps, "the wretch." The suppression of one's opponent's name was a norm in dialectical technique.

9. *sophist:* a hierocratic *topos.* Although sarcastic, this is not merely an *ad hominem* insult invented by Vernani. Based on Aristotle's *Nic. Ethics* 10:9, "the sophists who profess the art [of legislation] seem to be very far from teaching it" (1181a:13–14; cf. Barnes, 2:1866), the charge of being wordy sophists *("sophistici")* became the conventional *improperium* of papal writers against nonecclesiastical challengers to papal temporal plenitude of power. Ullmann remarks: "In whatever rational and scholarly manner the civilians might have replied to this vast and all-embracing claim [of the pope's claim to be *"rex omnium omnibus imperans"*] to papal jurisdiction, the canonists retorted by employing the ancient strategem of branding their ideological contestants as sophisticated speculators" (*Medieval Papalism*, p. 78 and n. 3). Such a derisive and taunting tone characterized some publicist polemics between the Guelphs and the Ghibellines. E.g., King Robert's countercharges against Henry VII in 1313, after Henry's condemnation of the Neapolitan king for lèse majesté, denounced the emperor as an enemy of the Church; Robert declared that he gave no care for the "fatuous verbosity" of Henry's sentences which were "the garrulity of an effeminate senescence" (Bowsky, *Henry VII*, pp. 185, 263). Such vituperations give historical and poetic context, for example, to our understanding of the jibes hurled during the Farinata-Cavalcante episode in *Inf.* 10.

10. Vernani's words echo those of his colleague at the *studium* of Bologna, Cecco d'Ascoli, in the latter's Boethian satire on Dante in *L'Acerba* 4:4669–46671: "Here we don't sing like frogs; / here we don't sing like the Poet / *who, imagining, feigns vain things.*" Vernani also reflects Dante's own biblical diatribe at the beginning of *Mon.* 2 where the poet cites Ps 2:1–3 concerning certain hierocrats "imagining vain things."

11. Boethius, *Consolation* 1:1. Note that Vernani has been using the language of painted whoredom in the preceding sentences.

12. The wording here and in the previous paragraph continues Vernani's calque on John XXII's *Quia quorundam mentes:* "In order to provide against those attempting such pernicious things, lest their pestiferous doctrine shape the souls of the simple and be able to lead them into the ways of their own error" (trans. Heft, *John XXII and Papal Teaching Authority*, p. 33).

13. *that screed: "illud scriptum."* Vernani avoids dignifying the *Mon.* anywhere in the *Ref.* with the philosophical term *tractatus*, "treatise," or even *liber*, "book."

14. *scoff with confidence, scrutinize with care, and with clear reasoning demolish: "irrideo fide, diligentia discutio et intelligentia clara dissolvo."* The phrase is calqued upon Augustine's *De agone christiano* 12[13] (*PL* 40:298): "But there are still a few grumblers who are troubled by unwarranted jealousy. They include: those who, while appearing to be Catholics, seek their own interests in the Church; heretics who look for glory in the very name of Christ; Jews eager to justify their impious crime; pagans fearful of losing their empty joy in ever curious satisfactions. *The Catholic Church*, however, spread over the length and breadth of the whole world, has turned back these assaults ... not by resistence, but by patient endurance: nowadays *She scoffs with confidence at their invidious questions, scrutinizes them with care and with clear reasoning demolishes them* [*invidiosas questiones fide irridet, diligentia discutit, intelligentia dissolvit*]" (trans. modified from *The Christian Combat*, trans. Robert P. Russell, in *The Writings of Saint Augustine* [New York: CIMA, 1947], 4:330–331). Since earlier editors failed to identify the source of this quotation, they did not realize that it further reveals Vernani's at once fearful, grandiose, and conflicted state of mind as he girds himself to refute Dante's treatise, addressing it to the powerful chancellor of the Bolognese court system: the friar poses as if he were the very Church herself speaking as a whole, a posture that fits also with his haughty stylistic and conceptual calques on Pope John XXII's bull *Quia quorundam mentes*, promulgated against the Franciscan ideal of apostolic poverty.

15. Reading *"hoc"* (Dolcini, p. 260), for *"hec"* (Käppeli, Matteini).

16. Reading *"et utilia et diligat"* (Dolcini, p. 260).

17. *screed:* see above, n. 13. Following Dante's model, Vernani divides his treatise into three parts.

18. Vernani cedes that Dante's arguments for a single world ruler have much truth; the friar agrees with the principle, of course, but for him that prince of temporal power must be the pope as Vicar of Christ.

19. Vernani is using subterfuge: he well knows why Dante does not clarify this, for it

would be to stress the imperfection of the individual apart from the community. For Dante, as for St. Augustine and St. Thomas Aquinas, the part is inferior to the whole. In the *Confessions* 3:8, St. Augustine says that there is "faultiness and deficiency in every part that does not fit into the whole, of which it is part." Likewise for St. Thomas Aquinas, in law "every part is ordained to the whole as imperfect to perfect" (*ST* I-II, q. 90, a. 2). Dante clarifies the ultimate end of mankind as his principle in *Mon.* 1:4:1, and 1:4:5.

20. See below, note 22.

21. "Whether the happiness of the state is to be pronounced the same as that of each individual man, or whether it is different. Here too the answer is clear: everybody would agree that it is the same. For all those who base the good life upon wealth in the case of the individual, also assign felicity to the state as a whole if it is wealthy; and all who value the life of the tyrant highest, would also say that the state which rules the widest empire is the happiest" (Aristotle, *Pol.* 7:2:1324a:5–10; trans. H. Rackham, LCL, pp. 538–539; cf. Barnes, 2:2101). See St. Thomas Aquinas, *In libros politicorum Aristotelis*, Lectio II, 1059–1060, ed. Spiazzi, pp. 342–343.

22. Such a choice between the goal of "all men" and the end of the "individual" is actually a creature of Vernani's own sophistry. Throughout his rebuttal, the friar stubbornly ignores the distinction between the ideal goal of attaining, ultimately, to God—the goal of all men (as St. Augustine says in his *Confessions* 1:1: "Our hearts shall not rest till they rest in Thee")—and the practical and doctrinal fact that, although Christ opened the choice of Heaven, some men will love lesser goods, and choose instead freely, willingly, and, eventually, impenitently, to go to Hell. In Florence, Remigio de' Girolami, who fairly represents, along with Dante, the Aristotelian tenor of that city, likewise cited Aristotle to the effect that the proper operation of man was to know; but he also realized that few followed this natural end: lured by ignorance, men pursued wealth, pleasure, and honors. Remigio, in fact, placed the common good on such a high level in the city-state and subordinated the citizens' welfare to it to the point that he affirmed, exaggerating rhetorically, that the individual citizen should prefer to see himself in Hell rather than allow his community be involved in inextricable error—although the higher love of God would prevent him from actually doing it (*De bono communi*, ed. De Matteis, pp. 20, 80).

23. Sancti Aureli Augustini, *De Genesi ad litteram libri duodecim* . . . , recensuit Josephus Zycha, CSEL 38, sect. 3, pt. 1 (Prague/Vienna/Leipzig: Tempsky & Freitag, 1893), p. 99.

24. Again Vernani glosses over the integrity of the context: St. Thomas Aquinas is speaking of man's ultimate felicity as his proper end, not the interim happiness attainable on earth. St. Thomas, in fact, adduces Aristotle: "[Aristotle] concludes that those men for whom such perfection in this life is possible are happy as *men*, as if they had not attained felicity absolutely, but merely in human fashion" (*Summa contra gentiles* 3:48, 9).

25. Vernani's refutation twists the poet's words; Dante would, in fact, agree. In *Par.* Dante provides just such a difference in degrees of beatitude as the very structural matrix of that canticle.

26. Dante argued for the full function of the possible intellect in peace and equity as a final goal (here on earth first, leading to the intellectual blessedness of heaven, the Sight of God, in the second spiritual realm); his argument on the necessity of the collectivity was not unlike St. Thomas Aquinas's in the *ST* I-II, q. 90, a. 2. In Purgatory, after having Virgilio crown and miter the Wayfarer over himself (*Purg.* 27:142), Dante has his Wayfarer enter the Earthly Paradise alone as an individual: suddenly Virgilio, his guide, has disappeared from his side (*Purg.* 30:49). Indeed, the whole drama of the separate and personal souls in the afterlife in Dante's poem shows the absurdity of Vernani's attempts to prove Dante a monopsychist. See Nardi, *Saggi di filosofia dantesca*, pp. 233–240; Gilson, *Dante and Philosophy*, pp. 169–170; J. De Raedemaeker, "Informations concernant quelques commentaires du *De Anima*," *Bulletin de Philosophie Médiévale édité par la Societe Internationale pour l'Etude de la Philosophie Médiévale* (S.I.E.P.M.), 8–9 (1966–1967): 102–104; C. J. Lohr, "Medieval Latin Aristotle Commentaries, Authors G–I," *Traditio* 24 (1968): 191–192; R. Macken, "Un apport important e l'ecdotique des manuscrits à pièces. A propos de l'édition léonin du Commentaire de Thomas d'Aquin sur la Politique d'Aristote et sa Tabula Libri Ethicorum," *Scriptorium* 27, no. 2 (1973): 319–327; Martin Grabmann, "Die Lehre vom *intellectus possibilis* und *intellectus agens* im *Liber de anima des Petrus Hispanus* des späteren Papstes Johannes XXI," *Archives d'histoire doctrinale et littérature du Moyen Age* 12–13 (1937–1938 [publ. 1938]): 167–208; Käppeli, *Scriptores Ordinis Prædicatorum Medii Ævi. II, G–I* (*Romæ ad S. Sabinæ 1975*), pp. 76–78; and Dolcini, "Guido Vernani e Dante. Note sul testo del *De reprobatione Monarchie*," in his *Crisi di poteri*, pp. 439–452; also see his corrections to Käppeli's ed. of the *Rep.*, p. 439, n. 4.

27. Aristotle, *Nic. Ethics* 6:6 (Barnes, 2:1801).

28. *Ars (technē)* is applied science. See Aristotle, *Nic. Ethics* 1:1 and 6:6 (Barnes, 2:1729, 1801). Also see St. Thomas Aquinas, *Commentary on the Nic. Ethics*, trans. Litzinger, pp. 5, 563.

29. *it says . . . that man is principally intellect:* "Life is defined . . . in the case of man, by the capacity for perception or thought. . . . It appears therefore that life in the full sense is perception or thought" (Aristotle, *Nic. Ethics* 9:9:1170a:15–18; trans. Rackham, LCL, pp. 560–561, also 562–563; cf. Barnes, 2:1849); see the version in St. Thomas Aquinas's *Commentary on the Nic. Ethics*, at 1170a 7: "For existence was defined as perception or thought" (trans. Litzinger, p. 839).

30. *The First Philosophy:* i.e., Aristotle's *Metaphysics* 12:3:1070a:25 (Barnes, 2:1690). Cf. Latin version in St. Thomas Aquinas, *In Metaph. Exp.*, ed. Cathala et Spiazzi, p. 573.

31. *clearly says:* In fact, Vernani knows very well that Aristotle is anything *but* intentionally clear in this regard! "*Whether* any form remains also afterwards *is another question. In some cases* there is nothing to prevent this, e.g., *the soul may be of this nature* (not all of it but the intelligent part; for *presumably* all of it cannot be)" (*Metaph.* 12:3:1070a:25–27, trans. Armstrong, LCL, pp. 130–131—my emphases; cf. Barnes, 2:1690).

32. Vernani refers to his *Expositio libri Aristotelis de anima*. See Chapter 2, p. 46, above.

33. Vernani again willfully ignores Dante's text: the poet, in fact, clearly states that "a

single prince, fittingly corresponds to the whole universe, or rather to *the prince of this universe who is God and Monarch*" (*Mon.* 1:7:2). Dante sees a bifurcation of such powers on earth where Vernani sees the pope as possessing both.

34. *a monarch must excel and exceed the whole multitude of his subjects:* Aristotle is actually discussing both monarchy and aristocracy in *Pol.* 3:17:1288a:15–19 (cf. Barnes, 2:2044); cf. St. Thomas Aquinas, *In Libros Politicorum Aristotelis Expositio*, ed. Spiazzi, pp. 183, 184.

35. See the chapter in F. Guidonis Vernani, *De potestate summi pontificis*, pp. 55–60, headed and affirming "That among the unbelievers there never was a true commonwealth or any kind of emperor."

36. St. Augustine, *Epistula* 137:17 (*CSEL* 44, p. 122).

37. Jn 17:11, 21–23.

38. This was the growing ecclesiological doctrine of the time: Peter, with his heirs the popes, alone receives the *auctoritas pastoralis* from Christ. Vernani is unnecessarily retreading a deeply rutted path; we can compare Guillaume de Pierre Godin (ca. 1260–1336), the staunch defender of papal monarchy and the faithful servant of Clement V and of John XXII at Avignon, as Guillaume asserts emphatically that Christ made Peter, and Peter *alone*, of the Apostles bishop and pope; the other eleven were simply priests, receiving their episcopacies not from Christ but from Peter (*Tractatus de causa immediata ecclesiastice potestatis* A: 576–599 ; ed. McReady, pp. 5, 21, 343, 347–348). Remigio de' Girolami, whose lectures Dante may have heard in Florence, makes much the same case as Vernani in his digression on papal power in *Contra falsos ecclesie professores* 18: "All Christians and the whole Church, according to the Apostle [Paul] in many passages, are one body; and this body is without spot, or wrinkle, or any defect, as he says himself in Ephesians 5[:27]. Therefore it is necessary that this body have a corporeal head joined to it . . . the supreme head on this body cannot be a secular prince . . . it is necessary that he be a cleric prince. And such a prince and such a head is Christ, as in Ephesians 1[:22]. . . . But inasmuch as this head has been separated from the body by corporal absence when He ascended into heaven, and lest any diminution be left in the body, it was necessary that a supreme head be joined to the body on earth. This head, then, is the pope and the Lord said that Peter was future pope: John 1[:42] 'Thou art Simon son of you will be called Cephas,' that is, 'head.'" (ed. Tamburini, cap. 18, pp. 44–45). In his vehemence, Vernani, of course, does not admit that Dante never denied, nor would deny, the supremacy of the office of the Roman pontiff *in the Church!*

39. In his chapter on the primacy of the Roman pontiff in *Against the Errors of the Greeks*, St. Thomas Aquinas cites Cyril of Alexandria's *Thesaurus* 98:17–23: "As Christ coming forth from Israel as leader and scepter of the Church of the Gentiles was granted by the Father the fullest power over every principality and power whatsoever, that all should bend the knee to him, so he entrusted most completely the fullest power to Peter and his successors." See *Contra errores Græcorum: Texte présenté et édité avec notes, références et documents connexes*, ed. Palémon Glorieux, in Monumenta Christiana Selecta (Tournai/Paris/New York: Desclée de Brouwer, 1957), p. 169.

40. Vernani, *De potestæ summi pontificis*, pp. 55–60; 64–66; 73–77; 79–80.

41. *man and the sun beget man:* See Aristotle, *Physics* 2:2:194b:13 (Barnes, 1:332); for Moerbeke's translation, see St. Thomas Aquinas, *In Phys. Exp.*, ed. Maggiòlo, p. 86. See Aquinas's exposition (179[10]), p. 88. Cf. *Mon.* 1:9:1.

42. The statement is found in chs. 17–18 of Gennadius Massiliensis's *Liber de ecclesiasticis dogmatibus* (*PL* 58:984–985).

43. Vernani skips over much of book 1 to come to censure Dante's metaphor in *Mon.* 1:9:1 concerning the human race as "the offspring of heaven," "for man and the sun beget man." Dante had cited Aristotle's *Physics* 2:4:194b:3 (Barnes, 1:332), but Vernani insists that this refers only to the body and not to the soul: the rational part of man does not come from the potentiality of matter but is created by God Almighty. Dante had, however, merely followed St. Thomas Aquinas's commentary on Aristotle's *De anima* 3:3:427a:25, lect. 4, no. 619, and had abridged the translated text by *omitting* the words concerning matter: "*homo enim hominem generat* [ex materia] *et sol*" (*In Aristotelis Librum de anima commentarium*, ed. Pirotta, p. 154). Thomas's citation in the *In libros Physicorum expositio* is, however, complete: "*homo enim hominem generat ex materia et sol*"; for Moerbeke's translation and Thomas's exposition, see St. Thomas Aquinas, *In octo libros Physicorum Aristotelis expositio*, ed. Maggiòlo, pp. 86, 88. Vernani is again blind to the meticulous way in which Dante followed his authorities. Vallone has amply shown and I have independently indicated that Dante is far more adherent to St. Thomas and Aristotle than any of the learned curialists such as Giles of Rome (whose *De regimine principum* of 1277–1279 Dante cites in *Conv.* 4:24:9), more so than Agostino d'Ancona (Augustinus "Triumphus"), and certainly far more so than Guido Vernani himself ("Dante, A. Trionfi, G. Vernani," p. 174). In a passage on papal power that runs in much the same order as Vernani's hastily spun arguments here, Remigio de' Girolami had given the complete citation from Aristotle in Moerbeke's translation: "*homo generat hominem ex materia et sol' ut dicitur in II Phisicorum.*" (man—and the sun—generates man *from matter* as it says in II of the *Physics*); *Contra falsos ecclesie professores* 18; ed. Tamburini, p. 45.

44. Vernani's reference is incorrect; he probably means Aristotle's *Pol.* 4:8:1294a:20–23 (Barnes, 2:2054); see the text [470] in St. Thomas Aquinas's *In libros Politicorum Aristotelis Expositio*, ed. Spiazzi, *Lectio* VII, no 612, p. 213. See note 11 above to *Mon.* 2:3:4.

45. Valerius Maximus, *Factorum et dictorum memorabilium* 1:1:8, ed. Kempf., p. 5.

46. St. Paul, in context, is really speaking of idolaters *in general*, and *not* merely about the Romans whom he is addressing.

47. St. Bernard, *De consideratione* 4:2 (*PL* 182:773); *On Consideration*, trans. Anderson and Kennan, p. 111.

48. St. Bernard, *De consideratione* 4:4 (*PL* 182:774); *On Consideration*, trans. Anderson and Kennan, p. 114.

49. Vernani is being again rather sly here: St. Jerome actually says that "Utaque autem *gens et Judæorum* et Romanorum *per hæc verba avaritiæ sugillatur*" (Both peoples, the Jews *and the*

*Romans* are sealed with that epithet of avarice; my emphasis). See Jerome, *Commentariorum in Isaiam Prophetam Libri* 1:8 (*PL* 24:48).

50. St. Thomas Aquinas explains how God permits evil that he does not will, despite his will that all men be saved, in *Scriptum super Libros Sententiarum* 1, Distinctio 45, q. 1, a. 4; Dist. 46, q. 1, a. 1; ed. P. Mandonnet (Paris: Lethielleux, 1929), pp. 1038–41, 1050–1052.

51. Vernani's belief in demons, though quaint to modern ears, was widely held. Though there was no fixed teaching in patristic times, early Church Fathers assumed that they were the sons of fallen angels and human mothers; St. Augustine posited that they had bodies. There was much speculation during Vernani's time. Duns Scotus, especially, among the Franciscans, believed that demons were the fallen angels (Jude 1:6; 2 Pt 2:4; Rv 12:7–9) who had followed Satan in desiring equality with God; Albert the Great and St. Thomas Aquinas, among the Dominicans, denied the desire for equality as motive and believed that demons sinned in believing that they could gain their own beatitude under their own powers.

52. St. Augustine, *De civitate Dei* 2:22; *The City of God*, LCL, 1:228–229. Cf. Livy, *Ab urbe condita* 5:37.

53. St. Augustine, *De Trinitate* 3:6–7 (*PL* 42:875).

54. Valerius Maximus, *Factorum et dictorum memorabilium* 3:2:2, ed. Kempf, p. 112. Valerius magnifies Cloelia's negligible actions as "unforgettable."

55. St. Augustine, *Epistula ad Volusianum* 137:17 (*CSEL* 44, p. 122).

56. Vernani either is quoting from a corrupt text or is citing by memory freely from St. Augustine, *De civitate Dei* 5:12; *The City of God*, LCL, 2:190–193.

57. "Ambition possessed all the rewards of virtues," cited by St. Augustine in *De civitate Dei* 5:12; *The City of God*, LCL, 2:202–203.

58. Valerius Maximus, *Factorum et dictorum memorabilium* 1:1:9; ed. Kempf, p. 5.

59. *things by which men arrive at happiness are not to be found in them by nature:* Aristotle, *Nic. Ethics* 2:1:1103a:19–20: "It is clear that moral virtue is not instilled in us by nature" (see St. Thomas Aquinas, *Commentary on the Nic. Ethics*, trans. Litzinger, p. 111; cf. Barnes, 2:1742).

60. Aristotle, *Nic. Ethics* 3:1:1110a:15–19: "Actions whose source is within man are in his power to do or not to do, and this belongs to the nature of the voluntary" (see St. Thomas Aquinas, *Commentary on the Nic. Ethics*, trans. Litzinger, p. 174; cf. Barnes, 2:1752).

61. Vernani's text [*"Scias quod excelsus dominatur in regno hominum, et cui volerit, tradet illud"*] is cited from memory. Dn 4:14 in the Vulgate reads: ". . . *donec cognoscant viventes quoniam dominatur Excelsus in regno hominum et cuicumque voluerit dabit illud et humillimum hominem constituet super eo"* (Douay-Rheims: ". . . till the living know that the most High ruleth in the kingdom of men; and he will give it to whomsoever it shall please him, and he will appoint the basest man over it").

62. Cf. St. Augustine, *De civitate Dei* 5:1; *The City of God*, LCL, 2:132–135.

63. Vernani takes Aristotle's antiphrasis-hyperbole seriously as justification for a hieratic political order; cf. Aristotle, *Pol.* 7:4:1326a:25–29: "Certainly experience shows that it is difficult and perhaps impossible for a state with too large a population to have good legal

government . . . an excessively large number cannot participate in order: *to give order would surely be a task for divine power, which holds even this universe together*" (my emphasis). Cf. Barnes, 2:2104–05. Cf. St. Thomas Aquinas, *In libros politicorum Aristotelis*, VII, Lectio III, 1096; Textus Aristotelis, 943–944, ed. Spiazzi, pp. 351, 354.

64. Aristotle, *Pol.*7:7:1327b:29; Latin text in St. Thomas Aquinas, *In Libros Politicorum Aristotelis Expositio*, ed. Spiazzi, pp. 361

65. *far more rightly: "magis de jure."*

66. The Ptolemaic-Aristotelian system held that the northern hemisphere of the earth's orb, consisting of dry land, was the "inhabitable," inhabited part. The southern hemisphere was barren except for water. Dante refers to the southern hemisphere through the pagan Ulysses' mouth as *"il mondo sanza gente"* (*Inf.* 26:117), but shows the heathen's limitation by citing Purgatory there.

67. St. Augustine, *De civitate Dei* 2:17, 18; *The City of God*, trans. McCracken, LCL, 1:196–207.

68. But see St. Augustine, *De civitate Dei* 5:22; *The City of God*, trans. Green, LCL, 2:252–257); see also notes to *Mon.* 2:9.

69. The *"per"* and *"hoc"* of the Latin here seem to be a corruption, although the sense seems fairly clear.

70. St. Augustine, *Contra Faustum Manichæum* 22:74 (*PL* 42:447).

71. Isidore of Seville, *Etymologiæ* 5:4 (*PL* 82:199).

72. *"Quid sit ius naturale"* (What natural law is), *Concordia discordantium canonum*, pt. I, d. 1, cap. 7; *CIC*, 1:2.

73. *the wretch: "iste homo."* The force of Vernani's contemptuous demonstrative is difficult to render adequately into English.

74. St. Anselmus, *Cur Deus homo* 1:9 (*PL* 158:370–373).

75. St. Anselmus, *Cur Deus homo* 2:13–14 (*PL* 158:413–414). Another inexact reference, however: 2:13 is not applicable; and in 2:14, Anselm proves that Christ's death outweighed the number and magnitude of all men's sins.

76. *"Quæ major injuiria quam justum innocentemque damnari,"* St. Augustine, *De vera religione* 16:31 (*PL* 34:135). Vernani here completely misreads and misrepresents Augustine's context. On the justice of Christ's death, see Chapter 3, above, pp. 81–82.

77. The Pseudo-Dionysius speaks of their cloudy and obscure nature (S. Dionysii Areopagitæ, *De mystica theologia* 1:1 [*PG* 3:997–1000]). Proofs from mystical theology are not conclusive; cf. the similar caution argued to the opposite end by John of Paris, *On Royal and Papal Power* 18 (trans. Watt, p. 196).

78. Vernani, as usual, cites from memory, here from Rv 13:8: "All that dwell upon the earth adored him, whose names are not written in the book of life of the Lamb, which was slain from the beginning of the world."

79. *"Vel occisus in agno mystice quem Abel obtulit, vel in ipso Abel a fratre occiso præfiguratus est"; Biblia cum Glossa.* 4:565 (col. 1).

80. St. Augustine comments on the cause of Cain's crime in *De civitate Dei* 15:7: "[Cain]

was a symbol of the Jews who slew Christ, shepherd of the flock of men, who was prefigured in Abel, shepherd of the flock of sheep"; see *The City of God*, trans. Levine, LCL, 4:446–447.

81. Vernani, *De potestate summi pontificis*, pp. 74–75.

82. S. Hieronymus, *Epistula* 53:7, in *Sancti Eusibii Hieronymi, Epistulæ*, pars I, ed. Isidorus Hilberg, CSEL 54, pp. 453–454.

83. *Biblia Sacra cum glossa ordinaria*, in I Reg. 8: 1, vol. 1, p. 13.

84. St. Augustine, *De vera religione* 31 (*PL* 34:148).

85. "In Novo Testamento . . ." *Concordia discordantium canonum*, pt. I, d. 21, cap. 2; *CIC*, 1:69. The apostles, whose heirs are the bishops, have, after Peter and his heirs, the popes, the power to bind and loose sins; thus, believed the hierocrats, the pope's jurisdiction *"ratione peccati."*

86. *"Iosephum in Bethleem alterum in Bersabe posuit"*; *Biblia Sacra cum glossa ordinaria* on Jn 21:17, 4:270.

87. On the commissioning of St. Peter, see Chapter 3, pp. 103.

88. For the problem of laws and repeal of laws "through contrary practice or through a certain rational cause," see Ennio Cortese, *La norma giuridica: Spunti teorici nel diritto comune classico*, 2 vols., Ius nostrum 6 (Milan: Giuffrè, 1962, 1964), ad indicem; also see Dolcini, "Note sul testo," p. 262.

89. Cf. St. Thomas Aquinas, *ST* I-II, q. 95, a. 2: "But it must be noted that something may be derived from natural law in two ways: first as a conclusion from premises; secondly, by way of determination of certain generalities. . . . Some things are therefore derived from the general principles of natural law, by way of conclusions . . . while some are derived there from by way of determination." Vernani the notary is demonstrating his juridical expertise in civil law by referring to a section of the *Corpus juris civilis* without any real specificity: the particular passage is difficult to pinpoint (as usual with the friar's references); he probably is alluding to *Novellæ* LXXXIII, 1, in *Corpus Iuris Civilis*, ed. Rudolfus Schoell and Guilelmus Wilhelm Kroll (Berlin: Weidmann, 1899), 3:410: "Nor do we wish our civil judges to have knowledge of such [ecclesiastical] matters in any way, since such matters must be examined and souls be corrected ecclesiastically through ecclesiastical penalty according to sacred and divine rules which indeed our [civil] laws are not worthy to pursue."

90. The passage is not to be found in St. Augustine's *Confessions*. On Vernani's mistaken references, see above, pp. 81, 100, and 343, n. 14.

91. The bull, *Venerabilem fratrem*, of March 1202, asserting that an imperial election must have the pope's endorsement, is given in *Decretales* 1:6:34, in *CIC*, 2:79–82; *Church and State through the Centuries*, ed. Ehler and Morrall, pp. 69–73; and Tierney, *Crisis*, pp. 133–134. Vernani—typically, in haste—does not seem to have read or remembered the decretal exactly, for, while *Venerabilem fratrem* cautions against the election of fools, heretics or pagans as emperor, it says nothing concerning the emperor's being "the advocate and defender of the

Church against heretics and schismatics," nor does *Per venerabilem;* Vernani is citing second-hand from Hostiensis's commentary on *Venerabilem fratrem* in his *Summa ("Qui filii sunt legiti-mi")*; see a partial text and commentary in Carlyle and Carlyle, 5:326–329. Vernani is insisting on the hierocratic theory of the derived *potestas indirecta*, with the "sword" of temporal power wielded by the emperor at the behest of the Church to defend it against schismatics and heretics—a commonplace in canonist writings.

92. Julianus Pomerius, *De vita contemplativa* 2:9 (*PL* 59:453).

93. Vernani cites his "Prosper," confusing the name of the author (actually Pomerius, see above, n. 92), in his typical lawyerly fashion not from the *De vita contemplativa,* but secondhand from Gratian's *Concordia discordantium canonum* p. 2, c. 12, q. 1, c. 13 (*CIC,* 1:681).

94. We must note that Vernani even cites St. Augustine's commentary on the Gospel of John here secondhand from Gratian's *Concordia discordantium canonum!* (see p. 2I c. 12, q. 1, c. 17; *CIC,* 1:683).

95. *"Odivi* ecclesiam *malignantium":* For the Vulgate's *"ecclesiam"* the Douay-Rheims version renders "I have hated the *assembly* of the malignant" (Ps 25:5); I thus cite the AV at this point.

96. Augustine, *De civitate Dei* 11:1: "I shall first tell how these two cities had their first origin in a parting of the ways among the angels" (*The City of God,* trans. Wiesen, LCL, 3:426–427). And in 18:1: "I would write about the origin, progress and appointed ends of the two cities, the one of God and the other of this world. . . . Yet the former city did not run its course alone in this world, but rather, as both cities began together, so together in their progress among men they have known the shifts of time and change" (*The City of God,* trans. Wiesen, LCL, 5:362–363).

97. St. Augustine, *De civitate Dei* 18:1; *The City of God,* trans. Wiesen, LCL, 5:364–365.

98. To assert the chronological precedence of the Church, in addition to theoretical and legal considerations, became a tenet of the canonists. Ullmann cites, e.g., Alvarus Pelagius: *"Ex his manifeste apparet, prius fuisse ecclesiam quam aliquod justum vel injustum imperium temporale"* (From these things it is patently clear that there was a Church before there was any kind of temporal empire, just or unjust) (*Medieval Papalism,* p. 120, n. 5).

99. Vernani, *De potestate summi pontificis,* pp. 56–60.

100. Aristotle, *Nic. Ethics* 2:1:1103a:26–1103b:1: "We become just by doing just actions; we become temperate by doing temperate actions; and we become courageous by doing courageous actions. . . . It is from playing the harp that good and bad harpists are made." Cf. Barnes, 2:1743. See text in St. Thomas Aquinas, *Commentary on the Nic. Ethics,* trans. Litzinger, pp. 112, 115.

101. Augustine, *De civitate Dei* 8:3; *The City of God,* trans. Wiesen, LCL, 3:12–13.

102. *On the Soul: De anima* 1:5:410b:6; Latin text in St. Thomas Aquinas, *In Aristotelis Librum de anima commentarium,* ed. Pirotta, p. 53.

103. *many other instances:* A boasting, childish exaggeration. In his *De potestate summi pontificis* 14, Vernani had merely written: "First I concede that both those powers come from

God, but it does not follow therefore that one does not depend on the other. . . . For that proposition which says that one thing does not depend upon another is true in many cases: stone does not depend on wood, nor an ox on a horse. But in many cases it is false, for the animated body depends on the soul, and yet the body and soul are of distinct nature, and the body comes from God by means of the soul; and medical science is distinct from natural science but it depends upon it . . . therefore although those two aforesaid two powers are distinct, one of them, however, namely the temporal, depends on the spiritual. . . . In the Highest Trinity in which there is a distinction of Persons, yet a single person proceeds from it" (pp. 62–64). Two instances of medical science and the Persons of the Trinity are his only two vaunted "many other" examples beyond those of the *Refutation!* Both of these, to boot, actually present entirely different instances from the argument he is confuting: medical science *is* (a branch of and not distinct from) natural science, and medicine itself was generally referred to as *physica* (Shakespeare's "physicke"); the Persons of the Trinity *are* severally and singly the *one* true God indivisible.

104. 1 Kgs 8:7.

105. Vernani retaliates rhetorically in this recounting of the deposition of King Saul by the priest, Samuel (1 Kgs 8–31), echoing Dante's verbs of "ousting" and "hurling forth" his hierocratic opponents from the wrestling ring of debate. It makes for a sour and awkward conclusion to his *Refutation.*

## NOTES TO JOHN XXII'S 'SI FRATRUM'

1. The translation is from the Latin text of *Extravagantes Iohannis XXII,* ed. Jacqueline Tarrant, *Monumenta iuris canonici,* ser. B: Corpus Collectiom 6 (Vatican City: Biblioteca Apostolica Vaticana, 1983), pp. 156–163. See also *CIC,* 2:1211–1212. The sentence-paragraph divisions have been numbered editorially for ease of reference. John XXII's very first sanctions in his war against Milan and the Ghibellines were directed against Matteo Visconti (who had assumed the title of duke), Can Grande della Scala, and Passerino Buonaccolsi. On December 16, 1317, the abbot of the Benedictine Monastery at St. Eufemia in Brescia, who was administrator of the diocese, began canonical charges against them; on April 6, 1318, the three were cited to appear in three months.

2. *disposition:* Latin *"dispositio."* The term could also signify "management" of the empire. However, the high papalists had firmly asserted that the Church disposed of the emperor and the empire in all senses of the verb. Cf. Hostiensis in his *Summa: "Imperator ab ecclesia Romana imperium tenet et potest dici officialis eius seu vicarius ab ecclesia Romana . . . et Papa ipsum confirmat, et inungit, et coronat, vel reprobat, et deponit, ut patet de ele. Venerabilem"* (The emperor holds his empire from the Roman Church and can be said to be its subaltern or vicar . . . *and the pope confirms him, and anoints him, and crowns him, or reproves him and deposes him, as is clear from the* [*bull*] *Venerabilem*). See *Summa una,* ff. 215$^r$–216$^v$, and *Summa aurea,* cols. 1385–1387.

3. The *podestà* was the equivalent, roughly, of mayor. In most Italian cities he was chosen from another commune or state to ensure impartiality, and given power for a certain period of office.

4. Reading *"patulo iudicio,"* instead of Tarrant's *"paculo iudicio,"* which is a simple misprint; *CIC* reads *"patenti iudicio,"* 2:1212.

5. In the first year of John XXII's reign: he was elected on August 7, 1316; the bull appears actually to have been issued March 31, 1317, during Holy Week. James A. Brundage gives a history of editions of John XXII's bulls in *Medieval Canon Law* (London: Longman, 1995); see esp. p. 199, n. 6.

# Bibliography

## WORKS OF DANTE ALIGHIERI

### Monarchia

[Bertalot]. *Dantis Alagherii De monarchia libri III.* Edited by Ludwig Bertalot. 2d ed. Geneva: Olschki, 1920.

[Henry]. *The "De Monarchia" of Dante Alighieri.* Edited and translated by Aurelia Henry. Boston and New York: Houghton, Mifflin, 1904.

[Imbach and Flüeler]. *Monarchia: Lateinisch-Deutsch Studienausgabe.* Translated by Ruedi Imbach, with an introduction by Christoph Flüeler and Ruedi Imbach. Universal-Bibliothek. Stuttgart: Reclam, 1989.

[Kay]. *Dante's "Monarchia."* Translated with a commentary by Richard Kay. Studies and Texts 131. Toronto: Pontifical Institute of Mediæval Studies, 1998.

[Meozzi]. *Monarchia: Commento storico comparativo.* Edited by Antero Meozzi. Milan: Vallardi, 1938.

[Nardi]. *Monarchia.* Edited by Bruno Nardi. In Dante, *Opere minori*, vol. 2. La letteratura italiana: Storia e testi 5. Milan and Naples: Ricciardi, 1979. [Rpt. of P. G. Ricci's text, with Nardi's amendments in the notes.]

[Nicholl]. *"Monarchy" and "Three Political Letters."* Translated with an introduction by Donald Nicholl, and with a "Note on the Chronology of Dante's Political Works" by Colin Hardie. Library of Ideas. London: Weidenfeld & Nicholson, 1954.

[Pizzica]. *Monarchia.* Translated by Maurizio Pizzica. Biblioteca Universale Rizzoli. Milan: Rizzoli, 1988.

[Ricci, P. G.]. *Monarchia.* Edited by Pier Giorgio Ricci. In *Le opere di Dante Alighieri*, Edizione nazionale 5. Milan: Mondadori, 1965.

[Rostagno]. *Monarchia.* Edited by Enrico Rostagno. In *Le opere di Dante: Testo critico della Società dantesca italiana*, pp. 355–412. Florence: Bemporad, 1921.

[Schneider, Friedrich]. *Die Monarchia Dantes aus der Berliner Handschrift Cod. Lat. Folio 437.* Edited by Friedrich Schneider. Weimar: Hermann Böhlaus Nachfolger, 1930.

[Schneider, Herbert]. *On World Government* [*De Monarchia*]. Translated by Herbert W. Schneider, with an introduction by Dino Bigongiari. 2d ed. Library of Liberal Arts 15. Indianapolis, Ind.: Bobbs-Merrill, 1949; rpt. 1957.

[Shaw]. *Monarchia.* Edited and translated by Prue Shaw. Cambridge Medieval Classics 4. Cambridge, U.K.: Cambridge University Press, 1995.

[Venice, 1740]. *Monarchia.* Venice, 1740. Title page gives false place and date: "Coloniæ Allobrogum Apud Henr. Albert. Gosse & Soc. MDCCXL," with the incipit "Dantis Aligherii Florentini MONARCHIA Scripta temporibus LUDOVICI BAVARI." Rpt., Venice: Zatta, 1757, 1758, 1760, and 1768.

[Vianello]. *Il trattato della "Monarchia" di Dante Alighieri.* Edited and translated by Natale Vianello. Genoa: Stabilimento Grafico Editore, 1921.

[Vinay]. *Monarchia: Testo, introduzione, traduzione e commento.* Edited and translated by Gustavo Vinay. Florence: Sansoni, 1950.

[Volpe]. *Monarchia: Versione col testo a fronte, introduzione e commento.* Edited and translated by Angelo Camillo Volpe. Istituto di filologia romanza della R. Università di Roma. Studi e testi. Modena: Società Tipografica Modense, 1946.

[Wicksteed]. *Monarchia.* Translated by Philip H. Wicksteed. In *A Translation of the Latin Works of Dante Alighieri,* pp. 125–292. Temple Classics. London: Dent, 1904.

[Witte]. *Dantis Alligherii De monarchia libri III.* Edited by Karl Witte. 2d ed. Vienna: Braumüller, 1874.

### Convivio

*Dante's "Convivio."* Translated by William W. Jackson. Oxford, U.K.: Clarendon Press, 1909.

*Il Convivio.* Edited by G. Busnelli and G. Vandelli. 2d ed. Revised by A. F. Quaglio. In *Opere di Dante,* edited by V. Branca et al., vols. 4–5. Florence: Le Monnier, 1964.

*Il Convivio.* Edited by Maria Simonelli. Testi e saggi di letterature moderne: Testi 2. Bologna: Pàtron, 1966.

*Convivio.* Edited by Cesare Vasoli and Domenico De Robertis. In *Opere minori,* tom. 1, pt. 2. La letteratura italiana: Storia e testi 5, tom. 1, pt. 2. Milan and Naples: Ricciardi, 1988.

[*Convivio*]. *The Banquet.* Translated by Christopher Ryan. Stanford French and Italian Studies 61. Saratoga, Calif.: ANMA Libri, 1989.

[*Convivio*]. *Dante's "Convivio" [The Banquet].* Translated by Richard H. Lansing. Garland Library of Medieval Literature, ser. B, vol. 65. New York: Garland, 1990. [Omits paragraph/sentence numbers.]

### Divina Commedia

[Grandgent]. *"La Divina Commedia" di Dante Alighieri.* Edited by C. H. Grandgent. 2d ed. Boston: D. C. Heath, 1933.

[Graziolo]. *Il Commento più antico [del Bambaglioli] e la versione latina dell'Inferno di Dante dal codice di Sandaniele del Friuli.* Edited by Antonio Fiammazzo. Udine: Doretti, 1892.

[Graziolo]. *Il Commento dantesco di Graziolo de' Bambaglioli dal "Colombino" di Siviglia con altri codici raffrontato.* Edited by Antonio Fiammazzo. Savona: Bertolotto, 1915.

Graziolo de' Bambaglioli. *Commento all'Inferno di Dante.* Edited by Luca Carlo Rossi. Pisa: Scuola Normale di Pisa, 1998.

Jacopo Alighieri. *Chiose all'Inferno.* Edited by Saverio Bellomo. Medioevo e Umanesimo 75. Padua: Antenore, 1990.

[Mazzoni]. Dante Alighieri. *La Divina Commedia. Inferno.* Con i commenti di Tommaso Casini-Silvio Adrasto Barbi e di Attilio Momigliano. Edited, with an introduction and bibliography, by Francesco Mazzoni. Florence: Sansoni, 1972.

———. Dante Alighieri. *La Divina Commedia. Purgatorio.* Con i commenti di Tommaso Casini-Silvio Adrasto Barbi e di Attilio Momigliano. Edited, with an introduction and bibliography, by Francesco Mazzoni. Florence: Sansoni, 1977.

[Ottimo]. *Ottimo commento della Divina Commedia.* Edited by Alessandro Torri. 2 vols. Pisa: N. Capurro, 1827–1829.

[Petrocchi]. *La Commedia secondo l'antica vulgata.* Edited by G. Petrocchi. 4 vols. In *Le opere di Dante
Alighieri*, Edizione nazionale 7. Milan: Mondadori, 1966–1967.

[Pietro Alighieri]. *Petri Allegherii super Dantis ipsius genitoris Comoediam Commentarium, nunc primum in
lucem editum.* Edited by Vincenzo Nannucci. Florence: Piatti, 1845.

[Pietro Alighieri]. *Il "Commentarium" di Pietro Alighieri nelle redazioni ashburnhamiana e ottoboniana.*
Edited by R. della Vedova and M. T. Silvotti, with an introduction by Egidio Guidubaldi.
Florence: Olschki, 1978.

[Sayers]. Dante Alighieri. *The Comedy of Dante Alighieri the Florentine: Cantica I. Hell (L'Inferno).*
Translated by Dorothy L. Sayers. Harmondsworth, Middlesex, U.K., and New York: Penguin Books, 1949; rpt. 1960. *Cantica II. Purgatory (Il Purgatorio).* Translated by Dorothy L. Sayers. Harmondsworth, Middlesex, U.K., and New York: Penguin Books, 1953; rpt. 1959. *Cantica III. Paradise (Il Paradiso).* Translated by Dorothy L. Sayers and Barbara Reynolds.
Harmondsworth, Middlesex, U.K., and New York: Penguin Books, 1962; rpt. 1973.

[Singleton]. *The Divine Comedy.* Translated with a commentary by Charles S. Singleton. 6 vols.
Bollingen Series 80. Princeton, N.J.: Princeton University Press, 1970–1975.

## Egloge

*Egloge.* Edited and translated by Enzo Cecchini. In *Opere minori*, vol. 2. La letteratura italiana:
Storia e testi 5. Milan and Naples: Ricciardi, 1979.

## Epistolæ

*Dantis Alagherii Epistolæ: The Letters of Dante.* Edited and translated by Paget Toynbee. Oxford, U.K.:
Clarendon Press, 1920. 2d ed., revised by Colin Hardie, Oxford, U.K.: Clarendon Press,
1966.

*Epistole.* Edited by Arsenio Frugoni and Giorgio Brugnoli. In *Opere minori*, vol. 2. La letteratura
italiana: Storia e testi 5. Milan and Naples: Ricciardi, 1979.

## Questio de aqua et terra [De situ et forma aque et terre]

*De situ et forma aque et terre.* Edited by Giorgio Padoan. Florence: Le Monnier, 1968.

*Questio de aqua et terra.* Edited and translated by Francesco Mazzoni. In *Opere minori*, vol. 2. La
letteratura italiana: Storia e testi 5. Milan and Naples: Ricciardi, 1979.

## Vita nuova

*Vita nuova.* Edited by Domenico de Robertis. In *Opere minori*, vol. 1, pt. 1. La letteratura italiana:
Storia e testi 5. Milan and Naples: Ricciardi, 1984.

## De vulgari eloquentia

*De vulgari eloquentia.* Edited by A. Mango. 3d ed. Revised by P. G. Ricci. In *Opere di Dante*, edited
by M. Barbi, vol. 6. Florence: Le Monnier, 1957.

*De vulgari eloquentia.* Edited and translated by Pier Vincenzo Mengaldo. In *Opere minori*, vol. 2. La
letteratura italiana: Storia e testi 5. Milan and Naples: Ricciardi, 1979.

*Other Translations and Editions*

Dante Alighieri. *A Translation of the Latin Works of Dante Alighieri*. Translated by A. G. Ferrers Howell [*De vulgari eloquentia*] and Philip H. Wicksteed [*De monarchia, Epistles, Eclogues, Quæstio de aqua et terra*]. Temple Classics. London: Dent, 1904.

———. *The Literary Criticism of Dante Alighieri*. Edited and translated by Robert S. Haller. Regents Critics Series. Lincoln: University of Nebraska Press, 1973.


PRIMARY SOURCES

[Agostino d'Ancona, Augustinus Triumphus]. Augustini Triumphi. *Tractatus brevis de duplici potestate prelatorum et laicorum*. In R. Scholz, *Die Publistik zur Zeit Philipps des Schönen und Bonifaz VIII*. Stuttgart: Ferdinand Enke, 1902.

Albertus Magnus. *De natura loci*. Edited by Paul Hossfeld. In *Opera omnia*, vol. 5, pt. 2, pp. 1–46. Monasterii Westfalorum in Ædibus Aschendorff, 1980.

———. *De unitate intellectus contra Averroistas*. Edited by Alfons Hufnagel. In *Opera omnia*, vol. 17, pt. 1, pp. 1–30. Monasterii Westfalorum in Ædibus Aschendorff, 1975.

———. *B. Alberti Magni Ratisbonensis Episcopi, Ordinis Prædicatorum, Opera Omnia*. Edited by August Borgnet. 38 vols. Paris: Vives, 1890–1895.

[Ambrose of Milan, St. *Hexæmeron*]. *Hexameron, Paradise, Cain and Abel*. Translated by John J. Savage. New York: Fathers of the Church, 1961.

[Anselm of Canterbury, St.]. *Saint Anselm: Basic Writings: Proslogium, Monologium, Gaunilons' On Behalf of the Fool, Cur Deus Homo*. Translated by S. N. Deane, with an introduction by Charles Hartshorne. LaSalle, Ill.: Open Court, 1903; 2d ed., 1962.

Anselm of Canterbury. *The Major Works*. Edited by Brian Davies and G. R Evans. Oxford, U.K., and New York: Oxford University Press, 1998.

*Antequam essent clerici*. [*Before There Were Clerics*]. In *Three Royalist Tracts, 1296–1302*, translated by R. W. Dyson, pp. 2–11. Bristol, U.K.: University of Durham Press and Thoemmes Press, 1999.

Aristotle. [*Categories*]. *Categoriæ vel Prædicamenta: Translatio Boethii-Editio Composita, Translatio Guillelmi de Moerbeka Lemmata e Simplicii Commentario Decerpta Pseudo-Augustini Paraphrasis Themistiana*. Edited by Lorenzo Mineo-Paluello. Aristoteles Latinus 1, 1–5. Bruges and Paris: Desclée de Brouwer, 1961.

———. *The Complete Works of Aristotle: The Revised Oxford Translation*. Edited by Jonathan Barnes. 2 vols. Bollingen Series 71. Princeton, N.J.: Princeton University Press, 1984.

———. *Metaphysics*. Translated by Hugh Tredennick (vol. 17) and by Hugh Tredennick and G. Cyril Armstrong (vol. 18). In *Aristotle*, vols. 17–18. LCL. Cambridge, Mass.: Harvard University Press, 1933; rpt. 1989–1990.

———. [*Nicomachean Ethics*]. *Ethica Nicomachea: Translatio Roberti Grosseteste Licolniensis sive "Liber Ethicorum."* Edited by René Antoine Gauthier. Aristoteles Latinus 26, 1–3. Leiden: Brill; Brussels: Desclée de Brouwer, 1973.

———. *Nicomachean Ethics*. Edited and translated by H. Rackham. *Aristotle*, vol 19. LCL. Cambridge, Mass., and London: Harvard University Press, 1926; rpt. 1994.

———. *The Physics*. Translated by P. H. Wicksteed and Francis M. Cornford. In *Aristotle*, vols. 4–5. LCL. Cambridge, Mass.: Harvard University Press, 1929–1934; rpt. 1995–1996.

————. [*Politics*]. *Politica*. Edited by Pierre Michaud-Quantin. Aristoteles Latinus 29, 1. Bruges and Paris: Desclée de Brouwer, 1961.

————. *Politics*. Translated by H. Rackham. In *Aristotle in Twenty-Three Volumes*, vol. 21. LCL. Cambridge, Mass., and London: Harvard University Press, 1932; rpt. 1990.

————. *The Politics*. Translated by T. A. Sinclair. Revised by Trevor J. Saunders. London and New York: Penguin Books, 1992.

————. [*Prior Analytics*]. *Analytica priora: Translatio Boethii (recensiones duæ), Translatio Anonyma, Pseudo-Philoponi Aliorumque Scholia, Specimina Translationum Recentiorum*. Edited by L. Minio-Paluello. Aristoteles Latinus 3, 1–4. Bruges and Paris: Desclée de Brouwer, 1962.

————. *Prior Analytics*. Translated with an introduction, notes, and commentary by Robin Smith. Indianapolis, Ind., and Cambridge, Mass.: Hackett, 1989.

————. [*Rhetoric*]. *Rhetorica: Translatio Anonyma sive Vetus et translatio Gullelmi de Moerbeke*. Edited by Bernhardus Schneider. Aristoteles Latinus 31, 1–2. Leiden: Brill, 1978.

————. *De Sophisticis elenchis*. Edited by Bernard G. Dod. Aristoteles Latinus 4, 1–3. Leiden: Brill; Brussels: Desclée de Brouwer, 1975.

[Augustine, St., Bishop of Hippo: Augustinus Aurelius Hipponensis]. *Augustine: Earlier Writings*. Translated by John H. S. Burleigh. Library of Christian Classics 6. London: SCM Press, 1953. Rpt., Philadelphia: Westminster Press, n.d.

————. *Augustine: Later Works*. Translated by John Burnby. Library of Christian Classics 8. London: SCM Press, 1955. Rpt., Philadelphia: Westminster Press, n.d.

————. [*De agone christiano*]. *The Christian Combat*. Translated by Robert P. Russell. *The Writings of Saint Augustine*, vol. 4. New York: CIMA, 1947.

————. *Confessions*. Translated by Rex Warner. New York: New American Library of World Literature, 1963.

————. *Confessions*. Translated by William Watts [1631]. LCL. Cambridge, Mass.: Harvard University Press; London: Heinemann, 1912; rpt. 1946.

————. [*De civitate Dei*]. *Sancti Aurelii Augustini episcopi de civitate Dei libri XXII*. Edited by Bernardus Dombart and Alfonsus Kalb. 5th ed. 2 vols. Biblioteca Scriptorum Græcorum et Romanorum Teubneriana. Stuttgart: Teubner, 1981.

————. [*De civitate Dei*]. *The City of God*. Translated by G. E. McCracken (vol. 1), William M. Green (vol. 2, vol. 7, and, with E. M. Sanford, vol. 5), David Wiesen (vol. 3), Philip Levine (vol. 4), E. M. Sanford (vol. 5), W. C. Greene (vol. 6), et al. 7 vols. LCL. Cambridge: Harvard University Press; London: Heinemann, 1957–1972.

————. [*De civitate Dei*]. *The City of God*. Edited and translated by R. W. Dyson. Cambridge, U.K.: Cambridge University Press, 1998.

————. [*De doctrina christiana*]. *On Christian Doctrine*. Translated by D. W. Robertson. Indianapolis, Ind., and New York: Bobbs-Merrill, 1958.

————. [*Enarrationes in Psalmos*]. *Expositions on the Book of Psalms*. Translated with notes and indices by A. Cleveland Coxe. A Select Library of the Nicene and Post-Nicene Fathers 8. Grand Rapids, Mich.: Eerdmans, 1974.

————. *Epistula ad Volusianum*. In *Sancti Aurelii Augustini Hipponensis Episcopi Epistulæ*, edited by A. Goldbacher, pt. 3. *CSEL* 44. Vienna: Tempsky; Leipzig: Freitag, 1904.

————. *Letters*. Translated by Sister Wilfred Parsons. The Fathers of the Church 12, 1. New York: Fathers of the Church, 1951.

————. *Sancti Aureli Augustini De Genesi ad litteram libri duodecim.* Edited by Josephus Zycha. *CSEL* 38. Sec. 3, pt. 1. Vienna: Tempsky; Leipzig: Freitag, 1893.

Averroës [Ibn Rushd]. [*Commentary on Aristotle's On the Soul*]. *Averrois Cordubensis Commentarium Magnum in Aristotelis De anima libros.* Edited by F. Stuart Crawford. Corpus commentariorum Averrois in Aristotelem 6, 1. Medieval Academy of America Publication no. 59. Cambridge, Mass.: Medieval Academy of America, 1953.

————. *Averroës' Middle Commentaries on Aristotle's Categories and De Interpretatione.* Translated with notes and an introduction by Charles E. Butterworth. Princeton, N.J.: Princeton University Press, 1983.

Baldwin of Ford. *Spiritual Tractates.* Translated by David Bell. 2 vols. Cistercian Fathers Series 38. Kalamazoo, Mich.: Cistercian Publications, 1986.

Benedict, St. *The Rule of St. Benedict.* Edited by Timothy Fry. New York: Vintage Books, 1981.

Bernard of Clairvaux, St. *De consideratione.* In *Opera omnia*, vol. 3, edited by J. Leclerq et al. Rome: Editiones Cistercienses, 1963.

————. [*De consideratione*]. *Five Books on Consideration.* Translated by John D. Anderson and Elizabeth T. Keenan. Cistercian Fathers Series 37. Kalamazoo: Cistercian Publications, 1976.

————. *On Consideration.* Translated by G. Lewis. Oxford, U.K.: Clarendon Press, 1908.

*Biblia Latina cum Glossa Ordinaria.* Facsimile reprint of the *Editio Princeps* by Adolph Rusch of Strassburg, 1480–1481. 4 vols. Turnhout: Brepols, 1992.

Boccaccio, Giovanni. *Trattatello in laude di Dante.* Edited by Pier Giorgio Ricci. In *Tutte le opere di Giovanni Boccaccio*, edited by Vittore Branca, vol. 3. Milan: Mondadori, 1974.

Boethius. *Consolation of Philosophy.* Translated with an introduction by Richard Green. The Library of Liberal Arts. Indianapolis, Ind., and New York: Bobbs-Merrill, 1962.

Bonaventure, St. [*Arbor vitæ*]. *Tree of Life.* In *Bonaventure*, translated by Ewert Cousins. New York: Paulist Press, 1978.

————. *De decem præceptis.* In *S. Bonaventuræ Opera Omnia*, vol. 5. Florence: Quarrachi, 1882–1902.

Branchazolus, Johannes. *De principio et origine et potencia imperatoris et pape.* Edited by Edmund F. Stengel. In *Nova Alamanniæ* 1, 2 vols., 1:44–52. Berlin: Weidmannsche Buchhandlung, 1921–1930.

[*Bullarium Romanum*]. *Bullarum Diplomatum et Privilegiorum Sanctorum Romanorum Pontificum Taurinensis Editio.* Edited by [Luigi] Aloysii Tomassetti. Tomo III: a Lucio III (an. MCLXXXI) ad Clementem IV (an. MCCLXVIII). Turin: Fory & Dalmazzo, 1858.

Cecco d'Ascoli [Francesco Stabili]. *L'Acerba.* Ed. Achille Crespi. Ascoli Piceno: Cesari, 1927.

Cicero, Marcus Tullius. *De inventione.* Translated by H. M. Hubbell. In *Cicero*, vol. 2. LCL. Cambridge, Mass.: Harvard University Press, 1949.

————. *De Officiis.* [*On Duties*]. Translated by Walter Miller. In *Cicero*, vol. 21. LCL. Cambridge, Mass.: Harvard University Press, 1913; rpt. 1997.

————. *First Rhetoric.* See *De inventione.*

————. *De Inventione, De Optime genere oratorium, Topica.* Translated by H. M. Hubbell. In *Cicero*, vol. 2. LCL. Cambridge, Mass.: Harvard University Press, 1949.

*The Church and State through the Centuries.* Edited and translated by Sidney Z. Ehler and John B. Morrall. Westminster, Md.: Newman Press, 1954. [Collection of primary documents in English translation.]

*Corpus iuris canonici.* Edited by Æmilius [Emil] Richter and Æmilius [Emil] Friedberg. 2 vols. Leipzig: Tauchnitz, 1879.

*Corpus Iuris Civilis.* Vol. 1: *Institutiones,* edited by P. Krueger; *Digesta,* edited by Theodor Mommsen. 3d ed. 1882. Vol. 2: *Codex Iustinianus,* edited by Paul Kreuger. 1880. Vol. 3: *Novellæ,* edited by Rudolfus Schoell and Guilelmus [Wilhelm] Kroll. Berolini [Berlin]: apud Weidmannos, 1880–1895.

[*Corpus Iuris Civilis, Digest*]. *The Digest of Justinian.* Edited by Theodor Mommsen with Paul Kreuger. Original texts with an English translation by Alan Watson. 4 vols. Philadelphia: University of Pennsylvania Press, 1985.

[*Corpus Iuris Civilis, Glossa Ordinaria*]. *Corpus iuris Iustinianei cum Accursii commentariis.* 5 vols. Cologne: Stephanus Gamonetus, 1612.

*Disputatio inter clericum et militem.* In *Three Royalist Tracts, 1296–1302,* translated by R. W. Dyson. Bristol, U.K.: University of Durham Press and Thoemmes Press, 1999.

Frederick II [of Hohenstaufen]. *The Liber Augustalis; or, Constitutions of Melfi Promulgated by the Emperor Frederick II for the Kingdom of Sicily in 1231.* Translated by James M. Powell. Syracuse, N.Y.: Syracuse University Press, 1971.

Galen. *De propriorum animi cuiuslibet affectuum dignotione et curatione* 10. Edited by Wilko De Boer. Corpus Medicorum Græcorum, vol. 5, no. 4, pt. 1, sec. 1. Leipzig and Berlin: Teubner, 1937.

Giles of Rome [Ægidius Romanus; Egidio Romano]. *De regimine principum libri III.* Edited by Girolamo Samaritano. Rome: Zannetti, 1607. Rpt. Darmstadt: Scientia Aalen, 1967.

———. *John Trevisa's Middle English Translation of the De Regimine Principum of Ægidius Romanus.* Edited by David C. Fowler, Charles F. Briggs, and Paul G. Remley. Garland Medieval Texts 19. Hamden, Conn.: Garland Press, 1997.

———. *Errores Philosophorum: Critical Text with Notes and Introduction.* Edited by Joseph Koch. Translated by John O. Riedl. Milwaukee, Wis.: Marquette University Press, 1944.

———. Ægidius Romanus. *De ecclesiastica potestate.* Edited by Richard Scholz. Leipzig: Böhlaus, 1929. Rpt., Darmstadt: Scientia Aalen, 1961.

———. *On Ecclesiastical Power: The "De Ecclesiastica Potestate" of Ægidius Romanus.* Translated with an introduction and notes by R. W. Dyson. Woodbridge, Suffolk, U.K.: Boydell Press, 1986.

———. Ægidius Romanus. *De renunciatione pape.* Texts and Studies in Religion 52. Lewiston, Queenston, and Lampeter: Edwin Mellen Press, 1992. [Latin text edited in German by John R. Eastman; with a summary in English, pp. 363–383.]

Giovanni di Calvaruso [attrib.]. *Memoriale* [*Quæstio an Romanus pontifex potuerit treguam inducere*] (*Memorialia et Disquisitiones, 1312–1313,* no. 1248C). Edited by J. Schwalm. *Monumenta Germaniæ Historica, Legum sectio IV.* Hannover and Leipzig, vol. 4, pt. 2, p. 1311.

Godfrey of Saint Victor. [*Fons Philosophiæ*]. *The Fountain of Philosophy.* Translated by E. A. Synan. Toronto: Pontifical Institute of Mediæval Studies, 1972.

Gugliemi Centeuri da Cremona. *Trattato "De iure Monarchiæ."* Edited by Cesare Cenci. Foreword by Gino Barbieri. Verona: Palazzo Giuliari, 1967.

[Guidonis, Bernardus]. Gui, Bernard. *Manuel de l'inquisiteur.* Edited and translated by G[uillaume] Mollat with the collaboration of G. Drioux. Classiques de l'Histoire de France au Moyen Âge 8–9. 2 vols. Paris: Champion, 1926. Rpt., New York: AMS, 1980.

Guillaume de Pierre Godin. *The Theory of Papal Monarchy in the Fourteenth Century: Guillaume de Pierre*

Godin, O.P., *Tractatus de causa immediata ecclesiastice potestatis*. Edited by W. D. McCready. Studies and Texts 56. Toronto: Pontifical Institute of Mediæval Studies, 1982.

Hervæus Natalis. *Liber de paupertate Christi et apostolorum*. Edited by J. G. Sikes. *Archives d'histoire doctrinale et littéraire du Moyen Âge* 12–13 (1937–1938): 209–297.

————. *The Poverty of Christ and the Apostles* [*Liber de paupertate Christi et apostolorum*]. Edited and translated by John D. Jones. Mediæval Sources in Translation 37. Studies in Mediæval Moral Teaching 2. Toronto: Pontifical Institute of Mediæval Studies, 1999.

Hobbes, Thomas. *Leviathan*. Edited by M. Oakeshott. Oxford, U.K.: Blackwell, 1946.

Horace. *Satires, Epistles, and Ars amatoria*. Translated by H. Rushtom Fairclough. LCL. Cambridge, Mass.: Harvard University Press; London: Heinemann, 1926; rpt. 1961.

————. *The Odes and Epodes*. Translated by C. E. Bennett. LCL. Cambridge, Mass.: Harvard University Press; London: Heinemann, 1914; rpt. 1978.

[Hostiensis, Henry of Susa, or Henry of Segusio. *Summa aurea*]. *Summa una*. Lyons, 1537. Rpt., Darmstadt: Scientia Aalen, 1962.

————. *Summa aurea*. Venice, 1574. Rpt., Turin: Bottega d'Erasmo, 1963.

Hugh of Saint Victor. *On the Sacraments of the Christian Faith*. Translated by Roy J. Deferrari. Cambridge, Mass.: Medieval Academy of America, 1951.

Innocent III. *Die Register Innocenz' III., 7:7. Pontifikatsjahr, 1204/1205, Texte und Indices*. Edited by Andrea Sommerlechner and Herwig Weigl, with Christoph Egger and Rainer Murauer. *Publicationen des Historischen Instituts beim Österreichischen Kulturinstitut in Rom*, II. Abt., 1. Reihe. Vienna: Österreichische Akademie der Wissenschaften, 1997.

James of Viterbo. *On Christian Government* [*De regimine Christiano*]. Edited, translated, and with an introduction by R. W. Dyson. Woodbridge, Suffolk, U.K.: Boydell Press, 1995.

Johannes Falkenberg, O.P. *De monarchia mundi*. Edited by W. Seńko. In *Materiały do historii filozofii średniowiecznej w Polsce* 20. Polska Akademia Nauk. Wrocław: Zaklad Narodowy im. Ossolinskich, 1975, n.s., 9 (1975).

[John of Paris; Jean Quidort de Paris]. [*On Royal and Papal Power*]. *De potestate regia et papali*. Edited by J. Leclerq. In *L'ecclésiologie du XIII* siècle. L'église et l'état au Moyen Âge 5. Paris: Vrin, 1942. [Text, pp. 173–260.]

————. *On Royal and Papal Power*. Translated with an introduction by J. A. Watt. Toronto: Pontifical Institute of Mediæval Studies, 1971.

————. *On Royal and Papal Power: A Translation, with Introduction of the De Potestate Regia et papali of John of Paris*. Translated by Arthur P. Monahan. The Records of Civilization: Sources and Studies 90. New York and London: Columbia University Press, 1974.

John of Salisbury. *The Metalogicon of John of Salisbury: A Twelfth-Century Defense of the Verbal and Logical Arts of the Trivium*. Translated by Daniel D. McGarry. Berkeley and Los Angeles: University of California Press, 1962.

————. *Policraticus*. Edited by M. F. Markland. Milestones of Thought in the History of Ideas. New York: Ungar, 1979.

[John XXII]. *Extravagantes Iohannis XXII*. Edited by Jacqueline Tarrant. Monumenta Iuris Canonici, Series B: Corpus Collectionum, vol. 6. Vatican City: Biblioteca Apostolica Vaticana, 1983.

[John XXII]. "Iohannis XXII. Papæ Primus processus contra Ludewicum Regem." In *MGH, Constitutiones*, edited by J. Schwalm, vol. 5, no. 792, p. 617.

[John XXII. *Quia quorundam mentes*]. English translation by James Heft in *John XXII and Papal Teaching Authority*. Texts and Studies in Religion 27. Lewiston, Queenston, and Lampeter: Edwin Mellen Press, 1986.

[Justinian]. *The Digest of Justinian*. Edited by Theodor Mommsen with Paul Kreuger. Original texts with an English translation by Alan Watson. 4 vols. Philadelphia: University of Pennsylvania Press, 1985.

Kant, Immanuel. *Critique of Pure Reason*. Translated by Norman Kemp Smith. London: Macmillan, 1929.

Lactantius, Lucius Cæcilius Firmianus. *Istitutiones divinæ. PL* 6:111–1016.

———. *Divine Institutions*. Translated by Mary Francis McDonald. The Fathers of the Church 49. Washington, D.C.: The Catholic University of America Press, 1964.

Latini, Brunetto. *Li livres dou Tresor*. Edited by F. Carmody. Berkeley and Los Angeles: University of California Press, 1948.

[*Liber de Causis*]. "*Le Liber de causis*. Édition établie à l'aide de 90 manuscrits avec introduction et notes." Edited by Adriaan Pattin. *Tijdschrift voor Filosofie* 28 (1966): 90–203.

[*Liber de Causis*]. *The Book of Causes*. Translated with an introduction by Dennis J. Brand. 2d ed. Milwaukee, Wis.: Marquette University Press, 1984.

Livy. *Ab urbe condita*. In *Livy with an English Translation in Thirteen* [actually fourteen] *Volumes*, translated by B. O. Foster, Frank Gardner Moore, et al. LCL. London: Heinemann; New York: Putnam, 1919–1967.

Lucan. *Pharsalia*. In *Lucan with an English Translation: The Civil War (Pharsalia)*, translated by J. D. Duff. LCL. Cambridge, Mass.: Harvard University Press; London: Heinemann, 1928; rpt. 1977.

[Marsiglio of Padua. *Defensor Pacis*]. *Marsilius of Padua*. Translated by Alan Gewirth. 2 vols. Records of Civilization. New York: Columbia University Press, 1956. Vol. 2 rpt. as Marsilius of Padua, *Defender of Peace: The Defensor Pacis*. Translated with an introduction by Alan Gewirth. New York: Harper & Row, 1956; rpt. 1965, 1967.

Marsilius of Padua. *Defensor minor*. Edited by C. Kenneth Brampton. Birmingham, U.K.: Cornish Brothers, 1922.

Martin of Braga. *Rules for an Honest Life*. Translated by Claude W. Barlow. In *Martin of Braga, Paschasius of Dumium, Leander of Seville*, pp. 87–97. In Iberian Fathers 1. Fathers of the Church 62. Washington, D.C.: The Catholic University of America Press, 1969.

Ockham, William of. *A Short Discourse on the Tyrannical Government*. Edited by Arthur Stephen McGrade. Translated by John Kilcullen. Cambridge, U.K.: Cambridge University Press, 1992.

———. *William of Okham: A Letter to the Friars Minor and Other Writings*. Edited by Arthur Stephen McGrade and John Kilcullen. Translated by John Kilcullen. Cambridge, U.K.: Cambridge University Press, 1995. [Contains the *Work of Ninety Days*, *Dialogues*, and *Eight Questions on the Power of the Pope*.]

———. *On the Powers of the Emperors and the Popes*. Translated and edited by Annabel S. Brett. Bristol, U.K.: University of Durham Press and Thoemmes Press, 1998.

[Orosius, Paulus. *Against the Pagans*]. *Paulus Orosius. Historia adversus paganos Libri VII*. Edited by Karl Zangemeister. Leipzig: Teubner, 1889.

———. *The Seven Books of History against the Pagans*. Translated by Roy J. Deferrari. Fathers of the Curch 50. Washington, D.C.: The Catholic University of America Press, 1964.

*Patrologiæ cursus completus . . .* , *series græca.* Edited by J.-P. Migne. 162 vols. Paris, 1886–1912. [*PG.*]

*Patrologiæ cursus completus . . .* , *series latina.* Edited by J.-P. Migne. 221 vols. Paris, 1844–1864. [*PL.*]

Peter Abelard. *Philosophische Schriften 1. Die Logica "Ingredientibus." 2 Die Glossen zu den Kategorien.* Edited by B. Geyer. Münster: Aschendorff, 1921.

Peter Lombard. *Liber sententiorum.* Paris: Vivès, 1892.

[Peter Lombard]. Petri Lombardi. *Libri IV sententiarum,* Liber III, et IV, tom. 2. 2d ed. Ad Claras Aquas [Quaracchi] prope Florentiam ex Typographia Collegii S. Bonaventuræ, 1916.

[Peter of Spain: Petrus Hispanus]. *Tractatus, Called Afterwards Summule logicales.* Edited by L. M. de Rijk. Philosophical Texts and Studies 22. Assen: Van Gorcum, 1972.

––––––. *The "Summulæ logicales" of Peter of Spain.* Edited and translated by Joseph P. Mullally. Publications in Medieval Studies: The University of Notre Dame 8. South Bend, Ind.: University of Notre Dame Press, 1945.

––––––. *Tractatus Syncategorematum.* Edited and translated by Joseph P. Mullally and Roland Houde. Milwaukee, Wis.: Marquette University Press, 1964.

[Petrarca, Francesco]. [*Familiares*]. Petrarch, Francis. *Letters on Familiar Matters: Rerum familiarium libri IX–XVI.* Translated by Aldo S. Bernardo. Baltimore and London: Johns Hopkins University Press, 1982.

––––––. [*Seniles*]. Petrarch, Francis. *Letters of Old Age: Rerum senilium libri I–XVIII.* Translated by Aldo S. Bernardo, Saul Levin, and Reta A. Bernardo. 2 vols. Baltimore and London: Johns Hopkins University Press, 1992.

––––––. *Petrarcas "Buch ohne Namen" Halle: und die päpstliche Kurie.* Edited by P. Piur. Halle: Niemeyer, 1925.

––––––. *Sine nomine: Lettere polemiche e politiche.* Edited by Ugo Dotti. Universale Laterza. Bari: Laterza, 1974.

––––––. [*Liber sine nomine*]. *Petrarch's "Book without a Name": A Translation of the "Liber sine nomine."* Translated by Norman P. Zacour. Toronto: Pontifical Institute of Mediæval Studies, 1973.

––––––. "On His Own Ignorance and That of Many Others." In *Renaissance Philosophy of Man,* edited and translated by Ernst Cassirer, Paul Oskar Kristeller, and John Herman Randall Jr., pp. 47–133. Chicago and London: University of Chicago Press, 1948.

[Porphyry]. *Categoriarum supplementa; Porphyrii Isagoge: Translatio Boethii et Anonymi Fragmentum vulgo vocatum "Liber sex principiorum."* Edited by Lorenzo Mineo Paluello with Bernard G. Dod. Bruges and Paris: Desclée de Brouwer, 1966.

Porphyry the Phoenician. *Isagoge.* Translated with an introduction and notes by Edward W. Warren. Toronto: Pontifical Institute of Mediæval Studies, 1975.

*Quæstio de Potestate Papæ (Rex Pacificus)/An Enquiry into the Power of the Pope: A Critical Edition and Translation.* Edited by R. W. Dyson. Texts and Studies in Religion 83. Lewiston, Queenston, and Lampeter: Edwin Mellen Press, 1999.

*Quæstio in utramque partem, pro et contra pontificiam potestatem* [*For and against Pontifical Power*]. In *Three Royalist Tracts, 1296–1302,* translated by R. W. Dyson, pp. 47–111. Bristol, U.K.: University of Durham Press and Thoemmes Press, 1999.

*Readings in Church History.* Edited by Colman J. Barry. 2 vols. Westminster, Md.: Newman Press, 1960.

Remigio de' Girolami. *Contra falsos ecclesie professores.* Edited by Filippo Tamburini. Rome: Libreria Editrice della Pontificia Università Lateranense, 1981.

[Remigio de' Girolami. *Contra falsos ecclesie professores*]. Emilio Panella. *Per lo studio di Fra Remigio dei Girolami (†1319): Contra falsos ecclesie professores cc. 5–37*, VII Centenario della Fondazione di S. Maria Novella in Firenze (1279–1979), vol. 1. Memorie Domenicane, n.s., 10. Pistoia: Memorie Domenicane, 1919. [Partial edition.]

———. [*De bono communi*]. Maria Consiglia De Matteis. "Il *De bono communi* di Remigio de' Girolami (†1319)." *Annali dell'Università degli Studi di Lecce*. Facoltà di lettere e filosofia e di magistero 3 (1965–1967): 13–86; text, pp. 53–86.

———. [*De bono pacis*]. Charles T. Davis. "Remigio de' Girolami and Dante: A Comparison of Their Conceptions of Peace." *Studi danteschi* 36 (1959): 105–136; text, pp. 123–136.

———. *Contra falsos professores ecclesie*. Edited by Filippo Tamburini. Preface by Charles T. Davis. Rome: Libreria Editrice della Pontificia Università Lateranense, 1981. [Complete edition.]

Scholz, Richard. *Unbekannte kirchenpolitische Streitschriften aus der Zeit Ludwigs des Bayern (1327–1354)*. 2 vols. Rome: Loescher, 1911–1914.

*Select Historical Documents of the Middle Ages*. Translated by Ernest F. Henderson. New York: Bilo & Tannen, 1965.

Seneca. *Epistulæ morales*. Edited by R. M. Gummere. 3 vols. LCL. Cambridge, Mass., and London: Harvard University Press, 1953.

[Magister *Sex principiorum; Six Principles*]. *Liber sex principiorum*. In *Categoriarum supplementa; Porphyrii Isagoge: Translatio Boethii et Anonymi Fragmentum vulgo vocatum "Liber sex principiorum."* Edited by Lorenzo Mineo-Paluello and Bernard G. Dod. Aristoteles Latinus. Bruges and Paris: Desclée de Brouwer, 1966.

*Summa parisiensis*. Edited by T. P. McLaughlin. Toronto: Pontifical Institute of Mediæval Studies, 1952.

Thomas Aquinas, St. *Against the Averroists on There Being Only One Intellect*. Edited and translated by Ralph McInerny. Purdue Series in the History of Philosophy. West Lafayette, Ind.: Purdue University Press, 1993.

———. [*Against the Errors of the Greeks*]. S. Thomas d'Aquin. *Contra errores Græcorum: Texte présenté et édité avec notes, références et documents connexes*. Edited by Palémon Glorieux. Monumenta Christiana Selecta. Tournai, Paris, Rome, and New York: Desclée de Brouwer, 1957.

———. [*Against the Errors of the Greeks*]. *Contra errores Græcorum*. Translated by James Likoudis. In James Likoudis, *Ending the Byzantine Greek Schism*. New Rochelle, N.Y.: Catholics United for the Faith, 1992.

———. *Aquinas: Selected Political Writings*. Edited by A. P. D'Entrèves. Translated by J. G. Dawson. Oxford, U.K.: Blackwell, 1948.

———. *Catena Aurea: Commentary on the Four Gospels Collected out of the Four Gospels*. 6 vols. Oxford and London: Parker, 1874.

———. [*Commentary on Aristotle's De anima*]. Sancti Thomæ Aquinatis. *In Aristotelis librum De Anima commentarium*. Edited by Angelo M. Pirotta. Turin: Marietti, 1959.

———. [*Commentary on Aristotle's De cælo et mundo*]. S. Thomæ Aquinatis. *In Aristotelis libros de cælo et mundo, De generatione et corruptione, Meteorologicorum expositio*. Edited by R. M. Spiazzi. Turin: Marietti, 1952.

———. [*Commentary on Aristotle's De generatione et corruptione*]. See St. Thomas Aquinas, *Commentary on Aristotle's De cælo et mundo*.

———. [*Commentary on Aristotle's Metaphysics*]. S. Thomæ Aquinatis. *In duodecim Libros Metaphysico-*

*rum Aristotelis Expositio.* Edited by M. R. Cathala and R. M. Spiazzi. Turin and Rome: Marietti, 1964.

———. [*Commentary on Aristotle's Meteorologica*]. See St. Thomas Aquinas, *Commentary on Aristotle's De cælo et mundo.*

———. [*Commentary on Aristotle's Nicomachean Ethics*]. S. Thomæ Aquinatis. *In decem libros Ethicorum Aristotelis ad Nicomachum Expositio.* Edited by R. M. Spiazzi. Turin and Rome: Marietti, 1949.

———. *Commentary on Aristotle's Nicomachean Ethics.* Translated by C. I. Litzinger. 2 vols. Library of Living Catholic Thought. Chicago: Regnery, 1964.

———. [*Commentary on Aristotle's Physics*]. S. Thomæ Aquinatis. *In octo libros Physicorum Aristotelis expositio.* Edited by P. M. Maggiòlo. Turin and Rome: Marietti, 1954.

———. [*Commentary on Aristotle's Politics*]. S. Thomæ Aquinatis. *In Libros Politicorum Aristotelis Expositio.* Edited by R. M. Spiazzi. Turin and Rome: Marietti, 1951.

———. *Commentary of the Book of Causes* [*Super librum De causis expositio*]. Translated by Vincent A. Guagliardo, Charles R. Hess, and Richard C. Taylor, with an introduction by Vincent A. Guagliardo. Thomas Aquinas in Translation. Washington, D.C.: The Catholic University of America Press, 1996.

———. *On Princely Government.* In *Aquinas: Selected Political Writings,* edited by A. P. D'Entrèves, translated by J. D. Dawson, pp. 2–83. Oxford, U.K.: Blackwell, 1948.

———. [*De regimine principum*]. St. Thomas Aquinas. *On Kingship, to the King of Cyprus.* Translated by Gerald B. Phelan (under the title *On the Governance of Rulers*). Revised with an introduction and notes by I. T. Eschmann, O.P. Toronto: Pontifical Institute of Mediæval Studies, 1949; rpt. 1989.

———. [*De regimine principum*]. In Ptolemy of Lucca, *On the Government of Rulers: De regimine principum, with Portions Attributed to Thomas Aquinas.* Translated by James M. Blythe. Philadelphia: University of Pennsylvania Press, 1997.

———. *S. Thomæ Aquinatis Scriptum super Libros Sententiarum Magistri Petri Lombardi Episcopi Parisiensis. Editio nova.* Edited by P. Mandonnet. 2 vols. Paris: Lethielleux, 1929.

———. [*Summa contra gentiles*]. Saint Thomas Aquinas. *On the Truth of the Catholic Faith: Summa contra gentiles.* Translated by Anton C. Pegis, Vernon J. Bourke, and Charles J. O'Neil. 4 books in 5 vols. Garden City, N.Y.: Doubleday, 1955–1957.

———. *Summa theologiæ.* Vol. 5: *God's Will and Providence* Ia, 19–26. Edited and translated by Thomas Gilby, with an introduction by Ian Hislop. New York: Blackfriars/McGraw-Hill; London: Eyre & Spottiswoode, 1967.

———. *Summa theologiæ.* Vol. 16: *Purpose and Happiness* Ia2æ, 1–5. Edited and translated by Thomas Gilby. New York: Blackfriars/McGraw-Hill; London: Eyre & Spottiswoode, 1969.

———. *Summa theologica.* Edited by Ottawa Institute of Medieval Studies. 4 vols. Ottawa: Impensis Studii Generalis Ordinis Prædicatorum, 1941–1944.

———. *Summa theologica.* Translated by Fathers of the English Dominican Province. 3 vols. New York: Benziger Brothers, 1947–1948.

———. [*De unitate intellectus contra Averroistas*]. St. Thomas Aquinas. *Against the Averroists: On There Being Only One Intellect against the Averroists.* Translated by Ralph McInerny. West Lafayette, Ind.: Purdue University Press, 1993.

*Three Royalist Tracts, 1296–1302.* Translated by R. W. Dyson. Bristol, U.K.: University of Durham Press and Thoemmes Press, 1999.

[Tolomeo da Lucca, Ptolemy of Lucca]. *Secunda vita Clementis V.* In *Vitæ paparum Avenionensium hoc est pontificum romanorum . . . ab anno Christ 1305 usque ad annum 1394,* edited by Etienne Baluze. Rev. ed., edited by Guillaume Mollat. 4 vols. Paris: Letouzey et Ané, 1914–1928.

—————. *On the Government of Rulers: De regimine principum, with Portions Attributed to Thomas Aquinas.* Translated by James M. Blythe. Philadelphia: University of Pennsylvania Press, 1997.

[Tolomeo da Lucca. *Short Determination*]. *Determinatio compendiosa de iurisdictione imperii auctore anonymo ut videtur Tholomeo Lucensi O.P.* Edited by Marius Krammer. Hannover and Leipzig: Hahn, 1909.

[Valerius Maximus. *Memorable Deeds and Sayings*]. *Valerii Maximi. Factorum et dictorum memorabilium: Libri Novem.* Edited by Carolus [Karl] Kempf. 2d ed. Stuttgart: Teubner, 1966.

Valla, Lorenzo. *The Treatise of Lorenzo Valla on the Donation of Constantine.* Edited and translated by Christopher B. Coleman. New Haven, Conn.: Yale University Press, 1922.

Vegetius. *De re militari: Epitome of Military Science (On the Military).* Translated by N. P. Milner. Translated Texts for Historians 16. Liverpool, U.K.: Liverpool University Press, 1993.

Vergil. *Æneid.* In *Virgil with an English Translation . . . in Two Volumes.* Translated by H. Rushton Fairclough. LCL. Cambridge, Mass.: Harvard University Press; London: Heinemann, 1967.

—————. *Eclogues.* In *Virgil with an English Translation.*

[Vernani, Guido]. [*De potestate* and *Reprobatio*]. *F. Guidonis Vernani Ariminensis Ordinis Prædicatorum. De potestate summi pontificis et De Reprobatione Monarchiæ compositæ a Dante Aligerio florentino tractatus duo nunc primum in lucem editi.* Bononiæ: apud Thomam Coli, ex Typographia S. Thomæ Aquinatis, 1746.

—————. [*Reprobatio*]. *Contro Dante (Contra Dantem): Fr. Guidonis Vernani Tractatus De Reprobatione "Monarchiæ" compositæ a Dante Aligherio Florentino,* rarissimo opuscolo del secolo XIV per la prima volta tradotto in italiano e ripubblicato da Jarro (R. Piccini). Florence, Rome, and Milan: Bemporad, 1906.

—————. [*Reprobatio*]. Käppeli, Thomas. "Der Dantegegner Guido Vernani O.P. von Rimini." *Quellen und Forschungen aus italienischen Archiven und Bibliotheken herausgegeben vom Deutschen Historischen Institut in Rom* 28 (Rome: 1938): 107–146.

—————. [*Reprobatio*]. Nevio Matteini. *Il più antico oppositore politico di Dante: Guido Vernani da Rimini: Testo Critico del "De Reprobatione Monarchiæ."* Il Pensiero medievale collana di Storia della Filosofia, ser. 1, vol. 6. Padua: CEDAM [Casa Editrice Dott. Antonio Milani], 1958.

—————. [*Commentary on Unam Sanctam*]. "Kommentar des Guido Vernani von Rimini O.P. zur Bulle *Unam Sanctam.*" In Martin Grabmann, "Studien über den Einfluss der aristotelischen Philosophie auf die mittelalterlichen Theorien über das Verhältnis von Kirche und Staat." *Sitzungsberichte der bayerischen Akademie der Wissenschaften,* Philosophisch-historische Abteilung, Heft 2 (1934): 1–163; text, pp. 144–157.

Villani, Giovanni. *Cronica.* Ristampa dell'Edizione Originale, Firenze 1823. 9 vols. Rome: Multigrafica Editrice, 1980.

SECONDARY SOURCES

Note: Authors are listed in alphabetical order; the studies under an author's name are listed chronologically.

Arquillière, Henri-Xavier. *L'Augustinisme politique: Essai sur la formation des théories politiques du Moyen-Âge.* Paris: Vrin, 1934.

Ascoli, Albert Russell. "The Vowels of Authority (Dante's *Convivio* IV.vi.3–4)." In *Discourses of Authority in Medieval and Renaissance Literature*, edited by Kevin Brownlee and Walter Stephens, pp. 23–46. Hanover, N.H., and London: Published for Dartmouth College by the University Press of New England, 1989.

———. "'Neminem ante nos': Historicity and Authority in the *De vulgari eloquentia.*" *Annali d'Italianistica* 8 (1990): 186–231.

———. "The Unfinished Author: Dante's Rhetoric of Authority in *Convivio* and *De vulgari eloquentia.*" In *The Cambridge Companion to Dante*, edited by Rachel Jacoff, pp. 45–66. Cambridge, U.K.: Cambridge University Press, 1993.

———. "Palinode and History in the Oeuvre of Dante." In *Dante Now: Current Trends in Dante Studies*, edited by Theodor J. Cachey Jr., pp. 155–186. South Bend, Ind., and London: University of Notre Dame Press, 1995.

Ashworth, Earline J. *The Tradition of Medieval Logic and Speculative Grammar from Anselm to the End of the Seventeenth Century: A Bibliography from 1836 Onwards.* Subsidia Mediævalia 9. Toronto: Pontifical Institute of Mediæval Studies, 1978.

*Atti del Congresso Internazionale di Studi Danteschi. A cura della Società dantesca italiana e dell'Associazione internazionale per gli studi di lingua et letteratura italiana e sotto il patrocinio dei Comuni di Firenze, Verona e Ravenna, 20–27 aprile 1965.* 2 vols. Florence: Sansoni, 1965.

*Atti del 1° Convegno di studi su Cecco d'Ascoli: Ascoli Piceno, Palazzo dei Congressi 23–24 novembre 1969.* Edited by B. Censori. Ascoli Piceno: Giunti Barbèra, 1976.

*Babylon on the Rhone: A Translation of Letters by Dante, Petrarch, and Catherine of Siena on the Avignon Papacy.* Edited and translated by Robert Coogan. Studia Humanitatis. Madrid and Potomac, Md.: José Porrúa Turanzas, 1983.

Baethgen, Friedrich. "Der Anspruch des Papsttums auf das Reichsvikariat: Untersuchung zur Theorie und Praxis der *potestas indirecta in temporalibus.*" In *Zeitschrift der Savigny-Stiftung für Rechtsgeschichte, Kanonistische Abteilung* 10 (Weimar: Hermann Böhlaus Nachfolger, 1920), 41:3:168–268.

———. "Die Entstehungszeit von Dantes *Monarchia.*" *Sitzungsberichte der Bayerische Akademie der Wissenschaften, Philosophisch-historische Klasse* 5 (1966): 1–34.

Bainton, Roland. *The Medieval Church.* Princeton, N.J.: Van Nostrand, 1962.

Balogh, J. "Romanum Imperium de Fonte nascitur pietatis." *Deutsches Dante-Jahrbuch* 10 (1928): 202–205.

Barbi, Michele. *Dante: Vita, opere e fortuna, con due saggi su Francesca e Farinata.* Florence: Sansoni, 1933.

———. "Nuovi problemi della critica dantesca, VI: L'ideale politico-religioso di Dante." *Studi danteschi* 23 (1938): 5–77.

Barraclough, Geoffrey. *The Origins of Modern Germany.* Oxford, U.K.: Blackwell, 1952.

Becker, Marvin B. "Dante and His Literary Contemporaries as Political Men." *Speculum* 41 (1966): 665–680.

Bemrose, Stephen. *A New Life of Dante*. Exeter, U.K.: University of Exeter Press, 2000.

Benson, R. L. *"Plenitudo potestatis:* Evolution of a Formula from Gregory to Gratian." *Studia Gratiana* 14 (1967): 196–217.

Benz, Ernst. *Ecclesia spiritualis. Kirchenidee und Geschichtstheologie der franziskanischen Reformation.* Stuttgart: Kohlhammer, 1934.

Bertelloni, C. Francisco. "Filosofia politica y teologia de la historia en la teoria dantesca del Imperio." *Patristica et Mediævalia* 2 (1981): 37–66.

———. "'Constitutum Constantini' y 'Romgedanke': La donacion constantiniana en el pensamiento de tres defensores del derecho imperial de Roma: Dante, Marsilio de Padua y Guillermo de Ockham." *Patristica et Mediævalia* 3 (1982): 21–46.

———. "'Constitutum Constantini' y 'Romgedanke': La donacion constantiniana en el pensamiento de tres defensores del derecho imperial de Roma: Dante, Marsilio de Padua y Guillermo de Ockham (2a parte)." *Patristica et Mediævalia* 4–5 (1984): 67–99.

Bigongiari, Dino. "The Text of Dante's *Monarchia*." *Speculum* 2 (1927): 457–462.

———. "Notes on the Text of Dante." *Romanic Review* 41 (1950): 3–13, 81–95.

———. *Essays on Dante and Medieval Culture: Critical Studies of Thought and Texts of Dante, St. Augustine, St. Thomas Aquinas, Marsilius of Padua and Other Medieval Subjects.* Biblioteca dell'Archivum Romanicum, ser. 1, vol. 71. Florence: Olschki, 1964.

Biscaro, G. "Le relazioni dei Visconti di Milano con la chiesa." *Archivio storico lombardo* 46 (1919): 84–229.

Blythe, James M. *Ideal Government and Mixed Constitution in the Middle Ages.* Princeton, N.J.: Princeton University Press, 1992.

Boffito, Giuseppe, and Ugo Oxilia. *Un trattato inedito di Egidio Colonna.* Florence: B. Seeber, 1908.

Boulet-Sautel, Marguerite. "Encore sur la bulle *Per venerabilem*." *Collecteana Stephan Kuttner* 3, in *Studia Gratiana* 13 (1967): 371–382.

Bowsky, William M. "Clement V and the Emperor-Elect." *Medievalia et Humanistica* 12 (1958): 52–96.

———. "Dante's Italy: A Political Dissection." *Historian* 21 (1958): 82–100.

———. "Florence and Henry of Luxembourg, King of the Romans: The Rebirth of Guelfism." *Speculum* 33 (1958): 177–203.

———. *Henry VII in Italy: The Conflict of Empire and City-State, 1310–1313.* Lincoln: University of Nebraska Press, 1960. Rpt., Westport, Conn.: Greenwood Press, 1974.

Boyde, Patrick. *Dante: Philomythes and Philosopher: Man in the Cosmos.* Cambridge, U.K.: Cambridge University Press, 1981.

———. *Perception and Passion in Dante's "Comedy."* Cambridge, U.K.: Cambridge University Press, 1993.

Brady, Ignatius. "Questions at Paris, c. 1260–1270." *Archivum Franciscanum historicum* 61 (1968): 434–461.

———. "Background to the Condemnation of 1270: Master William of Baglione, O.F.M." *Franciscan Studies* 30 (1970): 6–48.

Brezzi, Paolo. "Dante e la chiesa del suo tempo." In *Dante e Roma: Atti del Convegno di Studi a cura della "Casa di Dante," sotto gli auspici del Comune di Roma, in collaborazione con l'Istituto di Studi Romani, Roma, 8–9–10 aprile 1965,* pp. 97–113. Florence: Le Monnier, 1965.

———. "Dante e Roma." In *Filologia e critica dantesca: Studi offerti a Aldo Vallone,* Biblioteca dell'"Archivum Romanicum," ser. 1, Storia-Letteratura-Paleografia 224. Florence: Olschki, 1989.

Briggs, Charles F. *Giles of Rome's "De regimine principum": Reading and Writing Politics at Court and University, c. 1275–c. 1525.* Cambridge, U.K.: Cambridge University Press, 1999.

Brown, Oscar J. *Natural Rectitude and Divine Law in Aquinas.* Studies and Texts 55. Toronto: Pontifical Institute of Mediæval Studies, 1981.

Brundage, James A. *Medieval Canon Law.* London and New York: Longmans, 1995.

Buisson, Ludwig. *"Potestas" und "Caritas": Die päpstliche Gewalt im Spätmittelalter.* Cologne and Vienna: Böhlau, 1982.

Bulloch, James. *Adam of Dryburgh.* London: S.P.C.K., 1958.

Buti, Giovanni, and Renzo Bertagni. "Clima." In *Enciclopedia dantesca,* 2:43.

*The Cambridge Companion to Aquinas.* Edited by Norman Kretzmann and Eleonore Stump. Cambridge, U.K.: Cambridge University Press, 1993.

*The Cambridge Companion to Dante.* Edited by Rachel Jacoff. Cambridge, U.K.: Cambridge University Press, 1993.

*The Cambridge History of Medieval Political Thought, c. 350–c. 1450.* Edited by J. H. Burns. Cambridge, U.K.: Cambridge University Press, 1988.

Capitani, Ovidio. "L'incompiuto 'tractatus de iustitia' di fra' Remigio de' Girolami (1319)." *Bulletino dell'Istituto storico italiano per il medio evo e archivio muratoriano* 72, no. 2 (1960): 91–134.

———. "*Monarchia*: Il Pensiero politico." *Cultura e Scuola* 4 (1965): 722–738. Rpt. in *Dante nella critica d'oggi: Risultati e prospettive,* edited by Umberto Bosco, pp. 722–738. Florence: Le Monnier, 1965.

———. "Spigolature minime sul III della *Monarchia*." *Bullettino dell'Istituto Storico Italiano per il Medio Evo e Archivio Muratoriano* 87 (1978): 173–200. Rpt. in Ovidio, *Chiose minime dantesche.*

———. "Riferimento storico e pubblicista nel commento di Bruno Nardi alla *Monarchia* dantesca." *Letture classensi* 9–10 (1982): 217–245. Rpt. in *Chiose minime dantesche.*

———. *Chiose minime dantesche.* Bologna: Pàtron, 1983.

Carlyle, R. W., and A. J. Carlyle. *Mediæval Political Theory in the West.* 6 vols. Edinburgh, U.K.: William Blackwood, 1903–1936; rpt. 1950.

Carruccio, Ettore. "La logica nel pensiero di Dante." *Physis* 8, no. 3 (1966): 233–246.

Casini, Tommaso. "Intorno a Graziolo Bambaglioli." *Archiginnasio* 11 (1916): 146–170.

Cassell, Anthony K. *Lectura Dantis Americana: Inferno 1.* Philadelphia: University of Pennsylvania Press, 1989.

———. "'*Luna est ecclesia*': Dante and the 'Two Great Lights.'" *Dante Studies* 1119 (2001): 1–26.

———. "The Exiled Dante's Hope for Reconciliation: *Monarchia* 3:16:16–18." *Annali d'Italianistica* 20 (2002): 425–449.

Catalano, Gaetano. "Contributo alla biografia di Uguccione da Pisa." *Il diritto ecclesiastico* 65 (1954): 3–67.

———. *Impero, regni e sacerdozio nel pensiero di Uguccione da Pisa.* Milan: Giuffrè, 1959.

Cecchini, E. "Dante, *Mon.* II, x, 4–10." In *Miscellanea in onore di Vittore Branca,* Biblioteca dell'Archivum Romanicum, ser. 1, Storia-Letteratura-Paleografia 178–182, 5 vols., 1:177–184. Florence: Olschki, 1983.

Cheney, Christopher R. *Pope Innocent II and England.* Päpste und Papsttum 9. Stuttgart: Hiersemann, 1976.

Chiappelli, Luigi. "Ancora su Dante e il diritto." *Giornale dantesco* 20 (1912): 202–206.

*Church and State through the Centuries.* Translated and edited by Sidney Z. Ehler and John B. Morrall. Westminster, Md.: Newman Press, 1954.

Ciaccio, Lisetta. *Il cardinale legato Bertrando del Poggetto in Bologna (1327–1334).* Bologna: Zanichelli, 1905.

Cipolla, Carlo. "Il trattato *De Monarchia* di Dante Alighieri e l'opuscolo *De potestæ regia e papalis* di Giovanni di Parigi." In *Memorie dell'Accademia di Torino,* ser. 2, 42, pp. 325–419. Rpt. in *Gli studi danteschi,* pp. 175–300. Verona: La Tipografica Veronese, 1921.

Comoth, Katharina. "*Pax universalis:* Philosophie und Politik in Dantes *Monarchia.*" In *Soziale Ordnung im Selbstverständnis des Mittelalters, Akten des VI. Internaz. Kongress für Mittelaltische Philosophie der Société internationale pour l'étude de la philosophie mediévale, Bonn 29 August–3 September 1977,* 2 vols., edited by J. P. Beckmann et al. Berlin and New York: De Gruyter, 1981. In vol. 2, edited by Albert Zimmermann, pp. 341–350.

Comparetti, Domenico. *Vergil in the Middle Ages.* Translated by E. F. M. Benecke. London: Swan Sonnenschein; New York: Macmillan, 1895.

Consoli, Domenico. "Virgilio." In *Enciclopedia dantesca,* 5:1031.

Coogan, Robert, ed. and trans. *Babylon on the Rhone: A Translation of Letters by Dante, Petrarch, and Catherine of Siena on the Avignon Papacy.* Studia Humanitatis. Madrid and Potomac, Md.: José Porrúa Turanzas, 1983.

Cortese, Ennio. *La norma giuridica: Spunti teorici nel diritto comune classico.* 2 vols. Milan: Giuffrè, 1962, 1964.

Courtney, William J. "Between Pope and King: The Parisian Letters of Adhesion of 1303." *Speculum* 17, no. 3 (1996): 577–605.

Cram, Kurt Georg. *Judicium belli: Zum Rechtscharakter des Krieges im deutschen Mittelalter.* Münster and Cologne: Böhlau, 1955.

Cremascoli, Giuseppe. "Uguccione da Pisa: Saggio bibliografico." *Ævum* 42 (1968): 123–168.

Crosara, Fulvio. "Dante e Bartolo da Sassoferrato: Politica e diritto nell'Italia del Trecento." In *Bartolo da Sassoferrato: Studi e documenti per il VI centenario. Convegno commemorativo del VI centenario di Bartolo Perugia, 1959,* edited by Danilo Segolino, Università degli Studi di Perugia, 2:105–198. Milan: Giuffrè, 1962.

*Dante e Bologna nei Tempi di Dante a cura della Facoltà di Lettere e Filosofia dell'Università di Bologna. Comitato Nazionale per le Celebrazioni del VII Centenario della Nascita di Dante.* Bologna: Commissione per i Testi di Lingua, 1967.

*Dante e la cultura veneta. Atti del Convegno di Studi organizzato dalla Fondazione "Giorgio Cini" in collaborazione con l'Istituto universitario di Venezia, l'Università di Padova, il Centro scaligero di Studi Danteschi, e i Comuni di Venezia, Padova, Verona. Venezia, Padova, Verona, 30 marzo–5 aprile 1966.* Florence: Olschki, 1966.

*Dante e la scienza.* Edited by Patrick Boyde and Vittorio Russo. Ravenna: Longo, 1995.

*Dante nella critica d'oggi: Risultati e prospettive.* Edited by Umberto Bosco. Florence: Le Monnier, 1965. Rpt. of *Cultura e Scuola* 4 (1965).

*Dantis Alagherii Operum latinorum concordantiæ.* Edited by E. K. Rand and Ernest Hatch Wilkins. Oxford, U.K.: Clarendon Press, 1912.

Davidson, Herbert A. "Averroës on the Material Intellect." *Viator* 17 (1986): 91–137.

Davis, Charles Till. *Dante and the Idea of Rome.* Oxford, U.K.: Clarendon Press, 1957.

————. "Remigio de' Girolami and Dante: A Comparison of Their Conceptions of Peace." *Studi danteschi* 36 (1959): 105–136.

————. "An Early Political Theorist: Fra Remigio de' Girolami." *Proceedings of the American Philosophical Society* 104, no. 6 (1960): 662–676.

————. "Ptolemy of Lucca and the Roman Republic." *Proceedings of the American Philosophic Society* 118, no. 1 (1974): 30–50.

————. "Dante's Vision of History." *Dante Studies* 93 (1975): 143–160.

————. "Roman Patriotism and Republican Propaganda: Ptolemy of Lucca and Pope Nicholas III." *Speculum* 50 (1975): 411–433.

————. *Dante's Italy and Other Essays.* Philadelphia: University of Pennsylvania Press, 1984.

————. "Dante, Machiavelli, and Rome." *Dante Studies* 106 (1988): 43–60.

————. "The Florentine *Studia* and Dante's 'Library.'" In *"The Divine Comedy" and the Encyclopedia of Arts and Sciences, Acta of the International Dante Symposium, 13–16 November 1983, Hunter College, New York*, edited by Giuseppe Di Scipio and Aldo Scaglione, pp. 339–366. Amsterdam: Benjamins, 1988.

————. "Dante and Ecclesiastical Property." In *Law in Medieval Life and Thought*, Sewanee Medieval Studies 5, pp. 244–257. Sewanee, Tenn.: Press of the University of the South, 1990.

————. "Dante and the Empire." In *The Cambridge Companion to Dante*, edited by Rachel Jacoff, pp. 67–79. Cambridge, U.K.: Cambridge University Press, 1993.

Deane, Herbert A. *The Political and Social Ideas of St. Augustine.* New York and London: Columbia University Press, 1963.

De Angelis, Antonio. *Il Concetto d'imperium e la communità sopranazionale in Dante.* Milan: Giuffrè, 1965.

De Matteis, Maria Consiglia. "Il *De bono communi* di Remigio de' Girolami (†1319)." *Annali dell'Università degli Studi di Lecce. Facoltà di lettere e filosofia e di magistero* 3 (1965–1967): 13–86; text, pp. 53–86.

————. *La "Teologia politica comunale" di Remigio de' Girolami.* Bologna: Pàtron, 1977.

————. "Il mito dell'impero romano in Dante: A proposito di Monarchia II, i." *Letture classensi* 9–10 (1982): 247–256.

Dempf, A. *Sacrum Imperium.* Translated by C. Antoni. Messina: Principato, 1933.

d'Entrèves, Alexander Passerin. *The Medieval Contribution to Political Thought: Thomas Aquinas, Marsilius of Padua, Richard Hooker.* Oxford, U.K.: Oxford University Press, 1939.

————. *Dante as a Political Thinker.* Oxford, U.K.: Clarendon Press, 1952. Italian translation by author as "Alessandro Passerin d'Entrèves." *Dante politico e altri saggi.* Milan: Einaudi, 1955.

de Rijk, L. M. *Logica modernorum: A Contribution to the History of Early Terminist Logic.* Vol. 1: *On the Twelfth Century Theories of Fallacy.* Assen: Van Gorcum, 1962.

*Dictionary of the Middle Ages.* Edited by Joseph R. Strayer. 13 vols. New York: Charles Scribner's Sons, 1982–1989.

Di Giannatale, Giovanni. "Per una prospettiva della Monarchia di Dante: Appunti e problemi." *Ævum* 52, no. 2 (1978): 218–227.

————. "Alcune note a Mon. III, 4, 18, 20–21 e ad Ep. V, 30: Considerazioni sull'argomento della 'illuminatio' in Dante." *Ævum* 52, no. 2 (1978): 317–321.

————. "Papa e imperatore in Monarchia III, xii." *L'Alighieri: Rassena bibliografica dantesca* 22, no. 2 (1981): 46–60.

Di Scipio, Giuseppe. "Dante and Politics." In *"The Divine Comedy" and the Encyclopedia of Arts and Sciences, Acta of the International Dante Symposium, 13–16 November 1983, Hunter College, New York*, edited by Giuseppe Di Scipio and Aldo Scaglione, pp. 267–284. Amsterdam and Philadelphia: Benjamins, 1988.

Diurni, Giovanni. "Duello." In *Enciclopedia dantesca*, 2:605–607.

Dolcini, Carlo. *Crisi di poteri e politologia in crisi da Sinibaldo Fieschi a Guglielmo d'Ockham*. Il mondo medievale, Sezione di storia delle istituzioni, della spiritualità e delle idee 17. Bologna: Pàtron, 1988.

———. "Guido Vernani e Dante: Note sul testo del *De reprobatione Monarchiæ*." *Letture Classensi* 9–10 (1982): 257–262. Rpt. in his *Crisi di poteri*, pp. 439–444.

———. "*Eger cui lenia* (1245/46): Innocenzo IV, Tolomeo da Lucca e Guglielmo d'Ockham." *Rivista di Storia della Chiesa in Italia* 29 (1975): 127–148. Rpt. in his *Crisi di poteri*, pp. 119–146.

Dölger, Franz Joseph. *Die Sonne der Gerechtigkeit*. Münster in Westfalia: Aschendorff, 1918.

Domaneschio, F. P. M. *De rebus coenobii cremonensis ordinis prædicatorum, deque illustribus, qui ex eo prodiere viris commentarius*. Cremona: P. Richini, 1767.

Donlon, S. E. "Gelasian Letter." In *New Catholic Encyclopedia*, 6:315.

Douie, Decima L. *The Nature and Effect of the Heresy of the Fraticelli*. Manchester, U.K.: Manchester University Press, 1932.

———. "John XXII, Pope." In *New Catholic Encyclopedia*, 7:1014–1015.

Drake, H. A. *Constantine and the Bishops: The Politics of Intolerance*. Ancient Society and History. Baltimore and London: Johns Hopkins University Press, 2000.

Duggan, Charles. *Canon Law in Medieval England: The Becket Dispute and Decretal Collections*. London: Variorum Reprints, 1982.

Dupré Theseider, Eugenio. *L'idea imperiale di Roma nella tradizione del medioevo*. Milan: Istituto per gli Studi di Politica Internazionale, 1942.

———. *Roma dal comune di popolo alla signoria pontificia, 1252–1377*. Bologna: Licinio Cappelli, 1952.

———. "L'incoronazione imperiale e le reazioni curiali." In *Roma dal comune di popolo alla signoria pontificia, 1252–1377*, pp. 464–473. Bologna: Cappelli, 1952.

Dupuy, P. *Histoire du differend d'entre le Pape Boniface et Philippes le Bel Roy de France*. Paris, 1665. Rpt., Tucson: Audax Press, 1963.

Elmer, L. J. "Demons, Theology of." In *New Catholic Encyclopedia*, 4:752–756.

*Enciclopedia dantesca*. Edited by Umberto Bosco. 5 vols. Rome: Treccani, 1970–1975.

Engen, John Van. "The Donation of Constantine." In *Dictionary of the Middle Ages*, 4:257–259.

Ercole, Francesco. *Il pensiero politico di Dante*. 2 vols. Milan: Alpes, 1927–1928.

Evans, G. R. "The Use of Mathematical Method in Medieval Political Science: Dante's *Monarchia* and the *Defensor pacis* of Marsilius of Padua." *Académie Internationale d'Histoire des Sciences* 32, no. 108 (1982): 78–94.

Faral, Edmond. *Les arts poétiques du XII^e et du XIII^e siècle: Recherches et documents sur la technique littéraire du Moyen Âge*. Paris: E. Champion, 1924. Rpt., Paris: Librairie Honoré Champion, 1958, 1962.

Farnell, Stewart. *The Political Ideas of the "Divine Comedy": An Introduction*. Lanham, N.Y., and London: University Press of America, 1985.

Ferrante, Joan M. *The Political Vision of the "Divine Comedy"*. Princeton, N.J.: Princeton University Press, 1984.

Ferrari, Giuseppe. *Gli scrittori politici italiani*. Milan: Monanni, 1929.

Ferruolo, S. C. "Innocent III, Pope (1160/1161–16 July 1216)." In *Dictionary of the Middle Ages*, 6:464–465.

Filippini, Francesco. "Cecco d'Ascoli a Bologna." *Studi e memorie per la storia dell'Università di Bologna* 10 (1930): 8–9.

Fiorelli, Piero. "Sul senso del diritto nella *Monarchia*." *Letture classensi* 16 (1987): 79–97.

Folena, G. "La tradizione delle opere di Dante." In *Atti del Congresso Internazionale di Studi Danteschi a cura della Società dantesca italiana e dell'Associazione internazionale per gli studi di lingua et letteratura italiana e sotto il patrocinio dei Comini di Firenze, Verona e Ravenna, 20–27 aprile 1965*, 2 vols., 1:1–78. Florence: Sansoni, 1965.

Fortin, Ernest. *Dissidence et philosophie au Moyen Âge*. Institut d'études médiévales Université de Montréal, Cahiers d'Études Médiévales 6. Montreal: Bellarmin; Paris: J. Vrin, 1981.

Frati, Ludovico. "Notizie biografiche di rimatori italiani dei secoli XIII e XIV: VII, Graziolo Bambaglioli." *Giornale Storico della letterature italiana* 17 (1891): 367–380.

———. "Graziolo Bambaglioli esiliato a Napoli." *Giornale dantesco* 1 (1894): 212–216.

———. "La contesa fra Matteo Visconti ed il papa Giovanni XXII secondo i documenti dell'archivio vaticano." *Archivio Storico Lombardo* 15 (1888): 241–258.

Freccero, John. "Dante's Firm Foot and the Journey without a Guide." *Harvard Theological Review* 52, no. 3 (1959): 245–281. Rpt. as "The Firm Foot on a Journey without a Guide," in *Dante: The Poetics of Conversion*, edited by Rachel Jacoff, pp. 29–54. Cambridge, Mass.: Harvard University Press, 1986.

Freed, John B. "Elections, Royal." In *Dictionary of the Middle Ages*, 4:425–429.

Frugoni, Arsenio. "Dante e la Roma del suo tempo." In *Dante e Roma: Atti del Convegno di Studi a cura della "Casa di Dante," sotto gli auspici del Comune di Roma, in collaborazione con l'Istituto di Studi Romani, Roma, 8–9–10 aprile 1965*, pp. 73–96. Florence: Le Monnier, 1965.

———. "Le Epistole." *Cultura e Scuola* 4 (1965): 739–748. Rpt. in *Dante nella critica d'oggi: Risultati e prospettive*, edited by Umberto Bosco, pp. 739–748. Florence: Le Monnier, 1965.

Fuhrmann, Horst. "Konstantinische Schenkung." In *Lexikon des Mittelalters*, 5:1386–1387.

Fumagalli, Edoardo. "I condizionamenti del mondo ecclesiastico esemplificato attraverso Guido Vernani." In *Lectura Dantis mystica: Il Poema Sacro alla luce delle conquiste psicologiche odierne*, Atti della Settimana Dantesca 28 luglio–3 agosto 1968, pp. 286–300. Florence: Olschki, 1969.

Gauthier, René. "Notes sur les debuts (1225–1240) du premier 'Averroisme.'" *Revue des sciences philosophiques et theologiques* 66, no. 1 (1982): 321–373.

Gennaro, Maria Monti. *Cino da Pistoja giurista*. Città di Castello: "Il Solco" Casa Editrice, 1924.

Gewirth, Alan. "John of Jandun and the *Defensor pacis*." *Speculum* 23 (1948): 267–272.

Gierke, Otto. *Political Theories of the Middle Ages*. Translated with an introduction by Frederic William Maitland. Cambridge, U.K.: Cambridge University Press, 1900.

Gilbert, Alan H. "Had Dante Read the *Politics* of Aristotle?" *PMLA* 43 (1928): 602–613.

Gilson, Etienne. *Dante the Philosopher*. Translated by David Moore. New York: Sheed & Ward, 1949. Rpt. as *Dante and Philosophy*. New York: Harper & Row, 1963.

———. "L'impero universale." In *Scrittori e idee in Italia: Antologia della Critica: Dalle Origini al Trecento*, edited by P. Pullega, pp. 151–159. Bologna: Zanichelli, 1982.

Glutz, M. A. "Demonology." In *New Catholic Encyclopedia*, 4:756–757.

Gonnet, G. "La Donazione di Costantino in Dante e presso gli eretici medievali." In *Dante nel pensiero e nella esegesi dei secoli XIV e XV, Atti del III Congrsso Nazionale di Studi Danteschi. Convegno di Studi realizzato dal Comune di Melfi in collaborazione con la Biblioteca Provinciale di Potenza e il Seminario di Studi Danteschi di Terra di Lavoro. Melfi, 27 settembre–2 ottobre 1970*, edited by A. Borraro and P. Borraro, pp. 325–337. Florence: Olschki, 1975.

Gorra, Egidio. "Dante e Clemente V." *Giornale storico della letteratura italiana* 69 (1917): 193–216.

Grabmann, Martin. "Die Wege von Thomas von Aquin zu Dante." *Deutsches Dante-Jahrbuch* 9 (1925): 1–35.

————. *Mittelalterliches Geistesleben*. 2 vols. Munich: Heber, 1926.

————. *Studien über den Einfluss der aristotelischen Philosophie auf die mittelalterlichen Theorien über das Verhältnis von Kirche und Staat*. Sitzungsberichte der Bayerischen Akademie der Wissenschaften, Philosophisch-historische Abteilung 2. Munich: Bayerischen Akademie der Wissenschaften, 1934.

————. "Die Lehre vom *intellectus possibilis* und *intellectus agens* im *Liber de anima* des Petrus Hispanus des späteren Papstes Johannes XXI." *Archives d'histoire doctrinale et littérature du Moyen Âge* 12–13 (1937–1938): 167–208.

Gregory, T. "Intenzione." In *Enciclopedia dantesca*, 3:480–482.

Guerrini, Olindo, and Corrado Ricci. *Studi e polemiche dantesche*. Bologna: Zanichelli, 1853.

Gushee, Lawrence. "Augustinus Triumphus." In *Dictionary of the Middle Ages*, 2:1.

Hageneder, Othmar. "Das Sonne-Mond-Gleichnis bei Innocenz III.: Versuch einer teilweisen Neuinterpretation." *Mitteilungen des Instituts für Österreichische Geschichtsforschung* 65, nos. 1–2 (1957): 340–368.

Hampe, Karl. "Die Abfassung der *Monarchia* in Dantes letzten Lebensjahren." *Deutsches Dante-Jahrbuch*, n.s., 8, 17 (1935): 58–74.

Haskins, Charles Homer. *Renaissance of the Twelfth Century*. Cambridge, Mass.: Harvard University Press, 1927. Rpt., Cleveland and New York: World Publishing, 1968.

Heft, James. *John XXII and Papal Teaching Authority*. Texts and Studies in Religion 27. Lewiston, Queenston, and Lampeter: Edwin Mellen Press, 1986.

Herde, Peter. "Ein Pamphlet der päpstlichen Kurie gegen Kaiser Friedrich II. von 1245/46 (Eger cui lenia)." *Deutsches Archiv für Erforschung des Mittelalters* 23 (1967): 468–538.

Hoffmann, H. "Die beiden Schwerter im hohen Mittelalter." *Deutsches Archiv* 20 (1964): 78–114.

Hollander, Robert. *Dante's "Epistle to Cangrande."* Ann Arbor: University of Michigan Press, 1993.

Holmes, George. "Dante and the Popes." In *The World of Dante*, edited by Cecil Grayson, pp. 18–43. Oxford, U.K.: Clarendon Press, 1980.

————. "*Monarchia* and Dante's Attitude toward the Popes." In *Dante and Governance*, edited by John Woodhouse, pp. 46–57. Oxford, U.K.: Clarendon Press, 1997.

Hove, Alphonse van. *Prolegomena*. In *Commentarium Lovaniense in Codicem Iuris Canonici*, vol. 1, tom. 1, pp. 338–348. Mechlin and Rome: Dessain, 1928.

Hugelmann, Karl Gottfried. "Die Wirkungen der Kaiserweihe nach dem Sachsenspiegel." *Zeitschrift der Savigny-Stiftung für Rechtsgeschichte, Kanonistische Abteilung* 9 (Weimar: Hermann Böhlaus Nachfolger, 1919), 40:3:1–98.

Huillard-Bréholles, J.-L.-A., ed. *Historia Diplomatica Friderici Secundi*. Paris: Plon, 1857.

Hyde, Kenneth. "The Social and Political Ideal of the *Comedy*." In *Dante Readings*, edited by Eric Haywood, pp. 47–72. Dublin: Irish Academic Press, 1987.

Jacqueline, B. "Le pouvoir pontificale selon Saint Bernard: L'argument des deux glaives." *L'année canonique* 2 (1953): 197–201.

Joyce, George Hayward. *Principles of Logic*. London and New York: Longmans, Green, 1908. Rpt., 3d ed., 1949.

Kantorowicz, Ernst H[artwig]. *Frederick the Second, 1194–1250*. Translated by E. O. Lorimer. Makers of the Middle Ages. London: Constable, 1931.

———. "Dante's 'Two Suns.'" In *Semitic and Oriental Studies Presented to William Popper*, University of California Publications in Semitic Philology 11, pp. 217–231. Berkeley and Los Angeles: University of California Press, 1951. Rpt. in *Selected Studies by Ernst H. Kantorowicz*. Locust Valley, N.Y.: Augustin, 1965.

———. "Mysteries of State: An Absolutist Concept and Its Late Medieval Origins." *Harvard Theological Review* 48 (1955): 65–91. Rpt. in *Selected Studies by Ernst H. Kantorowicz*, pp. 381–398. Locust Valley, N.Y.: Augustin, 1965.

———. *The King's Two Bodies*. Princeton, N.J.: Princeton University Press, 1957. Rpt., with preface by William Chester Jordan, 1997.

Kantorowicz, Hermann. "*De pugna:* La letteratura langobardistica sul duello giudiziario." In Hermann Kantorowicz, *Rechtshistorische Schriften*, edited by H. Coing and G. Immel, Freiburger Rechts- und Staatswissenschaftliche Abhandlungen 30, pp. 255–271. Karlsruhe: Müller, 1970.

Käppeli, Thomas. *Scriptores Ordinis Prædicatorum Medii Ævi*. Vol. 2. Roma: Sabinæ, 1975.

Kay, Richard. "Hostiensis and Some Embrun Provincial Councils." *Traditio* 20 (1964): 503–513.

———. "The *Mentalité* of Dante's *Monarchia*." *Res Publica Litterarum* 9 (1986): 183–191.

———. "Roman Law in Dante's *Monarchia*." In *Law in Medieval Life and Thought*, edited by Edward B. King and Susan J. Ridyard, Sewanee Medieval Studies 5, pp. 259–268. Sewanee, Tenn.: Press of the University of the South, 1990.

———. "The Intended Reader of Dante's *Monarchia*." *Dante Studies* 110 (1992): 37–44.

Kelsen, Hans. *Die Staatslehre des Dante Alighieri*. Wiener staatswissenschaftlicher Studien 6. Vienna and Leipzig: Franz Deuticke, 1905. Italian translation by Wilifrido Sangiorgi. *La teoria dello stato in Dante*. Bologna: Massimiliano Boni, 1974.

Kennan, E. J. "The *De consideratione* of Saint Bernard and the Papacy in the Mid-Twelfth Century: A Review of Scholarship." *Traditio* 23 (1967): 73–115.

Kern, Fritz. *Humana Civilitas (Staat, Kirche, und Kultur): Eine Dante-Untersuchung*. Mittelalterliche Studien 1: 1. Leipzig: Koehler, 1913.

Koenig, John. "Guelphs and Ghibellines." In *Dictionary of the Middle Ages*, 6:6–7.

Kraus, Clara. "Garamanti." In *Enciclopedia dantesca*, 3:96.

Kuttner, Stephan. "The Father of the Science of Canon Law." *Jurist* 1 (1948): 2–19.

———. "Universal Pope or Servant of God's Servants? The Canonists, Papal Titles, and Innocent III." *Revue de droit canonique* 32 (1981): 109–149.

Lanzani, Francesco. *"La Monarchia" di Dante: Studi storici*. Milan: Tipografia del Pio Istituto di Patronato, 1864.

Lapparent, P., de. "L'oeuvre politique de François de Meyronnes et ses rapports avec celle de Dante." *Archives d'histoire doctrinale et littérature du Moyen Âge* 15–17 (1940–1942): 126–151.

*Law, Church, and Society: Essays in Honor of Stephan Kuttner*. Edited by Kenneth Pennington and Robert Somerville. Philadelphia: University of Pennsylvania Press, 1977.

Lea, Henry Charles. *The Duel and the Oath*. Philadelphia: University of Pennsylvania Press, 1974.

Lecler, Joseph. "L'argument des deux glaives (Luc XXII, 38) dans les controverses politiques du Moyen Âge: Ses origines et son développement." *Recherches de Science Religieuse* 21 (1931): 299–339.

———. "L'argument des deux glaives (Luc XXII, 38): Critique et déclin (XIVᵉ–XVIᵉ siècle)." *Recherches de Science Religieuse* 22 (1932): 151–177.

Leclerq, Jean. *Jean de Paris et l'ecclésiologie du XIIIe siècle*. Paris: Vrin, 1942.

———. *L'idée de la royauté du Christ au Moyen Âge*. Paris: Éditions du Cerf, 1959.

*Lectura Dantis [Californiana]: Inferno*. Edited by Allen Mandelbaum, Anthony Oldcorn, and Charles Ross. Berkeley, Los Angeles, and London: University of California Press, 1998.

Ledesma Uribe, J. J. "El Orden internacional en la *Monarquia* de Dante." *Juridica* 12 (1980): 375–403.

Legendre, Pierre. *La pénétration du droit romain dans le droit canonique classique de Gratien à Innocent IV, 1140–1254*. Paris: Imprimerie Jouve, 1964.

Lenkeith, Nancy. *Dante and the Legend of Rome: An Essay*. Edited by Richard Hunt and Raymond Klibansky. Medieval and Renaissance Studies, Supplement 2. Leiden: Brill, 1952.

Lewis, Ewart. *Medieval Political Ideas*. 2 vols. New York: Knopf, 1954.

Lewry, P. Osmund. "Dialectic." In *Dictionary of the Middle Ages*, 4:168–171.

*Lexikon des Mittelalters*. Edited by Robert Auty. 10 vols. Munich and Zurich: Artemis, 1937–1977.

Lindberg, David C., ed. *Science in the Middle Ages*. Chicago and London: University of Chicago Press, 1978.

Livi, Giovanni. *Dante: Suoi primi cultori, sua gente in Bologna con documenti inediti facsimili e illustrazioni figurate*. Bologna: Licinio Cappelli, 1918.

———. *Dante e Bologna. Nuovi Studi e documenti*. Bologna: Licinio Cappelli, 1921.

Lohr, C. J. "Medieval Latin Aristotle Commentaries, Authors G–I." *Traditio* 24 (1968): 191–192.

Lucas, Henry Stephen. "The Low Countries and the Disputed Imperial Election of 1314." *Speculum* 21 (1946): 72–114.

Maccarrone, Michele. *Chiesa e stato nella dottrina politica di papa Innocenzo III*. Rome: Facultas Theologica Pontificii Athenæi Lateranensis, 1940.

———. "Innocenzo III prima del pontificato." *Archivio Romano della Società Romana di Storia Patria* 66 (1943): 59–134.

———. "La teoria ierocratica e il canto XVI del *Purgatorio*." *Rivista di storia della Chiesa in Italia* 4 (1950): 359–398.

———. "Teologia e diritto canonico nella *Monarchia III, 3*." *Rivista di Storia della Chiesa* 5 (1951): 7–42.

———. *Vicarius Christi: Storia del titolo papale*. Lateranum, n.s., 18, nos. 1–4. Rome: Facultas Theologica Pontificii Athenæi Lateranensis, 1952.

———. "'Potestas directa' e 'potestas indirecta' nei teologi del XII e XIII secolo." In *Sacerdozio e regno da Gregorio VII a Bonifacio VIII: Studi presentati alla sezione storica del congresso della Pontificia Università Gregoriana, 13–17 ottobre 1953. Miscellanea Historiæ Pontificiæ* 18, pp. 27–47. Rome: Pontificia Università Gregoriana, 1954.

———. "Il terzo libro della *Monarchia*." *Studi Danteschi* 33 (1955): 5–142.

———. "Dante e i teologi del XIV–XV secolo." *Studi Romani* 5 (1957): 20–28.

———. "Nuovi studi su Innocenzo III." *Rivista di storia della Chiesa in Italia* 9 (1958): 40–46.

———. *Studi su Innocenzo III.* Italia sacra, Studi e documenti di storia ecclesiastica 17. Padua: Antenore, 1972.

———. "Papato e impero nella *Monarchia.*" *Nuove letture dantesche* 8 (1976): 259–332.

———. *Nuovi studi su Innocenzo III.* Edited by Roberto Lambertini, with an introduction by Ovidio Capitani. Nuovi Studi Storici 25. Rome: nella Sede dell'Istituto, Palazzo Borromini, 1995.

Macken, R. "Un apport important e l'ecdotique des manuscrits à pièces: À propos de l'édition léonin du Commentaire de Thomas d'Aquin sur la Politique d'Aristote et sa Tabula Libri Ethicorum." *Scriptorium* 27, no. 2 (1973): 319–327.

Maffei, Domenico. *La Donazione di Costantino nei giuristi medievali.* Milan: Giuffrè, 1964.

Mann, Horace K. *The Lives of the Popes in the Middle Ages: The Popes at the Height of Their Temporal Influence, Innocent II to Blessed Benedict XI.* Vol. 18: *Boniface VIII to Bl. Benedict XI, 1294–1304.* London: Kegan Paul, Trench Trubner; St. Louis, Mo.: Herder, 1932.

Manselli, Raoul. *Studi sulle eresie del secolo XII.* Istituto Storico Italiano per il Medio Evo: Studi storici 5. Rome: nella Sede dell'Istituto, 1953.

———. "Dante e l'*ecclesia spiritualis.*" In *Dante e Roma: Atti del Convegno di Studi a cura della "Casa di Dante." Sotto gli auspici del Comune di Roma, in collaborazione con l'Istituto di Studi Romani, Roma, 8–9–10 aprile 1965,* pp. 115–135. Florence: Le Monnier, 1965.

———. "Pietro di Giovanni Olivi ed Ubertino da Casale." *Sudi medievali,* n.s., 3, 6 (1965): 95–122.

———. "Cangrande e il mondo ghibellino nell'Italia settentrionale alla venuta di Arrigo VII." In *Dante e la cultura veneta. Atti del Convegno di Studi organizzato dalla Fondazione "Giorgio Cini" in collaborazione con l'Istituto universitario di Venezia, l'Università di Padova, il Centro scaligero di Studi Danteschi, e i Comuni di Venezia, Padova, Verona. Venezia, Padova, Verona, 30 marzo–5 aprile 1966,* pp. 39–49. Florence: Olschki, 1966.

Mariani, U. "La posizione di Dante fra i teologi dell'imperialismo ghibellino." *Giornale dantesco* 30 (1927): 111–117.

Markus, R. A. "Two Conceptions of Political Authority: Augustine, *De civitate Dei* XIX, 14–15, and Some Thirteenth-Century Interpretations." *Journal of Theological Studies,* n.s., 16, no. 1 ([Oxford, U.K.: Clarendon Press] April 1965): 68–100.

Marmura, Michael E. "Rushd, Ibn (Averroës)." In *Dictionary of the Middle Ages,* 10:571–575.

Martina, Antonio. "Uguccione nel proemio della *Monarchia* di Dante." *L'Alighieri* 13, no. 1 (1972): 69–74.

Martinelli, Bortolo. "Sul 'quodammodo' di *Monarchia* III, 15, 17." In *Miscellanea in onore di Vittore Branca,* 5 vols., Biblioteca dell'Archivum Romanicum, ser. 1, Storia-Letteratura-Paleografia 178–182, 1:193–214. Florence: Olschki, 1983.

Martini, G. "Regale sacerdotium." *Archivio della reale Deputazione romana di Storia patria,* n.s., 4, 61 (1938): 1–166.

Marx, C. W. *The Devil's Rights and the Redemption in the Literature of Medieval England.* Woodbridge, Suffolk, U.K., and Rochester, N.Y.: Boydell & Brewer, 1995.

Matteini, Nevio. *Il più antico oppositore politico di Dante: Guido Vernani da Rimini: Testo Critico del "De Reprobatione Monarchiæ."* Il Pensiero medievale collana di Storia della Filosofia, ser. 1, vol. 6. Padua: CEDAM [Casa Editrice Dott. Antonio Milani], 1958.

Mattingly, Garrett. *Renaissance Diplomacy.* Baltimore, Md.: Penguin Books, 1964.

Mazzeo, Felice. *Dante e Ravenna*. Bologna: Cappelli Editore, 1987.

Mazzoni, Francesco. "L'epistola a Cangrande." *Rendiconti della Accademia Nazionale dei Lincei*. Classe di Scienze morali, storiche e filologiche, ser. 8, 10 (1955): 157–198.

———. "Per l'epistola a Cangrande." In *Studi dedicati a Angelo Monteverdi*, pp. 3–21. Modena: STEM, 1959. Rpt. in *Contributi di filologia dantesca*. Florence: Sansoni, 1966.

———. "Le *Epistole* di Dante." In *Comitato Nazionale per le Celebrazioni del VII Centenario della Nascita Di Dante, Conferenze Aretine, 1965*, pp. 47–100. Arezzo: Accademia Petrarca-Bibbiena, Società Dantesca Casentinese, 1966.

———. "L'edizione delle opere latine minori." In *Atti del Convegno Internazionale di Studi Danteschi a cura del Comune di Ravenna and Società Dantesca Italiana, Ravenna, 10–12 September 1971*, pp. 129–143, 159–166. Ravenna: Longo, 1979.

———. "Bruno Nardi dantista." *L'Alighieri* 23 (1982): 8–28. Rpt. in Bruno Nardi, *"Lecturæ" e altri studi danteschi*, edited by Rudy Abardo, pp. 3–21. Florence: Casa Editrice le Lettere, 1990.

———. "Teoresi e prassi in Dante Politico." In *Monarchia, Epistole politiche*, con un saggio introduttivo di Francesco Mazzoni. Turin: Edizioni RAI Radiotelevisione Italiana, 1966.

McCready, William D. "The Problem of the Empire in Augustinus Triumphus and Late Medieval Papal Hierocratic Theory." *Traditio* 30 (1974): 325–349.

———. "Papalists and Anti-Papalists: Aspects of the Church-State Controversy in the Later Middle Ages." *Viator* 6 (1975): 241–273.

McInerny, Ralph M. *The Logic of Analogy: An Interpretation of St. Thomas*. The Hague: Martinus Nijhoff, 1961.

*Medieval and Renaissance Studies*. Edited by Eugene F. Rice Jr. Ithaca, N.Y.: Cornell University Press, 1959.

Mellone, Attilio. *"Liber de Causis."* In *Enciclopedia dantesca*, 2:327–329.

Menache, Sophia. "A Propaganda Campaign in the Reign of Philip the Fair, 1302–1303." *French History* 4 (1990): 427–454.

———. *Clement V*. Cambridge Studies in Medieval Life and Thought 36. Cambridge, U.K.: Cambridge University Press, 1998.

Meozzi, Antero. "I trattati politici di Guido Vernani e Dante Alighieri." *Giornale dantesco* (1930): 18–30.

Michaud-Quantin, P. *Universitas: Expressions du mouvement communautaire dans le Moyen-Âge latin*. Paris: Vrin, 1970.

Miething, Christoph. "Politeia und Utopia: Zur Epistemologie der literarischen Utopie." *Germanisch-Romanische Monatschrift* 37, no. 3 (1987): 247–263.

Mineo, Niccolò. *Profetismo e apocalittica in Dante*. Catania: Facoltà di Lettere e Filosofia, 1968.

Minio-Paluello, Lorenzo. "Tre note alla *Monarchia*." In *Medioevo e Rinascimento: Studi in onore di Bruno Nardi*, Pubblicazioni dell'Istituto di Filosofia dell'Università di Roma 2, 2:501–524. Florence: Sansoni, 1955.

———. "Remigio Girolami's *De bono communi*: Florence at the Time of Dante's Banishment and the Philosopher's Answer to the Crisis." *Italian Studies* 11 (1956): 56–71.

———. "Magister sex principiorum." *Studi medievali*, ser. 3, 6 (1965): 123–151.

Ministeri, P. B. "De Augustini de Ancona O.E.S.A. (†1328) vita et operibus." *Analecta Augustiniana* 22, no. 1 (1952): 148–262.

Mochi Onory, Sergio. *Fonti canonistiche dell'idea moderna dello stato (Imperium spirituale—iurisdictio di-*

*visa—sovranità*). Pubblicazioni dell'Università Cattolica del Sacro Cuore, n.s., vol. 38. Milan: Società Editrice "Vita e Pensiero," 1951.

Mollat, Guillaume. *Les papes d'Avignon (1305–1378)*. 7th ed. Paris: Librairie Lecoffre, J. Gabalda et Fils, 1930. English translation by Janet Love. *The Popes at Avignon, 1305–1387.* London, Edinburgh, Paris, and New York: Nelson, 1963.

———. "Bertrand du Poujet." In *Dictionnaire d'histoire et de géographie ecclésiastiques*, 8, col. 1068–1074. Paris: Librairie Letouzey, 1935.

Mommsen, Theodor E. "St. Augustine and the Christian Idea of Progress: The Background of the *City of God.*" In *Medieval and Renaissance Studies*, edited by Eugene F. Rice Jr., pp. 265–298. Ithaca, N.Y.: Cornell University Press, 1959.

Mongiello, Emilia. "Sulla datazione della *Monarchia* di Dante." *Le parole e le idee: Rivista internazionale di varia cultura* 11, nos. 43–44 (1969 [1971]): 290–324.

Moore, Edward. *Studies in Dante*. Oxford, U.K.: Clarendon Press, 1896. Rpt., New York: Haskell House, 1968.

Morais Barbosa, J. "A noçao de liberdade no *De Monarchia* de Dante." *Estudios de Filosofia medieval* 11, no. 32 (1984): 127–144.

Morris, Colin. *The Papal Monarchy: The Western Church from 1050 to 1250*. Oxford, U.K.: Clarendon Press, 1989.

Mozzillo-Howell, Elizabeth Marilyn. "Dialectic and the *Convivio.*" *Italian Culture* 9 (1991): 29–41.

———. "Dante's Art of Reason: A Study of Medieval Logic and Semantics in the *Monarchy.*" Ph.D. diss., Harvard University, 1998. Ann Arbor, Mich.: UMI, 1998.

Muldoon, James. *Empire and Order: The Concept of Empire, 800–1800*. New York: St. Martin's Press, 1999.

Müller, Carl. *Der Kampf Ludwigs des Baiern mit der römischen Curie: Ein Breitrag zur kirchlichen Geschichte des 14. Jahrhunderts*. 2 vols. Tübingen: Laupp, 1879–1880.

Müller, Wolfgang Peter. "Huguccio, Twelfth-Century Canonist and Author of the *Summa decretorum.*" Ph.D. diss., Syracuse University, 1991. Ann Arbor, Mich.: UMI, 1992.

———. *Huguccio: The Life, Works and Thought of a Twelfth-Century Jurist*. Washington, D.C.: The Catholic University of America Press, 1994.

Najemy, John M. "Dante and Florence." In *The Cambridge Companion to Dante*, edited by Rachel Jacoff, pp. 80–99. Cambridge, U.K.: Cambridge University Press, 1993.

Nardi, Bruno. *Nel mondo di Dante*. Rome: Edizioni di "Storia e Letteratura," 1944.

———. *Saggi di filosofia dantesca*. Milan: Società Anonima Editrice Dante Alighieri, 1930. 2d ed., Florence: La Nuova Italia, 1967.

———. *Dante e la cultura medievale: Nuovi saggi di filosofia dantesca*. 2d ed. Bari: Laterza, 1949.

———. *Dal Convivio alla Commedia (sei saggi danteschi)*. Rome: Istituto Storico Italiano per il Medio Evo, 1960; rpt. 1992.

———. "Di un'aspra critica di fra Guido Vernani a Dante." *L'Alighieri: Rassegna bibliografica dantesca* 6, no. 1 (1965): 42–47. Rpt. in *Saggi e note di critica dantesca*, pp. 377–385.

———. *Saggi e note di critica dantesca*. Milan and Naples: Riccardo Ricciardi Editore, 1966.

*New Catholic Encyclopedia*. 18 vols. New York: McGraw-Hill, 1967– .

Offler, Hilary Seton. "Empire and Papacy: The Last Struggle." *Transaction of the Royal Historical Society*, ser. 5, no. 6 (1956): 21–47.

Orioli, Emilio. *La cancelleria pepolesca: Atti e formule.* Bologna: Stabilimento Poligrafo Emiliano, 1910.

Ottokar, Niccolò. "Intorno a Farinata e alla sua famiglia." *Archivio storico italiano* 2 (1919): 159–163. Rpt. in *Studi comunali e fiorentini.* Florence: La Nuova Italia, 1948.

Padoan, Giorgio. *Introduzione a Dante.* 2d ed. Florence: Sansoni, 1981.

———. "Il Vicariato Cesareo dello Scaligero: Per la datazione dell'*Epistola a Cangrande.*" *Lettere italiane* 50, no. 2 (1998): 161–175.

———. "'*Alia utilia reipublice,*' la composizione della *Monarchia* di Dante." *Letture classensi* 28 (1999): 7–27. [Cited as "La composizione."]

Pagliaro, Antonio. "Ahi Costantin. . . ." In *Ulisse: Ricerche semantiche sulla Divina Commedia,* 1:253–291. Messina and Florence: D'Anna, 1966.

Palma di Cesnola, Maurizio. *Semiotica dantesca: profetismo e diacronica.* Ravenna: Longo, 1995.

Paratore, Ettore. "Il latino di Dante." *Cultura e Scuola* 4 (1965): 94–124. Rpt. in *Dante nella critica d'oggi: Risultati e prospettive,* edited by Umberto Bosco, pp. 94–124. Florence: Le Monnier, 1965.

———. "Stazio." In *Enciclopedia dantesca,* 5:419–425.

Partini, Anna Maria, and Vincenzo Nestler. *Cecco D'Ascoli: Un poeta occultista medievale.* Rome: Edizioni Mediterranee, 1979.

Pastore Stocchi, Manlio. "*Monarchia:* Testo e cronologia." *Cultura e Scuola* 4 (1965): 714–721. Rpt. in *Dante nella critica d'oggi: Risultati e prospettive,* edited by Umberto Bosco, pp. 714–721. Florence: Le Monnier, 1965.

Pattin, Adriaan, ed. "*Le Liber de causis:* Édition établie à l'aide de 90 manuscrits avec introduction et notes." *Tijdschrift voor Filosofie* 28 (1966): 90–203.

Pennington, Kenneth. *Pope and Bishops: The Papal Monarchy in the Twelfth and Thirteenth Centuries.* Philadelphia: University of Pennsylvania Press, 1984.

———. "Henry VII and Robert of Naples." In *Das Publikum politischer Theorie im 14. Jahrhundert,* edited by Jürgen Miethke and Arnold Bühler, Schriften des Historisches Kolleg, Kolloquien 21, pp. 81–92. Munich: Oldenbourg, 1992.

———. "The Legal Education of Pope Innocent III." *Bulletin of Medieval Canon Law* 4 (1974): 70–77. Rpt. in Kenneth Pennington, *Popes, Canonists and Texts, 1150–1550.* Aldershot, U.K.: Variorum Reprint Editions/Ashgate, 1993.

———. "Pope Innocent III's Views on Church and State: A Gloss to *Per Venerabilem.*" In *Law, Church, and Society: Essays in Honor of Stephan Kuttner,* edited by Kenneth Pennington and Robert Somerville, pp. 49–68. Philadelphia: University of Pennsylvania Press, 1977. Rpt. in Kenneth Pennington, *Popes, Canonists and Texts, 1150–1550.* Aldershot, U.K.: Variorum Reprint Editions/Ashgate, 1993.

———. *The Prince and the Law, 1200–1600: Sovereignty and Rights in the Western Legal Tradition.* Berkeley, Los Angeles, and Oxford, U.K.: University of California Press, 1993.

———. "Huguccio." In *Dictionary of the Middle Ages,* 6:327–328.

Pertile, Lino. "Dante Looks Forward and Back: Political Allegory in the Epistles." *Dante Studies* 115 (1997): 1–17.

Petrocchi, Giorgio. *Vita di Dante.* Bari: Laterza, 1984.

Pézard, André. *Dante sous la pluie de feu.* Etudes de Philosophie Médiévale 40. Paris: Vrin, 1950.

———. *"La rotta gonna": Gloses et corrections aux textes mineurs de Dante.* 3 vols. Florence and Paris: Sansoni-Didier, 1967–1979.

Pirie-Gordon, C. H. C. *Innocent the Great: An Essay on His Life and Times.* London and New York: Longmans, 1907.

Poletto, Giacomo. *La Santa Scrittura nelle opere di Dante Allighieri.* Siena: Tipografia Pontificio S. Bernardino, 1909.

*Il processo di Dante (Celebrato il 16 aprile 1966 nella Basilica di S. Francesco in Arezzo).* Edited by Dante Ricci. Florence: Edizioni Arnaud, 1967.

Proto, Enrico. *Scritti varii di erudizione e dicritica in onore di Rodolfo Renier.* Turin: Fratelli Bocca Editori, 1912.

Quaglioni, Diego. "Per una edizione critica e un commento moderno del *Tractatus de regimine civitatis* di Bartolo da Sassoferrato." *Il pensiero politico: Rivista di Storia, delle Idee Politiche e Sociali* 9, no. 1 (1976): 70–93.

Quarta, F. "Regalità di Cristo e del Papa in Innocenzo III." *Angelicum* 19 (1942): 227–288.

Queller, Donald. *The Office of Ambassador in the Middle Ages.* Princeton, N.J.: Princeton University Press, 1967.

Radding, Charles M. "Ordeals." In *Dictionary of the Middle Ages,* 9:259–260.

Raedemaeker, J. de. "Informations concernant quelques commentaires du *De Anima.*" *Bulletin de Philosophie Médiévale* (édité par la Société Internationale pour l'Etude de la Philosophie Médiévale [S.I.E.P.M.]) 8–9 (1966–1967): 102–104.

Reade, W. H. V. "Political Theory to ca. 1300." In *Cambridge Medieval History,* 6:629–632. Cambridge, U.K.: Cambridge University Press, 1929.

Reeves, Marjorie. "Marsiglio of Padua and Dante Alighieri." In *Trends in Medieval Political Thought,* edited by Beryl Smalley, pp. 86–104. Oxford, U.K.: Blackwell, 1965.

———. *The Prophetic Sense of History in Medieval and Renaissance Europe.* Variorum Collected Studies Series. Burlington, Vt.: Ashgate, 1999.

Ricci, Corrado, and Olindo Guerrini. *Studi e polemiche dantesche.* Bologna: Zanichelli, 1853.

Ricci, Pier Giorgio. "Primi approcci per l'edizione nazionale della *Monarchia.*" *Studi danteschi* 31 (1953): 31–58.

———. "Un codice della *Monarchia* mai utilizzato." *Studi danteschi* 31 (1953): 163–172.

———. "Il manoscritto Trivulziano della *Monarchia.*" *Studi danteschi* 32 (1954): 51–63.

———. "L'archetipo della *Monarchia.*" *Studi danteschi* 34 (1957): 127–162.

———. "Restauro di un luogo della *Monarchia.*" *Italia medioevale e umanistica* 2 (1959): 441–442.

———. "Il commento di Cola da Rienzo alla *Monarchia* di Dante." *Studi medievali,* ser. 3, vol. 6, pt. 2 (1965): 665–708.

———. "Donazione di Costantino." In *Enciclopedia dantesca,* 2:569–570.

———. "Vernani, Guido." In *Enciclopedia dantesca,* 5:986.

———. "L'ultima fase del pensiero politico di Dante e Cangrande vicario imperiale." In *Dante e la cultura veneta. Atti del Convegno di Studi organizzato dalla Fondazione "Giorgio Cini" in collaborazione con l'Istituto universitario di Venezia, l'Università di Padova, il Centro scaligero di Studi Danteschi, e i Comuni di Venezia, Padova, Verona. Venezia, Padova, Verona, 30 marzo–5 aprile 1966,* pp. 367–371. Florence: Olschki, 1966.

———. "La *Monarchia* dantesca e l'idea dell'impero nella sua realtà giuridica e politica al tempo di Dante." In *Il processo di Dante (Celebrato il 16 aprile 1966 nella Basilica di S. Francesco in Arezzo),* edited by Dante Ricci, pp. 67–71. Florence: Edizioni Arnaud, 1967.

———. "Dante e l'impero romano." In *Dante e Roma: Atti del Convegno di Studi a cura della "Casa di*

*Dante."* Sotto gli auspici del Comune di Roma, in collaborazione con l'Istituto di Studi Romani, Roma, 8–9–10 aprile 1965, pp. 137–149. Florence: Le Monnier, 1965.

Richter, M. "Dante the Philosopher-Historian in the *Monarchia*." In *Dante Soundings: Eight Literary and Historical Essays,* edited by D. Nolan, pp. 164–187. Dublin: Irish Academic Press; Totowa, N.J.: Rowman & Littlefield, 1981.

Rivière, Jean. *Le problème de l'Eglise et de l'état au temps de Philippe le Bel: Etude de théologie positive.* Université Catholique et Collèges Théologiques de Louvain, Spicilegium Sacrum Lovaniense, Etudes et Documents 8. Louvain: "Spicilegium Sacrum Lovaniense" Bureaux; Paris: Honoré Champion et Edouard Champion, 1926.

Rossi, Luca Carlo. "Tre dictamina inediti di Graziolo Bambaglioli con una nota biografica." *Italia medievale e umanistica* 31 (1988): 81–125.

Russell, Frederick H. *The Just War in the Middle Ages.* Cambridge, U.K.: Cambridge University Press, 1975.

Russo, Vittorio. "La *Monarchia* di Dante (diritto naturale e stato di diritto)." *Lavoro critico* 15–16 (1978): 167–208. Rpt. as "La *Monarchia* di Dante (tra utopia e progetto)." *Lettura Classensi* 7 (1978): 51–89.

———. *Impero e stato di diritto: Studio su "Monarchia" ed "Epistole" politiche di Dante.* Memorie dell'Istituto Italiano per gli Studi Filosofici 18. Naples: Bibliopolis, 1987.

Salman, D. H. "Jean de la Rochelle et les débuts de l'averroïsme latin." *Archives d'histoire doctrinale et litteraire du Moyen Âge* 22–23 (1947–1948): 133–144.

Salsano, Fernando. "Sciti." In *Enciclopedia dantesca,* 5:81.

Salvatorelli, Luigi. *L'Italia Communale dal secolo XI alla metà del secolo XIV.* Storia d'Italia 4. Milan: Mondadori, 1940.

Sandquist, T. A. "Inquest, English." In *Dictionary of the Middle Ages,* 6:481–482.

Sarubbi, Antonio. *Chiesa e stato communale nel pensiero di Remigio de' Girolami.* Nobilità dello Spirito 18. Naples: Morano, 1971.

Schizzerotti, G. "Uguccione." In *Enciclopedia dantesca,* 5:800–802.

Schneider, Fedor. *Rom und Romgedanke im Mittelalter: Die geistigen Grundlagen der Renaissance.* Cologne: Böhlau Verlag, 1925; rpt. 1959.

Schneider, Friedrich. "Neue Deutungen und Datierungen (Die Entwicklung des jungen Dante zu seiner künstlerischen und wissenschaftlichen Reife [B. Nardi]; Zur Entstehungszeit der *Monarchia* [M. Maccarrone, B. Nardi, P. R(G.). Ricci u. a.])." *Deutsches Dante-Jahrbuch* 36–37 (1958): 158–219.

Scholz, Richard. *Die Publizistik zur Zeit Philipps des Schönen und Bonifaz' VIII: Ein Beitrag zur Geschichte der politischen Anschauungen des Mittelalters.* Kirchenrechtlicher Abhandlungen. Edited by Ulrich Stutz. Stuttgart: Ferdinand Enke, 1903.

———. *Unbekannte kirchenpolitische Streitschriften aus der Zeit Ludwigs des Bayern (1327–1354).* 2 vols. Rome: Loescher, 1911–1914.

Schramm, Percy Ernst. *Kaiser, Rom und Renovatio: Studien und Texte zur Geschichte des romischen Erneuerungsgedankens vom Ende des Karolingischen Reiches bis zum Investiturstreit.* Edited by Fritz Saxl. 2 vols. Studien der Bibliothek Warburg. Leipzig and Berlin: Teubner, 1929.

*Science in the Middle Ages.* Edited by David C. Lindberg. Chicago and London: University of Chicago Press, 1978.

Scott, John A. "*Monarchia* III, iv, 10: Un leone tra le nuvole." In *Miscellanea in onore di Vittore Branca,*

5 vols., Biblioteca dell'Archivum Romanicum, ser. 1, Storia-Letteratura-Paleografia 178–182, 1:185–192. Florence: Olschki, 1983.

———. "Una contraddizione scientifica nell'opera dantesca: I *due soli* del *Purgatorio XVI 107.*" In *Dante e la scienza*, edited by Patrick Boyde and Vittorio Russo, pp. 149–155. Ravenna: Longo, 1995.

———. *Dante's Political Purgatory*. Philadelphia: University of Pennsylvania Press, 1996.

*Scrittori e idee in Italia: Antologia della Critica: Dalle Origini al Trecento*. Edited by P. Pullega. Bologna: Zanichelli, 1982.

Sebastio, L. "Il 'philosophus' e la 'monarchia' in Dante: Per una funzione sociale del sapiente." *Italianistica* 10 (1981): 323–347.

*The Seven Liberal Arts in the Middle Ages*. Edited by David L. Wagner. Bloomington: Indiana University Press, 1983.

Shannon, Albert Clement. *The Popes and Heresy in the Thirteenth Century*. Ph.D. diss., Columbia University. Villanova, Pa.: Augustinian Press, 1949.

Shaw, Prudence. "Il codice Uppsalense della *Monarchia.*" *Studi danteschi* 46 (1969): 293–331.

———. "Il Volgarizzamento inedito della *Monarchia.*" *Studi danteschi* 47 (1970): 59–224; her edition of the text is on pp. 127–224.

———. "La versione ficiniana della Monarchia." *Studi danteschi* 51 (1978): 289–408.

———. "Per l'edizione del volgarizzamento ficiniano della *Monarchia.*" In *Testi ed interpretazioni. Miscellanea in onore di Gianfranco Contini: Studi del Seminario di filologia dell'Università di Firenze*, pp. 927–939. Milan and Naples: Ricciardi, 1978.

———. "Sul testo della Monarchia." *Studi danteschi* 53 (1981): 187–217.

———. "Il manoscritto Q della *Monarchia.*" In *Miscellanea di studi danteschi in memoria di Silvio Pasquazi*, edited by Alfonso Paolella et al., 2:815–821. Naples: Ardia, 1993.

———. "Per un nuovo testo critico della *Monarchia.*" In *La Società dantesca italiana, 1888–1988: Convegno internazionale, Firenze, 24–26 novembre 1988, Atti*, edited by Rudy Abardo, pp. 435–444. Milan and Naples: Ricciardi, 1995.

———. "Some Proposed Emendations to the Text of Dante's *Monarchia.*" *Italian Studies* 50 (1995): 1–8.

———. "The *Stemma Codicum* of Dante's *Monarchia.*" *Italian Studies* 51 (1996): 5–26.

Silverstein, H. Theodore. "Dante and Virgil the Mystic." *Harvard Studies and Notes on Philology and Literature* 14 (1932): 51–82.

———. "On the Genesis of *De Monarchia* II, 5." *Speculum* 13 (1938): 326–329. Rpt. in *Dante in America: The First Two Centuries*, edited by A. Bartlett Giamatti, pp. 187–218. Binghamton, N.Y.: Center for Medieval and Early Renaissance Studies, 1983.

———. "The Throne of the Emperor Henry in Dante's Paradise and the Medieval Conception of Christian Kingship." *Harvard Theological Review* 32 (1939): 115–129.

Simonelli, Maria Picchio. "L'inquisizione e Dante: Alcune osservazioni." *Dante Studies* 97 (1979): 129–149. Rpt. in *Dante Studies* 118 (2000): 303–321.

———. *Lectura Dantis Americana: Inferno III*. Philadelphia: University of Pennsylvania Press, 1993.

Simonelli, Maria Sampoli. "G. Marcovaldo, *Aspetti dello spirito di Dante.*" *Studi danteschi* 33, no. 1 (1955): 239–240.

Singleton, Charles S. *Journey to Beatrice*. Cambridge, Mass.: Harvard University Press, 1958.

Sistrunk, Timothy G. "Obligations of the Emperor as the Reverent Son in Dante's *Monarchia.*" *Dante Studies* 105 (1987): 95–112.

Smalley, Beryl. *The Study of the Bible in the Middle Ages.* Oxford, U.K.: Blackwell & Mott, 1952. 2d ed., South Bend, Ind.: University of Notre Dame Press, 1964.

———, ed. *Trends in Medieval Political Thought.* Oxford, U.K.: Blackwell, 1965.

Solmi, Arrigo. "Stato e chiesa nel pensiero di Dante." *Archivio storico italiano,* ser. 6, 17–18 (1921): 9–75.

———. *Il pensiero politico di Dante.* Florence: La Voce, 1922.

———. "La *Monarchia* di Dante." *Nuova Antologia* 378 (1935): 321–331.

———. "L'idea imperiale di Dante." In *Studi su Dante,* Conferenze e letture dantesche tenuta a cura del Comitato milanese della Società Dantesca Italiana, 7:1–31. Milan: Hoepli, 1944.

Spicq, Ceslas. *Esquisse d'une histoire de l'exégèse latine au Moyen Âge.* Bibliothèque Thomiste 26. Paris: Vrin, 1944.

Steenberghen, Fernand van. *Thomas Aquinas and Radical Aristotelianism.* Washington, D.C.: The Catholic University of America Press, 1980.

Stickler, Alfons M. "Der Schwerterbegriff bei Huguccio." *Ephemerides iuris canonici* 3 (1937): 201–242.

———. "De potestate gladii materialis ecclesiæ secundum 'Quæstiones Bambergenses' ineditas." *Salesianum* 6 (1944): 113–140.

———. "Il potere coattiva materiale della Chiesa nella *Reforma Gregoriana* secondo Anselmo di Lucca." *Studi Gregoriani* 2 (1947): 235–285.

———. "Il 'gladius' nel registro di Gregorio VII." *Studi Gregoriani* 3 (1948): 88–103.

———. "Magistri Gratiani sententia de potestate ecclesiæ in statum." *Apollinaris* 21 (1948): 36–111.

———. "Sacerdotium et regnum nei decretisti e primi decretalisti: Considerazioni metodologiche di ricerca e testi." *Salesianum* 15 (1953): 575–612.

———. "Il 'gladius' negli atti dei concilii e dei RR. Pontefici sino a Graziano e Bernardo di Clairvaux." *Salesianum* 13 (1951): 414–445.

———. "Imperator vicarius Papæ." *Mitteilungen des Institut für Österreichische Geschichtsforschung* 62 (1954): 165–212.

———. "Alanus Anglicus als Verteidiger des monarchischen Papsttums." *Salesianum* 21 (1959): 361–363.

Strayer, Joseph R. *On the Medieval Origins of the Modern State.* Princeton, N.J.: Princeton University Press, 1970.

———. *The Reign of Philip the Fair.* Princeton, N.J.: Princeton University Press, 1980.

Stubbs, William, ed. *Select Charters and Other Illustrations of English Constitutional History from the Earliest Times.* 8th ed., rev. Edited by Henry William Carlos Davis. Oxford, U.K.: Clarendon Press, 1905.

Stump, Eleonore. "Dialectic." In *The Seven Liberal Arts in the Middle Ages,* edited by David L. Wagner, pp. 125–146. Bloomington: Indiana University Press, 1983.

Tabacco, Giovanni. *La casa di Francia nell'azione politica di Papa Giovanni XXII.* Istituto Storico per il Medio Evo, Studi storici, nos. 1–4. Rome: Istituto Storico per il Medio Evo, 1953.

Tateo, Francesco. "Marsiglio Ficino." In *Enciclopedia dantesca,* 2:853–854.

Taurisano, I. *Il canto di Dante nell'ordine domenicano.* Florence: Tipografia Domenicana, 1917.

Thompson, David. "Dante's Virtuous Romans." *Dante Studies* 96 (1978): 145–162.

Tierney, Brian. "Tria quippe Distinguit Iudicia . . .": A Note on Innocent III's Decretal *Per Venerabilem.*" *Speculum* 37 (1962): 48–59.

———. "*Natura id est Deus*: A Case of Juristic Pantheism?" *Journal of the History of Ideas* 24, no. 3 (1963): 307–322. Rpt. in *Church Law and Constitutional Thought*, 7:307–322.

———. *The Crisis of Church and State 1050–1300, with Selected Documents.* Englewood Cliffs, N.J.: Prentice-Hall, 1964. Rpt., Toronto, Buffalo, and London: University of Toronto Press and the Mediæval Academy of America, 1988, 1992.

———. "The Continuity of Papal Political Theory in the Thirteenth Century: Some Methodological Considerations." *Mediæval Studies* 27 (1965): 227–245. Rpt. in *Church Law and Constitutional Thought*, 5:227–245.

———. "'Sola scriptura' and the Canonists." In *Collecteana Stephan Kuttner*, edited by J. Forchielli and Alfons M. Stickler. In *Studia Gratiana* 11 (1967): 346–364. Rpt. in *Church Law and Constitutional Thought*, 9:345–366.

———. *Church Law and Constitutional Thought in the Middle Ages.* London: Variorum Reprints, 1979.

Tillmann, Helena. *Pope Innocent III.* Translated by Walter Sax. Europe in the Middle Ages 12. Amsterdam, New York, and Oxford, U.K.: North Holland, 1980.

Tocco, Felice. *La quistione della povertà nel secolo XIV, secondo nuovi documenti.* Naples: Perella, 1910.

Took, J. F. *Dante: Lyric Poet and Philosopher: An Introduction to the Minor Works.* Oxford, U.K.: Clarendon Press, 1990.

Torraca, Francesco. "A proposito d'un luogo della *Monarchia* (III, iii, 9–10)." *Atti della R. Accademia di archeologia, lettere e belle arti di Napoli*, n.s., 8 (1924): 149–163.

Toscano, A. "Dante: Il discorso aristotelico nella *Monarchia.*" *Forum Italicum* 15, nos. 2–3 (1981): 139–152.

Tosti, Luigi. *Storia di Bonifazio VIII e de' suoi tempi.* 2 vols. In *Opere Complete di D. Luigi Tosti*, 2–3. Rome: Tipografia della Camera dei Deputati, 1886.

Toynbee, Paget. *Dante Studies and Researches.* London: Methuen, 1902.

———. *A Dictionary of Proper Names and Notable Matters in the Works of Dante.* Revised by Charles S. Singleton. Oxford, U.K.: Oxford University Press, 1968.

*Trends in Medieval Political Thought.* Edited by Beryl Smalley. Oxford, U.K.: Blackwell, 1965.

Ullmann, Walter. *The Medieval Idea of Law as Represented by Lucas de Penna: A Study in Fourteenth-Century Legal Scholarship.* Introduction by Harold Dexter Hazeltine. London: Methuen; New York: Barnes and Noble, 1946; rpt. 1969.

———. *Medieval Papalism: The Political Theories of the Medieval Canonists.* Maitland Memorial Lectures. London: Methuen, 1949.

———. "The Development of the Medieval Idea of Sovereignty." *English Historical Review* 46 (1949): 1–33. Rpt. in *Law and Jurisdiction in the Middle Ages*, edited by George Garnett. London: Variorum Reprints, 1988.

———. *The Growth of Papal Government in the Middle Ages: A Study in the Ideological Relation of Clerical to Lay Power.* London: Methuen, 1955; rpt. 1970.

———. *A History of Political Thought in the Middle Ages.* Harmondsworth, Middlesex, U.K.: Penguin Books, 1965.

———. *A Short History of the Papacy in the Middle Ages.* London: Methuen, 1972.

————. *Law and Politics in the Middle Ages: An Introduction to the Sources of Medieval Political Ideas.* Ithaca, N.Y.: Cornell University Press, 1975.

————. *Scholarship and Politics in the Middle Ages.* London: Variorum Reprints, 1978.

————. *Law and Jurisdiction in the Middle Ages.* Edited by George Garnett. London: Variorum Reprints, 1988.

Vallone, Aldo. "Il pensiero politico di Dante dinanzi ad A. Trionfi e a G. Vernani da Rimini." In *Atti del Convegno Internazionale di Studi Danteschi a cura del Comune di Ravenna and Società Dantesca Italiana, Ravenna, 10–12 September 1971,* pp. 173–201. Ravenna: Longo, 1979. Rpt. as "A. Trionfi e G. Vernani da Rimini," in Aldo Vallone, *Antidantismo politico e dantismo letterario,* pp. 50–78. Rome: Bonacci, 1988.

————. "Di alcuni aspetti del pensiero politico-civile nel XIV secolo." In *Studi in onore di Antonio Corsano,* pp. 777–786. Bari: Laterza, 1970.

————. *Antidantismo politico nel XIV secolo: Primi contributi.* Naples: Liguori, 1973.

————. *Antidantismo politico e dantismo letterario.* Rome: Bonacci, 1988.

————. "A. Trionfi e G. Vernani da Rimini." In Aldo Vallone, *Antidantismo politico e dantismo letterario,* pp. 50–78. Rome: Bonacci, 1988.

————. "A proposito di *Monarchia* III, iii, 10." *Dante Studies* 113 (1995): 167–173.

van Cleve, T. C. *The Emperor Frederick of Hohenstaufen.* Oxford, U.K.: Clarendon Press, 1972.

Vasoli, Cesare. "La pace nel pensiero filosofico e teologico-politico da Dante a Okham." In *La Pace nel pensiero, nella politica, negli ideali del Trecento, 13–16 ottobre 1974. Centro di Studi sulla spiritualità medievale (Todi),* pp. 29–43. Rimini: L'Accademia tudertina, 1975.

————. "Filosofia e politica in Dante tra *Convivio* e *Monarchia.*" *Letture classensi* 9–10 (1982): 11–37.

————. "Note sul volgarizzamento ficiniano della *Monarchia.*" In *Miscellanea in onore di Vittore Branca,* 5 vols., Biblioteca dell'Archivum Romanicum, ser. 1, Storia-Letteratura-Paleografia 178–182, 3:451–474. Florence: Olschki, 1983.

————. "Papato e Impero nel tardo Medioevo: Dante, Marsilio, Ockham." In *Storia delle idee politiche economiche e sociali,* edited by L. Firpo, 2:543–649. Turin: UTET, 1985.

Veatch, Henry B. *Aristotle: A Contemporary Appreciation.* Bloomington and London: Indiana University Press, 1974.

Verlaque, Victor. *Jean XXII: Sa vie et ses oeuvres d'après des documents inédits.* Paris: Plon, 1883.

Vianello, Natale. "Il testo critico della *Monarchia* di Dante." *La Rassegna* 39 (1931): 89–111.

Vinay, Gustavo. *Interpretazione della Monarchia.* Lectura Dantis Scaligera. Florence: Le Monnier, 1962.

Viscardi, Antonio, and Gianluigi Barni. *L'Italia nell'età comunale.* Turin: UTET, 1966.

Vossler, Karl. *La Divina Commedia studiata nella sua genesi e interpretata, I, pt. 2 Storia dello svolgimento etico-politico.* Italian translation by S. Jacini. Bari: Laterza, 1910.

Waley, Daniel Philip. *The Papal State in the Thirteenth Century.* London: Macmillan; New York: St. Martin's Press, 1961.

Watt, John A. *The Theory of Papal Monarchy in the Thirteenth Century: The Contribution of the Canonists.* London: Burns & Oates, 1965.

————. "Hostiensis on *Per Venerabilem:* The Role of the College of Cardinals." In *Authority and Power: Studies in Medieval Law and Government Presented to Walter Ullmann on His Seventieth Birthday,* edited by Brian Tierney and Peter Linehan, pp. 99–113. Cambridge, U.K.: Cambridge University Press, 1980.

White, Donald A. *Medieval History: A Source Book.* Homewood, Ill.: Dorsey Press, 1965.

Whitfield, J. H. "Dante and the Roman World." *Italian Studies* 33 (1978): 1–19.

Wilks, Michael. *The Problem of Sovereignty in the Later Middle Ages: The Papal Monarchy with Augustinus Triumphus and the Publicists.* Cambridge, U.K.: Cambridge University Press, 1963.

Williamson, Edward. "De Beatitudine Huius Vite." *Annual Report of the Dante Society of America* 76 (1958): 1–22. Rpt. in *Dante Studies* 118 (2000): 109–127.

Woolf, Cecil N. Sidney. *Bartolus of Sassoferrato: His Position in the History of Medieval Political Thought.* Cambridge, U.K.: Cambridge University Press, 1913.

Ziegler, Aloysius P. "Pope Gelasius I and His Teaching on the Relation of Church and State." *Catholic Historical Review* 27 (1942): 412–437.

Zimmermann, Harald. *Papstabsetzungen des Mittelalters.* Graz, Vienna, and Cologne: Böhlaus, 1968.

Zingarelli, N. "La vita, i tempi e le opere di Dante." *Storia letteraria d'Italia* 3 (1931): 679–710.

# Index

All page numbers running between 111 and 159 refer to items in Dante's *Monarchia*; all pages between 174 and 197 refer to those in Vernani's *Refutation*; pages between 198 and 202 refer to those in John XXII's *Si fratrum*. Bible references to the translated texts are listed in the Notes.

*The* Monarchia *Controversy* was designed and composed in Monotype Centaur
by Kachergis Book Design, Pittsboro, North Carolina; printed on
60-pound Glatfelter Natural and bound by
Edwards Brothers, Inc., Lillington,
North Carolina.